Essentials of
WISC-V Assessment

Essentials

of WISC-V Assessment

Dawn P. Flanagan
Vincent C. Alfonso

WILEY

Library of Congress Cataloging-in-Publication Data

Names: Flanagan, Dawn P., author. | Alfonso, Vincent C., author.
Title: Essentials of WISC-V assessment / Dawn P. Flanagan, Vincent C. Alfonso.
Description: Hoboken : Wiley, 2017. | Series: Essentials of psychological assessment | Includes bibliographical references and index.
Identifiers: LCCN 2016055353 | ISBN 9781118980873 (paperback) | ISBN 9781118981009 (AdobePDF) | ISBN 9781118980996 (epub)
Subjects: LCSH: Wechsler Intelligence Scale for Children. | Wechsler Preschool and Primary Scale of Intelligence. | Children--Intelligence testing. | Ability--Testing. | BISAC: PSYCHOLOGY / Assessment, Testing & Measurement.
Classification: LCC BF432.5.W42 F583 2017 | DDC 155.4/1393--dc23 LC record available at https://lccn.loc.gov/2016055353

Cover Design: Wiley
Cover Image: ©Greg Kuchik/Getty Images

Printed in the United States of America

FIRST EDITION

PB Printing   10 9 8 7 6 5 4 3 2

CONTENTS

Acknowledgments xi

Series Preface xiii

Foreword xv
Susie Engi Raiford

One Overview of the WISC-V 1
*W. Joel Schneider, Dawn P. Flanagan, and
Vincent C. Alfonso*

Two How to Administer the WISC-V 53

Three How to Score the WISC-V 133

Four How to Interpret the WISC-V 167

Five Strengths and Weaknesses of the WISC-V 279

Six A Neuropsychological Approach to Interpretation
of the WISC-V 287
*George McCloskey, Jamie Slonim, Robert Whitaker,
Samantha Kaufman, and Naoko Nagoshi*

Seven   Use of the WISC-V in the Identification of
Specific Learning Disabilities   405

Eight   Illustrative Case Report   511
Erin M. McDonough

Nine   Assessment of English Learners With the WISC-V   539
Samuel O. Ortiz, Kristan E. Melo, and Meghan A. Terzulli

Ten   WISC-V and Q-interactive   591
Carlea Dries, Ron Dumont, and Kathleen D. Viezel

Epilogue   Dorothea McCarthy Remembered   617
Alan S. Kaufman

Appendices A–F can be accessed and downloaded from
http://www.wiley.com/go/flanaganWISCV

Appendix A   A Brief Overview of the Cattell-Horn-Carroll
(CHC) Theory

Appendix B   Norms Tables for New WISC-V
Clinical Composites

Appendix C   Case Reports
Gail Cheramie, Jamie Chaffin, and Robert Lichtenstein

Appendix D   Form for Manifestations of Cognitive Weaknesses

Appendix E   Definition of Terms and Clarification
of Concepts Used in the Dual Discrepancy/
Consistency Model of SLD and the Cross-Battery
Assessment Software System (X-BASS)

Appendix F   Task Characteristics of WISC-V Subtests
Marlene Sotelo-Dynega

About the Authors   621

Contributors   622

Index   623

Recently, each of us lost the second of the two most enduring mentors in our lives: our parents. We dedicate this book to them—Frank and Maryann Flanagan and Alfred and Mary Alfonso—for their unwavering belief in our capabilities, acceptance and support of our endeavors, and unconditional love.

We also dedicate this book to those who have mentored us in our professional lives, some who have come and gone but will never be forgotten, and some who remain in the wings, always willing to lend support and offer advice—we have benefited from and thank you for your wisdom and guidance.

And finally, we dedicate this book to all practitioners who use the WISC-V in a manner in which David Wechsler intended—that is, not only to understand the unique pattern of a child or adolescent's strengths and weaknesses, but to use that pattern to help him or her "act purposefully, think rationally and deal effectively with [his or her] environment (Wechsler, 1958, p. 7)."

ACKNOWLEDGMENTS

We acknowledge several people for their special and extraordinary contributions. We express our deepest appreciation to Tisha Rossi, Mary Ellen Schutz, Pam Suwinsky, Diane Turso, and Justin Frahm for supporting us through the publication process and for ensuring the quality of this book. We are also particularly grateful to Joel Schneider for contributing his expertise in writing Chapter 1; to George McCloskey, Jamie Slonim, Robert Whitaker, Samantha Kaufman, and Naoko Nagoshi for providing Chapter 6, on the use of the WISC-V in neuropsychological evaluation; to Samuel Ortiz, Kristan Melo, and Meghan Terzulli for providing Chapter 9, on assessing culturally and linguistically diverse individuals with the WISC-V; to Carlea Dries, Ron Dumont, and Kathleen Viezel for providing Chapter 10, on the WISC-V and Q-Interactive; and to Erin McDonough, who provided in Chapter 8 the case study that was used to demonstrate our interpretive method and approach to SLD identification and who provided us with valuable insight into the nuances of WISC-V interpretation based on her experience and clinical acumen.

We also thank Emma Hettrich, Caitlyn Hynes, Jennifer Mascolo, Carly Meyer, Kathleen Palma, Jaime Seaburg, John Willis, and Noelle Winter for their reviews of several chapters several times! In addition, we appreciate the tenacious efforts of Ou Zhang and Andrea Olson from Pearson, who provided us with norms and critical values for the clinical composites included in Appendix B; Gail Cheramie, Jamie Chaffin, and Robert Lichtenstein, who provided illustrative case studies in Appendix C; and Marlene Sotelo-Dynega, who compiled the WISC-V task characteristics found in Appendix F.

Finally, we recognize the contributions of our longtime colleague and friend, Samuel Ortiz, who spent countless hours incorporating new WISC-V components into X-BASS based on the interpretive method we espoused in this volume; Susie Engi Raiford, our new colleague, who supported our work from the beginning, carefully edited multiple chapters, and wrote the Foreword to this volume; and Alan Kaufman, our longtime mentor who taught us to test intelligently and who wrote the Epilogue to this volume.

SERIES PREFACE

I n the Essentials of Psychological Assessment series, we have attempted to provide the reader with books that will deliver key practical information in the most efficient and accessible style. The series features instruments in a variety of domains, such as cognition, personality, education, and neuropsychology. For the experienced clinician, books in the series offer a concise yet thorough way to master utilization of the continuously evolving supply of new and revised instruments as well as a convenient method for keeping up to date on the tried-and-true measures. The novice will find here a prioritized assembly of all the information and techniques that one must have at one's fingertips to begin the complicated process of individual psychological assessment and diagnosis.

Wherever feasible, visual shortcuts to highlight key points are utilized alongside systematic, step-by-step guidelines. Chapters are focused and succinct. Topics are targeted for an easy understanding of the essentials of administration, scoring, interpretation, and clinical application. Theory and research are continually woven into the fabric of each book but always to enhance clinical inference, never to sidetrack or overwhelm. We have long been advocates of what has been called "intelligent testing": the notion that a profile of test scores is meaningless unless it is brought to life by the clinical observations and astute detective work of knowledgeable examiners. Test profiles must be used to make a difference in the child's or adult's life, or why bother to test? We want this series to help our readers become the best intelligent testers they can be.

In *Essentials of WISC-V Assessment*, Dawn Flanagan and Vincent Alfonso provide practitioners with a complete, step-by-step approach to administering, scoring, and interpreting the most widely used intelligence test in the world: the WISC-V. Each chapter is chock-full of practical tips that make assessment of cognitive functions with the WISC-V efficient and informative. In addition, interpretation of the WISC-V is linked to X-BASS and applied to a case study in a step-by-step approach, highlighting the WISC-V in the identification of specific learning disabilities. This volume also includes chapters on use and interpretation of the

WISC-V in neuropsychological evaluation, use of the WISC-V in the assessment of culturally and linguistically diverse individuals, and how to administer and score the WISC-V on Q-Interactive. All told, Flanagan and Alfonso deliver a one-two knockout punch in this latest essentials volume.

Alan S. Kaufman and Nadeen L. Kaufman, Series Editors
University of Connecticut

FOREWORD

Susie Engi Raiford

In February 2015, the National Association of School Psychologists (NASP) held their first annual convention after the publication of the Wechsler Intelligence Scale for Children-Fifth Edition (WISC-V; Wechsler, 2014). The manuals and data were available, and many school districts had purchased the test. Drs. Dawn Flanagan and Vincent Alfonso were to give a talk about use of the WISC-V in the context of their cross-battery assessment (XBA) approach to interpretation.

I arrived late to a room with a capacity for 200 people. Every seat was full, and dozens of additional people stood in the back and sat crammed in the aisles on the floor. It was hot and crowded, but the room was buzzing with excitement and anticipation. Attendees delighted as Dawn and Vinny joked about the tight space and the fire code, but no attendees left and more hopefuls crowded around the door in the foyer. The school psychology field knew this was a big moment.

I sat quietly in the aisle, snapping pictures and awaiting their thoughts about use of the test that had been carefully and thoughtfully nurtured through a five-year revision process to publication. When you are involved in conceptualization and design of the WISC-V from beginning to end, you watch it take shape and pour your life into it on a daily basis. As its research director, you revise and write items, author the manuals, oversee data collection and scoring, ensure its technical integrity and quality, and help to launch and support it. The feeling is akin to bearing and raising a child, and NASP 2015 felt like the first day of kindergarten.

It was with good reason, then, that I was sitting on the edge of my metaphorical seat (since no real seats were available) awaiting their talk. XBA transcends individual instruments and focuses instead on comprehensively addressing referral questions (Flanagan, Ortiz, & Alfonso, 2013). However, XBA is highly relevant to the clinical utility of individual tests. The modern Wechsler scales are influenced by XBA and Dawn, Vinny, and colleagues' dual discrepancy/consistency pattern of strengths and weaknesses (PSW) method for learning disability identification (Flanagan, Alfonso, Mascolo, & Sotelo-Dynega, 2012). Using dialectical reasoning processes, the Wechsler theoretical framework of intelligence simultaneously considers these important works alongside other structural models of intellect, clinical utility evidence (e.g., clinical sensitivity, predictive validity, neuroscience), functional models of cognition (e.g., neuropsychological processing theory), and specific ability models (e.g., working memory). The Wechsler theoretical framework informs development to ensure each revision of the WISC is innovative, contemporary, and draws on the best that these different lines of inquiry have to offer.

Dawn, Vinny, and colleagues' collective writings also resonate with the modern Wechsler theoretical framework. They have sought in their own conceptualization of cognitive assessment to link and reconcile the same approaches to their own. For example, they have linked Cattell-Horn-Carroll with the Lurian and neuropsychological approaches (Flanagan, Alfonso, Ortiz, & Dynda, 2010) and have incorporated George McCloskey's neuropsychologically oriented process approach to psychoeducational evaluations (McCloskey, Hartz, & Slonim, 2016) into their own interpretive systems (Flanagan & Kaufman, 2005, 2009). *Essentials of WISC-V Assessment* features interpretation from the general to the specific in the spirit of Alan Kaufman's intelligent testing, beginning with global score selection (e.g., FSIQ, GAI, or NVI) and interpretation at the index score level. Their approach acknowledges that assessment is part science and part art: potentially clinically meaningful findings are investigated further. McCloskey's process approach (see Chapter 6) provides optional analyses that permit the test user to examine weaknesses through drilling down to the subtest and item level to examine the multiple processes involved in carrying out any WISC-V task.

Dawn and Vinny have the breadth and depth of knowledge and practicality that comes from devouring every article about assessment and test technical manual that was available and mentoring trainees and practitioners for decades. As a result, their thinking is steeped in psychometric knowledge and clinical utility, and seeks what will be useful in practice and clear to clinicians. Their approaches to interpretation of test results endeavor to link science to practice in ways that are understandable and useful. They don't just achieve this goal, they knock the ball out of the park. Their model is beautiful in its simplicity and sophistication; a masterpiece of practicality built on a strong theoretical foundation and psychometric excellence. Practitioners who follow their approach to comprehensive assessment and interpretation find it accessible and effective.

Research- and theory-based approaches to cognitive test interpretation now dominate the cognitive assessment scene (Kamphaus, Winsor, Rowe, Kim, & 2012), and they are here to stay. A systematic approach based firmly on research and theory helps us to make sense of the data we obtain so that we can explain assessment results to teachers and parents in a way that makes sense and that is defensible theoretically and empirically, and can help children to learn successfully. The sum total of human knowledge now doubles every 12 months and is projected soon to double every 12 hours (IBM, 2006). That knowledge is accessible to nearly everyone in the digital age, so teachers and parents expect answers that make sense and have scientific merit. Clinicians who approach test interpretation from sound underlying theoretical frameworks that stand up to psychometric investigations and are bolstered by neuroscience, such as the system presented in *Essentials of WISC-V Assessment*, are at a distinct advantage and are more likely to be able to help more children to learn effectively.

Remarkably, Dawn and Vinny don't rest on their laurels. They are keen to improve upon their methods. They seek criticism of their models and make refinements in response to new empirical findings. For example, *Essentials of WISC-IV Assessment* (Flanagan & Kaufman, 2005, 2009) recommended that if a 23-point discrepancy was present between the highest and lowest index scores, the FSIQ was to be considered invalid and should not be interpreted. *Essentials of WISC-V Assessment* marks a departure from this recommendation, in response to psychometric investigations demonstrating that such a discrepancy is quite common in both normative and clinical samples (Kaufman, Raiford, & Coalson, 2016; Orsini, 2014; Raiford & Coalson, 2014) and that cognitive ability composite scores show equal predictive validity in relation to achievement whether or not such a discrepancy is present between its component parts (Daniel, 2007, 2009). In response, *Essentials of WISC-V Assessment* features an updated interpretation approach to the WISC-V that relies on base rates to determine what is unusual, rather than using a cutoff of 23 points. Furthermore, the FSIQ is not considered invalid, but merely lacking sufficient detail to describe the child's abilities comprehensively.

Given their works' influence on the field in general and on the Wechsler theoretical framework in particular, it should come as no surprise that XBA, the dual-discrepancy PSW approach, and the modern WISC-V are highly compatible. The test was designed from the start to accommodate XBA and to complement cutting-edge achievement instruments such as the KTEA-3 (Kaufman & Kaufman, 2014) and the WIAT-III (Pearson, 2009) to optimize use within PSW approaches. When the WISC-V is administered with one of these measures, together they cover the major cognitive processes that have been shown to be important to learning and sensitive to learning problems and are necessary for PSW analyses (Breaux & Lichtenberger, 2016).

I held my breath as their presentation began. It quickly became apparent to me that they had detected the careful planning that went into the WISC-V. They discussed slide after slide that showed which WISC-V subtests and index scores would be appropriate measures of the constructs research had shown important to reading, math, and written expression skills. Their verdict? The new WISC-V has great utility within XBA. I looked around me at these school psychologists hanging on their every word and was overwhelmed with a sense of gratitude because Dawn and Vinny are helping clinicians to use the WISC-V well and impacting thousands of children by helping them to learn effectively. I exhaled as I remembered what I remind myself of on a daily basis: The test isn't my kid, it's for the kids. That's why we do what we do.

Because of the WISC-V's compatibility with XBA, this book provides interpretive assistance through a link with the XBA using the Cross-Battery Assessment Software System (X-BASS; Ortiz, Flanagan, & Alfonso, 2017). Administration and scoring are reviewed in depth in Chapters 2 and 3, with the helpful "Essentials" features and callout boxes that highlight important points to remember and provide strategies to avoid common errors. New clinical composites, exclusive analyses with the actual WISC-V standardization data, and a fresh approach to interpretation arm the reader with invaluable insights in the use and interpretation of the contemporary WISC-V.

REFERENCES

Breaux, K. C., & Lichtenberger, E. O. (2016). *Essentials of KTEA-3 and WIAT-III assessment.* Hoboken, NJ: Wiley.

Daniel, M. H. (2007). "Scatter" and the construct validity of FSIQ: Comment on Fiorello et al. (2007). *Applied Neuropsychology, 14*(4), 291–295.

Daniel, M. H. (2009). *Subtest variability and the validity of WISC–IV composite scores.* Blue ribbon paper presented at the annual meeting of the American Psychological Association, Toronto, Canada.

Flanagan, D. P., & Kaufman, A. S. (2005). *Essentials of WISC-IV assessment.* Hoboken, NJ: Wiley.

Flanagan, D. P., & Kaufman, A. S. (2009). *Essentials of WISC-IV assessment* (2nd ed). Hoboken, NJ: Wiley.

Flanagan, D. P., Alfonso, V. C., Mascolo, J. T., & Sotelo-Dynega, M. (2012). Use of ability tests in the identification of specific learning disabilities within the context of an operational definition. In D. P. Flanagan & P. L. Harrison (Eds.), *Contemporary intellectual assessment: Theories, tests, and issues* (pp. 643–669). Hoboken, NJ: Wiley.

Flanagan, D. P., Alfonso, V. C., Ortiz, S. O., & Dynda, A. M. (2010). Integrating cognitive assessment in school neuropsychological evaluations. In D. C. Miller (Ed.), *Best practices in school neuropsychology: Guidelines for effective practice, assessment, and evidence-based intervention* (pp. 101–140). Hoboken, NJ: Wiley.

Flanagan, D., Ortiz, S. O., & Alfonso, V. C. (2013). *Essentials of cross-battery assessment* (3rd ed.). Hoboken, NJ: Wiley.

IBM Global Technology Systems. (2006). *The toxic terabyte: How data dumping threatens business efficiency.* London, UK: IBM United Kingdom Limited. http://www-935.ibm .com/services/no/cio/leverage/levinfo_wp_gts_thetoxic.pdf.

Kamphaus, R. W., Winsor, A. P., Rowe, E. W., & Kim, S. (2012). A history of intelligence test interpretation. In D. P. Flanagan & P. L. Harrison (Eds.), *Contemporary intellectual assessment: Theories, tests, and issues* (pp. 56–70). Hoboken, NJ: Wiley.

Kaufman, A. S., & Kaufman, N. L. (2014). *Kaufman test of educational achievement* (3rd ed.). Bloomington, MN: NCS Pearson.

Kaufman, A. S., Raiford, S. E., & Coalson, D. L. (2016). *Intelligent testing with the WISC-V.* Hoboken, NJ: Wiley.

McCloskey, G., Hartz, E., & Slonim, J. (2016). Interpreting the WISC-V using George McCloskey's neuropsychological oriented process approach to psychoeducational evaluations. In A. S. Kaufman, S. E. Raiford, & D. L. Coalson (Authors), *Intelligent testing with the WISC-V* (pp. 493–548). Hoboken, NJ: Wiley.

Orsini, A., Pezzuti, L., & Hulbert, S. (2014). The unitary ability of IQ in the WISC-IV and its computation. *Personality and Individual Differences, 69,* 173–175.

Ortiz, S. O., Flanagan, D. P., & Alfonso, V. C. (2017). *The cross-battery assessment software system, version 2.0* (X-BASS v2.0). Hoboken, NJ: Wiley.

Pearson. (2009). *Wechsler individual achievement test* (3rd ed.) Bloomington, MN: Author.

Raiford, S. E., & Coalson, D. L. (2014). *Essentials of WPPSI-IV assessment.* Hoboken, NJ: Wiley.

Wechsler, D. (2014). *Wechsler Intelligence Scale for Children* (5th ed.). Bloomington, MN: Pearson.

Susie Engi Raiford
June 25, 2016

One

OVERVIEW OF THE WISC-V

W. Joel Schneider, Dawn P. Flanagan, and Vincent C. Alfonso

This book was written for assessment professionals who want to use the *Wechsler Intelligence Scale for Children-Fifth Edition* (WISC-V; Wechsler, 2014a) to help children and adolescents by understanding their cognitive strengths and weaknesses. Such a statement should be too obvious to mention, but it is not. Too often, in the public's eye, the purpose of intelligence tests is to assign labels to people, not to help them. Among some intellectuals, it is common to view intelligence tests as tools of oppression, designed to harm the least privileged and most vulnerable among us (Carroll, 1997).

Intelligence tests are—and have always been—powerful tools, and powerful tools can be used for good or for ill. People who are uneasy about the use of intelligence tests would likely be reassured if we clearly communicate to them what we actually do with intelligence tests: We use them as one tool among many to decide how best to help people. Professionals who use individually administered intelligence tests such as the WISC-V are not callous bureaucrats mechanically rendering judgments that decide the course of people's lives. Most of us sacrificed our twenties on the altar of graduate school. We did so gladly; becoming a member of the helping professions is a great honor. The thought of using intelligence tests to harm anyone, children in particular, is frightful.

Indeed, Alfred Binet and his colleagues developed modern intelligence tests because of their egalitarian ideals. They needed to find a fair and accurate method of identifying children and adolescents who needed additional help in school (Binet & Simon, 1916). This purpose continues to motivate most practitioners. Nevertheless, there is no denying that intelligence tests have been used to perpetrate injustice, particularly in their early history (Fancher, 1985). From the beginning, though, there were thoughtful and sophisticated theorists, practitioners,

1

and ordinary people who fought against these injustices (Lohman, 1997). Even the person who coined the term *intelligence quotient* or IQ, William Stern (1933), worked tirelessly to ensure that intelligence tests were used for preserving human dignity instead of degrading individuals:

> Under all conditions, human beings are and remain the centers of their own psychological life and their own worth. In other words, they remain persons, even when they are studied and treated from an external perspective with respect to others' goals.... Working "on" a human being must always entail working "for" a human being. (Trans. Lamiell, 2003, pp. 54–55)

FROM PREDICTION TO PREVENTION

Although it is true that intelligence tests are potent long-term predictors of a wide array of important life outcomes such as academic achievement, high school graduation, and income (Deary, Whiteman, Starr, Whalley, & Fox, 2004; Gottfredson, 1997), they do not speak with the authority of the white-robed Fates. Hardship is not inevitable, and success is never assured. Many people possess personal virtues that more than offset whatever weaknesses an IQ test might reveal. Some have liabilities that negate any intellectual advantages they might otherwise have enjoyed. Nevertheless, the forecast is still useful. The weather report is not always correct, but it helps us plan for the day.

DON'T FORGET

Performance on intelligence tests is a potent predictor of important life outcomes such as academic achievement, high school graduation, and income.

It is not difficult to identify struggling children and adolescents after they have already fallen behind in school—no IQ test is needed for that. What is difficult is to prevent problems before they occur. Intelligence or cognitive ability tests can help professionals prioritize scarce resources so that students most likely to fall behind are better able to keep up and succeed. As Kaufman (1979, p. 14) famously quipped, "Intelligence test scores should result ultimately in killing the prediction." That is, the proper role of cognitive ability tests is to predict problems that never happen—because skilled professionals, dedicated teachers, and loving parents make plans and labor long hours to prevent them.

Unfortunately, not all problems, such as traumatic brain injuries, can be foreseen. Cognitive ability tests are essential tools for evaluating the nature and severity of these injuries. Sometimes they are used to monitor the rate of an individual's recovery.

Even perfectly predicted problems cannot always be completely prevented. Much can be done to improve the lives of individuals with intellectual disabilities and learning disabilities, even if we cannot yet eliminate their cognitive deficits entirely (Patterson, Rapsey, & Glue, 2013). Intelligence tests help us identify children with intellectual disabilities and learning disabilities very early so that interventions can have maximal effect.

FROM EXPLANATION TO ENDURING EMPATHY

Alongside *prediction*, the second major function of intelligence tests is *explanation*. That is, intelligence tests play a role in informing comprehensive case conceptualizations, and thus are particularly useful when preventative efforts are not working. Understanding why a student is performing poorly in school despite the best efforts of all involved is often the first step toward finding a better approach. More than that, understanding a student's learning difficulties often results in greater empathy for him or her.

Many students who are performing poorly in school often work hard to avoid academic activities they find to be difficult and unpleasant, sometimes by making things difficult and unpleasant for the adults who are trying to help them. When parents and teachers understand why the tasks are difficult, they are likely to be more patient. It is for this reason that one of the most important goals of writing effective psychoeducational reports is to help foster in the reader an enduring sense of empathy for the student.

DON'T FORGET

An important goal of writing effective psychoeducational reports is to help foster in the reader an enduring sense of empathy for the student.

GENERAL TRENDS IN INTELLIGENCE TEST INTERPRETATION

Kamphaus and colleagues (1997, 2012) have outlined a number of long-term trends in how the use of cognitive ability tests has changed. Over the past 11 decades, there has been a shift away from the interpretation of a global IQ score toward the integrative understanding of how multiple factors of ability influence an individual's life. Multifactor tests are not exactly new, but recently developed tests are better grounded in strongly supported multifactor theories of cognitive abilities. Intuitively plausible, but haphazard and speculative interpretation systems are being replaced by systematic, empirically vetted, statistically sound approaches to interpretation. In this book, we strongly recommend one of these interpretive systems, the Cross-Battery Assessment approach (XBA; Flanagan, Ortiz, & Alfonso, 2013), which is closely aligned with the Cattell-Horn-Carroll Theory of Cognitive Abilities (CHC Theory; McGrew, 1997, 2005, 2009; Schneider & McGrew, 2012). (For a brief overview of CHC theory, including broad and narrow ability definitions, see Appendix A.)

DON'T FORGET
....

Appendix A includes a brief description of CHC theory, definitions of broad and narrow CHC abilities, and task examples of each narrow ability.

With each new edition, the WISC has become more amenable to the application of XBA and CHC Theory—changes we applaud! That said, progress is not always linear, and sometimes psychometric advances are dearly bought. There are subtests from previous editions of the WISC that sophisticated veteran users regret losing because they afforded opportunities to observe clinically rich samples of behavior. Thus, before talking about how the XBA approach can be applied to the WISC-V, we retrace our steps and perhaps recover some half-forgotten bits of wisdom from the creator of the original WISC, David Wechsler.

WHY THE HISTORY OF THE WECHSLER SCALES MATTERS

It is possible to administer the WISC-V competently without knowing much of anything about its history. Is it really necessary to become familiar with every twist and turn the evolution of the WISC has taken? Why not just study the most recent version?

The Wechsler scales are commercial products, and businesses respond to market demands. If practitioners are unaware of what made the original WISC great, they can clamor for changes that can inadvertently ruin the test. David Wechsler had a well-articulated vision for his instruments (Kaufman, 2009, pp. 29–54). Unless we come to know and appreciate what that vision was, the test's publishers will yield to pressures to give us more of what we think we want and less of what

David Wechsler thought we needed—to which, in our naiveté and ignorance, we will say, "Good riddance!"

For example, statistical training can sensitize us to the researcher's need for tests that cleanly measure unidimensional traits. From this perspective, the Wechsler scales are hopelessly messy. Why not make the Wechsler scales more like the relatively tidy tests from the Woodcock-Johnson cognitive batteries (e.g., *Woodcock-Johnson IV Tests of Cognitive Abilities* [WJ IV COG]; Schrank, McGrew, & Mather, 2014)? Because doing so would likely compromise what is special about the Wechsler scales, that they allow us to observe complex problem-solving processes as they unfold in real time. Unless we know more about what Wechsler was aiming for, we might not appreciate the fact that the "messiness" is a feature, not a bug. Wechsler did not create his tests to serve the needs of research. As he continually reminded Alan Kaufman, his former mentee, "First and foremost, the Wechsler scales are clinical tests—not psychometric tests but clinical tests" (Kaufman, 1994, p. xv).

With each revision of the WISC, *Wechsler Adult Intelligence Scale* (WAIS), and *Wechsler Preschool and Primary Scale of Intelligence* (WPPSI), old subtests are retired and new ones are added. The new developers of the Wechsler scales appear to be clearing away measures with clinical clutter to make room for tests that are more psychometrically sleek. There is a clear upside to this trend in that specific abilities are more easily isolated, but the downside is also very real. We are not making a plea for sloppy psychometrics, but for a diversity of options, including complex measures that allow for clinically rich observations. It is inevitable that Wechsler's tests should change with the times, but perhaps not too much, and not too soon. Likewise, it is probably better that the WJ tests stay true to Richard Woodcock's original vision; it is better for the field as a whole that we can choose among tests with complementary virtues.

Exposure to the history of the Wechsler scales not only broadens our knowledge of the tests, but often, in subtle ways, deepens our commitment to our field. When we learn about what mattered to David Wechsler as he constructed his tests, often we come to care about those things, too, to a degree that we did not before. Even learning about the weaknesses of the original tests is helpful. The missteps along the way as the tests evolved serve as cautionary tales, ultimately affirming what is most important to us as professionals.

DON'T FORGET

Exposure to the history of the Wechsler scales not only broadens our knowledge of the tests, but deepens our commitment to our field.

Sometimes simply learning about the humanizing details of important figures' lives changes our outlook on their work. For example, Alan Kaufman's (2009) moving tribute to his mentor reveals Wechsler to have been a kind, thoughtful person with a sometimes imposingly strong sense of personal dignity. He was passionate about his work, if somewhat out of step with the times; as they worked to revise the WISC in the early 1970s, he bristled at Kaufman's suggestion that the Comprehension item "Why should women and children be saved first in a shipwreck?" might be perceived as sexist. Kaufman was taken aback at the inordinate intensity of Wechsler's instant response. Flushed with emotion, Wechsler objected, "Chivalry may be dying! Chivalry may be dead! But it will not die on the WISC!" Kaufman was afraid he had crossed a line he did not know was there.

In time, though, Wechsler relented. Chivalry did not die, but it *was* retired from the WISC-R. This anecdote says little about the theorist, but it says something about the complexity of the man. From where did this passion for a test item about protecting women and children in times of crisis come? Probably it is a manifestation of his upbringing, his experiences, and his personality as a whole. It is interesting to note, though, that his first book, *The Range of Human Capacities*, published in 1935, was dedicated to "the undying memory of Florence Felske," a commercial artist who in 1934, just three weeks after becoming David Wechsler's bride, was killed in a vehicular accident (Carson, 1999).

Alfred Binet and the "First" Intelligence Tests

The fastest way to disabuse oneself of the false notion that Binet invented the first intelligence test is to read the works of Binet himself. He and his colleagues presented several attempts by previous scholars to measure intelligence and to identify children with intellectual disabilities (Binet & Simon, 1916, pp. 15–36). Indeed, it is clear that Binet's methods include many borrowings from these earlier scholars, including exact copies of specific test items. Though intelligence tests have many historical anticipations, stretching back to antiquity (Deary, 2000, p. 34), the tests designed by Binet and colleagues were superior to earlier tests along many dimensions. For example:

1. The procedures were standardized.
2. Test items were vetted by thousands of clinicians and refined over multiple editions.
3. The test scores were given proper norms.
4. The test scores were validated by correlations with multiple criteria and life outcomes (e.g., health, wealth, degrees, and grades).

Before Binet, it was common for doctors and other specialists to interview individuals suspected of having low intelligence, asking them to perform various tasks and answer test-like questions. The diagnosis of the condition now termed *intellectual disability* was then made based mostly on the holistic judgment of the interviewer. Binet was never against holistic judgment, just holistic judgment that was uninformed by high-quality data. The value of high-quality norms was not self-evident at the time; Binet and Simon (1905, 1916) had to write several persuasive papers and book chapters about the dangers of nonstandard procedures and the benefits of carefully compiled national norms. Although the standardization procedures used to create the norms for the Binet-Simon would be inadequate by today's standards, they were reasonably good—and vastly superior to no norms at all.

From Mental Ages to Intelligence Quotients to Standard Scores

If Binet's tests were good, why did Wechsler need to improve upon them? There were certain psychometric problems with Binet's idea of closely aligning test scores with the age of the child. Almost anyone can immediately understand what it means when we say that an 8-year-old child obtained a test score equal to that of the average 6-year-old—the child is 2 years behind the average. What is not immediately apparent is how unusual this is. No matter—norms can be compiled. Maybe 5% of 8-year-olds perform at this level or lower. Unfortunately, being 2 years behind does not mean the same thing, nor is it equally common at every age. Separate tables would need to be compiled for each age group. At some point there are too many tables. Some simplification is necessary to make the meaning of scores consistent.

CAUTION
. . . .

Being 2 years behind in ability does not mean the same thing at every age, nor is it equally common at every age.

William Stern (1914, p. 42) addressed this problem by inventing the *intelligence quotient* (IQ), which originally was a fractional quantity calculated like so:

$$IQ = \frac{Mental\,Age}{Chronological\,Age}$$

Later, this ratio was multiplied by 100 and rounded to the nearest integer. A child who is one year behind at age 4, two years behind at age 8, and three years at age 12 would at every age obtain an IQ of 75. A simple interpretation of this kind of IQ is that the mental capacities of a child with an IQ of 75 is advancing only three-quarters as fast as those of the average child. Stern knew that this was not strictly true, but believed that the IQ metric was a useful way of thinking about intellectual level.

The ratio of mental age to chronological age was more stable than Binet's measure of the difference of those values. However, the variability of intelligence quotients was not the same at all age levels (Wechsler, 1944, p. 25). For example, different percentages of children had IQs of 75 at different ages. Furthermore, the whole idea of *mental age* breaks down when intellectual growth tends to level off as adolescents approach adulthood. In late adulthood, intellectual decline is typical. An 80-year-old individual who scores as well as the average 40-year-old has performed better than the average 80-year-old. However, if the original IQ formula were mindlessly applied, this would result in a score of 50, which is absurd. Early test developers knew this and therefore applied other formulas for adults (e.g., comparing all adults to 14-year-olds), none of which were particularly satisfactory.

To address these problems, Wechsler reconceptualized *mental age* not as an age per se but as a score (i.e., the obtained score). From here, *chronological age* was also translated into a score (i.e., the expected mean score for a given age). Thus, the reconceptualized IQ:

$$IQ = 100 \times \frac{Obtained\ Score}{Mean\ Score}$$

Comparing obtained scores to mean scores like this is something of an improvement over the traditional IQ, especially for adults. Still, the problem with this method is that different score ratios would not always have the same meaning from test to test and from age to age. After a slight detour using a quirky type of deviation score, the Wechsler IQ scores eventually were expressed as *standard scores* instead of traditional intelligence quotients (Wechsler, 1958, pp. 241–242). Wechsler did not invent standard scores, but he adeptly adapted them for his tests and promoted their use.

Recall that Binet used the difference between mental age and chronological age. This tells us how far from the average a child performed. However, this distance does not have a consistent meaning. A *standard score*, in effect, puts this difference in the numerator and then gives it standardized meaning by dividing by the standard deviation, a measure of the typical distance a score is from the mean:

$$\frac{Deviation\ from\ the\ Mean}{Typical\ Deviation\ from\ the\ Mean}$$

More precisely,

$$\text{Standard Score} = \frac{\text{Obtained Score} - \text{Mean Score}}{\text{Standard Deviation}} \times 15 + 100$$

In this way, the Wechsler scales created intelligence scores that have a consistent meaning for all ages: They are standardized differences from the mean obtained by same-age peers. Wechsler Verbal IQ, Performance IQ, and Full Scale IQ were scaled to have means of 100 and standard deviations of 15 so that they would resemble traditional IQs. The Wechsler subtests are also standardized, but have means of 10 and standard deviations of 3.

DON'T FORGET

Standard intelligence scores are standardized differences from the mean obtained by same-age peers.

General Intelligence ≠ g

Binet invented a single-score test, but did not believe in general intelligence. Wechsler believed in general intelligence, but made multidimensional tests. What is going on here?

These scholars had complex views about intelligence and explicitly denied that their tests aligned perfectly with their respective definitions of intelligence (Wechsler, 1958, pp. 14–15). In fact, Binet denied that his tests measured intelligence at all! For him, intelligence was simply not amenable to measurement with the kinds of tests he and his colleagues developed (Binet & Simon, 1916):

> This scale properly speaking does not permit the measure of the intelligence, because intellectual qualities are not superposable, and therefore cannot be measured as linear surfaces are measured, but are on the contrary, a classification, a hierarchy among diverse intelligences; and for the necessities of practice this classification is equivalent to a measure. (p. 40)

Binet had a very particular purpose for his test, and the mental age concept accomplished its task reasonably well. When the goal is to identify children with intellectual disabilities quickly, a summary score was all that was needed.

In contrast, Wechsler wanted his instrument to be capable of revealing highly nuanced information about how people use their intellect (indeed, their whole personalities) to solve problems (Kaufman, 1994, pp. ix–xv). Wechsler made his scales to measure what he called *general intelligence*. Although many scholars use this term interchangeably with the first factor that emerges in a factor analysis of cognitive tests (i.e., Spearman's *g*), Wechsler did not. Although he admired Spearman's (1904, 1927) theories about the general factor of intelligence, Wechsler (1944) did not equate general intelligence with Spearman's *g*:

> We may say that "g" is a psychomathematical quantity which measures the mind's capacity to do intellectual work. Everybody will agree that the capacity to do intellectual work is a necessary and important sign of general intelligence. The question is whether it is the only important or paramount factor. In this writer's opinion it is not. (p. 8)

Truth be told, Spearman did not equate *g* with intelligence either (Spearman, 1927, pp. 75–76), though on this topic he was sometimes coy with his readers.

What did Wechsler mean when he used the term *general intelligence*? Certainly it included intellectual ability, but he asserted that it "must be regarded as a manifestation of the personality as a whole" (Wechsler, 1950, p. 83). Although general intelligence consists of many parts, it is the configuration of those parts that determines an individual's overall capacity "to act purposefully, to think rationally, and to deal effectively with [one's] environment" (Wechsler, 1958, p. 7). What were those parts? Wechsler did not claim to know precisely.

> We do not know what the ultimate nature of the "stuff" which constitutes intelligence but … we know it by the "things" it enables us to do—such as making appropriate associations between events, drawing correct inferences from propositions, understanding the meaning of words, solving mathematical problems or building bridges. (pp. 7–8)

To Wechsler, intelligence encompassed numerous primary mental abilities (as tentatively revealed by factor analysis) and also many non-intellective traits and abilities, including drive, persistence, self-control, and social adaptation (Wechsler, 1950, 1958, p. 13). These more subtle aspects of intelligence tend to be difficult to detect with factor analysis, but are nevertheless observable during testing and in other settings. It was one of Wechsler's great regrets that he never succeeded in developing good measures of these non-intellective factors of intelligence, despite several attempts and considerable effort (Tulsky, Saklofske, & Zhu, 2003).

Wechsler's tests yield many different kinds of scores, all of which could be considered carefully, but ultimately he wanted the test to be an index of the individual's global capacity:

> [The diverse tasks in intelligence tests] are only means to an end. Their object is not to test a person's memory, judgment or reasoning ability, but to measure something which it is hoped will emerge from the sum total of the subject's performance, namely, his general intelligence. (Wechsler, 1958, p. 9)

We begin with a series of aptitude measures, but somehow end up with an IQ. How is this possible? The suggested answer is that in the process we are using measures of ability primarily as a tool; that is, not as an end in itself but as a means for discovering something more fundamental. Then, when an examiner employs an arithmetic or a vocabulary test as part of an intelligence scale, the object of the examiner is not to discover the examinee's aptitude for arithmetic or extent of his word knowledge, although these are inevitably involved, but his capacity to function in overall areas that are assumed to require intelligence:

> While intellective abilities can be shown to contain several independent factors, intelligence cannot be so broken up. Hence, no amount of refinement of tests or addition of factors will account for the total variance of an intelligence test battery, because the variance in intelligence test performance is due not only to the direct contributions of the factors themselves but also to their collective behavior or integration. (Wechsler, 1958, p. 23)

Wechsler's Subtests

To say that David Wechsler did not invent new tests but merely adapted them is to fail to discern his genius. There were hundreds of tests available when he was developing his first battery, the Wechsler-Bellevue. It was not dumb luck that the Wechsler scales displaced the Stanford-Binet to become the dominant clinical measure of intelligence and retain that position for decades.

Wechsler believed that his first intelligence test was successful because it relied so heavily on the experience of others (Wechsler, 1944, p. 76). He found that it was nearly impossible to know whether a new test format or even a particular test item was going to be a good indicator of intelligence until it had been tried out clinically and evaluated statistically. As an example, he tells how when trying out items for the Information subtest, no one could predict which of two very similar items would be better: "How many pints make a quart?" or "How many feet make a yard?" The former item turned out to distinguish reliably among people at the low end of intelligence. The latter was practically worthless. "Certainly no one would have predicted this result in advance. Now that we have discovered it, we must frankly admit we can offer no good reason for the fact" (p. 75). This is not to say that good tests and good items are discovered purely by trial and error. Each test was carefully selected and each item was thoroughly scrutinized. Nevertheless, there are limits to how well one can reason one's way toward constructing a good test. In the end, each subtest had to correlate highly with established tests of intelligence and, more important, had to correlate with subjective ratings of intelligence by informed raters such as teachers, army officers, and business executives. Thus, it was something akin to natural selection—letting the data decide which items should live or die—that let the Wechsler scales climb Mount Improbable to become the most successful intelligence tests in history. If Wechsler had invented all of his tests from scratch, there would not have been enough time and resources to develop them properly, and they would most likely have failed to catch on, like so many other intelligence tests from his era that are now mostly forgotten.

Yerkes Point Scales

Binet's tests are delicious Sloppy Joes with diverse ingredients chopped up and thrown together. Wechsler's tests are well-structured sandwiches; the flavors blend nicely, but each layer is distinct.

In Binet-style tests, the diverse items are sequenced by difficulty, and item formats change frequently. Thus, if an individual answers a question incorrectly, it is difficult to know whether it was the item or the type of task that was too challenging for that individual. In contrast, Wechsler subtests generally hold the item format constant, ordering items from easy to difficult. This means that the diversity of tasks is reduced, but it allows clinicians to see which types of tasks are easy and which tasks are difficult for an individual, allowing clinicians to produce a more differentiated description of his or her intelligence.

This approach to constructing homogeneous subtests, termed *point scales*, was developed by Yerkes (1915) and then used to create new intelligence tests for the U.S. Army during World War I. One of these tests, the Army Alpha, was a battery of verbal tests, whereas the Army Beta was a battery of nonverbal performance tests. If this division between verbal and performance tests sounds familiar, you might be interested to know that on Yerkes's team of young psychologists was one David Wechsler.

Yerkes's use of diverse point scales with homogeneous items is now the dominant method of measuring intelligence. In a thoughtful essay, Lohman (1997) acknowledges that Yerkes's approach is a major advance, but one that seduces us into believing that because we control the format of the test we know what it measures. Wechsler (1958) was not fooled by this illusion. For him, the item content was not particularly important. Rather, what mattered was whether the individual responded to the item in a manner that was intelligent.

DON'T FORGET

For David Wechsler item content was not particularly important; what mattered was whether the individual responded to the item in a manner that was intelligent.

Previous Editions of the WISC

It is important to know the changes in previous editions of the WISC because it is common to see old scores from previous evaluations. Furthermore, research on previous editions of the WISC does not necessarily generalize to the newer editions if the scores have radically changed in their content (e.g., the WISC-III Perceptual Organization Index [POI] and the WISC-IV Perceptual Reasoning Index [PRI] only have Block Design in common). In Table 1.1, it is easy to see that the composition of the WISC was quite stable in the first three editions. The WISC-III retained the Verbal and Performance IQ, but introduced the factor index scores that were more psychometrically pure. The VIQ and PIQ were dropped on the WISC-IV, along with three of David Wechsler's subtests (Picture Arrangement, Object Assembly, and Mazes). Five new subtests were added to help refine and update the WISC-IV factor index scores.

DESCRIPTION OF THE WISC-V

Several issues prompted the revision of the WISC-IV. These issues are detailed clearly in the *WISC-V Technical and Interpretive Manual* (Wechsler, 2014b). Table 1.2 provides general information about the WISC-V, and Rapid Reference 1.1 lists the most salient changes from the WISC-IV to the WISC-V.

Table 1.1 Subtest Structure of Previous Editions of the WISC

	WISC/R/III			WISC-III					WISC-IV			
	FS	VIQ	PIQ	VC	PO	FD	PS	FS	VC	PR	WM	PS
Information	•	•		•				•	•			
Similarities	•	•		•				•	•			
Vocabulary	•	•		•				•	•			
Comprehension	•	•		•					o			
Word Reasoning									o			
Arithmetic	•	•				•					o	
Digit Span		o				•		•			•	
Letter-Number Sequencing								•			•	
Matrix Reasoning								•		•		
Picture Concepts								•		•		
Picture Completion	•		•		•					o		
Block Design	•		•		•			•		•		
Picture Arrangement	•		•		•							
Object Assembly	•		•		•							
Mazes			o		o							
Coding	•		•				•	•				•
Symbol Search							•	•				•
Cancellation												o

Note: o = Supplementary or conceptually related test. FS = Full Scale IQ; VIQ = Verbal IQ; PIQ = Performance IQ; VC = Verbal Comprehension; PO = Perceptual Organization; FD = Freedom From Distractibility; PS = Processing Speed; PR = Perceptual Reasoning; WM = Working Memory.

Table 1.2 The WISC-V At A Glance

GENERAL INFORMATION

Author:	David Wechsler (1896–1981)
Publication Date(s):	1949, 1974, 1991, 2003, 2014
Age Range:	6:0 to 16:11years
Administration Time:	48 to 65 minutes

GENERAL INFORMATION

Qualification of Examiners:	Graduate- or professional-level training in psychological assessment
Publisher:	Pearson
	Ordering Department
	P.O. Box 599700
	San Antonio, TX 78259
	800-629-7271
	http://www.pearsonclinical.com

Price   **WISC-V™ Basic Kit**

Includes Administration and Scoring Manual, Technical and Interpretive Manual, Stimulus Books 1-3, Record Forms (pkg. of 25), Response Booklets #1 (pkg of 25), Response Booklets #2 (pkg of 25), Symbol Search Scoring Key, Coding Scoring Key, Cancellation Scoring Template, and Wechsler Standard Block Design Set

$1,173.60 (in box) $1,235.10 (in soft bag) $1,245.35 (in hard case)

WISC-V™ Administration and Scoring Manual with Supplement	$220.35
WISC-V™ Q-Global Score Report	$2.00
WISC-V™ Q-Global Interpretive Report	$3.50
WISC-V™ Scoring with Score Report 1-Year Subscription	$35.00
WISC-V™ Scoring with Score Report 3-Year Subscription	$99.00
WISC-V™ Scoring with Score Report 5-Year Subscription	$149.00
WISC-V™ Scoring with Interpretive Report 1-Year Subscription	$45.00
WISC-V™ Scoring with Interpretive Report 3-Year Subscription	$129.00
WISC-V™ Scoring with Interpretive Report 5-Year Subscription	$199.00

COMPOSITE MEASURE INFORMATION

Global Ability:	Full Scale IQ (FSIQ)
	General Ability Index (GAI)
	Nonverbal Index (NVI)
Lower-Order Composites:	Verbal Comprehension Index (VCI)
	Visual Spatial Index (VSI)
	Fluid Reasoning Index (FRI)
	Working Memory Index (WMI)
	Processing Speed Index (PSI)
	Cognitive Proficiency Index (CPI)
	Quantitative Reasoning Index (QRI)

(continued)

(continued)

COMPOSITE MEASURE INFORMATION

	Auditory Working Memory Index (AWMI)
	Naming Speed Index (NSI)
	Symbol Translation Index (STI)
	Storage and Retrieval Index (SRI)
Number of Subtests	21

SCORE INFORMATION

Available Scores	Standard
	Scaled
	Percentile
	Age Equivalent
	Contrast

Range of Standard Scores for Global Ability Composites 40–160 (ages 6:0 to 16:11 years)

NORMING INFORMATION

Normative Sample Size	2,200
Sample Collection Dates	April 2013–March 2014
Average Number per Age Interval	200
Age Blocks in Norm Table	4 months (ages 6:0 to 16:11 years)
Demographic Variables:	Age
	Gender (male, female)
	Geographic region (four regions)
	Race/ethnicity (White; African American; Hispanic; Asian; other)
	Socioeconomic status (parental education)
Types of Validity Evidence in Test Manual	Test content
	Response processes
	Internal structure
	Relationships with other variables
	Consequences of testing

≡ *Rapid Reference 1.1*

. . . .

Changes From the WISC-IV to the WISC-V

- Addition of eight new subtests: Visual Puzzles, Figure Weights, Picture Span, Naming Speed Literacy, Naming Speed Quantity, Immediate Symbol Translation, Delayed Symbol Translation, and Recognition Symbol Translation

- Addition of Digit Span Sequencing to the Digit Span Subtest
- Word Reasoning and Picture Completion Subtests from the WISC-IV were not included in the WISC-V
- Q-interactive and Q-global online administration, scoring, and reporting options available
- Incorporated new research on intelligence, neurodevelopment, cognitive neuroscience, cognitive development, and processes important to learning
- Modified and new items added to subtests
- Scoring criteria for items revised for subtests
- Items added to improve floors and ceilings of subtests
- Provides standard scores for certain subtests (e.g., Naming Speed Literacy)
- No longer refers to subtests using the terms *supplemental* and *core*
- Substitution only permitted for FSIQ
- Provides global composite score options (NVI and GAI) in addition to the FSIQ
- PRI replaced by the VSI and the FRI
- Updated theoretical foundations
- Increased developmental appropriateness (instructions modified; teaching, sample, and/or practice items for each subtest)
- Shorter testing time to derive the FSIQ
- Replaced all WISC-IV items that were originally published on the WISC, WISC-R, or WISC-III
- More explicit and simple administration and scoring instructions to increase user-friendliness
- Substantially reduced discontinue rules
- Expanded significance level options for critical values: .01, .05, .10, .15
- Measures of processing speed modified
- Artwork updated to be more current, attractive, and engaging to children
- Estimate of overall ability (i.e., either the FSIQ or the mean primary index score [MIS]) can be used to evaluate strengths and weaknesses across primary index scores
- Addition of the NVI to provide more information about children with English as a second language and children with expressive language problems
- Expanded number of process scores
- Increased the number of special group studies during standardization to enhance clinical utility

Source: Information in this table was derived, in part, from the *WISC-V Technical and Interpretive Manual* (Wechsler, 2014b).

Table 1.3. New Subtests on the WISC-V

Index	Subtest
Visual Spatial	Visual Puzzles
Fluid Reasoning	Figure Weights
Working Memory	Picture Span
Naming Speed	Naming Speed Literacy
	Naming Speed Quantity
Symbol Translation	Immediate Symbol Translation
	Delayed Symbol Translation
	Recognition Symbol Translation

Note: The Digit Span subtest now includes Digit Span Sequencing.

Although users of the WISC-V will recognize many traditional WISC subtests on this latest edition of the Wechsler scales, users will also find eight new ones (see Table 1.3). The WISC-V has 21 subtests (see Table 1.4 for subtest descriptions) and 14 composites, including the FSIQ (see Figure 1.1 for composition of FSIQ) and five Primary Index Scales (see Figure 1.2), as well as five Ancillary Index Scales and three Complementary Index Scales (see Figure 1.3).

Table 1.4 Descriptions of WISC-V Subtests

Subtest	Description
1. Block Design (BD)*	The examinee is required to replicate a set of modeled and/or printed two-dimensional geometric patterns using red-and-white blocks within a specified time limit.
2. Similarities (SI)*	The examinee is required to describe how two words that represent common objects or concepts are similar.
3. Matrix Reasoning (MR)*	The examinee is required to complete the missing portion of a picture matrix or series by selecting one of five response options.
4. Digit Span (DS)*	On Digit Span Forward, the examinee is required to repeat numbers verbatim as stated by the examiner. On Digit Span Backward, the examinee is required to repeat numbers in the reverse order as stated by the examiner. On Digit Span Sequencing, the examinee is required to repeat numbers in ascending order as stated by the examiner.

Subtest	Description
5. Coding (CD)*	The examinee is required to copy symbols that are paired with either geometric shapes or numbers using a key within a specified time limit.
6. Vocabulary (VC)*	The examinee is required to name pictures or provide definitions for words.
7. Figure Weights (FW)*	The examinee is required to select a response option that will keep a scale with missing weights balanced within a specified time limit.
8. Visual Puzzles (VP)	The examinee is required to select three response options that combine to recreate a completed puzzle within a specified time limit.
9. Picture Span (PS)	The examinee is shown one or more pictures on a stimulus page and then required to select those pictures (in sequential order if possible) from a response page.
10. Symbol Search (SS)	The examinee is required to scan a search group and indicate the presence or absence of a target symbol(s) within a specified time limit.
11. Information (IN)	The examinee is required to answer questions that address a wide range of general-knowledge topics.
12. Picture Concepts (PC)	The examinee is required to choose one picture per row, from two or three rows of pictures presented, to form a group with a common characteristic.
13. Letter-Number Sequencing (LN)	The examinee is read a number and letter sequence and is required to recall numbers in ascending order and letters in alphabetical order.
14. Cancellation (CA)	The examinee is required to scan both a random and a nonrandom arrangement of pictures and mark target pictures within a specified time limit.
15. *Naming Speed Literacy (NSL)*	The examinee is shown arrays of objects of various colors, then various colors and sizes, or of letters and numbers and is required to name them as quickly as possible.
16. *Naming Speed Quantity (NSQ)*	The examinee is shown pictures of boxes and is required to name the number of squares within each box.
17. *Immediate Symbol Translation (IST)*	The examinee is taught visual-verbal pairs and then is required to translate strings of symbols into sentences or phrases.
18. Comprehension (CO)	The examinee is required to answer a series of questions based on his or her understanding of general principles and social situations.

(continued)

(continued)

Subtest	Description
19. Arithmetic (AR)	The examinee is required to mentally solve a variety of orally or visually presented arithmetic problems within a specified time limit.
20. *Delayed Symbol Translation (DST)*	The examinee is required to translate strings of symbols learned from the Immediate Symbol Translation subset into sentences or phrases.
21. *Recognition Symbol Translation (RST)*	The examinee is shown a symbol learned from the Immediate Symbol Translation subtest and is required to select the correct translation from a list of verbally presented response options.

Note: FSIQ subtests are denoted with an asterisk, primary subtests are printed in bold, secondary subtests appear in regular font, and complementary subtests appear in italics.

Source: Wechsler Intelligence Scale for Children-Fifth Edition (WISC-V). Copyright © 2014 NCS Pearson, Inc. Reproduced with permission. All rights reserved.

"Wechsler Intelligence Scale for Children" and *"WISC"* are trademarks, in the United States and/or other countries, of Pearson Education, Inc. or its affiliates(s).

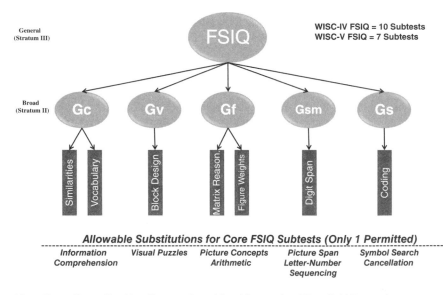

Note: Gc = Crystallized Intelligence; Gv = Visual Processing; Gf = Fluid Reasoning; Gsm = Short-Term Memory; Gs = Processing Speed.

Figure 1.1 Composition of the WISC-V Full Scale IQ

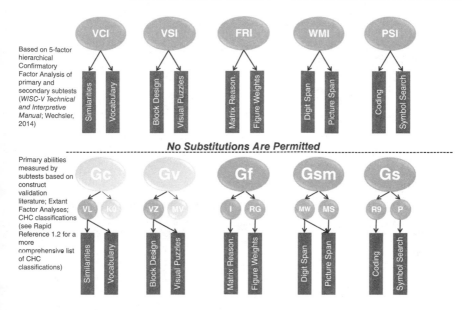

Based on 5-factor hierarchical Confirmatory Factor Analysis of primary and secondary subtests (*WISC-V Technical and Interpretive Manual*; Wechsler, 2014)

Primary abilities measured by subtests based on construct validation literature; Extant Factor Analyses; CHC classifications (see Rapid Reference 1.2 for a more comprehensive list of CHC classifications)

Note: VL = Lexical Knowledge; K0 = General (Verbal) Information; VZ = Visualization; MV = Visual Memory; I = Induction; RG = General Sequential Reasoning; MW = Working Memory Capacity; MS = Memory Span; R9 = Rate of Test-taking; P = Perceptual Speed.

Figure 1.2 WISC-V Primary Index Scales

Rapid Reference 1.2 includes the CHC broad ability classifications of the WISC-V according to multiple data sources. The first column shows the broad CHC classifications provided by the publishing company. All classifications based on other data sources listed in this rapid reference are highly consistent with the publisher's classifications. Differences across data sources appear to be related to two main questions: (1) Are Gf and Gv separate factors on the WISC-V?, and (2) What does Arithmetic measure? All the data sources listed in Rapid Reference 1.2 are based on within-battery factor analyses (excluding the complementary subtests), which may obscure information about the breadth of cognitive abilities measured by the WISC-V battery as well as its individual subtests (Woodcock, 1990). The classifications in the last column are based on a review of cross-battery factor analyses that included Wechsler subtests. Theory driven, cross-battery factor analyses are preferable because they assist in clarifying the range of abilities measured by batteries and individual subtests (Reynolds, Keith, Flanagan, & Alfonso, 2013; Woodcock). Therefore, the broad ability classifications reported in the last column of this rapid reference are the ones that are used throughout this book and in the Cross-Battery Assessment Software System (X-BASS v2.0; Ortiz, Flanagan, & Alfonso, 2017).

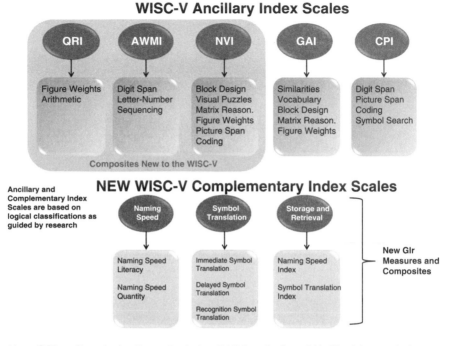

Note: QRI = Quantitative Reasoning Index; AWMI = Auditory Working Memory Index; NVI = Nonverbal Index; GAI = General Ability Index; CPI = Cognitive Processing Index; Glr = Long-Term Storage and Retrieval.

Figure 1.3   WISC-V Ancillary and Complementary Index Scales

Although broad CHC classifications provide information related to the cognitive abilities measured by the WISC-V subtests, they do not capture all the processes any given individual uses when answering questions and solving problems. Therefore, in addition to broad CHC classifications of subtests, Rapid Reference 1.3 provides narrow CHC classifications as well as information about other abilities and processes that may be involved in completing each subtest. Additionally, background and environmental factors that may facilitate or inhibit performance on a subtest are included in this rapid reference. The type of information included in this rapid reference is often used to generate hypotheses regarding why certain subtests differ significantly from one another. For example, it may not be expected that the Information and Comprehension subtests would differ significantly from one another because both measure Crystallized Intelligence (Gc) at the broad ability level and General (Verbal) Knowledge (K0) at the narrow ability level. Also, these subtests are highly correlated. Therefore, when they do

Rapid Reference 1.2

Broad CHC Classifications of WISC-V Subtests According to Various Data Sources

			Data Source			
Subtest	Wechsler (2014b)	Schneider (this chapter)	Sattler, Dumont, & Coalson (2016)	Canivez, Watkins, & Dombrowski (2016)	Reynolds & Keith (2016)	Ortiz, Flanagan, & Alfonso (2017)
Similarities	Gc	Gc	Gc	Gc	Gc	Gc
Vocabulary	Gc	Gc	Gc	Gc	Gc	Gc
Information	Gc	Gc	Gc	Gc	Gc	Gc
Comprehension	Gc	Gc	Gc	Gc	Gc	Gc
Block Design	Gv	Gv	Gv, Gf	Gv, Gf	Gv	Gv
Visual Puzzle	Gv	Gv	Gv, Gf	Gv, Gf	Gv	Gv
Matrix Reasoning	Gf	Gf, Gv	Gv, Gf	Gv, Gf	Gf	Gf
Picture Concepts	Gf	Gc/Gv	Gc, Gv, Gf	Gv, Gf	Gf	Gf
Figure Weights	Gf	Gf	Gv, Gf	Gv, Gf	Gf	Gf
Arithmetic	Gf, Gsm, Gc	Gsm, Gf, Gc	Gsm, Gc	Gsm	Gsm (g)*	Gsm, Gq
Digit Span	Gsm	Gsm	Gsm	Gsm	Gsm	Gsm
Picture Span	Gsm	Gsm	Gsm	Gsm	Gsm	Gsm
Letter-Number Sequencing	Gsm	Gsm	Gsm	Gsm	Gsm	Gsm
Coding	Gs	Gs	Gs	Gs	Gs	Gs
Symbol Search	Gs	Gs	Gs	Gs	Gs	Gs
Cancellation	Gs	Gs	Gs	Gs	Gs	Gs

*Arithmetic was primarily a direct indicator of g.

Note: Gf = Fluid Reasoning; Gq = Quantitative Knowledge; Gc = Crystallized Intelligence; Gsm = Short-Term Memory;
Gv = Visual Processing; Gs = Processing Speed.

differ unexpectedly, the information in the second and third columns of Rapid Reference 1.3 may assist the practitioner in understanding the difference. For instance, when Information is significantly higher than Comprehension, it may suggest that the individual's fund of knowledge is better developed than his or her social judgment and practical reasoning (Sattler, Dumont, & Coalson, 2016). In addition to the information in Rapid Reference 1.3, Chapters 4 and 6 provide information to assist in understanding unexpected variation in performance.

≡ Rapid Reference 1.3

Suggested Abilities and Processes Measured by WISC-V Subtests and Possible Influences on Subtest Performance

WISC-V Subtest	CHC Broad and Narrow Abilities Measured	Other Possible Abilities and Processes Measured	Possible Influences on Subtest Performance[a]
Similarities	Crystallized Intelligence (Gc) *Lexical Knowledge (VL)* Fluid Reasoning (Gf) *Induction (I)*	Language development Abstract reasoning Associative and categorical thinking Auditory comprehension Cognitive flexibility Concept formation Long-term memory Verbal comprehension Verbal expression Ability to separate essential from nonessential details Receptive/expressive language	Exposure to early education and quality of instruction Cultural opportunities Stimulating language environment in the early years Exposure to literacy Auditory acuity
Vocabulary	Crystallized Knowledge (Gc) *Lexical Knowledge (VL)*	Language development Fund of knowledge Learning ability Long-term memory Verbal comprehension Verbal concept formation Verbal fluency Expressive/receptive language	Exposure to early education and quality of instruction Cultural opportunities Stimulating language environment in the early years Exposure to literacy Intellectual curiosity Auditory acuity

WISC-V Subtest	CHC Broad and Narrow Abilities Measured	Other Possible Abilities and Processes Measured	Possible Influences on Subtest Performance[a]
Information	Crystallized Intelligence (Gc) *General (Verbal) Information (K0)*	Long-term memory Verbal comprehension Receptive/expressive language	Exposure to early education and quality of instruction Cultural opportunities Stimulating language environment in the early years Alertness to environment Intellectual curiosity Auditory acuity
Comprehension	Crystallized Intelligence (Gc) *General Information (K0)*	Language development Long-term memory Social judgment Common sense Logical reasoning Knowledge of societal and cultural mores Moral and ethical judgment Verbal comprehension Expression/receptive language Verbal reasoning and conceptualization	Exposure to early education and quality of instruction Cultural opportunities Stimulating language environment in the early years Development of conscience or moral sense Alertness to environment Auditory acuity
Block Design	Visual Processing (Gv) *Visualization (Vz)*	Ability to learn Nonverbal concept formation Visual-perceptual reasoning Visual-perceptual discrimination Visual-perceptual organization Simultaneous processing Visual-motor coordination Analysis and synthesis Speed of mental and visual-motor processing Planning ability Attention and concentration	Ability to work under time pressure Visual acuity Flexibility and trial and error learning Motivation, persistence, and effort Experience with puzzles and construction toys

(continued)

(continued)

WISC-V Subtest	CHC Broad and Narrow Abilities Measured	Other Possible Abilities and Processes Measured	Possible Influences on Subtest Performance[a]
Visual Puzzles	Visual Processing (Gv) *Visualization (Vz)*	Integration and synthesis of part-whole relationships Visual acuity Visual working memory Visual-perceptual discrimination Attention and concentration	Motivation, persistence, and effort Exposure to puzzles and construction toys Ability to work under time pressure Visual acuity
Matrix Reasoning	Fluid Reasoning (Gf) *Induction (I)*	Visual processing Classification ability Knowledge of part-whole relationships Simultaneous processing Spatial ability Visual-perceptual reasoning, discrimination, and organization Attention and concentration	Visual acuity Motivation, persistence, and effort
Figure Weights	Fluid Reasoning (Gf) *General Sequential Reasoning (RG) Quantitative Reasoning (RQ)*	Induction Working memory Visual processing Attention and concentration	Educational history and exposure to early number concepts and skills Visual acuity Motivation, persistence, and effort Ability to work under time pressure
Picture Concepts	Fluid Reasoning (Gf) *Induction (I)*	General information Lexical knowledge Conceptual thinking Visual-perceptual discrimination and reasoning Ability to separate essential from nonessential details	Cultural opportunities Stimulating language environment in the early years Quality of early education Motivation, persistence, and effort Visual acuity

WISC-V Subtest	CHC Broad and Narrow Abilities Measured	Other Possible Abilities and Processes Measured	Possible Influences on Subtest Performance[a]
Arithmetic	Working Memory (Gsm) *Working Memory Capacity (MW)* Quantitative Knowledge (Gq) *Math Achievement (A3)*	Applied computational ability Long-term memory Numerical reasoning ability Attention and concentration	Early exposure to numbers Quality of early instruction Auditory acuity Capacity to self-monitor
Digit Span	Working Memory (Gsm) *Memory Span (MS)* *Working Memory Capacity (MW)*	Auditory discrimination Auditory sequential processing Numerical ability Auditory rehearsal Mental manipulation Temporary storage Rote learning Attention and concentration	Auditory acuity Capacity to self-monitor Use of encoding and rehearsal strategies
Picture Span	Working Memory (Gsm) *Memory Span (MS)*	Visual working memory Visual sequential processing Rote learning Attention and concentration	Visual acuity Capacity to self-monitor Use of encoding and rehearsal strategies
Letter-Number Sequencing	Working Memory (Gsm) *Working Memory Capacity (MW)*	Memory span Auditory discrimination Rote learning Auditory sequential processing Mental manipulation Numerical ability Attention and concentration	Auditory acuity Capacity to self-monitor Use of encoding and rehearsal strategies

(continued)

(continued)

WISC-V Subtest	CHC Broad and Narrow Abilities Measured	Other Possible Abilities and Processes Measured	Possible Influences on Subtest Performance[a]
Coding	Processing Speed (Gs) *Rate of Test Taking (R9)*	Attention and concentration Associative memory Cognitive flexibility Fine motor coordination or dexterity Procedural and incidental learning ability Psychomotor speed Short-term visual memory Visual-motor coordination Scanning ability Visual-perceptual discrimination	Rate of motor activity Motivation, persistence, and effort Visual acuity Ability to work under time pressure Experience with paper and pencil tasks
Symbol Search	Processing Speed (Gs) *Perceptual Speed (P)*	Decision speed Inhibitory control Visual-perceptual discrimination Psychomotor speed and coordination Short-term visual memory Visual-motor and fine motor coordination Attention and concentration	Rate of motor activity Motivation, persistence, and effort Visual acuity Ability to work under time pressure Experience with paper and pencil tasks
Cancellation	Processing Speed (Gs) *Perceptual Speed (P)*	Decision speed Rate of test taking Visual-motor coordination or dexterity Visual processing Visual-perceptual recognition and discrimination Visual scanning ability Ability to maintain set Attention and concentration	Rate of motor activity Motivation, persistence, and effort Visual acuity Ability to work under time pressure Experience with paper and pencil tasks
Naming Speed Literacy	Long-term Storage and Retrieval (Glr) *Naming Facility (NA)*	Processing speed Rate of test taking Scanning ability Automaticity in visual-verbal associations Attention and concentration	Early and sustained exposure to letters and numbers Visual acuity Motivation, persistence, and effort Ability to work under time pressure

WISC-V Subtest	CHC Broad and Narrow Abilities Measured	Other Possible Abilities and Processes Measured	Possible Influences on Subtest Performance[a]
Naming Speed Quantity	Long-term Storage and Retrieval (Glr) *Naming Facility (NA)* Processing Speed (Gs) *Number Facility (N)*	Rate of test taking Visual-perceptual processing and discrimination Scanning ability Number sense Attention and concentration	Early and sustained exposure to numbers and quantities Quality of early instruction Visual acuity Motivation, persistence, and effort Ability to work under time pressure
Immediate Symbol Translation	Long-term Storage and Retrieval (Glr) *Associative Memory (MA)*	Visual memory Working memory capacity Visual-perceptual discrimination Learning ability Scanning ability Attention and concentration	Use of encoding strategies Motivation, persistence, and effort Visual acuity
Delayed Symbol Translation	Long-term Storage and Retrieval (Glr) *Associative Memory (MA)*	Visual memory Delayed visual recall Visual-perceptual discrimination Scanning ability Attention and concentration	Use of encoding strategies Motivation, persistence, and effort Visual acuity
Recognition Symbol Translation	Long-term Storage and Retrieval (Glr) *Associative Memory (MA)*	Visual memory Delayed visual recall Visual-perceptual discrimination Scanning ability Attention and concentration	Use of encoding strategies Motivation, persistence, and effort Visual acuity

Note: CHC narrow abilities are italicized. Information in this table was compiled from the following sources: *WISC-V Technical and Interpretive Manual* (Wechsler, 2014b); *Essentials of WISC-IV Assessment* (Flanagan & Kaufman, 2009); and the *Cross-Battery Assessment Software Program* (X-BASS; Ortiz et al., 2017).

[a]Information in this column adapted from Sattler et al. (2016).

No reader of this book should be under the illusion that administering the WISC-V without reading the manuals first is an option. However, it is easy to lose oneself in the psychometric details of the manuals' extensive discussions concerning the structure, reliability, and validity of the WISC-V. For this reason, we summarize key points found in the manuals, evaluating claims as we go.

The WISC-V is a carefully normed instrument suitable for children and adolescents in the United States ages 6:0–16:11 years. According to the *WISC-V Administration and Scoring Manual* (Wechsler, 2014c), the WISC-V is designed to identify intellectual giftedness, intellectual disability, and specific cognitive strengths and weaknesses for identification or diagnosis of specific learning disabilities in educational, clinical, and research settings. It is often used for the purpose of treatment planning and educational placement decisions. Also, the WISC-V can play a role in neuropsychological evaluations to help evaluate various aspects of neuropsychological functioning.

As seen in Table 1.5, the 21 WISC-V subtests (some of which have sub-subtests, e.g., Digit Span) can be combined in a variety of ways to estimate diverse aspects of cognitive functioning including verbal comprehension, visual spatial reasoning, fluid reasoning, working memory capacity, processing speed, general ability, and long-term storage and retrieval. The internal consistency reliability coefficients (found in Table 1.5) and the short-term stability coefficients of these scores are generally high, comparable to those of previous editions.

g-loadings of WISC-V Subtests

g-loadings are an important indicator of the degree to which a subtest measures general intelligence. Additionally, *g*-loadings aid in determining the extent to which a single subtest score can be expected to vary from other scores within the profile. The WISC-V subtest *g*-loadings were derived from a Principal Axis Factor Analysis reported in Sattler et al. (2016). WISC-V subtests that were found to be high, moderate, and low measures of *g*, based on this analysis, are reported in Table 1.6. These *g*-loadings may be useful in combination with other data (e.g., information reported in Rapid Reference 1.3) when generating hypotheses about fluctuations in a child's or adolescent's scaled score profile. For example, it would not be unusual to find that subtest scores with low *g*-loadings differ sometimes substantially from subtest scores with high *g*-loadings. More than 40% of individuals with GAIs of 120 or higher have CPIs that are a full standard deviation below their GAI. In other words, a standard deviation difference between a composite comprised of subtests with moderate to high *g*-loadings (i.e., GAI) and a composite comprised of mostly moderate to low *g*-loadings (i.e., CPI) is

Table 1.5 Structure of the WISC-V Composite Scores and Corresponding Internal Consistency Coefficients.

Subtest	Avg. Internal Consistency	Verbal Comprehension	Verbal Expanded Crystallized	Visual Spatial	Fluid Reasoning	Expanded Fluid	Quantitative Reasoning	Working Memory	Auditory Working Memory	Processing Speed	Full Scale	General Ability	Nonverbal Ability	Cognitive Proficiency	Naming Speed	Symbol Translation	Storage and Retrieval
(composite internal consistency)		.92	.95	.92	.93	.95	.95	.92	.93	.88	.96	.96	.95	.93	.90	.94	.94
Similarities	.87	•	•								•	•					
Vocabulary	.87	•	•								•	•					
Information	.86		•														
Comprehension	.83		•														
Block Design	.84			•							•	◦	•				
Visual Puzzles	.89			•									•				
Matrix Reasoning	.87				•	•					•	•	•				
Figure Weights	.94				•	•	•				•	•	•				
Picture Concepts	.83					•											
Arithmetic	.90					•	•										
Digit Span	.91							•	•		•			•			
Picture Span	.85							•					•	•			
Letter-Number Sequencing	.86								•								
Coding	.82										•		•	•			
Symbol Search	.81									•				•			
Cancellation	.82									•							
Naming Speed Literacy	.86														•		•
Naming Speed Quantity	.83														•		•
Immediate Symbol Trans.	.88															•	•
Delayed Symbol Trans.	.87															•	•
Recognition Symbol Trans.	.82															•	•

Note: Storage and Retrieval is calculated from the sum of the NSI and STI standard scores, not from the sum of the five Naming Speed and Symbol Translation subtests.

Table 1.6. Classification of WISC-V Subtest g-Loadings

Subtest	High Average g-loadings (.71–.78)	Moderate Average g-loadings (.56–.70)	Low Average g-loadings (.24–.49)
Vocabulary	✓		
Information	✓		
Similarities	✓		
Arithmetic	✓		
Digit Span	✓		
Letter-Number Sequencing	✓		
Visual Puzzles		✓	
Block Design		✓	
Comprehension		✓	
Matrix Reasoning		✓	
Figure Weights		✓	
Picture Span		✓	
Picture Concepts		✓	
Symbol Search			✓
Coding			✓
Cancellation			✓

Source: Sattler, J. M., Dumont, R., & Coalson, D. L. (2016). *Assessment of children: WISC-V and WPPSI-IV.* San Diego, CA: Jerome M. Sattler Publishing.

Note: Subtest *g*-loadings are also available in the *WISC-V Technical and Interpretive Manual* (Wechsler, 2014b, p. 84).

common among individuals with very high FSIQs. The opposite is true of individuals with very low GAIs. About 30% of individuals with GAIs below 80 have CPIs that are a full standard deviation above their GAIs.

Structure of the WISC-V

In order to use the interpretive approach we advocate, practitioners need to have a thorough understanding of the theoretical structure of the test batteries they use. Combining scores from subtests with diverse formats allows practitioners to be more confident that the ability estimates are reliable and valid. For this reason, the WISC-V offers two to four subtests with distinct formats for each of the six broad abilities (i.e., Gc, Gv, Gf, Gsm, Gs, Glr) that the WISC-V is designed to measure.

Verbal Comprehension Subtests: Similarities, Vocabulary, Information, and Comprehension

These subtests are measures of what in CHC Theory is called *Crystallized Intelligence* (Gc), or acquired knowledge and language comprehension. The VCI summarizes performance on the Similarities and Vocabulary subtests. When all four subtests are administered, the performance is summarized by the Verbal (Expanded Crystallized) Index (VECI; Raiford, Drozdick, Zhang, & Zhou, 2015; see Appendix B for the norms for this composite). Rapid Reference 1.4 provides new clinical composites that are made up of different combinations of subtests that measure Gc. The norms corresponding to these composites are located in Appendix B. These clinical composites are automatically generated in X-BASS, a program that is described in Chapter 4 and is used to assist in WISC-V interpretation.

≡ Rapid Reference 1.4

New Gc Clinical Composites for the WISC-V

Clinical Composite	Subtest Composition	Brief Description
Gc (Verbal Expression–Low) **Gc-VE/L**	Vocabulary Information	These two subtests form a broad Gc ability and require less verbal expression compared to the other Gc subtests (e.g., one- or two-word responses as compared to multiword responses or sentences). An alternative label for this composite is Retrieval from Remote Long-Term Storage (RFLT-Remote), which provides an estimate of an individual's ability to retrieve information from long-term storage that was encoded weeks, months, or years ago.
Gc (Verbal Expression–High) **Gc-VE/H**	Similarities Comprehension	These two subtests require greater verbal expression to earn maximum credit compared to the other Gc subtests and typically involve some degree of reasoning ability.
VECI	Similarities Vocabulary Information Comprehension	Provides a robust estimate of Gc as compared to the VCI, spanning two narrow ability domains (VL – Lexical Knowledge and K0 – General Information). Requires reasoning with verbal information. Involves tests that have low to high demands for verbal expression.

Note: Norms for Gc Clinical Composites are included in Appendix B and X-BASS (Ortiz et al., 2017). Norms for the VECI were also published in Raiford et al. (2015) and Kaufman et al. (2016).

In some ways, the Gc subtests are the crown jewels of the cognitive assessment field. To be sure, other batteries have tests of verbal knowledge and language ability. However, there is something special about these four subtests in that they tend to elicit particularly rich samples of verbal behavior. There is a feeling of knowing that experienced clinicians have with these tests that does not happen to the same degree with other verbal knowledge tests. Unquantifiable nuances in cognitive style are often discerned from listening closely to how children reason through items in their zone of proximal development. For example, some children answer only when they are sure they are right, whereas others say the first thing that pops into their heads with little hesitation and, right or wrong, with extreme self-confidence.

Wechsler selected verbal knowledge items that measured the sort of things that people could find out for themselves, even if they did not come from privileged backgrounds (though this undoubtedly is an advantage on at least some items). In particular, academic and specialized knowledge was avoided (Wechsler, 1944, p. 82). A close inspection of the verbal items from the WISC-V reveals that the easy items are not merely easy nor are the difficult items merely difficult. The easy items tend to be about practical knowledge and daily living skills and the more difficult items tend not to be about practical knowledge, but nevertheless topics one would wish well-informed voters knew something about.

In terms of CHC narrow abilities, Vocabulary is a measure of Lexical Knowledge and Information is a measure of General (Verbal) Information. Attempts have been made to fit Similarities and Comprehension in the CHC taxonomy, but it is not clear that they fit neatly into any narrow CHC domain. Similarities and Comprehension are probably best viewed as excellent measures of broad verbal comprehension (Gc) and as complex measures of several different narrow abilities. By way of example, consider the complexities of the Similarities subtest.

At first glance, Similarities appears to be similar to Vocabulary in that one must understand words to do well. However, even the most difficult items on the Similarities subtest consist of pairs of very easy words that are among the most frequently used words in the English language. It is not so much knowledge of word definitions that is required on the Similarities subtest, but a deeper understanding of how knowledge is structured in our culture. Flynn (2007b, p. 34) argues that it measures the degree to which a person sees the world with scientific spectacles, placing objects and ideas into abstract categories (e.g., hills and streams are both geographical features) instead of in functional relationships, as most people have done for most of human history (e.g., streams run down hills). It is likely that Similarities draws on reasoning ability (i.e., the narrow CHC factor Inductive Reasoning), but only on the more difficult items. It is easy to observe that most children are not really reasoning through the first few easy items. They are simply drawing on their background knowledge of how familiar items have been grouped in the past (e.g., blue and yellow are both colors). However, at some point the words are no longer paired in familiar ways, and figuring out how they are related requires careful thought. From this perspective, Similarities requires a complex mix of background knowledge retrieved from memory and on-the-spot reasoning.

Fluid Reasoning Subtests: Matrix Reasoning, Figure Weights, Picture Concepts, and Arithmetic

Fluid Reasoning is the ability to use logic to solve unfamiliar problems. Matrix Reasoning and Figure Weights compose the FRI and the four tests together make up the Expanded Fluid Index (EFI; see Appendix B or Raiford et al., 2015 for EFI norms). The EFI is described in Rapid Reference 1.5. Performance on the Figure Weights and Arithmetic subtests is summarized by the Quantitative Reasoning Index (QRI).

DON'T FORGET

An Expanded Fluid Index may be derived using four WISC-V subtests.

≡ Rapid Reference 1.5

New Gf Clinical Composite for the WISC-V

Clinical Composite	Subtest Composition	Brief Description
EFI	Matrix Reasoning Figure Weights Picture Concepts Arithmetic	Provides a more robust estimate of Gf as compared to the FRI, spanning three narrow ability domains, including Induction (I), General Sequential Reasoning (RG), and Quantitative Reasoning (RQ). Places more emphasis on quantitative reasoning as compared to FRI.

Note: Norms for the EFI are included in Appendix B and X-BASS (Ortiz et al., 2017). Norms for the EFI were also published in Raiford et al. (2015) and Kaufman et al. (2016).

In terms of an intuitive application of CHC Theory to these subtests, Matrix Reasoning and Picture Concepts are measures of Inductive Reasoning, Figure Weights measures General Sequential Reasoning, and Arithmetic is a measure of Quantitative Reasoning. Unfortunately, factor analytic evidence suggests that these intuitive classifications are perhaps a little simplistic. In Table 1.7, the loadings are displayed from a principal factors exploratory factor analysis (with oblimin rotation) of the correlation matrix in Table 5.1 from the *WISC-V Technical and Interpretive Manual* (Wechsler, 2014b).

As can be seen in Table 1.7, the Gc, Gsm, and Gs factors are very well defined, with fairly clean measures of each factor. However, the Gv and Gf factors are not clearly separate, a finding supported by Sattler et al. (2016, p. 78). Many subtests appear to be mixed measures of several factors, especially the subtests intended to measure fluid reasoning. Picture Concepts and Arithmetic have small loadings on the Verbal Comprehension (Gc) factor. Matrix Reasoning and Picture Concepts

Table 1.7 An Exploratory Factor Analysis of the WISC-V Subtests

Subtest	Gc	Gsm	Gs	Gv	Gf
Similarities	.75				
Vocabulary	.86				
Information	.77				
Comprehension	.70				
Block Design				.55	
Visual Puzzles				.81	
Matrix Reasoning				.23	.24
Figure Weights					.62
Picture Concepts	.26			.20	
Arithmetic	.22	.32			.27
Digit Span		.80			
Picture Span		.55			
Letter-Number Sequencing		.77			
Coding			.75		
Symbol Search			.76		
Cancellation			.45		

Note: Loadings less than .20 were omitted.

have small loadings on the Visual Spatial (Gv) factor. The Fluid Reasoning (Gf) factor does not seem to be well defined, a common finding with current and previous editions of the WISC (Canivez & Watkins, 2016; Weiss, Keith, Zhu, & Chen, 2013). Consider these facts from Table 5.1 of the *WISC-V Technical and Interpretive Manual* carefully:

- Although Matrix Reasoning and Picture Concepts are classified as measures of reasoning, their correlation is only 0.35.
- Matrix Reasoning's correlation with Picture Concepts is lower than its correlation with every other subtest, except for the three Processing Speed Subtests.
- Picture Concepts has a higher correlation with Vocabulary and Information than it does with any of the other Fluid Reasoning subtests.

What this means is that practitioners cannot apply test labels and CHC classifications from previous editions of the WISC unthinkingly. Expect Matrix Reasoning and Picture Concepts scores to diverge often.

Visual Spatial Processing Subtests: Block Design and Visual Puzzles

In terms of CHC Theory, these subtests measure Gv in general and visualization (Vz) in particular. That is, they measure the ability to perceive patterns and solve problems in the mind's eye by manipulating visual imagery.

After the Object Assembly subtest was dropped, Block Design was the only good measure of visual spatial ability on the WISC-IV. Visual Puzzles is therefore a welcome addition to the WISC-V. However, Visual Puzzles fits the trend in which the new tests are psychometrically clean, but do not permit the examiner to observe problem-solving behavior in real time.

Working Memory Subtests: Digit Span, Picture Span, and Letter-Number Sequencing

These subtests are measures of working memory capacity, the ability to maintain and manipulate information in short-term memory in order to solve multistep problems. Digit Span Forward is a measure of the CHC narrow ability Memory Span (MS). The remaining subtests are best conceptualized as measures of general working memory. Digit Span and Picture Span make up the WMI and Digit Span is paired with Letter-Number Sequencing to make up the Auditory Working Memory Index (AWMI). Rapid Reference 1.6 provides new clinical composites that are made up of different combinations of working memory subtests. The norms corresponding to these composites are located in Appendix B.

≣ *Rapid Reference 1.6*

New Gsm Clinical Composites for the WISC-V

Clinical Composite	Subtest Composition	Brief Description
Working Memory (Alternative) **Gsm-MW (Alt)**	Digit Span Backward Digit Span Sequencing Letter-Number Sequencing	Provides an alternative to the Auditory Working Memory Index (AWMI) by eliminating Digit Span Forward (a measure of memory span).
Memory Span-Working Memory **Gsm-MS,MW**	Digit Span Forward Digit Span Backward	Provides a balance of Memory Span and Working Memory Capacity and is consistent with the composition of the Digit Span subtest on the WISC-IV.
Working Memory (Cognitive Complexity— High) **WM-CC/H**	Arithmetic Picture Span	Provides an estimate of Working Memory Capacity with subtests that are more cognitively complex than Digit Span. Arithmetic involves Gf (e.g., Quantitative Reasoning), Gc, and Gsm (Working Memory Capacity). Picture Span involves Gv (Visual Memory), Memory Span, and Working Memory Capacity due to proactive interference.

Note: Norms for the new Gsm clinical composites are included in Appendix B and X-BASS (Ortiz et al., 2017).

Of the Working Memory subtests included on the WISC-V, only Digit Span was selected by Wechsler, and he did so reluctantly (Wechsler, 1958):

> To act intelligently one must be able to recall numerous items, i.e., have a retentive memory. But beyond a certain point this ability will not help much in coping with life situations successfully. (p. 7)

Although it is easy to give, score, and interpret, he claimed that Digit Span did not measure general intelligence very well, especially for high ability individuals (Wechsler, 1958, p. 71). Digit Span was retained mostly because it was extremely good at discriminating different levels of intelligence at the low end of the scale.

On the WISC-V, the nature of Digit Span has been changed by the inclusion of the Digit Span Sequencing sub-subtest, making it more of a measure of working memory capacity than a simple memory span subtest. It is difficult to know what David Wechsler would say about Picture Span and Letter-Number Sequencing. Most likely he would acknowledge their clinical utility but also fret that they, like Digit Span, do not capture what he meant by *general intelligence*.

Processing Speed Subtests: Coding, Symbol Search, and Cancellation

These three subtests are measures of Processing Speed (Gs), the ability to fluently deploy the focus of one's attention to process information quickly. Cancellation's loadings on Gs are considerably lower than those of Coding and Symbol Search. Nevertheless, if an "Expanded Processing Speed Index" (EPS) is desired, it can be calculated like so:

$$EPS = \frac{CD + SS + CA - 30}{0.4656} + 100$$

Rapid Reference 1.7 provides an alternative to the PSI and EPS. Specifically, it includes a new Perceptual Speed (Gs-P) clinical composite that reduces memory and motor dexterity demands.

DON'T FORGET

. . . .

Norms are also available for a new Gs clinical composite.

☰ Rapid Reference 1.7

. . . .

New Gs Clinical Composite for the WISC-V

Clinical Composite	Subtest Composition	Brief Description
Perceptual Speed **Gs-P**	Symbol Search Cancellation	Provides an alternative to the PSI, reducing the memory and motor dexterity demands inherent mainly in the Coding subtest.

Note: Norms for the new Gs clinical composite are included in Appendix B and X-BASS (Ortiz et al., 2017). Norms for this composite were first published in Kaufman et al. (2016).

Wechsler believed that the popularity of the digit-symbol paradigm was "fully merited" (Wechsler, 1958, p. 81), even though he did not give any explanation as to how it was a good measure of his definition of general intelligence. Even though it had the lowest loading on the general factor of his original tests, it was valuable because it was sensitive to a wide variety of outcomes, including brain injury, psychological disorders, and the general effects of aging. The newcomer subtests of Symbol Search and Cancellation continue the trend of reduced complexity, though Cancellation does reveal different uses of strategy in some individuals.

Long-Term Storage and Retrieval Subtests: Naming Speed Literacy, Naming Speed Quantity, Immediate Symbol Translation, Delayed Symbol Translation, and Recognition Symbol Translation

The five Long-Term Storage and Retrieval (Glr) subtests are new to the WISC-V. In terms of CHC theory, these subtests measure narrow aspects of Glr. Naming Speed Literacy and Naming Speed Quantity measure Naming Facility, or the ability to rapidly produce names of familiar concepts or common objects that are in the individual's long-term memory store. The Naming Speed Literacy subtest, for example, requires the individual to name pictures or letters and numbers rapidly. Immediate Symbol Translation, Delayed Symbol Translation, and Recognition Symbol Translation measure Associative Memory, or the ability to recall one part of a previously learned but unrelated pair of items (that may or may not be meaningfully linked) when the other part is presented. The addition of Glr subtests on the WISC-V was one of the most significant and positive revisions, particularly because Glr abilities are important for learning and academic success. Also, the Glr subtests on the WISC-V measure processes that are important in the evaluation and diagnosis of specific learning disabilities (e.g., Feifer, Gerhardstein Nader, Flanagan, Fitzer, & Hicks, 2014). A new clinical composite is available that is comprised of Delayed Symbol Translation and Recognition Symbol Translation. This composite is called Retrieval from Recent Long-Term Storage (RFLT-Recent; see Rapid Reference 1.8). Comparing this composite to the new Gc clinical composite comprised of Vocabulary and Information (or RFLT-Remote) may provide useful information about an individual's ability to retrieve recently encoded information compared to information that was encoded weeks, months, or years ago.

DON'T FORGET

Norms are also available for a new Glr clinical composite.

≡ *Rapid Reference 1.8*

New Glr Clinical Composite for the WISC-V

Clinical Composite	Subtest Composition	Brief Description
Retrieval from Recent Long-Term Storage **RFLT-Recent**	Delayed Symbol Translation Recognition Symbol Translation	Provides an estimate of an individual's ability to retrieve recently encoded information from long-term storage.

Note: Norms for the new Glr clinical composite are included in Appendix B and in X-BASS (Ortiz et al., 2017).

WISC-V Relations With Other Variables

In addition to structural validity, the WISC-V is supported by correlations with scores on other comprehensive measures of cognitive ability and achievement in normal and special groups (Wechsler, 2014b). Specifically, WISC-V criterion validity studies included the WISC-IV, WPPSI-IV, WAIS-IV, KABC-II, KTEA-3, WIAT-III, Vineland-II, and BASC-2. The relationships between the WISC-V Primary Index Scales and the scales of each of these instruments for normal and special groups are reported in Tables 1.8 and 1.9, respectively. Overall, these studies provide good support for the criterion validity of the WISC-V. However, it is important to note that all of the instruments included in these studies were published by Pearson. In addition, some of the special group studies included very small sample sizes (e.g., < 40 participants; see Sattler et al., 2016, for a more extensive review).

Wechsler's IQ vs. Spearman's *g*: Is the FSIQ the Only Score Worth Interpreting?

Shocking as it may seem, scholars disagree about things from time to time. This is a healthy state of affairs. Rivalries often inspire us to work at our peak capacity. There is a group of scholars who, unlike us, believes that the general factor of intelligence (*g*) is the only construct that should be interpreted on intelligence tests such as the WISC-V (Canivez, Watkins, & Dombrowski, in press; Glutting, Watkins, Konold, & McDermott, 2006; McDermott, Fantuzzo, & Glutting, 1990). They do not deny that other ability factors exist, nor that the general factor is the only score that predicts important outcomes. However, their

Table 1.8. Summary of Special Group Studies With the WISC-V for Primary Index Scales and FSIQ

Special Group	N	Verbal Comprehension Index M	SD	Visual Spatial Index M	SD	Fluid Reasoning Index M	SD	Working Memory Index M	SD	Processing Speed Index M	SD	FSIQ M	SD
Intellectually Gifted	95	127.7	12.3	121.2	11.5	120.3	12.0	117.9	11.7	112.9	13.5	127.5	8.8
Mild Intellectual Disability	74	66.0	10.9	66.0	9.9	67.0	11.0	65.1	10.5	71.6	16.2	60.9	8.9
Moderate Intellectual Disability	37	55.2	11.3	56.8	9.6	58.6	12.0	58.3	10.6	59.3	15.8	49.7	8.9
Borderline Intellectual Functioning	20	81.7	7.6	83.1	8.3	87.1	11.7	78.2	11.9	95.1	11.9	80.4	5.7
Specific Learning Disorder—Reading	30	89.1	11.2	93.3	14.1	92.5	10.8	87.8	10.1	93.0	15.3	88.9	10.5
Specific Learning Disorder—Reading and Written Expression	22	86.5	10.1	96.2	13.3	88.4	12.2	85.8	9.7	93.0	15.8	84.8	11.1
Specific Learning Disorder—Math	28	90.3	13.7	85.4	12.6	82.2	15.4	88.7	13.5	90.2	14.2	83.6	11.9
Attention-Deficit/Hyperactivity Disorder	48	97.8	11.4	97.3	16.7	97.6	13.4	94.8	13.3	94.2	13.9	95.6	11.7
Disruptive Behavior	21	94.1	11.8	97.1	13.9	94.4	15.2	95.3	13.7	92.8	17.1	93.3	12.4
Traumatic Brain Injury	20	88.9	12.9	87.5	15.9	88.4	18.0	86.2	15.5	84.1	22.2	83.3	14.1
English Language Learners	16	85.6	11.7	93.4	12.3	95.2	13.7	87.8	13.0	97.6	15.7	87.6	10.6
Autism Spectrum Disorder With Language Impairment	30	80.4	18.2	82.8	22.3	84.3	20.6	77.6	19.4	75.8	19.0	76.3	19.1
Autism Spectrum Disorder Without Language Impairment	32	102.5	14.4	100.7	17.1	100.9	17.5	95.4	16.8	89.4	18.4	98.3	17.4

Source: Adapted from *WISC-V Technical and Interpretive Manual* (Wechsler, 2014b) and reformatted by Sattler, Dumont, and Coalson in *Assessment of Children: WISC-V and WPPSI-IV* (2016), with permission of Jerome M. Sattler, Publisher, Inc.

Table 1.9 Summary of WISC-V Criterion Validity Studies for the Primary Index Scales and FSIQ

Criterion	Primary Index Scale					
	VCI	VSI	FRI	WMI	PSI	FSIQ
WISC-IV						
Verbal Comprehension	.81	--	--	--	--	--
Perceptual Reasoning	--	.62	.61	--	--	--
Working Memory	--	--	--	.59	--	--
Processing Speed	--	--	--	--	.70	--
Full Scale IQ	--	--	--	--	--	.81
WPPSI-IV						
Verbal Comprehension	.64	--	--	--	--	--
Visual Spatial	--	.57	--	--	--	--
Fluid Reasoning	--	--	.45	--	--	--
Working Memory	--	--	--	.46	--	--
Processing Speed	--	--	--	--	.34	--
Full Scale IQ	--	--	--	--	--	.74
WAIS-IV						
Verbal Comprehension	.80	--	--	--	--	--
Perceptual Reasoning	--	.78	.56	--	--	--
Working Memory	--	--	--	.72	--	--
Processing Speed	--	--	--	--	.79	--

(continued)

43

Primary Index Scale

Criterion	VCI	VSI	FRI	WMI	PSI	FSIQ
Full Scale IQ	--	--	--	--	--	.84
KABC-II						
Sequential/Gsm	.36	.20	.17	.63	-.06	.44
Simultaneous/Gv	.34	.53	.41	.27	.25	.55
Learning/Glr	.45	.33	.38	.43	-.19	.44
Planning/Gf	.44	.51	.50	.23	.05	.54
Knowledge/Gc	.74	.55	.52	.38	.06	.72
Fluid-Crystallized	.72	.65	.63	.63	.04	.81
Mental Processing	.64	.64	.60	.65	.04	.77
Nonverbal	.41	.60	.49	.41	.21	.64
KTEA-3						
Reading	.77	.47	.56	.54	.20	.75
Math	.67	.57	.66	.49	.32	.79
Written Language	.61	.39	.47	.51	.34	.69
Academic Skills Battery	.76	.54	.63	.58	.35	.82
Sound-Symbol	.55	.45	.48	.55	.15	.66
Decoding	.57	.43	.41	.52	.12	.63
Reading Fluency	.58	.43	.35	.48	.36	.65
Reading Understanding	.76	.47	.55	.50	.18	.74
Oral Language	.70	.47	.48	.62	.29	.69

Oral Fluency	.43	.28	.33	.36	.40	.49
Comprehension	.78	.48	.58	.49	.21	.75
Expression	.64	.42	.45	.45	.25	.66
Orthographic Processing	.51	.32	.34	.53	.39	.61
Academic Fluency	.42	.25	.23	.38	.47	.52
WIAT-III						
Oral Language	.78	.44	.33	.56	.22	.74
Total Reading	.65	.30	.32	.53	.29	.70
Basic Reading	.53	.24	.30	.54	.19	.61
Reading Comprehension and Fluency	.65	.30	.25	.40	.36	.65
Written Expression	.60	.39	.33	.47	.33	.68
Mathematics	.53	.44	.45	.46	.41	.71
Math Fluency	.36	.28	.31	.39	.51	.58
Total Achievement	.74	.46	.40	.63	.34	.81
Vineland-II						
Communication	.21	.09	.28	.41	-.02	.27
Daily Living Skills	.04	.03	-.05	-.01	.07	.02
Socialization	-.06	-.33	-.20	.11	-.16	-.12
Adaptive Behavior Composite	.04	-.12	-.04	.19	-.08	.01

(continued)

Primary Index Scale

Criterion	VCI	VSI	FRI	WMI	PSI	FSIQ
Maladaptive Behavior Index	.07	.06	.05	-.16	-.16	-.04
BASC-2 PRS						
Resiliency	.10	.07	.08	.10	.07	.12
Conduct Problems	-.16	-.10	-.13	-.12	-.08	-.17
Executive Functioning	-.11	-.07	-.10	-.08	-.08	-.14
Attention Problems	-.16	-.08	-.15	-.16	-.15	-.20

Note: Abbreviations for primary index scores: VCI = Verbal Comprehension Index, VSI = Visual Spatial Index, FRI = Fluid Reasoning Index, WMI = Working Memory Index, PSI = Processing Speed Index, FSIQ = Full Scale IQ. Abbreviations for tests: WISC-IV = *Wechsler Intelligence Scale for Children–Fourth Edition*, WPPSI-IV = *Wechsler Preschool and Primary Scale of Intelligence–Fourth Edition*, WAIS-IV = *Wechsler Adult Intelligence Scale–Fourth Edition*, KABC-II = *Kaufman Assessment Battery for Children–Second Edition*, KTEA-3 = *Kaufman Tests of Educational Achievement–Third Edition*, WIAT-III = *Wechsler Individual Achievement Test–Third Edition*, BASC-2 PRS = *Behavior Assessment System for Children–Second Edition, Parent Rating Scales.*

Source: Adapted from *WISC-V Technical and Interpretive Manual* (Wechsler, 2014b) and reformatted by Sattler, Dumont, and Coalson in *Assessment of Children: WISC-V and WPPSI-IV* (2016), with permission of Jerome M. Sattler, Publisher, Inc.

argument is that the general factor is the only construct that is measured well enough on intelligence tests such as the WISC-V to be of practical use with individuals. They contend that the other factors are so poorly measured that there is little reason to interpret them. Furthermore, even if they were measured well, these scholars cite and provide evidence that the smaller factors' effects on important outcomes is typically so small that it probably would not matter much in the best of circumstances (Glutting et al., 2006).

Are they right? Is the general factor the only construct worth considering on the WISC-V? A proper and complete answer to this question is probably too technical for a book with the word *Essentials* in its title. However, we give a brief explanation as to why we believe that this argument is overstated.

There are several points on which we agree with these scholars. First, professionals should be aware of the limitations of their instruments. It serves no purpose to make or believe in exaggerated claims about the utility of test scores. Second, we agree that measurement error is inherent in all psychological measures and that to the degree that a measure is unreliable, confidence in the validity of the measure may be compromised. We agree that the available reliability and validity evidence suggests that we should be cautious when interpreting the smaller factors of ability (e.g., visual spatial ability, working memory, processing speed) on intelligence tests such as the WISC-V. However, we believe that there are methods and guidelines by which one can responsibly use and interpret measures of these smaller factors. Indeed, we believe that in many cases it is our ethical responsibility to do so.

Even scholars who discourage the use of any scores beyond the FSIQ have shown that in earlier editions of the Wechsler scales, factor index scales have incremental validity in predicting academic outcomes (e.g., Canivez, 2013; Glutting et al., 2006; Nelson, Canivez, & Watkins, 2013). In many cases, the improvements in predictive validity were small (2% to 4% additional variance explained), but in some cases they were fairly large (9% to 30% additional variance explained). However, even when the improved prediction is small, why would one not make use of the improved prediction that comes with factor index scores if one has the means to do so? Who would want a worse prediction if a better one is easily available?

Looking beyond the FSIQ is not just a way of obtaining better predictions. Doing so allows for better explanations and case conceptualizations. We agree with James Flynn (2007a):

> Despite all the triumphs of the concept of general intelligence, I believe intelligence is like the atom: you have to know both why its parts cohere and why they sometimes fly apart. (n.p.)

There are some applications of intelligence testing in which it probably does little harm to fly low to the ground and stick with just the FSIQ. However, when faced with unusual profiles of ability in cases with documented brain injuries and neurological disorders, a straight-up interpretation of the FSIQ is just silly. Suppose that after a severe head injury a previously highly disciplined child has difficulty focusing on homework without becoming mentally fatigued and distracted. The WISC-V profile of scores suggests very low processing speed (PSI = 68) and low working memory (WMI = 79). The remaining scores are a bit above average and the FSIQ is in the average range. Are we to ignore this information and tell the child's parents that no cognitive deficits were detected? Should we not conduct follow-up tests to verify that the WMI and PSI scores are indeed much lower than expectations? We believe that not only can this be done, but it must.

We are not arguing that the FSIQ is bad and the factor index scores are good. FSIQ and the factor index scores are different tools for looking at abilities, and good practitioners can alternate between them flexibly. One tool is fairly accurate and has the virtue of simplicity. The other is more accurate, but the onus is on the user to manage the complexity of multiple scores properly. This is a real concern and we therefore appreciate that there are scholars who hold our feet to the fire and challenge our assumptions. However, we also believe that with rigorous training and a flexible mind-set, it is possible for practitioners to use both kinds of scores responsibly. It is our hope that the information and guidance presented in subsequent chapters of this book will assist practitioners in applying theory, research, and psychometric rigor to the test interpretation process, allowing for examination and interpretation of all scores.

🪶 TEST YOURSELF 🪶

1. **Performance on intelligence tests is a potent predictor of what important life outcomes?**
   a. Academic achievement
   b. High school graduation
   c. Income
   d. All of the above
2. **The Wechsler scales displaced the Stanford-Binet to become the dominant clinical measure of intelligence.**
   a. True
   b. False

3. **Why did David Wechsler create his tests?**
   a. For research use
   b. For clinical use
   c. For research use and clinical use
   d. To measure unidimensional traits

4. **How did Wechsler express IQ scores?**
   a. Standard scores
   b. Intelligence quotients
   c. Mental age
   d. Chronological age

5. **Which subtest remains constant in the WISC-III Perceptual Organization Index (POI), the WISC-IV Perceptual Reasoning Index (PRI), and the WISC-V Visual Spatial Index (VSI)?**
   a. Picture Completion
   b. Object Assembly
   c. Block Design
   d. Mazes

6. **Which of the following WISC-V composites allows one subtest substitution?**
   a. PRI
   b. FSIQ
   c. WMI
   d. PSI

7. **Wechsler selected verbal knowledge items that measured the sort of things that required academic and specialized knowledge.**
   a. True
   b. False

8. **Why was Digit Span retained in the WISC-V?**
   a. It is good at discriminating different levels of intelligence at the low end of the scale.
   b. It is good at discriminating different levels of intelligence at the high end of the scale.
   c. It is a good measure of general intelligence.
   d. It is the best measure of working memory capacity.

9. **Which of the following Glr subtests were included in the WISC-IV and WISC-V?**
   a. Naming Speed Quantity
   b. Naming Speed Literacy
   c. Immediate Symbol Translation
   d. No Glr subtests were included in the WISC-IV.

10. **Results of exploratory factor analysis show that two factors contain subtests that have significant loadings on another factor. Which two factors are these?**

a. Gf and Gv

b. Gsm and Gs

c. Gc and Gv

d. Gc and Gs

Answers: 1. d; 2. a; 3. b; 4. a; 5. c; 6. b; 7. b; 8. a; 9. d; 10. a

REFERENCES

Binet, A., & Simon, T. (1905). New methods for the diagnosis of the intellectual level of subnormals. *L'Année Psychologique, 12*, 191–244.

Binet, A., & Simon, T. (1916). *The development of intelligence in children: The Binet-Simon Scale.* Vineland, NJ: Williams & Wilkins.

Canivez, G. L. (2013). Incremental criterion validity of WAIS-IV factor index scores: Relationships with WIAT-II and WIAT-III subtest and composite scores. *Psychological Assessment, 25*(2), 484–495.

Canivez, G. L., & Watkins, M. W. (2016). Review of the Wechsler Intelligence Scale for Children–Fifth Edition: Critique, commentary, and independent analyses. In A. S. Kaufman, S. E. Raiford, & D. L. Coalson (Authors), *Intelligent testing with the WISC-V* (pp. 683–702). Hoboken, NJ: Wiley.

Canivez, G. L., Watkins, M. W., & Dombrowski, S. C. (in press). Factor structure of the Wechsler Intelligence Scale for Children–Fifth Edition: Exploratory factor analyses with the 16 primary and secondary subtests. *Psychological Assessment.* http://doi.org/10.1037/pas0000238

Carroll, J. B. (1997). Psychometrics, intelligence, and public perception. *Intelligence, 24*(1), 25–52.

Carson, J. (1999). David Wechsler. In J. A. Garraty & M. C. Carnes (Eds.), *American national biography* (Vol. 22). New York, NY: Oxford University Press.

Deary, I. J. (2000). *Looking down on human intelligence: From psychometrics to the brain.* New York, NY: Oxford University Press.

Deary, I. J., Whiteman, M. C., Starr, J. M., Whalley, L. J., & Fox, H. C. (2004). The impact of childhood intelligence on later life: Following up the Scottish mental surveys of 1932 and 1947. *Journal of Personality and Social Psychology, 86*(1), 130–147.

Fancher, R. E. (1985). *The intelligence men: Makers of the IQ controversy.* New York, NY: Norton.

Feifer, S. G., Gerhardstein Nader, R., Flanagan, D. P., Fitzer, K. R., & Hicks, K. (2014). Identifying specific reading disability subtypes for effective educational intervention. *Learning Disabilities: A Multidisciplinary Journal, 20*(1), 18–30.

Flanagan, D. P., & Kaufman, A. S. (2009). *Essentials of WISC-IV assessment* (2nd ed.). Hoboken, NJ: Wiley.

Flanagan, D. P., Ortiz, S. O., & Alfonso, V. C. (2013). *Essentials of cross-battery assessment* (3rd ed.). Hoboken, NJ: Wiley.

Flynn, J. R. (2007a, November 5). *Shattering intelligence: Implications for education and interventions.* http://www.cato-unbound.org/2007/11/05/james-r-flynn/shattering-intelligence-implications-education-interventions

Flynn, J. R. (2007b). *What is intelligence? Beyond the Flynn effect.* New York, NY: Cambridge University Press.

Glutting, J. J., Watkins, M. W., Konold, T. R., & McDermott, P. A. (2006). Distinctions without a difference: The utility of observed versus latent factors from the WISC-IV in estimating reading and math achievement on the WIAT-II. *Journal of Special Education, 40*(2), 103–114.

Gottfredson, L. S. (1997). Why *g* matters: The complexity of everyday life. *Intelligence, 24*(1), 79–132.

Kamphaus, R. W., Petoskey, M. D., & Morgan, A. W. (1997). A history of intelligence test interpretation. In D. P. Flanagan, J. L. Genshaft, & P. L. Harrison (Eds.), *Contemporary intellectual assessment: Theories, tests, and issues* (pp. 32–47). New York, NY: Guilford.

Kamphaus, R. W., Winsor, A. P., Rowe, E. W., & Kim, S. (2012). A history of intelligence test interpretation. In D. P. Flanagan & P. L. Harrison (Eds.), *Contemporary intellectual assessment: Theories, tests, and issues* (3rd ed., pp. 56–70). New York: Guilford.

Kaufman, A. S. (1979). *Intelligent testing with the WISC-R.* New York, NY: Wiley.

Kaufman, A. S. (1994). *Intelligent testing with the WISC-III.* New York, NY: Wiley.

Kaufman, A. S. (2009). *IQ testing 101.* New York, NY: Springer.

Kaufman, A. S., Raiford, S. E., & Coalson, D. L. (2016). *Intelligent testing with the WISC-V.* Hoboken, NJ: Wiley.

Lamiell, J. T. (2003). *Beyond individual and group differences: Human individuality, scientific psychology, and William Stern's critical personalism.* Thousand Oaks, CA: Sage.

Lohman, D. E. (1997). Lessons from the history of intelligence testing. *International Journal of Educational Research, 27*(5), 359–378.

McDermott, P. A., Fantuzzo, J. W., & Glutting, J. J. (1990). Just say no to subtest analysis: A critique on Wechsler theory and practice. *Journal of Psychoeducational Assessment, 8*(3), 290–302.

McGrew, K. S. (1997). Analysis of the major intelligence batteries according to a proposed comprehensive Gf-Gc framework. In D. P. Flanagan, J. L. Genshaft, & P. L. Harrison (Eds.), *Contemporary intellectual assessment: Theories, tests, and issues* (pp. 151–179). New York, NY: Guilford.

McGrew, K. S. (2005). The Cattell-Horn-Carroll theory of cognitive abilities: Past, present, and future. In D.P. Flanagan & P. L. Harrison (Eds.), *Contemporary intellectual assessment: Theories, tests, and issues* (2nd ed., pp. 136–181). New York, NY: Guilford.

McGrew, K. S. (2009). CHC theory and the human cognitive abilities project: Standing on the shoulders of the giants of psychometric intelligence research. *Intelligence, 37*(1), 1–10.

Nelson, J. M., Canivez, G. L., & Watkins, M. W. (2013). Structural and incremental validity of the Wechsler Adult Intelligence Scale–Fourth Edition with a clinical sample. *Psychological Assessment, 25*(2), 618–630.

Ortiz, S. O., Flanagan, D. P., & Alfonso, V. C. (2017). *Cross-battery assessment software system* (X-BASS v2.0). Hoboken, NJ: Wiley.

Patterson, T., Rapsey, C., & Glue, P. (2013). Systematic review of cognitive development across childhood in Down syndrome: Implications for treatment interventions. *Journal of Intellectual Disability Research, 57*(4), 306–318.

Raiford, S. E., Drozdick, L., Zhang, O., & Zhou, X. (2015). *Expanded index scores.* WISC-V Technical Report No. 1. Bloomington, MN: Pearson.

Sattler, J. M., Dumont, R., & Coalson, D. L. (2016). *Assessment of children: WISC-V and WPPSI-IV.* San Diego, CA: Jerome M. Sattler Publishing.

Schneider, W. J., & McGrew, K. S. (2012). The Cattell-Horn-Carroll model of intelligence. In D. P. Flanagan & P. L. Harrison (Eds.), *Contemporary intellectual assessment: Theories, tests and issues* (3rd ed., pp. 99–144). New York, NY: Guilford.

Schrank, F. A., McGrew, K. S., & Mather, N. (2014). *Woodcock-Johnson IV.* Rolling Meadows, IL: Riverside.

Spearman, C. E. (1904). "General intelligence," objectively determined and measured. *American Journal of Psychology, 15*(2), 201–292.

Spearman, C. E. (1927). *The abilities of man: Their nature and measurement.* London, UK: MacMillan.

Stern, W. (1914). *The psychological methods of testing intelligence.* Baltimore, MD: Warwick & York.

Stern, W. (1933). Der personale Faktor in Psychotechnik und praktischer Psychologie. *Zeitschrift Für Angewandte Psychologie, 44*, 52–63.

Tulsky, D. S., Saklofske, D. H., & Zhu, J. (2003). Revising a standard: An evaluation of the origin and development of the WAIS-III. In D. S. Tulsky, D. H. Saklofske, G. J. Chelune, R. K. Heaton, R. J. Ivnik, R. Bornstein,... M. F. Ledbetter (Eds.), *Clinical interpretation of the WAIS-III and WMS-III* (pp. 43–92). San Diego, CA: Academic Press.

Wechsler, D. (1944). *The measurement of adult intelligence* (3rd ed.). Baltimore, MD: Williams & Wilkins.

Wechsler, D. (1950). Cognitive, conative, and non-intellective intelligence. *American Psychologist, 5*(3), 78–83.

Wechsler, D. (1958). *The measurement and appraisal of adult intelligence* (4th ed.). Baltimore, MD: Williams & Wilkins.

Wechsler, D. (2014a). *Wechsler Intelligence Scale for Children* (5th ed.). Bloomington, MN: Pearson.

Wechsler, D. (2014b). *WISC-V technical and interpretive manual.* Bloomington, MN: Pearson.

Wechsler, D. (2014c). *WISC-V administration and scoring manual.* Bloomington, MN: Pearson.

Weiss, L. G., Keith, T. Z., Zhu, J., & Chen, H. (2013). WISC-IV and clinical validation of the four- and five-factor interpretative approaches. *Journal of Psychoeducational Assessment, 31*(2), 114–131.

Woodcock, R. W. (1990). Theoretical foundations of the WJ-R measures of cognitive ability. *Journal of Psychoeducational Assessment, 8*, 231–258.

Yerkes, R. M. (1915). A point scale for measuring mental ability. *Proceedings of the National Academy of Sciences of the United States of America, 1*, 114–117.

Two

HOW TO ADMINISTER THE WISC-V

Standardized and nonstandardized procedures should be used together to uncover an individual's true abilities as part of a comprehensive evaluation. Norm-referenced tests, such as the WISC-V, provide information that allows the examiner to compare an individual's performance to the performance of a norm group. In order to obtain accurate scores from a norm-referenced test, procedures and conditions must be followed under a set of standard conditions. When an examiner does so, a fair comparison of the examinee's level of ability can be made to the "normative sample"; that is, a representative group of same-age peers from the general population who were subject to the same procedures and conditions during data collection. The further an evaluation deviates from standardized procedures and conditions, the more error that is introduced into the results and subsequent interpretation of an examinee's performance; consequently, adhering to what is specified is critical. However, as is discussed throughout this book, other procedures, such as interviews, behavioral observations, and informal assessments, should be used alongside results of standardized tests to provide an integrated and complete picture of the examinee. Simply taking a snapshot of an individual's abilities through a time-limited sample of performance, as is done during the administration of any standardized test, including the WISC-V, does not provide sufficient information about the individual for the purposes of diagnosing and making recommendations.

APPROPRIATE TESTING CONDITIONS

The testing environment and testing materials necessary for quality administration are addressed in the sections below.

Testing Environment

There are some issues regarding the testing environment that are important to address when testing an individual of any age, but especially children or adolescents. For example, it is important to have a testing environment that is relatively bland and free of visual or auditory distractions. The optimal surroundings should not have toys or windows that can lead to distractions. However, the surroundings should not be so formal that the child or adolescent thinks he or she is in a medical examination room. The testing environment should be comfortable for the examiner and examinee. In most situations, only the examiner and the examinee should be in the testing room during the evaluation. In order to test an individual with the WISC-V in a manner consistent with standardized procedures, it is necessary to sit at a table. However, in some cases we have found that when testing a highly energetic young child, it may be advantageous to be prepared to move the testing materials to another location, such as the floor, where the child will best attend to the examiner. With some children it may be necessary to alternate between highly structured testing activities at a table and more informal activities that can be conducted on the floor. In any case, it is a good idea to use a clipboard throughout the testing session(s) as it provides a smooth writing surface and can be transported to the floor or other locations, if necessary. Any significant issues concerning the environment or changes such as testing on the floor should be described in the evaluation report so the reader knows the testing situation perhaps did not approximate standardized procedures.

Testing Materials

During testing, we recommend that that the examiner sit directly across from the examinee because the WISC-V is designed to be used from across a table. Having a square table edge (as contrasted with a round table edge) works well for subtests such as Block Design where alignment is critical. The testing manual may be propped up on the table and positioned to the side with the Record Form between the examiner and examinee. This positioning allows the examiner to read the directions easily, but does not construct an artificial "secrecy barrier" between the examiner and examinee. If it is distracting to the examinee to see the examiner writing, then the examiner can place the Record Form behind the manual or can use a clipboard.

Only the testing materials that are in immediate use should be visible to the examinee; therefore, the examiner should remove them immediately from the table top at the end of each subtest. Stimulus materials can easily distract any individual, especially a young child, if they are in view. It can also sometimes be difficult to take test materials away from a child if he or she is playing with them when moving to the next subtest. We recommend that the examiner keep testing materials on the floor or on a nearby chair so that they are readily available, but out of the child's view and reach.

Because the WISC-V test kit contains a variety of materials, including three stimulus books, two pencils, nine blocks, three manuals, two response booklets, three scoring keys, and one Record Form, we recommend that the examiner double-check that all necessary materials are present prior to beginning testing. A few necessary materials are not contained in the WISC-V test kit and, therefore, the examiner will need to bring these materials to the testing room. These items include a stopwatch, a clipboard, two no. 2 pencils with and without erasers, a red pencil without an eraser, and extra paper for taking notes. Rapid Reference 2.1 provides a list of things to remember when preparing to administer the WISC-V.

RAPPORT WITH EXAMINEE

The next two sections address establishing and maintaining rapport with the examinee.

Establishing Rapport

When working with children and adolescents, building rapport is critical to obtaining valid test results. Prior to test administration, examiners should ensure familiarity and comfort with the "mechanical aspects of test administration

≡ *Rapid Reference 2.1*

What to Remember When Preparing to Administer the WISC-V

- Quiet, distraction-free room with table and chairs
- Smooth writing surface
- Extra pencils (no. 2 and red) with and without erasers
- Stopwatch
- Clipboard, if desired
- Extra paper and writing instruments (for recording observations)

Sources: D. P. Flanagan & A. S. Kaufman, *Essentials of WISC-IV Assessment* (2nd ed.). Copyright © 2009 John Wiley & Sons, Inc.

A. S. Kaufman & E. O. Lichtenberger, *Essentials of WISC-III and WPPSI-R Assessment.* Copyright © 2000 John Wiley & Sons, Inc.

including giving directions to the examinee, handling materials, timing stimuli exposure, and timing and recording responses" (Wechsler, 2014a, p. 27). This familiarity allows the examiner to devote attention to the examinee while adhering to standard test administration. Even the most experienced examiners may find that it is challenging to juggle the maintenance of rapport with adherence to standardized procedures. When interacting with an examinee and especially with a child, it is important to allow him or her enough time to become accustomed to the examiner before beginning the test. Addressing the child by his or her name, telling the child the examiner's name, and spending a reasonable amount of time interacting with the child prior to formal testing (e.g., discussing the child's interests and hobbies) can aid in establishing rapport. When conversing with a child, the examiner should remember to be open, honest, and genuine. Any comments that the examiner makes upon initially meeting a child, or throughout testing, should be mildly positive. That is, too much interest in or praise of a child's conversation, appearance, and so on, may be viewed suspiciously.

In addition to time to accustom themselves to the examiner, children must be given time to acclimate to the testing environment itself. The manner in which the examiner, or in some cases a parent or caregiver, has introduced the child to the testing situation can have either positive or negative effects throughout testing. Therefore, we encourage examiners and parents to explain to children ahead of time what they should expect during the testing session(s). Such explanations can alleviate any anticipatory anxiety that the child may have and should vary according to the child's developmental level. For example, it is good to let the child know that the examiner will be showing him or her blocks and books containing pictures and words and will be asking some questions. We advise examiners (and parents) not to use the word *test* when introducing the situation to the child because the word has a negative connotation for many children and can elicit a fear reaction. However, if a child asks directly, "Am I going to take a test?" then it is best not to lie, but rather explain to the child, "Yes, but it is a different kind of test, not like a school test" (Wechsler, 2014a, p. 27). One technique is to ask the child if he or she knows why he or she is with the examiner. This can help directly address concerns or questions the child has. Examiners should also be sure to explain that no one answers all questions correctly, that some questions are easy and some are difficult for everyone, and that what may start off as a fairly easy task could become rather difficult.

Although an examiner should retain control of the testing situation at all times, it is important to structure the assessment sessions according to the child's needs. Some children may need frequent breaks due to a medical condition (e.g., cerebral palsy), and others may fatigue easily and require several short evaluation sessions (e.g., individuals with Attention-Deficit/Hyperactivity Disorder [ADHD]). Examiners should obtain sufficient information about a child's medical and behavioral history prior to the testing session to ensure the validity of the findings. Intermittent breaks and perhaps having a drink of water should be suggested if these may be helpful to the child, but not as suggestions given to each child as a routine. Examiners should also remember not to speak in a condescending, pejorative or lower-age-level manner to children of any age. Rather, they should try to adjust their vocabulary to the child's developmental level. Adolescents may become particularly uncooperative if they are treated like younger children. With adolescents it is important to try to initiate a conversation that is interesting to them but that does not appear overly invasive, showing respect for their boundaries. A balance between formality and informality—between being professional and being friendly—should be achieved when testing children and adolescents. Rapid Reference 2.2 provides a list of key points for establishing positive rapport with children and adolescents.

≡ Rapid Reference 2.2

Keys to Establishing Positive Rapport

- Effectively introduce the examinee to the testing activities.
- Avoid the word *test*.
- Introduce the assessment following the standardized instructions on page 77 of the *WISC-V Administration and Scoring Manual* (Wechsler, 2014a).
- Allow the examinee ample time to adjust to the testing situation.
- Achieve a balance between professional (formal) and friendly (informal) demeanor.
- Correct any misperceptions that the examinee may have about the purpose of testing.
- Describe the examiner's role clearly and maintain control of the testing situation.
- Tell examinees that the examiner may use a stopwatch and will record their answers.

Sources: D. P. Flanagan & A. S. Kaufman, *Essentials of WISC-IV Assessment* (2nd ed.). Copyright © 2009 John Wiley & Sons, Inc.

A. S. Kaufman & E. O. Lichtenberger, *Essentials of WISC-III and WPPSI-R Assessment*. Copyright © 2000 John Wiley & Sons, Inc.

Maintaining Rapport

Gaining the attention of a child and sometimes of an adolescent is often not as difficult as keeping his or her attention and motivating him or her. This is when the delicate balance between rapport and adherence to standardized test procedures becomes especially important. Providing frequent praise for an examinee's efforts is important for maintaining his or her attention and motivation. The examiner should pay close attention to signs of waning attention, frustration, or lack of motivation. Such signs may be verbal (e.g., "How much longer?" or "These are too hard") or nonverbal (e.g., increased fidgeting, sighing, grimacing). These observations are signals to the examiner that it may be necessary to increase encouragement and praise or perhaps to take a break. See Rapid Reference 2.3 for a list of ways to give appropriate feedback and encouragement.

Encouragement and praise may be delivered in many different ways (e.g., an understanding smile, statements such as, "I like the way you keep trying your best," "You're working hard," "Wow, you're a hard worker"). However, it is important that praise not be overly repetitive as it may lose its reinforcing effects. Likewise, examiners should be careful when praising an individual's efforts to ensure that feedback is not about whether his or her responses are correct; praise working hard without indicating if the response was correct or not. Encouragement should be given throughout administration of the items, not only when the

≡ Rapid Reference 2.3

Appropriate Feedback and Encouragement

- Praise frequently, but don't be repetitive, which may decrease the reinforcement value.
- Be aware that encouragement/feedback may be verbal or nonverbal. For example, smile or say "You sure are working hard," or "I can see you are trying your best," and so on.
- Praise and encourage the examinee's effort.
- Be careful *not* to give feedback on whether a particular response is right or wrong.
- Give encouragement *throughout* items, not just when the examinee is struggling.

Sources: D. P. Flanagan & A. S. Kaufman, *Essentials of WISC-IV Assessment* (2nd ed.). Copyright © 2009 John Wiley & Sons, Inc.

A. S. Kaufman & E. O. Lichtenberger, *Essentials of WISC-III and WPPSI-R Assessment*. Copyright © 2000 John Wiley & Sons, Inc.

examinee is struggling or giving incorrect responses. It is then important when writing the report to discuss the examinee's attention, focus, and length of time he or she is able to work, as a nonstandardized finding. It could be that the skill measured by the WISC-V subtests are average and unremarkable, but the examinee's ability to focus and stay on task during the evaluation is the most important detail to be reported.

Some individuals may require more than verbal and nonverbal praise to maintain motivation. In these cases, it may be useful to develop a reward system. For example, an agreement may be reached that the child can play with certain toys after a required number of tasks have been completed. Sometimes a small snack may be used as a reward, but this should always be discussed with the parent ahead of time (some parents disapprove of certain types of foods, don't want dinner spoiled, or will need to warn the examiner about their child's food allergies). As with taking breaks or having a drink of water, not all children need tangible rewards to work with and for the examiner. Adult attention is a powerful reinforcer and should be used often.

Maintaining the individual's motivational level requires consistent effort on the examiner's part. It is important to be able to remove materials skillfully and present the next item or task quickly, which creates a smooth and rapid administration pace. This is critical with younger children and individuals who have attention difficulties, for whom considerable time between subtests may be distracting. It is wise to continue small talk while recording behavioral observations between subtests, as this helps maintain an examinee's attention, but it is important to limit such conversation to the time between subtests. Frequent eye contact also helps maintain rapport; thus, it is critical for the examiner to be familiar with the standardized instructions. If considerable effort is needed to read the material, the examiner is probably not adequately observing the examinee. This is not to say that the test instructions should not be read verbatim, they must be; but knowing the instructions well allows the examiner to pay attention to the individual being tested.

Children and especially adolescents may occasionally refuse to cooperate, be easily fatigued, or become too anxious to continue. In such situations it is appropriate to give several breaks throughout the session or to reschedule for another day, keeping in mind that a second session should occur as soon as possible, preferably within one week. However, examiners should be aware that many children are skilled in "testing" them as examiners and may try to distract him or her from the task at hand. Attending to such behavior helps to keep the session flowing. When individuals of any age indicate that they do not want to continue with a subtest (e.g., a challenging task or item), provide encouragement such as "Just

≡ *Rapid Reference 2.4*

· ·

Keys to Maintaining Rapport

- Provide frequent praise and encouragement.
- Praise examinees for their effort rather than the correctness of their responses.
- Record all responses, not just incorrect responses, to avoid giving inadvertent cues that a response is incorrect.
- Set up a reward system if necessary.
- Give frequent breaks if necessary.
- Reschedule testing if the examinee is too tired, anxious, or uncooperative.
- Make eye contact.
- Make smooth and rapid transitions *between* subtests.
- Use small talk *between* subtests, but not *during* subtests.
- Familiarize yourself ahead of time with test directions and test materials.
- Be subtle, not distracting, when using a stopwatch.

Sources: D. P. Flanagan & A. S. Kaufman, *Essentials of WISC-IV Assessment* (2nd ed.). Copyright © 2009 John Wiley & Sons, Inc.

A. S. Kaufman & E. O. Lichtenberger, *Essentials of WISC-III and WPPSI-R Assessment.* Copyright © 2000 John Wiley & Sons, Inc.

try your best" or "Give it your best shot." To prevent undue frustration during subtests with strict time limits, it may be useful to allow the individual to work for a few moments after the time limit has expired if he or she is actively involved in the task. Although any response given on timed tests after the time limit has expired is not counted toward the score, allowing extra time under these circumstances may decrease discouragement. Another technique could be to administer two subtests per day for five days in a row; five short sessions to mitigate the examinee's difficulty with attention. Rapid Reference 2.4 provides a list of ideas to help you maintain rapport with examinees.

Any changes to the typical test administration should be addressed in the written report. In addition, it is important to report the examinee's behavior during the testing; for example, the examinee's attention to the task, how long he or she can work, how hard he or she worked, verbalizations in an attempt to stop the testing or particular subtests. Also report if testing occurred over multiple days, if the session or sessions were unusually long or short, etc. Similarly, if the examinee is particularly hard working, say so in the report. These nonstandardized observations can be significant and can be more valuable than the particular index or subtest scores.

TESTING INDIVIDUALS WITH SPECIAL NEEDS

Children or adolescents with special needs—including those with speech, language, or hearing deficits; visual impairments; intellectual disability; sensory, or neurological physical disabilities; or behavioral disorders—may require certain modifications during an evaluation to ensure the evaluation results reflect their abilities accurately. Therefore, it is important to obtain thorough information about any of these conditions from the caregiver prior to beginning the evaluation. The caregiver may be able to suggest the best way to elicit a response from the child when he or she is presented with verbal and nonverbal stimuli. This information is likely to lead to the most appropriate modifications or accommodations during an evaluation for a child with special needs. Examiners should be prepared to be flexible with regard to the types of accommodations that may be needed for any individual with specific impairments or disabilities, and should be aware of conditions that may occur earlier than are typical, such as fatigue or distraction. In short, the examiner must understand the specific needs of any child or adolescent, make appropriate modifications or accommodations as necessary, and pay close attention to signs of inattention, tiredness, fatigue, and the like to make sure that the evaluation constitutes a fair assessment of the individual's cognitive abilities. As noted in the *WISC-V Administration and Scoring Manual* (Wechsler, 2014a), "Any and all modifications from the standard administration and scoring instructions (e.g., nonstandard administration order, substitutions, translations) should be documented on the Record Form and considered when interpreting test results" (p. 18). It is very common and appropriate that accommodations are made because of an examinee's disability or needs. The extent and types of accommodations are based on the examiner's clinical judgment. But the extent and types of accommodations made must be extensively explained in the written report, as this allows the reader to judge the validity of the findings based on the extent of the accommodations made.

As stated previously, when modifications are made to the standardized testing procedures for any reason, test scores may be altered in an unknown way and use of the test's norms may be invalid. Clinical judgment must be exercised in determining whether modifications to the test or the impact of the specific impairment itself prevent the calculation of valid standard scores. All modifications must be described in the written report to allow the reader to judge the extent of the modifications or accommodations as they relate to test validity. Modifications may include the following:

1. Administer only the Verbal Comprehension Index and Auditory Working Memory Index subtests and Arithmetic (a Fluid Reasoning Subtest) to an examinee with a visual impairment. However, for Vocabulary (a primary subtest) the first four items (pictorial stimuli) cannot be given to individuals with visual impairments who are ages 6–7 years who begin with Item 1, or examinees ages 8–16 years who do not earn perfect scores on Items 5 and 6. For Arithmetic the first five items, which include pictorial stimuli, cannot be administered. Individuals ages 6–7 years begin the Arithmetic subtest with Item 3, so this secondary subtest is not recommended for children age 6–7 years who have visual impairments.

2. For individuals who are deaf or hard of hearing, administer the test in his or her preferred mode of communication (e.g., American Sign Language) or allow him or her to lip-read if he or she is able. Examiners who are skilled in testing children or adolescents who are deaf or hard of hearing are encouraged to study WISC-V Technical Report 2 (Day, Costa, & Raiford, 2015). The Nonverbal Index is an option for this population, with the understanding that the index is not language-free, but language-reduced.

3. Provide an appropriate translation or adaptation for an individual who is an English Learner (EL) by using an interpreter, administering the test bilingually or in the individual's native language, or using an adapted or translated version of the test. It is noteworthy, however, that all of these methods pose interpretive challenges, particularly for verbal subtests (e.g., Verbal Comprehension Subtests) because the difficulty level of words is often not equivalent across languages. Further, individuals who are bilingual can differ in levels of language proficiency and preference across tasks. Finally, beyond linguistic factors, cultural variables must be considered when assessing ELs (Ortiz, Ochoa, & Dynda, 2012; Wechsler, 2014a).

4. Consider administering only the Verbal Comprehension, Visual Spatial, Fluid Reasoning, Working Memory, Naming Speed, and Symbol Translation subtests that require minimal or no motor skills to individuals with motor impairments. Cancellation, which involves less fine motor skill, may serve as a substitute for Coding in deriving the FSIQ (Full Scale IQ).

5. Extend testing, as necessary, over more than one session for individuals with special needs.

It is important to realize that successful evaluation of any individual with special needs may require the use of supplemental measures or another instrument altogether. Careful consideration of the individual's needs, coupled with astute observations of his or her range of verbal and nonverbal capabilities, will help to determine what types of modifications are best.

DON'T FORGET

The extent and types of accommodations made must be explained in the written report, as this allows the reader to judge the validity of the findings based on the accommodations made.

ADMINISTRATION CONSIDERATIONS

In the next sections we address administration considerations for testing children at the extreme ends of the age range, rules for starting and discontinuing subtests, recording responses, timing, querying, and repeating items.

Special Considerations for Testing Children at the Extreme Ends of the Age Range

The WISC-V may be administered to children as young as age 6 years 0 months and as old as age 16 years 11 months. When testing children or adolescents at these lower and upper limits of the WISC-V age range, examiners must decide whether this instrument is the most appropriate or whether, for example, the WPPSI-IV or WAIS-IV, respectively, may be preferable. When making this determination, it is recommended that examiners use the WISC-V with 6-year-olds who are considered to be of average intelligence (or higher). Otherwise, the WPPSI-IV or another instrument with norms for children ages 6 years and younger should be used as deemed appropriate. A good gauge of the need to use the WPPSI-IV or another instrument is the number of subtests on which the examinee establishes a sufficient basal. If multiple subtests do not have a clear basal, another instrument would probably provide a more valid picture of the

Table 2.1 Deciding on the WISC-V versus Another Battery for 6- and 16-Year-Olds

Age	Estimated Level of Ability	Battery to Administer
6–0 to 7–7	Below Average	WPPSI-IV or an appropriate alternative battery
	Average	WISC-V
	Above Average	WISC-V
16–0 to 16–11	Below Average	WISC-V
	Average	WISC-V
	Above Average	WAIS-IV or an appropriate alternative battery

Note: WPPSI-IV = *Wechsler Preschool and Primary Scale of Intelligence–Fourth Edition*; WAIS-IV = *Wechsler Adult Intelligence Scale–Fourth Edition.*

examinee's abilities. Likewise, it is recommended that examiners use the WISC-V with 16-year-olds who are considered to be within the average range or below. Otherwise, the WAIS-IV or another instrument with norms for adolescents and adults should be used. A good gauge of the need to use the WAIS-IV or another instrument is the number of subtests on which the examinee does not establish a ceiling. That is, to ensure the availability of a sufficient number of items to assess an examinee's ability adequately, the WPPSI-IV should be used with 6-year-olds who are below the average range because it provides significantly easier items than the WISC-V, and the WAIS-IV should be used with 16-year-olds who are above the average range because it provides significantly more difficult items than the WISC-V. These recommendations are summarized in Table 2.1.

RULES FOR STARTING AND DISCONTINUING SUBTESTS

The administration rules of the WISC-V are detailed in the *WISC-V Administration and Scoring Manual* (Wechsler, 2014a) and are also located on the Record Form. In this section we highlight the general administration rules. Some of the WISC-V subtests start at predetermined items according to the examinee's age, whereas other subtests begin at Item 1 regardless of age. These start points are easily found on the Record Form at the beginning of each subtest. Rapid Reference 2.5 identifies which subtests have age-appropriate start points (denoted by checkmarks) and reverse rules and also provides the start points for specific age categories throughout the entire age range of the battery. Table 2.2 summarizes WISC-V subtest reverse rules.

≡ Rapid Reference 2.5

. . . .

WISC-V Subtest Starting Points and Whether Reverse Rules Apply

Subtest	Age-Appropriate Start Point (Reverse Rule)	Age and Start Point
1. Block Design	✓ (Yes)	6–7: Item 1 8–16: Item 3
2. Similarities	✓ (Yes)	6–7: Sample, then Item 1 8–11: Sample, then Item 5 12–16: Sample, then Item 8
3. Matrix Reasoning	✓ (Yes)	6–8: Samples A & B, then Item 1 9–11: Samples A & B, then Item 5 12–16: Samples A & B, then Item 9
4. Digit Span	✓ (No)	Forward Ages 6–16: Item 1 Backward Ages 6–16: Sample Item Trial 1 & 2, then Item 1 Sequencing Ages 6–7: Qualifying Items; Sample Item A Trials 1 & 2 and then Sample Item B Trials 1 & 2, then Item 1; Ages 8–16: Sample Item A Trials 1 & 2 & Sample Item B Trial 1 & 2 then Item 1
5. Coding	✓ (No)	Ages 6–7: Form A Demonstration Items, Sample Items, then Test Items Ages 8–16: Form B Demonstration Items, Sample Items, then Test Items
6. Vocabulary	✓ (Yes)	6–7: Item 1 8–11: Item 5 12–16: Item 9
7. Figure Weights	✓ (Yes)	Ages 6–8: Sample A, then 1 Ages 9–16: Sample B, then 4
8. Visual Puzzles	✓ (Yes)	Ages 6–8: Demonstration, Sample, then Item 1 Ages 9–11: Demonstration, Sample, then Item 5 Ages 12–16: Demonstration, Sample, then Item 8

(continued)

(continued)

Subtest	Age-Appropriate Start Point (Reverse Rule)	Age and Start Point
9. Picture Span	✓ (Yes)	Ages 6–16: Samples B & C then Item 4
10. Symbol Search	✓ (No)	Ages 6–7: Form A Demonstration Items, Sample Items, then Test Items Ages 8–16: Form B Demonstration Items, Sample Items, then Test Items
11. Information	✓ (Yes)	6–8: Item 1 9–16: Item 8
12. Picture Concepts	✓ (Yes)	Ages 6–8: Samples A & B, then Item 1 Ages 9–11: Samples A & B, then Item 4 Ages 12–16: Samples A & B, then Item 7
13. Letter-Number Sequencing	✓ (No)	Ages 6–7: Qualifying Items, Demonstration A, Sample A, then Item 1 Ages 8–16: Demonstration A, Sample A, then Item 1
14. Cancellation	(No)	6–16: Demonstration Item, Sample Item, then Item 1
15. Naming Speed Literacy	✓ (No)	Age 6: Demonstration A, Sample A, then Item 1 Ages 7–8: Demonstration B, Sample B, then Item 2 Ages 9–16: Sample C, then Item 3
16. Naming Speed Quantity	✓ (No)	Age 6: Sample A, then Item 1 Ages 7–16: Sample B, then Item 2
17. Immediate Symbol Translation	(No)	Ages 6–16: Item 1
18. Comprehension	✓ (Yes)	6–11: Item 1 12–16: Item 3
19. Arithmetic	✓ (Yes)	6–7: Item 3 8–9: Item 8 10–16: Item 11
20. Delayed Symbol Translation	(No)	6–16: Item 1

Subtest	Age-Appropriate Start Point (Reverse Rule)	Age and Start Point
21. Recognition Symbol Translation	(No)	6–16: Item 1

Note: ✓ = Subtest has age-based start point. (Yes) = subtest has reversal rule. (No) = subtest does not have reversal rule.

Note: Examinees suspected of developmental delay or cognitive impairment may begin subtests at earlier items.

Source: D. Wechsler, *WISC-V Administration and Scoring Manual.* Copyright © 2014 NCS Pearson, Inc. Adapted and reproduced by permission. All rights reserved.

Table 2.2 Summary of WISC-V Subtest Reverse Rules

Subtest	Reverse Rule
1. Block Design	Ages 8–16: Imperfect score on either of the first two items given, administer preceding items in reverse order until two consecutive perfect scores are obtained.
2. Similarities	Ages 8–16: Imperfect score on either of the first two items given, administer preceding items in reverse order until two consecutive perfect scores are obtained.
3. Matrix Reasoning	Ages 9–16: Imperfect score on either of the first two items given, administer preceding items in reverse order until two consecutive perfect scores are obtained.
4. Digit Span	None
5. Coding	None
6. Vocabulary	Ages 8–16: Imperfect score on either of the first two items given, administer preceding items in reverse order until two consecutive perfect scores are obtained.
7. Figure Weights	Ages 9–16: Imperfect score on either of the first two items given, administer preceding items in reverse order until two consecutive perfect scores are obtained.
8. Visual Puzzles	Ages 9–16: Imperfect score on either of the first two items given, administer preceding items in reverse order until two consecutive perfect scores are obtained.
9. Picture Span	Ages 6–16: Imperfect score on either of the first two items given, administer preceding items in reverse order until two consecutive perfect scores are obtained.

(continued)

(*continued*)

Subtest	Reverse Rule
10. Symbol Search	None
11. Information	Ages 9–16: Imperfect score on either of the first two items given, administer preceding items in reverse order until two consecutive perfect scores are obtained.
12. Picture Concepts	Ages 9–16: Imperfect score on either of the first two items given, administer preceding items in reverse order until two consecutive perfect scores are obtained.
13. Letter-Number Sequencing	None
14. Cancellation	None
15. Naming Speed Literacy	None
16. Naming Speed Quantity	None
17. Immediate Symbol Translation	None
18. Comprehension	Ages 12–16: Imperfect score on either of the first two items given, administer preceding items in reverse order until two consecutive perfect scores are obtained.
19. Arithmetic	Ages 6–16: Imperfect score on either of the first two items given, administer preceding items in reverse order until two consecutive perfect scores are obtained.
20. Delayed Symbol Translation	None
21. Recognition Symbol Translation	None

Source: D. Wechsler, *WISC-V Administration and Scoring Manual.* Copyright © 2014 NCS Pearson, Inc. Adapted and reproduced by permission. All rights reserved.

A basal level of functioning for all primary subtests is established upon obtaining two consecutive perfect scores in the subtest, regardless of the start point, with the exception of Digit Span, Coding, and Symbol Search. Regardless of the start point (with the exception of Digit Span, Coding, and Symbol Search), if the examinee does not receive a perfect score on the first two items, the examiner administers preceding items in reverse order until two consecutive perfect scores are obtained. The examinee receives full credit for all items below the basal.

CAUTION

A common error is to establish a basal, but not to give full credit for all items below the basal when calculating the total raw score for that subtest. When multiple issues of establishing a basal are encountered, this may be a sign that the test may not be the appropriate instrument for the individual.

For an individual suspected of intellectual disability or low cognitive ability, the examiner may administer any subtest starting with the first item, regardless of the recommended age-based start point. This is an acceptable practice and helps reduce the likelihood of encountering the awkwardness of administering items in reverse order until a basal is established. However, there is no merit in starting below the suggested start point unless an intellectual disability or low cognitive ability is suspected or for another clinically relevant reason. To give the examinee more practice or to have him or her receive more success (or other such reasoning) on easy items is not helpful as there is generally sufficient practice in the instructions of the subtest to ensure the examinee understands the task. Starting early on each subtest lengthens the entire test which introduces an unintended variable into the test: extended testing time. It is recommended that examiners begin subtests at the recommended start point unless there is a good clinical reason to deviate from this general rule.

If an examiner opts to begin a subtest with an item before the age-appropriate start point, but then the examinee receives full credit on the first two items at the age-appropriate start point, full credit must be given to all previous items even if one or more of those items were answered incorrectly. Remain aware of this scoring rule while administering subtests to prevent a premature discontinuation of the subtest prior to the age-appropriate start point. This scoring rule can be a little confusing, but it makes sense because if the examiner had begun administering at the age-appropriate start point, then the examiner would not have known that there was an easier item that the examinee would have missed. This rule is consistent with standardized procedures.

In addition to start points and reverse rules, subtests also have *discontinue rules*. Start points and discontinue rules were developed to minimize testing time and maintain rapport. Similar to start points, discontinue rules differ across subtests. These rules typically require that a certain number of consecutive zero-point responses be obtained prior to discontinuing the subtest. If a discontinue criterion is met while reversing, points are not awarded for items beyond the discontinue point, even if they were originally earned by the examinee (provided the scoring rule described in the previous paragraph regarding age-appropriate start points has also been followed). Discontinue points are easily found in the Record Form at the beginning of each subtest. Table 2.3 lists the discontinue rules for the WISC-V subtests.

Table 2.3 Summary of WISC-V Subtest Discontinue Rules

Subtest	Discontinue Rule
1. Block Design	After 2 consecutive scores of 0
2. Similarities	After 3 consecutive scores of 0
3. Matrix Reasoning	After 3 consecutive scores of 0
4. Digit Span	*Forward* After scores of 0 on both trials of at item *Backward* After scores of 0 on both trials of at item *Sequencing* Ages 6–7: After an incorrect response to Qualifying Item or after scores of 0 on both trials of an item Ages 8–16: After scores of 0 on both trials of at item
5. Coding	After 120 seconds
6. Vocabulary	After 3 consecutive scores of 0
7. Figure Weights	After 3 consecutive scores of 0
8. Visual Puzzles	After 3 consecutive scores of 0
9. Picture Span	After 3 consecutive scores of 0
10. Symbol Search	After 120 seconds
11. Information	After 3 consecutive scores of 0
12. Picture Concepts	After 3 consecutive scores of 0
13. Letter-Number Sequencing	Ages 6–7: After an incorrect response to either Qualifying Item OR after scores of 0 on all three trials of an item Ages 8–16: After scores of 0 on all three trials of an item
14. Cancellation	After 45 seconds for each item
15. Naming Speed Literacy	Age 6: After administering Item 2, Trial 2 Ages 7–16: After administering Item 3, Trial 2
16. Naming Speed Quantity	Age 6: After administering Item 1, Trial 2 Ages 7–16: After administering Item 2, Trial 2
17. Immediate Symbol Translation	If the examinee's cumulative raw score is less than or equal to the value specified at decision point: Decision Point A: Raw score less than or equal to 9 Decision Point B: Raw score less than or equal to 20 Decision Point C: Raw score less than or equal to 30
18. Comprehension	After 3 consecutive scores of 0
19. Arithmetic	After 3 consecutive scores of 0
20. Delayed Symbol Translation	At the same decision point as Immediate Symbol Translation
21. Recognition Symbol Translation	At the same decision point as Immediate Symbol Translation

Source: D. Wechsler, *WISC-V Administration and Scoring Manual.* Copyright © 2014 NCS Pearson, Inc. Adapted and reproduced by permission. All rights reserved.

When administering a subtest, examiners may occasionally find that they are unsure of how to score a response and, therefore, whether a subtest should be discontinued or not. Most often this uncertainty may arise during Verbal Comprehension subtests that have some subjectivity in scoring, most notably Similarities and Vocabulary. If it is not possible to determine quickly whether a response is correct, it is best to continue administering further items until the examiner is certain that the discontinue rule has been met. This procedure is the safest because scores can be reviewed later and items that are passed after the discontinue criterion has been met can be excluded from the examinee's total raw score on that subtest. There is no penalty or standardization error for over-querying. When in doubt . . . query. Also, the information obtained on the items that were accidentally administered beyond the discontinue criterion may provide valuable *clinical* information. If the examiner does not follow the procedure just described, and notes later that he or she did not administer enough items to meet the discontinue rule, then the subtest should be considered spoiled. Examiners should *not* go back and administer the items in an attempt to meet the discontinue rule. If an examiner needs to derive a scaled score based on the total raw score on this subtest, he or she would need to explain that the scaled score most likely underestimates the examinee's ability.

A noteworthy exception to discontinue rules occurs on the Immediate Symbol Translation, Delayed Symbol Translation, and Recognition Symbol Translation subtests. For Immediate Symbol Translation, the discontinue criterion is based on the examinee's cumulative raw score after a specific number of items has been administered. At each possible decision point, the examinee's cumulative raw score is calculated and a determination is made as to whether it is less than or equal to a specified value. Immediate Symbol Translation is discontinued when a cumulative score is less than or equal to a specified value. If the score exceeds the value, testing is continued through to the next decision point. Though it was noted previously that additional items can be administered when the discontinue criterion is questionable, an examiner would not routinely administer additional items on Immediate Symbol Translation, because doing so provides additional exposure to the visual-verbal pairs (Wechsler, 2014a).

RECORDING RESPONSES

The manner in which responses are recorded during paper-and-pencil administration of the WISC-V is very important. Examiners should be careful to write down responses verbatim for all items administered or attempted. This recording is especially important for Similarities, Vocabulary, Information, and

Comprehension (i.e., subtests that tend to elicit a good amount of verbiage). It is sometimes difficult to write down all responses of very verbal examinees, but examiners must try their best. Even when only brief verbal responses are given, such as during the Digit Span and Arithmetic subtests, they should be recorded, because they may prove useful in the interpretation process. It is tempting to write down only an examinee's score, rather than the exact response, but this practice is discouraged. If only a 0, 1, or 2 is recorded on the Record Form, then irretrievable clinical information may be lost. Recording all responses affords the examiner an opportunity to note patterns in responding that may be useful in interpretation. Very frequently what the examinee says and how he or she behaves during the testing is more important than the specific subtest or index scores. For these reasons, it is important to attempt to capture most of what is said verbatim. The use of abbreviations can make the process of recording information easier, and can also help to balance the maintenance of rapport with the gathering of essential information. Rapid Reference 2.6 lists commonly used abbreviations.

As noted in the *WISC-V Administration and Scoring Manual* (Wechsler, 2014a), "Some types of responses and testing behaviors can yield process observations, or raw scores that are based on the examiner's observations of such responses and testing behaviors" (p. 50). For instance, a DK may be used to denote that an examinee noted that he or she did not know a response to a specific item. Appendix D of the *WISC-V Technical and Interpretive Manual* (Wechsler, 2014b) provides normative data (e.g., base rates) for specific process observations. To obtain a raw score for a process observation, the examiner must record an appropriate abbreviation (e.g., DK, IR, SC) on the Record Form for each item or trial during which the behavior of interest was observed. Following this, the examiner tallies the number of times the abbreviation is recorded to obtain a raw score for the process observation of interest and compares that score to base rate data provided in Appendix D of the *WISC-V Technical and Interpretive Manual* (Wechsler, 2014b).

In addition to recording what an examinee says, examiners might find it appropriate to record his or her own statements. For example, if an examiner probes to clarify an answer by saying "Tell me more about it," the letter Q should be recorded in parentheses on the Record Form directly after the queried response. During the process of interpretation of an individual's performance, it may be of clinical interest to note whether many of the responses were elicited by querying, or whether they were produced spontaneously. Beyond noting the level of querying typically required for the individual, it

≡ Rapid Reference 2.6

Abbreviations for Recording Responses on WISC-V Subtests

Abbreviation	Description
@	at
ABT	about
B	both
BC	because
C	see
DK	don't know
EO	everyone
-G	ing
INC	incomplete (response wasn't completed within the time limit)
IR	item repeated
LL	looks like
NR	no response
P	prompt
PPL	people
(Q)	query administered
RR	child requested repetition, but item was not repeated
SC	child self-corrected
Shd	should
SO	someone
ST	something
SV	child used observable subvocalization
↓	decrease
↑	increase
U	you
w/	with
w/o	without
W/d	would
Y	why

Sources: D. P. Flanagan & A. S. Kaufman, *Essentials of WISC-IV Assessment* (2nd ed.). Copyright © 2009 John Wiley & Sons, Inc.
A. S. Kaufman & E. O. Lichtenberger, *Essentials of WISC-III and WPPSI-R Assessment.* Copyright © 2000 John Wiley & Sons, Inc.
A. S. Kaufman, S. E. Raiford, & D. L. Coalson, *Intelligent Testing with the WISC-V.* Copyright © 2016 John Wiley & Sons, Inc.

may be useful to determine whether the quality of response improved after the individual was queried. Some individuals may tend not to add anything to their first responses (e.g., they may respond to most queries with "I don't know"); others may elaborate a great deal after a query, but may not necessarily improve their scores; and some individuals will improve their scores most of the time when queried.

TIMING

Precision is necessary for administration of subtests that require timing. The examiner must be prepared to utilize his or her stopwatch to monitor strict time limits for 9 of the 21 WISC-V subtests. The use of a stopwatch should be unobtrusive so that it is not distracting to the examinee. If possible, examiners should use a stopwatch that does not make beeping sounds. If examinees ask whether they are being timed, examiners may want to respond, "Yes, but you don't need to worry about that." The WISC-V Record Form contains a picture of a clock at the beginning of each timed subtest as a reminder to examiners that a stopwatch is required. Some subtests have no time limits, but are subject to a 30-second guideline. The 30-second guideline should not be rigidly applied and a stopwatch should not be used to mark response time. This guideline should be used to maintain administration pace and decrease the potential for fatigue. Therefore, if the examinee is spending an extended amount of time considering responses without benefit to performance, a 30-second estimate before moving on is appropriate. However, if the examinee is performing well and taking extra time to consider responses, the examiner should be more generous with the time limit. During the examinee's "thinking time," the examiner can maintain eye contact, smile, and look expectantly at the examinee.

As the examiner states the directions to the timed subtests, he or she should already have the stopwatch out and ready for use. This is especially helpful when testing examinees who are impulsive and may want to begin testing earlier than expected. Also, there are subtests such as Block Design and Picture Span that require very precise timing. The examiner must not expose the stimulus page and then fumble in starting the stopwatch, since this increases the time in which the examinee sees the stimulus card, and this is not how the subtests were normed. Rapid Reference 2.7 lists some important points to remember when timing an examinee's performance.

DON'T FORGET
. . . .

The nine timed subtests on the WISC-V are the following:

1. Block Design
2. Coding
3. Figure Weights
4. Visual Puzzles
5. Symbol Search
6. Cancellation
7. Arithmetic
8. Naming Speed Literacy
9. Naming Speed Quantity

Note: Although Picture Span does not have strict time limits for the examinee to provide a response, this subtest does require a stopwatch to time accurately stimulus exposure.

≡ *Rapid Reference 2.7*
. . . .

Important Points to Remember When Using a Stopwatch on Timed Tests

1. If an examinee asks for clarification or repetition of an item after timing has begun, the examiner will generally continue timing while repeating the item. However, Arithmetic allows the examiner to pause the timer in order to repeat *some* items *once* upon request. Follow the specific guidelines for this subtest to see when to cease timing for item repetition.

2. When an examinee appears to have completed a timed item, but does not provide a clear indication that he or she is finished, ask "Are you done?"

3. If the examiner stops timing because an examinee appears to have completed an item, he or she should restart the stopwatch immediately upon recognizing that the examinee is still working and record the entire time that he or she worked on that item. The examiner should then estimate the number of seconds that the stopwatch was stopped, and add that estimated number of seconds to the time reflected on the running stopwatch to determine when the time limit has elapsed (and enforce the time limit accordingly). The examiner should also remember to add the estimated number of seconds to the completion time reflected on the stopwatch when the examinee is finished with the item.

4. In the interest of maintaining rapport, a child may be given a few extra seconds to complete an item if he or she is nearing completion when the time limit expires. However, do not award credit for these items completed after the time limit.

QUERYING

Examiner judgment often comes into play during subtests that allow a wide variety of responses, such as many of the Verbal Comprehension subtests. If an examinee's response appears too vague or ambiguous to score, examiners must decide whether to query or prompt for clarification. But in general, if the examiner does not understand what the examinee is saying, how can he or she score the response? The *WISC-V Administration and Scoring Manual* (Wechsler, 2014a) lists responses to Similarities, Vocabulary, Information and Comprehension, items that should be queried. However, the responses in the manual are only illustrative, leaving the examiner to decide whether to query other responses that are not represented. The key to deciding whether to query a response is its ambiguity or incompleteness. The manner in which examinees are queried may impact how they respond. Therefore, it is important that querying be done with neutral, non-leading questions. Good queries include, "Tell me more about it" or "Explain what you mean." The examiner should avoid providing any hints or clues to the answer and should use only the queries listed in the manual. A query should be noted on the Record Form with a (Q).

Examiners should be careful not to ask, "Can you tell me more?" because a likely response is "No." A better technique is for the examiner to show that he or she expects a response from the examinee and say simply some variation of, "Tell me more." This is a soft demand for more information, instead of a question. This subtle difference in the approach can make a big difference in the quantity and quality of the examinee's response.

I Don't Know

Frequently, examinees may say "I don't know" when asked a question on a subtest (especially on Similarities and Vocabulary). This does not necessarily mean that he or she does not know the correct answer. It could mean that the examinee does not know with 100% certainly, so may not wish to be wrong. It might mean that he or she is unsure and doesn't know to "give it their best try." It could mean that the examinee does not know that guessing is acceptable. He or she may know some part of an answer, but not the whole answer. Finally, the examinee may just be tired of trying or of talking to the examiner, and trying to finish the subtest as quickly as possible. So an examiner query at this point is very appropriate: "Well what do you think though?" "Give it your best try," "I know you don't completely know, but what do you think?," or "Give your best thought." Examiners should not assume that when an examinee says, "I don't know," that he or she does not know.

DON'T FORGET

Whenever the examiner queries an examinee, he or she should record "(Q)" on the Record Form next to the response that is queried. The examiner should not query an examinee if he or she spontaneously produced an incorrect or zero-point response, unless a "(Q)" appears next to the same or a similar response in the manual.

Repeating Items

Occasionally, an examinee may not completely hear or understand the instructions or a question that was read. In some cases, the examinee may ask the examiner to repeat the question. Generally, it is okay to repeat a question or set of instructions; however, for the Digit Span, Picture Span, and Letter-Number Sequencing subtests, an item or trial may not be repeated. Additionally, repetitions are not allowed on the Immediate Symbol Translation subtest. Further, on the Arithmetic subtest, item repetition is not allowed for Items 1–20. When an examinee requests to have instructions or an item repeated, the examiner repeats the entire set of instructions or the entire item, not just a portion of it and uses a notation on the Record Form such as IR to see if there is a pattern of frequent requests for repeating certain statements. It is possible that the examinee has a hearing impairment or maybe the question just buys time for the examinee to think more. Nevertheless, it is an examinee behavior and should be recorded.

Another situation that may warrant a repetition of items is a pattern of responding in which the examinee provides correct answers to difficult items and incorrect or "I don't know" responses to easier items. That is, if the examiner believes that the examinee may have known the answers to earlier, easier items, then it is acceptable and desirable to readminister these items, as responses to these testing-of-the-limits procedures may prove useful in interpretation. An examinee may have received a zero on initial items due to anxiety or insecurity, leading to an incorrect response. Testing the limits may reveal that the examinee actually knew the answers to these questions. Although examiners are not permitted to change 0-point responses to 1- or 2-point responses in this situation, information from the testing-of-the-limits procedure may be used, for example, to support an interpretation of a subtest score's reflecting an underestimate of ability due to anxiety. It is important to note, however, that an incorrect response that is *spontaneously* corrected at any time during the evaluation session should be changed from a raw score of 0 to a raw score of 1 or 2 as appropriate.

SUBTEST-BY-SUBTEST RULES OF ADMINISTRATION OF THE WISC-V PRIMARY SUBTESTS

What follows below are step-by-step rules for administering the WISC-V primary subtests.

1. Block Design (Visual Spatial Index and FSIQ)

The WISC-V Block Design subtest requires the examinee to replicate a set of modeled or printed two-dimensional geometric patterns using red-and-white blocks within a specified time limit. The stimulus materials for the Block Design subtest consist of nine cubes, each having two red sides, two white sides, and two red-and-white sides. A stopwatch, the *WISC-V Administration and Scoring Manual* (Wechsler, 2014a), Stimulus Book 1, the blocks, and the Record Form are needed for this subtest.

The WISC-V Block Design subtest administration is based on age-appropriate start points. An examinee age 6–7 years begins with Item 1; an examinee age 8–16 years begins with Item 3. If an examinee age 8–16 does not receive credit on either trial of Item 3 as well as Item 4, the examiner should administer Items 1 and 2 in reverse sequence until the examinee obtains a perfect score on two consecutive items. The Block Design subtest is discontinued after two consecutive zero-point responses.

The WISC-V Block Design subtest, like the WISC-IV Block Design subtest, provides two trials for Items 1, 2, and 3. The examinee works directly from models and pictorial models constructed by the examiner on Items 1–3 and constructs the remaining designs based on the pictorial models presented in the Stimulus Book. If the examinee attempts to duplicate the sides of the model, the examiner should tell the examinee to match only the tops of the blocks. Demonstrations are provided by the examiner on both trials of Items 1–3. The second trial of each of these three items is administered only if the examinee does not assemble the blocks correctly within the time limit during the first trial. Item 1 has a 30-second time limit, Items 2–5 have a 45-second time limit, Items 6–9 have a 75-second time limit, and Items 10–13 have a 120-second time limit. Item 1 utilizes two blocks, Items 2–9 utilize four blocks, and the remaining items include all nine blocks.

Similar to the rotation rules on the WISC-IV Block Design subtest, any rotation of 30 degrees or more is considered an error. The examiner is allowed to correct only the first rotation ("See, it goes this way") and no credit is to be awarded for that item. When the correction is made, the examiner moves the blocks slowly so the examinee sees the subtle change being made. Having the examinee sit up square to the table edge and aligning the Stimulus Book and blocks squarely in front of the examinee can all assist in reducing careless errors which are, regardless of the reason, considered an error and no points are awarded. When an examinee makes a rotation error, the examiner should pay close attention to determine if the error happened because the examiner did not align the materials properly. All incorrect responses, including rotations, should be recorded on the Record Form by sketching the design constructed by the examinee. Correct responses are indicated by placing a checkmark over the grid of stimulus blocks associated with those items on the Record Form. List 2.1 provides

LIST 2.1

Changes in Administration From the WISC-IV to the WISC-V: Subtest 1, Block Design

- Stimulus book images are shown for all items (previously, Items 1 and 2 used the model only). Now, for Items 1 to 3 the examiner constructs a model and places it to the side of the stimulus book that corresponds to the examinee's dominant hand.
- The Block Design ceiling item is now shaped like an X as opposed to the square or diamond design.
- If an examinee tries to duplicate the *sides* of the examiner's model, the examiner should indicate to him or her that only the *tops* need to be the same. Timing continues during the provision of this new prompt.
- If an examinee tries to construct his or her design on *top* of the Stimulus Book, the examiner is required to point and direct the examinee to make his or her design in the area *next* to the Stimulus book.
- Examiners can calculate a *Block Design Partial* score, which credits the examinee for each correctly placed block in his or her design. This score cannot be used in the calculation of the VSI or FSIQ.
- A base rate score is provided for *Rotation Errors*, which are recorded for each item and summed to derive a total raw score.
- A base rate score is provided for *Dimension Errors*, which occur when the examinee breaks the standard organization of blocks for an item (e.g., constructs three rows for a 2 × 2 design). A dimension error occurs if the examinee exhibits this behavior at *any time* during the construction.
- Discontinue after two consecutive scores of 0.

a description of the changes in the administration of the Block Design subtest from WISC-IV to WISC-V. The Don't Forget "Behaviors to Note on Block Design" provides a description of behaviors that the examiner should note during the administration of the Block Design subtest. It is important to note that the behaviors outlined in this Don't Forget box (and in subsequent Don't Forget boxes outlining "behaviors" to note for each WISC-V subtest) provide information that may aid in hypothesis generation. Any hypotheses that are generated from this list, however, must be tested with other methods and data sources. Consistent findings from multiple data sources are necessary to retain or reject hypotheses.

DON'T FORGET

Behaviors to Note on Block Design

- Problem-solving styles while the examinee is manipulating the blocks. Some examinees use a trial-and-error approach, whereas others appear to approach the construction of a design haphazardly, seemingly without learning from earlier errors. Other examinees develop a strategy and use it consistently throughout the subtest.
- The level of planning involved. Does the examinee review the problem systematically and appear to plan carefully before arranging the blocks, or does he or she approach the task impulsively?
- How the examinee arranges the blocks to form a correct response. For example, does he or she work from the outside in, constructing the corners first and then the center of the design, or vice versa? Such approaches may provide information about the examinee's visual analytic style.
- Be aware that motor coordination and hand preference may be apparent during this task. Note whether the examinee seems clumsy in the manipulation of the blocks, has hands that are noticeably trembling, or move very quickly and steadily.
- During Items 1 to 3, which use the model and the pictorial stimuli, displays a preference to use the model or picture as a guide.
- Whether the examinee refers back to the model while working. This could indicate a visual memory difficulty, cautiousness, or other factors.
- Whether the examinee tends to be obsessively concerned with details (e.g., lining up the blocks perfectly). Such behaviors may negatively affect his or her speed.

- How well the examinee persists, especially when the task becomes more difficult. Note how well he or she tolerates frustration. Does he or she persist past the time limit, or give up with time to spare?
- Whether the examinee commits a break-in-configuration error at any time, or seems to understand that items are constrained within a predictable structural matrix. A break-in configuration error occurs when the maximum dimension of the design is exceeded while assembling a construction.
- Commits an uncorrected rotation error (i.e., the construction remains rotated upon completion).
- Performs better on items with model and pictorial stimuli as compared to items with pictorial stimuli only.
- Whether the examinees loses the square shape of some designs (violation of the matrix), even if he or she managed to recreate the overall pattern. This kind of response may indicate figure-ground problems.
- Whether the examinee is noticeably twisting his or her body to obtain a different perspective on the model or is rotating his or her own designs. Such behaviors may indicate visual-perceptual difficulties.
- Whether the examinee fails to recognize that his or her designs look different from the model, as this may indicate visual-perceptual difficulties.

Sources: D. P. Flanagan & A. S. Kaufman, *Essentials of WISC-IV Assessment* (2nd ed.). Copyright © 2009 John Wiley & Sons, Inc.

A. S. Kaufman & E. O. Lichtenberger, *Essentials of WISC-III and WPPSI-R Assessment.* Copyright © 2000 John Wiley & Sons, Inc.

A. S. Kaufman, S. E. Raiford, & D. L. Coalson, *Intelligent Testing with the WISC-V.* Copyright © 2016 John Wiley & Sons, Inc.

Gap and misalignment errors are less common. These occur when gaps in the blocks or misalignments of the designs are greater than about ¼ inch. Gaps are easier to see than the 30-degree rotation errors, but are not corrected as the first rotation error is. For Items 4–13 the presentation sequence is "scramble then show"; the examiner scrambles the blocks, makes sure the correct sides are showing, then shows the stimulus page. If the sequence is reversed and the examinee sees the stimulus page before the blocks are arranged by the examiner, then the examinee is allowed to see the stimulus page for an extra amount of time before timing begins. This leads to inaccurate and inconsistent timing. Also, the examiner should not present the blocks to the examinee in a square; he or she should pick up the blocks a few inches above the table top and drop them so they scatter a little.

CAUTION

· ·

Seating Arrangement for the Block Design Subtest

When administering Block Design, a square table works best. Square examinee's body with the table edge and then present the stimulus book parallel with the table edge. These techniques assure that the examinee is not viewing the stimulus book from an angle, which could elicit rotation errors.

---

2. Similarities (Verbal Comprehension Index and FSIQ)

The WISC-V Similarities subtest requires the examinee to describe how two words that represent common objects or concepts are similar. Unlike Block Design and many other WISC-V subtests, there is no separate stimulus material for the Similarities subtest. The *WISC-V Administration and Scoring Manual* (Wechsler, 2014a) and Record Form are the only materials needed for this subtest.

The WISC-V Similarities subtest item administration is based on age-appropriate start points. Examiners who were familiar with the WISC-IV should be cautioned that the age ranges for each start point vary slightly from previous versions of the test so care should be taken to ensure that the examiner begins with the appropriate item. An examinee age 6–7 years begins with the sample item, then Item 1; an examinee age 8–11 years begins with the sample item, then Item 5; and an examinee age 12–16 years begins with the sample item, then Item 8. If an examinee age 8–16 does not obtain a perfect score on either of the first two administered items, the preceding items should be administered in reverse order until a perfect score on two consecutive items is obtained. The Similarities subtest is discontinued after three consecutive zero-point responses. It should be noted that this again represents a difference from the WISC-IV, where five consecutive zero-point responses were needed to discontinue. If the examiner is unsure about a score on one of the items that may count toward the 3 consecutive zero-point responses, the examiner should administer more items until he or she is sure that a proper discontinue point has been reached. The discussions above concerning "Querying," "I don't know," and "Repeating Items" applies to administering the Similarities subtest.

The first two items of each age-appropriate start point are scored, but they also serve as teaching items. Thus, if the examinee does not provide a 2-point response for either of the first two items administered for his or her age, the examiner provides a correct 2-point response. This is done in order to teach the examinee the type of response expected for each item. However, if an examinee fails to

LIST 2.2

Changes in Administration From the WISC-IV to the WISC-V: Subtest 2, Similarities

- The introduction has been shortened and no longer includes the statement "I am going to say two words and ask you how they are alike."
- There are revised age-appropriate start points.
- Additional teaching items have been added for each age-appropriate start point to ensure that all examinees receive similar opportunity for corrective feedback.
- Discontinue after three consecutive scores of 0.

provide a correct response on the remaining items no further assistance is given. The questions may be repeated as many times as necessary without changing the wording. List 2.2 provides a description of the changes in the administration of the Similarities subtest from WISC-IV to WISC-V. The Don't Forget "Behaviors to Note on Similarities" provides a description of behaviors that the examiner should note during the administration of the Similarities subtest.

DON'T FORGET

Behaviors to Note on Similarities

- Whether the examinee responded more readily to Block Design, which involves pictorial stimuli and manipulatives and can be responded to nonverbally, and then has more difficulty with Similarities, which involves only verbal stimuli and requires a verbal response. Because this is the first subtest with expressive requirements, it can provide important cues about the examinee's ability to respond verbally.
- Whether the examinee provides complete responses or must be repeatedly queried as a cue to give all pertinent information.
- Whether the examinee benefits from feedback (if it is given) on items that allow the examiner to provide an example. Examinees who learn from the example may have flexibility, whereas those who do not may be more rigid or concrete.
- Be aware that length of verbal responses gives important behavioral clues. Overly elaborate responses may suggest obsessiveness. Of course, data from other sources are necessary to support or rule out this hypothesis.
- Be aware that quick responses or abstract responses to easy items *may* indicate overlearned associations rather than higher-level abstract reasoning.

- How the examinee manages frustration on this subtest. For example, some examinees may give up when faced with frustration by repeatedly responding "I don't know," or stating that the two items are not alike. Although these responses may indicate difficulty with conceptualization or categorization, they may also indicate defensiveness or avoidance, especially when seen in older examinees.
- Spontaneous corrections during the administration of this subtest and remember to give credit for them.
- Whether the examinee seems to not know answers to items that might be more closely related to cultural opportunities and educational background (e.g., Items 12, 14, 15, 18, and 23). This information may be important for interpretation.
- Whether the examinee performs better on Similarities than on Picture Concepts. This comparison may provide information about the examinee's reasoning ability from the perspective of different stimulus modalities and response formats.

Sources: D. P. Flanagan & A. S. Kaufman, *Essentials of WISC-IV Assessment* (2nd ed.). Copyright © 2009 John Wiley & Sons, Inc.

A. S. Kaufman & E. O. Lichtenberger, *Essentials of WISC-III and WPPSI-R Assessment.* Copyright © 2000 John Wiley & Sons, Inc.

A. S. Kaufman, S. E. Raiford, & D. L. Coalson, *Intelligent Testing with the WISC-V.* Copyright © 2016 John Wiley & Sons, Inc.

3. Matrix Reasoning (Fluid Reasoning Index and FSIQ)

The WISC-V Matrix Reasoning subtest requires the examinee to complete the missing portion of a picture matrix or series by selecting one of five response options. Administration materials used for the Matrix Reasoning subtest consist of the *WISC-V Administration and Scoring Manual* (Wechsler, 2014a), the Record Form, and Stimulus Book 1.

The WISC-V Matrix Reasoning subtest administration is based on age-appropriate start points. As with many of the subtests on the WISC-V, these starting points vary slightly from the WISC-IV so it is important for examiners to ensure they are starting with the appropriate item. A child age 6–8 years is administered Sample Item A and B, followed by Item 1; a child age 9–11 years is administered Sample Item A and B, followed by Item 5; and a child age 12–16 years is adminis-tered Sample Item A and B, followed by Item 9. If the examinee does not obtain a perfect score on either of the first two items administered, the preceding items should be administered in reverse order until a perfect score on two consecutive items is obtained. The Matrix Reasoning subtest is discontinued after three

LIST 2.3

Changes in Administration From the WISC-IV to the WISC-V: Subtest 3, Matrix Reasoning

- Now there are only two sample items as opposed to three. One sample introduces the examinee to matrix items (2 × 2 or 3 × 3), the other introduces the examinee to serial order items (1 × 6).
- There are revised age-appropriate start points.
- There is a revised prompt given in response to *self-corrections or multiple responses* (e.g., "You [said, pointed to], and you [said, pointed to]. Which one did you mean?").
- Discontinue after three consecutive scores of 0.

consecutive zero-point responses. This represents a change from the WISC-IV, where Matrix Reasoning could be discontinued after either four consecutive zero-point responses or four zero-point responses on five consecutive items.

It is essential that the examiner point to the visual stimuli, the response options, and the box with the question mark as instructed in the administration directions in the manual. The examiner may provide assistance on the sample items only. It should be noted that explicit feedback is given on the sample items regardless of whether or not the examinee chose the correct response to the item. When answering, the examinee should indicate his or her response by pointing to the picture in the Stimulus Book or by stating the number associated with the desired answer. For young examinees it may be appropriate to be sure their hands are clean so the Stimulus Book does not become smudged. List 2.3 provides a description of the changes in administration of the Matrix Reasoning subtest from WISC-IV to WISC-V. The Don't Forget "Behaviors to Note on Matrix Reasoning" provides a description of behaviors that the examiner should note during the administration of the Matrix Reasoning subtest.

DON'T FORGET

Behaviors to Note on Matrix Reasoning

- The level of planning involved. Does the examinee systematically study the problem and appear to carefully plan before providing an answer, or does the examinee appear to be impulsive?

- The examinee completes items relatively quickly or slowly. Note if the examine frequently and repeatedly studies the matrix or series to confirm an answer or rarely glances at the matrix or series then checks after selecting a response to confirm. These observations can be informative about visual memory.
- Shows different performance and response times on the matrix items than on the series items. Preference for the series items may indicate a greater comfort with increasing confirmation of hypotheses or anxiety. Preference for the matrix items may indicate efficient reasoning ability or a preference for fewer examples in problem solving and tasks.
- Be aware that the eye movements of the examinee may be informative, providing information about a systematic versus random approach to problem solving.
- The examinee appears to give up easily on more difficult items by stating "I don't know" before examining the item. This type of behavior may indicate that the examinee has become frustrated with the task.
- Spontaneous corrections during the administration of this subtest and remember to give credit for them.

Sources: D. P. Flanagan & A. S. Kaufman, *Essentials of WISC-IV Assessment* (2nd ed.). Copyright © 2009 John Wiley & Sons, Inc.

A. S. Kaufman & E. O. Lichtenberger, *Essentials of WISC-III and WPPSI-R Assessment.* Copyright © 2000 John Wiley & Sons, Inc.

A. S. Kaufman, S. E. Raiford, & D. L. Coalson, *Intelligent Testing with the WISC-V.* Copyright © 2016 John Wiley & Sons, Inc.

4. Digit Span (Working Memory Index and FSIQ)

The WISC-V Digit Span subtest consists of three tasks: Digit Span Forward, Digit Span Backward, and Digit Span Sequencing. All three tasks must be administered to the examinee. Digit Span Forward requires the examinee to repeat numbers verbatim as they were stated by the examiner. Digit Span Backward requires the examinee to repeat numbers in the reverse order as they were stated by the examiner. Digit Span Sequencing requires the examinee to put the numbers in sequential order, beginning with the smallest number. There are no stimulus materials for the WISC-V Digit Span subtest. The only materials needed to administer the WISC-V Digit Span subtest are the *WISC-V Administration and Scoring Manual* (Wechsler, 2014a) and Record Form.

There are no age-appropriate start points for the WISC-V Digit Span subtest; all examinees begin with Digit Span Forward, Item 1. Each item has two trials. If an examinee fails both trials of a Digit Span Forward item, testing for that task is discontinued and the examiner proceeds to the sample item of Digit Span

Backward. Examiners should proceed to Item 1 even if the examinee is not able to respond correctly to any trial of the sample items. The Digit Span Backward task should be discontinued after a score of zero is obtained on both trials of an item. For examinees ages 6-7 years, a qualifying item must be administered before proceeding to Digit Span Sequencing. If the examinee does not count correctly to at least 3, the subtest should be discontinued, as the examinee may not have the requisite knowledge to perform the task. If the child correctly counts to at least 3 or is age 8 or older, the examiner may proceed to Sample Item A of the Digit Span Sequencing task. Examiners should proceed to Item 1 even if the examinee does not respond correctly to any trial of the sample items. If an examinee fails both trials of a Digit Span Sequencing item, testing is discontinued.

The rate and intonation of the examiner's speech are important during this subtest. Each of the numbers must be read at a rate of one per second, and at the end of the sequence of numbers, the examiner's voice should drop slightly, indicating the end of a sequence. It is also helpful if the examiner looks up expectantly at the examinee at the end of the sequence. The primary examiner error on this subtest is saying the numbers too quickly or too slowly. Practice is critical on this point. It is important not to "chunk" the numbers into small groups while reading them, because this may provide extra help. If an examinee begins to respond before a trial is completely presented, the examiner should not pause. Instead, the examiner should continue reading the sequence, allow the examinee to respond, and give the proper score. Afterward, give the prompt for the examinee to wait until the entire sequence is complete before responding. Examiners may repeat task instructions, but may not readminister trials. If the examinee asks for the sequence to be repeated, the examiner gives the prompt that a trial can be read only once; for example, "I can't say it again, but let's try another one." List 2.4 provides a description of the changes in the administration of the Digit Span subtest from WISC-IV to WISC-V. The Don't Forget "Behaviors to Note on Digit Span" provides a description of behaviors that the examiner should note during the administration of the Digit Span subtest.

LIST 2.4

Changes in Administration From the WISC-IV to the WISC-V: Subtest 4, Digit Span

- A Sequencing task has been added to the Forward and Backward conditions and is required to obtain the Digit Span scaled score.

- Digit Span Sequencing contains a qualifying item for examinees ages 6-7 years. Examinees who do not pass the item are not administered this condition and receive a raw score of 0.

- If an examinee responds before the examiner has finished reading a trial, the response is scored and a new prompt, "Wait until I stop before you start," is provided.

- There is a prompt given in response to *self-corrections* or *multiple responses* (e.g., "You said [insert examinee's response], and you said [insert examinee's response]. Which one did you mean?").

- For the Sequencing task only, the same number may be included more than once in a single trial. For the Forward task, a number is repeated for each trial of Item 9. If the examinee asks if he or she is required to repeat the same number, give the following prompt, "You may have to say the same number more than one time."

DON'T FORGET

Behaviors to Note on Digit Span

- The examinee attempts to use a problem-solving strategy such as "chunking." Some examinees use such a strategy from the beginning; others learn a strategy as they progress through the task.

- Whether errors are due simply to transposing numbers or to completely forgetting numbers.

- Be aware that inattention, a hearing impairment, or anxiety can influence performance on this subtest; therefore, such difficulties should be noted if present. Clinical judgment must be exercised in determining whether one or more of these factors is responsible for a spuriously low score.

- Interference with the quality of the testing conditions (e.g., noise outside the testing room) should be noted. Such interference may spoil the subtest, rendering it uninterpretable.

- Watch for rapid repetition of digits or beginning to repeat the digits before the examiner has completed the series. Such behavior may indicate impulsivity.

- Whether there is a pattern of failing the first trial and then correctly responding to the second trial. Such a pattern may indicate learning or may simply be a warm-up effect.

- Easily learns the Digit Span Forward task but has more difficulty with the Digit Span Backward and/or Digit Span Sequencing tasks, which are more cognitively complex and require resequencing of the stimuli to provide a response.

Sources: D. P. Flanagan & A. S. Kaufman, *Essentials of WISC-IV Assessment* (2nd ed.). Copyright © 2009 John Wiley & Sons, Inc.

5. Coding (Processing Speed Index and FSIQ)

The WISC-V Coding subtest requires the examinee to copy symbols that are paired with either geometric shapes or numbers using a key within a specified time limit. Response Booklet 1 is presented to the examinee as the stimulus material for the Coding subtest. A stopwatch, the *WISC-V Administration and Scoring Manual* (Wechsler, 2014a), the Record Form, and a pencil without an eraser are also needed to administer this subtest.

The WISC-V has two different Coding forms: Form A for children ages 6–7 years and Form B for children ages 8–16 years. The different Coding forms have their own separate pages in the Response Booklet. If the examinee is left-handed, an extra Coding response key should be placed to the right of his or her Response Booklet so that he or she may have an unobstructed view of the Coding key (some left-handers' hand positions obstruct the key on the Record Form). There are no reverse rules for the Coding subtest. The subtest is discontinued after 120 seconds. *Note:* 120 seconds is 2 minutes, not 1 minute and 20 seconds.

The directions for Coding are lengthy and contain much important detail. Examiners should read slowly with inflection, pausing to give emphasis to important points in the instructions and must be prepared to look up from reading the directions to check that the examinee is following what is being said. Therefore, the directions should be rehearsed and read carefully to each examinee. During administration of the sample items, if the examinee makes any mistake it should be corrected immediately. If the examinee does not appear to understand the task after the sample items have been completed, further instruction should be given until he or she clearly understands the task. If it is clear that the examinee will not understand the task with further instruction, the examiner should discontinue the subtest. When the examinee has successfully completed the sample items, the examiner may proceed to the Test Items. The Test Items include additional directions that must be given before examiners begin timing the task. If the examinee attempts to begin the items before the instructions are finished, the examiner should instruct him or her, "Wait until I say 'Go' to start."

Once the subtest has begun, examiners should be astute observers. Examinees are not permitted to omit any item or to complete all items of one type at a time; if they are observed doing this they need to be told "Do them in order. Don't skip

LIST 2.5

. . . .

Changes in Administration From the WISC-IV to the WISC-V: Subtest 5, Coding

- New symbols allow a child to recreate each symbol without having to lift his or her pencil.
- All number-symbol associations are represented on every row, as opposed to the WISC-IV where only some of the symbol-number associations appeared in the first few rows.
- If an examinee begins the task before instructions are read, a new prompt, "Wait until I say 'Go' to start," is given.
- There are not any time-bonus scores for Coding A or B, whereas the WISC-IV provided a potential time bonus for Coding A.
- Examiners can record and sum symbol rotations greater than 90 degrees. This score is converted to a base rate score that describes the total number of rotations that occurred.

any." Some examinees appear to stop midway through the task; the examiner should remind them to continue until told to stop. The pencil the examinee uses does not have an eraser and if he or she attempts to erase an answer and looks confused the examiner should say, "That's okay, just keep working as fast as you can." Occasionally, examinees appear frustrated at the end of the test because they are able to complete only a few lines. If this behavior is observed, examiners may want to reassure the examinee that most individuals are not able to complete the entire sheet. Any of these behaviors are worthy of noting. List 2.5 provides a description of the changes in the administration of the Coding subtest from WISC-IV to WISC-V. The Don't Forget "Behaviors to Note on Coding" provides a description of behaviors that the examiner should note during the administration of the Coding subtest.

DON'T FORGET

. . . .

Behaviors to Note on Coding

- Be aware that the eye movements of examinees can be informative. Frequent use of the Coding key may indicate poor memory or insecurity. In contrast, an examinee who uses the key infrequently may have good memory span, visual memory, and/or associative memory. Examiners should check to see where on the key the examinee's eyes are focused, especially with older examinees. Failing to recognize that the key is numerically ordered (i.e., from 1 through 9) not only suggests poor visual memory, but may also suggest difficulty with number concepts.

- Whether the examinee quickly, but carelessly fills in symbols across the rows. This behavior may suggest impulsivity.
- Whether an examinee attempts to fill in the symbol for the number 1s first, followed by the symbol for the number 2s. This behavior may suggest good planning ability.
- Watch for shaking hands, a tight grip on the pencil, or pressure on the paper when writing. These behaviors may indicate anxiety.
- Observe as the subtest progresses. Noting the number of symbols copied during 3-second intervals provides helpful behavioral information in this regard.
- Whether examinees spend a significant amount of time trying to perfect each of the symbols that are drawn. This behavior may suggest obsessiveness, excessive attention to detail, or perfectionism.

Sources: D. P. Flanagan & A. S. Kaufman, *Essentials of WISC-IV Assessment* (2nd ed.). Copyright © 2009 John Wiley & Sons, Inc.

A. S. Kaufman & E. O. Lichtenberger, *Essentials of WISC-III and WPPSI-R Assessment*. Copyright © 2000 John Wiley & Sons, Inc.

6. Vocabulary (Verbal Comprehension Index and FSIQ)

The WISC-V Vocabulary subtest requires the examinee to name pictures or provide definitions for words. Administration of the Vocabulary subtest requires the *WISC-V Administration and Scoring Manual* (Wechsler, 2014a), the Record Form, and Stimulus Book 1. Whereas in the WISC-IV the picture items (Items 1–4) were administered only as reversal items, all examinees ages 6–7 years now begin with these items. Picture items require the examinee to be able to name the item pictured. Items 5–29 are verbal items; the examiner reads the word printed in the manual aloud and asks the examinee to provide a definition. Note that the words are no longer printed in the Stimulus Book and are not visually presented to the examinee when administering each item. The Stimulus Book is only used for the picture items in the WISC-V.

For all Verbal items, read the item stimuli verbatim as it is printed in the manual. Do not merely say the word once. Adhering to this guideline ensures the examinee hears the word twice and thus reduces the likelihood he or she will Mishear it and define a different word that sounds similar.

The WISC-V Vocabulary subtest administration is based on age-appropiate start points. An examinee age 6–7 years begins with Item 1, an examinee age 8–11 years begins with Item 5, and an examinee age 12–16 years begins with Item 9. If an examinee age 8–16 fails to obtain a perfect score on either of the first two items administered, the preceding items should be administered in reverse order until a perfect score on two consecutive items is obtained. It is important to note that the first picture item and the first two verbal items at each age-appropriate start point

LIST 2.6

Changes in Administration From the WISC-IV to the WISC-V: Subtest 6, Vocabulary

- There are revised age-appropriate start points.
- Teaching items have been added for each age-appropriate start point to ensure that all examinees receive similar opportunity for corrective feedback.
- Words are not printed on a stimulus page for any age range.
- The administration has changed to include a reading of the word, followed by a request to define the word (e.g., "LEAVE. What does LEAVE mean?").
- The manual and Record Form contain asterisks for words likely to be misheard. Upon mishearing a word, the examiner says to the examinee, "Listen carefully" and repeats the item being sure to emphasize the misheard word.
- Discontinue after three consecutive scores of 0.

on the WISC-V Vocabulary subtest require the examiner to provide an example of a specified full-credit response (i.e., a 1-point response for picture items and a 2-point response for verbal items) if the child does not spontaneously give a full-credit response. If the child does not obtain a perfect score on any teaching item at any point during the subtest, the teaching feedback should be given. The Vocabulary subtest is discontinued after three consecutive zero-point responses. If the examiner is unsure about an examinee's score on one of the items that may count toward the discontinue rule, he or she should administer more items until a proper discontinue point has been reached. The discussion above concerning "Querying," "I don't know," and "Repeating Items" applies to administering the Vocabulary subtest.

The questions may be repeated as many times as necessary without changing the wording. List 2.6 provides a description of the changes to administration of the Vocabulary subtest from WISC-IV to WISC-V. The Don't Forget "Behaviors to Note on Vocabulary" provides a description of behaviors that the examiner should note during the administration of the Vocabulary subtest.

DON'T FORGET

Behaviors to Note on Vocabulary

- Whether the examinee responds more readily to the picture items, which require only 1-word verbal responses, then has more difficulty with Items 5 and 6, which require more lengthy verbal responses (for younger children or other children who begin with Item 1).

- Whether the examinee appears to benefit from the feedback provided on teaching items, giving correct responses after learning the task.
- Whether the examinee provides complete definitions or must be repeatedly queried as a cue to give all pertinent information.
- Whether the examinee provides additional information about responses upon query or tends to say he or she does not know any more.
- Whether the examinee continues to provide complete answers throughout the subtest, or if responses become briefer or vaguer as the subtest progresses.
- Whether the examinee seems to not know answers to items that might be more closely related to cultural opportunities and educational background (e.g., Items 10, 14, 17, and 25). This information may be important for interpretation.
- Whether the examinee has difficulties pronouncing words or seems uncertain about how to express what they think.
- Some examinees supplement what they say with gesturing; others rely on verbal expression more than nonverbal communication.
- "I don't know" responses or the "tip of the tongue" phenomenon, as these responses and behaviors may indicate word retrieval problems. A lack of rapidity and efficiency in retrieving words from the lexicon can influence test performance negatively, leading to an underestimate of the examinee's actual word knowledge.
- Hearing difficulties may be apparent on this subtest. The Vocabulary words are not presented in a meaningful context. Note behaviors such as leaning forward during administration to hear better, as well as indications of auditory discrimination problems (e.g., defining *line* rather than *lied*).
- Verbosity in the examinee's responses. He or she may be attempting to compensate for insecurity about his or her ability or may be obsessive or inefficient in verbal expression.
- Spontaneous corrections during the administration of this subtest and remember to give credit for them.

Sources: D. P. Flanagan & A. S. Kaufman, *Essentials of WISC-IV Assessment* (2nd ed.). Copyright © 2009 John Wiley & Sons, Inc.

A. S. Kaufman & E. O. Lichtenberger, *Essentials of WISC-III and WPPSI-R Assessment.* Copyright © 2000 John Wiley & Sons, Inc.

A. S. Kaufman, S. E. Raiford, & D. L. Coalson, *Intelligent Testing with the WISC-V.* Copyright © 2016 John Wiley & Sons, Inc.

7. Figure Weights (Fluid Reasoning Index and FSIQ)

The new WISC-V Figure Weights subtest requires the examinee to view a scale with a missing weight(s) and select the appropriate option that will keep the scale balanced within a specified time limit. The stimulus material for the Figure

Weight subtest is Stimulus Book 1. A stopwatch, the *WISC-V Administration and Scoring Manual* (Wechsler, 2014a), and the Record Form are also needed to administer this subtest.

The WISC-V Figure Weights subtest administration follows age-appropriate start points. An examinee age 6–8 years begins with Sample Item A followed by Item 1, and an examinee age 9–16 years begins with Sample Item B followed by Item 4. If an examinee age 9–16 fails to obtain a perfect score on either of the first two items administered, the preceding items should be administered in reverse order until a perfect score on two consecutive items is obtained. The examiner does not administer Sample Item A in this situation. The Figure Weights subtest is discontinued after three consecutive zero-point responses.

For Sample Item A and Sample Item B, explicit feedback is given as to whether the examinee's answer was correct or incorrect. Examiners should note that if the examinee's answer is incorrect, specific feedback is given, based upon the type of error. Pages 164–165 of the *WISC-V Administration and Scoring Manual* (Wechsler, 2014) provide the explicit feedback that must be given. These sample items must be administered correctly to assure that the examinee understands the task fully. The examinee must indicate his or her choice by either pointing to or saying the number of their response. If the examinee responds by naming the shapes in their selected response, the examiner stops the timer to ask him or her to indicate which numbered response is the desired option. The time limit for Items 1–18 is 20 seconds per item. The time limit for Items 19–34 is 30 seconds per item. A thick black line on the Record Form is a visual reminder for the examiner of the change in time limit. If the examinee has not responded when only 10 seconds remain in the time limit for a given item, the examiner should prompt him or her for a response. If the examinee does not give a correct response within the time limit and the discontinue criterion has not been met, the examiner may prompt him or her before proceeding to the next appropriate item. The examinee must indicate the selection before the time limit runs out, or the response is incomplete. Examiners should be aware that Item 27 has a specific set of instructions to introduce the examinee to items with three sets of scales. As a reminder, this item is marked with a double asterisk in both the Record Form and manual. The Don't Forget "Behaviors to Note on Figure Weights" provides a description of behaviors that the examiner should note during the administration of the Figure Weights subtest.

DON'T FORGET

. . . .

Behaviors to Note on Figure Weights

- Whether the examinee verbalizes during problem solving.
- Whether the examinee initially approaches items by studying the scales or begins searching the response options and comparing with the final scale.
- Whether the examinee calculates the correct answer with mathematical calculation.
- Whether the examinee selects responses impulsively, based on color or shape, but misses other important features that make the response incorrect.
- Whether the examinee frequently self-corrects on items initially responded to correctly.
- Whether the examinee finishes items relatively quickly or slowly. Note if the examinee frequently studies the pieces and complete pictures to confirm an answer.
- Whether the examinee gives up easily on more difficult items or persists in studying them.

Sources: A. S. Kaufman, S. E. Raiford, & D. L. Coalson, *Intelligent Testing with the WISC-V.* Copyright © 2016 John Wiley & Sons, Inc.

E. O. Lichtenberger & A. S. Kaufman, *Essentials of WAIS-IV Assessment.* Copyright © 2009 John Wiley & Sons, Inc.

8. Visual Puzzles (Visual Spatial Index)

The new WISC-V Visual Puzzles subtest requires the examinee to view a completed puzzle and select three options within a specified time limit that would reconstruct the puzzle when combined. The stimulus material for the Visual Puzzles subtest is Stimulus Book 1. A stopwatch, the *WISC-V Administration and Scoring Manual* (Wechsler, 2014a), and the Record Form are also needed to administer this subtest.

The WISC-V Visual Puzzles subtest administration is based on age-appropriate start points. All examinees are first administered the Demonstration Item and the Sample Item. After the Demonstration Item and Sample Item are completed, an examinee age 6–8 years proceeds to Item 1, an examinee age 9–11 years proceeds to Item 5, and an examinee age 12–16 years proceeds to Item 8. If a child age 9–16 fails to obtain a perfect score on either of the first two items administered, the preceding items should be administered in reverse order until a perfect score on two consecutive items is obtained. The Visual Puzzles subtest is discontinued after three consecutive zero-point responses.

Each item on the Visual Puzzles subtest is timed, and has a time limit of 30 seconds. The examiner should begin timing immediately after the saying the last word in the instructions for a given item and stop timing immediately after an examinee responds or 30 seconds have elapsed. If the examinee has not provided a response after 20 seconds have elapsed, the examiner should prompt him or her by asking if he or she has an answer. If the examinee does not give a correct response within the time limit and the discontinue criterion has not been met, the examiner alerts the examinee before proceeding to the next appropriate item. The manual describes several situations in which the examiner may respond to questions from the examinee about the nature of the questions, including if he or she asks whether responses must be selected in numerical order (answer: no) and if response options may be rotated to fit the puzzle (answer: yes). The Don't Forget "Behaviors to Note on Visual Puzzles" provides a description of behaviors that the examiner should note during the administration of the Visual Puzzles subtest.

DON'T FORGET

Behaviors to Note on Visual Puzzles

- Whether the examinee verbalizes during problem solving.
- Whether the examinee initially approaches items by studying the pieces or begins impulsively.
- Whether the examinee asks if a piece can be flipped.
- Whether the examinee turns his or her head or twists his or her body to rotate the pieces rather than mentally rotating the pieces.
- Whether the examinee selects responses impulsively, based on color or shape, but misses other important features that make the response incorrect.
- Any patterns in the errors.
- Whether the examinee frequently self-corrects on items initially responded to correctly.
- Whether the examinee finishes items relatively quickly or slowly. Note if the examinee frequently studies the pieces and complete pictures to confirm an answer.
- Whether the examinee gives up easily on more difficult items or persists in studying them.

Sources: A. S. Kaufman, S. E. Raiford, & D. L. Coalson, *Intelligent Testing with the WISC-V.* Copyright © 2016 John Wiley & Sons, Inc.

E. O. Lichtenberger & A. S. Kaufman, *Essentials of WAIS-IV Assessment.* Copyright © 2009 John Wiley & Sons, Inc.

9. Picture Span (Working Memory Index)

The new WISC-V Picture Span subtest requires the examinee to select one or more target pictures in order from options on a response page after viewing a stimulus page for a specific amount of time. The stimulus material for the Picture Span subtest is Stimulus Book 2. A stopwatch, the *WISC-V Administration and Scoring Manual* (Wechsler, 2014a), and the Record Form are also needed to administer this subtest.

There are no age-appropriate start points for the WISC-V Picture Span subtest; all examinees begin with Sample Items B & C followed by Item 4. Examinees suspected of having an intellectual disability or low cognitive ability may start with Sample Item A followed by Item 1. If an examinee fails to obtain a perfect score on either of the first two items administered, the preceding items should be administered in reverse order until a perfect score on two consecutive items is obtained. However, Sample Item A should not be administered to examinees who started with Item 4 if under any circumstances. The Picture Span subtest is discontinued after three consecutive zero-point responses.

It is important to adhere to the exposure times for each stimulus page before turning to the response page. Sample Item A and Items 1–3 have an exposure time of 3 seconds. Sample Items B–C and Items 4–26 have an exposure time of 5 seconds. It is important not to expose the stimulus page, read the verbal directions and then start timing because this will add 3–4 seconds of exposure time. Instead, begin timing immediately upon exposure of the stimulus page, regardless of when the verbal instructions are spoken. Do not permit the examinee to turn the stimulus book pages before the exposure time has ended. Provide the given prompt if the examinee attempts to turn the page. Direct the examinee back to the task if he or she seems to be looking away from the stimuli during exposure. Adhering to these guidelines ensures the exposure time remains consistent with standardized procedures.

Sample Item A has two trials and is designed to teach the task for Items 1–3, which require the examinee to view a single picture and subsequently identify that picture in a larger group of pictures. Sample Items B and C each has two trials and are designed to teach the task for Items 4–26, which require the examinee to view multiple pictures and subsequently identify those pictures in a larger group of pictures. Items 1, 2, 4, and 5 are teaching items and corrective feedback should be given on these items if the examinee does not obtain a perfect response. Corrective feedback should not be offered and stimuli may not be re-exposed on any other test items. However, if the examinee is identifying the correct pictures in reverse order then the examiner may remind him or her to remember the pictures in order from left to right. One point is awarded if the examinee selects all of the stimulus pictures in reverse order (or any other order). The examiner should note any interruptions or distractions that occur during timed stimulus exposure and if repeated interruptions occur, the subtest may be considered spoiled and uninterpretable. The Don't Forget "Behaviors to Note on Picture Span" provides a description of behaviors that the examiner should note during the administration of the Picture Span subtest.

DON'T FORGET

Behaviors to Note on Picture Span

- Whether the examinee is attending during the exposure time. Length of exposure affects the ease or difficulty with which stimuli can be remembered.
- The order in which the examinee is attempting to remember items. Examinees are instructed to memorize stimulus images from left to right, but some may reverse this.
- Though the stimulus page can only be shown once, requests for repetition are noteworthy and should be recorded.
- Strategies used to facilitate memorization (e.g., verbally coding items versus visually tracking items).
- Whether the examinee gives up easily or responds impulsively on more difficult items, or appears determined to respond correctly.
- Whether the examinee hesitates to respond resulting in decay of the encoded memory and increased errors. These are qualitatively different errors from those due to inattention during stimulus exposure.
- Whether the examinee scores 1 point on items scored 2, 1, or 0 points because he or she swaps the order of only two pictures or chooses the correct responses in the incorrect order more haphazardly.
- Whether the examinee has incorrect responses that correctly include some of the first or last pictures in the array but omit those in the middle of the array; or if the incorrect responses include mostly incorrect objects.
- Whether the examinee tends to respond incorrectly to the first item of a new span length or new number of response options, then experiences later success on similar items. This is in contrast to a child who responds correctly to sets of similar items, then discontinues quickly after reaching his or her maximum span length.

Sources: A. S. Kaufman, S. E. Raiford, & D. L. Coalson, *Intelligent Testing with the WISC-V.* Copyright © 2016 John Wiley & Sons, Inc.

J. T. Mascolo (personal communication, September 24, 2015).

10. Symbol Search (Processing Speed Index)

The WISC-V Symbol Search subtest requires the examinee to scan a search group and indicate the presence or absence of a target symbol or symbols within a specified time limit. The stimulus material for the Symbol Search subtest is Response Booklet 1. A stopwatch, the *WISC-V Administration and Scoring Manual* (Wechsler, 2014a), the Record Form, and a pencil without an eraser are also needed to administer this subtest. The Symbol Search Scoring Key is needed for scoring.

The Symbol Search subtest has two forms that are found within the same Response Booklet: Symbol Search A for examinees ages 6–7 years and Symbol Search B for examinees ages 8–16 years. There are no reverse rules for the Symbol Search subtest. The subtest is discontinued after 120 seconds.

Although the Symbol Search subtest has a time limit of 120 seconds, prior to beginning the subtest examinees must be administered demonstration items and sample items that are not timed. It is important not to skip any of the demonstration or sample items, even if the examinee appears to understand the task. The directions to the demonstration, sample, and test items have been somewhat simplified from the previous version of this subtest in the WISC-IV; however, they still require multiple rehearsals in order to be able to communicate them while maintaining rapport with the examinee. Examiners should read slowly with inflection, pausing to give emphasis to important points in the instructions. The task should not begin until it is clear that the examinee understands what is required.

The timing of 120 seconds must be exact. Please note that 120 seconds is 2 minutes, not 1 minute and 20 seconds. Some examinees may purposefully or inadvertently skip items; they should be reminded to complete items in order and not skip any. Other examinees may appear to stop the task before the 120-second time limit expires and must be reminded to continue. If the examinee indicates his or her response with something other than one slash mark or marks the target symbol, prompt him or her to draw only one line to make each mark. If the examinee completes the task in less than 120 seconds, stop timing and record the completion time in seconds. List 2.7 provides a description of the changes in the administration of the Symbol Search subtest from WISC-IV to WISC-V. The Don't Forget "Behaviors to Note on Symbol Search" provides a description of behaviors that the examiner should note during the administration of the Symbol Search subtest.

LIST 2.7

Changes in Administration From the WISC-IV to the WISC-V: Subtest 10, Symbol Search

- New symbols and distractor items are included that allow for the observation of different types of errors, namely, Rotation Errors and Set Errors. A *rotation error* is scored when an examinee selects a response option that matches the correct design, but is rotated. A *set error* occurs when an examinee selects a symbol that looks similar to the target symbol.
- Rather than selecting Yes or No to denote the presence or absence of a symbol, examinees are now asked to select the matching symbol if it is present and to select No only if the symbol is not present.
- Several new prompts have been added, including when an examinee marks a target symbol as a response, when an examinee uses anything other than a single slash to mark their answer, and when an examinee attempts to begin the task before the instructions are completed. Timing continues through any prompt.

DON'T FORGET

Behaviors to Note on Symbol Search

- Watch for shaking hands, a tight pencil grip, or pressure on the paper when writing. These behaviors may indicate anxiety.
- Observe attention and concentration. Is the examinee's focus consistent throughout the task, or does it wane as the task progresses?
- Whether the examinee checks each row of symbols only once, or whether he or she rechecks the row of symbols in an item more than once. Obsessive concern with detail may be noted.
- Whether the examinee quickly, but carelessly identifies a symbol or its absence in a row. This behavior may suggest impulsivity.
- Be aware that eye movements of examinees taking the subtest can be informative. Consistent glancing back and forth between the target and search groups before making a choice may indicate poor memory. In contrast, an examinee who refers to the target symbol infrequently may have a good memory span and/or visual memory.
- Watch for signs of fatigue, boredom, or inattention as the subtest progresses. Noting the number of items answered during each of the four 30-second intervals with the 120-second time limit may provide helpful behavioral information in this regard.
- Whether an examinee is identifying rotations of the target symbol or symbols similar to the target in his or her response.

SUBTEST-BY-SUBTEST RULES OF ADMINISTRATION OF THE WISC-V SECONDARY AND COMPLEMENTARY SUBTESTS

What follows below are step-by-step rules for administering the WISC-V secondary and complementary subtests.

11. Information (Verbal Comprehension Subtest, Secondary)

The WISC-V Information subtest requires the examinee to answer questions that address a wide range of general-knowledge topics. To administer this subtest, the examiner needs only the *WISC-V Administration and Scoring Manual* (Wechsler, 2014a) and the Record Form.

The WISC-V Information subtest administration follows age-appropriate start points. An examinee age 6–8 years begins with Item 1, and an examinee age 9–16 years begins with Item 8. If an examinee age 9–16 does not obtain a perfect score on either of the first two items administered, the preceding items should be administered in reverse order until a perfect score on two consecutive items is obtained. The Information subtest is discontinued after three consecutive zero-point responses. If the examiner is unsure about an examinee's score on one of the items that count towards the discontinue rule, he or she should administer more items until a proper discontinue point has been reached. The prior discussion concerning "Querying," "I don't know," and "Repeating Items" applies to administering the Information subtest.

The first two items at each start point on the WISC-V Information subtest require the examiner to provide corrective feedback if the examinee provides an incorrect answer. This is done in order to teach him or her the type of response expected for each item. In terms of item repetition, each item may be repeated as often as necessary, as long as the examiner does not reword the original item in any manner. If the examinee mishears a word and provides an incorrect answer, the examiner should repeat the entire item with emphasis on the misheard word. Items with sample responses that require a specific query are identified with an asterisk in the Record Form and the manual. List 2.8 provides a description of

LIST 2.8

Changes in Administration From the WISC-IV to the WISC-V: Subtest 11, Information

- There are revised age-appropriate start points for the WISC-V.
- Teaching items have been added for each age-appropriate start point to ensure that all examinees receive similar opportunity for corrective feedback.
- Beyond general queries, several *specific* queries are included and marked with an asterisk in the manual and on the Record Form.
- Discontinue after three consecutive scores of 0.

the changes in the administration of the Information subtest from WISC-IV to WISC-V. The Don't Forget "Behaviors to Note on Information" provides a description of behaviors that the examiner should note during the administration of the Information subtest.

DON'T FORGET

Behaviors to Note on Information

- Whether the examinee appears to benefit from the feedback provided on teaching items, giving correct responses after learning the task.
- Whether the examinee provides complete responses or must be repeatedly queried as a cue to give all pertinent information about the response.
- Whether the examinee provides additional information about responses upon query or tends to say he or she does not know any more.
- Whether the examinee continues to provide complete answers throughout the subtest, or if responses become briefer or vaguer as the subtest progresses.
- Whether the examinee provides multiple correct answers for items where this is appropriate (e.g., Items 3, 6, 8, 10, 11, 12, 15, 16, 19, 24, 25, 26, 28) versus only the single requisite answer.
- Any observable patterns in an examinee's responses. Patterns of responding such as missing early, easy items and having success on difficult items may suggest anxiety, poor motivation, or retrieval difficulties.
- Consider whether incorrect responses are related to the examinee's cultural background (e.g., on questions about a character in U.S. history at a certain time or about the geography of a specific location). Such observations should be incorporated into interpretation.
- Whether the examinee provides unnecessarily long responses. Long responses filled with excessive detail may be indicative of obsessiveness, a desire to

impress the examiner, or an attempt to cover up for not knowing the correct response.

- Whether the content of failed items consistently owes to lack of knowledge in a specific area (e.g., numerical information, history, or geography); an error analysis may be useful in this regard.
- Spontaneous corrections during the administration of this subtest and remember to give credit for them.

Sources: D. P. Flanagan & A. S. Kaufman, *Essentials of WISC-IV Assessment* (2nd ed.). Copyright © 2009 John Wiley & Sons, Inc.

A. S. Kaufman & E. O. Lichtenberger, *Essentials of WISC-III and WPPSI-R Assessment.* Copyright © 2000 John Wiley & Sons, Inc.

A. S. Kaufman, S. E. Raiford, & D. L. Coalson, *Intelligent Testing with the WISC-V.* Copyright © 2016 John Wiley & Sons, Inc.

12. Picture Concepts (Fluid Reasoning Subtest, Secondary)

The WISC-V Picture Concepts subtest requires the examinee to choose one picture from each of the two or three rows of pictures to form a group with a common characteristic. The materials necessary for the administration of WISC-V Picture Concepts comprise the *WISC-V Administration and Scoring Manual* (Wechsler, 2014a), Stimulus Book 2, and the Record Form.

The WISC-V Picture Concepts subtest administration is based on age-appropriate start points. An examinee age 6–8 years begins with Sample Items A and B and then Item 1; an examinee age 9–11 years begins with Sample Items A and B and then Item 4; and an examinee age 12–16 years begins with Sample Items A and B and then Item 7. If an examinee age 9–16 fails to obtain a perfect score on either of the first two items administered, the preceding items should be administered in reverse order until a perfect score on two consecutive items is obtained. The Picture Concepts subtest is discontinued after three consecutive zero-point responses. The examinee must show his or her response by pointing to or saying the number of the selections, rather than responding by naming a pictured option or with any other verbal response.

Items 1–7 of the WISC-V Picture Concepts subtest are two-row items; Items 8–27 are three-row items. The manual suggests a general 30-second guideline for each item, but emphasizes that this subtest is not timed and that additional time can and should be granted if the examinee has established a pattern of providing delayed, but correct responses as the items become more difficult.

LIST 2.9

. . . .

Changes in Administration From the WISC-IV to the WISC-V: Subtest 12, Picture Concepts

- Images never repeat across items.
- There is a prompt given in response to *self-corrections* or *multiple responses* (e.g., "You [said, pointed to], and you [said, pointed to]. Which one did you mean?").

List 2.9 provides a description of the changes in the administration of the Picture Concepts subtest from WISC-IV to WISC-V. The Don't Forget "Behaviors to Note on Picture Concepts" provides a description of behaviors that the examiner should note during the administration of the Picture Concepts subtest.

DON'T FORGET

. . . .

Behaviors to Note on Picture Concepts

- Whether the examinee frequently requests the names of objects.
- Whether the examinee selects responses impulsively, but misses other important features that make the responses incorrect.
- Whether the examinee finishes items relatively quickly or slowly, frequently and repeatedly studies all options to confirm an answer, or glances at the rows initially then rechecks them after selecting a response to confirm.
- Whether the examinee gives up easily on more difficult items or persists in studying them and appears determined to understand the item and respond correctly.
- Be aware that quick responses to easy items may indicate overlearned associations rather than higher-level abstract reasoning.
- How the examinee manages frustration on this subtest. For example, the examinee may respond by saying "Nothing is alike," indicating defensiveness or avoidance. Other examinees may give up when faced with frustration by repeatedly responding "I don't know."
- Whether the examinee studies the pictures for a few seconds prior to answering. Such behavior may indicate a reflective style.

- Whether there is verbalization during problem solving.
- Any behaviors that give clues to whether errors relate to social or cultural misinterpretation, as opposed to visual-perceptual difficulties.
- Spontaneous corrections during the administration of this subtest and remember to give credit for them.

Sources: D. P. Flanagan & A. S. Kaufman, *Essentials of WISC-IV Assessment* (2nd ed.). Copyright © 2009 John Wiley & Sons, Inc.

A. S. Kaufman & E. O. Lichtenberger, *Essentials of WISC-III and WPPSI-R Assessment.* Copyright © 2000 John Wiley & Sons, Inc.

A. S. Kaufman, S. E. Raiford, & D. L. Coalson, *Intelligent Testing with the WISC-V.* Copyright © 2016 John Wiley & Sons, Inc.

13. Letter-Number Sequencing (Working Memory Subtest, Secondary)

The WISC-V Letter-Number Sequencing subtest requires the examinee to listen to a sequence of numbers and letters presented orally by the examiner and to recall the numbers in ascending order followed by the letters in alphabetical order. Administration materials consist of the *WISC-V Administration and Scoring Manual* (Wechsler, 2014a) and the Record Form.

The WISC-V Letter-Number Sequencing subtest administration is based on age-appropriate start points. An examinee age 6–7 years is presented with the qualifying items (counting numbers and reciting the alphabet at least to C), Demonstration Item A, Sample Item A, and then Item 1. An examinee age 8–16 years is presented with Demonstration Item A, Sample Item A, and then Item 1. If the examinee provides an incorrect response on Sample Item A, the examiner should provide the correct response before moving on to Item 1. Items 1–2 are teaching items and corrective feedback should be provided if the examinee responds incorrectly or does not respond in an appropriate timeframe. The WISC-V version of this subtest includes an additional demonstration and sample item (Demonstration Item B and Sample Item B) after Items 1–2 are administered. If the examinee provides an incorrect response on either trial of Sample Item B, the examiner should provide the correct response before proceeding.

Each item except for the Sample Items is composed of three trials and each trial is presented only one time. The examiner may repeat item instructions, but does not re-administer trials. As in Digit Span, the letters and numbers are read at the rate of one per second, dropping the voice at the end of the sequence. If the examinee responds before the sequence is fully read, continue presenting

LIST 2.10

. . . .

**Changes in Administration From the WISC-IV to the WISC-V:
Subtest 13, Letter-Number Sequencing**

- For Items 1 and 2, there is one letter and one number per trial and a demonstration and sample item precede these items. For incorrect responses where a letter is provided before the number, corrective feedback is provided and credit is *not* given.
- Items 1 and 2 are followed by another demonstration and sample item before test items 3–10 are started.
- Rhyming letters and numbers (e.g., E and 3, E and P) do not appear on the same trial.
- The prompt for item repetition requests is, "I can only say them one time. Just take your best guess."
- If an examinee responds before the examiner finishes reading a trial, accept the response, then say, "Wait until I stop before you start."
- A longest span score can be calculated by counting up the number of digits and letters from the longest correct sequence (e.g., A – B – 4 – 5 = raw score of 4).

the sequence, allow him or her to respond, and assign the proper score to the trial. After the trial is completed, the examiner gives the prompt to wait to respond until he or she has stopped reading the sequence. The Letter-Number Sequencing subtest is discontinued if an examinee age 6–7 years does not respond correctly to either qualifying item, or if he or she obtains zero-point responses on all three trials of an item. The number zero (0) and the letter O are not included in any trials as they are frequently confused. The letters I and L are not included in any trial as they are often misread as the number 1. List 2.10 provides a description of the changes in the administration of the Letter-Number Sequencing subtest from WISC-IV to WISC-V. The Don't Forget "Behaviors to Note on Letter-Number Sequencing" provides a description of behaviors that the examiner should note during the administration of the Letter-Number Sequencing subtest.

DON'T FORGET

. . . .

Behaviors to Note on Letter-Number Sequencing
- Whether the examinee learns from errors made during the sample items.

- Whether the examinee attempts to use a problem-solving strategy such as "chunking." Some examinees use such a strategy from the beginning; others learn a strategy as they progress through the task.
- Whether errors are due to the failure to reorder the letter-number sequence, with the sequence being repeated verbatim (which is still credited as correct on certain items) versus the sequences having been forgotten (which is scored 0).
- Whether the examinee responds by providing the letters before the numbers despite attempts to teach the reverse response requirement.
- Whether the examinee shows a pattern of forgetting only numbers or only letters more frequently. Such a pattern could indicate a greater relative comfort with the favored stimuli or stimulus overload. Forgetting letters is more typical because they must be held in memory longer and are repeated last, with more opportunity for the memory trace to decay.
- Whether the examinee repeats numbers or letters rapidly or before the stimuli has been read completely. These behaviors may be indicators of impulsivity.
- Whether the examinee shows a pattern of failing the first trial and then correctly responding to the second and/or third trial of a given span length, which may indicate learning or a warm-up effect. If this occurs, consider interpreting the Longest Letter-Number Sequencing score for this subtest.
- Be aware that inattention, a hearing impairment, or anxiety can influence performance on this subtest.
- Interference with the quality of the testing conditions (e.g., noise outside the testing room) should be noted. Such interference may spoil the subtest, rendering it uninterpretable.
- How well examinees persist, noting how well they tolerate frustration.
- Whether there is a pattern of failing the first trial and then correctly responding to the second trial. Such a pattern may indicate learning or may simply be a warm-up effect.
- Whether the examinee treats the task as digits forward or digits backward. Remember that when an examinee gives only verbatim responses (as opposed to the appropriate reordered responses), the examiner cannot draw valid inferences about his or her working memory.
- Spontaneous corrections during the administration of this subtest. Remember to give credit for them.

Sources: D. P. Flanagan & A. S. Kaufman, *Essentials of WISC-IV Assessment* (2nd ed.). Copyright © 2009 John Wiley & Sons, Inc.

A. S. Kaufman & E. O. Lichtenberger, *Essentials of WISC-III and WPPSI-R Assessment.* Copyright © 2000 John Wiley & Sons, Inc.

A. S. Kaufman, S. E. Raiford, & D. L. Coalson, *Intelligent Testing with the WISC-V.* Copyright © 2016 John Wiley & Sons, Inc.

14. Cancellation (Processing Speed Subtest, Secondary)

The WISC-V Cancellation subtest requires the examinee to scan a random and a structured arrangement of pictures and mark target pictures within a specified time limit. The stimulus material for the Cancellation subtest is Response Booklet 2. A stopwatch, the *WISC-V Administration and Scoring Manual* (Wechsler, 2014a), the Record Form, and a red pencil without an eraser, are also needed to administer this subtest.

There are no age-appropriate start points for the WISC-V Cancellation subtest; all examinees begin with the demonstration item, the sample item, and then Item 1. There are no reverse rules on this subtest. The items are discontinued after 45 seconds have elapsed.

There are two types of items contained within the Response Booklet: random (i.e., the target pictures and distractors are scattered across the page) and structured (i.e., the target pictures and distractors are arranged in rows). Each target picture is an animal. If the examinee fails to mark a target or mistakenly marks a distractor picture during the practice items, the examiner should provide corrective feedback. It is important not to proceed to Item 1 until the examinee fully understands the task. Spontaneous corrections should not be discouraged, unless such corrections occur frequently enough to impede performance. Do not permit the examinee to begin the test items early. Provide necessary prompts during the administration, such as prompting to draw one slash mark to make each mark, rather than something other than one slash mark; for example, "Don't make an X, make a slash." List 2.11 provides a description of the changes in the administration of the Cancellation subtest from WISC-IV to WISC-V. The Don't Forget "Behaviors to Note on Cancellation" provides a description of behaviors that the examiner should note during the administration of the Cancellation subtest.

LIST 2.11

Changes in Administration From the WISC-IV to the WISC-V: Subtest 14, Cancellation

- If an examinee marks his or her answer using anything other than a single slash, say, "Draw *one* line to make each mark." Timing continues through the provision of this prompt.
- No time-bonus score.

DON'T FORGET

Behaviors to Note on Cancellation

- Watch for shaking hands, a tight grip on the pencil, or pressure on the paper when writing. These behaviors may indicate anxiety.
- Whether the examinee has difficulty understanding that he or she is expected to work quickly. This behavior may relate to immaturity.
- Observe attention and concentration. Is the examinee's focus consistent throughout the task, or does it wane as the task progresses?
- Observe signs of fatigue, boredom, or inattention as the subtest progresses. Noting the number of responses produced during each of the 45-second item intervals may provide helpful behavioral information in this regard.
- Whether the examinee's response rate is consistent throughout the subtest.
- Whether the examinee quickly but carelessly circles responses. This behavior may suggest impulsivity.
- The effect of distractors on the examinee's performance. Remember that the target items are identically placed on the randomized and nonrandomized forms.

Sources: D. P. Flanagan & A. S. Kaufman, *Essentials of WISC-IV Assessment* (2nd ed.). Copyright © 2009 John Wiley & Sons, Inc.

A. S. Kaufman & E. O. Lichtenberger, *Essentials of WISC-III and WPPSI-R Assessment.* Copyright © 2000 John Wiley & Sons, Inc.

15. Naming Speed Literacy (Complementary)

The new WISC-V Naming Speed Literacy subtest requires the examinee to name elements, such as objects of various size and color, letters, and numbers as quickly as possible within a given time limit. The stimulus material for the Naming Speed Literacy subtest is Stimulus Book 3. A stopwatch, the *WISC-V Administration and Scoring Manual* (Wechsler, 2014a), and the Record Form are also needed to administer this subtest.

The WISC-V Naming Speed Literacy subtest administration is based on age-appropriate start points. An examinee age 6 years begins with Demonstration Item A and Sample Item A, followed by Item 1; an examinee age 7–8 years begins with Demonstration Item B and Sample Item B, followed by Item 2; an examinee age 9–16 years begins with Sample Item C, followed by Item 3. The WISC-V Naming Speed Literacy subtest administration also has age-appropriate stop points. Examiners should end the subtest after administering

Item 2, Trial 2 for examinees age 6 and after administering Item 3, Trial 2 for examinees ages 7–16. If an examinee age 6 does not understand Sample Item A and Item 1 is not administered, the examiner does not administer Demonstration or Sample Item B or Item 2. If an examinee age 7–8 does not understand Sample Item B and Item 2 is not administered, the examiner administers Sample Item C and Item 3 to obtain some measure of rapid automatized naming, as he or she may be able to name numbers and letters. Stop points for each age are indicated in the Record Form as a reminder for examiners not to continue testing.

Demonstration Items A–B each consists of one row of elements to teach the names of the attributes of the elements the examinee will be expected to identify. Sample Items A–C each consists of two rows of elements to introduce the task for the corresponding items. Examinees age 6 years will be asked to identify the name and color of various objects, then the size, name, and color of the various objects; while examinees ages 7–8 years will be asked to identify the size, name, and color of the various objects. Synonyms for the attributes can be accepted. Examinees ages 7–16 years will be asked to identify numbers and letters. Test Items 1, 2, and 3 have two trials each with four rows of elements per trial. Synonyms are acceptable for Items 1 and 2.

Examinees ages 6–8 are required to keep track of their progress across the rows of elements using their finger and should be reminded to do so. Examinees ages 9–16 are not required to keep track of their progress using their finger, but should not be discouraged from doing so. To follow where the examinee is on the page and ensure that he or she and the examiner are referencing the same stimulus, clarification may be necessary. If the examinee misnames two stimuli consecutively, the examiner points to the second misnamed stimulus and provide the appropriate prompt to keep going from that point. If the examinee hesitates, either at the end of a row or on a single stimulus, the examiner gives the prompt to go on to the next row or stimulus.

The time limit for each trial is 300 seconds (5 minutes). The examiner stops timing when the examinee completes the trial or when the time limit expires. Because some examinees respond so quickly and recording can be overwhelming, the examiner marks only incorrect responses with a single slash mark through the misnamed element. A response is not considered complete until the examinee has said an entire word in an attempt to name the stimulus and self-corrections are acceptable and should be noted. Self-corrections are not considered errors. The Don't Forget "Behaviors to Note on Naming Speed Literacy" provides a description of behaviors that the examiner should note during the administration of the Naming Speed Literacy subtest.

DON'T FORGET

Behaviors to Note on Naming Speed Literacy

- Whether the examinee misnames stimuli more frequently on Trial 1 than on Trial 2 of an item.
- Pay attention to wandering attention during the task.
- Whether the examinee loses time by checking and rechecking answers before moving on.
- Whether the examinee appears to benefit from ongoing experience with items, becoming faster as items progress.

Source: A. S. Kaufman, S. E. Raiford, & D. L. Coalson, *Intelligent Testing with the WISC-V.* Copyright © 2016 John Wiley & Sons, Inc.

16. Naming Speed Quantity (Complementary)

The new WISC-V Naming Speed Quantity subtest requires the examinee to name the quantity of squares inside a series of boxes as quickly as possible. The stimulus material for the Naming Speed Quantity subtest is Stimulus Book 3. A stopwatch, the *WISC-V Administration and Scoring Manual* (Wechsler, 2014a), and the Record Form are also needed to administer this subtest.

The WISC-V Naming Speed Quantity subtest administration is based on age-appropriate start points. An examinee age 6 years begins with Sample Item A followed by Item 1, and an examinee age 7–16 years begins with Sample Item B followed by Item 2. The WISC-V Naming Speed Quantity subtest administration also has age-appropriate stop points. Examiners should end the subtest after administering Item 1, Trial 2 for examinees age 6 and after administering Item 2, Trial 2 for examinees ages 7–16.

Sample Items A–B each includes two rows of boxes to introduce the task. Test Items 1 and 2 each has two trials with four rows of boxes per trial. The examinee must name the quantity of squares in each box moving from left to right and down the page. If an examinee skips a row or begins to complete a row in reverse order, the examiner points to the first box in the row and instructs him or her to continue from there. If an examinee hesitates to name a single quantity for more than 5 seconds, the examiner should instruct him or her to move to the next box.

Examinees ages 6–8 years are required to keep track of their progress across the rows of elements using their finger and should be reminded to do so. Examinees ages 9–16 years are not required to keep track of their progress using their finger, but should not be discouraged from doing so. Examiners should mark only incorrect responses with a single slash mark, as examinees respond quickly and recording everything can be too much. Self-corrections also occur frequently because the pace is fast and these should be noted. Self-corrections are not considered errors. A response is not complete until the examinee has said an entire word in an attempt to name the quantity and self-corrections should only be marked if made after a complete word was said. The time limit for each trial is 300 seconds (5 minutes). The examiner stops timing when the examinee completes the trial or when the time limit expires. The Don't Forget "Behaviors to Note on Naming Speed Quantity" provides a description of behaviors that the examiner should note during the administration of the Naming Speed Quantity subtest.

DON'T FORGET

Behaviors to Note on Naming Speed Quantity

- Whether the examinee misnames stimuli more frequently on Trial 1 than on Trial 2 of an item.
- Pay attention to wandering attention during the task.
- Whether the examinee loses time by checking and rechecking answers before moving on.
- Whether the examinee appears to benefit from ongoing experience with items, becoming faster as items progress.

Source: A. S. Kaufman, S. E. Raiford, & D. L. Coalson, *Intelligent Testing with the WISC-V.* Copyright © 2016 John Wiley & Sons, Inc.

---

17. Immediate Symbol Translation (Complementary)

The new WISC-V Immediate Symbol Translation subtest requires the examinee to translate symbol strings into phrases or sentences after learning visual-verbal pairs. The stimulus material for the Immediate Symbol Translation subtest is Stimulus Book 3. The *WISC-V Administration and Scoring Manual* (Wechsler, 2014a) and the Record Form are also needed to administer this subtest.

There are no age-appropriate start points for the WISC-V Immediate Symbol Translation subtest; all examinees begin with Item 1. Discontinue rules for this subtest are based on an examinee's cumulative performance at specific decision points. The examiner should discontinue testing if the examinee's raw score is less than or equal to 9 at Decision Point A, if the examinee's raw score is less than or equal to 20 at Decision Point B, or if the examinee's raw score is less than or equal to 30 at Decision Point C. If the examinee's raw score is high enough to continue past all three decision points, the examiner continues through the end of the subtest.

The examinee is introduced to the visual-verbal pairs needed to translate symbol strings into phrases or sentences in a stepwise manner, with new pairs being presented periodically throughout the subtest. Twenty-nine of the symbols represent words and five of the symbols represent modifiers that indicate a change in the tense or plurality of the word or require the examinee to add a suffix to the word. The examiner should follow the instructions for each item carefully, as some items require the examiner to review previously learned visual-verbal pairs. Items 1–3 each allows for two trials if the examinee does not provide the correct answer on the first trial. If the examinee responds correctly to the second trial, full credit is received. If the examinee does not translate a symbol after approximately 5 seconds, the examiner should prompt him or her to go on to the next symbol. The examiner records the subtest stop time at the end of the administration as approximately 20 to 30 minutes should elapse before administering Delayed and/or Recognition Symbol Translation. The Don't Forget "Behaviors to Note on Immediate Symbol Translation" provides a description of behaviors that the examiner should note during the administration of the Immediate Symbol Translation subtest.

DON'T FORGET

Behaviors to Note on Immediate Symbol Translation
- Whether the examinee hesitates before responding or answers immediately.
- Whether the examinee uses a form of the correct word or a word that is the same part of speech as the correct response when responses are incorrect.
- Whether the examinee forms sentences and phrases that represent coherent thoughts even if they are not completely correct.
- Whether the examinee repeats incorrect translations made on earlier items, indicating that meaning was encoded incorrectly and retention is good.

Source: A. S. Kaufman, S. E. Raiford, & D. L. Coalson, *Intelligent Testing with the WISC-V.* Copyright © 2016 John Wiley & Sons, Inc.

18. Comprehension (Verbal Comprehension Subtest, Secondary)

The WISC-V Comprehension subtest requires the examinee to answer a series of questions based on his or her understanding of general principles and social situations. The *WISC-V Administration and Scoring Manual* (Wechsler, 2014a) and Record Form are the only items needed for the administration of this subtest.

The WISC-V Comprehension subtest administration is based on age-appropriate start points. An examinee age 6–11 years begins with Item 1, and an examinee age 12–16 years begins with Item 3. If a child age 12–16 does not obtain a perfect score on either of the first two items, the preceding items should be administered in reverse order until a perfect score on two consecutive items is obtained. The Comprehension subtest is discontinued after three consecutive zero-point responses.

The WISC-V Comprehension subtest questions should be read at such a pace that examinees find it easy to follow the examiner, but do not become distracted because of the speed. The questions may be repeated as many times as necessary without changing the wording, which is logical since this is not a memory test. It is important to note Items 1–4 on the WISC-V Comprehension subtest require the examiner to provide an example of a 2-point response if the examinee does not spontaneously give a 2-point response. This is done in order to teach the examinee the type of response expected for each item. On Items 5, 7, and 18, the examinee is required to give two general concepts in response to the question in order to receive full credit (i.e., 2 points). On these items, the examiner is required to prompt the examinee for another response if only one general concept is reflected in the response. Items 11, 15, and 19 involve sayings and proverbs from other cultures that are outdated and adapted for the WISC-V. Concrete responses are scored as incorrect and abstract proverb interpretations receive more credit. These items require familiarity with general principles and social situations and they correlate highly with the remaining items on the subtest. If the examinee's first spontaneous response is incorrect, examiners should not prompt for a second response unless it is followed by (Q) in the sample responses. The earlier discussion concerning "Querying," "I don't know," and "Repeating Items" all apply to administering the Comprehension subtest. List 2.12 provides a description of the changes in the administration of the Comprehension subtest from WISC-IV to WISC-V. The Don't Forget "Behaviors to Note on Comprehension" provides a description of behaviors that the examiner should note during the administration of the Comprehension subtest.

LIST 2.12
. . . .

Changes in Administration From the WISC-IV to the WISC-V: Subtest 18, Comprehension

- The introduction to the subtest has been shortened such that the phrase "Now I am going to ask you some questions, and I would like for you to tell me the answers" is eliminated.
- There are four teaching items, two for each of the start points.
- If an examinee offers only one concept for an item response requiring two general concepts (e.g., "Tell me some *reasons* why we go to the doctor."), the examiner provides only *one* prompt for a second concept. If the examinee's extended response refers to the *same* concept *initially* given, the item is scored and an additional prompt is *not* given.

DON'T FORGET
. . . .

Behaviors to Note on Comprehension

- Whether the examinee appears to benefit from the feedback provided on teaching items, giving correct responses after learning the task.
- Whether the examinee provides complete responses or must be repeatedly queried as a cue to give all pertinent information about the response.
- Whether the examinee provides additional information about responses upon query or tends to say he or she does not know any more.
- Whether the examinee continues to provide complete answers throughout the subtest, or responses become briefer or vaguer as the subtest progresses.
- Observe whether unusually long verbal responses are an attempt to cover up for not actually knowing the correct response, or an indication that the examinee tends to be obsessive about details.
- Be aware that Comprehension requires a good amount of verbal expression; therefore word-finding difficulties, articulation problems, circumstantiality, tangentiality, or circumlocutions (e.g., verbal discourse that is overly detailed, irrelevant, or convoluted, respectively) may be apparent during this subtest.
- Note whether defensiveness is apparent in responses to some Comprehension items. For example, when asked about doctors, if the examinee's response does not really answer the question and is something like "We shouldn't have to go to the doctor," this may be defensive responding. Although such responses are scored 0, it is recommended that you follow up if you believe that the child knows the answer.

- Whether the examinee needs consistent prompting when a second response is required or whether he or she spontaneously provides enough information in the initial answer.
- Whether incorrect responses are a result of poor verbal ability or poor social judgment.
- How the examinee responds to queries and requests for elaboration (e.g., "Give me another reason"). Some examinees may be threatened or frustrated by the interruptions, and others may seem comfortable with the added structure. Some examinees, when asked for "another reason," simply restate the first reason in different words or otherwise do not give a second idea.
- Spontaneous corrections during the administration of this subtest and remember to give credit for them.

Sources: D. P. Flanagan & A. S. Kaufman, *Essentials of WISC-IV Assessment* (2nd ed.). Copyright © 2009 John Wiley & Sons, Inc.

A. S. Kaufman & E. O. Lichtenberger, *Essentials of WISC-III and WPPSI-R Assessment.* Copyright © 2000 John Wiley & Sons, Inc.

A. S. Kaufman, S. E. Raiford, & D. L. Coalson, *Intelligent Testing with the WISC-V.* Copyright © 2016 John Wiley & Sons, Inc.

19. Arithmetic (Fluid Reasoning Subtest, Secondary)

The WISC-V Arithmetic subtest requires the examinee to mentally solve a variety of visually (and orally) or orally presented arithmetic problems within a specified time limit. The materials necessary for the administration of the WISC-V Arithmetic subtest comprise the *WISC-V Administration and Scoring Manual* (Wechsler, 2014a), the Record Form, Stimulus Book 2, and a stopwatch.

The WISC-V Arithmetic subtest administration is based on age-appropriate start points. An examinee age 6–7 years begins with Item 3, an examinee age 8–9 years begins with Item 8, and an examinee age 10–16 years begins with Item 11. If the examinee does not obtain a perfect score on either of the first two items administered, the preceding items should be administered in reverse order until a perfect score on two consecutive items is obtained. If an examinee provides an incorrect answer or does not respond within 30 seconds to Items 1–3, the examiner should provide the correct response. The Arithmetic subtest is discontinued after three consecutive zero-point responses.

It is important to note that the Arithmetic items are timed. The examiner should begin timing immediately after each item presentation and stop timing

LIST 2.13

Changes in Administration From the WISC-IV to the WISC-V: Subtest 19, Arithmetic

- Item repetitions are disallowed for Items 1–19.
- For Items 20–34, alert the examinee that a single repetition will be allowed for remaining items and pause the timer while the item is repeated. Timing begins again immediately after the last word of the repeated item is said.
- Prompt the child for a response after 20 seconds have elapsed by asking, "Do you have an answer?" Timing continues during the provision of this prompt.
- Item 31 includes a specific query.

immediately after an examinee responds or 30 seconds have elapsed. If the examinee has not provided a response after 20 seconds have elapsed, the examiner may prompt for an answer. The examiner may not repeat Items 1–19. If an examinee requests repetition of one of these items, the examiner does not stop the timer, but says "I can't say it again." However, repetition is allowed if requested for Items 20–34. For Items 20–34, the timer should be paused immediately when the examinee requests a repetition and timing should be resumed after the last word of the item is repeated. Only a single repetition per item is permitted.

There are corresponding pictures in the Stimulus Book for Items 1–5; Items 6–34 are presented orally to the examinee. The examinee must not use a pencil or paper for this subtest. If the examinee provides a spontaneous second answer within the 30-second time limit, score the second response. List 2.13 provides a description of the changes in the administration of the Arithmetic subtest from WISC-IV to WISC-V. The Don't Forget "Behaviors to Note on Arithmetic" provides a description of behaviors that the examiner should note during the administration of the Arithmetic subtest.

DON'T FORGET

Behaviors to Note on Arithmetic

- Observe the examinee for signs of anxiety. Some examinees who view themselves as "poor at math" may be anxious during this task. Be aware of statements such as "I was never taught that in school" or "I can't do math in my head."

- Whether the examinee appears to be focusing on the stopwatch. This may be a sign of anxiety, distractibility, or competitiveness. Watch for statements such as "How long did that take me?"
- Watch for signs of distractibility or poor concentration.
- Be aware that finger counting may occur in an examinee of any age. This may be indicative of insecurity about math skills or may be an adaptive problem-solving tool for younger examinees. Note if the examinee attempts to hide finger counting from the examiner, is brazen about finger counting, or is nonchalant about finger counting.
- Whether the examinee asks for repetition of a question, as it may indicate several things, including poor hearing, inattention, or stalling.
- The examinee's response style. Does he or she respond quickly, or is he or she methodical and careful in his or her responding?

Sources: D. P. Flanagan & A. S. Kaufman, *Essentials of WISC-IV Assessment* (2nd ed.). Copyright © 2009 John Wiley & Sons, Inc.

A. S. Kaufman & E. O. Lichtenberger, *Essentials of WISC-III and WPPSI-R Assessment.* Copyright © 2000 John Wiley & Sons, Inc.

20. Delayed Symbol Translation (Complementary)

The new WISC-V Delayed Symbol Translation subtest requires the examinee to recall the visual-verbal pairs taught in the Immediate Symbol Translation subtest in order to translate symbols into words, phrases, and sentences. The stimulus material for the Immediate Symbol Translation subtest is Stimulus Book 3. The *WISC-V Administration and Scoring Manual* (Wechsler, 2014a) and the Record Form are also needed to administer this subtest.

There are no age-appropriate start points for the WISC-V Delayed Symbol Translation subtest; all examinees begin with Item 1. Discontinue rules for this subtest are based on the examinee's performance on the Immediate Symbol Translation Subtest, so the examiner should stop testing at the same decision point as Immediate Symbol Translation. If the examinee did not discontinue on the Immediate Symbol Translation subtest, do not discontinue.

Delayed Symbol Translation cannot be administered without first administering Immediate Symbol Translation. There should be approximately a 20–30-minute gap between the administrations of these two subtests. Examiners follow the instructions provided in the manual to introduce the examinee to the task. If the examinee does not translate a symbol after approximately 5 seconds, the examiner should prompt them to go on to the next symbol. Apart from reminding the examinee to translate symbols from left to right if necessary, no feedback should be provided during this subtest. Examiners administer Recognition Symbol Translation immediately after this subtest if it is given. The Don't Forget "Behaviors to Note on Delayed Symbol Translation" provides a description of behaviors that the examiner should note during the administration of the Delayed Symbol Translation subtest.

DON'T FORGET

Behaviors to Note on Delayed Symbol Translation

- Whether the examinee hesitates before responding or immediately answers.
- Whether the examinee uses a form of the correct word or a word that is the same part of speech as the correct translation when response is incorrect.
- Whether the examinee forms sentences and phrases that represent coherent thoughts even if they are not completely correct.
- Pay attention to repeated incorrect translations that may indicate that the meaning was initially encoded incorrectly, but retention is good.
- Whether the examinee frequently self-corrects on translations that were initially correct.

Source: A. S. Kaufman, S. E. Raiford, & D. L. Coalson, *Intelligent Testing with the WISC-V.* Copyright © 2016 John Wiley & Sons, Inc.

---

21. Recognition Symbol Translation (Complementary)

The new WISC-V Recognition Symbol Translation subtest requires the examinee to view a symbol and select the correct translation from a series of orally presented response options using recalled visual-verbal pairs from the Immediate Symbol Translation subtest. The stimulus material for the Immediate Symbol Translation subtest is Stimulus Book 3. The *WISC-V Administration and Scoring Manual* (Wechsler, 2014a) and the Record Form are also needed to administer this subtest.

There are no age-appropriate start points for the WISC-V Recognition Symbol Translation subtest; all examinees begin with Item 1. Discontinue rules for this subtest are based on the examinee's performance on the Immediate Symbol Translation Subtest, so the examiner should stop testing at the same decision point as Immediate Symbol Translation. If the examinee did not discontinue on the Immediate Symbol Translation subtest, do not discontinue.

The Recognition Symbol Translation subtest may be administered regardless of the examinee's performance on Delayed Symbol Translation. Recognition

Symbol Translation should be administered immediately after Delayed Symbol Translation if both subtests are given. If Delayed Symbol Translation was not administered, administration of the Recognition Symbol Translation should begin approximately 20–30 minutes after the completion of Immediate Symbol Translation. When reading the response options aloud to the examinee, the examiner should not include the letter that identifies the response option (i.e., A, B, C, D). Each item may be repeated as many times as necessary without changing the wording. No feedback should be given during this subtest. The Don't Forget "Behaviors to Note on Recognition Symbol Translation" provides a description of behaviors that the examiner should note during the administration of the Delayed Symbol Translation subtest.

DON'T FORGET

Behaviors to Note on Recognition Symbol Translation

- Whether the examinee hesitates before responding or immediately answers.
- Whether the examinee uses process of elimination to determine the answer versus guessing the same incorrect translations repeatedly.
- When responding incorrectly, note if the examinee selects response options that are from the same part of speech as those of the correct item.
- Whether the examinee repeats errors made on Immediate Symbol Translation and Delayed Symbol Translation.
- Whether the examinee frequently self-corrects on translations that were initially correct.

Source: A. S. Kaufman, S. E. Raiford, & D. L. Coalson, *Intelligent Testing with the WISC-V.* Copyright © 2016 John Wiley & Sons, Inc.

CAUTION

Common Errors in WISC-V Subtest Administration

Verbal Subtests

Common Errors on the Similarities Subtest

- Forgetting to provide the correct response if the examinee fails to respond or the response is incorrect on Items 1, 2, 5, 6, and 9

- Forgetting to administer previous items in *reverse sequence* if an examinee age 9–16 years does not obtain a perfect score on either of the first two items administered
- Over-querying or under-querying vague responses

Common Errors on the Vocabulary Subtest

- Forgetting to give an example of a 1-point response if the examinee's response to Item 1 is not perfect
- Forgetting to give an example of a 2-point response if the examinee's response to Item 5, 6, 9, or 10 is not perfect
- Forgetting to administer previous items in *reverse sequence* if the examinee does not obtain a perfect score on either of the first two items administered
- Not correcting the examinee if he or she mishears items, especially Items 9, 13, 15, 17, 19, 23, 25, and 28
- Not recording verbal responses verbatim
- Not querying vague or incomplete responses as indicated in the *WISC-V Administration and Scoring Manual* (Wechsler, 2014a)

Common Errors on the Comprehension Subtest

- Forgetting to give an example of a 2-point response if the examinee's response to Item 1–4 is not perfect
- Forgetting to administer previous items in *reverse sequence* if an examinee age 9–16 years does not obtain a perfect score on either of the first two items administered
- Forgetting to query for a second response if necessary on Items 5 and 7
- Not recording verbal responses verbatim
- Defining words if asked by child
- Neglecting to query sample responses followed by a Q
- Not providing the specific query for sample responses noted with an asterisk (*)
- Not providing corrective feedback on teaching items marked with a dagger (†) in response to an imperfect score

Common Errors on the Information Subtest

- Forgetting to provide the correct response if the examinee fails to respond or responds incorrectly to Items 1, 2, 8, and 9
- Forgetting to administer previous items in *reverse sequence* if the examinee does not obtain a perfect score on either of the first two items administered
- Defining words if asked by the examinee
- Forgetting to query an incomplete answer as indicated in the *WISC-V Administration and Scoring Manual* (Wechsler, 2014a)
- Being unaware that neutral queries may be given to responses that are incomplete or ambiguous

Visual Spatial Subtests

Common Errors on the Block Design Subtest

- Forgetting to time the examinee
- Improper use of the stopwatch: allowing too little or too much time
- Forgetting to administer previous items in *reverse sequence* if an examinee age 8–16 years fails the second trial of Item 3 or provides an incorrect response to Item 4
- Neglecting to make sure that the proper variety of block faces is showing before an item has been started
- Neglecting to give the five extra blocks on Items 11 through 14
- Placing the model or stimulus book in an incorrect position
- Correcting block rotations more than once
- Forgetting to leave the examiner's model intact when the child constructs his or her designs for Item
- Presenting the wrong blocks for a given item
- Not penalizing rotation and discontinuing too late
- Forgetting to correct the first rotation
- Not following the guidelines about a variety of block faces being presented face up

Common Errors on the Visual Puzzles Subtest

- Failing to administer the demonstration and sample item
- Allowing additional time beyond the time limit to provide a response
- Failing to prompt the examinee to select three response options if he or she selects fewer or more than three

Fluid Reasoning Subtests

Common Errors on the Matrix Reasoning Subtest

- Forgetting to provide the correct response and point to the correct corresponding pictures in Sample Items A and B
- Forgetting to administer previous items in *reverse sequence* if the examinee does not obtain a perfect score on either of the first two items administered
- Forgetting to point to the pictured responses and the box with the question mark as often as needed when presenting test items
- Failing to administer the sample items
- Rigidly applying the 30-second guideline as a strict time limit
- Failing to circle the selected response option

Common Errors on the Figure Weights Subtest

- Not administering the items prior to the start point in reverse sequence if the examinee obtains an imperfect score on either start-point item
- Failing to administer sample items
- Allowing additional time beyond the time limit to provide a response
- Forgetting to provide the verbatim instruction required on the first three-scale item
- Failing to identify the intended response when multiple response options are given

Common Errors on the Picture Concepts Subtest

- Not administering the items prior to the start point in reverse sequence if the examinee obtains an imperfect score on either start-point item
- Failing to prompt the examinee to select one response option from each row, if needed
- Failing to circle all selected response options
- Failing to identify the intended response when multiple response options are given

Common Errors on the Arithmetic Subtest

- Forgetting to time the examinee
- Stopping the stopwatch when a question is repeated
- Repeating an item more than one time
- Allowing paper and pencil to be used
- Forgetting to provide the correct response to Items 1, 2, and 3 if the examinee does not respond within 30 seconds or responds incorrectly
- Forgetting to administer previous items in *reverse sequence* if the examinee does not obtain a perfect score on either of the first two items administered
- Forgetting to remove the Stimulus Booklet after administering Item 5
- Forgetting to give credit for spontaneous corrections within the time limit
- Forgetting to record completion times for every item
- Providing repetition of the item for Items 1 to 19
- Pausing timing of an item for anything other than a permitted repetition of the item stimulus
- Allowing additional time beyond the time limit to provide a response
- Failing to provide repetition of the item or pause timing while providing the repetition for Items 20 to 24

Working Memory

Common Errors on the Digit Span Subtest

- Inadvertently "chunking" the numbers when reading them
- Repeating a digit sequence if asked
- Giving extra help beyond the sample item on Digits Backward
- Forgetting to administer Digits Backward to a child who receives 0 points on Digits Forward
- Forgetting to administer *both* trials of an item
- Failing to administer all demonstration and sample items
- Forgetting to administer the qualifying items to examinees ages 6 and 7 years
- Administering the qualifying items to children ages 8 to 16 years
- Failing to read the stimuli at a rate of one per second and/or in a consistent tone and failing to drop tone of voice only on the last letter or number read
- Discontinuing after consecutive trials are missed across two items rather than only after all trials are missed on a single item
- Failing to administer all three tasks

Common Errors on the Letter-Number Sequencing Subtest

- Administering the subtest if an examinee age 6–7 years fails the qualifying items
- Forgetting to remind the examinee of the correct order on all trials of Item 1 and Item 2
- Repeating a letter-number sequence if asked
- Forgetting to administer all three trials of an item
- Failing to read the stimuli at the rate of one per second and/or in a consistent tone and failing to drop tone of voice only on the last letter or number read
- Discontinuing after consecutive trials are missed across two items rather than only after all trials are missed on a single item

Common Errors on the Picture Span Subtest

- Neglecting to use the stopwatch to track stimulus exposure time
- Failing to record all selected response options in the order they were given
- Neglecting to administer Sample Items A and/or B
- Administering Sample Item A to a child who does not start with Item 1
- Forgetting to increase stimulus exposure time from 3 seconds to 5 seconds, beginning with Sample Item B
- Failing to re-expose stimulus pages to identify correct response on Sample Items and Items 1, 2, 4, and 5

Processing Speed

Common Errors on the Coding Subtest

- Forgetting to administer the correct form, based on the examinee's age (e.g., Coding A: 6–7; Coding B: 8–16)
- Forgetting to time the examinee
- Forgetting to correct errors on sample items immediately
- Not paying attention to the child and allowing him or her to skip over items or complete a row in reverse order
- Forgetting to turn the Response Booklet pages for the examinee
- Stopping administration after 1 minute and 20 seconds rather than 120 seconds (2 minutes)

Common Errors on the Symbol Search Subtest

- Forgetting to administer the correct form, based on the examinee's age (e.g., Symbol Search A: 6–7; Symbol Search B: 8–16)
- Forgetting to time the examinee
- Proceeding with the task before the examinee clearly understands what is required
- Burying your head in the manual while reading directions
- Not paying attention to the examinee and allowing him or her to skip over items
- Neglecting to provide prompt if examinee marks a stimulus with something other than a single slash
- Forgetting to turn the Response Booklet pages for the examinee
- Stopping administration after 1 minute and 20 seconds rather than 120 seconds (2 minutes)

Common Errors on the Cancellation Subtest

- Forgetting to time the examinee
- Forgetting to discontinue after a 45-second interval
- Forgetting to provide corrective feedback when the examinee marks incorrect responses during the practice items
- Forgetting to provide further explanation as needed when presenting Items 1 and 2
- Neglecting to provide prompt if the examinee marks a stimulus with something other than a single slash
- Failing to open the response booklet to expose the entire spread
- Stopping the administration at 120 seconds rather than 45 seconds for each item

Complementary Subtests

Common Errors on the Naming Speed Literacy Subtest

- Failing to record completion times for every trial administered.
- Recording correct responses; only incorrect responses are recorded
- Penalizing responses that were self-corrected
- If the final response (i.e., named element, aspect of an element) is correct, credit is awarded accordingly
- Administering unnecessary or wrong tasks to an examinee, or not administering all of the age-appropriate tasks to an examinee
- Penalizing the use of appropriate synonym to name an aspect of an element on Item 1 or Item 2; the use of reasonable synonyms is acceptable

Common Errors on the Naming Speed Quantity Subtest

- Failing to record completion times for every trial administered
- Recording correct responses; only incorrect responses are recorded
- Penalizing responses that were self-corrected
- If the final response (i.e., named element, aspect of an element, quantity) is correct, credit is awarded accordingly

Common Errors on the Immediate Symbol Translation Subtest

- Recording incorrect responses; only correct responses are recorded
- Providing additional instruction to assist the examinee in learning the visual-verbal pair
- Discontinuing administration too early or too late; at each decision point, sum the total number of correct responses and discontinue if the sum is less than or equal to the value provided for that decision point

Common Errors on the Delayed Symbol Translation Subtest

- Recording incorrect responses; only correct responses are recorded
- Failing to allow approximately 20 to 30 minutes after the end of Immediate Symbol Translation administration before commencing administration of Delayed Symbol translation
- Providing assistance to the examinee in remembering the visual-verbal pairs; no assistance should be provided
- Discontinuing administration too early or too late; discontinue at the same decision point A, B, or C as on Immediate Symbol Translation. If the examinee did not discontinue on Immediate Symbol Translation, administer all items and do not discontinue.

Common Errors on the Recognition Symbol Translation Subtest

- Failing to allow approximately 20 to 30 minutes after the end of Immediate Symbol Translation administration before commencing administration of Recognition Symbol translation

- Providing assistance to the examinee in remembering the visual-verbal pairs; no assistance should be provided
- Discontinuing administration too early or too late; discontinue at the same decision point A, B, or C as on Immediate Symbol Translation. If the examinee did not discontinue on Immediate Symbol Translation, administer all items and do not discontinue.
- Failing to circle the selected response option; this is particularly important for items to which the examinee does not respond correctly

Sources: D. P. Flanagan & A. S. Kaufman, *Essentials of WISC-IV Assessment* (2nd ed.). Copyright © 2009 John Wiley & Sons, Inc.

A. S. Kaufman & E. O. Lichtenberger, *Essentials of WISC-III and WPPSI-R Assessment.* Copyright © 2000 John Wiley & Sons, Inc.

A. S. Kaufman, S. E. Raiford, & D. L. Coalson, *Intelligent Testing with the WISC-V.* Copyright © 2016 John Wiley & Sons, Inc.

Note: The WISC-V allows examinees to correct responses spontaneously at *any* time during the administration of the entire test and receive the appropriate credit on any subtest with the exception of memory tasks, processing-speed tasks, and timed tasks (i.e., Block Design, Visual Puzzles, Figure Weights, Arithmetic, Coding, Symbol Search, Cancellation, Naming Speed Literacy, and Naming Speed Quantity), which allow for spontaneous correction only during the specified time limits of each subtest. Some subtests (i.e., Similarities, Vocabulary, Information, Comprehension, Matrix Reasoning, and Picture Concepts) also allow for the examiner to return to the item immediately prior to the present item and readminister it if the examiner believes that the examinee knows the answer and may reward credit if it is earned. The only exception to this, of course, is if the answer to that item is addressed elsewhere on the test.

FREQUENTLY ASKED QUESTIONS: SUBTEST ADMINISTRATION

Pearson Education® has provided information on its website to respond to frequently asked questions (FAQs) regarding the WISC-V. One category on this website reflects FAQs related to subtest administration. The information contained in this category has been reproduced for the benefit of practitioners and is presented in Rapid Reference 2.8

Rapid Reference 2.8

. . . .

Frequently Asked Questions: Subtest Administration

- How does Block Design work with children with motor deficits (such as cerebral palsy)? Is there an alternative test?

Whether Block Design is appropriate depends on the severity of the motor impairment. Unless the child has severe motor impairment, he or she may be able to complete the task. You will need to evaluate the severity and impact of the motor impairment for each case. If Block Design cannot be administered, the Visual Puzzles subtest can be substituted to obtain the FSIQ. The VSI and some ancillary index scores may not be obtained in this situation.

- Is teaching allowed on the sample items to ensure that children understand the expectations of the subtests?

Yes, many of the subtests have demonstration, sample, and teaching items built in to ensure the child understands the task. These items were added in response to the needs of thousands of children who participated in the development of the scale. Children with special needs were included among these participants.

- How is color-blindness being handled in Naming Speed Literacy?

Individuals with color-perception differences are a group that encompasses greater than 10% of the general population. These issues are much more common in males. We have made every effort to ensure our items, including those on the WAIS-IV, WISC-V, WPPSI-IV, and WASI-II, are free of bias against these individuals. Items are reviewed by color-perception differences experts, as well as individuals with color-perception differences, during the early stages of the test development process. In addition, acetate overlays have been utilized so that the test developers can understand the appearance of the stimuli to individuals with various color-perception differences. Items are also copied in black and white to check appearance to those with monochromatic color perception. All items are also subjected to an electronic "color-blindness" simulator to check item appearance with every type of color-perception difference and ensure that the intensity and saturation of colors are not confused or result in different responses. For the WISC-V, the colors are yellow, blue, and red; green is not included. This means that for the most common color blindness (green/red, which is 7%–10% of boys), the children will be able to take it without a problem. Children with monochromacy (0.00001% of children) should not be administered the WISC-V Naming Speed Literacy items that involve colors; however, they could take Item 3 (Letter-Number) and the Naming Speed Quantity subtest. For children with deuteranopia (1%), the simulation, template, and expert review indicate that they should be able to see the differences between the yellow and blue.

- Should I provide teaching on any teaching item to which the child responds incorrectly, or only for the first two items administered?

When the child responds incorrectly to a teaching item, teaching is provided regardless of the start point used or the child's age.

- Is the WISC-V quicker to administer than the WISC-IV?

Yes. Substantial efforts were made during development to achieve the shortest testing time possible and still offer greater construct coverage and flexibility. As a result, administration time is shorter than that of the WISC-IV. For the heart of the test, the primary index scores, the subtests take less time (about 10 minutes) to administer than the WISC-IV. The FSIQ can be obtained about 25–30 minutes faster than the WISC-IV. Because administration time is determined by the composite scores desired, it varies based on the practitioner's choices. The WISC-V measures a number of other related constructs (e.g., rapid automatized naming, visual-verbal associative memory). If you opt to administer the measures related to these constructs, the testing time will somewhat longer.

- What are the recommendations for using the WISC-V over the WAIS-IV when evaluating examinees age 16?

Because the age ranges of the WISC-V and the WAIS-IV overlap for examinees age 16, practitioners have the option of choosing the appropriate measure for an examinee this age. For examinees suspected of intellectual disability or low cognitive ability, the WISC-V should be administered because of its lower floor at this age range. For examinees of high ability, however, the WAIS-IV should be considered because of its higher ceiling. For the examinee of average ability, the choice between the WISC-V and the WAIS-IV requires clinical judgment from the educational and/or psychological professional. Both tests require the administration of 10 subtests to calculate the FSIQ and primary index scores, but examinees who have difficulty completing a lengthier assessment may benefit if the WISC-V is used because it is somewhat faster to obtain the primary index scores and the FSIQ. The WISC-V provides a Nonverbal Index that requires no expressive responses, which may be useful for examinees who are English language learners or who have expressive difficulties. The WISC-V provides some additional composite scores and more links to achievement tests that may be informative for certain referral questions (e.g., specific learning disability). The reasons for referral, familiarity with the tests, and knowledge of the examinee's characteristics (e.g., attention span) should be taken into consideration.

- On Visual Puzzles, some children seem confused by the instructions that refer to a piece being on top of another piece. They seem to think that a piece cannot appear above another piece on the puzzle, rather than thinking that the instruction refers to stacking the pieces in layers. Can I give them additional help?

The demonstration and the sample item are used together to teach how the task and items are completed. The "on top of" direction is to teach the child not to stack the pieces on top of each other in layers to complete it, but that the pieces have to fit next to each other. In the demonstration item you are actually teaching the child what "next to" means when you show them the correct response, because there is one piece that is above another. The child also gets additional feedback during the sample item explicitly if he or she is stacking the pieces "on top of" each other to get a solution.

If, after you show them on the demonstration item that choosing those three answers constitute "next to," and the child asks what "on top of" means, it's fine to explain more using the demonstration and the sample item. The demonstration item would be a perfect place to emphasize this point. Page 47 of the *WISC-V Administration and Scoring Manual* states that demonstration and sample items are used to explain the task and allow the child to practice.

Sources: http://www.pearsonclinical.com/psychology/products/100000771 /wechsler-intelligence-scale-for-childrensupsupfifth-edition--wisc-v.html#tab-faq

TEST YOURSELF

1. **Which of the following subtests require the use of a stopwatch?**
   a. Block Design, Picture Concepts, Coding, Symbol Search, Cancellation
   b. Cancellation, Coding, Symbol Search
   c. Block Design, Picture Concepts, Coding
   d. Block Design, Coding, Symbol Search, Cancellation, Arithmetic

2. **On a subtest with age-appropriate start points, when the examinee receives full credit on the first item administered but not the second, the first item is used to meet the reversal criteria of two consecutive perfect scores.**
   a. True
   b. False

3. **Which of the following subtests does not have reverse rules?**
   a. Digit Span
   b. Picture Concepts
   c. Block Design
   d. Similarities

4. **Which of the following subtests requires the use of a Response Booklet?**
   a. Matrix Reasoning
   b. Coding
   c. Arithmetic
   d. Block Design

5. **If a child asks for clarification or repetition of an item after timing has begun, the examiner should discontinue timing.**
   a. True
   b. False

6. **When an examinee requests to have instructions or an item repeated, the examiner must**
   a. repeat the entire set of instructions or item, not just a portion of it.
   b. repeat only the portion of instructions that the child requested repetition for.
   c. tell the examinee that you are unable to repeat any instructions.
   d. repeat the entire set of instructions or item, with the exception of trials on Letter-Number Sequencing and Digit Span.

7. **Which of the following subtests can serve as a substitute for Digit Span to derive the FSIQ?**
   a. Arithmetic
   b. Coding
   c. Symbol Search
   d. Letter-Number Sequencing

8. **Which of the following subtests can serve as a substitute for Block Design to derive the FSIQ?**
   a. Visual Puzzles
   b. Picture Concepts
   c. Immediate Symbol Translation
   d. Cancellation

9. **When administering the Naming Speed subtests, the examiner is allowed to tell the examinee to continue reading from the second misnamed consecutive element in a row.**
   a. True
   b. False

10. **The Comprehension subtest has four teaching items in the WISC-V, as compared to two teaching items in the WISC-IV.**
   a. True
   b. False

11. **You are advising a parent how to describe testing to her 6-year-old child. Which of the following is a good example of what the parent might say?**
   a. "You are going to take a test with a lot of questions, just try your best."
   b. "You are going to play with some blocks, look at books with pictures and words, complete some puzzles, and answer some questions."
   c. "The doctor is going to test you for about 2 or 3 hours to try to find out why you have problems in school."
   d. "You are going to play with the doctor for a while; it will be a lot of fun."

12. **When assessing an individual with a visual impairment, it may be advisable to administer the Verbal Comprehension subtests, Digit Span, and Letter-Number Sequencing only.**
   a. True
   b. False

13. **In which of the following situations can an examiner query a response?**
   a. The response is vague.
   b. The response is ambiguous.
   c. The response is incomplete.
   d. All of the above.

14. If an examiner finds that he or she did not administer enough items to meet the discontinue rule for a subtest, the subtest should be considered spoiled.

a. True

b. False

15. Which of the following can aid in establishing rapport with an examinee?

a. Telling the examinee your name.

b. Addressing the examinee by his or her name.

c. Spending a reasonable amount of time interacting with the examinee prior to testing.

d. All of the above.

Answers: 1. d; 2. a; 3. a; 4. b; 5. b; 6. d; 7. d; 8. a; 9. a; 10. b; 11. b; 12. a; 13. d; 14. a; 15. d

REFERENCES

Day, L. A., Costa, E. B. A., & Raiford, S. E. (2015). *Testing children who are deaf or hard of hearing* (WISC-V Technical Report no. 2). Bloomington, MN: Pearson.

Flanagan, D. P., & Kaufman, A. S. (2009). *Essentials of WISC-IV assessment* (2nd ed.). Hoboken, NJ: Wiley.

Kaufman, A. S., & Lichtenberger, E. O. (2000). *Essentials of WISC-III and WPPSI-R assessment.* New York, NY: Wiley.

Kaufman, A. S., Raiford, S. E., & Coalson, D. L. (2016). *Intelligent testing with the WISC-V.* Hoboken, NJ: Wiley.

Lichtenberger, E. O., & Kaufman, A. S. (2009). *Essentials of WAIS-IV assessment.* Hoboken, NJ: Wiley.

Ortiz, S. O., Ochoa, S. H., & Dynda, A. M. (2012). Testing with culturally and linguistically diverse populations: Moving beyond the verbal-performance dichotomy into evidence-based practice. In D. P. Flanagan & P. L. Harrison (Eds.), *Contemporary intellectual assessment: Theories, tests, and issues* (3rd ed., pp. 526–552). New York, NY: Guilford.

Wechsler, D. (2003). *Wechsler Intelligence Scale for Children* (4th ed.). San Antonio, TX: Pearson.

Wechsler, D. (2008). *Wechsler Adult Intelligence Scale* (4th ed.). San Antonio, TX: Pearson.

Wechsler, D. (2012). *Wechsler Preschool and Primary Scale of Intelligence* (4th ed.). Bloomington, MN: Pearson.

Wechsler, D. (2014a). *WISC-V administration and scoring manual.* Bloomington, MN: Pearson.

Wechsler, D. (2014b). *WISC-V technical and interpretive manual.* Bloomington, MN: Pearson.

Three

HOW TO SCORE THE WISC-V

TYPES OF SCORES

Administration of the WISC-V results in several types of scores, comprising item scores, total raw scores, primary and secondary subtest and process scaled scores, which are typically standard scores with mean = 10 and standard deviation = 3, complementary subtest, Index, Full Scale IQ (FSIQ), and process standard scores with mean = 100 and standard deviation = 15, raw process scores, and contrast scores. All of these scores are described in this chapter and some of them (e.g., process, contrast) are described further in Chapter 6 of this volume.

The first score calculated by the examiner is the *total raw score,* which is the total number of points earned on a single subtest (i.e., the sum of the item scores) or the total completion time for the Naming Speed subtests. The raw score by itself is largely meaningless because it is not norm referenced. That is, it has no meaning with respect to the examinee's level of functioning compared to the general population. It is, however, associated with an examinee's age equivalent. Although age equivalents have serious psychometric limitations, they are found in Table A.9 of the *WISC-V Administration and Scoring Manual* (Wechsler, 2014a).

In order to interpret an examinee's performance on a subtest relative to the general population (and more specifically, to same-age peers), total raw scores must be converted to *standard scores* (i.e., a subtest scaled or standard score, process scaled or standard score, index score, or FSIQ). The metrics for the various Wechsler standard scores are given in Rapid Reference 3.1.

≡ Rapid Reference 3.1

The primary and secondary subtest raw scores are converted to scaled scores (ranging from 1 to 19) with a mean (**X**) of 10 and a standard deviation (SD) of 3. The complementary subtests, Primary, Ancillary, and Complementary Index Scales, and Full Scale IQ have an **X** = 100 and an SD = 15. Unlike the WISC-IV, where each Primary Index Scale had different standard score ranges, the VCI (Verbal Comprehension Index), VSI (Visual-Spatial Index), FRI (Fluid Reasoning Index), WMI (Working Memory Index), and PSI (Processing Speed Index) have a standard score range of 45 to 155. The FSIQ has a standard score range of 40 to 160. The standard score range for two of the Ancillary Index Scales, namely, QRI (Quantitative Reasoning Index) and AWMI (Auditory Working Memory Index) is 45–155. The standard score range for the remaining three Ancillary Index Scales, namely, NVI (Nonverbal Index), GAI (General Ability Index), and CPI (Cognitive Proficiency Index), is 40–160. The standard score range for the Complementary Index Scales, namely, NSI (Naming Speed Index), STI (Symbol Translation Index), and SRI (Storage and Retrieval Index), is 45–155.

Intellectual abilities are distributed along the normal probability curve in the general population. Most examinees earn scores within 1 SD below and above the mean on measures of these abilities. That is, about 68 out of every 100 individuals tested obtain an FSIQ or Index scores between 85 and 115. A greater number of individuals, about 96%, obtain these scores ranging from 70 to 130 (2 SDs below and above the mean, respectively). The number of individuals earning extremely high scores (i.e., above 130) is about 2%, and the number earning very low scores (i.e., less than 70) is about 2%. With regard to Index scores, Crawford, Garthwaite, and Gault (2007) found that it is not unusual for individuals from the normal population to exhibit at least one abnormal Index score (i.e., below the 5th percentile).

STEP BY STEP: HOW THE WISC-V IS SCORED

The sections below discuss in greater depth all WISC-V scores, special considerations regarding these scores, prorating, scoring subtests requiring judgment, subtest-by-subtest scoring keys, and frequently asked questions regarding scoring.

Subtest Raw Scores and Raw Process Scores

Each of the items of a subtest contributes directly to the total raw score. The scoring of most subtests is not complicated. Simple arithmetic is all that is necessary to calculate the subtests' total raw scores, but examiners must remember to include raw score points earned for reversal items and unadministered items prior to the start point, if applicable. There are a few subtests, however, in which some element of subjectivity presents a challenge to the examiner during the scoring process. Tips for scoring responses that clearly involve subjectivity are discussed later in this chapter. The Caution "Common Errors in Calculating Total Raw Scores" presents common errors that examiners make in calculating total raw scores. Examiners should note that for the Digit Span, Picture Span, and Letter-Number Sequencing subtests raw process scores are available. There are 6 memory, 10 error, and nearly 4 dozen process observation raw scores for which base rates are available (Kaufman, Raiford, & Coalson, 2016) but do not involve summing item-level scores (Wechsler, 2014a). Memory base rate data are found in Table C.17 and error base rate data are found in Table C.18 of the *WISC-V Administration and Scoring Manual Supplement* (Wechsler, 2014b). Process observation base rate data are found in Appendix D of the *WISC-V Technical and Interpretive Manual* (Wechsler, 2016c). Subtest raw process scores are discussed further in Chapter 6, Kaufman et al. (2016), and Wechsler (2016a, c). Total raw and process scores are transferred to the "Total Raw Score to Scaled Score Conversion" table on the Summary page of the Record Form.

CAUTION

Common Errors in Calculating Total Raw Scores

- Neglecting to include points from the items below the basal (i.e., items that were not administered) to the total raw score
- Neglecting to add the points recorded on one page of the Record Form to the points recorded on the next
- Forgetting to subtract the number of incorrect responses from the number of correct responses on the Symbol Search and Cancellation subtests
- Transferring total raw scores incorrectly from inside the Record Form to the front page of the Record Form
- Miscalculating the total raw score sum
- Including points earned on items that were presented after the discontinue criterion was met
- Forgetting to attend closely to items that are scored 0, 1, or 2 rather than 0 or 1 only
- Awarding points for sample items

Sources: D. P. Flanagan & A. S. Kaufman, *Essentials of WISC-IV Assessment* (2nd ed.). Copyright © 2009 John Wiley & Sons, Inc.

Subtest Scaled, Subtest Standard, Standardized Process Scores, and Contrast Scores

After the raw scores have been transferred to the Total Raw Score to Scaled Score Conversion table on the Summary page of the Record Form, they are converted to scaled or standard scores. To convert the examinee's total raw scores to scaled or standard scores, the examiner needs the following: (1) the examinee's chronological age at the time of testing, (2) the examinee's total raw scores on all subtests, (3) Table A.1 from the *WISC-V Administration and Scoring Manual* (Wechsler, 2014a) for primary and secondary subtests, and (4) Table C.6 from the *WISC-V Administration and Scoring Manual Supplement* (Wechsler, 2014b) for the complementary subtests. In the section of Table A.1 or Table C.6 that has the examinee's chronological age, find his or her total raw score for each subtest and the corresponding scaled or standard score. Record the scaled score equivalents for primary and secondary subtests in the appropriate boxes in two separate places on the Summary Page of the Record Form, one labeled "Total Raw Score to Scaled Score Conversion," and another labeled "Subtest Scaled Score Profile." Record the standard score equivalents for complementary subtests in the appropriate boxes on the "Total Raw Score to Standard Score Conversion" table of the Ancillary and Complementary Analysis page located on the back side of the Summary page of the Record Form. The Caution "Most Frequent Errors in Obtaining Scaled Scores" lists the most frequent errors that examiners make in obtaining scaled scores.

CAUTION

Most Frequent Errors in Obtaining Scaled Scores

- Using a score conversion table that references the wrong age group
- Misreading across the rows of the score conversion tables
- Transferring scaled scores incorrectly from the conversion table to the Record Form
- Using the wrong panel of a page
- Mistakenly confusing total raw scores with scaled or standard scores when they are within the same range

- Recording the scaled or standard score from a different subtest in a given row

Sources: D. P. Flanagan & A. S. Kaufman, *Essentials of WISC-IV Assessment* (2nd ed.). Copyright © 2009 John Wiley & Sons, Inc.

A. S. Kaufman & E. O. Lichtenberger, *Essentials of WISC-III and WPPSI-R Assessment.* Copyright © 2000 John Wiley & Sons, Inc.

A. S. Kaufman, S. E. Raiford, & D. L. Coalson, *Intelligent Testing with the WISC-V.* Copyright © 2016 John Wiley & Sons, Inc.

Four subtests (Block Design, Digit Span, Cancellation, and Naming Speed Literacy) also allow for the calculation of 10 scaled or standard process scores that provide more detailed information relevant to subtest performance and involve calculating raw scores for specific items or portions of a subtest. These scores, which are discussed further in Chapter 6 of this volume, "may not be substituted for any scaled or standard subtest score and may not contribute to the FSIQ" (Wechsler, 2014a, p. 7). Tables C.6 and C.14 of the *WISC-V Administration and Scoring Manual Supplement* (Wechsler, 2014b) contain the scaled and standard process score equivalents for the subtests noted above. Examiners who desire to calculate scaled or standard process scores should transfer the corresponding raw scores to the "Total Raw Score to Scaled/Standard Process Score Conversion" table at the top of the Process Analysis page located on the back of the Primary Analysis page.

Contrast scores provide information regarding an examinee's performance on a task compared to others of the same age from the norm group who earned scores at the same level on another, related task (Kaufman et al., 2016). Contrast scores are found in Appendix C of the *WISC-V Technical and Interpretive Manual* (Wechsler, 2016c) and are dependent on the scaled or standard scores already calculated on the subtests involved. Contrast scores are available for the following: Digit Span Forward versus Digit Span Backward and Digit Span Sequencing; Digit Span Sequencing versus Letter-Number Sequencing; Cancellation Structured versus Cancellation Random; Immediate Symbol Translation versus Delayed Symbol translation; and Recognition Symbol Translation versus Delayed Symbol Translation.

Indexes and FSIQ

Converting scaled scores to Indexes and the FSIQ is the next step in the WISC-V scoring process. The following steps are necessary to convert subtest scaled scores to the Primary Index scores and the FSIQ. The Don't Forget lists the subtests that compose the WISC-V Primary Indexes and the FSIQ.

DON'T FORGET

. . . .

Subtests Composing WISC-V Primary Indexes and FSIQ

VCI	VSI	FRI	WMI	PSI
Similarities	**Block Design**	**Matrix Reasoning**	**Digit Span**	**Coding**
Vocabulary	Visual Puzzles	**Figure Weights**	Picture Span	Symbol Search

Note: Subtests in bold compose the FSIQ.

1. Calculate the Sum of Scaled Scores for each Primary Index and the FSIQ. To accomplish this, add the scaled scores of the two primary Verbal Comprehension subtests (i.e., Similarities and Vocabulary). Next, add the scaled scores of the two primary Visual Spatial subtests (i.e., Block Design and Visual Puzzles). Do this also for the Fluid Reasoning, Working Memory, and Processing Speed indexes. The Primary Index scores are made up of the first 10 subtests, but the Full Scale Sum of Scaled Scores is calculated only from the first seven subtests, not the 10 that make up the five Primary Index scores. This is a common point of confusion in calculating the Sum of Scaled Scores of the FSIQ.

   Unlike the WISC-IV, there is no subtest substitution allowed *for the calculation of any of the Index scores, only the FSIQ.* The Secondary subtests (i.e., Information, Picture Concepts, Letter-Number Sequencing, Cancellation, Comprehension, and Arithmetic) are not used in the Sum of Scaled Scores for Primary Index scores, but may be used in the calculation of the FSIQ as a substitute. Subtest substitutions are discussed later in this chapter and are presented in Table 3.1. It is important to note that only *one* subtest substitution is permitted in the calculation of the FSIQ. Subtest substitution is not the norm and usually the first 10 subtests of the WISC-V will comprise the Primary Index scores. Subtest substitution is a result of a spoiled or invalid administration of a subtest, rather than examiner preference for subtests. Scaled scores can also be calculated for the five Ancillary Index scores, which are derived from combinations of primary subtests or primary and secondary subtests, and three Complementary Index scores, which are derived from the complementary subtests.

Table 3.1   Allowable Subtest Substitutions for Deriving the FSIQ

Primary Subtest	Acceptable Substitution
Similarities	Information, Comprehension
Vocabulary	Information, Comprehension
Block Design	Visual Puzzles
Matrix Reasoning	Picture Concepts
Figure Weights	Picture Concepts or Arithmetic
Digit Span	Picture Span or Letter-Number Sequencing
Coding	Symbol Search or Cancellation

2. Transfer the Sum of Scaled Scores from the section titled Total Raw Score to Scaled Score Conversion to the section titled Sum of Scaled Scores to Composite Score Conversion. In these sections, the boxes in which the Sums of Scaled Scores are placed are shaded light green.
3. In the section titled Sum of Scaled Scores to Composite Score Conversion, convert the Sum of Scaled Scores for Verbal Comprehension, Visual Spatial, Fluid Reasoning, Working Memory, Processing Speed, and Full Scale to the appropriate Composite Score, Percentile Rank and Confidence Interval (the scaled score range), using Tables A.2, A.3, A.4, A.5, A.6, and A.7, respectively, in the *WISC-V Administration and Scoring Manual* (Wechsler, 2014a). Examiners determine the confidence interval they would like to use for the primary index scores and the FSIQ (either 90% or 95%) and circle that number to show which is chosen.
4. Plot scaled scores and composite scores on Subtest Scaled Score Profile and Composite Score Profile, respectively. These graphs are helpful when explaining test results to interested parties. The Composite Score Profile is especially valuable since this profile also shows the confidence intervals, and the subsequent overlap of the Index scores ranges.

Special Considerations for Calculating WISC-V Index Scores and FSIQ Using Substitution

According to the *WISC-V Administration and Scoring Manual* (Wechsler, 2014a), some subtests can be substituted for calculating the FSIQ under certain conditions. For example, an examiner may choose to substitute the Cancellation subtest for the Coding subtest for an individual with fine motor difficulties because, like the Symbol Search subtest, Cancellation requires making slash marks rather than drawing specific shapes. Likewise, the examiner may choose to substitute the Visual Puzzles subtest for Block Design for the same examinee because Visual Puzzles requires either a verbal or a pointing response rather than the manual manipulation of objects. Another situation in which a substitution may be warranted is when an FSIQ subtest is spoiled or invalidated for some reason. For example, when an examinee clearly misunderstands the directions for the Coding subtest, rendering the results uninterpretable, the Symbol Search or Cancellation subtest may be used.

There are nine subtests available for substitution when deriving the FSIQ (see Table 3.1). The substitution of only one of these subtests is permitted to calculate the FSIQ. It should be noted that this substitution will allow only the calculation of the FSIQ, not the calculation of other composite scores. The FSIQ is the only composite score on the WISC-V that allows any subtest substitutions.

In general, although there may be many situations in which substitutions for FSIQ subtests or proration is judged appropriate, this should be done cautiously and in accordance with the guidelines established by the test publisher. It is important to remember that when FSIQ subtests are replaced, the underlying construct intended to be measured by the FSIQ may change. All subtest substitutions are made for clinical reasons, not based on examinee preference.

Beyond the calculation of the Primary Index Scales and FSIQ, the WISC-V also allows for the calculation of additional Index scores that may be helpful to the clinician. The Ancillary Indexes Scales and the Complementary Index Scales contain subtest and Index scores that address specific issues that may be relevant to understanding the cognitive abilities of the examinee. These are optional scales that depending upon the referral question or needs of the examinee can be obtained in addition to the Primary Index Scales. The Ancillary Index Scales are Quantitative Reasoning, Auditory Working Memory, Nonverbal, General Ability and Cognitive Proficiency. The Complementary Index Scales are Naming Speed, Symbol Translation, and Storage and Retrieval. There are no subtest substitutions allowed in calculating any of these Index scores and no Ancillary or Complementary Index Scales can substitute for the Primary Index Scales. The two Don't Forgets below list the subtests that compose the WISC-V Ancillary and Complementary Index Scales, respectively.

DON'T FORGET

Subtests That Compose the WISC-V Ancillary Indexes

QRI	AWMI	NVI	GAI	CPI
Figure Weights	Digit Span	Block Design	Similarities	Digit Span
Arithmetic	Letter-Number Sequencing	Visual Puzzles	Vocabulary	Picture Span
		Matrix Reasoning	Block Design	Coding
		Figure Weights	Matrix Reasoning	Symbol Search
		Picture Span	Figure Weights	
		Coding		

DON'T FORGET

Subtests That Compose the WISC-V Complementary Indexes

NSI	STI	SRI
Naming Speed Literacy	Immediate Symbol Translation	Naming Speed Index
Naming Speed Quantity	Delayed Symbol Translation	Symbol Translation Index
	Recognition Symbol Translation	

Note: The SRI is derived from two other index scores (i.e., the NSI and the STI). The standard scores from Complementary subtests are not summed to derive the SRI.

Special Considerations for Indexes and the FSIQ with Subtest Total Raw Scores of Zero

Subtest total raw scores of zero deserve special consideration when being converted to scaled scores and then included in the conversion to Index scores, and the FSIQ. The problem with a total raw score of zero is that the examinee's true ability cannot be determined. A zero total raw score does not mean that an individual lacks a certain ability. Rather, it means that the particular subtest did not have enough low-level (or easy) items (called *floor items*) to assess adequately the individual's skills. If the examinee receives a total raw score of zero, it may mean that the WISC-V is not the right test for the examinee and another test, such as the WPPSI-IV, may assess the examinee's abilities more accurately. The Don't Forget lists the only situations in which it is permitted to calculate Index scores and a FSIQ when one or more total raw scores of zero are obtained.

DON'T FORGET

Appropriate Situations for Calculating Index Scores and an FSIQ When Total Raw Scores of Zero Are Obtained on Subtests

- *For any Index score derived from two subtests, only one subtest with a raw score of zero is allowed.*

  This includes the VCI, VSI, FRI, WMI, PSI, QRI, and AWMI. If both of the contributing subtests have total raw scores of zero, then the composite score is not valid and should not be derived.

- *For index scores derived from more than two contributing subtests, the number of allowable subtests with raw scores of zero varies with the number that contribute to the score.*

  For Index scores composed of three or four subtests (i.e., the STI and CPI), total raw scores of zero on no more than two of the contributing subtests are allowed. For Index scores derived from five or more subtests (i.e., the GAI and NVI), no more than three of the contributing subtests may have a total raw score of zero.

- *For the FSIQ, no more than four of the seven contributing subtests can have total raw scores of zero.*

  This includes the one allowable substitution permitted when deriving the FSIQ. If the FSIQ is prorated to six subtests, no more than three of the contributing subtests may have total raw scores of zero.

Prorating the FSIQ on the WISC-V

Prorating the FSIQ sum of Scaled Scores is allowed in specific instances. However, due to the multitude of problems associated with this technique, examiners are advised to avoid it whenever possible (see *WISC-V Administration and Scoring Manual*, Wechsler, 2014a, pp. 60–61). If an examiner determines through his or her sound clinical judgment that prorating is required, the following should be noted:

1. Proration is only allowed for the FSIQ and not for any of the Index scores. Table A.8 in the *WISC-V Administration and Scoring Manual* (Wechsler, 2014a) provides prorated sums of scaled scores.
2. A prorated sum of scaled scores can be used only to derive the FSIQ if six of the seven FSIQ subtests are available.
3. Proration cannot be combined with subtest substitution when deriving the FSIQ.
4. The examiner should always clearly record the term "PRORATED" next to the FSIQ on the Record Form. This term should be explained fully in the written psychological report.

Scoring Subtests Requiring Judgment

While administering the WISC-V examiners will likely find that the verbal subtests (e.g., Similarities and Vocabulary) elicit many more responses than listed in the manual. The multitude of responses given by an examinee, although interesting, may cause frustration for the examiner during the scoring process because of the time needed to learn the nuances of using the scoring criteria, a skill that takes practice and experience. The general scoring criteria are found on pages 51–54 in the *WISC-V Administration and Scoring Manual* (Wechsler, 2014a).

In addition to these criteria, there are some basic rules to consider when scoring Verbal Comprehension subtests. First, an examinee must not be penalized for poor grammar or improper pronunciation. Although grammar and pronunciation are important to note for clinical reasons, it is the *content* of what the examinee says that is most important for scoring a response. Second, long and elaborate answers are not necessarily worth more points than short, concise ones. Some examinees have a tendency to respond in paragraph form, which may lead to two or three answers given within the context of a single response. If this occurs, either spontaneously or after a query, it is the examiner's responsibility to determine two things, namely, (1) which part of the response was intended as the final response, and (2) whether the response has been spoiled. A response is considered spoiled when the examinee's elaboration reveals a fundamental misconception about the item.

If an examinee's response contains many answers, but none that spoil the response, further querying may be necessary. Sometimes it is clear that in a series of responses, the last answer is the final response. In that case, the final response should be the one scored. At other times it is unclear whether the second or third response is intended as the actual response. For clarification purposes you may ask, "You said, 'We wear bicycle helmets because our parents want us to wear them, they look cool, and they protect you.' Which one did you mean?" In some instances examinees say that their *entire* long response was what they intended the answer to be, and embedded in that long response are 0-, 1-, and 2-point answers. In such a case, if no response spoils part of the long response, then simply score the *best* response (i.e., the response that would allow the maximum number of points to be awarded to the examinee).

Subtest-by-Subtest Scoring Keys

The following sections provide important points to remember when scoring the respective WISC-V subtests. We do not review all nuances of scoring each subtest here, but rather cover areas that commonly cause difficulty for examiners. Additionally, tables outlining the most salient scoring revisions from the WISC-IV to the WISC-V are presented after each subtest, where applicable.

It is important to note that in addition to the subtest total raw score calculations, four WISC-V subtests presented in this section (i.e., Block Design, Digit Span, Cancellation, and Naming Speed Literacy) allow for the calculation of *scaled or standard process scores.* According to the test author, process scores are designed to provide more detailed information about subtest performance (*WISC-V Administration and Scoring Manual*, Wechsler, 2014a, p.7). The procedures for calculating scaled or standard process scores for the Block Design, Digit Span, Cancellation, and Naming Speed Literacy subtests appear in the sections that follow.

Each subtest is listed along with its cognitive domain. Subtests used to calculate the FSIQ are denoted FSIQ. Subtests that contribute to a primary index score are designated as primary.

1. **Block Design (Visual Spatial, FSIQ, and Primary)**
   - For each item, record the completion time in seconds.
   - For Items 1–3, successful completion on Trial 1 earns 2 points, successful completion on Trial 2 earns 1 point.
   - 0 points are scored if the examinee either does not construct the design correctly or exceeds the time limit.
   - For Items 4–9, successful completion of the designs (within the time limit) earns 4 points. An incorrect construction earns 0 points.
   - For Items 10–13, bonus points (either 0, 1, 2, or 3 bonus points) are awarded for successfully completed designs on the basis of completion time. Award 0 points for incorrect construction.

- Rotated designs of 30 degrees or more (that are not corrected within the time limit) are scored 0 points. For rotated designs, the degree of rotation and the number of degrees rotated can be noted on the Record Form.

- Dimension errors occur when the maximum dimension for a square- or diamond-shaped design is exceeded at any time during the construction and remains uncorrected at the time limit. Dimension errors are scored 0 points.

- Gaps and/or misalignments between blocks that exceed ¼ inch and that remain uncorrected at the time limit are also penalized and are scored 0 points.

- Partially completed or incorrect designs are scored 0 points. Incorrect or partially complete designs should be drawn in the Constructed Design column of the protocol. This allows the examiner to inspect the errors later and see if there is a pattern to the errors that is clinically significant.

- If an examinee correctly completes a design after the time limit has expired, then no points are awarded (although a note should be made that the examinee constructed the design correctly).

- Include early unadministered items (as correct) and reversal items when calculating the total raw score.

- Block Design No Time Bonus (BDn) is a scaled process score and is calculated by scoring 0, 1, or 2 on Items 1–3, and 4 points for *correct* designs completed within the time limit on Items 4–13.

- Block Design Partial (BDp) is a scaled process score and is based on the sum of the total number of correctly placed blocks for all items (including reversal items), and time-bonus points awarded for Items 10–13.

- Block Design Dimension Errors (BDde) is a raw process score for which base rates are available and is derived from the total number of constructions with dimension errors made at any time during the examinee's construction. There is a maximum of one dimension error per item. To calculate the BDde raw score, count the number of items with dimension errors (except items 1 and 13).

- Block Design Rotation Errors (BDre) is a raw process score for which base rates are available and based on the total number of constructions with rotations of 30° or more at the time limit. There is a maximum of one rotation error per item. To calculate the BDre raw score, count the number of items with rotation errors.

- A maximum of 58 raw score points for standard administration (with bonus points) may be obtained.
- The maximum "Block Design No Time Bonus" total raw score is 46 points.
- The maximum "Block Design Partial Total" total raw score is 82 points with time bonuses.
- The maximum "Block Design Dimension Errors" raw score is 11 points.
- The maximum "Block Design Rotation Errors" raw score is 13 points.

Table 3.2 provides Block Design scoring revisions from the WISC-IV to the WISC-V.

Table 3.2 Changes in Scoring: Subtest 1, Block Design (Visual Spatial, FSIQ, and Primary)

WISC-IV	WISC-V
Maximum total raw score 68 points	Maximum total raw score 58 points
No partial scoring	Partial scaled process scores
No error scores	Dimension and rotation error process scores

2. Similarities (Verbal Comprehension, FSIQ, and Primary)

- For all Similarities items, use the specific sample responses and the general 0-, 1-, or 2-point scoring criteria as a guide (see *WISC-V Administration and Scoring Manual,* Wechsler, 2014a, pp. 89–112).
- Responses listed in the manual are not all-inclusive. Give credit for responses that are of the same caliber as those in the manual.
- The key to scoring Similarities items is the *degree of abstraction* evident in the response. Responses that reflect a relevant general categorization earn 2 points, whereas responses that reflect only one or more common properties or functions of the members of an item pair earn 0 or 1 point.
- For multiple responses, score the best response as long as no portion of the examinee's answer spoils the response.
- Include early unadministered items (as correct) and reversal items when calculating the total raw score.
- A maximum of 46 raw score points may be obtained.

Table 3.3 provides Similarities scoring revisions from the WISC-IV to the WISC-V.

Table 3.3 Changes in Scoring: Subtest 2, Similarities (Verbal Comprehension, FSIQ, and Primary)

WISC-IV	WISC-V
Items 1–2 score 0 or 1 point	All items score 0, 1, or 2 points
Items 3–23 score 0, 1, or 2 points	
Maximum total raw score 44 points	Maximum total raw score 46 points
	Sample responses for all items revised or new

3. Matrix Reasoning (Fluid Reasoning, FSIQ, and Primary)

- Circle the numbers that correspond to the examinee's responses for each item on the Record Form. Correct answers are printed in color.
- Score 1 point for a correct response and 0 points if the examinee gives an incorrect response, says he or she does not know the answer, or does not give a response.
- Include early unadministered items (as correct) and reversal items when calculating the total raw score.
- A maximum of 32 raw score points may be obtained.

Table 3.4 provides Matrix Reasoning scoring revisions from the WISC-IV to the WISC-V.

Table 3.4 Changes in Scoring: Subtest 3, Matrix Reasoning (Fluid Reasoning, FSIQ, and Primary)

WISC-IV	WISC-V
Circle DK on the Record Form when the examinee does not respond or states that he or she does not know the answer	Circle 0 on the Record Form when the examinee does not respond or states that he or she does not know the answer
Maximum total raw score 35 points	Maximum total raw score 32 points

4. Digit Span (Working Memory, FSIQ, and Primary)

- For each trial, record the examinee's response verbatim. For each trial, score 1 point for correct responses and 0 points for incorrect responses (or no response).
- The item score is the sum of the two *trial scores* for each item.
- Final Digit Span total raw score is the sum of the total raw scores for Digit Span Forward, Digit Span Backward, and Digit Span Sequencing.

- Digit Span Forward (DSf) is a scaled process score and the total raw score is obtained by summing all item scores on DSf (Maximum of 18 points).
- Digit Span Backward (DSb) is a scaled process score and the total raw score is obtained by summing all item scores on DSb, excluding the sample (Maximum of 18 points).
- Digit Span Sequencing (DSs) is a scaled process score and the total raw score is obtained by summing all item scores on DSs, excluding the samples (Maximum of 18 points).
- Longest Digit Span Forward (LDSf), Longest Digit Span Backward (LDSb), and Longest Digit Span Sequencing (LDSs) are raw process scores for which base rates are available. These indicate the number of digits recalled on the last Digit Span trial (Forward, Backward, or Sequencing, respectively). For instance, if an examinee correctly recalls five digits forward once and misses both trials of six digits forward, the LDSf is 5.
- If an examinee age 6–7 years gives an incorrect response to the Sequencing Qualifying Item, the Digit Span total raw score and the Digit Span Sequencing total raw score are invalid and missing; no total raw score may be obtained. In this case, the Digit Span Forward and Digit Span Backward total raw scores may still be calculated.
- A maximum of 54 raw score points may be obtained for Digit Span.

Table 3.5 provides Digit Span scoring revisions from the WISC-IV to the WISC-V.

Table 3.5   Changes in Scoring: Subtest 4, Digit Span (Working Memory, FSIQ, and Primary)

WISC-IV	WISC-V
Maximum total raw score 32 points	Maximum total raw score 54 points
	Digit Span Sequencing is required to obtain an overall scaled score for Digit Span

5. Coding (Processing Speed, FSIQ, and Primary)

- When 120 seconds have elapsed, tell the examinee to stop working and record the completion time as 120 seconds, even if the examinee has not completed all of the items.
- Do not score any items that may have been completed beyond the time limit (e.g., if the examinee attempts to finish an item after he

or she has been told to stop, or if an examiner allows an examinee to continue working on a nearly finished item in the interest of maintaining rapport). If the examinee completes all of the items before the 120-second time limit, stop timing and record the completion time in seconds.

- Careful placement of the Coding scoring template is necessary for accurate scoring. Be sure to use the appropriate side of the scoring template depending on the form (A or B) administered.
- Score 1 point for each symbol drawn correctly within the 120-second time limit. *Note:* Incorrectly drawn symbols are not subtracted from the total score as occurs with Symbol Search and Cancellation.
- Do not penalize an examinee for an imperfectly drawn symbol. Symbols do not have to be perfectly drawn to obtain credit, but symbols must be recognizable.
- If an examinee spontaneously corrects his or her drawing, give credit to the corrected drawing.
- Items that an examinee did not attempt (e.g., skipped or did not reach before the time limit expired) should not be counted when calculating the total raw score.
- Do not count sample items toward the final total raw score.
- A symbol is considered rotated if the examinee's drawing is rotated 90° or more in either direction, relative to the keyed symbol. Rotated symbols are not scored as correct.
- Coding Rotation Errors (CDRe) is a raw process score for which base rate date are available and is obtained by summing the total number of symbols judged as rotated. Because rotations are not possible on circles, a maximum of 60 raw score points may be obtained for CDRe for Coding A and a maximum of 104 raw score points may be obtained for CDRe for Coding B.
- A maximum of 75 raw score points may be obtained for Coding A; a maximum of 117 raw score points may be obtained for Coding B.
- If the examinee does not understand the task, does not complete any test items, or simply draws a line through the subtest, the total raw score is 0.

Table 3.6 provides Coding scoring revisions from the WISC-IV to the WISC-V.

Table 3.6 Changes in Scoring: Subtest 5, Coding (Processing Speed, FSIQ, and Primary)

WISC-IV	WISC-V
Maximum total raw score of 65 points with time bonus for Coding A	Maximum total raw score of 75 points for Coding A
Maximum total raw score of 119 points for Coding B	Maximum total raw score of 117 points for Coding B
Six time-bonus points for Form A	No time-bonus points available for either form
No process scores available	Rotation errors process score available

6. Vocabulary (Verbal Comprehension, FSIQ, and Primary)

- Picture Items 1–4 are scored either 0 or 1 point and Verbal Items 5–29 are scored either 0, 1, or 2 points (see the *WISC-V Administration and Scoring Manual,* Wechsler, 2014a, pp. 134–161).
- Responses listed in the manual are not all-inclusive. Give credit for responses that are of the same caliber as those in the manual.
- On Picture Items 1–4, score 0 points for the following responses:
  - Inappropriate marginal responses (e.g., saying "engine" for a pictured fire truck)
  - Generalized responses (e.g., saying "drink" for a pictured milk container)
  - Functional responses (e.g., saying "It's a money holder" for a pictured wallet)
  - Hand gestures (e.g., pretending to pedal in response to a pictured bicycle)
  - Personalized responses (e.g., saying "I have one in front of my house" when shown a picture of a tree)
- Do not penalize an examinee for articulation errors or poor grammar if it is clear that he or she knows the correct name of an object (for Picture Items) or is able to define it (for Verbal Items).
- In general, any recognized word meaning is acceptable, but a response that lacks significant content (e.g., a response that indicates only a vague knowledge of the word's meaning) should be penalized.
- If an examinee makes a remark that is clearly not part of his or her response it should not affect the score.
- Regionalisms and slang definitions should be scored 0 points if not improved upon inquiry.

- For multiple responses, score the best response as long as no portion of the examinee's answer spoils the response.
- Include early unadministered items (as correct) and reversal items when calculating the total raw score.
- A maximum of 54 raw score points may be obtained.

Table 3.7 provides Vocabulary scoring revisions from the WISC-IV to the WISC-V.

Table 3.7 Changes in Scoring: Subtest 6, Vocabulary (Verbal Comprehension, FSIQ, and Primary)

WISC-IV	WISC-V
Maximum total raw score 68 points	Maximum total raw score 54 points
	Sample responses for all items revised or new

7. Figure Weights (Fluid Reasoning, FSIQ, and Primary)
- Record the completion time in seconds for each item.
- Circle the examinee's response for each item. Correct answers are printed in color.
- Score 1 point if an examinee correctly responds within the time limit.
- Score 0 points if the examinee gives an incorrect response, states that he or she does not know the answer, or does not provide a response within the time limit.
- A maximum of 34 raw score points may be obtained.

8. Visual Puzzles (Visual Spatial, Primary)
- Record the completion time in seconds for each item.
- Circle the examinee's response for each item. Correct answers are printed in color.
- Score 1 point if the examinee selects all three correct responses within the time limit.
- Score 0 points if the examinee does not select all three correct responses, selects more than three responses, states that he or she does not know the answer, or does not respond within the time limit.
- A maximum of 29 raw score points may be obtained.

9. Picture Span (Working Memory, Primary)
- Items 1–3 are scored either 0 or 1 point and Items 4–26 are scored 0, 1, or 2 points.

- Items 1–3: Score 1 point if the examinee gives a correct response and score 0 points if the examinee does not select the stimulus picture, selects an incorrect picture, states that he or she does not know the answer, or does not respond within approximately 30 seconds.
- For Items 4–26: Score 2 points if the examinee selects all of the stimulus pictures in the correct order, score 1 point if the child selects all of the stimulus pictures in the incorrect order, and score 0 points, if the child does not select all of the stimulus pictures, selects an incorrect picture, states that he or she does not know the answer, or does not respond within approximately 30 seconds.
- The Longest Picture Span Stimuli (LPSs) is a raw process score for which base rates are available and is the number of pictures on the stimulus page for the last item assigned a perfect score. A maximum of 8 raw score points may be obtained for the LPSs.
- The Longest Picture Span Response (LPSr) is a raw process score for which base rates are available and is the number of pictures on the response page for the last item assigned a perfect score. A maximum of 12 raw score points may be obtained for the LPSr.
- For each item, record the examinee's response verbatim.
- A maximum of 49 raw score points may be obtained.

10. **Symbol Search (Processing Speed, Primary)**
    - When 120 seconds have elapsed, tell the examinee to stop working and record the completion time as 120 seconds, even if the examinee has not completed all of the items.
    - Do not score any items that may have been completed beyond the time limit (e.g., if the examinee attempts to finish an item after he or she has been told to stop, or if an examiner allows an examinee to continue working on a nearly finished item in the interest of maintaining rapport).
    - If the examinee completes all of the items before the 120-second time limit, stop timing and record the time. This is important as bonus points may be awarded.
    - Careful placement of the Symbol Search scoring key is necessary for accurate scoring. Be sure to use the appropriate side of the scoring key depending on the form (A or B) administered. Side A and Side B depict the correct scoring responses for Form A and Side C, Side D, and Side E indicate the correct scoring responses for Form B.
    - Score 0 points if an examinee marks multiple responses to one item.

- On items where there is a clear indication of self-correction (e.g., the examinee crossed out one answer and endorsed another), score the latter response.
- Unanswered items (i.e., skipped or not reached before the time limit) do count toward either the correct or the incorrect total.
- Sum the number of correct items and the number of incorrect items separately.
- Symbol Search Set Errors (SSse) is a raw process score for which base rates are available and is the total number of set errors an examinee marked. A maximum of 20 raw score points may be obtained for SSse on Symbol Search A and a maximum of 30 raw score points may be obtained for SSse on Symbol Search B. A maximum of 1 set error per item is allowed.
- Symbol Search Rotation Errors (SSre) is a raw process score for which base rates are available and is the total number of rotated symbols an examinee selected in error. A maximum of 20 raw score points may be obtained for SSre on Symbol Search A and a maximum of 30 raw score points may be obtained for SSre on Symbol Search B. A maximum of 1 rotation error per item is allowed.
- Calculate the total raw score by subtracting the number of incorrect items from the number correct. *Note:* This is different from the Coding subtest where the incorrect items are not subtracted from the correct items to obtain the total raw score.
- A maximum of 42 raw score points may be obtained for Symbol Search A with time bonus; a maximum of 60 raw score points may be obtained for Symbol Search B. There is no time bonus available for Symbol Search B.

Table 3.8 provides Symbol Search scoring revisions from the WISC-IV to the WISC-V.

Table 3.8 Changes in Scoring: Subtest 10, Symbol Search (Processing Speed, Primary)

WISC-IV	WISC-V
Maximum total raw score 45 points on Symbol Search A	Maximum total raw score 42 points on Symbol Search A
No time-bonus points available for either form	Maximum of two time-bonus points available for Form A with perfect performance
No process scores available	Set errors and rotation errors process score available

11. **Information (Verbal Comprehension, Secondary)**
   - Record the examinee's responses verbatim.
   - Score 1 point for a correct response and score 0 points for either an incorrect response or no response (see *WISC-V Administration and Scoring Manual,* Wechsler, 2014a, pp. 189–203).
   - Responses listed in the manual are not all-inclusive. Give credit for responses that are of the same caliber as those in the manual.
   - For multiple responses, score the best response as long as no portion of the examinee's answer spoils the response. A 1-point response accompanied by a spoiled response is scored as 0 points.
   - Include early unadministered items (as correct) and reversal items when calculating the total raw score.
   - If the examinee makes a remark that is clearly not part of his or her response it should not affect the score.
   - A maximum of 31 raw score points may be obtained.

Table 3.9 provides Symbol Search scoring revisions from the WISC-IV to the WISC-V.

Table 3.9   Changes in Scoring: Subtest 11, Information (Verbal Comprehension, Secondary)

WISC-IV	WISC-V
Maximum total raw score 33 points	Maximum total raw score 31 points
	Sample responses for all items revised or new

12. **Picture Concepts (Fluid Reasoning, Secondary)**
   - Circle the numbers that correspond to the examiner's responses for each item. Correct answers are printed in color.
   - One point is awarded *only* if the examinee chooses the correct pictures from *all* rows of an item; 0 points are earned for incorrect responses or no response.
   - If an examinee offers more than one combination of selected pictures as a response or they self-correct and it is unclear which is the selected response, say, "You said (insert examinee's response) and you said (insert examinee's response). Which one did you mean?"
   - Include early unadministered items (as correct) and reversal items when calculating the total raw score.
   - A maximum of 27 raw score points may be obtained.

Table 3.10 provides Picture Concepts scoring revisions from the WISC-IV to the WISC-V.

Table 3.10   Changes in Scoring: Subtest 12, Picture Concepts (Fluid Reasoning, Secondary)

WISC-IV	WISC-V
Maximum total raw score of 28 points	Maximum total raw score of 27 points

13. **Letter-Number Sequencing (Working Memory, Secondary)**
    - Record the examinee's responses verbatim.
    - For the qualifying items, circle Y or N to indicate whether the examinee age 6–7 years correctly counted to *at least* three and recited *at least* the first three letters of the alphabet in order.
    - For each trial of Items 1–2, score 1 point if the examinee gives the correct response.
    - For each trial of Items 3–10, score 1 point if the examinee recalls all the numbers and letters in their correct sequence, *even if the examinee recalls the letters before the numbers.* Score 0 points for incorrect items.
    - If the standardized prompt reminding the examinee to say the numbers first, then the letters is given on Items 1–2 and the examinee subsequently corrects his or her previous answer, do not award credit.
    - Sum the scores on the three trials for each item to calculate the item score. An examinee can score up to 3 points (i.e., all three trials correct) on each item.
    - Longest Letter-Number Sequence (LLNs) is a raw process score for which base rates are available and is equal to the number of letters and numbers that were recalled on the last Letter-Number Sequencing trial that was scored 1 point. The maximum raw score is 8 points.
    - If an examinee ages 6–7 gives an incorrect response to *either* Qualifying Item, the total raw score is invalid and missing; no total raw score may be obtained.
    - A maximum of 30 raw score points may be obtained.

14. **Cancellation (Processing Speed, Secondary)**
    - When 45 seconds have elapsed, tell the examinee to stop working and record the completion time as 45 seconds, even if the examinee has not completed the item.
    - Do not score any response that may have been completed beyond the time limit (e.g., if the examinee attempts to finish a response after he or she has been told to stop, or if an examiner allows an examinee to continue working on a nearly finished response in the interest of maintaining rapport).

- If the examinee completes an item before the 45-second time limit, stop timing and record the time.
- Careful placement of the Cancellation Scoring Template is essential for accurate scoring.
- When using the scoring template, marks on target objects are scored as correct; marks on non-target objects are scored as incorrect. Consider objects as marked *only* if it is clear that the examinee intended to mark them (see the *WISC-V Administration and Scoring Manual,* Wechsler, 2014a, p. 216).
- Add the total number of correct responses and incorrect responses separately.
- Calculate the item score by subtracting the total number of incorrect responses from the total number of correct responses for a given item. If there are more incorrect responses than correct responses, record an item score of 0.
- The total raw score for Cancellation is the sum of the item scores for *both* Items 1 and 2.
- It is also possible to obtain scaled process scores for this subtest. The total raw scores for Cancellation Random (CAr) and Cancellation Structured (CAs) are the total item scores for Items 1 and 2, respectively. A maximum of 64 total raw score points is available for each of these items.
- A maximum of 128 raw score points may be obtained.

Table 3.11 provides Cancellation scoring revisions from the WISC-IV to the WISC-V.

Table 3.11   Changes in Scoring: Subtest 14, Cancellation (Processing Speed, Secondary)

WISC-IV	WISC-V
Time bonus available	No time bonus available
Maximum total raw score of 136 points	Maximum total raw score of 128 points

15. Naming Speed Literacy (Complementary)

- For examinees ages 6–8 years, the Naming Speed Literacy total raw score is the sum of the completion times for all administered trials (i.e., the sum of the total raw score for each item administered). For examinees ages 9–13 years, it is the completion time for Item 3.
- The error scores do not affect the total raw score, but they must be used to inform interpretation. Therefore, it is important to record

completion time and errors for every trial of every item administered.

- Synonyms are considered acceptable responses and should not be classified as errors. Table 3.1 in the *WISC-V Administration and Scoring Manual* provides common synonyms for naming speed attributes (Wechsler, 2014a, p. 221).
- Because of the rapid pace of administration, do not record correct responses.
- Errors should be noted by recording a slash mark through each misnamed attribute (e.g., big, red, or dog) or element (e.g., 9, T, or 5). Each slash mark represents one error. Because the elements for Items 1 and 2 each have multiple attributes, it is possible on Items 1 and 2 for the examinee's response to contain multiple errors for a single element.
- The examinee may self-correct at any time during administration. Self-corrections are not classified as errors. If the examiner wishes to obtain a self-corrections score, record SC next to the slash mark that identifies the previously misnamed attribute or element. Remember that corrections to incomplete names of attributes or elements (e.g., examinee says, "Yel . . . blue") are not considered self-corrections.
- Record the completion time for each trial in seconds. If a trial is not completed before the time limit, record the completion time as 300 seconds.
- To obtain the total raw score for a test item, sum the completion times for each trial of the item.
- Each trial of the age-appropriate item(s) must be administered or no Naming Speed Literacy subtest-level scores can be obtained.
- The Naming Speed Literacy total raw score is calculated differently based on the age of the examinee. For examinees age 6, the Naming Speed Literacy total raw score is the sum of the Item 1 and Item 2 total raw scores; for examinees ages 7–8, the Naming Speed Literacy total raw score is the sum of the Item 2 and Item 3 total raw scores; for examinees ages 9–16, the Naming Speed Literacy total raw score is the same as the Naming Speed Letter-Number total raw score (i.e., Item 3).
- Naming Speed Literacy Color-Object (NSco) is a standard process score for examinees age 6 and is the sum of the completion times for each trial of Item 1. A maximum of 600 raw score points may be obtained for NSco.

- Naming Speed Literacy Size-Color-Object (NSsco) is a standard process score for examinees ages 6–8 and is the sum of the completion times for each trial of Item 2. A maximum of 600 raw score points may be obtained for NSsco.
- Naming Speed Literacy Letter-Number (NSln) is a standard process score for examinees ages 7–16 and is the sum of the completion times for each trial of Item 3. A maximum of 600 raw score points may be obtained for NSln.
- Naming Speed Literacy Color-Object Errors (NScoe) is a raw process score for which base rates are available for examinees age 6 years. It is the total number of errors made on both trials of Item 1. A maximum of 80 raw score points may be obtained for the NScoe.
- Naming Speed Literacy Size-Color-Object Errors (NSscoe) is a raw process score for which base rates are available for examinees ages 6–8 years. It is the total number of errors made on both trials of Item 2. A maximum of 120 raw score points may be obtained for NScoe.
- Naming Speed Letter-Number Errors (NSlne) is a raw process score for which base rates are available for examinees ages 7–8 years. It is the total number of errors made on each trial of Item 3. A maximum of 80 raw score points may be obtained for NScoe.
- Naming Speed Literacy Errors (NSLe) is a raw process score for which base rates are available. For examinees age 6 it is the sum of the errors for Item 1 and Item 2. The NSLe raw score for examinees ages 7–8 is the sum of the errors for Item 2 and Item 3. For examinees ages 9–16, the NSLe raw score is the total number of errors for Item 3. A maximum of 200 raw score points may be obtained for NSLe.
- For examinees ages 6–8 years, a maximum of 1200 raw score points may be obtained; for examinees ages 9–16 years, a maximum of 600 raw score points may be obtained.

16. **Naming Speed Quantity (Complementary)**
    - The Naming Speed Quantity total raw score is equal to the completion time of the administered item.
    - The error score does not affect the total raw score, but it should be used to inform interpretation. Therefore, it is important to record completion time and errors.
    - Because of the rapid pace of administration, do not record correct responses.

- Errors should be noted by recording a slash mark through each misnamed attribute. Each slash mark represents one error. It is possible for the examiner's response to contain multiple errors for a single item.
- The examinee may self-correct at any time during administration. Self-corrections are not classified as errors. If the examiner wishes to obtain a self-corrections score, record SC next to the slash mark that identifies the previously misnamed quantity. Remember that corrections to incomplete responses (e.g., examinee says, "Fo . . . Three") are not considered self-corrections.
- Record the completion time for each trial in seconds.
- Naming Speed Quantity Errors (NSQe) is a raw process score for which base rates are available and is the sum of the errors for each trial of the item administered. A maximum of 40 raw score points for the NSQe may be obtained. Both trials must be administered to obtain NSQe.
- The maximum of 600 raw score points may be obtained.

17. Immediate Symbol Translation (Complementary)

- Credit for each item is based on the number of correct translations. For each correct translation, record a checkmark in the corresponding box.
- Score 1 point for each correct translation. Score 0 points for an incorrect translation, a skipped translation, or failure to respond after approximately 5 seconds.
- Synonyms and unindicated changes in tense, plurality, or sounds at the end of the word are incorrect. However, errors in word forms are not penalized (e.g., translating *ran* as *runned*).
- The inclusion of extraneous or additional words in the translation does not affect the score.
- Incorrect or skipped translations are not recorded and the corresponding boxes should be left empty.
- Incorrect responses may be noted to provide qualitative information relevant to interpretation if desired.
- Record the cumulative raw score at each decision point to determine if the discontinue criterion has been met.
- The total raw score for the Immediate Symbol Translation subtest is the sum of the item scores.
- For Items 1–3, score only the last completed trial of each item.
- For Items 7–21, correct translations of *the* and *and* do not receive credit. For these items, the boxes above these words on the Record Form are filled as a visual reminder that those translations are not scored.
- A maximum of 108 raw score points may be obtained.

18. **Comprehension (Verbal Comprehension, Secondary)**
   - For all Comprehension items, use the general 0-, 1-, or 2-point scoring criteria and specific sample responses as a guide (see *WISC-V Administration and Scoring Manual,* Wechsler, 2014a, pp. 252–273).
   - Responses listed in the manual are not all-inclusive. Give credit for responses that are of the same caliber as those in the manual.
   - For items that contain more than one general concept, the examiner's response must reflect at least two different concepts to earn 2 points. If the examinee's response reflects only one concept, score the item 1 point and prompt for another concept. If the examinee's second response reflects the same concept as his or her first response, do not prompt for an additional response.
   - If an examinee improves an answer spontaneously or after a query, give credit for the improvement (e.g., when asked why people should brush their teeth, the examinee responds "It's good for them" [1-point response requiring a query] and then, when queried, says "To keep them healthy" [2-point response]).
   - If an examinee provides several responses that vary in quality, but nevertheless does not spoil his or her response, then score the best response (i.e., the response that will result in the maximum number of score points being awarded).
   - Include early unadministered items (as correct) and reversal items when calculating the total raw score.
   - If the examinee makes a remark that is clearly not part of his or her response, it should not affect the score.
   - A maximum of 38 raw score points may be obtained.

Table 3.12 provides Comprehension scoring revisions from the WISC-IV to the WISC-V.

Table 3.12 Changes in Scoring: Subtest 18, Comprehension (Verbal Comprehension, Secondary)

WISC-IV	WISC-V
Maximum total raw score 42 points	Maximum total raw score 38 points
	Sample responses for all items revised or new
Part of FSIQ	No longer a part of FSIQ and now a secondary subtest

19. **Arithmetic (Fluid Reasoning, Secondary)**
   - Score 1 point for a correct response given within the 30-second time limit.
   - Score 0 points for an incorrect response if the examinee says he or she does not know the answer, or for a response given after the time limit has expired.
   - If the examinee provides a numerically correct response, but leaves out the units (or states the units incorrectly) that appeared in the question (e.g., says "five" rather than "five *crayons*" or "six" rather than "six *minutes*"), score the response correct. The only exception to this is on items where money or time is the unit; on such items, *alternate* numerical responses must be accompanied by the correct unit (e.g., if the answer is "one hour," saying "one" is correct; however, if the examinee transforms the units to minutes, he or she must say "sixty minutes," rather than just "sixty" to receive credit).
   - If the examinee spontaneously provides a correct response in place of an incorrect response within the time limit, score 1 point.
   - Include early unadministered items (as correct) and reversal items when calculating the total raw score.
   - A maximum of 34 raw score points may be obtained.

20. **Delayed Symbol Translation (Complementary)**
   - Credit for each item is based on the number of correct translations. For each correct translation, record a check mark in the corresponding box.
   - Score 1 point for each correct translation. Score 0 points for an incorrect translation, a skipped translation, or failure to respond after approximately 5 seconds.
   - Synonyms and unindicated changes in tense, plurality, or sounds at the end of the word are incorrect. However, errors in word forms are not penalized (e.g., translating *ran* as *runned*).
   - The inclusion of extraneous or additional words in the translation does not affect the score.
   - Incorrect or skipped translations are not recorded and the corresponding boxes should be left empty.
   - Incorrect responses may be noted to provide qualitative information relevant to interpretation if desired.
   - Record the cumulative raw score at each decision point to determine if the discontinue criterion has been met.

- For Items 7–21, correct translations of *the* and *and* do not receive credit. For these items, the boxes above these words on the Record Form are filled as a visual reminder that those translations are not scored.
- A maximum of 81 raw score points may be obtained.

21. Recognition Symbol Translation (Complementary)
- Score 1 point for each correct response. Score 0 points for an incorrect response, a skipped translation, or failure to respond after approximately 5 seconds.
- A maximum of 34 raw score points may be obtained.

Frequently Asked Questions: Subtest Scoring

Pearson has provided information on its website regarding the WISC-V. Among the questions included in the FAQs is a number of questions related to the scoring of WISC-V subtests. Some of the information contained in this category has been reproduced for the benefit of practitioners and is presented in Rapid Reference 3.2.

≋ *Rapid Reference 3.2*

· ·

Frequently Asked Questions: Scoring

- <u>I have noticed children getting correct answers but just after the time limit has expired. These children had the correct answers but were just somewhat slower in responding. Are these children penalized because of their slow processing speed rather than their cognitive abilities on these higher-level cognitive reasoning tasks? For any of the subtests, did the WISC-V standardization research compare the accuracy of answers versus just their time-based raw scores?</u>

  In early research phases of the project, data were collected with extended time limits. Analyses indicated the children who answered correctly after the time limit were of lower ability than children who answered before the time limit. There was often little benefit to extending the time, as few children could answer correctly after the time limit expired. Data were not collected with extended time limits at standardization because that would've given children more exposure to the items which could result in some additional procedural learning or practice that is not standard. Process observations to test the limits can be done at the end of all testing and described qualitatively in the report. Figure Weights Process Approach and Arithmetic Process Approach will be offered with the WISC-V Integrated. Those are standardized subtests that offer additional time for items that were missed.

- <u>Why was Comprehension not chosen as a primary subtest? From a language perspective, it provides a richer sense of the child's ability to answer open-ended questions, a more authentic skill for real life.</u>

In the online basic training that is included with each kit, we describe in more detail the types of analyses that were conducted to make the decisions regarding which subtests would be primary and which would be secondary. To summarize, the team looked at psychometric properties such as floors, ceilings, reliability, validity, and construct coverage; clinical utility; demographic differences; user-friendliness; and feedback from practitioners and customers. There is nothing that precludes administration of secondary subtests if a practitioner believes that useful information will be gathered for a particular child.

- Did you consider removing the time bonuses for Block Design?

  If the time limits are removed, children who do not have the commensurate intellectual ability complete more items correctly. Removing the time bonuses on this subtest would result in a loss of the ceiling, greatly reduced reliability, and a much lower correlation with general intelligence. These issues greatly reduce the meaningfulness of scores that could be derived from the results. For practitioners who are interested in a score without time bonuses, a Block Design No Time Bonus (BDn) process score is available and can be compared with Block Design.

- How does Block Design work with children with motor deficits such as cerebral palsy? Is there an alternative test?

  Whether Block Design is appropriate depends on the severity of the motor impairment. Unless the child has severe motor impairment, they may be able to complete the task. You will need to evaluate the severity and impact of the motor impairment for each case. If Block Design cannot be administered, the Visual Puzzles subtest can be substituted to obtain the FSIQ. The VSI and some ancillary index scores may not be obtained in this situation.

- I tested a child age (6, 7, or 8) and the Naming Speed Quantity score came out unusually high. Did I make a scoring error?

  Check to ensure you are in the NSQ column in the norms table in the *WISC-V Administration and Scoring Manual Supplement*. Some examiners mistakenly apply the column from the NSco, NSsco, or NSln process scores to their NSQ results and obtain unusually high scores as a result.

- For the BDp score, if a child has to take both trials of an item, do you use the correct placement of blocks on Trial 2 only to get the optional partial score for that item?

  Only the last trial administered is counted.

- For the BDp score, if a child has the correct design but rotates it 30 or more degrees, is the optional partial score for that item equal to 0?

  Yes.

- For the BDp score, if a child commits a dimension error, which blocks are counted as correct?

  Count the blocks that are in the correct position, but not the ones involved in the dimension error.

- For Naming Speed Literacy, the top table on the Process Analysis page of the Record Form provides a space to complete the NSLn raw score and scaled score. However, it indicates that this is for ages 7–8 in light blue ink within the boxes. Is this also where the NSL raw score for ages 9–16 is converted for this age group? If not, where else on the Record Form would you convert the NSL raw score for ages 9–16?

The NSL score is converted on the top right corner of the Ancillary and Complementary Analysis page using the Total Raw Score to Standard Score Conversion table. Refer to Steps 3–4 on pages 70–71 of the *WISC-V Administration and Scoring Manual.*

- On the sheet that was inserted into the WISC-V Administration and Scoring Manual Supplement to display the LPSr scores on Table C.17, are the numbers displayed for the median at ages 15 and 16 correct? It seems odd that it would decrease with age.

Yes, the median is correct. The median for age 16 is 9. The 50th percentile is midway between scores of 8 and 10, so the median is correctly calculated by dividing the difference. This slight age-based decrease across some ages occurs because the LPSr is calculated based on the last item with a perfect score. There are some later items that have fewer response options relative to the earlier ones; hence there is a decrease in the measures of central tendency. The LPSr score should be reported alongside LPSs for context.

- In testing a child between the ages of 6:0 and 7:11, I have obtained an extremely low score on the NSQ score that doesn't make any sense. Is there a problem with this score?

Check to be sure that you are looking at the correct column in Table C.6 of the WISC-V Administration and Scoring Manual Supplement. These ages have process scores for NSsco and NSln, and the columns are between the NSL and NSQ columns. Using the incorrect column can result in erroneous, abnormally high scores on NSQ.

Source: http://www.pearsonclinical.com/psychology/products/100000771/wechsler-intelligence-scale-for-childrensupsupfifth-edition—wisc-v.html#tab-faq

🖎 TEST YOURSELF 🖎

1. **Which subtests allow for the calculation of scaled process scores?**
   a. Block Design, Digit Span, Symbol Search, and Naming Speed Literacy
   b. Block Design, Digit Span, Cancellation, and Naming Speed Literacy
   c. Coding, Symbol Search, Digit Span, and Naming Speed Quantity
   d. Block Design, Arithmetic, Symbol Search, and Coding

2. **On a Similarities subtest item, Jessica, age 7, provides several responses that vary greatly in quality, but do not spoil her response. The examiner should**

   a. score Jessica's best response.

   b. score the last response given by Jessica.

   c. score the first response given by Jessica.

   d. query Jessica for further information.

3. **If an examinee obtains total raw scores of 0 on two of the subtests that compose the Verbal Comprehension Index (VCI), no VCI can be derived.**

   a. True

   b. False

4. **Susan, age 12, attempts to self-correct an item on the Coding subtest. The examiner should**

   a. query Susan as to which response is her intended response.

   b. score Susan's first response, ignoring her self-correction attempt.

   c. score the last response given by Susan within the time limit.

   d. score Susan's best response.

5. **A *poor* response is an elaboration that does not improve the examinee's spontaneous response, whereas a *spoiled* response is an elaboration that reveals a fundamental misconception about the item.**

   a. True

   b. False

6. **If an examiner administered additional items to an examinee beyond the point at which testing should have discontinued, the examiner should**

   a. include all additional items in the total raw score.

   b. include the additional items in the total raw score only if they are correctly answered.

   c. award no points for items beyond the correct discontinue point.

   d. include the additional items in the total raw score by deducting points for incorrect responses that occurred after the discontinue point.

7. **Samuel, age 10, is suspected to have an intellectual disability. Therefore, the examiner administers him items prior to his age-appropriate start point. Samuel answered these items incorrectly, but obtained perfect scores on his age-appropriate start point and subsequent item. In this case, the examiner should**

   a. consider the subtest spoiled and do not calculate a raw score.

   b. include the incorrect responses in the calculation of the total raw score.

   c. award partial credit for each incorrect item that precedes the age-appropriate start point.

   d. award full credit for all items preceding the age-appropriate start point.

8. **Prorating sum of scaled scores is encouraged as often as is needed.**
   a. True
   b. False

9. **Information should be included in the calculation of which WISC-V Index?**
   a. VCI
   b. VSI
   c. PSI
   d. None of the above.

10. **When scoring the Symbol Search subtest, the examiner notices that Angela, age 9, skipped some items. The examiner should count the items that she skipped in the incorrect total.**
    a. True
    b. False

Answers: 1. b; 2. a; 3. a; 4. c; 5. a; 6. c; 7. d; 8. b; 9. d; 10. b

REFERENCES

Crawford, J. R., Garthwaite, P. H., & Gault, C. B. (2007). Estimating the percentage of the population with abnormally low scores (or abnormally large score differences) on standardized neuropsychological test batteries: A generic method with applications. *Neuropsychology, 21,* 419–430.

Flanagan, D. P., & Kaufman, A. S. (2009). *Essentials of WISC-IV assessment* (2nd ed.). Hoboken, NJ: Wiley.

Kaufman, A. S., & Lichtenberger, E. O. (2000). *Essentials of WISC-III and WPPSI-R assessment.* New York, NY: Wiley.

Kaufman, A. S., Raiford, S. E., & Coalson, D. L. (2016). *Intelligent testing with the WISC-V.* Hoboken, NJ: Wiley.

Wechsler, D. (2014a). *WISC-V administration and scoring manual.* Bloomington, MN: Pearson.

Wechsler, D. (2014b). *WISC-V administration and scoring manual supplement.* Bloomington, MN: Pearson.

Wechsler, D. (2014c). *WISC-V technical and interpretive manual.* Bloomington, MN: Pearson.

Four

HOW TO INTERPRET THE WISC-V

This chapter is designed to simplify the daunting task of generating psychometrically sound and clinically meaningful interpretations of individuals' performance on the WISC-V. A series of steps is provided that allows the practitioner to organize WISC-V data in efficient ways and interpret performance within the context of contemporary theory and research. Our systematic method of interpretation begins with an analysis of the WISC-V Full Scale IQ (FSIQ) and other global composites (i.e., the Nonverbal Index [NVI] and General Ability Index [GAI]) to determine the most defensible *and* meaningful estimate(s) of the individual's general intellectual ability. Next, Primary, Ancillary, and Complementary Index Scales are examined to determine whether they are cohesive and, therefore, considered good summaries of the theoretically related abilities they were intended to measure. Analysis of variability in scaled scores within Index Scales along with a consideration of where these scores fall relative to same-age peers is conducted to determine whether there is a need to follow up (e.g., conduct additional testing) in an ability domain, such as Fluid Reasoning (Gf) or Processing Speed (Gs).

As an interpretive option, practitioners may identify Normative and Personal Strengths and Weaknesses as well as Key Assets and High Priority Concerns among the Primary Index Scales. Interpretation of fluctuations in the individual's Index profile offers meaningful information about WISC-V performance because it identifies strong and weak areas of cognitive functioning relative to same-age peers from the general population (inter-individual comparison) and the individual's own overall ability level (intra-individual comparison). We also offer optional interpretive steps involving several new WISC-V composites (which we call *Clinical Composites*) for examiners who choose to go beyond the FSIQ and Index Scales in an attempt to uncover additional information about the individual's cognitive abilities as well as generate hypotheses about areas of integrity or dysfunction.

Our interpretive method (a) de-emphasizes individual subtest interpretation; (b) uses statistical significance and base rate data to evaluate cohesion and the clinical meaningfulness of variability within indexes; (c) grounds interpretation mainly in the CHC theory of the structure of cognitive abilities and processes; and (d) provides guidance on the use of secondary WISC-V subtests and supplemental measures to test hypotheses about significant and unusual subtest variation within Index Scales, particularly when lower subtest scaled scores are indicative of a weakness or deficit relative to same-age peers. When follow-up assessment is considered necessary, guidance is offered following the principles and procedures of the Cross-Battery Assessment (XBA) approach. To assist in all aspects of psychometrically and theoretically defensible interpretation of the WISC-V, the Cross-Battery Assessment Software System (X-BASS v2.0; Ortiz, Flanagan, & Alfonso, 2017), which automates the interpretive method outlined in this chapter, is introduced and its application is demonstrated throughout.

DON'T FORGET

After WISC-V scores have been entered, X-BASS automates WISC-V interpretation and provides the user with a summary of the results.

In addition to a *quantitative* analysis of WISC-V data, practitioners are encouraged to consider a variety of *qualitative* factors that may help to explain an individual's test performance. This information is discussed in terms of its utility in interpreting WISC-V performance and in selecting supplemental measures to augment the WISC-V when deemed necessary. *In the end, any and all interpretations of test performance gain diagnostic meaning when they are corroborated by other data sources and when they are empirically or logically related to the area or areas of difficulty specified in the referral.* Rapid Reference 4.1 provides a summary of the interpretive steps for the WISC-V.

≡ *Rapid Reference 4.1*

Summary of WISC-V Interpretation Step by Step

Step 1. Determine the best way(s) to describe overall intellectual ability.
Step 2. Conduct an analysis of the Primary index scores.
Step 3. If applicable, conduct an analysis of the Ancillary index scores.
Step 4. If applicable, conduct an analysis of the Complementary index scores.

Step 5. Determine normative strengths and normative weaknesses in the index score profile.

Step 6. (Optional) Determine personal strengths, personal weaknesses, key assets, and high-priority concerns among Primary index scores.

Step 7. (Optional) Determine whether the new Clinical Composites are cohesive and add clinically relevant information beyond that provided by the Primary, Ancillary, and Complementary index scores.

The interpretive steps listed in Rapid Reference 4.1 are illustrated using the WISC-V profile of Amanda, an 8-year-old girl referred for a possible reading disability. Amanda's full case report is included in Chapter 8. Excerpts from other case reports are also used to demonstrate specific interpretive features of the WISC-V.

GETTING STARTED

A table of Amanda's standard scores (e.g., FSIQ, Primary index scores) as well as her subtest scaled scores that make up the five Primary index scores are included in Rapid Reference 4.2. As may be seen in this rapid reference, confidence intervals, percentile ranks, and descriptive categories or classifications associated with Amanda's obtained scores are also reported. Rapid Reference 4.2 is similar to the type of table that typically is included in most psychoeducational reports. The information in this rapid reference was derived from various tables in the WISC-V manuals. Rapid Reference 4.3 is a handy guide to locating the tables in the *WISC-V Administration and Scoring Manual* (Wechsler, 2014a), and *WISC-V Administration and Scoring Manual Supplement* (Wechsler, 2014b) that the examiner will need to convert raw scores to scaled scores and standard scores, to convert sums of scaled scores to Global Composites and index scores, and to obtain confidence intervals and percentile ranks.

≡ *Rapid Reference 4.2*

Amanda's Performance on the WISC-V

Composites Subtest	Score	Percentile Rank	Confidence Interval	Classification
Full Scale IQ Score	91	27	87–96	**Average**
Verbal Comprehension Index (VCI)	100	50	94–106	**Average**

(continued)

(continued)

Composites Subtest	Score	Percentile Rank	Confidence Interval	Classification
Similarities	10	50		Average
Vocabulary	10	50		Average
Fluid Reasoning Index (FRI)	**97**	**42**	**91–103**	**Average**
Matrix Reasoning	9	37		Average
Figure Weights	10	50		Average
Visual Spatial Index (VSI)	**81**	**10**	**76–89**	**Low Average**
Block Design	6	9		Below Average
Visual Puzzles	7	16		Low Average
Working Memory Index (WMI)	**85**	**16**	**80–93**	**Low Average**
Digit Span	8	25		Average
Picture Span	7	16		Low Average
Processing Speed Index (PSI)	**92**	**30**	**85–100**	**Average**
Coding	8	25		Average
Symbol Search	9	37		Average
Naming Speed Index (NSI)	**99**	**47**	**92–106**	**Average**
Naming Speed Literacy	98	45		Average
Naming Speed Quantity	102	55		Average
Symbol Translation Index (STI)	**102**	**55**	**96–108**	**Average**
Immediate Symbol Translation	102	55		Average
Delayed Symbol Translation	102	55		Average
Recognition Symbol Translation	104	61		Average
Storage and Retrieval Index (SRI)	**100**	**50**	**94–106**	**Average**

Note: Confidence Interval is reported at 90%.

≡ Rapid Reference 4.3

Location of Information in WISC-V Manuals Needed for Score Conversions

Conversion Type	Manual	Location	Page(s)
Total Raw Scores to Scaled Scores for Primary and Secondary Subtests	A&S	Table A.1	298–330
Sum of Scaled Scores for VCI	A&S	Table A.2	331
Sum of Scaled Scores for FRI	A&S	Table A.4	332
Sum of Scaled Scores for VSI	A&S	Table A.3	331
Sum of Scaled Scores for WMI	A&S	Table A.5	332
Sum of Scaled Scores for PSI	A&S	Table A.6	333
Sum of Scaled Scores for FSIQ	A&S	Table A.7	334–335
Sum of Scaled Scores for NVI	A&S-S	Table C.3	4–5
Sum of Scaled Scores for GAI	A&S-S	Table C.4	6
Sum of Scaled Scores for CPI	A&S-S	Table C.5	7
Sum of Scaled Scores for QRI	A&S-S	Table C.1	2
Sum of Scaled Scores for AWMI	A&S-S	Table C.2	3
Sum of Scaled Scores for NSI	A&S-S	Table C.7	74–75
Sum of Scaled Scores for STI	A&S-S	Table C.8	76–77
Sum of Scaled Scores for SRI	A&S-S	Table C.9	78–79

Note: A&S = WISC-V Administration and Scoring Manual (Wechsler, 2014a); A&S-S = WISC-V Administration and Scoring Manual Supplement (Wechsler, 2014b).

A Note About Classification Systems

Notice that the qualitative descriptors (i.e., classifications) of scores reported in Rapid Reference 4.2 are not those that are associated with the WISC-V as reported in the *WISC-V Technical and Interpretive Manual* (Wechsler, 2014c, p. 153). Practitioners who have experience in administration, scoring, and interpretation of a wide variety of instruments have undoubtedly noticed, and indeed may have become frustrated by, the lack of consistency in classification systems across batteries. For example, the new classification system for the WISC-V, reported in Rapid Reference 4.4, is different from the one used for the WISC-IV. Of note, the descriptor "Borderline," used on the WISC-IV to describe the standard score range of 70–79, was replaced with "Very Low," a more value-neutral term. Incidentally, the term Borderline has been used in classification systems since the early 1900s. For example, "Borderline" was sandwiched between "Dullness" (80–90) and "Definite Feeble-mindedness" (Below 70) on the Stanford-Binet (Terman, 1916); it was just below the term "Backward" (80–89) in Pintner's (1923) classification system; and just above "Morons" in Levine and Marks's (1928) IQ classification system. The new classification system for the WISC-V is a welcome change indeed.

However, when conducting comprehensive evaluations of children and adolescents, the WISC-V is seldom the only cognitive battery administered or the only battery from which subtests are drawn. More commonly, when a WISC-V is selected as the core battery in an evaluation, it is often supplemented with other batteries (e.g., a memory battery, a phonological processing battery) or with subtests from other batteries, and it is often administered along with a comprehensive test of achievement, such as the *Wechsler Individual Achievement*

≡ Rapid Reference 4.4

WISC-V Classification System

Standard Score Range for Composites	Scaled Score Range for Subtests	Percentile Ranks	Classification
> 130	16–19	> 98th	Extremely High
120–129	14–15	91st–97th	Very High
110–119	13	75th–90th	High Average
90–109	8–12	25th–74th	Average
80–89	7	9th–24th	Low Average
70–79	5–6	2nd–8th	Very Low
< 69	1–4	< 2nd	Extremely Low

Source: Wechsler Intelligence Scale for Children-Fifth Edition (WISC-V). Copyright © 2014 NCS Pearson, Inc. Reproduced with permission. All rights reserved.

"Wechsler Intelligence Scale for Children" and "WISC" are trademarks, in the U.S. and/or other countries, of Pearson Education, Inc. or its affiliates(s).

Test-Third Edition (WIAT-III; Pearson, 2009), *Kaufman Test of Educational Achievement-Third Edition* (KTEA-3; Kaufman & Kaufman, 2013), or *Woodcock-Johnson IV Tests of Achievement* (2014; Schrank, Mather, & McGrew, 2014). Herein lies the classification problem: different batteries have different classification systems. As such, the same standard score may be classified in two or even three different ways in the same psychoeducational report if the examiner used the battery-specific classification systems.

Consider two tests that are often used together: the WISC-V and KTEA-3. Rapid Reference 4.5 shows one classification system for the KTEA-3. Notice that the Average range of ability on the KTEA-3 (85–115) differs from the Average range on the WISC-V (90–109; Rapid Reference 4.4). Neither classification system is wrong; they are just different. However, such differences lead to confusion among readers of psychoeducational reports. How is a parent to understand that her son's ability to reason and solve novel problems is Low Average, as represented by an FRI of 85, but his ability to solve math problems is Average, as represented by the *same score* of 85 on the Math Concepts and Applications subtest? Which is it? Average or Low Average?

≡ *Rapid Reference 4.5*

KTEA-3 Classification System

Standard Score Range for Composites	Percentile Ranks	Classification
146–160	>99th	Very High
131–145	98th–99th	High
116–130	86th–98th	Above Average
85–115	16th–84th	Average
70–84	2nd–14th	Below Average
55–69	0.1–2nd	Low
40–54	< 0.1	Very Low

Source: *Kaufman Test of Educational Achievement, Third Edition (KTEA-3).* Copyright © 2014 NCS Pearson, Inc. Reproduced with permission. All rights reserved.

"Kaufman Test of Educational Achievement" and "KTEA" are trademarks, in the U.S. and/or other countries, of Pearson Education, Inc. or its affiliates(s).

In light of the confusion that arises when multiple classification systems are used in the same psychoeducational report, it is recommended that the practitioner select one classification system and use it to describe all score performances. We prefer the classification system included in Rapid Reference 4.6. However, any classification system may be used. What is most important is that all scores be classified based only on one classification system to avoid confusion.

≡ Rapid Reference 4.6

Generic Classification System That May Be Used to Classify All Scores in a Psychoeducational Report

Standard Score	Scaled Score	Percentile Range	Classification
<70	1–3	<2nd	Normative Weakness/ Extremely Below Average
70–79	4–5	2nd–8th	Normative Weakness/ Well Below Average
80–84	6	9th–4th	Normative Weakness/Below Average
85–89	**7**	**16th–23rd**	**WNL/Low Average**
90–109	**8–11**	**25th–73rd**	**WNL/Average**
110–115	**12–13**	**75th–84th**	**WNL/High Average**
116–119	—	86th–90th	Normative Strength/Above Average
120–129	14–15	91st–97th	Normative Strength/ Well Above Average
≥130	16–19	≥98th	Normative Strength/ Extremely Above Average

Note: On standardized norm-referenced tests, most people (almost 70%) perform *within normal limits* (WNL; standard scores of 85 to 115, inclusive). This range is highlighted in bold.

DON'T FORGET

Select one classification system and use it to describe scores obtained from all subtests administered to the individual as well as corresponding composites.

A Note About Confidence Intervals

An obtained score should always be reported with a confidence interval because it is not the individual's true score. Confidence intervals provide a range of scores in which the true score is expected to fall based on a specified probability. Most practitioners were taught to use the 95% confidence interval. This interval allows us to say that we are 95% confident that the individual's true score is within a specified interval. That is, hypothetically, if the individual were tested 100 times, 95 out of 100 of those times her score would be within the confidence interval. Because the true score is unknown, however, we actually do not know if it is in the 5% range (i.e., outside of the confidence interval) or the 95% range (i.e., within the confidence interval), but 95% is good, allowing us to be quite confident in our prediction. Confidence intervals serve as a reminder that all obtained scores are imprecise, containing at least some degree of measurement error. The higher the reliability of the score, the narrower the confidence interval (less error associated with the score); the lower the reliability of the score, the wider the confidence interval (more error associated with the score). Confidence intervals ensure greater accuracy of test score interpretation. The WISC-V manuals report confidence intervals at 90% and 95%. Why use 90% if we could be more accurate? Why not use 99%?

The reason we do not use 99% is because the margin of error increases as the confidence level increases. As the confidence level increases, it may become so large that it is in effect useless. For example, what if a parent or teacher were told that Johnny's reasoning ability is between 80 (Below Average) and 110 (High Average)? How useful is this information in predicting Johnny's reasoning ability or planning an educational program for Johnny? Not useful at all. In fact, we don't know if Johnny needs any assistance with tasks that involve novel problem solving! This example demonstrates that some confidence intervals are simply too wide to be of practical utility. For this reason, 90% or 95% confidence intervals are preferred.

X-BASS allows the user to select the 68%, 90%, or 95% confidence interval, depending on the level of precision desired, although the program defaults to 68%. At the bottom of each individual test tab in X-BASS is a box for selecting the desired confidence interval (see Figure 4.1). Figure 4.2 shows Amanda's WISC-V score graph produced by X-BASS with 68% confidence intervals and Figure 4.3 shows the same graph with 95% confidence intervals. A comparison of these two figures shows that the larger confidence intervals (95%) are much more likely to span different classification categories as compared to the smaller confidence intervals (68%). Rapid Reference 4.7 provides a few reasons why we opt to report scores using 68%. However, practitioners may choose whatever confidence interval they are most comfortable with for the types of decisions they need to make.

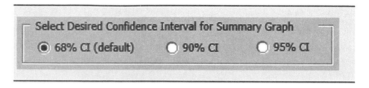

Figure 4.1 Bottom Portion of Test-Specific Tabs on X-BASS: Confidence Interval for Score Reporting

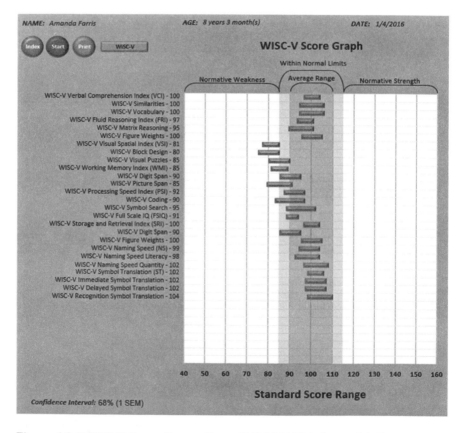

Figure 4.2 WISC-V Score Report From X-BASS With Amanda's Data Displayed With 68% Confidence Intervals

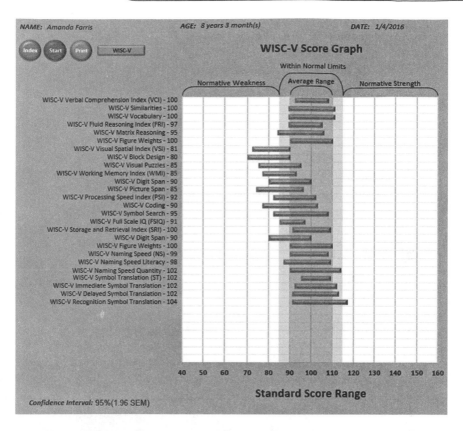

Figure 4.3 WISC-V Score Report From X-BASS with Amanda's Data Displayed with 95% Confidence Intervals

---

≡ *Rapid Reference 4.7*

● ●

Some Reasons for Using 68% Confidence Intervals for Score Reporting

- 68% represents +/- 1 Standard Error of Measurement (SEM), which is considered sufficient for making the clinical types of decisions that are often made based on test scores (e.g., determining areas of strength and weakness; Mather & Wendling, 2014; McGrew, Werder, & Woodcock, 1991).

- The scores that are relied on most in the interpretive steps for the WISC-V are the global scores (most reliable), followed by the index scores (also highly reliable). In addition, these scores are considered suitable for interpretation in our system only when they are cohesive and supported by other data sources, the latter of which bolster their ecological validity, suggesting that they are likely to be accurate indications of the individual's actual ability.

- 68% confidence intervals are less likely to span more than one classification category as compared to 90% and 95% confidence intervals, which may improve upon the practical utility of the scores for informing intervention planning.

DON'T FORGET

The WISC-V manuals provide confidence intervals at 90% and 95%. X-BASS graphs scores using 68%, 90%, or 95% confidence intervals, but defaults to 68%. Determining which confidence interval to use requires balancing *level of precision* with *practical utility*. Using 90% confidence intervals appears to strike a comfortable balance between the two.

Once a table of the individual's scores has been created, either by hand, or using X-BASS, interpretation begins. In many cases, the fact that the 10 WISC-V primary subtests were administered does not mean that assessment of cognitive abilities and processes has been completed. Upon a review of the results of an individual's performance on these 10 subtests, the practitioner may generate hypotheses that will need to be tested by gathering other data sources, which may include additional assessment. This process is demonstrated in the interpretive steps included in this chapter.

WISC-V INTERPRETATION STEP BY STEP

Allowing yourself to be wrong allows you to be right . . . eventually.

—*W. J. Schneider, 2013, p. 322*

Before we present the first step of the WISC-V interpretive system, which is related to the FSIQ, a little recent history is in order. Flanagan and colleagues have written about the importance of "unitary" or "cohesive" composites in test interpretation for a number of years (e.g., Flanagan, McGrew, & Ortiz, 2000; Flanagan & Ortiz, 2001; Flanagan, Ortiz, & Alfonso, 2013; McGrew & Flanagan, 1998). When a composite is cohesive, variability between or among the scores that compose it is not considered unusual or rare, indicating that it likely provides a good summary of the theoretically related abilities it was intended to represent and should be interpreted. Thus, when the FSIQ is cohesive, it means that it provides a good summary of the individual's overall intellectual ability.

The FSIQ is the most reliable score on the WISC-V and therefore is usually reported and interpreted, often regardless of the variability among the scores that compose it. However, when the scores that comprise the FSIQ vary greatly, say from Well Below Average to High Average, most practitioners would agree that it does not provide a very good summary of overall intellectual ability because it obscures differences in the individual's range of cognitive capabilities. Nearly 30 years ago Kaufman (1990) stated:

> The individual tested makes an unspoken plea to the examiner not to summarize his or her intelligence in a single, cold number; the goal of profile interpretation should be to respond to the pleas by identifying hypothesized strengths and weaknesses that extend well beyond the limited information provided by the FS-IQ and that will conceivably lead to practical recommendations that help answer the referral question. (p. 422)

In *Essentials of WISC-IV Assessment*, Flanagan and Kaufman's (2004) response to the individual's unspoken plea was to create a rule of thumb by which to judge whether the FSIQ was likely to be a good summary of the individual's overall intellectual ability, thereby rendering this score "interpretable." Specifically, when the difference between the lowest Index and the highest Index on the WISC-IV was ≥ 23 points (or ≥ 1.5 SDs), they stated, "The variation in the Indexes that compose the FSIQ is considered too great . . . for the purpose of summarizing global intellectual ability in a single score" (p. 140) and their software program marked the FSIQ as "uninterpretable." An uninterpretable FSIQ meant that interpretation focused squarely on the Indexes.

As it turns out, Flanagan and Kaufman's (2004) rule of thumb was much more practical than it was psychometrically defensible. In other words, most practitioners would find a 23-point discrepancy between two indexes (e.g., Verbal Comprehension Index [VCI] = 105 and Working Memory Index [WMI] = 82) to be *clinically meaningful* and worthy of consideration within the context of the referral. Furthermore, most practitioners would probably not want to summarize the individual's cognitive ability as Average, based on an aggregate of the VCI and WMI (i.e., 94) and call it a day. This rationale was part of the thinking behind the ≥ 23 point rule of thumb. To be clear, there was nothing at all wrong with "flagging" a ≥ 1.5 SD difference between Indexes and considering its meaningfulness within the context of the case, especially when the lower score in the comparison was suggestive of a normative weakness. The first author (DPF) who was involved in the selection of the ≥ 23-point rule of thumb still stands behind that line of thinking. Nevertheless, the rule of thumb, albeit practical, was not defensible from a psychometric standpoint.

Research conducted after the publication of *Essentials of WISC-IV Assessment* showed that a difference of 23 points between an individual's highest and lowest Indexes was quite common in the general population. For example, about 50% of the Italian WISC-IV standardization sample had differences of ≥ 23 points between the highest and lowest Index score (Orsini, Pezzuti, & Hulbert, 2014). The same is true for the WISC-V standardization sample. That is, about 57% of the WISC-V normative sample had ≥ 23 points between the highest and lowest Index scores (Kaufman, Raiford, & Coalson, 2016). We therefore know *now* that it doesn't make "psychometric sense" to state that an FSIQ is uninterpretable when the difference between or among the scores that make it up is common in the general population.

To make matters a little bit worse, as they pertain to Flanagan and Kaufman's (2004) rule of thumb, it is not a good idea to classify the FSIQ as "uninterpretable" in any instance. This is because the FSIQ does not lose its predictive validity, even when the variability among the scores that make it up is rare in the standardization sample. According to Daniel (2007), the FSIQ's construct and predictive validity are independent of the variability in scores that compose it. It seems clear that Flanagan and Kaufman produced a rule that had more *clinical* than *psychometric* relevance. Test interpretation is part art and part science, and it is often difficult to strike a balance between the two. Notwithstanding, it is our intention to do so here by revisiting the practical and psychometric issues that are relevant to interpreting the WISC-V FSIQ.

Flanagan and Kaufman's (2004) method, the research that followed their method, and the wealth of information reported in the WISC-V manuals were all stepping stones to the interpretive approach presented here. And this interpretive approach will eventually become yet another stepping stone on the path of successive approximations to getting it "right."

Rapid Reference 4.8 lists "what is known" and "what we want to know" about the FSIQ and other global ability scores on the WISC-V. Note that what we know as well as what we want to know involve the practical/art and psychometric/science of test interpretation. The first step in our WISC-V interpretive system provides the answers to the "what we want to know" questions through a better balance of art and science than that offered by Flanagan and Kaufman (2004, 2009).

≋ Rapid Reference 4.8

The Art and Science of What We Know and What We Want to Know About WISC-V Global Ability Scores

What We Know

- WISC-V global ability scores (i.e., FSIQ, NVI, GAI) are highly reliable [psychometric/"science"].
- The FSIQ is the most comprehensive global ability score on the WISC-V and, therefore, is arguably the best estimate of overall intellectual ability and should be reported and interpreted unless otherwise indicated [psychometric/"science"].
- The FSIQ does not lose its construct or predictive validity when the variability among the scores that comprise it is unusual or rare in the general population [psychometric/"science"].
- The FSIQ may obscure important information about an individual's strengths and weaknesses, even when the variability in scores that compose it is common in the general population [practical/"art"].

What We Want to Know

- Is the FSIQ cohesive? [psychometric/"science"]
- Is the FSIQ clinically meaningful? [practical/"art"]
- When is it appropriate to interpret the NVI in lieu of the FSIQ? [art and science]
- When is it appropriate to interpret the GAI in lieu of the FSIQ? [art and science]
- Is it ever appropriate to interpret more than one global ability score? [art and science]

DON'T FORGET

Base rate refers to the frequency with which test score differences of various magnitudes occur in the general population. Base rate data assist in answering the question: *Is the size of the difference between two scores rare in the general population?* Typically, score differences that occur in < 10% of the population are considered rare.

　　Commonly used terms to describe statistical rarity: uncommon, unusual, infrequent, abnormal, and *rare*. All of these terms are used in this book with the exception of abnormal. The term *abnormal* is avoided and should be dropped from the statistical rarity vernacular because it has a negative connotation. Not all statistical rarities are abnormal or "bad." Many statistical rarities are "good" and are *valuable deviations* that should be recognized as such.

Step 1. Determine the Best Way to Describe Overall Intellectual Ability

> *The FSIQ is the most comprehensive and reliable of all of the global scores. A large body of research accrued across 75 years supports its predictive validity and clinical utility. Unless there is a compelling reason to deviate, the FSIQ is the default global score of choice.*
>
> —Kaufman et al., 2016, p. 234

As you will see in the pages that follow, there may very well be compelling reasons to deviate from the FSIQ as the global score of choice. But prior to doing so, a number of factors must be considered.

Surgeon General's Warning

This step is long. It contains many permutations. Conducting all the substeps within this step by hand will lead to an unnecessarily long day and may result in undue stress. To avoid stress-related health problems associated with conducting these substeps by hand, enter WISC-V scores into X-BASS and allow the program to provide a recommendation for you automatically.

Although it is certainly wise to heed the obviously fictitious Surgeon General's Warning and use a computer program to *assist* with interpretation of the WISC-V, it is also helpful to know how the decision-making process is carried out by X-BASS to generate recommendations regarding interpretation of global ability scores on a case-by-case basis. This step describes the decisions that were involved in making a determination of the best way to describe overall intellectual ability.

The WISC-V contains three global ability scores that provide a summary of overall intellectual ability, namely the FSIQ, the NVI, and the GAI. The composition of these global ability scores is found in Rapid Reference 4.9 along with selected Primary (VCI, WMI, PSI) and Ancillary (CPI) Index Scales that are referenced in this step.

≡ *Rapid Reference 4.9*

Composition of the FSIQ and Selected Primary and Ancillary Index Scores That Are Considered When Making Decisions About the Best Way to Describe Overall Intellectual Ability

Subtest	CHC Broad: Narrow Ability	FSIQ	NVI	VCI	GAI	CPI	WMI	PSI
Similarities	Gc:VL, Gf: I	√		√	√			
Vocabulary	Gc:VL	√		√	√			
Block Design	Gv:Vz	√	√		√			
Visual Puzzles	Gv:Vz		√					
Matrix Reasoning	Gf:I	√	√		√			
Figure Weights	Gf:RG, RQ	√	√		√			
Digit Span	Gsm:MW,MS	√				√	√	
Picture Span	Gsm:MS,MW		√			√	√	
Coding	Gs:R9	√	√			√		√
Symbol Search	Gs:P					√		√

Note: FSIQ = Full Scale IQ; NVI = Nonverbal Index; VCI = Verbal Comprehension Index; GAI = General Ability Index; CPI = Cognitive Proficiency Index; WMI = Working Memory Index; PSI = Processing Speed Index; Gc:VL = Crystallized Intelligence: Lexical Knowledge; Gv:Vz = Visual Processing: Visualization; Gf:I = Fluid Reasoning: Induction; RG = General Sequential Reasoning or Deduction; RQ = Qualitative Reasoning; Gsm: MW = Short-Term Memory: Working Memory; MS = Memory Span; Gs:R9 = Processing Speed: Rate of Test Taking; P = Perceptual Speed.

As may be seen in Rapid Reference 4.9, the FSIQ is the most comprehensive estimate of overall ability because it is based on seven subtests that measure aspects of five cognitive constructs (Gc, Gv, Gf, Gsm, and Gs), whereas the NVI and GAI are made up of subtests that measure four and three cognitive constructs, respectively.

Why did the authors of the WISC-V provide other global ability scores when the FSIQ is a comprehensive, highly reliable (.96; Wechsler, 2014c, p. 57), and valid estimate of overall intellectual ability? The answer is that despite the seeming superiority of the FSIQ over the NVI and GAI, there are indeed times that one of the latter two scores may be more useful or meaningful as an estimate of overall intellectual ability.

The NVI as an Alternative to the FSIQ

A careful look at Rapid Reference 4.9 shows that the subtests that make up the NVI do not require a verbal response from the examinee. The NVI includes measures of four cognitive constructs. Specifically, this global ability score eliminates Gc and places more weight on Gv, making it qualitatively different from the FSIQ. However, like the FSIQ, the NVI is highly reliable (.95; Wechsler, 2014c, p. 57) and has a high correlation with the FSIQ (i.e., .93; p. 74).

Because the NVI is a reliable and valid estimate of overall intellectual ability that minimizes expressive language demands, it is suitable for consideration as a summary score for English Learners (ELs), individuals who are deaf or hard of hearing, and individuals who are suspected of having speech/language impairment, expressive language disorder, or any other disorder that may compromise expressive language (e.g., autism spectrum disorder; see also Kaufman et al., 2016; Raiford & Coalson, 2014; Weiss, Saklofske, Holdnack, & Prifitera, 2016). Therefore, when testing an examinee with any of these characteristics, the NVI should be considered as an alternative to the FSIQ.

DON'T FORGET

The NVI is an estimate of overall intellectual ability that minimizes expressive language demands for individuals who have expressive language difficulties or who are learning English. It provides a better choice for estimating ability for these individuals than the VSI or FRI because it is more comprehensive, including subtests from every Primary Index Scale except the VCI.

CAUTION

The NVI is not a *language-free* index because it requires receptive language (i.e., understanding test directions), but it is *language-reduced.*

It should not be assumed, however, that the NVI will always be the best estimate of overall intellectual ability for all ELs or all individuals with suspected language-related disorders, for example. It is necessary to determine which one (NVI *or* FSIQ) may be the best estimate or whether both estimates offer important information about the individual's overall intellectual ability. To determine the best estimate, it is necessary to consider whether the NVI and the FSIQ are cohesive and clinically meaningful. These terms are defined in Rapid Reference 4.10.

≡ Rapid Reference 4.10

Definition of Cohesion and Clinical Meaningfulness

Cohesion

A composite is considered cohesive when the variation in the scores that comprise it is not unusual in the general population. Common variation in scores making up a composite suggests that the composite provides a good summary of the theoretically related abilities it was intended to represent. Determination of composite cohesion is based on statistical rarity. Variability of scores within composites that occurs in less than about 10% of the general population is considered rare and indicates that the composite is not cohesive. The test for statistical rarity for composite cohesion is discussed in Step 2.

Clinical Meaningfulness

There are instances in which a composite may be cohesive, and also obscure information about the individual's range of cognitive capabilities. Rather than relying on results of cohesion analysis only, evaluation of where scores within a composite fall relative to most people are examined to determine whether the summary score (in this step, a global ability score) may obscure important information about an individual's strengths and weaknesses.

Cohesion analysis is part of the science of interpretation; judging the clinical meaningfulness of summary scores is part of the art of interpretation.

There are other factors that go beyond examining cohesion and clinical meaningfulness that are necessary to consider, such as evaluating NVI-FSIQ and NVI-VCI differences, prior to making a "best estimate" determination. Based on the number of permutations involved in answering the question, "NVI, FSIQ, or both?" X-BASS produces more than 20 different summary statements that provide the practitioner with a defensible rationale for reporting either the NVI or FSIQ as the individual's best estimate. In some instances, the summary statements leave the decision of whether to report both the NVI and the FSIQ up to the practitioner's best judgment given the uniqueness of the case. Space limitations preclude the reproduction of all summary statements here. A sample summary statement related to the "NVI or FSIQ" question is found in Rapid Reference 4.11.

≡ Rapid Reference 4.11

Sample Statement Produced by X-BASS When the Practitioner Is Interested in Understanding Which Summary Score Is the Best to Report for an Individual Who Is an EL or Suspected of Having a Language-Related Disorder

The difference between the FSIQ and NVI is not statistically significant ($p < .05$). However, the difference between the NVI and VCI is statistically significant ($p < .05$) and the NVI is higher than the FSIQ and the VCI. These findings suggest that the subtests with the highest language demands may have attenuated the FSIQ. In this case, the NVI should be reported and interpreted as the best estimate of the individual's overall intellectual ability. If a global ability score is needed in a formula or when diagnostic criteria include a cut score, then the NVI should be used. Use index and subtest level analysis to assist in understanding the NVI > FSIQ difference.

A review of the statement in Rapid Reference 4.11 should provide a general understanding of the type of information that X-BASS provides when a practitioner is interested in the utility of the NVI as an estimate of overall ability. Nevertheless, the practitioner may still be wondering how is it possible that there are more than 20 statements like the one reported in Rapid Reference 4.11 that may be produced by X-BASS, depending on the data entered (i.e., FSIQ, NVI, and the 10 subtest scaled scores that make up the Primary Index Scores). The steps outlined in Rapid Reference 4.12 may provide some insight.

≡ Rapid Reference 4.12

Summary of Some of the Steps Involved in Determining Whether the NVI or FSIQ Is the Best Estimate of Overall Intellectual Ability for ELs or Individuals Suspected of Having a Language-Related Disorder

Step 1.1. Is the NVI cohesive?

- If the difference between the highest and lowest subtest scaled scores that make up the NVI is < 9 points, *then the NVI is cohesive.* Determine its clinical meaningfulness (go to Step 1.2).
- If the difference between the highest and lowest subtest scaled scores that make up the NVI is ≥ 9 points, *then the NVI is not cohesive.* Determine whether the FSIQ is cohesive (go to Step 1.3).

Step 1.2. Is the NVI clinically meaningful?

- If the difference between the highest and lowest subtest scaled scores that make up the NVI is < 5 points, *then the NVI is clinically meaningful.* Determine whether the FSIQ is cohesive and clinically meaningful to understand whether it represents a viable alternative to the NVI or offers additional information to aid in understanding the individual's overall intellectual ability (go to Step 1.3).

- If the difference between the highest and lowest subtest scaled scores that comprise the NVI is ≥ 5 points, then the NVI *might not be clinically meaningful.* To determine if the NVI is clinically meaningful when the difference between the highest and lowest scaled scores that make up the NVI is ≥ 5 points, do the following:

  For the subtests that make up the NVI (BD, VP, MR, FW, PS, CD),

- Report the *highest* score here: _____ and the *lowest* score here: _____
- Report the *difference* between these scores here: _____
- Using the following table, determine whether the high and low score pair is listed in the column associated with the difference between these scores (e.g., suppose the highest score is 10, the lowest score is 4, and the difference between them is 6. Go to the "Difference = 6" column, and look for the score pair, "10–4." It is listed.) (See following for interpretation.)

Highest-Lowest Scaled Score Ranges That Render the NVI Not Clinically Meaningful

	Difference Between Highest and Lowest Scores That Make Up the NVI			
	Difference = 5	Difference = 6	Difference = 7	Difference = 8
Score Range	9 – 4	9 – 3	9 – 2	9 – 1
	10 – 5	10 – 4	10 – 3	10 – 2
	11 – 6	11 – 5	11 – 4	11 – 3
	12 – 7	12 – 6	12 – 5	12 – 4
		13 – 7	13 – 6	13 – 5
			14 – 7	14 – 6
				15 – 7

- If the *score pair is not reported* in the table, then the NVI is *clinically meaningful.*
- If the *score pair is reported* in the table, then the NVI is *not clinically meaningful.*
- In either case, it is necessary to understand whether the FSIQ is cohesive and clinically meaningful to determine the best estimate of global ability (go to Step 1.3).

(continued)

(continued)

Step 1.3. Is the FSIQ cohesive?

- If the difference between the highest and lowest subtest scaled scores that make up the FSIQ is < 9 points, *then the FSIQ is cohesive.* Determine its clinical meaningfulness (go to Step 1.4).
- If the difference between the highest and lowest subtest scaled scores that make up the FSIQ is ≥ 9 points, *then the FSIQ is not cohesive* (go to Output 1.1).

Step 1.4. Is the FSIQ clinically meaningful?

- If the difference between the highest and lowest subtest scaled scores that make up the FSIQ is ≥ 5 points, then the FSIQ *might not be clinically meaningful.* To determine if the FSIQ is clinically meaningful when the difference between the highest and lowest scaled scores that make up the FSIQ is ≥ 5 points, do the following:

  For the subtests that make up the FSIQ (SI, VC, BD, MR, FW, DS, CD),
- Report the *highest* score here: _____ and the *lowest* score here: _____
- Report the *difference* between these scores here: _____
- Using the following table, determine whether the high and low score pair is listed in the column associated with the difference between these scores.

Highest-Lowest Scaled Score Ranges That Render the FSIQ Not Clinically Meaningful

	Difference Between Highest and Lowest Scores That Make Up the FSIQ		
	Difference = 5	**Difference = 6**	**Difference = 7**	**Difference = 8**
Score Range	9 – 4	9 – 3	9 – 2	9 – 1
	10 – 5	10 – 4	10 – 3	10 – 2
	11 – 6	11 – 5	11 – 4	11 – 3
	12 – 7	12 – 6	12 – 5	12 – 4
		13 – 7	13 – 6	13 – 5
			14 – 7	14 – 6
				15 – 7

- If the *score pair is not reported* in the table, then the FSIQ *is clinically meaningful.*
- If the *score pair is reported* in the table, then the FSIQ *is not clinically meaningful.*
- In either case, go to Output 1.1.

Output 1.1

Based on the Steps 1.1 to 1.4, the NVI and FSIQ have been classified according to cohesion and clinical meaningfulness. Thus, the following classifications of NVI and FSIQ are possible:

Global Composite Classification	All Possible Classifications
Cohesive (C) and Clinically Meaningful (CM)	NVI C + CM and FSIQ C + CM
Cohesive (C) and Not Clinically Meaningful (NCM)	NVI C + CM and FSIQ C + NCM
Not Cohesive (NC)	NVI C + CM and FSIQ NC
	NVI C + NCM and FSIQ C + CM
	NVI C + NCM and FSIQ C + NCM
	NVI C + NCM and FSIQ NC
	NVI NC and FSIQ C + CM
	NVI NC and FSIQ C + NCM
	NVI NC and FSIQ NC

The information in the preceding table is considered along with information about differences between the NVI and FSIQ and the NVI and VCI. For example, if the NVI and FSIQ were cohesive and clinically meaningful and the differences between the NVI and the FSIQ and NVI and VCI were not statistically significant ($p < .05$), then X-BASS would produce a statement for those findings. The following table includes this scenario along with a few others to demonstrate how X-BASS was programmed to provide a recommendation regarding whether the NVI or FSIQ is considered the best estimate of overall intellectual ability. Note that the following scenarios have been simplified for inclusion here.

Score Cohesion and Clinical Meaningfulness	Statistical Analysis of Score Differences	X-BASS Output
If NVI C + CM and FSIQ C + CM **(A1)** Or If NVI C + NCM and FSIQ C + CM **(A2)** Or If NVI NC and FSIQ C + CM or C + NCM **(A3)**	AND if NVI-FSIQ < 9 and NVI-VCI < 10, *then FSIQ best estimate* **(O1)**	**A1 + O1:** The differences between the FSIQ and NVI and the NVI and VCI are not statistically significant ($p < .05$), suggesting that language demands most likely did not affect the individual's performance to a substantial degree. Although the FSIQ and the NVI each provides a good summary of the individual's cognitive abilities, the FSIQ is considered the best estimate of overall intellectual ability because it summarizes a broader range of abilities as compared to the NVI.

(continued)

(continued)

Score Cohesion and Clinical Meaningfulness	Statistical Analysis of Score Differences	X-BASS Output
		The NVI may be reported along with the FSIQ and both may be used to inform diagnosis. Although the FSIQ is considered the best score to use when a global ability score is needed for a formula or when diagnostic criteria include a cut score, there may be instances when the NVI is selected over the FSIQ based on clinical judgment. **A2 + O1:** The differences between the FSIQ and NVI and the NVI and VCI are not statistically significant ($p < .05$), suggesting that language demands most likely did not affect the individual's performance to a substantial degree. Because the NVI may obscure important information about the individual's strengths and weaknesses, the FSIQ is considered the best estimate of overall intellectual ability because it has less variability among the scores that compose it compared to the NVI. If the examiner chooses to report the NVI along with the FSIQ, then index and subtest level analysis should be used to assist in explaining the variability in the scores that compose the NVI. The FSIQ is considered the best score to use when a global ability score is needed for a formula or when diagnostic criteria include a cut score unless clinical judgment suggests otherwise. **A3 + O1:** The differences between the FSIQ and NVI and the NVI and VCI are not statistically significant ($p < .05$), suggesting that language demands most likely did not affect the individual's performance to a substantial degree. Because the NVI

Score Cohesion and Clinical Meaningfulness	Statistical Analysis of Score Differences	X-BASS Output
		very likely obscures important information about the individual's strengths and weaknesses, the FSIQ is considered the best estimate of overall intellectual ability because it has less variability among the scores that compose it compared to the NVI. The FSIQ is considered the best score to use when an overall intellectual ability score is needed for a formula or when diagnostic criteria include a cut score unless clinical judgment suggests otherwise.

Note: The information contained in this rapid reference demonstrated only a small part of the logic behind considering whether the NVI offers a viable alternative to the FSIQ. X-BASS is needed for all possible outcomes based on the 10 subtests that make up the Primary Index Scales.

The information in Rapid Reference 4.12 should make it clear that there are many possible permutations regarding cohesion, clinical meaningfulness, and NVI-FSIQ and NVI-VCI differences, including the direction of score differences (e.g., NVI > FSIQ or NVI < FSIQ). For example, this rapid reference showed that when the FSIQ is cohesive and clinically meaningful, and the FSIQ-NVI and NVI-VCI differences are not statistically significant, meaning that any differences between these scores are not real (but rather, likely due to chance), then regardless of how the NVI is classified in terms of cohesion and clinical meaningfulness, the FSIQ is probably the best estimate of overall intellectual ability. However, if the NVI was cohesive and the FSIQ was not cohesive, and the NVI-FSIQ and NVI-VCI score differences were not statistically significant, then the NVI might be considered the best estimate of global ability. Individual subtest level performance guides this decision-making process as well. Given the number of factors that we believe are necessary to consider when determining the best overall ability estimate to report and interpret on the WISC-V, it was necessary to automate our interpretive method in X-BASS rather than provide a lengthy paper-and-pencil worksheet.

Why Are Detailed Analyses Necessary to Determine the Best Estimate of Global Ability?

Seasoned practitioners may wonder why it is necessary to conduct or consider analyses at the level of detail suggested in Rapid Reference 4.12. For example, a seasoned practitioner might test an EL, look at the FSIQ and NVI, note that the NVI is higher, glance at the VCI and other Primary index scores and see that the VCI is lower than the rest and intuit that the NVI is the best estimate of overall ability because it is less "language loaded" than the FSIQ. We have observed practitioners who are among *the best* clinicians we know do just that; we have worked on cases in which we have done just that; "that" is what clinicians do. They have an excellent sense of the child, because they tested the child, observed the child, met with his or her parents and teachers, and interacted with the child over the course of many hours. They have a sense of who the child is and how he or she behaves and solves problems and performs academic tasks relative to the hundreds of children they have encountered over the years of the same age and grade, both typical and atypical. Seasoned clinicians take a set of data from one child and filter it through everything they know about that child, other children, the tests administered, theory, research, and the suspected disorder(s) and referral questions and within minutes are indeed confident with their decision to use either the NVI or FSIQ without ever having looked up a critical value to determine if the difference between any two scores is significant or rare, for example. They know what global ability score is the best estimate for the child who stands before them. Why? *Experience.*

Nevertheless, even seasoned practitioners find themselves in due process hearings, serving as expert witnesses, or otherwise in a position in which they are asked to demonstrate accountability for the decisions they made about a child based on the test data they gathered. In these situations, and indeed in all situations involving decisions drawn from test data that affect how, when, and where a child will be educated and in what way, the science behind the decisions must be evident. For this reason, our interpretive approach is systematic, taking into consideration the psychometric properties of the test, in this case the WISC-V, and the manner in which the test publisher recommended its use. We build on that foundation with a thoughtful and deliberate set of steps to aid all users of the WISC-V (first-year graduate students and seasoned practitioners) to make important decisions, such as selecting the best global ability score for use in a required formula for identification of specific learning disability. And, because many factors need to be considered to provide a *defensible* basis for using one global ability score over another (particularly for diagnostic purposes), the process is necessarily complex, but simplified greatly by software.

Seasoned practitioners make good decisions, sometimes without looking up critical values or using software programs like X-BASS, because they have internalized sound assessment principles and procedures. They have stepped on many stones along the test interpretation path, perhaps having taken their first step after reading Alan Kaufman's *Intelligent Testing with the WISC-R* in 1979 or *Intelligent Testing with the WISC-III* in 1994. Nevertheless, they know that a systematic, psychometrically and theoretically sound approach to test interpretation *and clinical judgment* are necessary to draw defensible conclusions from WISC-V data—their approach to test interpretation may simply be more eclectic and integrate aspects of different interpretive methods. For example, they may not be wedded to all the steps presented here or to X-BASS, but they may find some of the steps and some features of X-BASS valuable.

New practitioners will likely follow the steps outlined here (or in another book on WISC-V interpretation) routinely and rely heavily on X-BASS for assistance with test interpretation with the goal of internalizing sound assessment principles and procedures. However, it is important to understand that no matter how detailed a set of interpretive steps and how precisely they may have been automated, neither a test nor a software program like X-BASS capture the intricacies of every individual.

A Note About Clinical Meaningfulness

Rapid Reference 4.12 provided an operationalization of the clinical meaningfulness of the NVI and FSIQ, which is evaluated even when these global ability scores are cohesive. To review, when the difference between the highest and lowest scaled scores that make up the NVI and FSIQ is < 9, indicating that it is not uncommon in the general population, the global ability score is considered cohesive. However, the difference between the highest and lowest scaled scores may be 8, for example, which represents a 2 and 2/3rds SD difference between the highest and lowest scaled scores. Though this difference is not unusual, occurring in a little more than 20% of the normative sample (see Rapid Reference 4.13), a global ability score made up of scores that vary by 2 and 2/3rds SD may very well obscure important information about the individual's strengths and weaknesses, rendering the global ability score a less meaningful representation of the individual's cognitive capabilities as compared to the Primary Index Scores, for example. For this reason, we created guidelines for judging the clinical meaningfulness of global ability scores, even when the global ability score is cohesive.

≡ Rapid Reference 4.13

Percentages of the WISC-V Normative Sample Obtaining High Minus Low Scaled Score Differences Between 5 and 9, Inclusive

Difference Between Highest and Lowest Subtest Scaled Score	FSIQ	NVI	GAI
5	77	72	55
6	59	54	35
7	39	36	19
8	24	22	10
9	< 10	< 10	5

Note: Differences associated with ≤ 10% (shaded in the figure) are considered unusual and indicate that the global ability score is not cohesive.

In our operationalization of the clinical meaningfulness of the NVI and FSIQ (and GAI, discussed later in this step), when differences between the highest and lowest scaled scores that make up these global scores are < 5, they are considered clinically meaningful. In other words, it is very likely that the global score does not obscure important information about the individual's strengths and weaknesses, rendering the score a good estimate of the individual's overall intellectual ability. However, when the difference between the highest and lowest scaled scores that make up a global ability score differ by 1 and 2/3rds SDs or more (i.e., 5 or more points), the global ability score may begin to obscure some important information about the individual's strengths and weaknesses, *despite how common that difference may be in the general population* (as reported in Rapid Reference 4.13). Therefore, when differences between the highest and lowest scaled scores that make up the NVI or the FSIQ are between 5 and 8, inclusive—that is, the range in which differences are not unusual, but are nevertheless substantial from a clinical perspective—a consideration of where the high and low scores fall relative to the general population is necessary to inform the meaningfulness of the global composite as a summary of the individual's overall intellectual ability.

Consider an NVI wherein the difference between the highest and lowest scaled scores that make it up is 6 points. Rapid Reference 4.13 shows that a difference of this magnitude occurs in 54% of the WISC-V normative sample—a common finding. However, what if the highest score is 11 (Average; 63rd percentile) and the lowest score is 5 (Well Below Average; 8th percentile)? It seems clear that if the scaled score of 5, in particular, is a valid representation of the individual's ability in that cognitive domain, as corroborated by Primary Index level analysis (Step 2), other data sources, and ecological validity (discussed in Step 2 and in Chapter 7), then an Average summary score, such as an NVI of 98 (45th percentile), obscures this normative weakness. For this reason, operationalization of clinical meaningfulness (as presented in Tables 1 and 2 in Rapid Reference 4.12) "flags" those ranges of scaled scores that, although common in the general population, may in fact obscure important information about the individual's weaknesses, in particular. It is important to understand that when substantial variation among the scores that make up a global ability obscures important information about an individual's strengths and weaknesses, it does not invalidate the estimate. It simply means that (1) another global ability estimate may provide a better summary of overall intellectual ability; and (2) more attention should be given to the individual's performance on the Primary Index Scales.

Examples of FSIQs That Are Cohesive, but Not Considered Clinically Meaningful

There are times when the FSIQ, although cohesive, masks an individual's unique strengths and/or weaknesses. Consider the two examples reported in Rapid Reference 4.14. Alessandra and Jonathan both have FSIQs of 100. In each case, the difference between the highest and lowest scaled scores that make up the FSIQ is less than 9, indicating that the FSIQ for these children is cohesive, reliable, and valid. Furthermore, in each case the FSIQ is expected to be an accurate predictor of a variety of outcomes for these children, such as overall academic performance. However, upon close examination, it is clear that Alessandra's and Jonathan's scaled scores are quite different from each other.

Alessandra's scaled scores fall within the Average to High Average range of ability and her highest and lowest scaled scores differ only by 1 and 2/3rds standard deviations (5 points), which is common (i.e., occurring in approximately 77% of the population). On the other hand, Jonathan's scaled scores range from Well Below Average to High Average and his highest and lowest scaled scores differ by 2 and 2/3rds standard deviations (8 points), a difference that occurs in about 24%

≡ Rapid Reference 4.14

Two Children With the Same FSIQ but Different Scaled Scores

Composite Subtest	Alessandra	Jonathan
	Standard Score Scaled Score	
FSIQ	**100**	**100**
Vocabulary	11	13
Similarities	9	12
Matrix Reasoning	10	11
Figure Weights	9	10
Block Design	8	13
Digit Span	10	6
Coding	13	5
Difference between highest and lowest scaled score	**5**	**8**

Note: A difference between highest and lowest scaled scores of ≥ 9 occurs in less than 10% of the WISC-V standardization sample and, therefore, is considered rare.

of the population, which is not so common as the difference demonstrated by Alessandra, but it is still considered common. Furthermore, while none of Alessandra's scaled scores suggest a cause for concern, two of Jonathan's do (i.e., 6 on Digit Span and 5 on Coding). Jonathan's low scores on Digit Span and Coding may manifest as weaknesses in working memory and processing speed, respectively, or lower ability to process information efficiently. Weaknesses in working memory and processing speed may interfere with Jonathan's daily academic activities in the classroom, and therefore may require interventions (e.g., accommodations, compensatory strategies) to minimize their effects on his ability to access the curriculum and perform grade level work. Thus, a FSIQ can be reliable and valid, but at the same time mask important differences within and between children.

For this reason, we argue that Alessandra's FSIQ is clinically meaningful (or a good summary of her overall cognitive ability), whereas Jonathan's is much less so. Therefore, the interpretation of his FSIQ should be tempered and his range of cognitive abilities should be understood, reported, and perhaps given more weight than his FSIQ, particularly when addressing specific referral concerns. In other words, despite the fact that the FSIQs for these children are the same (100) *and cohesive*, more weight should be placed on Alessandra's FSIQ as compared to Jonathan's FSIQ because, from a clinical perspective, it is a more *meaningful* summary of her cognitive capabilities as compared to his. From a psychometric perspective, both FSIQs are reliable and valid. Variability in the subtest scaled scores that make up the FSIQ, even when extremely rare, does not alter its reliability or validity, from a *psychometric* perspective, but it does alter the meaning of the FSIQ, from a clinical perspective. The information in Rapid Reference 4.15 is intended to demonstrate this point.

≡ *Rapid Reference 4.15*

Nature and Meaning of Global Ability Composites

Nature of Composite	Reliable[1]	Valid[2]	Meaning
Cohesive; Clinically Meaningful	√	√	The global ability composite provides a good summary of the individual's overall intellectual ability. **FSIQ:** Provides the *best estimate* of overall intellectual ability and is composed of five areas of cognitive ability (i.e., Gc, Gv, Gf, Gsm, and Gs).

Nature of Composite	Reliable[1]	Valid[2]	Meaning
			NVI: Provides an estimate of overall intellectual ability, which minimizes expressive language demands, and is composed of four cognitive abilities (i.e., Gv, Gf, Gsm, and Gs).
			GAI: Provides an estimate of overall intellectual ability, which minimizes working memory and processing speed demands, and is composed of three cognitive abilities (i.e., Gc, Gv, and Gf).
Cohesive; Not Considered Clinically Meaningful	√	√	The variability in scores that make up the global ability composite may obscure meaningful differences in the cognitive abilities that make it up. Global composite may be insufficient to summarize the individual's range of intellectual abilities. Use index and subtest level analysis to assist in understanding strengths and weaknesses.
Not Cohesive	√	√	The variability in scores that make up the global ability composite very likely obscures meaningful differences in the cognitive abilities that make it up. Global composite is insufficient to summarize the individual's range of intellectual abilities. Use index and subtest level analysis to assist in understanding strengths and weaknesses.

[1] The average reliability coefficients for the global ability composites are the highest of all WISC-V scores (i.e., .95 for NVI and .96 for FSIQ and GAI; Wechsler, 2014c, p. 57).

[2] The predictive validity of the global ability composites remains strong regardless of the magnitude of the difference between the highest and lowest scores that make them up (Kaufman, Raiford, & Coalson, 2016; Weiss, Saklofske, Holdnack, & Prifitera, 2016).

DON'T FORGET

Substantial variability among the scaled scores that make up the FSIQ may obscure important information about an individual's strengths and weaknesses. Nevertheless, it is a reliable and valid estimate of overall intellectual ability.

Example of the Decision-Making Process for NVI Versus FSIQ

The WISC-V data reported in Rapid Reference 4.16 were entered into X-BASS for an individual, Alysia, who has difficulties in expressive language and generally below average academic performance relative to same age peers.

Based on these data, X-BASS evaluated cohesion and clinical meaningfulness of the FSIQ and NVI, differences between FSIQ-NVI and NVI-VCI, as well as the direction of those differences (e.g., FSIQ < NVI) and provided a recommendation regarding the best estimate of global ability for Alysia. Alysia's FSIQ is cohesive, but not clinically meaningful and her NVI is cohesive and clinically meaningful. Also, the NVI-FSIQ and NVI-VCI differences are statistically significant and the NVI is higher than the FSIQ and VCI. Given this set of permutations (along with a consideration of which subtest scaled scores may have contributed to these differences), X-BASS provided a recommendation that indicated that the NVI should be considered the best estimate of global ability for Alysia. An example of X-BASS output regarding the best estimate of global ability for Alysia is shown in Figure 4.4.

In summary, there are times when the NVI should be considered in lieu of the FSIQ for some individuals, especially individuals who are ELs, have expressive language difficulties, or are suspected of having a language-related disorder. Deciding on the best estimate of overall intellectual ability for these individuals, NVI or FSIQ, involves a consideration of many factors, such as composite cohesion, clinical meaningfulness of the composite, and differences between

⟰ Rapid Reference 4.16

WISC-V Data for Alysia

FSIQ = 73		NVI = 84	
Similarities	1	Visual Puzzles	9
Vocabulary	3	Picture Span	8
Block Design	8	Block Design	8
Matrix Reasoning	7	Matrix Reasoning	8
Figure Weights	6	Figure Weights	6
Digit Span	8	Coding	9
Coding	9		
Sum of Scaled Scores	**42**	**Sum of Scaled Scores**	**47**

Note: VCI = 55.

Cross-Battery Assessment Software System (X-BASS®) WISC-V® Interpretive Output

NAME: Alysia
DATE OF BIRTH: 5/4/2007
DATE OF EVALUATION: 5/12/2016
GRADE: 4
EVALUATOR: Dr. Smith

DATE OF REPORT: 6/1/2016
SCHOOL: Appleby Elementary
ETHNICITY: Caucasian
FIRST LANGUAGE: English
SECOND LANGUAGE:

GENERAL ABILITY SCORE(S)

Index or Subtest	Score	PR	Normative Category
Full Scale IQ (FSIQ)	73		Well Below Average
Nonverbal Index (NVI)	84		Below Average

RECOMMENDATIONS AND INTERPRETATION: GENERAL ABILITY

The difference between the FSIQ and NVI is statistically significant (p < .05) and the NVI is higher than the FSIQ. The difference between the NVI and the VCI is also significant (p < .01) and the NVI is higher than the VCI. The difference between the NVI and VCI is rare, occuring in only about 1% of the general population. These findings suggest that the subtests with the highest language demands very likely attenuated the FSIQ. Therefore, the NVI should be reported and interpreted as the best estimate of the individual's overall intellectual ability. If a global ability score is needed in a formula or when diagnostic criteria include a cut score, then the NVI should be used. Consider the results of index and subtest level analysis to assist in understanding the NVI > FSIQ difference.

Figure 4.4 Example of X-BASS Output for Determining the Best Estimate of Global Ability for Alysia

composites. Because of the number of permutations involved in considering these factors, only a few examples were presented. The determination of the best estimate of overall intellectual ability is automated in X-BASS.

The GAI as an Alternative to the FSIQ

Just as there are circumstances in which the NVI is considered a viable alternative to the FSIQ as an estimate of overall intellectual ability, there are circumstances in which the GAI may provide a viable alternative to the FSIQ. These circumstances are (1) specific learning disability (SLD) classification and eligibility decisions; (2) gifted and talented placement decisions; and (3) identification of Intellectual Disability (ID). Rapid Reference 4.17 shows that the GAI is made up of five subtests, including all of the subtests that make up the FSIQ, except Digit Span and Coding. The GAI includes measures of three cognitive constructs (Gc, Gv, and Gf), whereas the FSIQ includes measures of five (Gc, Gv, Gf, Gsm, and Gs). Therefore, the GAI may be interpreted as an estimate of overall intellectual ability that minimizes the demands of working memory and processing speed.

Like the NVI, the GAI is highly reliable (.96; Wechsler, 2014c, p. 57) and has a high correlation with the FSIQ (i.e., .96; p. 74).

The GAI and Specific Learning Disability

The GAI was originally developed for use in an ability-achievement discrepancy analysis to minimize the effects of lower cognitive proficiency relative to higher level thinking and reasoning abilities for individuals suspected of having an SLD. Children with neurodevelopmental disorders often have difficulties with cognitive proficiency and frequently demonstrate a GAI > CPI profile (Raiford, Weiss, Rolfhus, & Coalson, 2005, 2008). In general, when cognitive proficiency is lower relative to higher level abilities, the GAI will be higher than the CPI and FSIQ. Therefore, when testing an examinee with lower working memory and/or processing speed relative to crystallized intelligence, visual processing, fluid reasoning, and the GAI should be considered as an alternative to the FSIQ, particularly for use in an ability-achievement discrepancy formula should one be required for SLD determination. That is not to say that lower cognitive proficiency relative to higher level thinking abilities should be ignored, or even that the magnitude of the difference between lower cognitive proficiency compared to other abilities is unusual for a given individual. When the GAI > CPI difference is significant and the GAI > FSIQ difference is significant or unusual, the GAI is simply considered the better score to use in a discrepancy formula if SLD is suspected. Whenever the GAI is selected as an alternative to the FSIQ, the GAI and CPI should be reported and used to explain the GAI > FSIQ difference. Note that the WMI and PSI may also be helpful in explaining GAI > CPI and GAI > FSIQ differences.

DON'T FORGET

Many independent researchers have found that *working memory* displays sensitivity to specific learning disorders, attention-deficit/hyperactivity disorder (ADHD), language disorders, and autism spectrum disorder, and *processing speed* displays sensitivity to specific learning disorders, ADHD, and autism spectrum disorder (e.g., Kaufman et al., 2016, p. 230).

The GAI and Students Who Are Gifted and Talented

Another circumstance in which the GAI may be considered a viable alternative to the FSIQ is for placement decisions for gifted and talented programs. Individuals of high ability often perform *relatively* lower on measures of working memory and processing speed. For example, in the Intellectually Gifted special group study included in the *WISC-V Technical and Interpretive Manual* (Wechsler, 2014c), 34% had GAI > FSIQ discrepancies and 72% had GAI > CPI discrepancies (p. 167). These data show that working memory and processing speed are not typically the strongest areas of performance for individuals of high intellectual ability. Base rates for the WISC-V normative sample obtaining PSI < FSIQ and WMI < FSIQ also support this finding. For example, Rapid Reference 4.17 shows that at lower levels of ability, small differences between PSI and FSIQ (i.e., 2 points) and WMI and FSIQ (i.e., 4 points) are unusual, occurring in about 10% or less of the normative sample. However, at higher ability levels, much larger differences are needed to be considered unusual for these same comparisons—that is, approximately 25–30 points! For example, for an individual whose overall ability is ≥ 120, a PSI that is 30 points lower than the FSIQ is unusual. This means that *large PSI < FSIQ differences of 20–25 points, for example, are common among high ability individuals.* Rapid Reference 4.17 shows the same trend for WMI < FSIQ differences. That is, the higher the overall ability level, the greater the variability between the WMI and the FSIQ. Therefore, the finding of a FSIQ of 125 and a PSI and WMI of 106 and 107, respectively, is not atypical and should not be construed as anything other than *normal variation* because large PSI < FSIQ and WMI < FSIQ differences are common among high functioning individuals in the WISC-V standardization sample.

≡ *Rapid Reference 4.17*

Standard Score Differences Between Selected Composites Occurring in ≤ 10% of the WISC-V Normative Sample

FSIQ Ability Level	PSI < FSIQ	WMI < FSIQ	GAI > CPI	GAI > FSIQ
≤ 79	2	4	6	6
80–89	9	7	8	4
90–109	15	14	16	6
110–119	21	17	24	7
≥ 120	30	23	28	6
Overall Sample	**18**	**15**	**18**	**6**

Source: WISC-V Administration and Scoring Manual (Wechsler, 2014a); *WISC-V Administration and Scoring Manual Supplement* (Wechsler, 2014b).

Rapid Reference 4.17 also shows that relatively large GAI > CPI differences are common in individuals of high intellectual ability. That is, the higher the individual's ability level, the more common it is to find large GAI > CPI differences. Interestingly, however, the same trend is not seen for GAI > FSIQ differences. That is, regardless of ability level, a GAI > FSIQ difference of around 6 points is unusual. Taken together, however, it seems clear that in many circumstances use of a FSIQ instead of a GAI might exclude an individual from a gifted and talented program due to the attenuating effects of relatively lower Gs and Gsm on the FSIQ, which is not something we support if the GAI meets the cut off for program inclusion. Our rationale follows.

There are likely many plausible reasons for relatively lower Gs and Gsm performance as compared to Gf, Gc, and Gv performance for individuals of high intellectual ability. For example, many of these individuals have a methodical and reflective approach to tasks and often value accuracy over speed (despite the test directions' implied need for speed), which may affect their performance on processing speed tasks in particular. Notwithstanding, the best explanation for the larger PSI < FSIQ, WMI < FSIQ, and CPI < GAI patterns in individuals of high intellectual ability as compared to lower levels of ability is related to a *threshold effect*. That is, a certain amount of working memory and processing speed is necessary to perform higher-level thinking and reasoning tasks reasonably well to exceedingly well. However, beyond that threshold, working memory and processing speed add little to the individual's capacity to think and reason. Richard Woodcock described this effect nearly 30 years ago when he likened Gs to a valve in a water pipe (Woodcock, 1990). The inference was that the valve did not need to be wide open for the individual to think and reason well, but if the valve was not open *wide enough*, thinking and reasoning abilities would be compromised. Thus, it would appear that when Gsm and Gs (or the CPI) are at least solidly Average (at the threshold), higher-level thinking and reasoning abilities are likely not compromised. The normative data for the WISC-V appear to support this threshold effect.

Many individuals with overall intellectual ability estimated to be greater than 120 perform in the Average range on tests of cognitive proficiency. About 40% of the of the normative sample with overall ability of ≥ 120 has a GAI > CPI difference of 1SD (or 15 points). Nevertheless, there is a tendency to believe that individuals of high intellectual ability who have a significant GAI > CPI discrepancy are somehow impaired, even when the CPI is solidly Average (see Lovett & Sparks, 2010). Any deviation from an *average* CPI in the positive direction (i.e., a higher GAI) is a *valuable* deviation. Such discrepancies are not indicative of impairment. *Impairment* would typically be a hypothesis only when either

Gsm Gs, or both fell below average relative to same age peers in the general population.

Based on the data related to individuals who are of high ability, it seems reasonable to allow the use of a GAI instead of a FSIQ for gifted and talented placement decisions when they demonstrate a GAI > CPI and GAI > FSIQ pattern *and* their PSI and WMI are at least average. In fact, some test developers provide an overall intellectual ability score that *deliberately* emphasizes problem-solving and deemphasizes processing speed and memory for the reasons stated here. For example, the *Reynolds Intellectual Ability Scales-Second Edition* (RIAS-2; Reynolds & Kamphaus, 2016) provides a Composite Intelligence Index (CIX) based on four subtests only, two that measure reasoning with visual information (Gf) and two that measure reasoning with verbal information (Gc). The CIX is conceptually similar to the GAI and is used in SLD identification and gifted placement decisions (Reynolds & Kamphaus).

DON'T FORGET

Use GAI instead of FSIQ for gifted and talented placement decisions when the individual demonstrates a GAI > CPI and GAI > FSIQ pattern and his or her PSI and WMI are at least solidly average.

The GAI and Students with Intellectual Disability

In addition to suspected learning disability identification decisions and gifted and talented placement decisions, for example, the GAI may be considered a viable alternative to the FISQ in cases of suspected intellectual disability (ID). The WMI-FSIQ and PSI-FSIQ differences reveal an opposite pattern for individuals at the lower end of the ability continuum as compared to the higher end. For example, although it is common to see large PSI < FSIQ differences in individuals with high ability, it is common to see large PSI > FSIQ in individuals with low ability. A PSI > FSIQ difference of approximately 20 points occurs in about one out of every four individuals at the lowest ability level in the normative sample (i.e., $\leq$ 79) and therefore is quite common. Likewise, a WMI > FSIQ difference of about 15 points occurs in about one out of every five individuals in the same low ability range and is also common (Wechsler, 2014a, Table B.2, p. 344). A review of the literature on Wechsler subtest scores for individuals with ID showed that their highest scores are often on Processing Speed subtests, as well as tasks requiring rote recall of information (e.g., Digit Span; see Kaufman et al., 2016), which is consistent with the WISC-V normative base rates. For example, approximately 30% of individuals with a low FSIQ (i.e., ≤ 79) have a 15-point CPI > GAI difference as compared to only 13% of individuals with Average ability (90–109) and less than 1% of individuals with high ability (i.e., ≥ 120). These findings suggest that individuals of low ability may have a significant or unusual FSIQ > GAI difference (i.e., 3 points at $p < .05$, 6 points at about a 10% base rate, respectively) due to relatively higher performance on Gsm and Gs subtests, which have relatively lower g-loadings, especially Gs subtests. In order to avoid a situation where an ID or other developmental disorder is missed, when the FSIQ > GAI difference is significant, the GAI should be considered a reliable and valid estimate of overall intellectual ability for the individual (see McGrew, 2015, for a thorough discussion of part scores as they relate to the identification of ID).

The manner in which this first interpretive step evaluates WISC-V data to determine whether the GAI may be a viable alternative to the FSIQ takes into consideration the issues just raised (e.g., differences in performance on Gsm and Gs for individuals of different ability levels). Additionally, like the steps outlined for determining whether the NVI may be a viable alternative to the FSIQ, the steps for considering the viability of the GAI as an alternative to the FSIQ evaluate cohesion and clinical meaningfulness and take into account differences between composites (e.g., FSIQ, GAI, CPI) and the direction of those differences. Therefore, there are well over 20 possible summary statements produced by X-BASS to assist the user in making decisions with regard to the best estimate of overall ability, FSIQ or GAI (or both), when these two composites, the CPI, and the 10 subtests that make up the Primary Index Scales are entered into the program. The steps outlined in Rapid Reference 4.12 are quite similar to those involved when considering whether the GAI is a viable alternative to the FSIQ. Therefore, similar steps will not be repeated here. Rather, WISC-V data for four students, Amanda (from Rapid Reference 4.2), Rhonda, Omar, and Beth (from Rapid Reference 4.18) are used to demonstrate the decision-making process regarding the viability of the GAI as an alternative estimate of overall intellectual ability and the summary statement produced by X-BASS is displayed.

Amanda: Referred for Suspected Learning Disability
Based on the data in Rapid Reference 4.18, X-BASS classified Amanda's FSIQ and GAI according to cohesion and clinical meaningfulness. For the FSIQ and GAI, the difference between Amanda's highest scaled score of 10 and her lowest scaled score of 6 (i.e., 4 points) meets criteria for cohesion (i.e., < 9 points for FSIQ and < 8 points for GAI) and clinical meaningfulness (i.e., < 5 points). Also, the differences between Amanda's GAI and CPI and GAI and FSIQ are not

≡ Rapid Reference 4.18

WISC-V Data for Four 8-year-olds Referred for Different Reasons

Subtest Composite	Amanda	Rhonda	Omar	Beth
			Scaled Scores Composites (90% Confidence Interval)	
Vocabulary	10	4	12	15
Similarities	10	3	10	16
Block Design	6	5	10	14
Matrix Reasoning	9	3	9	13
Figure Weights	10	4	8	16
Digit Span	8	9	6	10
Coding	8	10	8	9
Picture Span	7	6	7	12
Symbol Search	9	8	9	11
FSIQ	91	70 (66–76)	93 (89–98)	124 (118–128)
GAI	94	63 (60–69)	99 (94–104)	130 (124–134)
CPI	85	87 (82–94)	82 (77–89)	104 (98–110)
Visual Puzzles[1]	7	5	10	13

Note: Shaded area includes subtests that are part of the CPI.
[1]This subtest is not included in the calculation of any composite listed in this table.

statistically significant. Her GAI > CPI difference occurs in about 25% of the population of individuals at her ability level and the GAI > FSIQ difference occurs in almost 30% of the population. Based on these data, there is little justification for using the GAI over the FSIQ as the best estimate of Amanda's overall intellectual ability. As such, the interpretation statement produced by X-BASS for Amanda is as follows:

The FSIQ and GAI each provides a good summary of Amanda's cognitive abilities. However, the FSIQ-GAI difference is not unusual and the GAI-CPI difference is not statistically significant. Therefore, the FSIQ is considered the best estimate of Amanda's overall intellectual ability because it summarizes a broader range of abilities as compared to the GAI. If a global ability score is needed in a formula or when diagnostic criteria include a cut score, then the FSIQ should be used.

Rhonda: Referred for General Learning Difficulties

Based on the data in Rapid Reference 4.18, X-BASS classified Rhonda's FSIQ and GAI according to cohesion and clinical meaningfulness. For the FSIQ, the difference between Rhonda's highest scaled score of 10 and her lowest scaled score of 3 (i.e., 7 points) meets criteria for cohesion (i.e., < 9), but not clinical meaningfulness. That is, although a difference of 7 points between Rhonda's highest and lowest scaled scores that make up the FSIQ is common, occurring in almost 40% of the population, it is not considered clinically meaningful (see second table in Rapid Reference 4.12). This is because important information about Rhonda's strengths are obscured by her FSIQ of 70. Rhonda's GAI is cohesive and clinically meaningful. Rhonda's CPI > GAI and FSIQ > GAI differences are statistically significant and unusual, occurring in less than 10% of the population. Based on these data, it appears that Coding, a low *g*-loaded subtest, contributed to the FSIQ > GAI difference. To avoid a Type 2 error (not identifying ID when, in fact, it is present), the GAI is considered the best estimate of overall intellectual ability in this case. As such, the interpretation statement produced by X-BASS for Rhonda is as follows:

> The variability among the scores that comprise the FSIQ may obscure important information about Rhonda's strengths and weaknesses. By comparison, the variation in scores that comprise the GAI is not substantial, indicating that it is a good summary of Rhonda's overall intellectual ability. Performance on a test of processing speed and/or working memory led to more substantial variation in scores that comprise the FSIQ as compared to the GAI. This finding is supported by the statistically significant CPI > GAI difference ($p < .01$) and the unusual FSIQ > GAI difference, which occurs in less than 10% of same age peers from the general population. These findings indicate that relatively higher performance on one or more tests of cognitive proficiency resulted in a higher FSIQ as compared to GAI. However, because Rhonda's performance on lower *g*-loaded tests (mainly processing speed) as compared to higher g-loaded tests, like the ones that make up the GAI led to a higher FSIQ than GAI. In order to avoid a situation where an intellectual disability or other developmental disorder is missed, the GAI is considered the best estimate of Rhonda's overall intellectual ability. When an overall intellectual ability score is needed for a formula or when diagnostic criteria include a cut score, the GAI should be used unless clinical judgment suggests otherwise. Index level analysis should also be used to assist in understanding FSIQ > GAI and CPI > GAI differences.

Omar: Referred for Suspect Learning Disability

Based on the data in Rapid Reference 4.18, X-BASS classified Omar's FSIQ and GAI according to cohesion and clinical meaningfulness. For the FSIQ, the difference between Omar's highest scaled score of 12 and his lowest scaled score of 6 (i.e., 6 points) meets criteria for cohesion (i.e., < 9), but not clinical meaningfulness. That is, although a difference of 6 points between Omar's highest and lowest scaled scores that make up the FSIQ is common, occurring in almost 60% of the population, it is not considered clinically meaningful (see second table in Rapid Reference 4.12). This is because important information about Omar's weaknesses is obscured by his FSIQ of 93. Omar's GAI of 99 is cohesive and clinically meaningful. Furthermore, his GAI > CPI and GAI > FSIQ differences are statistically significant and unusual, occurring in less than 10% of the population. Based on these data, it is clear that Omar's lower cognitive proficiency attenuated his FSIQ. To avoid a Type 2 error (not identifying SLD when, in fact, it is present), the GAI is considered the best estimate of overall intellectual ability in this case. As such, the interpretation statement produced by X-BASS for Omar is as follows:

> The variability among the scores that comprise the FSIQ may obscure important information about Omar's strengths and weaknesses. By comparison, the variation in scores that comprise the GAI is not substantial, indicating that it is a good summary of Omar's overall intellectual ability. Performance on a test of processing speed and/or working memory led to more substantial variation in scores that comprise the FSIQ as compared to the GAI. This finding is supported by the statistically significant difference ($p < .01$) between the GAI and CPI. Because the difference between the FSIQ and GAI is unusual, occurring in less than 10% of same age peers from the general population, and the FSIQ is lower than the GAI, cognitive proficiency (estimated by the CPI to be below average) constrained the FSIQ. Analysis of the WMI and PSI will assist in understanding Omar's cognitive proficiency and how it may affect his general reasoning ability adversely. The GAI is considered the best estimate of Omar's overall intellectual ability. Nevertheless, the FSIQ should be reported and the GAI and CPI should be used, along with the results of index and subtest level analysis, to assist in explaining the FSIQ < GAI difference. The GAI should be used for diagnostic decisions, specifically when an overall intellectual ability score is needed for a formula or when diagnostic criteria include a cut score, unless clinical judgment suggests otherwise.

Beth: Referred for Gifted and Talented Program

Based on the data in Rapid Reference 4.18, X-BASS classified Beth's FSIQ and GAI as cohesive and clinically meaningful. This indicates that both composites provide a good summary of Beth's overall intellectual ability, with the FSIQ representing a broader range of abilities as compared to the GAI. Furthermore, Beth's GAI > CPI and GAI > FSIQ differences are statistically significant ($p < .01$), but not unusual. The significant differences between Beth's GAI of 130 and her CPI (106) and FSIQ (125) are the result of *relatively* lower cognitive proficiency performance as compared to higher level thinking and reasoning performance. However, it seems clear that Beth's cognitive proficiency enables her to think and reason at a level that is Extremely Above Average relative to her same-age peers (GAI of 130). Because Beth demonstrates a GAI > CPI and GAI > FSIQ pattern *and* her PSI (100) and WMI (110) are at least average, the GAI is considered a viable alternative to the FSIQ for summarizing overall intellectual ability, particularly for the purpose of gifted and talented placement decisions. Use of the GAI may serve to reduce a Type 2 error (not identifying Gifted and Talented, when in fact, it is present). As such, the interpretation statement produced by X-BASS for Beth is as follows:

> The FSIQ and the GAI each provides a good summary of Beth's cognitive abilities, although her FSIQ summarizes a broader range of abilities as compared to her GAI. Beth demonstrated GAI > CPI and GAI > FSIQ differences that were statistically significant ($p < .01$), although not unusual. These findings indicate that relatively lower performance on one or more tests of cognitive proficiency resulted in a lower FSIQ as compared to GAI. Nevertheless, Beth's cognitive proficiency performance, including processing speed (PSI of 100) and working memory (WMI of 110) ranged from Average to High Average, respectively. This pattern of performance suggests that, although Beth's CPI is relatively lower than her GAI, she is proficient at processing information necessary for learning, problem-solving, and higher level thinking and reasoning, as demonstrated by her GAI of 130. To avoid a situation where intellectually gifted is missed, the GAI should be used when an overall intellectual ability score is needed. Index and subtest level analysis should also be used to assist in understanding FSIQ > GAI and CPI > GAI differences.

CAUTION

The first step of the WISC-V interpretive approach focused on the global ability scores only and referenced which ones may make the most sense to consider when individuals are referred due to suspicion of various disorders, mainly SLD and ID, or when an individual is referred for consideration for placement in a gifted and talented program. However, one or two global scores will never (and should never) be sufficient to identify any disorder or make any placement decision. Multiple data sources, gathered through multiple methods, must be compiled and demonstrate a convergence of indicators that support the practitioner's or team's decision.

Analysis of WISC-V data for the purpose of determining the best estimate of overall ability was presented in this step. In the process of determining whether either the NVI or the GAI may be considered a viable alternative to the FSIQ in certain circumstances, we attempted to blend the art and science of interpretation. Specifically, we adhered closely to issues of reliability, validity, composite cohesion, and statistical significance and rarity of score differences. In addition, we attended to the variability among the scores that comprise the global ability composites. In this regard, we provided criteria for determining whether the difference between the highest and lowest scaled scores that comprise the composite is clinically meaningful, indicating that the composite is not likely to obscure important information about an individual's strengths and weaknesses. Nevertheless, determining which global ability score(s) to report is a first step on the road to understanding an individual's cognitive capabilities. Many of the summary statements produced by X-BASS with regard to global ability scores suggested that differences between composites be explained using the results of index level analysis, which is the next step in our interpretive method.

Step 2. Analyze the Primary Index Scores

Analysis of the Primary index scores is a critical, and arguably necessary, component of WISC-V interpretation. Rapid Reference 4.19 summarizes the WISC-V's five Primary Index Scales, namely Verbal Comprehension, Visual Spatial, Fluid Reasoning, Working Memory, and Processing Speed, which yield the following scores, VCI, VSI, FRI, WMI, and PSI, respectively.

≡ Rapid Reference 4.19

Summary of the Five Primary Index Scores on the WISC-V

Index	Subtests	Reliability of Composite
Verbal Comprehension	Similarities Vocabulary	.92
Visual Spatial	Block Design Visual Puzzles	.92
Fluid Reasoning	Matrix Reasoning Figure Weights	.93
Working Memory	Digit Span Picture Span	.92
Processing Speed	Coding Symbol Search	.88

Note: Substitutions are not permitted for any of the primary index scores. Overall average reliability coefficients are reported in this table (*WISC-V Technical and Interpretive Manual*, Wechsler, 2014c, p. 57).

Analysis of the Primary index scores involves a consideration of three main factors. First, it is important to consider what the Primary Index Scales measure from a theoretical standpoint. Based on the underlying construct measured and the breadth of that measurement, it is necessary to decide if additional measures might be necessary to broaden the evaluation of a particular cognitive construct in a manner that may more adequately address the referral. Second, when the two subtests that make up a scale are administered, it is important to consider whether their respective scaled scores form a cohesive composite. Third, regardless of index cohesion, it is important to consider whether follow up assessment is necessary based on an analysis of where scaled scores within an index fall relative to each other and to most people. X-BASS analyzes each of these factors and then provides guidance regarding Primary index score interpretation. These factors are discussed next.

CHC Broad and Narrow Abilities Measured by Primary Index Scales

As stated at the outset of this book, our interpretation of the WISC-V is based primarily on CHC theory. A brief summary of CHC theory is found in Appendix A. Rapid Reference 4.20 shows the broad and narrow CHC abilities that are measured by the Primary Index Scales along with a brief definition of each broad ability. A composite or index provides an estimate of a *broad* ability when it consists of two or more measures that represent two or more qualitatively different aspects of the broad ability. A composite provides an estimate of a *narrow* ability when it is made up of two or more measures of the same narrow ability. Generally speaking, subtests represent narrow abilities and composites represent broad abilities. Although subtests are never really "pure" measures of any one ability, they are typically designed to measure mainly one, such as Induction (I) or General Sequential (Deductive) Reasoning (RG). The aggregate of subtest scaled scores that purport to measure *different* narrow abilities within the *same* broad cognitive ability domain yields a broad ability composite (e.g., Fluid Reasoning [Gf]). For example, because Matrix Reasoning measures mainly the narrow ability of I and Figure Weights (FW) measures mainly the narrow ability of RG, the FRI is best interpreted as a measure of the broad ability of Gf. However, because Block Design and Visual Puzzles each measures the narrow ability of Visualization (Vz), the VSI is best interpreted as a measure of the narrow Vz ability, rather than the broad ability of Visual Processing (Gv).

≡ *Rapid Reference 4.20*

CHC Broad and Narrow Abilities Measured by Primary Index Scales

Index Subtest	Broad Ability Narrow Ability	Description of Broad Ability[1]
VCI	**Gc**	*Crystallized intelligence* (Gc) refers to a person's knowledge base (or general fund of information) that has built up over time, beginning in infancy. It is like your own personal library or everything you know. Crystallized intelligence involves knowledge of one's culture (e.g., Who is the president of the United States?) as well as verbal- or language-based knowledge that has been developed during general life experiences, and formal schooling (e.g., understanding
Similarities	**VL, Gf: I**	
Vocabulary	**VL**	

(continued)

(continued)

Index Subtest	Broad Ability Narrow Ability	Description of Broad Ability[1]
		words and their meaning; understanding street signs, knowledge of current events and the history of the United States). Having well developed or good Crystallized intelligence means that one understands and uses language well, has an average or better vocabulary, has good listening skills, and is able to use language well via verbal expression. These abilities are important for reading, particularly reading comprehension. Children with below average Crystallized intelligence may have a hard time understanding what they read because they don't know what the words mean or they haven't had the life experiences that are needed to understand the words. It is important for children who are below average in this ability to work on improving it. The best way to do this is through activities that involve reading, such as going to the library. Also helpful are activities such as watching educational programs, playing educational games, and listening and following along to others reading. When children read, they build their vocabulary and knowledge base. When vocabulary and knowledge grows, reading improves.

Index Subtest	Broad Ability Narrow Ability	Description of Broad Ability[1]
FRI	**Gf**	***Fluid Intelligence*** (Gf) refers to a type of thinking that an individual may use when faced with a relatively new task that cannot be performed automatically. This type of thinking includes such things as forming and recognizing concepts (e.g., How are a dog, cat, and cow alike?), identifying and perceiving relationships (e.g., Sun is to morning as moon is to *night*), drawing inferences (e.g., after reading a story, answering the question "What will John do next?"), and reorganizing or transforming information (e.g., selecting one of several pictures to complete a puzzle). Overall, this ability can be thought of as a *problem-solving* type of intelligence. Problem solving is important for reading comprehension (e.g., making inferences from text), math (e.g., figuring out how to set up a math problem by using information provided in a word problem), and writing (e.g., a persuasive essay).
Matrix Reasoning	I	
Figure Weights	RG, RQ	
VSI	**Gv**	***Visual processing*** (Gv) is an individual's ability to think about visual patterns (e.g., What is the shortest route from your house to school?) and visual images (e.g., What would this shape look like if I turned it upside down?). This type of ability also involves generating, perceiving, and analyzing visual patterns and visual information (e.g., Which three shapes go together to make this shape?). Additional examples of this
Block Design	Vz	
Visual Puzzles	Vz	

(continued)

(continued)

Index Subtest	Broad Ability Narrow Ability	Description of Broad Ability[1]
		type of ability include putting puzzles together, completing a maze (such as the ones often seen on children's menus in restaurants), and interpreting a graph or chart. This type of visual processing is important when doing advanced math (e.g., geometry). But, visual processing is also important for reading because it is the type of ability that helps us automatically say "T" when we see that letter, and say "ball" when we see that word. Understanding what we see (letters and words on a page) is the part of visual processing that is important for reading.
WMI Digit Span Picture Span	**Gsm** MW,MS MS,MW	**Short-term memory** (Gsm) is the ability to hold information in one's mind and then use it within a few seconds. The most common example of short-term memory is holding a phone number in one's mind long enough to dial it. Working memory is also part of the short-term memory system and involves manipulating or transforming information and using it in some way (e.g., saying the months of the year backwards). A child with short-term memory difficulties may have a hard time following directions, understanding long reading passages (e.g., a story read aloud by the teacher), spelling, sounding out words, and doing math problems (e.g., remembering the steps required to solve long math problems: first multiply, then

Index Subtest	Broad Ability Narrow Ability	Description of Broad Ability[1]
		add, then subtract). Children who have difficulties with short-term memory do better when they are taught how to use strategies to help them remember things. For example, if a child has difficulty remembering the order of operations in a long division math problem, teach the child to say "Dad, Mom, Sister, and Brother." The first letter of each person represents an operation for long division in the correct order (i.e., Divide, Multiply, Subtract, Bring-down).
PSI Coding Symbol Search	**Gs** R9 P	***Processing speed*** (Gs) refers to an individual's ability to perform simple clerical tasks quickly, especially when under pressure to maintain attention and concentration. It can also be thought of as how quickly one can think or how quickly one can take simple tests that require simple decisions. For example, how quickly an individual can cross out all of the letter A's when they are embedded in multiple rows of scrambled letters is a measure of processing speed. Processing speed in important during all school years, particularly the elementary school years. Slow processing speed may interfere with reading because the rapid processing of letters and words is necessary for fluent reading. Slow processing speed may also lead to difficulties in math and writing because basic skills in these areas must

(continued)

(continued)		
Index Subtest	**Broad Ability Narrow Ability**	**Description of Broad Ability[1]**
		be automatic (i.e., performed without much thought) before higher level skills in these areas can be carried out effectively (e.g., understanding what you read).

Note: I = Induction; RG = General Sequential Reasoning; RQ = Quantitative Reasoning; MS = Memory Span; MW = Working Memory; Vz = Visualization; P = Perceptual Speed; R9 = Rate-of-Test-Taking; VL = Lexical Knowledge; K0 = General (Verbal) Information.

[1]These descriptions are general and purposefully simplistic so as to be relevant for a wide audience (e.g., parents, teachers). In some cases, the Primary Index Scales will need to be expanded upon with other measures to align more closely with the definition presented or the definition will need to be scaled back to align more closely with the specific aspects of the broad abilities the Primary Index Scales measure. For example, expanding upon the VCI via the administration of the Information and Comprehension subtests would result in the Verbal (Expanded Crystallized) Index (VECI), which is a much better estimate of Gc than the VCI. Therefore, the Gc definition in this table is a better description of the VECI as compared to the VCI.

It is important to understand that broad ability classifications are driven mainly by factor analysis and narrow ability classifications are driven mainly by expert consensus (or content validity studies; see Flanagan, Alfonso, & Reynolds, 2013, for a discussion). While these classifications assist in generating hypotheses about an individual's functioning in important cognitive domains, they are only really starting points—indeed valuable and necessary starting points—and mainly serve to guide our understanding of an individual's cognitive functioning.

Because CHC classifications are based on *group* data (e.g., large standardization samples), they may not be true to form for an *individual.* The cognitive abilities and processes that an examinee brings to bear on his or her approach to solving items on a given subtest may contraindicate group data. For example, an examinee with an average vocabulary, but a Well Above Average ability to reason, may perform in the Average range on the Vocabulary subtest, but in the Well Above Average range on the Similarities subtest. Why didn't this examinee perform about the same on Vocabulary *and* Similarities? After all, they are both measures of the Gc narrow ability of Lexical Knowledge (VL) and the VCI is interpreted mainly as an estimate of word knowledge (Wechsler, 2014a). To answer this question, the task demands of each subtest should be considered carefully.

As items on the Similarities subtest become more difficult, it is not necessarily because the vocabulary increased in difficulty but rather because the level of abstraction required to answer the question "How are these two things similar?" increased in difficulty. An examinee who can reason exceptionally well may earn a much higher scaled score on Similarities compared to Vocabulary because he or she brings much more to the Similarities task than his or her word knowledge. For example, he or she may bring an excellent ability to reason abstractly and form concepts as well as cognitive flexibility and well-developed associative and categorical thinking. To treat both subtests (Vocabulary and Similarities) as largely measures of VL for this examinee is to fail to understand why Similarities was significantly higher than Vocabulary. Indeed, this examinee's performance on the Similarities subtest is described best as his or her ability to *reason* with verbal information, rather than simply to understand words and their meaning. Although for some examinees, the underlying construct for the Similarities subtest may indeed be VL. When tests do not necessarily behave in a manner suggested by group data, it is the job of the practitioner to figure out why. This quest leads us away from the subtest classification per se (i.e., Gc:VL) and forces us to consider the individual's functioning across a broad range of abilities and processes in an attempt to understand the difference. This process is explained well in Chapter 6. By understanding the reason(s) for unexpected findings, we gain insight into how the individual is smart as well as why the individual may struggle in the learning process—a primary reason for administering the WISC-V.

Rapid Reference 4.20 shows that Similarities has a secondary classification of Gf:I, which makes sense given the demands of the task, particularly at higher item difficulty levels. When scaled scores on Vocabulary and Similarities do not converge as expected, then a logical hypothesis would be related to the individual's ability to reason inductively. However, in the multitude of exploratory and confirmatory factor analytic studies that have been conducted over several decades, Similarities has never loaded on a Gf factor (see Flanagan et al., 2013, for a review). This finding does not mean that Similarities does not require inductive reasoning for optimal performance. Rather, it means that different sources of validity evidence are necessary to assist in understanding what abilities and processes are involved in answering subtest items correctly (e.g., content validity, response processes), along with a qualitative analysis of the individual's responses (see Chapter 6 for numerous examples of the latter).

A Note About Construct Representation

Classifications of cognitive ability tests according to content, format, and task demand at the narrow ability level improve upon the validity of intellectual assessment and interpretation (see Messick, 1989). In other words, narrow ability classifications of subtests are important. Specifically, narrow ability classifications help to ensure that the CHC constructs that underlie assessments are adequately represented (Flanagan et al., 2013; McGrew & Flanagan, 1998). According to Messick (1995), *construct underrepresentation* is present when an "assessment is too narrow and fails to include important dimensions or facets of the construct" (p. 742).

Interpreting the VSI, which is made up of the Block Design and Visual Puzzles subtests—each a measure of the narrow Gv ability of Visualization (Vz)—as a measure of Visual Processing (i.e., the *broad* Gv ability) is an example of construct underrepresentation. This is because Vz measures one narrow aspect of Gv. At least one additional Gv measure (i.e., subtest) that is qualitatively different from Vz is necessary to include in an assessment to ensure adequate representation of the Gv construct (e.g., a measure of Visual Memory [MV]). Two or more qualitatively different indicators (i.e., measures of two or more narrow abilities subsumed by the broad ability) are needed for *adequate construct representation* (see Comrey, 1988; Keith & Reynolds, 2012; McGrew & Flanagan, 1998; Messick, 1989, 1995). Rapid Reference 4.21 provides information about the construct representation of the Primary Index Scales.

It has been many years since we began recommending that assessments include measure of *broad* CHC abilities (e.g., Flanagan & McGrew, 1997; Flanagan & Oritz, 2001; Flanagan, Oritz, & Alfonso, 2007; McGrew & Flanagan, 1998; McGrew, Flanagan, & Ortiz, 2000). We have continued in our writings to emphasize the importance of adequate representation of broad CHC ability domains in comprehensive evaluations, particularly because it is important to sample functioning broadly across many cognitive domains in an attempt to understand whether cognitive abilities and processes are impacting real-world activities (e.g., reading, math, writing, learning) adversely. In other words, a broad sampling of functioning that includes a measure of Induction and a measure of General Sequential (Deductive) Reasoning that reveals average ability on both measures most likely suggests that the broad ability of Gf is at least average and therefore the individual's ability to reason probably does not inhibit learning and achievement. However, if the individual was referred in the 5th grade for a suspected learning disability in math, such an evaluation may have missed something. Specifically, a thorough assessment of Gf in this case would require evaluation of the individual's Quantitative Reasoning (RQ)—another narrow Gf ability. Evaluation of RQ may be necessary in this case to tease out whether the individual's math difficulties are related to basic skills acquisition and development, fluency with numbers, or higher level *thinking and reasoning* with numbers, the latter of which was not initially included in the assessment of Gf in this example. This example suggests that attention to both the broad and narrow abilities measured by a battery like the WISC-V is important to ensure that referral questions are addressed sufficiently.

≡ Rapid Reference 4.21

Construct Representation of the WISC-V Primary Index Scales

Index	Construct Representation	Comment
VCI	VL only; Underrepresented	The WISC-V contains two secondary subtests, Information and Comprehension, that when administered can be used to derive a *broad* estimate of Crystallized Intelligence (Gc). These subtests measure General (Verbal) Information (K0) and are used to derive the Verbal (Expanded Crystallized) index (VECI), the Verbal Expression-Low (Gc-VE/L) clinical composite and the Verbal Expression-High (Gc-VE/H) clinical composite. The VECI provides the broadest and most comprehensive estimate of Gc. Importantly, while the VCI may underrepresent the Gc construct, the WISC-V does not.
VSI	Vz only; Underrepresented	Vz is the most commonly assessed narrow Gv ability among tests of intelligence and cognitive abilities. If a broad Gv composite is desired, then it is necessary to administer a test or tests from another battery. Although the broad ability of Gv consists of many narrow abilities (see Appendix A), the most commonly measured Gv narrow ability, second to Vz, is Visual Memory. A list of all Gv subtests, including those that measure Visual Memory, is found on the "XBA-CHC Test List" tab of X-BASS[1]. Expanding upon the VSI by administering measures of Gv other than Vz *may not* be necessary in all assessments. Consideration of the reason for referral and the relations between Gv narrow abilities and specific academic skills, for example, is necessary to determine whether measurement of Gv should be expanded. See Chapter 7 for more guidance.

(continued)

(*continued*)

Index	Construct Representation	Comment
FRI	I, RG, RQ; Adequate Representation	The WISC-V contains two subtests that are also classified as Gf by the test authors, namely Picture Concepts and Arithmetic. These subtests along with Matrix Reasoning and Figure Weights may be used to derive the Expanded Fluid Index (EFI). However, Picture Concepts also involves Gc to a substantial degree and Arithmetic involves working memory and math achievement. Therefore, the FRI is very likely a purer measure of Gf as compared to the EFI. For most purposes, the FRI should be considered the best estimate of Gf on the WISC-V.
WMI	MS, WM; Adequate Representation	Though the WMI provides an adequate representation of Gsm, there are alternative clinical composites that may enhance an examiner's understanding of the examinee's memory. An alternative working memory composite (Gsm-MW [Alt]) may be derived from Digit Span Backward (DSb), Digit Span Sequencing (DSs), and Letter-Number Sequencing (LNS), in cases where Digit Span Forward (DSf) is significantly higher than DSb and DSs. A Memory Span-Working Memory (Gsm-MS, MW) clinical composite may be derived from DSf and DSb. And, a working memory composite made up of memory tests that appear to have the highest degree of cognitive complexity may be derived from Arithmetic and Picture Span. The latter clinical composite is called Working Memory (Cognitive Complexity-High) or WM-CC/H.
PSI	R9, P; Adequate Representation	Though the PSI provides an adequate representation of Gs, there is an alternative Perceptual Speed (Gs-P) clinical composite that may be derived from Symbol Search and Cancellation. This clinical composite reduces the memory and motor dexterity demands inherent mainly on the Coding subtest.

Note: The clinical composites referenced in this rapid reference are discussed in the last step of the WISC-V interpretive approach.

[1]The XBA-CHC Test List tab includes more than 1,000 subtests classified according CHC broad and narrow ability domains.

When intelligence tests and cognitive batteries began providing better representation of broad CHC abilities (see Alfonso, Flanagan, & Radwan, 2005, for a discussion), research was mounting, showing that specific narrow abilities were related to specific skills in reading, math, and writing, for example (see summaries by Flanagan, Alfonso, Mascolo, McDonough, & Sotelo-Dynega, in press; McDonough, Flanagan, Sy, & Alfonso, in press; McGrew & Wendling, 2010; Niileksela, Reynolds, Keith, & McGrew, 2016). In light of this research, it no longer seems critically important that *all* the major cognitive domains assessed by intelligence and cognitive batteries (i.e., Gc, Gf, Gv, Gsm, Glr, Gs, Ga) be represented *broadly* via at least two subtests that measure qualitatively different aspects of the cognitive domain. Rather, it seems more important to understand (1) whether composites represent a broad or a narrow ability such that appropriate inferences may be drawn from test scores; and (2) whether the battery provides adequate measurement of the abilities and processes that research shows are important for understanding referrals, particularly those related to suspected learning disability (see Chapter 7). With an understanding of the constructs underlying the WISC-V Primary Index Scales (Rapid Reference 4.21), interpretation of the results of cohesion analysis is facilitated.

Primary Index Scale Cohesion

Whenever two tests that purport to measure the same aspect of a broad ability domain (e.g., two tests of I in the Gf domain) or two different, but related aspects of that domain (e.g., one test of I and one test of RG) are administered to an individual, it is expected that the individual will perform about the same on both tasks. The construct validation research suggests that individuals who perform well on one aspect of a psychological construct (e.g., Gf) ought to perform well on all aspects of that construct (e.g., I, RG, RQ; Messick, 1995). Generally speaking then, it is expected that composites, or in the case of the WISC-V, primary index scores, will be cohesive, indicating that the index is a good summary of the theoretically related abilities it was intended to represent.

X-BASS evaluates cohesion of a two-subtest composite by considering whether the two scores are statistically significantly different at the $p < .05$ level as well as the magnitude of that difference for statistical rarity (i.e., $\leq$ 10% of the population). Rapid Reference 4.22 demonstrates the manner in which the interpretations regarding cohesion are derived in X-BASS. Figures 4.5 and 4.6 show excerpts of cohesion analysis output from X-BASS for Amanda (see Rapid Reference 4.2 for her WISC-V scores), including the VCI,

VSI, FRI and WMI, respectively. Note that the output found in Figure 4.5 and Figure 4.6 is transferred to a summary page that may be printed directly from X-BASS. The first page of the output summary is found in Figure 4.6. Due to space limitations, these figures only include the output for some of the Primary Index Scales. The WISC-V interpretive output summary (shown in part in Figure 4.7) is not intended to replace a psychoeducational report. Instead, it is intended to facilitate test interpretation.

CAUTION

The summary of WISC-V performance provided in X-BASS (see Figure 4.6 for a portion of the summary) should not replace a psychoeducational report. It is only intended to facilitate test interpretation.

≡ Rapid Reference 4.22

Cohesion Analysis of the Primary Index Scales Using X-BASS

Finding	Interpretation
The difference between scaled scores is not statistically significant or rare.	The difference between the scaled scores that make up the index is not statistically significant and a difference of this size occurs in more than 10% of the general population which makes it relatively common. The composite is, therefore, **cohesive** and considered to be a good summary of the theoretically related abilities it was intended to represent.
The difference between scaled scores is statistically significant but not rare.	Although the difference between the scaled scores that make up the index is statistically significant, a difference of this size occurs in greater than 10% of the general population, which makes it relatively common. Therefore, **clinical judgment** is needed to determine whether the composite is cohesive and likely to provide an adequate summary of the theoretically related abilities it was intended to represent.
The difference between scores is statistically significant and rare.	The difference between the scaled scores that make up the index is statistically significant and considered rare, occurring in about 10% (or less) of the general population. Therefore, the index is **not cohesive,** meaning that it most likely is not a good summary of the theoretically related abilities it was intended to represent.

Cross-Battery Assessment Software System (X-BASS® v2.0)

WISC-V® Data Analysis
(age range = 6.0 – 16:11)

Name: Amanda Farris   **Grade:** 2   **Age:** 8 years 3 month(s)   **Date:** 1/4/2016

XBA Analyzer	WISC-V Graph
Data Organizer	Integrated Graph
C-LIM Summary	C-LIM Analyzer

Start   Index

WISC-V | WAIS-IV | WPPSI-IV | WIAT-III | WJ IV CCG | WJ IV ACH | WJ IV OL | KABC-II | KTEA-3 | CAS2 | DAS-II | SBS

Index Name (check box for integrated graph)	Enter scores	PR	Transfer scores	Cohesion and Interpretation: Is variability...		Follow up Recommendations
				significant or substantial?	infrequent or uncommon?	Do the results suggest a need for follow up?
Subtest Name				No	No	No, not considered necessary
Verbal Comprehension Index (VCI/Gc)	100	50	☐	**COHESIVE - AVERAGE**		*Gc:VL = 100* Transfer to Data Organizer
Similarities (Gc:VL,Gf:I)	10	50	☐	The difference between the scores that comprise the VCI is not significant and a difference of this size is considered common in the general population. This means that the VCI is a good summary of Amanda's Crystallized Intelligence, particularly her word knowledge (Vocabulary) and her ability to reason with words (Similarities). Amanda's VCI of 100 (95 - 105) is classified as Average and is ranked at the 50th percentile, indicating that she performed as well as or better than 50% of same age peers from the general population. Amanda's word knowledge and ability to reason with words should enable learning.		Because the difference between the scores that comprise the VCI is not substantial and both scores are at least average, follow up is not considered necessary.
Vocabulary (VL)	10	50	☐			
Information (K0)			☐			
Comprehension (K0)			☐			

Fluid Reasoning Index (FRI/Gf)	97	42	☐	**COHESIVE - AVERAGE**		*Gf = 97* Transfer to Data Organizer
Matrix Reasoning (I)	9	37	☐	The difference between the scores that comprise the FRI is not significant and a difference of this size is considered common in the general population. This means that the FRI is a good summary of Amanda's Fluid Reasoning, particularly her ability to reason inductively (Matrix Reasoning) and deductively (Figure Weights) with visual information. Amanda's FRI of 97 (91 - 103) is classified as Average and is ranked at the 42nd percentile, indicating that she performed as well as or better than 42% of same age peers from the general population. Amanda's general reasoning ability should enable learning.		Because the difference between the scores that comprise the FRI is not substantial and both scores are at least average, follow up is not considered necessary.
Figure Weights (RG,RQ)	10	50	☐			
Picture Concepts (I)			☐			
Arithmetic (Gsm:MW,Gq:A3)			☐	No, not considered necessary		

Figure 4.5 Example of Cohesion and Follow-Up Statements for Amanda's VCI and FRI in X-BASS

223

Visual Spatial Index (VSI/Gv) — 81 | 10

☐ Block Design* (Vz)	6	9
☐ Visual Puzzles (Vz)	7	16

Additional process scaled scores can be generated for Block Design (see WISC-V Administration and Scoring Manual Supplement). These subtest processes are available in the XBA Analyzer Gv drop down menu.

No	No	No, not considered necessary

COHESIVE - HIGH PRIORITY CONCERN Gv-Vz = 81 [Transfer to Data Organizer]

The difference between the scores that comprise the VSI is not significant and a difference of this size is considered common in the general population. This means that the VSI is a good summary of Amanda's Visual Processing, particularly her ability to perceive complex patterns and mentally simulate how they might look when transformed in some way (e.g., rotated). Amanda's VSI of 81 (76 - 89) is classified as Below Average and is ranked at the 10th percentile, indicating that she performed as well as or better than 10% of same age peers from the general population. Amanda's difficulty with analyzing and synthesizing visual information is not only a personal weakness for her, but it is also a weakness relative to her same age peers. The difference between her VSI and the average of all of her primary index scores is so large that it is not commonly found in the general population (i.e., < 10%). Taken together, these results suggest that Amanda's visual processing difficulty may contribute to learning difficulties and is, therefore, a high priority concern. Minimizing the effects of Amanda's visual processing difficulties on learning should play an essential role in intervention planning.

Working Memory Index (WMI/Gsm) — 85 | 16

☐ Digit Span* (MW, MS)	8	25
☐ Picture Span (MS, MW)	7	16
☐ Letter-Number Sequencing (MW)		

Additional process scaled scores can be generated for Digit Span (see WISC-V Administration and Scoring Manual Supplement). These subtest processes are available in the XBA Analyzer Gsm drop down menu.

No	No	No, not considered necessary

COHESIVE - LOW AVERAGE Gsm = 85 [Transfer to Data Organizer]

The difference between the scores that comprise the WMI is not significant and a difference of this size is considered common in the general population. This means that the WMI is a good summary of Amanda's Working Memory Capacity or her ability to hold information in immediate awareness and use it within a few seconds. For example, some of the memory tasks performed by Amanda required her to manipulate or transform information in immediate awareness (e.g., repeating numbers backwards). Amanda's WMI of 85 (80 - 93) is classified as Low Average and is ranked at the 16th percentile, indicating that she performed as well as or better than 16% of same age peers from the general population. Amanda performed better on auditory memory tasks (Picture Span; Low Average) as compared to the visual memory task (Picture Span; Average), although the difference is not significant. Overall, it appears that Amanda's working memory capacity is somewhat limited as compared to same age peers, which may contribute to academic difficulties. Minimizing the effects of working memory demands on learning should play an essential role in intervention planning.

Because the difference between the scores that comprise the VSI is not substantial, indicating similar subtest performances, follow up is not considered necessary.

Because the difference between the scores that comprise the WMI is not substantial, indicating similar subtest performances, follow up is not considered necessary.

Figure 4.6 Example of Cohesion and Follow-Up Statements for Amanda's VSI and WMI in X-BASS

Cross-Battery Assessment Software System (X-BASS®) WISC-V® Interpretive Output

NAME: Amanda Farris
DATE OF BIRTH: 10/1/2007
DATE OF EVALUATION: 1/4/2016
GRADE: 2
EVALUATOR: Dr. Erin McDonough

DATE OF REPORT: 1/24/2016
SCHOOL: Washington Elementary
ETHNICITY: Eastern European-American
FIRST LANGUAGE: English
SECOND LANGUAGE: none

GENERAL ABILITY SCORE(S)

Index or Subtest	Score	PR	Normative Category
Full Scale IQ (FSIQ)	91	27	Average
General Ability Index (GAI)	94	34	Average

RECOMMENDATIONS AND INTERPRETATION: GENERAL ABILITY

The FSIQ and the GAI each provides a good summary of the Amanda's overall intellectual ability. Her FSIQ is significantly higher than her GAI (p < .05). Howerever, this difference is not considered unusual, as it occurs in almost 30% of the population. Therefore, the FSIQ is considered the best estimate of Amanda's overall intellectual ability because it summarizes a broader range of abilities as compared to the GAI. If a global ability score is needed in a formula or when diagnostic criteria include a cut score, then the FSIQ should be used, unless clinical judgement suggests otherwise.

SUMMARY DESCRIPTION OF PRIMARY INDEXES AND SUBTESTS

Index or Subtest	Score	PR	Classification	Normative S or W?	Personal S or W?	Asset/High Priority Concern?
Verbal Comp Index	100	50	Average			
Similarities	10	50				
Vocabulary	10	50				
Fluid Reasoning Index	97	42	Average			
Matrix Reasoning	9	37				
Figure Weights	10	50				
Visual-Spatial Index	81	10	Below Average	Normative Weakness	Personal Weakness	High Priority Concern
Block Design	6	9				
Visual Puzzles	7	16				
Working Memory Index	85	16	Low Average			
Digit Span	8	25				
Picture Span	7	16				
Processing Speed Index	92	30	Average			
Coding	8	25				
Symbol Search	9	37				

Figure 4.7 Portion of the Interpretive Output Summary for Amanda from X-BASS

When subtest scores that are expected to converge do not, there is either a real difference between the individual's cognitive abilities as represented by the subtest scaled scores or influences other than the cognitive construct intended to be measured by the subtests may have resulted in a significant difference between the scores (see Rapid Reference 1.3 in Chapter 1 for a summary of potential influences on WISC-V performance). Without generating and testing those hypotheses, however, the confidence a practitioner can place in his or her interpretation of a noncohesive index is *typically* not as high as when the index is cohesive. To demonstrate, consider the examples in Rapid Reference 4.23.

≡ Rapid Reference 4.23

Examples of Cohesion Analysis for the Fluid Reasoning Index (FRI)

Scores and Results of Cohesion Analysis for FRI	Sheena	Marie	Antonio	Alan
Matrix Reasoning	10	11	8	5
Figure Weights	9	16	6	2
FRI	**97**	**121**	**82**	**64**
Results of Cohesion Analysis	Difference is not statistically significant; *Cohesive*	Difference is statistically significant and rare; *Not Cohesive*	Difference is not statistically significant; *Cohesive*	Difference is statistically significant but not rare; *Clinical Judgment Needed*

Sheena's FRI performance is straightforward. The difference between her Matrix Reasoning (MR) and Figure Weights (FW) scaled scores is not significant and both scaled scores are within the Average range. Therefore, her FRI is a good summary of the theoretically related abilities it was intended to represent. Unless referral concerns or clinical judgment suggest otherwise, there is little need to expand upon the assessment of Gf for Sheena. The remaining examples are not as straightforward. Marie's performance shows that the FRI is not cohesive because the difference between the scores that make it up is statistically significant and unusual. However, the FRI scaled scores range from Average to Extremely Above Average and the FRI of 121 is Well Above Average. Therefore, although not cohesive, the FRI and its component parts do not suggest any evidence of weakness. Marie's FRI should be reported and interpreted. While the variability in the Gf scaled scores for Marie is unusual, it is related to her very high score on FW, which is a normative strength for her and should be highlighted as such. Figure 4.8 provides a summary statement for Marie's FRI based on X-BASS output. To obtain information about possible reasons for the unusually large difference between the MR and FW subtest scaled scores, a consideration of task demands and task characteristics may be helpful. This information for all WISC-V subtests is provided in Appendix F.

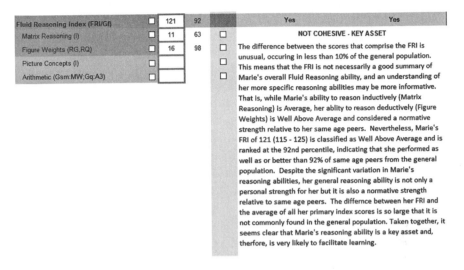

Fluid Reasoning Index (FRI/Gf)	☐	121	92		Yes	Yes
Matrix Reasoning (I)	☐	11	63	☐		NOT COHESIVE - KEY ASSET
Figure Weights (RG,RQ)	☐	16	98	☐		The difference between the scores that comprise the FRI is
Picture Concepts (I)	☐			☐		unusual, occuring in less than 10% of the general population.
Arithmetic (Gsm:MW;Gq:A3)	☐			☐		This means that the FRI is not necessarily a good summary of

The difference between the scores that comprise the FRI is unusual, occuring in less than 10% of the general population. This means that the FRI is not necessarily a good summary of Marie's overall Fluid Reasoning ability, and an understanding of her more specific reasoning abilities may be more informative. That is, while Marie's ability to reason inductively (Matrix Reasoning) is Average, her ability to reason deductively (Figure Weights) is Well Above Average and considered a normative strength relative to her same age peers. Nevertheless, Marie's FRI of 121 (115 - 125) is classified as Well Above Average and is ranked at the 92nd percentile, indicating that she performed as well as or better than 92% of same age peers from the general population. Despite the significant variation in Marie's reasoning abilities, her general reasoning ability is not only a personal strength for her but it is also a normative strength relative to same age peers. The differnce between her FRI and the average of all her primary index scores is so large that it is not commonly found in the general population. Taken together, it seems clear that Marie's reasoning ability is a key asset and, therfore, is very likely to facilitate learning.

Figure 4.8 Example of a Noncohesive Composite That Was Reported and Interpreted for Marie

DON'T FORGET

Information about the task demands and task characteristics of all WISC-V subtests is found in Appendix F.

Rapid Reference 4.23 shows that Antonio's FRI of 82 is cohesive, indicating that it is a good summary of the theoretically related abilities it was intended to represent. However, an examination of his MR and FW scaled scores shows that MR is Average and FW is Below Average and considered a normative weakness. Therefore, despite the fact that the FRI is cohesive, further investigation of Antonio's deductive and quantitative reasoning (the abilities presumed to be measured by the FW subtest) may be warranted.

Rapid Reference 4.23 also shows that the difference between Alan's MR and FW scaled scores is statistically significant but not unusual, indicating that clinical judgment is needed to determine whether the FRI appears to provide a good summary of the theoretically related abilities it was intended to represent. Because the scaled scores that make up Alan's FRI in this example ranged from Well Below Average to Extremely Below Average and his FRI of 64 is Extremely Below Average, it seems clear that Gf is a normative weakness or deficit for this individual. As such, it appears to be a good summary of the theoretically related abilities it was intended to represent. However, a review of task demands and task characteristics (Appendix F) may reveal hypotheses about reasons for the substantial difference that may warrant additional assessment in the judgment of the practitioner. This information may be particularly relevant for instructional planning (Mascolo, Alfonso, & Flanagan, 2014).

The data for Marie, Antonio, and Alan in Rapid Reference 4.23 make it clear that despite the results of cohesion analysis (i.e., the science of test interpretation), judgment is involved in score interpretation (i.e., the art of test interpretation). For this reason, we developed a set of criteria for assisting practitioners in determining whether follow up assessment may be warranted regardless of the results of the cohesion analysis. Essentially, in addition to understanding cohesion, an examination of where the scaled scores that make up a Primary index score fall relative to most people provides additional, necessary information to ensure that practitioners are aware of differences that may warrant follow up assessment.

Follow Up Assessment

Rapid Reference 4.24 provides examples of what is meant by follow up when it is recommended in X-BASS. As may be seen in this rapid reference, follow up does not always mean administering more tests. There may very well be times that follow up involves a review of previous evaluations, a review of work

≡ Rapid Reference 4.24

Examples of What Is Meant by "Follow up" in X-BASS (v2.0)

Additional Data Collection	Review of Existing Data
Investigation of narrow ability performance via administration of standardized, norm-referenced tests	Evaluation of existing data to determine if it corroborates current test performance (e.g., classroom work samples reveal manifestations of current cognitive ability weakness or deficit).
Informal assessment of the manifestations of an ability weakness or deficit (e.g., curriculum-based measures, state/local exams)	Outside evaluation corroborates current findings.
Formal and informal testing of hypotheses regarding variation in task characteristics and task demands	Professional, teacher, parent, and/or student report corroborates current findings.

Additional Data Collection	Review of Existing Data
Outside evaluation of disorder or condition that may adversely affect test performance (e.g., neuropsychological evaluation of attention deficit/hyperactivity disorder; psychological evaluation of emotional or personality functioning; functional behavioral assessment)	Error analysis explains inconsistencies in current data or reasons for weak or deficient performance.
Consultation with parents, teachers, or other professionals	Demand analysis explains inconsistencies in current data or reasons for weak or deficient performance.
Classroom observations in areas of concerns	Review attempted interventions.

samples, or an evaluation of the types of errors made, for example. Therefore, when follow up is recommended, practitioners should consider all data sources in an attempt to support or refute initial findings.

Table 4.1 and corresponding Rapid Reference 4.25 provide further information about follow up assessment for two-subtest composites. Specifically, Table 4.1 provides the criteria used in X-BASS to determine whether follow up is necessary for any of the Primary Index Scales. These criteria take into consideration the relative value and location (with respect to classification and meaning of performance) of the scaled scores (e.g., ≤ 5; ≥ 8) that make up the composite as well as the difference between them. The cells in Table 4.1 represent every possible combination of scaled score variation for a two-subtest composite. Each cell contains the word "Yes," "No," or "Maybe," indicating that follow up assessment is recommended, not recommended, or may be helpful, respectively. The number/letter code (e.g., 1A, 1B, 1C) in each cell corresponds to the interpretive statement that is provided in X-BASS for that particular subtest scaled score configuration. Specific examples of each cell are provided in Rapid Reference 4.25. Note that the matching shaded areas in Table 4.1 indicate identical scenarios. Examples of the subtest scaled score configurations in these shaded areas are reported in the same shade of gray in Rapid Reference 4.25.

Rapid Reference 4.26 provides some of the information that is produced by X-BASS with regard to follow-up analysis. Specifically, when X-BASS indicates

Table 4.1 Criteria Used in X-BASS for Follow-Up Analysis for Composites That Are Made Up of Two Scores

	Subtest A Scaled Score		
Subtest B Scaled Score	**SS ≤ 5**	**SS = 6 or 7**	**SS ≥ 8**
SS ≤ 5	HI-LO > 2 _YES_ (1A) · HI-LO < 2 _NO_ (1B) · HI-LO = 2 _MAYBE_ (1C)	HI-LO > 2 _YES_ (2A) · HI-LO < 2 _NO_ (2B) · HI-LO = 2 _MAYBE_ (2C)	HI-LO is always > 2 _YES_ (3A)
SS = 6 or 7	HI-LO > 2 _YES_ (4A) · HI-LO < 2 _NO_ (4B) · HI-LO = 2 _MAYBE_ (4C)	HI-LO is always < 2 _NO_ (5B)	HI-LO > 2 _YES_ (6A) · HI-LO < 2 _NO_ (6B) · HI-LO = 2 _MAYBE_ (6C)
SS ≥ 8	HI-LO is always > 2 _YES_ (7A)	HI-LO > 2 _YES_ (8A) · HI-LO < 2 _NO_ (8B) · HI-LO = 2 _MAYBE_ (8C)	HI-LO > 2 _YES_ (9A) · HI-LO < 2 _NO_ (9B) · HI-LO = 2 _MAYBE_ (9C)

Note: HI = the highest score in the composite; LO = the lowest score in the composite. "Yes," "No," and "Maybe" are produced in X-BASS in answer to the question "Is follow up necessary?" Number/letter codes (e.g., 1A, 1B, 1C) correspond to X-BASS interpretive output and follow-up recommendations, which are described in Rapid Reference 4.25.

Rapid Reference 4.25

Two-Subtest Composites: Determining Whether Follow up Is Necessary, Regardless of Composite Cohesion

Criterion Used by X-BASS v2.0 as Reported in Table 4.1	Interpretive Output by X-BASS v2.0	WISC-V Example	Examples of Practitioner Decision and General Interpretation
1A	Although both scores that make up the composite are indicative of a deficit, the difference between them is at least 1 SD. Therefore, to gain a better understanding of the individual's performance in this ability domain, it is considered necessary to follow up on the lower score and consider the differences that specific task characteristics and demands may have had on performance.	**Working Memory Index = 65** Digit Span = 5 Picture Span = 2	The practitioner followed up and found supporting evidence from previous evaluation results. In addition, followup included further discussion with the student's teachers and parents. No further standardized, norm-referenced assessment in short-term memory was considered necessary. Practitioner's general conclusion: **Robert has a deficit in Gsm based on his performance on auditory-verbal and visual-spatial tasks, namely Digit Span and Picture Span. Of note, his performance on memory span tasks (Digit Span Forward) is significantly better than his performance on working memory tasks. This finding is supported by previous psycho-educational evaluations and is corroborated by teacher reports and parent report (e.g., BRIEF). Previous evaluation results also support higher memory span than working memory performance when the tasks were auditory-verbal (as opposed to visual-spatial) in nature.**

(continued)

Criterion Used by X-BASS v2.0 as Reported in Table 4.1	Interpretive Output by X-BASS v2.0	WISC-V Example	Examples of Practitioner Decision and General Interpretation
1B	Because the difference between the scores that make up the composite is not substantial (i.e., less than ⅔ SD) and both scores are indicative of a deficit, follow-up is not considered necessary.	**Fluid Reasoning Index = 64** Matrix Reasoning = 4 Figure Weights = 3	Following the recommendation of the X-BASS, the practitioner did not follow up. Practitioner's general conclusion: **Makayla's performance on tasks that measured Fluid Reasoning (Gf) was Extremely Below Average and is considered a normative deficit. The difference between her performance on a task that required her to reason inductively (Matrix Reasoning) and her performance on a task that required her to reason deductively and quantitatively (Figure Weights) was not statistically significant, indicating that she performed about the same on these tasks. Overall, this finding indicates that Makayla either cannot solve or has considerable difficulty solving novel problems that cannot be performed automatically, as compared to same-age peers. When Makayla enters third grade in the fall, she very likely will have extreme difficulty forming and recognizing concepts, perceiving relationships among patterns, and drawing inferences. Therefore, these reasoning processes must be externalized for Makayla whenever possible via explicit strategy instruction with many opportunities for practice.**
1C	Although both scores that make up the composite are indicative of a deficit,	**Naming Speed Index = 67** Naming Speed	The practitioner did not follow up but instead considered the differences in task demands to assist in understanding variability in performance. Evaluator's general conclusion:

	the difference between them is considered substantial (i.e., at least ⅔ SD). Therefore, to gain a better understanding of the individual's performance in this ability domain, it *may* be helpful to follow up on the lower score and consider the specific task characteristics and demands that may have had on performance.	Literacy = 75 Naming Speed Quantity = 65	*Zion's performance on tasks that measured Long-term Storage and Retrieval (Glr), particularly Naming Facility or Speed of Lexical Access, was Extremely Below Average and is considered a normative deficit. Zion's performance on these tasks suggests that he has difficulty rapidly producing names for concepts when presented with a pictorial cue. This finding is supported by Zion's interventionist's observations that when asked to name letters and object quickly, Zion needs much more time to complete tasks than same-age peers. Based on specific task demands, it appears that naming numbers quickly, using and manipulating numbers rapidly and accurately, number sense, and subitizing are very difficult for Zion.*	
2A, 4A	Because the difference between the scores that comprise the composite is at least 1 SD and the lower score is indicative of a deficit, follow up on the lower score is considered necessary to determine if it is an accurate and valid representation of ability.	**Working Memory Index = 74** Digit Span = 7 Picture Span = 4		Following the recommendations of X-BASS, the practitioner followed up on test performance in the area of Gsm. When following up, some issues the practitioner considered were: (1) the examinee earned a significantly higher Digit Span Forward scaled score than Digit Span Backward or Digit Span Sequencing; and (2) the nature of the stimuli (i.e., auditory-verbal versus visual-spatial). The practitioner followed up with another measure of working memory, namely the DAS-II Recall of Sequential Order—a subtest that involves visual-spatial stimuli, like Picture Span. In addition, a measure of memory span was administered from the DAS-II (Recall of Digits-Forward). The WISC-V/DAS-II cross-battery data were entered into the XBA tab of X-BASS for further analysis. X-BASS output revealed Average memory span and Well Below Average working memory capacity with no difference in verbal versus visual-spatial content in either domain.

(continued)

(continued)

Criterion Used by X-BASS v2.0 as Reported in Table 4.1	Interpretive Output by X-BASS v2.0	WISC-V Example	Examples of Practitioner Decision and General Interpretation
2B, 4B	Because the difference between the scores that make up the composite is not substantial (i.e., less than ⅔ SD), indicating similar subtest performances, follow up is not considered necessary.	**Fluid Reasoning Index = 74** Matrix Reasoning = 6 Figure Weights = 5	This scenario is nearly identical to 1B above. The only difference is in terms of the severity of the deficit. Specifically, the scaled scores in 1B are ≤ 5 (e.g., 1 and 2; 3 and 4; 3; 2 and 2), whereas in this scenario, one scaled score is 6 and the other is 5. Following the recommendation of the X-BASS, the practitioner did not follow up. Practitioner's general conclusion: *Cathy's performance on tasks that measured Fluid Reasoning (Gf) was Well Below Average and is considered a normative deficit. The difference between her performance on a task that required her to reason inductively (Matrix Reasoning) and her performance on a task that required her to reason deductively and quantitatively (Figure Weights) was not statistically significant, indicating that she performed about the same on these tasks. Overall, this finding indicates that Cathy has considerable difficulty solving novel problems that cannot be performed automatically, as compared to same-age peers. Because it is very likely that Cathy will have difficulty forming and recognizing concepts, perceiving relationships among patterns, drawing inferences, extrapolating, and reorganizing or transferring information, these reasoning processes must be externalized for her whenever possible.*

| 2C, 4C | **Visual Spatial Index = 78**
Block Design = 7
Visual Puzzles = 5 | The difference between the scores that make up the composite is considered substantial (i.e., at least ≥ $\frac{2}{3}$ SD). Therefore, to gain a better understanding of the individual's performance in this ability domain, it may be helpful to follow up on the lower score and consider the specific task characteristics and demands may have had on performance. | This scenario is nearly identical to 1C above. The only difference is in terms of the severity of the deficit. Specifically, the scaled scores in 1C are both ≤ 5 and differ by 2 scaled score points (i.e., 1 and 3; 2 and 4; 3 and 5), whereas in this scenario, the scaled scores are either 7 and 5 or 6 and 4.

The practitioner generated the following information upon which she based her follow up assessment decisions and *a posteriori* hypotheses in the area of Visual Processing (Gv): (a) Block Design is likely higher than Visual Puzzles for Louis because performance is facilitated by experience with blocks and other-like manipulatives. Louis told the practitioner that he likes blocks when testing began; and (b) Block Design was the first subtest administered and Visual Puzzles was the last subtest administered on the first day of testing. Louis appeared tired and less interested in Visual Puzzles and his attention appeared to wander throughout.

The practitioner opted to administer WJ IV Visualization because it is similar to Visual Puzzles. This was the second test administered on day two of testing. The practitioner hypothesized that Louis's performance on Visualization would be higher than on Visual Puzzles because Louis would be attentive and engaged early in the day. The practitioner entered the WISC–V/WJ IV cross-battery data into the XBA tab of X-BASS for further analysis. Specifically, Louis received a standard score of 95 on the Visualization test. X-BASS reported an XBA Gv:Vz composite of 88 based on the Block Design and Visualization tests. This composite is considered the best estimate of Gv:Vz for Louis and was used in place of the VSI. Behavioral observations were used to explain the divergent, spuriously low Visual Puzzles scaled score. |

(continued)

Criterion Used by X-BASS v2.0 as Reported in Table 4.1	Interpretive Output by X-BASS v2.0	WISC-V Example	Examples of Practitioner Decision and General Interpretation
3A	Because one score in the composite is indicative of average or better performance and the other score is indicative of a deficit, follow up on the lower score is considered necessary to determine if it is an accurate and valid representation of ability.	**Auditory Working Memory Index = 89** Letter-Number Sequencing = 6 Digit Span = 10	The practitioner generated the following information upon which he based his follow-up assessment decisions and *a posteriori* hypotheses in the area of Short-Term Memory (Gsm): (a) Jayla demonstrated significantly better performance on Digit Span Forward (DSf) as compared to Digit Span Backward (DSb) and Digit Span Sequencing (DSs), suggesting that her registration of digits in short-term memory is similar to that of her peers whereas her ability to manipulate numbers in working memory is more problematic; (b) Jayla's performance on the Letter-Number Sequencing subtest, a more demanding auditory working memory task, as compared to DSb and DSs, supports difficulties in her ability to manipulate information in working memory; and (c) Jayla's Picture Span performance was consistent with her DSf performance. Based on this information, it was hypothesized that Jayla's visual working memory is better than her auditory working memory. To understand Jayla's memory difficulties better, the Spatial Span subtest from the WISC-V Integrated was administered. The practitioner entered the WISC-V/WISC-V Integrated data into the XBA tab of X-BASS for further analysis. Specifically, the Visual Working Memory Index from WISC-V Integrated was compared to the working Memory (Alternative) clinical composite made up of LNS, DSb, and DSs. The practitioner's hypothesis was supported. Jayla's visual working memory is Average compared to same age peers, a finding that should play an important role in intervention planning.

| 5B | Because the difference between the scores that make up the composite is not substantial (i.e., less than ⅔ SD), indicating similar subtest performances, follow up is not considered necessary. | **_Processing Speed Index = 83_** Coding = 7 Symbol Search = 7 | Following the recommendation of X-BASS, the practitioner did not follow up. Practitioner's general conclusion: **_Alberto's performance on tasks that measured Processing Speed (Gs) was Below Average and is considered a normative weakness. The variability among the scores on the subtests that make up this scale was not statistically significant, indicating that he performed about the same on these tasks. Overall, this finding indicates that Alberto has difficulty carrying out simple, repetitive cognitive tasks quickly and accurately, especially when sustained and focused attention are required. Therefore, it is hypothesized that Alberto may have difficulty in school when he is required to quickly perceive relationships between stimuli (e.g., attending to signs in math speed drills), and work within time parameters._** Prior to making recommendations, the practitioner will test this hypothesis by reviewing Alberto's work samples, talking to his teachers, and examining how he performs on tasks of reading, math, and writing fluency. |
| 6A, 8A | Because the difference between the scores that make up the composite is at least 1 SD, and the lower score is indicative of a weakness or deficit, follow-up on the lower score is considered necessary to determine if it is an accurate and valid representation of ability. | **_Working Memory Index = 88_** Digit Span = 6 Picture Span = 10 | Following the recommendations of X-BASS, the practitioner followed up on Mateo's performance in the area of Short-Term Memory (Gsm). However, rather than following up on the lower score and administering another measure of Memory Span (MS) or Working Memory (limited complexity), the practitioner followed up with WISC-V Arithmetic (a more complex task than either Digit Span or Picture Span and one that requires increased working memory capacity). The rationale for using the Arithmetic subtest was based on the following: (a) there was no indication of memory difficulties, based on referral information and interviews with teacher and parent; and (b) it is hypothesized that if Mateo's Gsm performance improves |

(continued)

Criterion Used by X-BASS v2.0 as Reported in Table 4.1	Interpretive Output by X-BASS v2.0	WISC-V Example	Examples of Practitioner Decision and General Interpretation
			as the context of task demands becomes more meaningful, he ought to perform better on WISC-V Arithmetic. The practitioner hypothesized that Mateo's performance on WISC-V Arithmetic would be well within the normal limits of functioning.
6B, 8B	Because the difference between the scores that make up the composite is not substantial (i.e., less than ⅔ SD), indicating similar subtest performances, follow up is not considered necessary.	*Quantitative Reasoning Index = 85* Arithmetic = 8 Figure Weights = 7	Following the recommendation of the X-BASS, the practitioner did not follow up. Practitioner's general conclusion: *Scott's performance on tasks that measured Fluid Reasoning (Gf) was Low Average, but within the normal limits of functioning relative to same-age peers. The difference between his performance on a task that required him to reason inductively and deductively with numbers (Arithmetic) and his performance on a task that required him to reason deductively with visual information (Figure Weights) was not statistically significant, indicating that he performed about the same on these tasks. Overall, although within normal limits, Scott's Quantitative Reasoning Index is ranked at the 16th percentile compared to same-age peers, suggesting that he will likely have difficulty solving novel problems that cannot be performed automatically. It is likely that explicit strategy instruction will be necessary to assist Scott in solving problems, drawing inferences, extrapolating, and reorganizing or transferring information.*

6C, 8C	**Visual Spatial Index = 89** Block Design = 7 Visual Puzzles = 9	The practitioner generated the following information upon which she based her follow-up assessment decision and *a posteriori* hypothesis in the area of Visual Processing (Gv): ***Rick's lower Block Design performance appeared to be less related to difficulty problem-solving or poor visual perceptual capacity but, rather, difficulties in figuring out how to orient diagonal blocks in asymmetrical designs in order to get his design to match the model. It was hypothesized that Rick would do better with regard to visual integration and mental construction of designs without the impact of motor planning and execution.*** To test this hypothesis, the practitioner opted to administer the WISC-V Integrated Block Design Multiple Choice (BDMC) subtest. Rick performed significantly better on BDMC as compared to BD. X-BASS was used to calculate a Gv:Vz composite, which fell well within the Average range—a finding that supported the practitioner's hypothesis.
	The difference between the scores that make up the composite is considered substantial (i.e., at least ≥ ⅔ SD). Therefore, to gain a better understanding of the individual's performance in this ability domain, it may be helpful to follow up on the lower score and consider the differences that specific task characteristics and demands may have had on performance.	
7A (same as 3A)	**Quantitative Reasoning Index = 88** Arithmetic = 11 Figure Weights = 5	Following the recommendation of X-BASS, the practitioner followed up on the lower score. The practitioner generated the following information upon which she based her follow up assessment decision and *a posteriori* hypothesis in the area of Quantitative Reasoning (RQ; a narrow Gf ability): (a) While these subtests involve quantitative reasoning to some extent, Figure Weights requires visual discrimination, deductive reasoning, and perceptual reasoning all of which are not involved (or not as much involved) on the Arithmetic subtest; (b) Nina's visual processing (Gv) is below average and may nave affected her performance on the Figure Weights subtest negatively and (c) Nina will likely perform better on quantitative reasoning tasks that do not rely heavily on visualization.
	Because one score in the composite is indicative of average or better performance and the other score is indicative of a deficit, follow up on the lower score is considered necessary to determine if it is an accurate and valid representation of ability.	

(continued)

239

Criterion Used by X-BASS v2.0 as Reported in Table 4.1	Interpretive Output by X-BASS v2.0	WISC-V Example	Examples of Practitioner Decision and General Interpretation
			To test her hypothesis that Nina's quantitative reasoning ability is within normal limits when visualization is reduced, the practitioner opted to administer the SB:5 Verbal Quantitative Reasoning subtest. This subtest measures RQ, but uses an auditory-verbal format and relies less on visual discrimination as compared to the WISC-V Figure Weights subtest.
9A	Although both scores that make up the composite are indicative of average or better ability, the difference between them is at least 1 SD. Therefore, to gain a better understanding of the individual's performance in this ability domain, it may be helpful to follow up on the lower score and consider the differences that specific task characteristics and demands may have had on performance.	**Fluid Reasoning Index = 103** Matrix Reasoning = 13 Figure Weights = 8	Following the recommendation of X-BASS, the practitioner followed up on the lower score. The practitioner generated this information upon which she based her follow up assessment decision and *a posteriori* hypothesis in the area of Fluid Reasoning (Gf): *Bai was born in China and moved to the United States three years ago. While he is behind his classmates in reading comprehension and written language, he excels in other areas (e.g., mathematics) and performs significantly above his peers who have a similar culture and language background. Bai was referred to determine whether he qualifies for placement in his school's gifted and talented program. It is possible that the cultural demands (even though minimal) of the Figure Weights subtest, in particular, attenuated Bai's performance, rendering his scaled score of 8 an underestimate of his ability to reason deductively and quantitatively.*

To test this hypothesis, the practitioner opted to give the CTONI-2 Geometric Sequences subtest. This subtest, like Figure Weights, measures general sequential (deductive) reasoning. However, performance on the Geometric Sequences subtest is negligibly influenced by cultural and language differences. Therefore, it is expected that Bai's performance on Geometric Sequences will be similar to his performance on the Matrix Reasoning subtest. The practitioner entered the WISC-V/CTONI-2 cross-battery data into the XBA tab of X-BASS for further analysis.

Following the recommendation of X-BASS, the practitioner did not follow up. Practitioner's general conclusion:

Tanya's performance on tasks that measured her ability to process or manipulate abstractions, rules, generalizations, and logical relationships was Average as compared to same-age peers from the general population. The difference between her performance on a task that required her to reason inductively (Matrix Reasoning) and her performance on a task that required her to reason deductively and quantitatively (Figure Weights) was not statistically significant, indicating that she performed about the same on these tasks. Overall, this finding indicates that Tanya is able to solve novel problems that cannot be performed automatically at least as well as most of her same-age peers. Her reasoning ability should facilitate her academic performance in all areas.

9B	Because the difference between the scores that make up the composite is not substantial (less than $2/3$ SD) and both scores are at least average, follow-up is not considered necessary.	**Fluid Reasoning Index = 109** Matrix Reasoning = 11 Figure Weights = 12

(continued)

Criterion Used by X-BASS v2.0 as Reported in Table 4.1	Interpretive Output by X-BASS v2.0	WISC-V Example	Examples of Practitioner Decision and General Interpretation
9C	Although both scores that make up the composite are indicative of average or better performance, the difference between them is considered substantial (i.e., at least ⅔ SD). Therefore, to gain a better understanding of the individual's performance in this ability domain, it may be helpful to follow up on the lower score and consider the specific task characteristics and demands may have had on performance.	**Verbal Comprehension Index = 123** Vocabulary = 13 Similarities = 15	The practitioner did not find a need to follow up on Gary's performance in the area of Crystallized Intelligence (Gc) and, therefore, concluded: *On tasks that involved Gary's lexical knowledge, vocabulary development, and inductive reasoning with verbal stimuli, he performed in the Well Above Average range (92nd percentile). Gary's lexical knowledge, as acquired through reading, school, and daily life experiences, is considered a significant strength when compared to his same-age peers from the general population and should prove to be an asset to his learning.*

that follow-up assessment is necessary or may be necessary, the program provides guidance on how to proceed. Rapid Reference 4.27 provides some of the guidelines that are offered by X-BASS when both cohesion and follow up are taken into consideration. Figure 4.9 provides an excerpt from X-BASS that shows recommendations for follow up based on Antonio's FRI (reported in Rapid Reference 4.23).

≡ Rapid Reference 4.26

Guidance Provided by X-BASS Based on Follow up Analysis

Index	Is Follow up Necessary? No	If Yes or Maybe, Consider the Following:
VCI	Interpret Index	• Consider whether IN or CO would provide useful additional information. • If IN and CO are administered, consider the new clinical composite, Verbal (Expanded Crystallized) Index (VECI). • Consider whether the Gc clinical composites (e.g., Gc-Verbal Expression Low; Gc–Verbal Expression High) would provide useful additional information. • Consider whether there is a difference between Retrieval from Remote Long-Term Storage (Vocabulary + Information) and Retrieval from Recent Long-Term Storage (Delayed Symbol Translation + Recognition Symbol Translation) (See Chapter 6 for more information). • Consider task characteristics and response demands.
FRI	Interpret Index	• If MR < FW and MR is suggestive of a weakness or deficit, consider obtaining more information about the individual's ability to reason inductively (e.g., Picture Concepts; subtest from another cognitive battery). • If FW < MR and FW is suggestive of a weakness or deficit, consider (a) obtaining more information about the individual's ability to reason deductively (e.g., subtest from another battery) and/or (b) obtaining information about the individual's ability to reason quantitatively (e.g., Arithmetic; quantitative reasoning subtest from another battery; Applied Math Problems or Math Problem Solving subtests from an achievement battery).

(continued)

(*continued*)

Index	No	Is Follow up Necessary? If Yes or Maybe, Consider the Following:
		• If AR is administered, determine whether QRI is cohesive. • Consider task characteristics and response demands. • If Picture Concepts and Arithmetic were administered, consider the Expanded Fluid Index (EFI).
VSI	Interpret Index	• If BD is the lower score, consider the BD process scores. • Consider broader measurement of Gv (e.g., Visual Memory), as may be warranted by referral concerns. • Consider task characteristics and response demands.
WMI	Interpret Index	• If DS < PS and suggestive of a weakness or deficit, consider administering LNS. If LNS is administered, evaluate AWMI for cohesion. • If DS < PS, consider differences among process scores. • If PS < DS, consider administering another test of visual working memory to explore hypotheses about verbal-visual differences in working memory capacity. • If DSf is significantly higher or lower than DSb and DSs, consider the new clinical cluster, Gsm-Working Memory (Alternative).
PSI	Interpret Index	• If CD < SS or SS < CD, consider task characteristics and response demands. • If CD < SS or SS < CD, consider whether CA will provide additional information. • If CA is administered, consider the new clinical composite, Gs-Perceptual Speed.

≡ Rapid Reference 4.27

. . . .

Guidelines for Index Score Interpretation Based on Cohesion and Follow up Analysis

Result of Cohesion Analysis	Result of Follow-up Analysis[1]	Interpret Index Score?	Comments
Cohesive	No Follow Up	**Yes**	The Index is a good summary of the theoretically related abilities it was intended to represent.

Result of Cohesion Analysis	Result of Follow-up Analysis[1]	Interpret Index Score?	Comments
Cohesive	Yes or Maybe Follow Up	**Yes,** if clinical judgment suggests that follow up is not considered necessary; **No,** if clinical judgment suggests that follow up is considered necessary.	Follow up assessment is usually considered necessary when the lower score falls below average, suggesting a weakness or deficit and the higher score is at least average. Note that follow up on the lower score often leads to derivation of an alternative composite, which may replace the WISC-V Index (see Rapid Reference 4.25; 2C, 4C scenario).
Clinical Judgment	No Follow Up	**Yes.** In most cases the index score is a good summary of the theoretically related abilities it was intended to represent.	Although the difference between the scaled scores that make up the index is statistically significant, the difference is not unusual. The index may be interpreted if converging data sources support such an interpretation. In cases where the lower score is suggestive of a weakness or deficit and the higher score is at least average, a decision may be made to follow up on the lower score.
Clinical Judgment	Yes or Maybe Follow Up	**No.** If the lower score is suggestive of a weakness or deficit and the higher score is at least average, then follow up is recommended. **Yes.** If the lower score is not considered a weakness or deficit (or if both scores are in the weakness or deficit range), then in most cases the composite likely provides good summary of the	Follow up assessment on lower score often leads to derivation of an alternative composite, which may replace the WISC-V Index (see Rapid Reference 4.25; 2C, 4C scenario).

(continued)

Result of Cohesion Analysis	Result of Follow-up Analysis[1]	Interpret Index Score?	Comments
		theoretically related abilities it was intended to represent.	
Not Cohesive	Follow Up	**No.** In most cases the index score is not a good summary of the theoretically related abilities it was intended to represent. If follow up resulted in an alternative composite, then interpret the alternative composite.	Note that in some instances, clinical judgment may suggest that there is no need to follow up even when the index is not cohesive; for example, when the Index is made up of scores that range from average to above average or higher or when the index is made up of scores that range from below average to well below average or lower. Although such indexes may not be cohesive, they do convey that performance reflects intact or deficient ability, respectively, indicating that further testing may not be warranted, especially when other data sources are consistent with performance on the index.

[1]The results of follow-up analysis in X-BASS provide suggestions only. The practitioner is free to override any X-BASS recommendations based on his or her clinical judgment as it pertains to the nuances inherent in each individual case.

Step 2 described Primary Index Scale interpretation based on cohesion and follow up criteria. Steps 3 and 4 of the WISC-V interpretive approach involve the same type of analyses, but only for Ancillary and Complementary Index Scales. Because the rationale behind these analyses are the same, the description of Steps 3 and 4 are brief.

			No	No	Maybe for lowest score
					Gf = 82 Transfer to Data Organizer
Fluid Reasoning Index (FRI/Gf)	82	12			
Matrix Reasoning (I)	8	25			
Figure Weights (RG,RQ)	6	9			
Picture Concepts (I)					
Arithmetic (Gsm:MW;Gq-A3)					

COHESIVE - BELOW AVERAGE

The difference between the scores that comprise the FRI is not significant and a difference of this size is considered common in the general population. This means that the FRI is a good summary of Antonio's Fluid Reasoning, particularly his her ability to reason inductively (Matrix Reasoning) and deductively (Figure Weights) with visual information. Antonio's FRI of 82 (77 - 89) is classified as Below Average and is ranked at the 12th percentile, indicating that he performed as well as or better than 12% of same age peers from the general population. Antonio's weakness in Fluid Reasoning may contribute to learning difficulties. Minimizing the effects of Antonio's reasoning difficulties on learning should play an essential role in intervention planning.

The difference between the scores that comprise the composite is considered substantial (i.e., at least 2/3 SD). Therefore, to gain a better understanding of Antonio's performance in this domain, consider the following:

• If MR < FW and MR is suggestive of a weakness or deficit, consider obtaining more information about Antonio's ability to reason inductively (e.g., Picture Concepts; subtest from another cognitive battery)

• If FW < MR and FW is suggestive of a weakness or deficit, consider a) obtaining more information about Antonio's ability to reason deductively (e.g., subtest from another battery) and/or b) obtaining information about Antonio's ability to reason quantitatively (e.g., Arithmetic; quantitative reasoning subtest from another battery; Applied Math Problems or Math Problem Solving subtests on from an achievement batteryies)

• If AR is administered, determine whether QRI is informative

• Consider task characteristics and response demands

• If Picture Concepts and Arithmetic were administered, consider the Expanded Fluid Index (EF)

Figure 4.9 Example of X-BASS Output When Follow up May Be Necessary for the FRI

Step 3. Analyze the Ancillary Index Scores: Quantitative Reasoning Index (QRI), Auditory Working Memory Index (AWMI), and Cognitive Proficiency Index (CPI)

According to Weiss et al. (2016), the Ancillary Index Scales "allow the clinician to explore specific cognitive hypotheses related to children's WISC-V scores in the context of their performance in the real world of the classroom" (p. 15). Rapid Reference 4.28 summarizes the Ancillary Index Scores that were not evaluated in prior steps, namely the QRI (Quantitative Reasoning), AWMI, and CPI. As may be seen in this rapid reference, these Ancillary Index Scores are highly reliable and may provide important information about an individual's cognitive capabilities beyond that which is provided by the Primary Index Scores. The clinical utility of the Ancillary Index Scales is summarized in Rapid Reference 4.29. Note that this rapid reference does not include the NVI or GAI, as the clinical utility of these indexes was discussed in Step 1. Like the Primary Index Scores, the Ancillary Index Scores are evaluated in X-BASS according to cohesion and follow up.

≡ Rapid Reference 4.28

Summary of the Three Ancillary Indexes on the WISC-V

Index	Subtests	CHC Ability Measured	Reliability of Index
Quantitative Reasoning	Figure Weights Arithmetic[1]	Gf:RG, RQ Gsm:MW; Gq:A3	.95
Auditory Working Memory	Digit Span Letter-Number Sequencing	Gsm:MW, MS Gsm: MW	.93
Cognitive Proficiency	Digit Span Picture Span Coding Symbol Search	Gsm:MW, MS Gsm:MS, MW Gs:R9 Gs:P	.93

Note: Substitutions are not permitted for any of the Ancillary Index Scores. Overall average reliability coefficients are reported in this table (*WISC-V Technical and Interpretive Manual*, Wechsler, 2014c, p. 57).

[1] The CHC ability classifications for Arithmetic in column three of this rapid reference are based on the present authors' review of the extant literature and their own review of the demands of this subtest. However, in the *WISC-V Technical and Interpretive Manual* it is also considered a measure of Gf.

≡ *Rapid Reference 4.29*

Clinical Utility of Selected Ancillary Index Scales

Scale	Clinical Utility
Quantitative Reasoning	• May be useful in assessing individuals who may have giftedness or attention deficit/hyperactivity disorder with comorbid learning disorders, such as specific learning disability and giftedness. • Provides additional information regarding an individual's reasoning skills, specifically those involving numeric information, when the reason for referral is in the learning disability area of math problem solving.
Auditory Working Memory	• Allows for a comparison with the Working Memory Index which assesses complex visual-spatial working memory versus auditory-verbal working memory. • Auditory working memory tasks are generally more related to academic achievement than are visual working memory tasks, especially for reading, math problem solving, and written expression. The two modalities of working memory may be differentially sensitive to specific learning disorders.
Cognitive Proficiency	• Proficient processing facilitates fluid reasoning and the acquisition of new material by reducing the cognitive demands of novel or higher order tasks. • Provides an estimate of cognitive information processing efficiency. • Quick processing speed facilitates information processing before decay from working memory occurs. • Most useful in the context of a pairwise difference comparison with the General Ability Index.

Sources: D. P. Flanagan, S. O. Ortiz, & V. C. Alfonso (2013). *Essentials of cross-battery assessment* (3rd ed.). Hoboken, NJ: Wiley.

A. S. Kaufman, S. E. Raiford, & D. L. Coalson (2016). *Intelligent testing with the WISC-V.* Hoboken, NJ: Wiley.

J. M. Sattler, R. Dumont, & D. L. Coalson (2016). *Assessment of children: WISC-V and WPPSI-IV.* San Diego, CA: Jerome M. Sattler Publishing.

D. Wechsler (2014). *WISC-V technical and interpretive manual.* Bloomington, MN: Pearson.

L. G. Weiss, D. H. Saklofske, J. A. Holdnack, & A. Prifitera (Eds.) (2016). *WISC-V clinical use and interpretation: Scientist-practitioner perspectives.* Amsterdam, The Netherlands: Elsevier Academic.

Step 4. Analyze the Complementary Index Scores: Naming Speed Index (NSI), Symbol Translation Index (STI), and Storage and Retrieval Index (SRI)

Rapid Reference 4.30 summarizes the Complementary Index Scores. As may be seen in this rapid reference, these Complementary Index Scores are highly reliable and may provide important information about an individual's cognitive capabilities beyond that which is provided by the Primary and Ancillary Index Scores. In fact, given the importance of Long-Term Storage and Retrieval in understanding learning and achievement, it is our recommendation that the subtests comprising the NSI and STI be administered routinely to individuals referred for suspected learning disability or other neurodevelopmental disorders. Others also agree with this recommendation (e.g., Kaufman et al., 2016).

The clinical utility of the Complementary Index Scores is summarized in Rapid Reference 4.31. Like the Primary and Ancillary Index Scores, the Complementary Index Scores are evaluated in X-BASS according to cohesion and follow up. Because the Storage and Retrieval Index provides an estimate of the CHC broad ability of Long-Term Storage and Retrieval (Glr), to be consistent with the broad ability definitions presented in Rapid Reference 4.20 (i.e., Gc, Gv, Gf, Gsm, and Gs), the following definition is offered for Glr. It too is intentionally simplistic so as to be understood by a wide audience, including parents and teachers.

> Long-term storage and retrieval (Glr) refers to an individual's ability to take in and store a variety of information (e.g., ideas, names, concepts) in one's mind and then retrieve it quickly and easily at a later time by using association (e.g., remembering nonsense names that are given to a variety of silly-looking robots). This ability does not represent *what* is stored in long-term memory or what you know. Rather, it represents the *process* of storing information, which is related to learning efficiency, and retrieving information quickly. When someone says, "It's on the tip of my tongue," he or she is having a hard time retrieving something that the individual knows. Sometimes children have difficulty "finding" information that they know and, therefore, cannot come up with a word or phrase that they learned. Long-term retrieval is important for learning in general and, therefore, affects specific areas of achievement. For example, children who have difficulty naming letters quickly may have difficulty in reading and therefore need to practice this task to the point where it becomes a skill. Although long-term retrieval is critical for overall learning and academic success in school, there are compensatory strategies, accommodations, and instruc-

tional modifications that can minimize the effects of a Glr deficit thereby allowing the student to perform certain academic tasks more efficiently.

DON'T FORGET

Because Glr tasks are related to reading and writing skills and to learning disorders in reading, writing, and math, the subtests that make up the Complementary Index Scales should be administered routinely to individuals suspected of having a specific learning disability.

☰ Rapid Reference 4.30

Summary of the Three Complementary Indexes on the WISC-V

Index	Subtests	Reliability of Composite
Naming Speed	Naming Speed Literacy Naming Speed Quantity	.90
Symbol Translation	Immediate Symbol Translation Delayed Symbol Translation Recognition Symbol Translation	.94
Storage and Retrieval	Naming Speed Index Symbol Translation Index	.94

Note: Overall average reliability coefficients are reported in this table (*WISC-V Technical and Interpretive Manual,* Wechsler, 2014c, p. 57).

☰ Rapid Reference 4.31

Clinical Utility of Complementary Index Scales

Scale	Clinical Utility
Naming Speed	• Provides a broad estimate of automaticity (fluency) which is important for early learning in reading, math, and writing • Sensitive to reading and written expression skills, specific learning disorders in reading and written expression, mathematics skills, and specific learning disorders in mathematics

(*continued*)

(continued)

Scale	Clinical Utility
Symbol Translation	• Involves visual-verbal associative memory tasks that are closely associated with reading decoding skills, word reading accuracy and fluency, text reading, reading comprehension, math calculation skills and math reasoning • Enhances the assessment of children suspected of having learning problems or declarative memory impairment • Offers a strong measure of learning especially in the early years
Storage and Retrieval	• Provides an overall measure of the individual's ability to store and retrieve learned information quickly and efficiently • May be useful in a pattern of strengths and weaknesses model for individuals suspected of having a learning disability (e.g., naming facility versus associative memory)

Sources: D. P. Flanagan, S. O. Ortiz, & V. C. Alfonso (2013). *Essentials of cross-battery assessment* (3rd ed.). Hoboken, NJ: Wiley.

A. S. Kaufman, S. E. Raiford, & D. L. Coalson (2016). *Intelligent testing with the WISC-V.* Hoboken, NJ: Wiley.

J. M. Sattler, R. Dumont, & D. L. Coalson (2016). *Assessment of children: WISC-V and WPPSI-IV.* San Diego, CA: Jerome M. Sattler Publishing.

D. Wechsler (2014c). *WISC-V technical and interpretive manual.* Bloomington, MN: Pearson.

L. G. Weiss, D. H. Saklofske, J. A. Holdnack, & A. Prifitera (Eds.). (2016). *WISC-V clinical use and interpretation: Scientist-practitioner perspectives.* Amsterdam, The Netherlands: Elsevier Academic.

Step 5. Determine Normative Strengths and Weaknesses in the Index Scale Profile

Based on the previous steps, it is likely that practitioners now have an understanding of the individual's performance across a variety of Index Scales. In addition, by this step, it is likely that any follow-up assessment deemed necessary was conducted and alternative composites were generated (e.g., if the Information and Comprehension subtests were administered, the VECI may be used in place of the VCI). As such, it makes sense to evaluate the individual's pattern of *normative* strengths and weaknesses. This is considered necessary to understand where the individual is functioning across a range of cognitive abilities and processes relative to same age peers. Rapid Reference 4.32 includes a chart that may be replicated and filled out by the practitioner. Similar charts are generated automatically in X-BASS (e.g., see Figure 4.7).

Rapid Reference 4.32

Chart for Categorizing Index Scale Scores From a Normative Perspective

Index	Standard Score Normative Weakness < 85	Within Normal Limits 85–115			Normative Strength >115
		Low Average 85–89	Average 90–109	High Average 110–115	
VCI or alternative Gc composite					
FRI or alternative Gf composite					
VSI or alternative Gv composite					
WMI or alternative Gsm composite					
PSI or alternative Gs composite					
QRI					
AWMI					
CPI					
NSI					
STI					
SRI or Alternative Glr Composite					

Note: Nearly 70% of the population obtains standard scores on norm-referenced tests that fall *within normal limits.* Therefore, scores that fall in this range represent expected performance relative to most people. However, scores that fall at the lower end of this range (i.e., 85–89) *may* represent areas of difficulty for the individual. As such, other data sources should be considered prior to suggesting that a Low Average score is problematic for the individual.

253

To determine normative strengths and normative weaknesses in an individual's index profile, review the individual's scores and consider the exact value of the index. If the index is greater than 115, then the ability measured by the index is a *normative strength*. If the index is less than 85, then the ability measured by the index is a *normative weakness*. If the index is between 85 and 115 (inclusive), then the ability measured by the index is *within normal limits*.

Step 6 (Optional). Determine Personal Strengths, Personal Weaknesses, Key Assets, and High Priority Concerns Among the Primary Index Scores

Tables 4.2 to 4.7 may be used to determine personal strengths, personal weaknesses, key assets, and high priority concerns. However, only one of these tables is necessary to conduct the analysis. These tables vary by ability level. That is, practitioners may choose to conduct this analysis based on reference to the *overall WISC-V normative sample* (using Table 4.2) or in reference to the overall ability level of individuals included in the normative sample. Our preference is to conduct the analysis by using the data that were derived from those in the normative sample with a similar ability level as the individual evaluated. Also, we agree with the recommendation in the *WISC-V Technical and Interpretive Manual* (Wechsler, 2014c) and prefer the *Mean of the Index Scores* (MIS) over the FSIQ to conduct this intra-individual analysis because it is based on more subtests and a broader sample of performance than the FSIQ. Therefore, X-BASS carries out this strengths and weaknesses analysis by ability level using the MIS. Figure 4.10 provides an example of the results of this level of analysis for Amanda. Because Amanda's FSIQ was 91, the comparison group used was individuals from the normative sample with FSIQs between 90 and 109 (i.e., Table 4.5). Rapid Reference 4.33 provides a description of terms associated with the strengths and weaknesses analysis of the Primary Index Scales.

A Note About Personal Strengths and Weaknesses
Truth be told, we find limited value in conducting this level of analysis, particularly as it applies to personal strengths and weaknesses, which is why we include it as an optional step. Certainly personal strengths and weaknesses provide information that is useful for intervention planning (see Mascolo et al., 2014); however, they are often misinterpreted, particularly personal weaknesses.

Misinterpretation often results from failure to consider where scores fall relative to most people. For example, for a very bright individual, an Index of 100 may emerge as a personal weakness and the difference between that Index and the MIS

Table 4.2 Determination of Strengths and Weaknesses Using Overall Sample Comparison

Index	Standard Score (SS)	Mean Primary Index Score (MIS)[1]	Difference (indicate "+" for a positive difference and "–" for a negative difference)	Critical Value for Statistical Significance at .05/.01 Level	Personal Strength or Weakness?	Base Rate at 15%/10% Index < MIS (–)	Base Rate at 15%/10% Index > MIS (+)	Key Asset (KA) or High Priority Concern (HPC)? W and difference meets or exceeds base rate and SS ≤ 85 = HPC S and difference meets or exceeds base rate and SS ≥ 115 = KA
VCI				10/12	S or W	9/12	9/12	
VSI				10/12	S or W	9/11	9/12	
FRI				9/11	S or W	9/11	9/11	
WMI				10/12	S or W	10/12	10/12	
PSI				12/14	S or W	12/15	12/15	

Note: If the FSIQ is preferred over the MIS, see Table B.1 and B.2 (*WISC-V Administration and Scoring Manual;* Wechsler, 2014a).

[1] Mean = Sum of VCI + VSI + FRI + WMI + PSI Divided by 5.

255

Table 4.3 Determining Strengths and Weaknesses Using FSIQ Less Than 80 Comparison

Index	Standard Score (SS)	Mean Primary Index Score (MIS)[1]	Difference (indicate "+" for a positive difference and "−" for a negative difference)	Critical Value for Statistical Significance at .05/.01 Level	Personal Strength or Weakness?	Base Rate at 15%/10%		Key Asset (KA) or High Priority Concern (HPC)? W and difference meets or exceeds base rate and SS ≤ 85 = HPC; S and difference meets or exceeds base rate and SS ≥ 115 = KA
						Index < MIS (−)	Index > MIS (+)	
VCI				10/12	S or W	10/13	7/9	
VSI				10/12	S or W	9/11	5/8	
FRI				9/11	S or W	9/11	6/8	
WMI				10/12	S or W	8/9	10/12	
PSI				12/14	S or W	6/9	16/18	

Note: If the FSIQ is preferred over the MIS, see Table B.1 and B.2 (*WISC-V Administration and Scoring Manual*; Wechsler, 2014a).

[1] Mean = Sum of VCI + VSI + FRI + WMI + PSI Divided by 5

Table 4.4 Determining Strengths and Weaknesses Using FSIQ 80–89, Inclusive, Comparison

Index	Standard Score (SS)	Mean Primary Index Score (MIS)[1]	Difference (indicate "+" for a positive difference and "−" for a negative difference)	Critical Value for Statistical Significance at .05/.01 Level	Personal Strength or Weakness?	Base Rate at 15%/10%		Key Asset (KA) or High Priority Concern (HPC)? W and difference meets or exceeds base rate and SS ≤ 85 = HPC S and difference meets or exceeds base rate and SS ≥ 115 = KA
						Index < MIS (−)	Index > MIS (+)	
VCI				10/12	S or W	9/11	8/10	
VSI				10/12	S or W	9/11	8/11	
FRI				9/11	S or W	11/12	7/8	
WMI				10/12	S or W	9/11	9/12	
PSI				12/14	S or W	10/12	15/18	

Note: If the FSIQ is preferred over the MIS, see Table B.1 and B.2 (*WISC-V Administration and Scoring Manual;* Wechsler, 2014a).

[1] Mean = Sum of VCI + VSI + FRI + WMI + PSI Divided by 5.

Table 4.5 Determining Strengths and Weaknesses Using FSIQ 90 – 109, inclusive, Comparison

Index	Standard Score (SS)	Mean Primary Index Score (MIS)[1]	Difference (indicate "+" for a positive difference and "−" for a negative difference)	Critical Value for Statistical Significance at .05/.01 Level	Personal Strength or Weakness?	Base Rate at 15%/10% Index < MIS (−)	Index > MIS (+)	Key Asset (KA) or High Priority Concern (HPC)? W and difference meets or exceeds base rate and SS ≤ 85 = HPC	S and difference meets or exceeds base rate and SS ≥ 115 = KA
VCI				10/12	S or W	10/12	9/12		
VSI				10/12	S or W	10/12	10/12		
FRI				9/11	S or W	10/12	9/11		
WMI				10/12	S or W	10/12	11/14		
PSI				12/14	S or W	12/15	13/16		

Note: If the FSIQ is preferred over the MIS, see Table B.1 and B.2 (*WISC-V Administration and Scoring Manual*; Wechsler, 2014a).

[1] Mean = Sum of VCI + VSI + FRI + WMI + PSI Divided by 5.

Table 4.6 Determining Strengths and Weaknesses Using FSIQ 110 – 119, Inclusive, Comparison.

Index	Standard Score (SS)	Mean Primary Index Score (MIS)[1]	Difference (indicate "+" for a positive difference and "–" for a negative difference)	Critical Value for Statistical Significance at .05/.01 Level	Personal Strength or Weakness?	Base Rate at 15%/10% Index < MIS (–)	Index > MIS (+)	Key Asset (KA) or High Priority Concern (HPC)? W and difference meets or exceeds base rate and SS ≤ 85 = HPC S and difference meets or exceeds base rate and SS ≥ 115 = KA
VCI				10/12	S or W	8/12	10/12	
VSI				10/12	S or W	8/10	10/12	
FRI				9/11	S or W	7/9	10/12	
WMI				10/12	S or W	10/12	10/11	
PSI				12/14	S or W	13/16	8/11	

Note: If the FSIQ is preferred over the MIS, see Table B.1 and B.2 (*WISC-V Administration and Scoring Manual*; Wechsler, 2014a).

[1] Mean = Sum of VCI + VSI + FRI + WMI + PSI Divided by 5.

Table 4.7 Determining Strengths and Weaknesses Using FSIQ 120 or higher Comparison

Index	Standard Score (SS)	Mean Primary Index Score (MIS)[1]	Difference (indicate "+" for a positive difference and "−" for a negative difference)	Critical Value for Statistical Significance at .05/.01 Level	Personal Strength or Weakness?	Base Rate at 15%/10%		Key Asset (KA) or High Priority Concern (HPC):
						Index < MIS (−)	Index > MIS (+)	W and difference meets or exceeds base rate and SS ≤ 85 = HPC / S and difference meets or exceeds base rate and SS ≥ 115 = KA
VCI				10/12	S or W	7/9	14/16	
VSI				10/12	S or W	8/10	11/12	
FRI				9/11	S or W	6/9	13/14	
WMI				10/12	S or W	13/15	9/10	
PSI				12/14	S or W	18/19	6/9	

Note: If the FSIQ is preferred over the MIS, see Table B.1 and B.2 (*WISC-V Administration and Scoring Manual*; Wechsler, 2014a).

[1] Mean = Sum of VCI + VSI + FRI + WMI + PSI Divided by 5.

Index	Standard Score (SS)	Mean Primary Index Score (MIS)[1]	Difference (indicate "+" for a positive difference and "−" for a negative difference)	Critical Value for Statistical Significance at .05/.01 Level	Personal Strength or Weakness?	Base rate at 15% / 10% Index<MIS (−)	Index>MIS (+)	Key Asset (KA) or High Priority Concern (HPC)? W and difference meets or exceeds base rate and SS ≤ 85 = HPC S and difference meets or exceeds base rate and SS ≥ 115 = KA
VCI	100	-91	-9	10/12	S or W	10/12	9/12	
VSI	81	-91	-10	(10)/12	S or (W)	(10)/12	10/12	High Priority Concern
FRI	-97	-91	6	9/11	S or W	10/12	9/11	
WMI	85	-91	-6	10/12	S or W	10/12	11/14	
PSI	-92	-91	1	12/14	S or W	12/15	13/16	

[1] Mean = Sum of VCI + VSI + FRI + WMI + PSI Divided by 5

Note: If the FSIQ is preferred over the MIS, see Table B.1 and B.2 (*WISC-V Administration and Scoring Manual;* Wechsler, 2014a).

Figure 4.10 Determining Amanda's Primary Index Strengths and Weaknesses Using FSIQ 90–109 Comparison

may be rare in the general population. In such circumstances, there is a tendency to attach terms like *abnormality, dysfunction, deficit,* and *impairment* to the Index of 100. None of these terms is accurate. In fact, the only way in which these terms could conceivably be accurate is when, for example, the Index of 100 was obtained following a closed head injury and there was evidence of premorbid functioning in the above average or higher range of functioning in the cognitive domain represented by that Index (e.g., Lezak, 1995). Otherwise, average ability is just that—average. And, when an Index of 100 emerges as a personal weakness (regardless of whether the difference between the Index and the MIS is rare in the general population), it simply means that the individual has valuable deviations (i.e., higher scores in other areas). To illustrate, consider the following analogy.

Michael Jordan has been called the greatest basketball player of all time. He also played minor league baseball. He was never called the best baseball player of all time—certainly not as a minor leaguer. Jordan has a personal weakness in his baseball ability because his basketball ability is far superior. Despite these differences, Jordan was an exceptional athlete. He did not have a deficit in baseball ability simply because he was not as good at baseball as he was at basketball. Instead, his basketball ability was a valuable deviation, not only relative to his baseball ability, but also to other NBA basketball players (a highly skilled population). His personal weakness in baseball ability relative to basketball ability could never be construed as a "deficit" in athletic ability. The same logic applies to psychoeducational test interpretation.

Anytime a norm-referenced test is administered, it is expected that the examinee will perform within normal limits (i.e., standard score range of 85–115, inclusive). Why? Because nearly 70% of the population performs within that range. As such, when the finding of a personal weakness is not also considered in terms of where the score falls relative to most people, misinterpretations may result.

To circumvent the misinterpretations that often result from analysis of personal strengths and weaknesses without consideration of where scores fall relative to most people, it is important to consider the following. First, personal strengths and weaknesses are often common in the general population. Therefore, base rate data should always be considered when ascribing meaning to personal strengths and weaknesses. Second, because personal weaknesses that are also uncommon in the general population may not interfere with learning, academic performance, or activities of daily living, meaning should not be ascribed to a personal weakness without first considering where the score falls relative to most people. Third, Key Assets (KA) and High Priority Concerns (HPC) should be given the most weight when ascribing meaning to strengths and weaknesses in an individual's Primary Index Score profile. This is because KA and HPC take into consideration base rate data as well as where scores fall relative to most people (see Rapid Reference 4.33). Finally, any score that emerges as a personal weakness, a personal weakness that is uncommon, or a HPC should not be interpreted as limiting the individual in any way without evidence of its ecological validity (i.e., how the weakness manifests in real world performances, such as classroom activities; see Rapid Reference 7.5 in Chapter 7 for examples).

≡ Rapid Reference 4.33

Terms Used in the Strengths and Weaknesses Analysis of the Primary Index Scores

Term (Abbreviation)	Definition
Normative Strength (NS)	An Index that is above 115.
Normative Weakness (NW)	An Index that is below 85.
Within Normal Limits (WNL)	An Index ranging from 85 to 115, inclusive.
Personal Strength (PS)	An Index that is significantly higher than the MIS (using either .05 or .01 level of significance).
Personal Weakness (PW)	An Index that is significantly lower than the MIS (using either .05 or .01 level of significance).
Uncommon Personal Strength (PS/Uncommon)[1]	A Personal Strength that is also substantially different from the individual's MIS. That is, the size of the difference between the Index and the MIS is unusually large, occurring less than 10% of the time in the WISC-V normative sample.
Uncommon Personal Weakness (PW/Uncommon)[1]	A Personal Weakness that is also substantially different from the individual's MIS. That is, the size of the difference between the Index and the MIS is unusually large, occurring less than 10% of the time in the WISC-V normative sample.
Key Asset (KA)	An Index that is an uncommon Personal Strength and a Normative Strength.
High Priority Concern (HPC)	An Index that is an uncommon Personal Weakness and a Normative Weakness.

Note: MIS-Mean of the index scores.

[1] Determination of an uncommon or unusual difference is typically associated with a base rate of 10%. However, a base rate of 15% may also be used at the discretion of the practitioner, diagnostic team members, district guidelines for eligibility for special education services, and the like.

Rapid Reference 4.34 provides examples of interpretive output from X-BASS regarding strengths and weaknesses in an individual's Primary Index Score profile.

≡ *Rapid Reference 4.34*

Interpretation of Strengths and Weaknesses in the Primary Index Score Profile

Index Scores That Are Classified as Strengths

1. Key Asset (Normative Strength and Personal Strength/Uncommon)

Interpretation: Jessica's processing speed is considered a significant strength as compared to other individuals her age in the general population. In addition, her ability in this area is significantly higher than her abilities in other areas. In fact, the difference between Jessica's processing speed and her abilities in other areas is so large that it is not commonly achieved by other children her age in the general population. Therefore, Jessica's processing speed is a Key Asset and a notable integrity, a finding that should play an essential role in developing educational interventions. [Note that the latter part of this interpretive statement may be germane only when other abilities (cognitive or academic) are either in the lower end of the Average range or lower, suggesting that intervention may be warranted.]

2. Normative Strength and Personal Strength/Not Uncommon

Interpretation: Jessica's processing speed is considered a significant strength as compared to other individuals her age in the general population. In addition, her ability in this area is significantly higher than her abilities in other areas. Therefore, Jessica's processing speed is a notable integrity, a finding that may play an essential role in developing educational interventions. [Note that the latter part of this interpretive statement may be germane only when other abilities (cognitive or academic) are either in the lower end of the Average range or lower, suggesting that intervention may be warranted.]

3. Normative Strength but Not a Personal Strength

Interpretation: Jessica's processing speed is considered a significant strength compared to other children her age in the general population. Her processing speed is a notable integrity, a finding that may play an essential role in developing educational interventions. [Note that the latter part of this interpretive statement may be germane only when other abilities (cognitive or academic) are either in the lower end of the Average range or lower, suggesting that intervention may be warranted.]

4. Personal Strength/Uncommon but Not a Normative Strength

Interpretation: Jessica's processing speed is considered a significant strength compared to her abilities in other areas. In fact, the difference between her processing speed and her abilities in other areas is so large that it is not commonly achieved by other children her age in the general population.

Therefore, Jessica's processing speed is a notable Personal Strength, a finding that should play an essential role in developing educational interventions. [Note that the latter part of this interpretive statement may be germane only when other abilities (cognitive or academic) are either in the lower end of the Average range or lower, suggesting that intervention may be warranted. Also, in this scenario, Jessica's processing speed may be considered a notable integrity, as it was in the first two scenarios, if her Processing Speed standard score is at the upper end of the Average range (i.e., 110 to 115). Finally, it is also possible for Jessica's processing speed to be a Personal Strength/ Uncommon but a Normative Weakness (i.e., if the Personal Strength/ Uncommon is associated with a standard score of < 85).]

5. **Personal Strength/Not Uncommon but Not a Normative Strength**

Interpretation: Jessica's processing speed is considered a significant strength compared to her abilities in other areas. Her processing speed is a notable Personal Strength, a finding that should play an essential role in developing educational interventions. [Note that the latter part of this interpretive statement may be germane only when other abilities (cognitive or academic) are either in the lower end of the Average range or lower, suggesting that intervention may be warranted. Also, it is possible for Jessica's processing speed to be a Personal Strength/Not Uncommon but a Normative Weakness (i.e., if the Personal Strength/Not Uncommon is associated with a standard score of < 85).]

Index Scores That Are Classified as Weaknesses

6. **High-Priority Concern (Normative Weakness and Personal Weakness/Uncommon)**

Interpretation: Jessica's processing speed is considered a significant weakness as compared to other individuals her age in the general population. In addition, her ability in this area is significantly lower than her abilities in other areas. In fact, the difference between her processing speed and her abilities in other areas is so large that it is not commonly found in the general population. Therefore, Jessica's processing speed is a High-Priority Concern, a finding that should play an essential role in developing educational interventions.

7. **Normative Weakness and Personal Weakness/Not Uncommon**

Interpretation: Jessica's processing speed is considered a significant weakness as compared to other individuals her age in the general population. In addition, her ability in this area is significantly lower than her abilities in other areas. Therefore, Jessica's processing speed may be an area of concern and may have significant implications with regard to her ability to perform basic skills/ tasks quickly and automatically.

8. **Personal Weakness/Uncommon but Not a Normative Weakness**

Interpretation: Jessica's processing speed is considered a significant weakness compared to her abilities in other areas. In fact, the difference between her processing speed and her abilities in other areas is so large that it is not

(continued)

commonly found in the general population. Therefore, Jessica's processing speed is a notable Personal Weakness, a finding that may play a role in developing educational interventions. [Note that the latter part of this interpretive statement may be germane only when the actual Processing Speed standard score is in the lower end of the Average range (i.e., 85–90), suggesting that interventions or accommodations may be warranted. The finding of a Personal Weakness that is uncommon in the normal population does not provide de facto evidence of a processing disorder. This is because it is feasible for an individual to have a Personal Weakness/Uncommon that is associated with a standard score that falls in the Average range or higher.]

9. Normative Weakness but Not a Personal Weakness

Interpretation: Jessica's processing speed is considered a significant weakness compared to other children her age in the general population. Her processing speed is a notable weakness, a finding that should play an essential role in developing educational interventions.

10. Personal Weakness/Not Uncommon but Not a Normative Weakness

Interpretation: Jessica's processing speed is considered a significant weakness compared to her abilities in other areas. Her processing speed is a notable Personal Weakness. However, the finding of a Personal Weakness, in and of itself, does not provide de facto evidence of a processing disorder. A Personal Weakness that is associated with a standard score that falls Within Normal Limits or higher does not, in and of itself, provide evidence of a disorder. Also, it is feasible for a child to have a Personal Weakness/Not Uncommon that is associated with a standard score that falls in the Above Average range, for example.

11. Index is cohesive but is neither a strength nor a weakness

Interpretation: The Processing Speed Index (PSI), a measure of Processing Speed (Gs), represents Jessica's ability to fluently and automatically perform cognitive tasks, especially when under pressure to maintain focused attention and concentration. Jessica's Gs was assessed by tasks that required her to copy a series of symbols that are paired with numbers using a key (Coding) and indicate the presence or absence of a target symbol within a search group (Symbol Search). Jessica obtained a PSI standard score of 100, which is ranked at the 50th percentile and is classified as Average.

Step 7 (Optional). Determine Whether the New Clinical Composites Are Cohesive and Add Clinically Relevant Information Beyond That Provided by the Primary, Ancillary, and Complementary Scales

Analysis of the new clinical composites is optional and this step is meant to guide the interpretation of these composites should they offer important information beyond the WISC-V Index Scores. Rapid Reference 4.35 summarizes the new clinical composites for the WISC-V. We generated these composites based on clinical considerations that we believed extended beyond what the WISC-V

≡ Rapid Reference 4.35

Summary of New Clinical Composites for the WISC-V

Clinical Composite	Subtest Composition	Brief Description
Gc (Verbal Expression – Low) **Gc-VE/L**	Vocabulary Information	These two subtests form a broad Gc ability and require less verbal expression compared to the other Gc subtests (e.g., one-or two-word responses as compared to multi-word responses or sentences). An alternative label for this composite is Retrieval from Remote Long-Term Storage (**RFLT-Remote)**, which provides an estimate of an individual's ability to retrieve information from long-term storage that was encoded weeks, months, or years ago.
Gc (Verbal Expression – High) **Gc-VE/H**	Similarities Comprehension	These two subtests require greater verbal expression to earn maximum credit compared to the other Gc subtests and typically involve some degree of reasoning ability.
Fluid-Crystallized **Gf-Gc**	Vocabulary Information Matrix Reasoning Figure Weights	Provides an alternative to the FSIQ and GAI. Balances Gf and Gc about equally. Contains only subtests with high *g* loadings. Because Gf and Gc are highly correlated with *g* and are considered to be the cornerstones of general intelligence, research supports use of a Gf-Gc composite as an estimate of general ability (e.g., McGrew, LaForte, & Schrank, 2014).
Working Memory (Alternative) **Gsm-MW (Alt)**	Digit Span Backwards + Digit Span Sequencing + Letter-Number Sequencing	Provides an alternative to the Auditory Working Memory Index (AWMI) by eliminating Digit Span Forward (a test of memory span).
Memory Span-Working Memory **Gsm-MS,MW**	Digit Span Forward + Digit Span Backward	Provides a balance of Memory Span and Working Memory and is consistent with the composition of the Digit Span subtest on the WISC-IV.

(continued)

(continued)

Clinical Composite	Subtest Composition	Brief Description
Working Memory (Cognitive Complexity – High) **WM-CC/H**	Arithmetic Picture Span	Provides an estimate of working memory with tests that are more cognitively complex than Digit Span. Arithmetic involves Gf (i.e., Quantitative Reasoning), Gc, and Gsm (Working Memory Capacity). Picture Span involves Memory Span and Working Memory (due to proactive interference) and may involve Gv (Visual Memory).
Verbal (Expanded Crystallized) Index **VECI***	Similarities Vocabulary Information Comprehension	Provides a robust estimate of Gc as compared to the Verbal Comprehension Index (VCI), spanning two narrow ability domains (VL – Lexical Knowledge and K0 – General Information). Requires reasoning with verbal information. Involves subtests that have low to high demands for verbal expression.
Expanded Fluid Index **EFI***	Matrix Reasoning Figure Weights Picture Concepts Arithmetic	Provides a more robust estimate of Gf as compared to the Fluid Reasoning Index (FRI), spanning three narrow ability domains, including Induction (I), General Sequential Reasoning (RG), and Quantitative Reasoning (RQ).
Perceptual Speed **Gs-P****	Symbol Search Cancellation	Provides an alternative to the PSI, eliminating the memory and motor dexterity demands inherent mainly in the Coding subtest.
Retrieval From Recent Long-Term Storage **RFLT-Recent**	Delayed Symbol Translation Recognition Symbol Translation	Provides an estimate of an individual's ability to retrieve recently encoded information from long-term storage.

Sources: *S. E. Raiford, L. Drozdick, O. Zhang, & X. Zhou, Expanded index scores. Technical Report #1. Retrieved from http://downloads.pearsonclinical.com /iimagesw/Assets/WISC-V/WISC-VTechReport1_FNL_v2.pdf.

**A. S. Kaufman, S. E. Raiford, & D. L. Coalson, Intelligent Testing with the WISC-V. Copyright © 2016 John Wiley & Sons, Inc.

Primary, Ancillary, and Complementary Index Scales offer. The reliability and SEMs for the new clinical composites are provided in Table 4.8. Although carried out by X-BASS, Table 4.9 and Table 4.10 provide the critical values necessary to determine whether the clinical composites are cohesive. When the subtests that make up the clinical composites are administered and the scaled scores are entered into X-BASS, the program automatically provides the composite. Nevertheless, the norms for the clinical composites are also found in Appendix B.

CONCLUSION

A WISC-[V] detective strives to use ingenuity, clinical sense, a thorough grounding in psychological theory and research, and a willingness to administer supplementary cognitive tests to reveal the dynamics of a child's scaled-score profile.

—*Alan S. Kaufman, 1994, P. 23*

The above quote summarizes beautifully the art and science that is part and parcel of Kaufman's *Intelligent Testing* approach. In this chapter, our goal was to blend art and science in a manner that intelligent testing clearly requires and that Kaufman continues to espouse (Kaufman et al., 2016). Although our approaches differ with regard to specific criteria used to draw conclusions from test data, in the end each approach places cognitive assessment upon a solid theoretical, psychometric, and research-based foundation and results in very similar summaries of an individual's cognitive capabilities. This chapter set forth a step-by-step approach for interpreting an individual's cognitive score profile from the most global and reliable scores, namely, the FSIQ, NVI, and GAI, to the Primary, Ancillary, and Complimentary Index Scores, to an individual's normative and relative strengths and weaknesses. In addition, we provided normative data for 10 new clinical composites that may be helpful to the practitioner in understanding more thoroughly an individual's profile of scores. Given the comprehensiveness and complexity of the WISC-V, as described in this chapter and in Chapter 1, the use of manual worksheets for interpretation was no longer an option. Instead, we automated our interpretive steps in X-BASS, a sophisticated software system that aids in understanding an individual's WISC-V cognitive score profile, provides guidance for use of the WISC-V in the identification of specific learning disabilities, and provides guidance in the use of the WISC-V in the assessment of individuals from culturally and linguistically diverse backgrounds.

Table 4.8 Internal Consistency Reliability Coefficients and SEMs for the WISC-V Clinical Composites, by Age and Overall Sample

Composite	Age											All
	6	7	8	9	10	11	12	13	14	15	16	
Gc-VE/L or RFLT-Remote												
Reliability	.89	.92	.89	.92	.91	.91	.94	.92	.92	.93	.94	.92
SEM	4.97	4.24	4.97	4.24	4.50	4.50	3.67	4.24	4.24	3.97	3.67	4.24
Gc-VE/H												
Reliability	.88	.91	.89	.91	.91	.87	.92	.91	.92	.90	.90	.90
SEM	5.20	4.50	4.97	4.50	4.50	5.41	4.24	4.50	4.24	4.74	4.74	4.74
Gf-Gc												
Reliability	.94	.95	.95	.95	.95	.94	.97	.95	.95	.96	.96	.95
SEM	3.67	3.35	3.35	3.35	3.35	3.67	2.59	3.35	3.35	3.00	3.00	3.35
Gsm-MW [Alt]												
Reliability	.95	.92	.90	.90	.89	.90	.92	.90	.92	.92	.92	.91
SEM	3.35	4.24	4.74	4.74	4.97	4.74	4.24	4.74	4.24	4.24	4.24	4.50
Gsm-MS, MW												
Reliability	.87	.84	.86	.83	.83	.87	.88	.87	.86	.88	.88	.86
SEM	5.41	6.00	5.61	6.18	6.18	5.41	5.20	5.41	5.61	5.20	5.20	5.61
WM-CC/H												
Reliability	.90	.89	.91	.92	.91	.90	.92	.92	.92	.91	.92	.91
SEM	4.74	4.97	4.50	4.24	4.50	4.74	4.24	4.24	4.24	4.50	4.24	4.50

VECI										
Reliability	.93	.95	.94	.95	.95	.95	.95	.95	.94	.94
SEM	3.97	3.35	3.67	3.35	3.35	3.35	3.35	3.35	3.67	3.38
EFI										
Reliability	.95	.94	.95	.95	.94	.96	.95	.95	.95	.95
SEM	3.35	3.67	3.35	3.35	3.67	3.00	3.35	3.35	3.35	3.44
Gs-P										
Reliability	.85	.80	.87	.81	.85	.88	.86	.88	.87	.86
SEM	5.81	6.71	5.41	6.54	5.81	5.20	5.61	5.20	5.41	5.70
RFLT-Recent										
Reliability	.93	.90	.92	.90	.92	.91	.91	.91	.90	.91
SEM	3.97	4.74	4.24	4.74	4.24	4.50	4.50	4.50	4.74	4.50

A. S. Kaufman, S. E. Raiford, & D. L. Coalson, *Intelligent Testing with the WISC-V.* Copyright © 2016 John Wiley & Sons, Inc.

S. E. Raiford, L. Drozdick, O. Zhang, & X. Zhou, *Expanded index scores.* Technical Report #1. http://downloads.pearsonclinical.com/iimagesw/Assets/WISC-V/WISC-VTechReport1_FNL_v2.pdf

Note: SEM = standard error of measurement; Gc = Crystallized Intelligence; Gc-VE/L = Gc Verbal Expression-Low; Gc-VE/H = Gc Verbal Expression-High; Gf-Gc = Fluid Reasoning-Crystallized Intelligence; Gsm = Short-Term Memory; Gsm-MW [Alt] = Working Memory (Alternative); Gsm-MS, MW = Memory Span-Working Memory; WM-CC/H = Working Memory (Cognitive Complexity-High); VECI = Verbal (Expanded Crystallized) Index; EFI = Expanded Fluid Index; Gs = Processing Speed; Gs-P = Perceptual Speed; RFLT-Recent = Retrieval from Long-Term Storage-Recent.

Table 4.9 Cohesion Analysis for New WISC-V Clinical Composites Made Up of Two Subtests

Index	Highest Subtest Scaled Score	Lowest Subtest Scaled Score	Difference Between Highest and Lowest Subtest Scaled Score	Critical Value Needed for Statistical Difference at .05 Level	Is Difference Statistically Significant? Y/N	Critical Value Needed for Rare Difference (10% of population)	Is Difference Rare? Y/N	Is Index Cohesive? *For Information reported in shaded Columns:* N + N = Cohesive Y + Y = Not Cohesive Y + N = Use Clinical Judgment
Gc-VE/L			=	3		4		
Gc-VE/H			=	3		4		
Gsm-MS,MW			=	4		5		
Gwm-CC/H			=	3		5		
Gs-P			=	4		6		
RFLT-Recent			=	16		16		

Note: Gc-VE/L = Verbal Expression Low (also Retrieval From Remote Long-Term Stores); Gc-VE/H = Verbal Expression High; Gwm-CC/H = Working Memory with Cognitive Complexity High; Gs-P = Perceptual Speed; RFLT-Recent = Retrieval From Recent Long-Term Stores.

Table 4.10 Cohesion Analysis for New WISC-V Clinical Composites Made up of Three or More Subtests

Index	Highest Subtest Scaled Score	Lowest Subtest Scaled Score	Difference Between Highest and Lowest Subtest Scaled Score	Critical Value Needed for Rare Difference (10% of population)	Is Difference Rare? Y/N	Is Index Cohesive? *For Information reported in shaded Column:* N = Cohesive Y = Not Cohesive
Gf-Gc			=	7		
Gsm-MW ALT			=	6		
VECI			=	6		
EFI			=	8		

Note: Gf-Gc = Fluid-Crystallized; Gsm-MW ALT = Working Memory Alternative; VECI = Verbal Expanded Crystallized Index; EFI = Expanded Fluid Index.

🪶 TEST YOURSELF 🪶

. . . .

1. **Michaela obtained scaled scores of 8 and 9 on the WISC-V Coding and Symbol Search subtests, respectively. When interpreting her PSI of 92, the practitioner should consider the Index as representing**

   a. a cohesive index.

   b. a noncohesive index.

   c. a normative strength.

   d. a key asset.

2. **The approach to test interpretation presented in this chapter emphasizes the importance of featuring the**

   a. Subtest profile.

   b. Primary Index profile.

   c. Ancillary Index profile.

   d. FSIQ only.

3. **For most individuals, the FSIQ is the best estimate of their overall cognitive ability.**

   a. True

   b. False

4. **Using the normative descriptive classification system to describe WISC-V index scores, a standard score of 119 should be described as**

   a. a Normative Weakness.

   b. within Normal Limits.

   c. a Normative Strength.

   d. none of the above.

5. **Juanita is a 10-year-old Hispanic female referred for a cognitive evaluation. The best estimate of her overall cognitive ability will be**

   a. the FSIQ.

   b. the NVI.

   c. the GAI.

   d. determined by an examination of her FSIQ and NVI.

6. **The FSIQ is always the best estimate of overall intellectual ability for individuals suspected of having an intellectual disability.**

   a. True

   b. False

7. **The X-BASS may be used for the following:**
   a. Understanding an individual's index score profile
   b. Guidance in the use of the WISC-V with individuals suspected of having a learning disability
   c. Interpretation of WISC-V score profiles for individuals who are culturally and linguistically diverse
   d. All of the above

8. **The new WISC-V Clinical Composites should be used in all evaluations.**
   a. True
   b. False

9. **Which of the following is not true of the interpretive method presented in this book?**
   a. Individual subtest interpretation is featured.
   b. Base rate data are used to evaluate cohesion of scores.
   c. Interpretation is grounded firmly in CHC theory.
   d. Guidance regarding the use of supplemental measures to test hypotheses about significant subtest variation is provided.

10. **The foundation of WISC-V interpretation advocated in Chapter 4 is that in order to understand well an individual's cognitive profile of scores, the practitioner must blend the art and the science of test interpretation.**
    a. True
    b. False

Answers: 1. a; 2. b; 3. a; 4. c; 5. d; 6. b; 7. d; 8. b; 9. a; 10. a

REFERENCES

Alfonso, V. C., Flanagan, D. P., & Radwan, S. (2005). The impact of Cattell-Horn-Carroll (CHC) theory on test development and the interpretation of cognitive and academic abilities. In D. P. Flanagan & P. L. Harrison (Eds.), *Contemporary intellectual assessment: Theories, tests, and issues* (2nd ed., pp. 185–202). New York, NY: Guilford.

Comrey, A. L. (1988). Factor-analytic methods of scale development in personality and clinical psychology. *Journal of Consulting and Clinical Psychology, 56,* 754–761.

Daniel, M. H. (2007). "Scatter" and the construct validity of FSIQ: Comment on Fiorello et al. (2007). *Applied Neuropsychology, 14,* 291–295.

Flanagan, D. P., Alfonso, V. C., Mascolo, J. T., & McDonough, E. M. (in press). A CHC-based operational definition of SLD: Integrating multiple data sources and multiple data gathering methods. In D. P. Flanagan & V. C. Alfonso (Eds.), *Essentials of specific learning disability identification* (2nd ed.). Hoboken, NJ: Wiley.

Flanagan, D. P., Alfonso, V. C., & Reynolds, M. R. (2013). Broad and narrow CHC abilities measured and not measured by the Wechsler Scales: Moving beyond within-battery factor analysis. *Journal of Psychoeducational Assessment, 31,* 202–223.

Flanagan, D. P., & McGrew, K. S. (1997). A cross-battery approach to assessing and interpreting cognitive abilities: Narrowing the gap between practice and cognitive science. In D. P. Flanagan, J. L. Genshaft, & P. L. Harrison (Eds.), *Contemporary intellectual assessment: Theories, tests, and issues* (pp. 314–325). New York, NY: Guilford.

Flanagan, D. P., & Ortiz, S. O. (2001). *Essentials of cross-battery assessment.* New York, NY: Wiley.

Flanagan, D. P., Ortiz, S. O., & Alfonso, V. C. (2007). *Essentials of cross-battery assessment* (2nd ed.). New York, NY: Wiley.

Flanagan, D. P., Ortiz, S. O., & Alfonso, V. C. (2013). *Essentials of cross-battery assessment* (3rd edition). Hoboken, NJ: Wiley.

Kaufman, A. S., & Kaufman, N. L. (2014a). *Kaufman Test of Educational Achievement* (3rd ed.). Bloomington, MN: Pearson.

Kaufman, A. S., & Kaufman, N. L. (2014b). *KTEA-3 technical and interpretive manual.* Bloomington, MN: Pearson.

Kaufman, A. S., Raiford, S. E., & Coalson, D. L. (2016). *Intelligent testing with the WISC-V.* Hoboken, NJ: Wiley.

Keith, T. Z., & Reynolds, M. R. (2010). Cattell-Horn-Carroll abilities and cognitive tests: What we've learned from 20 years of research. *Psychology in the Schools, 47,* 635–650. doi:10.1002/pits 20496

Levine, A. J., & Marks, L. (1928). *Testing intelligence and achievement.* New York, NY: Macmillan.

Mather, N., & Wendling, B. J. (2014). Examiner's Manual. *Woodcock-Johnson IV Tests of Cognitive Abilities.* Rolling Meadows, IL: Riverside.

McDonough, E. M., Flanagan, D. P., Sy, M., & Alfonso, V. C. (in press). Specific learning disorder. In S. Goldstein & M. DeVries (Eds.), *Handbook of DSM-5 disorders in children.* New York, NY: Springer.

McGrew, K. S. (2015). Intellectual functioning. In E. A. Polloway (Ed.), *The death penalty and intellectual disability* (pp. 85–111). Washington, DC: American Association on Intellectual and Developmental Disabilities.

McGrew, K. S., & Flanagan, D. P. (1998). *The intelligence test desk reference (ITDR): Gf-Gc cross-battery assessment.* Needham Heights, MA: Allyn & Bacon.

McGrew, K. S., Flanagan, D. P., & Ortiz, S. O. (2000). *The Wechsler intelligence scales and Gf-Gc theory: A contemporary approach to interpretation.* Boston, MA: Allyn & Bacon.

McGrew, K. S., & Wendling, B. J. (2010). Cattell-Horn-Carroll cognitive-achievement relations: What we have learned from the past 20 years of research. *Psychology in the Schools, 47,* 651–675. doi:10.1002/pits.20497

McGrew, K. S., Werder, J. K., & Woodcock, R. W. (1991). *Woodcock-Johnson Psycho-Educational Battery-Revised technical manual.* Chicago, IL: Riverside.

Messick, S. (1989). Validity. In R. Linn (Ed.), *Educational measurement* (3rd ed., pp. 104–131). Washington, DC: American Council on Education.

Messick, S. (1995). Validity of psychological assessment: Validation of inferences from persons' responses and performances as scientific inquiry into score meaning. *American Psychologist, 50,* 741–749. http://dx.doi.org/10.1037/0003-066X.50.9.741

Niileksela, C. R., Reynolds, M. R., Keith, T. Z., & McGrew, K. S. (2016). A special validity study of the WJ IV: Acting on evidence for specific abilities. In D. P. Flanagan & V. C. Alfonso (Eds.), *WJ IV clinical use and interpretation: Scientist-practitioner perspectives* (pp. 65–106). Amsterdam, The Netherlands: Elsevier Academic Press.

Orsini, A., Pezzuti, L., & Hulbert, S. (2014). The unitary ability of IQ in the WISC-IV and its computation. *Personality and Individual Differences, 69*, 173–175. doi:10.1016/j.paid .2014.05.023

Ortiz, S. O., Flanagan, D. P., & Alfonso, V. C. (2017). *Cross-Battery Assessment Software System (X-BASS)* (Version 2.0) [Computer software]. Hoboken, NJ: Wiley.

Pearson. (2009). *Wechsler Individual Achievement Test* (3rd ed.). Bloomington, MN: Author.

Pintner, R. (1923). *Intelligence testing.* New York, NY: Holt, Rinehart, & Winston.

Raiford, S. E., & Coalson, D. L. (2014). *Essentials of WPPSI-IV assessment.* Hoboken, NJ: Wiley.

Raiford, S. E., Weiss, L. G., Rolfhus, E., & Coalson, D. (2005/2008). *General Ability Index. WISC-IV Technical Report #4* (updated December 2008). San Antonio, TX: Pearson Education. http://images.pearsonclinical.com/images/assets/WISC-IV/80720 _WISCIV_Hr_r4.pdf

Reynolds, C. R., & Kamphaus, R. W. (2016). *Reynolds Intellectual Assessment Scales* (2nd ed.). Lutz, FL: PAR.

Sattler, J. M., Dumont, R., & Coalson, D. L. (2016). *Assessment of children: WISC-V and WPPSI-IV.* San Diego, CA: Jerome M. Sattler Publishing.

Schneider, W. J. (2013). Principles of assessment of aptitude and achievement. In D. Saklofske, C. Reynolds, & V. Schwean (Eds.), *The Oxford handbook of child psychological assessment* (pp. 286–330). New York, NY: Oxford University Press.

Schrank, F. A., Mather, N., & McGrew, K. S., (2014). *Woodcock-Johnson IV Tests of Achievement.* Rolling Meadows, IL: Riverside.

Terman, L. M. (1916). *The measurement of intelligence: An explanation of and a complete guide for the use of the Stanford revision and extension of the Binet-Simon Intelligence Scale.* Boston, MA: Houghton Mifflin.

Wechsler, D. (2014a). *WISC-V administration and scoring manual.* Bloomington, MN: Pearson.

Wechsler, D. (2014b). *WISC-V administration and scoring manual supplement.* Bloomington, MN: Pearson.

Wechsler, D. (2014c). *WISC-V technical and interpretive manual.* Bloomington, MN: Pearson.

Weiss, L. G., Saklofske, D. H., Holdnack, J. A., & Prifitera, A. (Eds.). (2016). *WISC-V clinical use and interpretation: Scientist-practitioner perspectives.* Amsterdam, The Netherlands: Elsevier Academic Press.

Five

STRENGTHS AND WEAKNESSES OF THE WISC-V

The WISC-V has far more strengths than limitations and is a substantial revision of the previous edition of the instrument. Some of the WISC-V's most salient strengths include (1) a robust five-factor structure across the age range of the test; (2) improved measurement of cognitive constructs (i.e., Gf, Gsm) and coverage of Long-Term Storage and Retrieval (Glr); (3) greater alignment with CHC theory; (4) exemplary psychometric properties; (5) greater clinical utility for special populations; and (6) greater applicability to neuropsychological assessment.

Rapid References 5.1 through 5.4 include the strengths and weaknesses of the WISC-V that we consider most important for practitioners to know. These strengths and weaknesses are organized into four categories: (1) test development and content (Rapid Reference 5.1); (2) administration and scoring (Rapid Reference 5.2); (3) psychometric properties (Rapid Reference 5.3); and (4) interpretation (Rapid Reference 5.4).

Rapid Reference 5.1

Strengths and Weaknesses of the WISC-V: Test Development and Content

Strengths

- The WISC-V surpasses WISC-IV in *substantial improvements* and close adherence to theory.
- The WISC-V FSIQ includes measures that span five cognitive domains, yielding a broader representation of general intellectual functioning than the WISC-IV FSIQ.

(continued)

(continued)

- The number of subtests required to derive the FSIQ decreased from 10 on the WISC-IV to 7 on the WISC-V, thereby reducing the amount of time needed to derive an overall score.
- The WISC-IV PRI was replaced with the VSI and FRI on the WISC-V, resulting in more precise measurement and interpretation of and differentiation between visual processing and fluid reasoning, respectively, and greater adherence to Cattell-Horn-Carroll (CHC) theory.
- Several new ancillary indexes (e.g., Auditory Working Memory Index [AWMI] and complementary indexes (i.e., Naming Speed Index [NSI], Symbol Translation Index [STI], and [Storage and Retrieval Index [SRI]) improve on the test's clinical utility in neuropsychological and educational assessment.
- The addition of Figure Weights (FW) improves measurement of fluid reasoning.
- The addition of Visual Puzzles improves measurement of visual processing.
- The assessment of working memory capacity has been expanded through the inclusion of Digit Span Sequencing and Picture Span. Arithmetic also has increased working memory demands.
- Classification categories for score ranges were revised to be more comprehensible and less pejorative (e.g., the term *borderline* was dropped).
  - *The WISC-V Technical and Interpretive Manual* (Wechsler, 2014a) clearly states, "Qualitative descriptors are only suggestions and are not evidence-based; alternate terms may be used as appropriate" (p. 152).
- The Nonverbal Index (NVI) provides an alternative measure of overall cognitive ability that does not require verbal responses.
- The General Ability Index (GAI) and Cognitive Proficiency Index (CPI) are available with norms provided in the test manuals and may have clinical utility for identification and diagnosis of specific learning disabilities and intellectual disability.
- Primary and secondary subtests are designed to measure complex cognitive processes, while complementary subtests are designed to measure processes related to learning difficulties, particularly in reading and math.
- Subtest instructions have been shortened and are simpler.
- Demonstration, sample, and teaching items have been added to increase the examinee's understanding of task demands.
- New or revised test items were added to increase the security of the test and update items dependent on current culture; artwork was updated to be more engaging for children.
- The Pearson WISC-V Web page makes available free interpretive information, including a *Technical and Interpretive Manual Supplement* (Wechsler, 2014b), technical reports that include norms for two expanded index scores, detailed information on testing children who are deaf or hard of hearing and a special group study with this population, instructions and technical information on using the WASI-II with the WISC-V, and several papers on digital versions of WISC-V subtests.

Weaknesses

- Ga is not represented, although it is measured to some extent by the *Wechsler Individual Achievement Test–Third Edition* (WIAT-III; Pearson, 2009) and more extensively by the *Kaufman Test of Educational Achievement–Third Edition* (KTEA-3; Kaufman & Kaufman, 2014), both of which are statistically linked to the WISC-V through a common sample.
- Gv is underrepresented, as the VSI is derived via two tests of Visualization (Vz); the VCI is an underrepresentation of Gc because it is derived via two tests of Lexical Knowledge. However, Similarities also involves fluid reasoning.
- No rationale is given for including two VCI and two FRI subtests, but only one VSI subtest in the GAI and FSIQ.
- Subtests that make up the NVI require receptive language, calling into question the name of this index.
- No substitutions are allowed for the five Primary Index Scales and prorating is not permissible, which may limit the clinical utility of the instrument.
- The NSI and the STI make up the SRI but are not well integrated with the other indexes of the WISC-V or incorporated into its overall factor structure.

≡ *Rapid Reference 5.2*

. . . .

Strengths and Weaknesses of the WISC-V: Administration and Scoring

Strengths

- Discontinue rules were modified to reduce testing time and examinee discouragement.
- Improvements were made to the instructions of many subtests (e.g., Block Design, Picture Concepts), making them more explicit and simple.
- Ample use of queries and prompts improves the individual's understanding of the task.
- Rapid completion of tasks was deemphasized by reducing the number of subtests with time bonus points.
- Includes an expanded number of process scores.
- Continues the practice of giving full credit to any failed items below the age-appropriate starting point if the examiner begins testing below that point and the child then earns perfect scores on the first two items at the age-appropriate starting point. (Similarly, no credit is given for passed items beyond the correct discontinue point.)

(continued)

(continued)

- Offers Q-global scoring, but retains the option of hand-scoring for those who want it or who cannot access the Internet.

Weaknesses

- The directions for the Letter-Number Sequencing subtest indicate that the examinee must first recall the numbers followed by the letters. However, if the opposite occurs, the examinee is given credit.
- Audio recordings are not used for memory tests, which would have provided a more reliable means of administering the Digit Span and Letter-Number Sequencing subtests, in particular.
- Examiner training activities are not included in the WISC-V manuals.
- The organization of subtests into three stimulus books is handy, but it may encourage examiners to "travel light" and not be able to administer secondary and complementary subtests if they might be called for.
- The Record Form may be overwhelming and cumbersome to some practitioners.
- The Record Form makes it too easy for examiners accustomed to the WISC-IV to add 10 rather than 7 scaled scores for the FSIQ.
- Examiners and examinees have reported irritation with and distraction from the Figure Weights and Visual Puzzles requirement to ask "Do you have an answer?" if the examinee has not responded 10 seconds before the time limit.

≡ *Rapid Reference 5.3*

. . . .

Strengths and Weaknesses of the WISC-V: Psychometric Properties

Strengths

- The WISC-V has a large, demographically representative normative sample that allows generalizability of individual test performance to the U.S. population.
- High internal consistency reliability estimates. The average internal consistency estimates for the five Primary Index Scales are generally high, ranging from .88 (PSI) to .93 (FRI); reliabilities of subtests are generally medium to high (i.e., .81–.94) across the age range. The average internal consistency estimate for the FSIQ and the GAI is .96.

- Preliminary test-retest reliability (mean interval = 26 days) was provided for 218 children across the age range of the test and appears to generally support the stability of WISC-V performance. Subtest stability correlations ranged from .71 (Picture Concepts) to .90 (Vocabulary). All other subtest stability correlations were in the .80s, except Matrix Reasoning (.78). The stability coefficients for the FSIQ and GAI were .92 and .91, respectively. For the Primary Index Scales, the VCI had the highest stability coefficient (.94) and the FRI had the lowest (.75).

- High interscorer agreement.

- Exemplary subtest floors, ceilings, and item gradients.

- The WISC-V Technical and Interpretive Manual (Wechsler, 2014a) includes information on response processes.

- Construct validity of the five Primary Indexes is supported by confirmatory factor analysis (CFA) in the WISC-V Technical and Interpretive Manual (Wechsler, 2014a) and independent research (Reynolds & Keith, 2017).

- Global and primary index scores correlated as expected with other variables, providing strong preliminary validity evidence for the WISC-V.

- In general, subtests correlate more highly with subtests purported to measure the same construct as compared to subtests that measure different constructs. For example, this was true of the 10 subtests that make up the Primary Index Scales.

- The WISC-V Technical and Interpretive Manual (Wechsler, 2014a) provides initial clinical validity data by offering index and subtest profiles for 13 clinical groups, with sample sizes ranging from $N = 16$ (English Language Learners) to $N = 95$ (Intellectually Gifted).

Weaknesses

- Poor correspondence between the normative sample and the U.S. population by special education classification: Intellectual Disability, Specific Learning Disability, Speech/Language Impairment, Attention-Deficit/Hyperactivity Disorder, Intellectually Gifted.

- Correlational studies are provided between the WISC-V and several other instruments (e.g., WISC-IV, KTEA-3, WIAT-III), which are all published by Pearson. It would have been desirable for Pearson to report correlations with a more diverse group of cognitive and achievement tests, including measures from other publishers.

- It was assumed that Arithmetic would correlate more highly with Gf subtests (i.e., Figure Weights, Matrix Reasoning) as compared to subtests that measured other constructs. However, Arithmetic had similar correlations with Gf, Gsm (e.g., Digit Span), and Gc (e.g., Similarities) subtests. Likewise, Picture Concepts was expected to correlate more highly with Gf subtests as compared to subtests that measure other constructs. Instead, the correlations between Picture Concepts and Gc and Gv subtests were about as high as or

(continued)

(continued)

higher than those between Picture Concepts and Gf subtests (i.e., Figure Weights and Matrix Reasoning). Arithmetic and Picture Concepts are factorially complex, making interpretation of performance on these measures difficult.

- Score differences between groups defined by ethnic, gender, and socioeconomic status are not mentioned in the manuals. This omission is curious, given the debate that was sparked by research on ethnic group differences with previous editions of the WISC (Braden & Niebling, 2005). However, these analyses are available in Kaufman, Raiford, and Coalson (2016).
- Some of the stability coefficients are relatively low (e.g., FRI = .75, Picture Concepts = .71), although still in the adequate range.

Rapid Reference 5.4

Strengths and Weaknesses of the WISC-V: Interpretation

Strengths

- More guidance is provided in the WISC-V manuals than in the WISC-IV manuals.
- Critical value significance level options for various score comparisons have been expanded (i.e., .01, .05, .10, and .15 are provided).
- Base rates for several qualitative behaviors have been included. Also, critical values and base rates are available for all process score comparisons.
- The inclusion of multiple process scores and subtests that measure long-term storage and retrieval enhances depth of interpretation and understanding of performance.
- Closer adherence to CHC theory facilitates integration of data from the WISC-V with data from other measures that are based on CHC theory.
- Inclusion of alternative global scores (e.g., GAI, NVI), ancillary indexes (e.g., AWMI), and complementary indexes (e.g., SRI) offer greater interpretive options that may enhance diagnostic decision making.
- The AWMI permits direct comparison with Working Memory Index (WMI) on an examinee's previous WISC-IV performance.
- The prohibition of substitutions on the Primary Index Scales and limitation to one substitution on the FSIQ facilitate accurate comparison of scores across repeated administrations and limit "examiner roulette."

Weaknesses

- Because there are no substitutions permitted for the Primary Index Scales, interpretive options are limited.

- Limited information is available to describe how process scores aid in diagnostic decision making.
- Limited information is provided on interpreting patterns of strengths and weaknesses within the context of a referral for suspected learning disability.
- The number of scores available as well as the number of score comparisons are legion and there is limited information about their utility.
- Limited information is available to assist in understanding the meaning of differences in response processes.
- No guidance is given on how to integrate information about performance on subtests that do not contribute to any index.
- Although the WISC-V is more closely aligned with CHC theory, there is limited emphasis on CHC theory in the *WISC-V Technical and Interpretive Manual* (Wechsler, 2014a).
- There is limited information on the differences between processes and abilities, which interferes with accurate interpretation.
- Case studies were not provided in the manuals to demonstrate the recommended approach to interpretation and the clinical utility of the test.

TEST YOURSELF

1. **The WISC-V is the first revision of the WISC to include meaures of Long-Term Storage and Retrieval (Glr).**
   a. True
   b. False
2. **Which of the following statements is not true of the WISC-V?**
   a. The WISC-V FSIQ is made up of subtests that span five cognitive domains.
   b. The WISC-V has high internal consistency reliability estimates.
   c. The WISC-V includes measures of phonological processing.
   d. The WISC-V adheres more closely to CHC theory than its predecessor.
3. **Modification of the discontinue rules on the WISC-V may lead to increased testing time.**
   a. True
   b. False
4. **Which of the following subtests may be difficult to interpret because it measures more than one broad cognitive ability to a substantial degree?**
   a. Vocabulary
   b. Figure Weights
   c. Block Design
   d. Arithmetic

5. Which of the following is not considered an exemplary psychometric characteristic of the WISC-V?

a. Internal consistency reliability

b. Correspondence between the normative sample and the U.S. population by special education classification

c. Subtest floors and ceilings

d. Factor structure

Answers: 1. a; 2. c; 3. b; 4. d; 5. b

REFERENCES

Braden, J. P., & Niebling, B. C. (2005). Evaluating the validity evidence for intelligence tests using the joint test standards. In D. P. Flanagan & P. L. Harrison (Eds.), *Contemporary intellectual assessment: Theories, tests, and issues* (2nd ed., pp. 615–630). New York, NY: Guilford.

Kaufman, A. S., & Kaufman, N. L. (2014). *Kaufman Test of Educational Achievement* (3rd ed.). Bloomington, MN: Pearson.

Kaufman, A. S., Raiford, S. E., & Coalson, D. L. (2016). *Intelligent testing with the WISC-V.* Hoboken, NJ: Wiley.

Pearson. (2009). *Wechsler Individual Achievement Test* (3rd ed.). Bloomington, MN: Author.

Reynolds, M. R., & Keith, T. Z. (2017). *Multi-group and hierarchical confirmatory factor analysis of the Wechsler Intelligence Scale for Children–Fifth Edition: What does it measure?* Manuscript submitted for publication.

Wechsler, D. (2003). *Wechsler Intelligence Scale for Children* (4th ed.). Bloomington, MN: Pearson

Wechsler, D. (2014a). *Technical manual for the Wechsler Intelligence Scale for Children* (5th ed.). Bloomington, MN: Pearson.

Wechsler, D. (2014b). *Wechsler Intelligence Scale for Children* (5th ed.). *Technical and interpretive manual supplement.* Bloomington, MN: Pearson.

Six

A NEUROPSYCHOLOGICAL APPROACH TO INTERPRETATION OF THE WISC-V

George McCloskey, Jamie Slonim, Robert Whitaker,
Samantha Kaufman, and Naoko Nagoshi

This chapter applies neuropsychological concepts to the interpretation of performance on the WISC-V. The approach described here is an extension of the process-oriented approach that has been applied to the interpretation of the *Wechsler Intelligence Scale for Children-Fourth Edition* (WISC-IV; Wechsler, 2003), *Wechsler Adult Intelligence Scale-Fourth Edition* (WAIS-IV; Wechsler, 2009) (McCloskey, 2009a, 2009b; McCloskey & Maerlender, 2005), and, more recently, to the WISC-V (McCloskey, Slonim, & Hartz, 2015). This approach incorporates many of the clinical interpretation methods proposed by Edith Kaplan (Kaplan, 1988; Kaplan, Fein, Kramer, Delis, & Morris, 1999, 2004) and draws on the Lurian tradition in neuropsychology (Korkman, Kirk, & Kemp, 1998; Luria 1973, 1980) and developmental cognitive neuropsychology (Arnsten & Robbins, 2002; Berninger, 1994; Berninger & Richards, 2002; Dehaene, 1997, 2009, 2011, 2014; Kosslyn & Koenig, 1992; Levine, 1994; Levine, Gordon, & Reed, 1998; Posner & Raichle, 1994; Posner & Rothbart, 2007; Sporns, 2011; Stuss & Knight, 2002, 2013; Temple, 1997). The approach described here also is highly compatible with the cognitive hypothesis testing model offered by Hale and Fiorello (2004) and to some degree with the neuropsychological frameworks proposed by Miller (2013) and Dehn (2013) and the Cattell-Horn-Carroll (CHC) framework proposed by Flanagan and colleagues (Flanagan, Alfonso, & Ortiz, 2012; Flanagan, Alfonso, Ortiz, & Dynda, 2010). The focus of this process-oriented approach is on how the examinee executes the items of each WISC-V subtest as well as the scores earned on each of those subtests. The key to effective interpretation of test performance *after* administration, therefore, is careful observation of test performance *during* administration. Integration of what was observed during administration with what is scored after administration enables the clinician to characterize more accurately the specific cognitive strengths and weaknesses of the examinee.

LEVELS OF INTERPRETATION

The approach presented in this chapter is best summarized through the Interpretive Levels Framework shown in Figure 6.1. Interpretation of the WISC-V can occur on multiple levels. Each of these levels represents a particular degree of aggregation, or disaggregation, of the information gathered during administration and evaluated after administration. While moving through the levels (from top to bottom), it can be seen how each successive level represents an aggregation of information that obscures the details revealed by the levels below it. The Full Scale IQ (FSIQ) obscures variability that may be present at the Index level. Each index score obscures the contribution of individual subtest scores to the Index. Each subtest score obscures the contribution of individual item scores to the subtest. Each item score obscures the contributions of specific cognitive constructs as observed during item administration. Although interpretation at each level can be viewed from a neuropsychological perspective, some levels are more suited to the application of a wider range of neuropsychological concepts than others, as discussed in Rapid References 6.1 through 6.5. While there may be merit in the interpretation of Full Scale IQ and index scores, the premise of this chapter is that the most effective neuropsychological interpretation of WISC-V performance is found at the subtest, item, and cognitive constructs levels. This chapter, therefore,

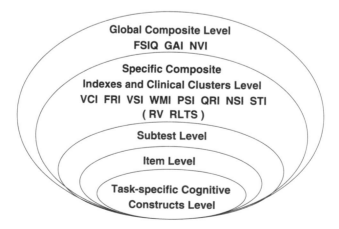

Figure 6.1 Interpretive Levels Framework Applied to the WISC-V

focuses on WISC-V interpretation at the subtest, item, and cognitive constructs levels with some treatment of subtest clusters at the specific composite level.

Global Level of Interpretation

At the global composite level, subtests from multiple indexes are summed together to yield a broader composite score. The WISC-V offers three such global-level composite scores: Full Scale IQ, General Ability Index (GAI), and Nonverbal Index (NVI). Global composite interpretations assume that performance across the multiple indexes from which subtests were drawn was relatively uniform and that a closely related group of cognitive constructs was used by the examinee while performing the index-specific tasks comprising the global composite. A global composite standard score is thought to be a homogeneous indication of the examinee's degree of capability, relative to a standardization sample comparison group, in using the cognitive constructs thought to be assessed by the index-specific tasks aggregated to form the global composite. Global composite-level interpretation obscures the contribution of the separate indexes and subtests to the global score.

DON'T FORGET
. . . .

The WISC-V offers three global-level composite scores, namely, the Full Scale IQ (FSIQ), the Nonverbal Index (NVI), and the General Ability Index (GAI). All 10 primary subtests must be administered in order to derive the FSIQ, NVI, and GAI scores.

≡ *Rapid Reference 6.1*
. . . .

Key Facts About the Global Composite Level of Interpretation

- Multiple subtests from two or more specific composites are summed together to yield a broader composite score.
- The WISC-V offers three global composites: the FSIQ, the GAI, and the NVI.
- When there are statistically significant and uncommonly large differences among the subtests that comprise the FSIQ, GAI, or NVI, these composites are masking information that is critical to a neuropsychological interpretation of performance.

Specific Composite (Index and Subtest Cluster) Level of Interpretation

At the specific composite level, various subtest scaled score triads and dyads are aggregated to form composite scores called Indexes that are represented normatively by standard scores. Each index standard score represents an aggregation of performance across multiple subtests. Index-level interpretation assumes that performance on the subtests comprising the Index was relatively uniform and that a closely related group of cognitive constructs was used by the examinee while performing these subtests. An index standard score is thought to be a homogeneous indication of the examinee's degree of capability, relative to a standardization sample comparison group, in using the cognitive constructs thought to be assessed by the cluster of subtests that form the index. However, when the scores of subtests that make up the Index differ significantly, Index-level interpretation obscures the contribution of individual subtests to the Index, assuming that variations in subtest-level performance represent random fluctuations that are unimportant or impossible to interpret meaningfully.

WISC-V index-level interpretation provides a more varied perspective on cognitive functioning than the FSIQ, GAI, or NVI. Index-level interpretation acknowledges that performance can be interpreted in a meaningful way by examining performance on the specific cognitive domains referred to as Primary Indexes (Verbal Comprehension [VCI], Fluid Reasoning [FRI], Visual-Spatial [VSI], Working Memory [WMI], and Processing Speed [PSI]). Additionally, the WISC-V offers a Quantitative Reasoning Index (QRI), an Auditory Working Memory Index (AWMI), a Cognitive Proficiency Index (CPI), a Naming Speed Index (NSI), a Symbol Translation Index (STI), and a Storage and Retrieval Index (SRI), all of which can further assist in differentiating interpretation at this level.

DON'T FORGET

When the scores of subtests that comprise the index differ significantly, Index-level interpretation obscures the contribution of individual subtests to the index.

It is interesting to note that some subtests contribute to more than one index (i.e., Figure Weights and Digit Span) and that a subtest traditionally considered a measure of working memory (i.e., Arithmetic) is now listed as a Fluid Reasoning subtest and included in the Quantitative Reasoning Index. These manipulations of the index configuration implicitly acknowledge the fact that subtests are multifactorial and assess more than one cognitive construct. Additionally, some subtests (i.e., Comprehension, Information, Picture Concepts, and Cancellation) do not contribute to any global or specific indexes and therefore must be interpreted at the subtest level when administered unless they are used as replacement tasks for subtests that are spoiled or unusable or as part of a new clinical cluster (see Chapter 4).

Contrasting performance on multiple indexes is certainly a step in the right direction in acknowledging the need for a neuropsychological perspective on interpretation. Stopping at this level of analysis, however, even when significant and unusual differences among index scores are found would significantly limit the potential effectiveness of a neuropsychological interpretation of WISC-V test performance. The seemingly unitary nature of each of the primary indexes is not an accurate representation of the multiple cognitive constructs that are needed to perform the aggregated tasks of each of these indexes. This is especially apparent in cases where significant differences are found between the subtest scores within an Index.

A more valid approach to aggregation of subtest score information at the specific composite level is the subtest cluster method, which combines scores from one or more subtests only after interpretive analyses support the hypothesis that the clustered subtests are measuring similar cognitive constructs at the level of specificity needed for effective interpretation. Table 6.1 shows the subtest composition and structure of the Indexes of the WISC-V and a proposed alternate subtest clusters structure based on neuropsychological constructs. A subtest cluster can be considered appropriate for interpretation when an examinee's performance on the subtests that comprise the cluster is relatively homogeneous (subtest scores do not vary by more than 2 scaled score points) and process-oriented observations offer support for the hypothesis that the subtests are assessing the same constructs for this examinee.

≡ *Rapid Reference 6.2*

. . . .

Key Facts About the Specific Composite (Index and Clinical Cluster) Level of Interpretation

- Subtest scaled score triads and dyads form composite scores called Indexes that are represented normatively by Standard Scores.
- Index-level interpretation assumes that performance across multiple subtests was relatively uniform.
- Index-level interpretation assumes that the examinee used a closely related group of cognitive constructs while performing the subtests that make up the Index.
- Clinical clusters involve combining subtests to form meaningful composites after interpretive analyses indicate that specific subtests are measuring similar cognitive constructs.

Table 6.1 WISC-V Indexes and an Alternate Subtest Clinical Clusters Model Based on Neuropsychological Constructs

WISC-V Index	Subtest Clinical Clusters Based on Neuropsychological Constructs
Verbal Comprehension (VCI) Similarities Vocabulary	Reasoning with Language (RL) Similarities Comprehension Retrieval from Remote Long-Term Storage (RLTS-Remote) Vocabulary Information
Fluid Reasoning (FRI) Matrix Reasoning Figure Weights	Reasoning with Nonverbal Visual (RNV) Matrix Reasoning Picture Concepts Figure Weights Block Design
Quantitative Reasoning (QRI) Figure Weights Arithmetic	Reasoning with Quantity (RQ) Figure Weights Arithmetic
Visual Spatial (VSI) Block Design Visual Puzzles	Visual Spatial (VS) Block Design Visual Puzzles Matrix Reasoning Coding Symbol Search Cancellation
Working Memory (WMI) Digit span Picture Span Auditory Working Memory (AWMI) Digit Span Letter-Number Sequencing	Working Memory (WM) Digit Span Picture Span Letter-Number Sequencing Arithmetic Immediate Symbol Translation
Symbol Translation (STI)	Retrieval from Recent Long-Term Storage (RLTS-Recent) Delayed Symbol Translation Recognition Symbol Translation
Naming Speed (NSI) Naming Speed Literacy Naming Speed Quantity	Naming Speed (NS) Naming Speed Literacy Naming Speed Quantity

Note: The Cognitive Proficiency Index and Symbol Recognition Index are not included in this table because they represent aggregations of Indexes rather than unique aggregations of subtests.

Subtest Level of Interpretation

Individual subtest scores are obtained by summing performance across all the items of the subtest producing an aggregate raw score that is converted into a norm-referenced scaled score. Subtest-level interpretation assumes that performance across the multiple items of the subtest was relatively uniform in the sense that the same set of task-specific cognitive constructs was used by the examinee while performing all of the items comprising the subtest. A subtest scaled score is thought to be a homogeneous indication of the examinee's degree of capability, relative to a standardization sample comparison group, in using the task-specific cognitive constructs thought to be assessed by the items of that subtest. Clinicians seeking to interpret WISC-V assessment results from a neuropsychological perspective are on somewhat firmer ground when attention is focused at the subtest level. The need for subtest-level interpretation is clear when significantly large differences are present between or among the subtests that comprise an index. In these instances, a clear pattern of difference in the use of cognitive constructs might be readily apparent when considering the examinee's approach to performing subtest items. The WISC-V manual provides additional norm-referenced interpretive information at the subtest level in the form of Subtest Scaled Score Pairwise Comparisons and Subtest Scaled Score Contrast Scores for selected subtests. Table 6.2 lists the specific subtest pairwise comparisons and subtest scaled score contrasts that are available as well as their table locations in the various WISC-V manuals.

The WISC-V provides additional process approach interpretive information that can enhance subtest level score interpretation or extend below the subtest level to characterize performance on item clusters within subtests (for example, providing scaled scores for Digit Span Forward, Digit Span Backward, and Digit Span Sequencing). The various process approach aids to interpretation and their locations within the various WISC-V manuals are listed in Table 6.3.

Although subtest-level interpretation can be more specific than index- or global-level interpretation, clinicians attempting to interpret the WISC-V from a neuropsychological perspective using the subtest scaled score profile are at risk of missing important aspects of performance that would significantly alter interpretation. In the majority of cases, interpretation of subtest differences is not particularly straightforward due to the fact that performance on each of the subtests of the WISC-V always involves the use of multiple cognitive constructs. Additionally, the multiple cognitive constructs used to perform a subtest can vary from one examinee to another. Because subtest-level performance involves multiple cognitive constructs, it is necessary to test hypotheses on a case-by-case basis in order to develop and test reasonable

Table 6.2 Subtest Scaled Score Pairwise Comparisons and Subtest Scaled Score Contrast Scores Available in the WISC-V Manuals

Subtest Scaled Score Pairwise Comparison Base Rates	
Similarities vs Vocabulary	Table B.8
Block Design vs Visual Puzzles	Administration and Scoring Manual
Matrix Reasoning vs Figure Weights	
Digit Span vs Picture Span	
Coding vs Symbol Search	
Figure Weights vs Arithmetic	
Digit Span vs Letter-Number Sequencing	
Complementary Subtest Scaled Score Pairwise Comparison Base Rates	
Naming Speed Literacy vs Naming Speed Quantity	Table C.13
Immediate Symbol Translation vs Delayed Symbol Translation	Administration and Scoring Manual Supplement
Immediate Symbol Translation vs Recognition Symbol Translation	
Delayed Symbol Translation vs Recognition Symbol Translation	
Complementary Subtest Scaled Score Contrast Scores	
Immediate Symbol Translation vs Delayed Symbol Translation	Tables C.5 and C.6 Technical and Interpretive Manual
Recognition Symbol Translation vs Delayed Symbol Translation	

Table 6.3 Process Score Scaled Score and Raw Score Norms Available in the WISC-V Manuals

Process Raw Score to Scaled Score Conversions	
Block Design No Time Bonus (BDn)	Table C.14
Block Design Partial Score (BDp)	Administration and Scoring Manual Supplement
Digit Span Forward (DSf)	
Digit Span Backward (DSb)	
Digit Span Sequencing (DSs)	
Cancellation Random (CAr)	
Cancellation Structured (CAs)	

Process Raw Score to Scaled Score Conversions	
Naming Speed Color-Object (NSco) (Ages 6-0 to 6-11 only)	Table C.6
Naming Speed Size-Color-Object (NSsco) (Ages 7-0 to 8-11 only)	Administration and Scoring Manual Supplement
Naming Speed Letter-Number (NSln) (Ages 7-0 to 8-11 only)	
Process Scaled Score Pairwise Comparison Base Rates	
Block Design (BD) vs BDn	Table C.16
BD vs BDp	Administration and Scoring Manual Supplement
DSf vs DSb	
DSf vs DSs	
DSb vs DSs	
Letter-Number Sequencing (LNS) vs DSs	
CAr vs CAs	
NSco vs NSsco (Ages 6-0 to 6-11 only)	Table C.13
NSsco vs NSln (Ages 7-0 to 8-11 only)	Administration and Scoring Manual Supplement
Process Raw Score Base Rates	
Longest Digit Span Forward (LDSf)	Table C.17
Longest Digit Span Backward (LDSb)	Administration and Scoring Manual Supplement
Longest Digit Span Sequence (LDSs)	
Longest Picture Span Stimulus (LPSs)	
Longest Picture Span Response (LPSr)	
Longest Letter-Number Sequence (LLNs)	
Process Error Score Base Rates	
Block Design Dimension Errors (BDde)	Table C.18
Block Design Rotation Errors (BDre)	Administration and Scoring Manual Supplement
Coding Rotation Errors (CDre)	
Symbol Search Set Errors (SSse)	
Symbol Search Rotation Errors (SSre)	
Naming Speed Literacy Errors (NSLe)	
Naming Speed Color-Object Errors (NScoe)	
Naming Speed Size-Color-Object Errors (NSscoe)	
Naming Speed Letter-Number Errors (NSlne)	
Naming Speed Quantity Errors (NSQe)	

(continued)

(continued)

Process Raw Score Difference Base Rates	
LDSf vs LDSb	Tables C.19, C.20, and
LDSf vs LDSs	C.21
LDSb vs LDSs	Administration and Scoring Manual Supplement

Process Score Scaled Score Contrast Scores	
DSf vs DSb	Tables C.1 through C.4
DSf vs DSs	Technical and
DSs vs LNS	Interpretive Manual
CAs vs Car	

Process Observation Base Rates	
Don't Know Responses (SI, VC, IN, CO, VP, MR, FW, PC, AR, PS, RST)	Tables D.1 through D.6 Technical and
No Responses (SI, VC, IN, CO, VP, MR, FW, PC, AR, PS, RST)	Interpretive Manual
Item Repetitions (when allowed) (SI, VC, IN, CO, AR)	
Requests for Item Repetition (when not allowed) (DS, LNS)	
Subvocalizations (VP, MR, FW, PC, AR, PS)	
Self-Corrections (VP, MR, FW, PC, AR, DS, PS, LNS, NSL, NSQ)	

Note: SI = Similarities; VC = Vocabulary; IN = Information; CO = Comprehension; V = Visual Puzzles; MR = Matrix reasoning; FW = Figure Weights; PC = Picture Concepts; AR = Arithmetic; PS = Picture Span; RST = Recognition Symbol Translation; DS = Digit Span; NSL = Naming Speed Literacy; NSQ = Naming Speed Quantity

hypotheses about how specific cognitive constructs are affecting subtest performance.

If interpretation remains focused solely on the subtest score level, then the clinician must use additional subtests to test hypotheses about the contributions of various cognitive constructs to task performance. The greater the number of possible cognitive constructs required for subtest performance, the greater the number of competing hypotheses that may require further testing.

≡ Rapid Reference 6.3

Key Facts About the Subtest Level of Interpretation

- A subtest score is a sum (aggregate) of item scores that is converted into a norm-referenced scaled score.
- Interpretation at the subtest level assumes that the same set of cognitive constructs was used by the examinee while performing the items making up the subtest.
- The contribution of item response patterns, item clusters, or individual items to subtest performance is obscured at this level of interpretation.
- Subtest-level performance involves multiple cognitive constructs; hypotheses about how specific cognitive constructs affected test performance must be tested on a case-by-case basis.

Item Level of Interpretation

All WISC-V items are scored individually using predetermined criteria. Each item score represents an aggregate statement about the cognitive capacities used to perform the item. The methods used to assign scores to items assume that only the cognitive capacities thought to be required for item performance are being assessed as intended and are contributing equally to the performance of each item. An assumption is made that the correct response indicates that the examinee demonstrated effective use of the cognitive capacities intended to be assessed with the item. Conversely, it is assumed that an incorrect response indicates the ineffective use of the cognitive capacities intended to be assessed with the item. It is also assumed that an examinee's item responses will follow a specific pattern throughout the subtest where consistently correct performance on a subset of items in the "easy range" will be followed by variable performance on a subset of items in the "challenging range" which will be followed by incorrect responses on a subset of items in the "too difficult range."

Taken at face value, item scores obscure the possible differential contribution of multiple cognitive constructs to item success or item failure, and deviations from the expected pattern of item performance represent random fluctuations that are unimportant or impossible to interpret meaningfully in an empirically valid manner. In contrast to the standard assumptions, item level interpretation attempts to identify and understand unusual patterns of item performance, such as easy items answered incorrectly or difficult items answered with ease, or performance on a cluster of items that is inconsistent with the expected pattern. When performed effectively, item-level interpretation will draw on knowledge obtained at the Task Cognitive Constructs Level to generate hypotheses about the cognitive constructs that are, or are not, being used in the performance of individual items or subsets of items.

Although subtest-level interpretation is much more likely to yield valuable information from a neuropsychological perspective than Index scores, specific subtests that can be used to test hypotheses about the contribution of different cognitive constructs to WISC-V subtest performance are not always available and/or clinicians often cannot devote the time needed to test thoroughly every hypothesis using additional subtests. In these instances, neuropsychological interpretation of subtest performance can be greatly enhanced through careful observation of item-level performance during test administration and subsequent analysis and interpretation of performance patterns. Item-level analysis focused on item response patterns, item cluster performance, and individual item performance often will yield information that can be very useful in testing hypotheses about the specific cognitive constructs likely to be involved in subtest performance.

≡ *Rapid Reference 6.4*

Key Facts About the Item Level of Interpretation

- Item scores are aggregate statements about the cognitive constructs used to perform the item.
- An examinee's response indicates whether he or she effectively used the cognitive constructs intended to be assessed with the item.
- An item score may obscure the possible differential contributions of multiple cognitive constructs to item success or item failure.
- Deviations from the expected pattern of item performance often represent important variations in task performance that can be interpreted meaningfully in an empirically valid manner.
- Analyzing item response patterns, item cluster performance, and individual item performance often will yield information useful in testing hypotheses about the specific cognitive constructs involved in subtest performance.

Task-Specific Cognitive Construct Level of Interpretation

The task-specific cognitive constructs level of interpretation acknowledges the fact that an examinee's attempt to complete any item from any subtest of the WISC-V will require an attempt to make use of multiple cognitive constructs. Although each item is constructed in a manner that assumes that the use of a specific cognitive construct, or set of constructs, will be the most efficient and effective way to perform the item, there is no guarantee that examinees will choose to use those specific cognitive constructs in their efforts to complete an item. Examinees use their own decision-making processes to determine what cognitive constructs they draw on to perform an item. The cognitive constructs chosen by the examinee are likely to reflect inherent preferences or biases of the examinee, and may not be consistent with the cognitive constructs the item was intended to assess. Careful observation of how the examinee performs an item, therefore, is critical to the accurate understanding of what cognitive constructs are being assessed by that item. No matter what efforts are made to try to ensure that a specific task is assessing a specific cognitive construct, most examinees' specific neural capabilities will enable them to choose for themselves the cognitive constructs they wish to employ in their efforts with a task. This fact will continue to frustrate the efforts of researchers and clinicians who desire to identify and make use of tasks that are "pure" measures of a single cognitive construct. This fact also confounds the standard view of subtest reliability in which all sources of unexplained variability in task performance are considered "measurement error." Unfortunately, such misguided conceptions of reliability are used to support the argument against the use of subtest-level interpretation of test performance and to discourage clinicians from attempting to understand the individual variations observed in task performance. In many cases, careful clinical observation of task performance can identify and explain how examinees are, or are not, using cognitive constructs, thereby increasing the interpretive validity as well as the reliability of the assessment process by explaining the unexplained sources of variability in performance that would have been identified only as measurement error.

A cognitive neuropsychological approach to WISC-V interpretation requires a solid understanding of the various cognitive constructs that could be involved in the performance of the individual items of each subtest and knowledge of the kinds of behaviors that are most likely to indicate the use of these cognitive constructs. This level of analysis requires more than simply looking for item response patterns, performance on item clusters, or knowing whether a specific item was scored as right or wrong. As noted earlier, examinees determine for themselves what cognitive constructs they choose to use to perform test items, necessitating careful observation of examinee performance and an understanding of how specific behaviors can reflect the use of specific cognitive constructs. Effective interpretation of the cognitive constructs used during individual items increases the likelihood of an accurate characterization of examinee performance from a neuropsychological perspective.

≡ Rapid Reference 6.5

Task-Specific Cognitive Constructs Level of Interpretation

- Individual examinees determine what cognitive constructs they draw on to perform an item.
- Careful observation of how the examinee performs an item is critical to the accurate understanding of what cognitive constructs are actually being assessed by that item.
- The interpretive validity and the reliability of the assessment process are increased by illuminating the unexplained sources of variability in performance that may be inferred from careful clinical observations of how examinees are using cognitive constructs.
- Effective interpretation of the cognitive constructs used during individual items informs all subsequent levels of interpretation, thereby increasing the likelihood of an accurate characterization of the examinee from a neuropsychological perspective.

NEUROPSYCHOLOGICAL INTERPRETATION OF WISC-V PERFORMANCE

In order to use and interpret the WISC-V effectively from a neuropsychological perspective, it is necessary to have an understanding of the multifactorial nature of the WISC-V subtests in terms of the cognitive constructs they assess and how these cognitive constructs are reflected in item-level performance and subtest and composite-level scores. Although many examiners are now likely to administer only the core seven WISC-V subtests that comprise the FSIQ or the 10 subtests that constitute the five Primary Indexes, cognitive neuropsychological interpretation can be greatly enhanced when three or more of the remaining 11 subtests also are administered, as the additional subtests offer a more varied perspective on an examinee's use of cognitive constructs. This section discusses subtest, item, and construct-level interpretation following the Index and domain organization of the WISC-V, but alternate subtest cluster formats also will be suggested to align more closely specific composite-level interpretation with a neuropsychological cognitive construct perspective. As noted earlier, Table 6.1 shows the subtest composition and cognitive domain structure of the indexes of the WISC-V and a proposed alternate subtest clusters structure based on neuropsychological constructs. Contrasting the WISC-V index structure with the subtest clusters will enable clinicians to see more clearly how the WISC-V Primary Index scores can mask important variations in test performance and how information gathered at the subtest cluster, subtest, item, and cognitive construct levels can be used to enhance test interpretation from a neuropsychological perspective.

Verbal Comprehension Domain

The WISC-V manual lists four subtests within the Verbal Comprehension Domain: Similarities, Vocabulary, Information, and Comprehension. Two of these subtests (Similarities and Vocabulary) are included in the FSIQ and the GAI and form the Verbal Comprehension Primary Index Scale (VCI). The additional two subtests (Information and Comprehension) do not contribute to any Index score and are not discussed as an intricate part of the WISC-V interpretive framework.

The subtests listed within the WISC-V Verbal Comprehension Domain were designed to assess the use of specific cognitive constructs applied with orally presented verbal content. These constructs are the focus of interpretation of the VCI and include retrieval of verbal information from remote long-term storage and reasoning with verbal information. The roles of these primary cognitive constructs in Verbal Comprehension Domain Subtest performance are described in detail in Appendix 6.A.

DON'T FORGET

Subtest Composition of the Verbal Comprehension Index (VCI)
Similarities and Vocabulary must be administered in order to derive a VCI.

It is important to note that with the relegation of the Comprehension subtest to supplementary status, many examiners will be less likely to administer this subtest. This would be unfortunate since the Comprehension subtest is the only subtest other than Similarities that attempts to assess reasoning with verbal information. Clinicians who are interested in knowing more about an examinee's ability to reason with verbal information are strongly encouraged to administer the Comprehension subtest and examine the relationship between the scores on the Comprehension and Similarities subtests from the perspective of the Reasoning with Language (RL) subtest cluster. Similarly, clinicians who are interested in knowing more about an examinee's ability to retrieve information from remote long-term storage are strongly encouraged to administer the Information subtest and interpret the relationship between the scores on the Vocabulary and Information subtests from the perspective of the Retrieval from Remote Long-Term Storage (RLTS-Remote) subtest cluster.

Beyond the two primary cognitive constructs targeted for assessment, the specific formats of each of the four Verbal Comprehension Domain subtests make demands on the examinee that require the engagement of additional cognitive constructs for successful performance. While these constructs are required for effective subtest performance, they are not considered to be the primary target of assessment; that is, the intention of the subtest is not to assess quantitatively the examinee's use of these cognitive constructs. These secondary cognitive constructs are Auditory Attention, Auditory Discrimination, Auditory Comprehension, Expressive Language, Working Memory applied to verbal content, and multiple Executive Functions applied to cue and direct the mental processing of language and working with verbal content. The roles of these secondary cognitive constructs in subtest performance are described in detail in Appendix 6.A. Rapid Reference 6.6 provides an interpretive summary table that can be used to assist with the analysis of Verbal Comprehension Domain subtests in terms of the cognitive constructs that could be contributing to performance on each subtest.

≡ Rapid Reference 6.6

Cognitive Constructs Likely to Be Assessed by Verbal Comprehension Domain Subtests

Cognitive Construct	SI	VC	IN	CO
Retrieval of verbal knowledge	XX	XXX	XXX	X
Reasoning with verbal content	XXX			XXX
Auditory acuity		X	X	X	X

Cognitive Construct	SI	VC	IN	CO
Auditory attention	X	X	X	X
Auditory discrimination	XX	XX		XX
Auditory comprehension	X	X	XX	XX
Auditory processing speed			XX	XX
Initial registration of auditorily presented information	X	X	X	X
Working memory	X		X	X
Expressive language production	XX	XXX	X	XXX
EF – Cueing appropriate consideration of the cognitive capacities and mental effort required to perform a task	XX	XX	XX	XX
EF – Directing Auditory Perception, Discrimination, and Comprehension	XX	XX	XX	XX
EF – Cueing the focusing and sustaining of attention to auditory details	X	X	X	X
EF – Directing Processing Speed			XX	XX
EF – Directing Retrieval	X	XX	X	X
EF – Directing Reasoning	XX			XX
EF – Directing Language Expression	XX	XX	X	XX
EF – Directing Flexible Shifting of Reasoning Mindset	XXX			XX
EF – Directing Working Memory	X		X	X
EF – Recognizing and Responding to Prompts for More Information	X	X	X	X
EF – Coordinating the Use of Multiple Capacities Simultaneously	XX	XX	XX	XX
EF – Cueing the inhibition of impulsive responding	X	X	X	X

Note: SI = Similarities; VC = Vocabulary; IN = Information; CO = Comprehension; EF = Executive Function. XXX = Primary Construct targeted for assessment with the task; XX = Secondary Construct highly likely to affect task performance; X = Secondary Construct possibly affecting task performance.

When Verbal Comprehension Domain subtest scores are interpreted, either collectively using the VCI or individually, it is often assumed that the subtests are measuring the primary constructs intended to be assessed. The secondary constructs required for effective performance are either ignored or assumed to be intact and functioning as expected allowing the focus of interpretation to be on the primary constructs. For example, if an examinee cannot respond effectively on the Similarities subtest, the assumption often is that the examinee has poor reasoning abilities; if the examinee cannot provide adequate responses for the Vocabulary subtest, the assumption is that the examinee does not know the meanings of the words. That is, the examinee has not stored, and therefore cannot retrieve, the required knowledge. In many cases where low performance is observed, however, such assumptions are not necessarily warranted. To know whether these assumptions about the primary constructs are valid, the role of the secondary cognitive constructs in task performance must be understood and examined in detail. When secondary cognitive constructs are not being accessed or applied effectively, they can significantly interfere with an individual's performance. Therefore, it would be inappropriate to focus interpretations solely on primary constructs that are thought to be assessed by particular subtests—especially when poor performance may in fact be due to deficits in secondary constructs.

When low scores or scores that are not consistent with what is known about the examinee are obtained with one or more of the Verbal Comprehension Domain subtests, careful analysis of the shared and/or unique contributions of secondary cognitive constructs and more detailed analysis of item responses and the ways in which the responses were delivered should be undertaken. As indicated in the previous discussion, poor performance on the Verbal Comprehension Domain subtests is thought to reflect a lack of reasoning and/or a lack of stored knowledge (i.e., a lack of verbal intelligence). Clinicians who appreciate that a low score on one or more verbal comprehension subtests could be due to many different sources can draw on their knowledge of cognitive constructs shared by subtests and observations about the manner in which the responses were delivered to help obtain a better understanding of the cognitive constructs most likely to have contributed to the poor performance. Appendix 6.B provides a summary of the interpretations associated with behaviors observed during administration of the Verbal Comprehension Domain subtests that can be used to enhance hypothesis testing about what cognitive constructs are, or are not, being used to perform subtests (see also Chapter 2). Examiners also can use the process observation base rate tables in the *Technical and Interpretation Manual* (Wechsler, 2014a) to obtain base rates for specific behaviors such as the number of times the examinee offers no response or a "Don't Know" response, or the number of times the examinee asks for repetition of items (see Table 6.3 for the list and location of these process observation base rate tables).

When verbal comprehension subtest scores vary greatly and/or when the examiner observes behaviors that suggest that secondary cognitive constructs are influencing task performance, subtest cluster analysis may be helpful in identifying specific strengths and weaknesses in the use of various cognitive constructs. Appendix 6.C illustrates the application of the cluster analysis interpretation with the Verbal Comprehension Domain subtests.

When an examiner is engaged in subtest interpretation at the composite level with cluster analysis or at the subtest level, subtest comparisons should include the determination of whether a statistically significant difference exists between the scores earned on the subtests being compared. A value of 3 scaled score points can be used to signify a statistically significant difference for the comparisons between pairs of Verbal Comprehension Domain subtests. Appendix 6.D provides a worksheet to aid in the interpretation of Verbal Comprehension Domain Subtest scaled score comparisons.

Fluid Reasoning and Visual Spatial Domains

Perhaps the most substantial change in the interpretive structure of the WISC-V involves the replacement of the Perceptual Reasoning Domain with two new construct domains: Fluid Reasoning and Visual Spatial. The content of the Perceptual Reasoning Domain was split between these two domains and additional subtests were added in each of the new domains. The Matrix Reasoning and Picture Concepts subtests are joined by the Arithmetic subtest (moved here from the Working Memory domain) and the Figure Weights subtest to form the Fluid Reasoning Domain. Two of these subtests (Matrix Reasoning and Figure Weights) are included in the FSIQ, the GAI, and the NVI and form the Fluid Reasoning Primary Index Scale (FRI). The Arithmetic subtest joins the Figure Weights subtest to form the Quantitative Reasoning Index, which is labeled as an Ancillary Index Scale rather than a Primary Index Scale. The Picture Concepts subtest does not contribute to any Index score and is not discussed as an intricate part of the WISC-V interpretive framework.

The subtests listed within the WISC-V Fluid Reasoning Domain were designed to assess the use of reasoning with nonverbal abstract visual images and reasoning with quantitative information. These reasoning constructs are the focus of interpretation of the FRI. When the Arithmetic subtest is combined with the Figure Weights subtest to form the QRI the primary constructs targeted for assessment are reasoning with orally presented quantitative information and reasoning with visually presented quantitative information, respectively. The roles of these primary cognitive constructs in Fluid Reasoning Domain subtest performance are described in detail in Appendix 6.A.

The Block Design Subtest is joined by the Visual Puzzles Subtest to form the Visual Spatial Domain. One of these subtests (Block Design) is included in the FSIQ, the GAI, and the NVI. Block Design is joined by Visual Puzzles (the only other subtest in this domain) to form the VSI.

The subtests listed within the WISC-V Visual Spatial Domain were designed to assess the use of reasoning with nonverbal abstract visual images and integrating visual images to match a visual model. These constructs are the focus of interpretation of the VSI. The roles of these primary cognitive constructs in Visual Spatial Domain subtest performance are described in detail in Appendix 6.A.

Beyond the primary cognitive constructs targeted for assessment with the Fluid Reasoning Domain and the Visual Spatial Domain subtests, the specific formats of each subtest make demands on the examinee that require the engagement of additional cognitive constructs in order to achieve success. While these constructs typically are required for effective subtest performance, they are not considered to be the primary target of the assessment; that is, the intention of the subtest is not to assess quantitatively the examinee's use of these cognitive constructs. These secondary cognitive constructs comprise Visual Perception and Representation; Visual Discrimination; Visualization; Motor Dexterity; Mental, Visual, and Motor Processing Speeds; Working Memory applied to visual nonverbal content; Language Representation of Visual Stimuli; and multiple Executive Functions applied to cue and direct the mental processing of nonverbal visual stimuli. The roles of these secondary cognitive constructs in subtest performance are described in detail in Appendix 6.A. Rapid Reference 6.7 provides an interpretive summary table that can be used to assist with the analysis of Fluid Reasoning and Visual Spatial Domain subtests in terms of cognitive constructs thought to be assessed by each subtest.

≡ Rapid Reference 6.7

Cognitive Constructs Likely to Be Assessed by Fluid Reasoning Subtests,* Visual Puzzles (VP), and Picture Span (PS) Subtests

Cognitive Construct	MR	FW	PCn	BD	VP	PS**
Visual acuity	XX	XX	XX	XX	XX	XX
Visual discrimination	XX	XX	XX	XX	XX	XX
Visual perception	XX	XX	XX	XX	XX	XX
Attention to visual stimuli	XX	XX	XX	XX	XX	XX
Reasoning with nonverbal visual materials	XXX	XXX	XXX	XXX	XXX	

Cognitive Construct	MR	FW	PCn	BD	VP	PS**
Reasoning with quantity		XXX				
Visualization	X	X		X	XX	
Use of working memory with visually presented material	X	XX	X	X	X	XXX
Motor dexterity				XX		
Mental processing speed	X	XX	X	XX	XX	XX
Visual processing speed	XX	XX	X	XX	XX	X
Motor processing speed				XX		
Visual-motor processing speed				XX		X
Language representation of visual stimuli	X	X	X			X
Executive functions:						
EF – Cueing and directing efficient perception of visual stimuli	XX	XX	XX	XX	XX	XX
EF – Cueing the appropriate consideration of the cognitive demands of a task and the amount of mental effort required to effectively perform the task	XX	XX	XX	XX	XX	XX
EF – Cueing and directing the focusing of attention to visual details and task demands	XX	XX	XX	XX	XX	XX
EF – Cueing and directing sustained attention to task	XX	XX	XX	XX	XX	XX
EF – Cueing and directing the use of reasoning abilities (generating novel solutions or making associations with prior knowledge that lead to problem solutions)	XX	XX	XX	X	X	
EF – Cueing and directing the inhibition of impulsive responding	XX	XX	XX	XX	XX	X
EF – Cueing and directing the flexible shifting of cognitive mindset to consider and respond to the specific demands of the task	X	XX	X	X	X	
EF – Cueing and directing the use of working memory resources	X	XX	X	X	X	XX
EF – Cueing and directing the execution of motor routines				XX		X
EF – Cueing and directing mental, visual, motor, and visual-motor processing speed		XX		XX	XX	XX
EF – Cueing and directing the balance between pattern (global) and detail (local) processing	X	X		XX	XX	

(continued)

(continued)

Cognitive Construct	MR	FW	PCn	BD	VP	PS**
EF – Cueing and directing the monitoring of work and the correcting of errors	XX	XX	XX	XX	XX	XX
EF – Cueing and directing the coordination of the use of multiple mental capacities simultaneously	XX	XX	XX	XX	XX	X

Note: MR = Matrix Reasoning; FW = Figure Weights; PCn = Picture Concepts; BD = Block Design; EF = Executive Function. XXX = Primary Capacity targeted for assessment with the task; XX = Secondary Capacity highly likely to affect task performance; X = Secondary Capacity possibly affecting task performance.

* The mental constructs most likely to be assessed by the Arithmetic Subtest are listed in Rapid Reference 6.8.

** The Picture Span Subtest is listed here due to the nature of the cognitive constructs it is likely to assess.

Note that Rapid Reference 6.7 does not include the Arithmetic Subtest. The Arithmetic Subtest is included with the Working Memory Domain tasks based on the majority of the cognitive constructs that it assesses. The Arithmetic Subtest is an excellent example of why it is necessary to interpret tasks based on the cognitive constructs that they assess for the individual rather than their placement within domains or indexes. On the WISC-V, the Arithmetic Subtest has been moved to the Fluid Reasoning Domain and contributes to the QRI but not to the WMI. Although the Arithmetic Subtest has changed positions within the overall interpretive configuration of the WISC-V, the cognitive constructs likely to be involved in performance of the Arithmetic Subtest items have not changed. While the change in location serves to highlight the Arithmetic Subtest's focus on reasoning with quantity (a focus that was always present despite its placement within the Working Memory Domain), the location change now serves to obscure the major contribution that the Arithmetic Subtest can make to the assessment of working memory when interpretive efforts focus on index scores rather than neuropsychological-based subtest clusters.

It is important to note the specific wording being used here to describe the primary cognitive construct that most Fluid Reasoning and Visual Spatial tasks are attempting to assess (i.e., reasoning with nonverbal, visual stimuli). Reasoning with nonverbal visual stimuli is not synonymous with the term nonverbal reasoning. Placing nonverbal visual materials in front of an examinee is not a guarantee that the examinee will engage only nonverbal reasoning with those materials, especially when clinicians use standardized directions that include verbal explanations and model verbal strategies of how to perform items. While it may be advantageous to reason without engaging language abilities when attempting Fluid Reasoning and Visual Spatial subtests, it is not necessary to do so. Clinicians are likely to observe examinees who engage language abilities to "talk themselves through" some or all aspects of specific Matrix Reasoning, Figure Weights or Picture Concepts items. Such verbal mediation can be helpful, or even essential, to the success of an examinee's efforts with these tasks. Less likely to be observed are examinees who attempt to mediate verbally most or all of their work with the Block Design and/or Visual Puzzles subtests, but even such a mismatched allocation of mental resources, though unusual, is not entirely without occurrence.

The Fluid Reasoning and/or Visual Spatial tasks are interpreted based on the assumption that scores reflect nonverbal reasoning or reasoning with nonverbal, visual material. When this assumption is made, the secondary constructs required for effective performance are either ignored or assumed to be intact and functioning as expected thereby allowing the focus of interpretation to be on reasoning. From this perspective, if an examinee cannot respond effectively to Visual Puzzles, Block Design, Matrix Reasoning, and/or Figure Weights subtest items, the assumption is that the examinee has poor nonverbal reasoning ability. In many cases where low performance is observed, however, such an assumption is not necessarily warranted. To know if the assumption about the primary construct is valid, the role of the secondary cognitive constructs in task performance must be understood and explored in more detail. When not accessed, or when applied ineffectively, these secondary cognitive constructs can interfere with task performance to a significant degree, making it inappropriate to focus subtest score interpretation exclusively on the primary construct thought to be assessed.

Clinicians should take note of the variety of secondary cognitive constructs assessed with the Picture Concepts Subtest. Knowing how an examinee performs with this supplemental subtest can greatly enhance interpretation of Fluid Reasoning Domain performance. Examiners are strongly encouraged to include Picture Concepts as part of their standard administration of the WISC-V even though it is not a core Fluid Reasoning Domain subtest.

When low scores or scores that are not consistent with what is known about the examinee are obtained with one or more of the Fluid Reasoning or Visual Spatial Domain subtests, careful analysis of the shared and/or unique contributions of the secondary cognitive constructs and more detailed analysis of item responses and the ways in which responses were delivered should be undertaken. As indicated in the discussion above, poor performance on the Fluid Reasoning and Visual Spatial Domain subtests is thought to reflect a lack of reasoning with nonverbal visual material or a lack of nonverbal reasoning. Clinicians who appreciate that a low score on one or more Fluid Reasoning and/or Visual Spatial subtests could be due to many different sources can draw on subtest cluster, item, and cognitive construct-level analyses to help obtain a better understanding of why the examinee performed poorly and the implications of such poor performance. Appendix 6.B provides a summary of the interpretations associated with behaviors observed during administration of the Fluid Reasoning and Visual Spatial subtests that can be used to enhance hypothesis testing about what cognitive constructs are, or are not, being used to perform subtests.

Examiners also can make use of the various process scores available for enhancing interpretation of the Block Design Subtest such as scaled scores based on completion of items without time bonus (Block Design No Time Bonus scaled score) and the number of blocks placed correctly (Block Design Partial Scaled Score) and base rate tables for scores comparisons (Block Design vs Block Design No Time Bonus and Block Design vs Block Design Partial Score) and base rate tables for the number of different types of errors made with Block Design items (Dimension Errors and Rotation Errors). Also available are tables providing base rates for process observations including the number of "Don't Know" responses, or the number of times an examinee provides no response, subvocalizes, or self-corrects responses. These process observation base rates are provided for many of the Fluid Reasoning and Visual Spatial Domain subtests (see Table 6.3 for the list and location of these process score and process observation tables).

When Fluid Reasoning and/or Visual Spatial Domain subtest scores vary greatly and/or when the examiner observes behaviors that suggest secondary cognitive constructs are influencing task performance, subtest cluster analysis may be helpful in identifying specific strengths and weaknesses in the use of various cognitive constructs. Appendix 6.C illustrates the application of cluster analysis interpretation with the Fluid Reasoning and Visual Spatial Domain subtests.

When examiners are engaged in interpretation at the subtest cluster analysis level or at the subtest level, subtest score comparisons should include the determination of whether a statistically significant difference exists between the scores earned on the subtests being compared. Use a value of 3 scaled score points to signify a statistically significant difference for the comparisons between pairs of Fluid Reasoning and/or Visual Spatial Domain subtests. Appendix 6.D provides a worksheet to aid in the interpretation of Fluid Reasoning and Visual Spatial Domain subtest scaled score comparisons.

Working Memory Domain (Including the Arithmetic and Immediate Symbol Translation Subtests)

The Working Memory Domain Subtests are primarily designed to assess the constructs involved in the initial registration and holding of information (sometimes referred to as short-term memory) and the mental manipulation of information that is being held in mind (often referred to as working memory). Traditionally, the Working Memory Domain of the Wechsler Scales was made up only of tasks that used auditory verbal input (Digit Span, Letter-Number Sequencing, and Arithmetic). The WISC-V breaks with that tradition by adding the Picture Span Subtest, a task that uses visual nonverbal input (pictures of objects).

The WISC-V Working Memory Domain is comprised of three subtests: Digit Span, Picture Span, and Letter-Number Sequencing. The major changes in this domain are the inclusion of the new Picture Span Subtest and the addition of a new item type to the Digit Span Subtest (Digit Span Sequencing). The Digit Span Subtest is included in the FSIQ and is paired with the Picture Span Subtest to form the WMI. The Digit Span Subtest also is paired with the Letter-Number Sequencing Subtest to form the AWMI.

Although the Arithmetic subtest is now included as part of the Fluid Reasoning Domain, reassignment to a new domain has not changed the cognitive constructs likely to be involved in the performance of this subtest; success with the Arithmetic Subtest continues to require effective use of working memory along with knowledge of math computation operations and math problem-solving skills. For this reason, the Arithmetic Subtest will be included here as a task that primarily assesses working memory.

Following this same logic, a new subtest called Immediate Symbol Translation is also here as a task that primarily assesses initial registration and working memory. The Immediate Symbol Translation Subtest has been added to the WISC-V as one of five new subtests referred to as Complementary subtests (Immediate Symbol Translation, Delayed Symbol Translation, Recognition Symbol Translation, Naming Speed Literacy, and Naming Speed Quantity). These Complementary subtests do not contribute to the Full Scale or the Primary or Ancillary Index Scales, and are referred to in the *WISC-V Technical and Interpretive Manual* (Wechsler, 2014a) as tasks that do not assess intelligence but nevertheless are important in learning.

The Immediate Symbol Translation Subtest uses a combination of visual non-verbal and auditory verbal input and requires the use of initial registration and working memory for successful performance. The Immediate Symbol Translation Subtest is a rebus learning task that requires the examinee to learn associations between abstract symbols and words that they are intended to represent. The examinee must hold in mind these symbol-word associations as they are presented in successive item sets and also apply them to read short sentences.

Appendix 6.A discusses in detail the role of the primary cognitive constructs assessed by the Digit Span, Picture Span, Letter-Number Sequencing, Arithmetic, and Immediate Symbol Translation Subtests.

Beyond the primary cognitive constructs targeted for assessment with these subtests, the specific formats of each subtest make demands on the examinee that require the engagement of additional cognitive constructs for successful performance. Though these constructs are required for effective subtest performance, they are not considered to be the primary target of the assessment (i.e., the intention of the subtest is not to quantitatively assess the examinee's use of these cognitive constructs). The secondary cognitive constructs and their roles in subtest performance are described in detail in Appendix 6.A. Rapid Reference 6.8 provides an interpretive summary table that can be used to assist with the comparison of the subtests discussed in this section in terms of the cognitive constructs that may be involved in the performance of test items.

≡ Rapid Reference 6.8

Cognitive Constructs Likely to Be Assessed by Working Memory Domain Tasks and the Arithmetic (AR) and Immediate Symbol Translation (IST) Subtests

Cognitive Construct	DS						
	DSf	DSb	DSs	PS	LNS	AR*	IST*
Initial registration of auditory stimuli	XXX	XXX	XXX		XXX	XXX	XXX
Initial registration of visual stimuli				XXX			XXX
Mental manipulation of auditory stimuli		XXX	XXX		XXX	XXX	XXX

Cognitive Construct	DS			PS	LNS	AR*	IST*
	DSf	**DSb**	**DSs**	**PS**	**LNS**	**AR***	**IST***
Mental manipulation of visual stimuli				XXX			XXX
Visual acuity				X			X
Auditory discrimination	XX	XX	XX		XX	XX	XX
Visual representation/ discrimination				XX			XX
Attention to auditory stimuli	XX	XX	XX		XX	XX	XX
Attention to visual stimuli				XX			XX
Auditory processing speed	XX	XX	XX		XX	XX	XX
Visual processing speed				XX			XX
Mental processing speed	X	X	X	X	X	X	X
Retrieval of verbal information from remote long-term storage			XX		XX	XX	
Retrieval of information from recent long-term storage							XX
Sequencing ability	XX	XX	XX	XX	XX	XX	
Math skills						XX	
Expressive language ability	X	X	X		X	X	X
EF – Direct perception and registration of stimuli	XX	XX	XX	XX	XX	XX	XX
EF – Cueing appropriate consideration of the cognitive capacities and mental effort required to perform a task	XX	XX	XX	XX	XX	XX	XX
EF – Cueing the modulation of effort	XX	XX	XX	XX	XX	XX	XX
EF – Direct mental manipulation	X	X	X	X	X	X	X
EF – Direct attention to details of stimuli being presented	XX	XX	XX	XX	XX	XX	XX
EF – Cueing the shift to an imbalanced emphasis on processing details over patterns	XX	XX	XX	XX	XX	XX	XX

(continued)

(continued)

Cognitive Construct	DS						
	DSf	**DSb**	**DSs**	**PS**	**LNS**	**AR***	**IST***
EF – Direct sustained attention to task	XX	XX	XX	XX	XX	XX	XX
EF – Cueing the inhibition of impulsive responding				XX			XX
EF – Cueing the use of reasoning abilities						XX	
EF – Cueing the organization of information			XX		XX	XX	XX
EF – Directing the retrieval of information from recent/ remote long-term storage			XX		XX	XX	XX
EF – Cueing the execution of sequencing routines	XX	XX	XX	XX	XX	X	
EF – Cueing and directing of processing speed	XX	XX	XX	XX	XX	XX	XX
EF – Coordinating use of multiple capacities simultaneously	X	X	XX	XX	XX	XX	
EF – Cueing the monitoring of responses and the correcting of errors	X	X	X	X	X	XX	

Note: DS = Digit Span; DSf = Digit Span Forward; DSb = Digit Span Backward; DSs = Digit Span Sequencing; PS = Picture Span; LNS = Letter-Number Sequencing; EF = Executive Function. XXX = Primary Capacity targeted for assessment with the task; XX = Secondary Capacity highly likely to affect task performance; X = Secondary Capacity possibly affecting task performance.

*The Arithmetic and Immediate Symbol Translation Subtests are included in this table due to the nature of the cognitive constructs they are likely to assess.

WMI subtests, a generalized assumption of poor initial registration and/or poor working memory capacities is not necessarily warranted. To know if the assumption about these primary constructs is valid, the role of the secondary cognitive constructs in task performance and the effect of input and response formats must be understood and explored in more detail. When not assessed, or when applied ineffectively, secondary cognitive constructs can interfere with task performance to a significant degree, making it inappropriate to focus index or subtest score interpretation exclusively on the primary constructs that are thought to be assessed.

Additionally, without knowing how the examinee performs when input and response formats are varied, the clinician is in danger of over-interpreting the generalizability of the WMI score. The WMI is now comprised of one subtest that uses auditorily presented verbal information for input and one subtest that uses visually presented nonverbal images for input. Beyond initial registration of the input, examinees can adopt various approaches to represent and transform the input as they hold and manipulate it. As described in detail in Rapid Reference 6.8, visual input can be transformed and represented auditorily and manipulated through verbal rehearsal strategies; auditory input can be transformed and represented visually and manipulated with visualization strategies. It is not possible to know exactly how an examinee will attempt to perform these tasks prior to subtest administration. This variability in task approach may lead some clinicians to believe that the WMI score is the best way to represent the examinee's working memory capacity because it takes into account performance with the Digit Span and the Picture Span Subtests regardless of what input transformations may have been used by the examinee. Such thinking will serve only to cloud the picture rather than to clarify it. Digit Span and Picture Span represent two very different ways to assess initial registration and working memory, and combining scores from these two tasks will not help a clinician understand how the examinee approaches tasks that require the use of these mental constructs.

Understanding of performance comes only from careful observation of item responses and behaviors reflecting the use of mental strategies employed by the examinee and careful analysis of the shared and/or unique contributions of the secondary cognitive constructs. Although such close analysis is critical when an examinee earns significantly different scores on the Digit Span and Picture Span Subtests, it is also important in cases where scores do not differ significantly.

Similarly, although poor performance on Working Memory Domain subtests is thought to reflect a lack of effective use of initial registration and working memory capacities, clinicians who appreciate that a low score on one or more of the Working Memory Domain subtests could be due to many different sources can draw on item and cognitive construct-level analyses to help obtain a better understanding of why the examinee performed poorly and the implications of such poor performance. Appendix 6.B provides a summary of the interpretations associated with behaviors observed during administration of these subtests that can be used to enhance hypothesis testing about what cognitive constructs are, or are not, being used to perform subtests.

Examiners also can make use of the various process scores available for enhancing interpretation of the Digit Span Subtest such as separate scaled scores for Digit Span Forward, Digit Span Backward, and Digit Span Sequencing, multiple tables reporting base rates and contrast scores for comparisons among the three different Digit Span formats, and base rate tables for longest spans forward, backward, and sequenced. Base rates for longest Picture Span Stimulus and longest Picture Span Response also are provided as well as tables providing base rates for process observations including the number of "Don't Know" responses, or the number of times an examinee provides no response, subvocalizes, self-corrects responses, or asks for repetitions (see Table 6.3 for the list and location of these process score and process observation tables).

When working memory subtest scores are interpreted either collectively using the WMI or individually using subtest scores, information such as that provided in Rapid Reference 6.8 and Appendices 6.A and 6.B often is not applied effectively to enhance interpretation. It is typically assumed that the WMI score reflects a general level of working memory capacity. The secondary constructs required for effective performance are either ignored completely or assumed to be intact and functioning as expected to allow for the focus of interpretation to be on the primary constructs of initial registration and mental manipulation of stimuli.

When the subtest scores of tasks designed to assess working memory vary greatly and/or when the examiner observes behaviors that suggest that secondary cognitive constructs are influencing task performance, subtest cluster analysis may be helpful in identifying specific strengths and weaknesses in the use of various cognitive constructs. Appendix 6.C illustrates the application of cluster analysis interpretation with the Digit Span, Picture Span, Letter-Number Sequencing, Arithmetic, and Immediate Symbol Translation Subtests.

When examiners are engaged in interpretation at the cluster analysis level or at the subtest level, subtest score comparisons should include the determination of whether a statistically significant difference exists between the scores earned on the subtests being compared. Clinicians can use a value of 3 scaled score points to signify a statistically significant difference for comparisons among pairs of working memory subtests. Appendix 6.D also provides a worksheet to aid in the interpretation of working memory subtest scaled score comparisons.

It should be noted that the addition of Digit Span Sequencing to the Digit Span Subtest and the pairing of the Digit Span Subtest with the Picture Span Subtest were intended to increase the likelihood that performance on the WMI would reflect the use of working memory. Although this is a reasonable hypothesis, clinicians need to let the data they collect drive their interpretation of what the Digit Span tasks and the Picture Span Subtest are measuring for a particular examinee. When scores on Digit Span Forward and Picture Span are similar, but differ significantly from scores on Digit Span Backward, Digit Span Sequencing, Letter-Number Sequencing, Arithmetic and Immediate Symbol Translation, it is reasonable to hypothesize that Digit Span Forward and Picture Span are primarily reflecting the use of initial registration and short-term (immediate) memory whereas the other subtests are more likely to be reflecting the use of working memory capacities beyond the initial registration stage.

Without an understanding of the role that secondary cognitive constructs play in task performance, clinicians frequently will have difficulty effectively interpreting an examinee's performance on this collection of working memory subtests. For example, it is a neuropsychological fact that stimuli must be effectively registered before they can be manipulated in mind (i.e., no manipulation of information can occur if the information was not initially registered and/or is no longer being held in mind). How then does a clinician explain the performance of an examinee who repeats only 4 digits forward, but is able to repeat 6 digits in reverse? The former result suggests a capacity for initially registering and holding only 4 digits, but in order to perform Digit Span Backward, the examinee had to first register and hold 6 digits, and then mentally manipulate those 6 digits to provide a correct response. In such cases, although the examinee has the capacity to register and hold 6 digits initially, difficulties in the use of one or more secondary constructs (most likely one or more executive functions) reduced the examinee's ability to demonstrate that capacity in a consistent manner, when attempting digits forward, thereby resulting in fewer digits being repeated forward than digits being repeated backward.

Clinicians interested in examining in more detail the relationship between performance on Digit Span Forward, Digit Span Backward, and Digit Span Sequencing will find scaled score norms and cumulative frequency (Base Rate) tables in Appendix C of the *WISC-V Administration and Scoring Manual Supplement* (Wechsler, 2014b). These scaled scores along with the base rate information can be used to understand the relationships among these three digit span process tasks.

Processing Speed Domain

The Processing Speed Subtests were designed primarily to assess processing speed with nonverbal, visual stimuli. Assessment of visual processing speed, therefore, is the primary focus of interpretation of the Processing Speed Index as well as for each of the individual Processing Speed subtests as discussed in detail in

Appendix 6.A. The WISC-V Processing Speed Domain has three subtests: Coding, Symbol Search and Cancellation. The Coding Subtest is included as part of the FSIQ as well as the NVI and the Cognitive Proficiency Index (CPI). The Symbol Search Subtest also contributes to the CPI and joins the Coding Subtest to form the PSI. The Cancellation Subtest in not included in any of the WISC-V Indexes.

Beyond the primary cognitive construct of visual processing speed targeted for assessment with the Processing Speed Domain subtests, the specific formats of each subtest make demands on the examinee that require the engagement of additional cognitive constructs in order to achieve success. While these constructs typically are required for effective subtest performance, they are not considered the primary target of the assessment; that is, the intention of the subtest is not to quantitatively assess the examinee's use of these cognitive constructs. These secondary cognitive constructs include visual acuity, visual perception/representation, attention to visual stimuli, visual discrimination, grapho-motor functioning, visualization, working memory applied with visual stimuli, language representation of visual stimuli and multiple executive functions applied to cue and direct the use of visual processing and processing speed resources. The roles of these secondary cognitive constructs in subtest performance are described in detail in Appendix 6.A. Rapid Reference 6.9 provides an interpretive summary table that can be used to assist with the comparison of Processing Speed Domain subtests in terms of the cognitive constructs that may be involved in the performance of test items.

≡ Rapid Reference 6.9

Cognitive Constructs Likely to Be Assessed by Processing Speed Subtests

Cognitive Construct	CD	SS	CA
Visual Processing Speed	XXX	XXX	XXX
Motor and/or Grapho-motor Processing Speed	XXX	XX	XX
Attention to Visual Stimuli Details	XX	XX	XX
Visual Perception/Representation	XX	XX	XX

Cognitive Construct	CD	SS	CA
Visual Discrimination	XX	XX	XX
Multitasking	XXX		X
Organization Skills	X		
Grapho-motor Functioning	XX	X	X
Use of Working Memory With Visual Material	X	X	X
Language Representation of Visual Stimuli	X	X	X
EF – Cueing and directing efficient perception of visual stimuli	XX	XX	XX
EF – Cueing the appropriate consideration of the cognitive demands of a task and the amount of mental effort required to effectively perform the task	XX	XX	XX
EF – Cueing and directing the focusing of attention to visual details and task demands	XX	XX	XX
EF – Cueing and directing sustained attention to task	XX	XX	XX
EF – Cueing and directing the execution of motor routines	XX	X	X
EF – Cueing and directing visual, motor, and visual-motor processing speed	XX	XX	XX
EF – Cueing and directing a work pace that can achieve a balance between speed and accuracy	XX	XX	XX
EF – Cueing and directing the monitoring of work and the correcting of errors	XX	XX	XX
EF – Cueing and directing the coordination of the use of multiple mental capacities simultaneously	XX	XX	XX
EF – Cueing and directing the inhibition of impulsive responding		X	XX
EF – Cueing and directing the use of working memory resources	X	X	X
EF – Cueing and directing the organization of work strategies	X		
EF – Cueing and directing the generating of novel solutions or retrieving associations to improve performance	X		XX

Note: CD = Coding; SS = Symbol Search; CA = Cancellation; EF = Executive Function. XXX = Primary Capacity targeted for assessment with the task; XX = Secondary Capacity highly likely to affect task performance; X = Secondary Capacity possibly affecting task performance.

It is important to recognize that the Processing Speed Index Scale comprised of the Coding and Symbol Search Subtests offers a fairly limited measure of processing speed. All three of the Processing Speed Domain subtests employ a visual presentation format that requires the processing of nonverbal visual stimuli and grapho-motor responses. The WISC-V Processing Speed subtests do not address processing speed directly applied to academic tasks such as the fluent reading or writing of words or the completion of math calculations. As a result of this narrow focus of input, processing and output demands, PSI scores have limited generalizability to academic or work settings involving these academic skills. For example, clinicians who wish to know about an examinee's processing speed for tasks involving reading or mathematics cannot infer this from the PSI score or the individual Symbol Search, Coding, or Cancellation Subtest scores. Such information needs to be obtained from one or more speeded measures involving reading or mathematics. From a neuropsychological perspective, however, there is a link between performance on the Coding Subtest and written expression production. Because effective performance of Coding and written expression tasks involve basic grapho-motor functioning, an examinee who experiences extreme difficulties with grapho-motor production on the Coding Subtest may experience somewhat similar difficulties with the grapho-motor demands of written expression tasks. Additionally, the multitasking demands of the Coding Subtest are somewhat similar to the multitasking demands of written expression tasks, and both require the effective use of executive functions to direct and coordinate such multitasking performance. When an examinee earns a low score on the Coding Subtest, speeded performance of written expression production should be assessed. A high score on the Coding Subtest, however, is no guarantee that an examinee will not experience grapho-motor or other kinds of difficulties with written expression tasks. This is because of the increased complexity involved in producing words and sentences when performing written expression tasks.

When Processing Speed subtest scores are interpreted, either collectively using the PSI or individually, it is typically assumed that score levels reflect a general level of processing speed. It is often the case that the secondary constructs required for effective performance are either ignored completely or assumed to be intact and functioning as expected to allow for the focus of interpretation to be on the primary constructs. For example, if an examinee earns a low score on the Coding Subtest, the assumption often is that the examinee's processing speed is slower than that of same age peers. In many cases where low performance is observed, such an assumption is not necessarily warranted. To know if the assumption about the primary construct is valid, the role of the secondary cognitive constructs in task performance must be understood and explored in detail. When secondary cognitive constructs are not being accessed or applied effectively, they can significantly interfere with an individual's performance. Therefore, it would be inappropriate to focus interpretations solely on primary constructs that are thought to be assessed by particular subtests—especially when poor performance may in fact be due to deficits in secondary constructs.

When low scores or scores that are not consistent with what is known about the examinee are obtained from one or more of the Processing Speed subtests, careful analysis of the shared and/or unique contributions of the secondary cognitive constructs and more detailed analysis of item responses and the ways in which responses were delivered should be undertaken. Appendix 6.B provides a summary of the interpretations associated with behaviors observed during administration of the Processing Speed subtests that can be used to enhance hypothesis testing about what cognitive constructs are or are not being used to perform subtests.

Examiners also can make use of the various process scores available for enhancing interpretation of the Cancellation Subtest, such as separate scaled scores for the Cancellation Random and Cancellation Structured scores and a base rate table for the comparison of these scores. Tables providing base rates for the frequency of Coding Subtest rotation errors and Symbol Search Subtest set errors and rotation errors are also available (see Table 6.3 for the list and location of these process score and process observation tables).

When examiners are engaged in interpretation at the subtest level, subtest score comparisons should include the determination of whether a statistically significant difference exists between the scores earned on the subtests being compared. Clinicians can use a value of 3 scaled score points to signify a statistically significant difference for comparisons among pairs of processing speed subtests. Appendix 6.D provides a worksheet to aid in the interpretation of processing speed subtest scaled score comparisons.

WISC-V COMPLEMENTARY SUBTESTS

The WISC-V comprises five new tasks referred to as Complementary subtests: Naming Speed Literacy, Naming Speed Quantity, Immediate Symbol Translation, Delayed Symbol Translation, and Recognition Symbol Translation. These subtests are not included in the FSIQ or any of the Primary or Ancillary Index Scales. Rather, these five subtests form a set of Complementary Indexes: Naming Speed Literacy and Naming Speed Quantity are combined to form the

Naming Speed Index (NSI); the Immediate, Delayed, and Recognition Symbol Translation Subtests are combined to form the Symbol Translation Index (STI); and the NSI and STI scores are combined to produce a Storage and Retrieval Index (SRI).

Naming Speed Subtests

The Naming Speed Literacy Subtest is intended to assess the automaticity of retrieval of visual-verbal associations (often referred to as rapid automatic naming). Specifically, examinees are required to state quickly object colors and names, object sizes, colors and names, and/or letter and number names. The Naming Speed Quantity Subtest also is intended to assess the automaticity of retrieval, but rather than object attributes and names of letters and number names, the examinee retrieves the number names associated with the visual representations of small quantities of objects. Assessment of automaticity of retrieval of different types of visual-verbal associations, therefore, is the primary focus of interpretation of the NSI as well as the individual Naming Speed Subtests. The roles of these primary cognitive constructs in task performance are described in detail in Appendix 6.A.

Clinicians must be careful in the interpretation of the Rapid Naming tasks due to the varying nature of the visual stimuli used to elicit verbal labels. As noted in the *WISC-V Technical and Interpretation Manual* (Wechsler, 2014a), Naming Speed Literacy is more closely associated with reading and writing and Naming Speed Quantity is more closely associated with mathematics. When the Naming Speed Literacy and Quantity subtest scores differ significantly, it is imperative that the focus of interpretation be at the subtest, item, and task specific construct levels rather than at the Index level.

CAUTION

Clinicians must be careful in the interpretation of the Rapid Naming tasks due to the varying nature of the visual stimuli used to elicit verbal labels.

The Naming Speed Quantity Subtest is uniform in its task demands for all ages; 6-year-olds identify quantities comprised of one to four elements; children older than 6 identify quantities comprised of one to five elements. Interpretation of the Naming Speed Quantity Subtest, therefore, is relatively straightforward in that visual-verbal associations between quantity and number are being assessed at all age levels.

In contrast, interpretation of the Naming Speed Literacy Subtest is much more convoluted due to the changing nature of task demands at various age levels. For children age 6 years, Naming Speed Literacy requires identification of object colors and names for two trials and identification of object sizes, colors, and names for two trials; children ages 7–8 years identify object sizes, colors, and names for two trials and then name series of randomly alternating letters and numbers for two trials; children ages 9–16 years name only series of randomly alternating letters and numbers. Although the Naming Speed Literacy Subtest is intended to assess automaticity of visual-verbal associations for all examinees, the fact of the matter is that the cognitive constructs being assessed by this subtest change for each age group. The interpretive implications of the changing nature of task demands and the cognitive constructs being assessed are discussed in detail in Appendix 6.A. Rapid Reference 6.10 provides an interpretive summary table that can be used to assist with the comparison of Naming Speed subtests in terms of the cognitive constructs that may be involved in the performance of test items.

≡ Rapid Reference 6.10

Cognitive Constructs Likely to Be Assessed by the WISC-V Complementary Subtests

| Cognitive Construct | Naming Speed | | | | |
	NSL	NSQ	IST	DST	RST
Initial registration of auditory stimuli			XXX		X
Initial registration of visual stimuli	X	X	XXX	X	X
Working Memory – Auditory			XXX		
Working Memory – Visual			XXX		
Retrieval of verbal labels and/or visual-verbal associations – Objects & Attributes	XXX 6-8*				
Retrieval of verbal labels and/or visual verbal associations – Numbers & Letters	XXX 7-16*				

(continued)

(continued)

Cognitive Construct	Naming Speed		IST	DST	RST
	NSL	NSQ			
Retrieval of verbal labels and/or visual-verbal associations – Quantities		XXX			
Retrieval of visual-verbal associations from recent long-term storage			XX	XXX	XXX
Auditory acuity			X		X
Visual acuity	X	X	X	X	X
Auditory discrimination			XX		X
Visual representation/discrimination			XX	X	X
Attention to auditory stimuli			XX		X
Attention to visual stimuli	X		XX	X	X
Auditory processing speed			XX		X
Visual processing speed	X	X	XX		X
Oral-motor sequencing	X	X			
Expressive language ability	X	X	X	X	X
EF – Direction of shifting between automatic retrieval of number names and automatic retrieval of letter names	XXX 7-16*				
EF – Direct perception and registration of stimuli			XX		
EF – Cueing appropriate consideration of the cognitive capacities and mental effort required to perform a task			XX		
EF – Cueing the modulation of effort			XX		
EF – Direct mental manipulation			X		
EF – Direct attention to details of stimuli being presented			XX		
EF – Direct sustained attention to task			XX		
EF – Cueing the inhibition of impulsive responding			XX		
EF – Directing the retrieval of information from recent/remote long-term storage			XX		
EF – Cueing the execution of sequencing routines					
EF – Cueing and directing of processing speed	XX	XX	XX		

| | Naming Speed | | | | |
Cognitive Construct	NSL	NSQ	IST	DST	RST
EF – Coordinate use of multiple capacities simultaneously					
EF – Cueing the monitoring of responses and the correcting of errors	X	X	X		

Note: NSL = Naming Speed Literacy; NSQ = Naming Speed Quantity; IST = Immediate Symbol Translation; DST = Delayed Symbol Translation; RST = Recognition Symbol Translation; EF = Executive Function. XXX = Primary Capacity targeted for assessment with the task; XX = Secondary Capacity highly likely to affect task performance; X = Secondary Capacity possibly affecting task performance

* Indicates the age range for which this cognitive construct is likely to be assessed.

When interpreting performance on the Naming Speed Literacy and Naming Speed Quantity Subtests, it is critical to keep in mind that item (Trial) raw scores only reflect the amount of time spent naming the objects/attributes, letters/numbers, or quantities. The number of errors made while naming does not factor into the raw score. As a result, subtest scaled scores may be based on fast but highly inaccurate naming. When administering the trials of the Naming Speed Literacy and Quantity Subtests, examiners should always record the number of errors. The total number of errors made across all trials administered can be compared to the standardization sample base rate totals by age that are provided in Table C.18 of the *Administration and Scoring Manual Supplement* (Wechsler, 2014b). When an examinee's error total drops below the lower end of the average range (base rate < 25 percent), statements about naming speed performance should note that the examinee made more errors than was typical among same-age peers in the standardization sample, and that naming speed, therefore, was achieved at the cost of naming accuracy. In such cases, the resulting scaled score should not be considered an accurate characterization of the examinee's level of automaticity of retrieval of visual-verbal associations and the implications of the high rate of naming speed errors should be ascertained and discussed.

When interpreting Naming Speed, either collectively using the Naming Speed Index or individually using the Naming Speed Literacy and Naming

Speed Quantity Subtests, it is typically assumed that score levels reflect a general level of automaticity of retrieval of verbal labels associated with visual stimuli. The secondary cognitive constructs required for effective performance may be ignored completely or assumed to be intact and functioning as expected to allow for the focus of interpretation to be on the primary construct. For example, if an examinee earns a low score on the Naming Speed Literacy Subtest, the assumption is likely to be that the examinee's capacity for quick retrieval of verbal labels for visual stimuli is poor relative to same age peers. In some cases where low performance is observed, such an assumption may not be warranted. To know if the assumption about the primary construct is valid, the role of the secondary cognitive constructs in task performance must be understood and explored in detail. When secondary cognitive constructs are not being assessed or applied effectively, they can significantly interfere with an individual's performance. Therefore, it would be inappropriate to focus interpretations solely on primary constructs that are thought to be assessed by particular subtests—especially when poor performance may in fact be due to deficits in secondary constructs.

When low scores or scores that are not consistent with what is known about the examinee are obtained from one or both of the Naming Speed subtests, careful analysis of the shared and/or unique contributions of the secondary cognitive constructs and more detailed analysis of item responses and the ways in which responses were delivered should be undertaken. Appendix 6.B provides a summary of the interpretations associated with behaviors observed during administration of the Naming Speed subtests that can be used to enhance hypothesis testing about what cognitive constructs are, or are not being used to perform subtests.

Examiners also can make use of the various process scores available for enhancing interpretation of the Naming Speed subtests such as Naming Speed Literacy scaled scores based on type of stimulus used (Color-Object for ages 6-0 through 6-11, Size-Color-Object, or Letter-Number for ages 7-0 through 8-11) and base rate tables for score comparisons (Color-Object vs Size-Color-Object for ages 6-0 through 6-11 and Size-Color-Object vs Letter-Number for ages 7-0 through 8-11). Base rate tables also are provided for the number of errors made with each type of Naming Speed stimulus (Color-Object, Size-Color-Object, Letter-Number, and Quantity). The interpretive implications of naming errors was discussed in detail earlier in this section. Table 6.3 provides the list and location of these process score and error frequency base rate tables.

When examiners are engaged in interpretation at the subtest level, subtest score comparisons should include the determination of whether a statistically significant difference exists between the scores earned on the subtests being compared.

Clinicians can use a value of 3 scaled score points to signify a statistically significant difference for comparisons of the naming speed subtest scores. Appendix 6.D also provides a worksheet to aid in the interpretation of naming speed subtest scaled score comparisons.

Symbol Translation Subtests

The Symbol Translation subtests were designed primarily to assess the constructs involved in the retrieval of visual-verbal associations and the strength of verbal-visual associative memory in the form of retrieval from recent long-term storage. The Symbol Translation subtests assess these constructs utilizing an array of pictographic representations that are associated with verbal labels, namely words. Assessment of these constructs is the primary focus of interpretation of the STI as well as the individual Symbol Translation subtests. The roles of these primary cognitive constructs in task performance are described in detail in Appendix 6.A.

In addition to the primary cognitive constructs targeted for assessment with the Symbol Translation subtests, the specific formats of the Immediate, Delayed, and Recognition Symbol Translation subtests make demands on the examinee that require the engagement of secondary cognitive constructs in order to achieve success. While these secondary constructs are required for effective subtest performance, they are not considered to be the main construct targeted for assessment. These secondary cognitive constructs include Auditory Discrimination, Auditory Processing Speed, Attention to Visual and Verbal Stimuli, Encoding of Visual-Verbal Pairings, Working Memory, Expressive Language, and a number of Executive Functions applied to cue and direct the processes of focused attention, sustained effort, shifting cognitive resources, monitoring response accuracy, inhibiting erroneous responding, and efficiently placing information in long-term storage and retrieving such information on demand. The roles of these secondary cognitive constructs in subtest performance are described in detail in Appendix 6.A. Rapid Reference 6.10 provides an interpretive summary table that can be used to assist with the comparison of Symbol Translation and Naming Speed subtests in terms of the cognitive constructs that may be involved in the performance of test items.

In many instances where low performance is observed on one or more of the Symbol Translation subtests, the generalized assumption of poorly developed visual-verbal associative memory consolidation and/or retrieval efficiency is not necessarily accurate. In order to determine whether assumptions about the primary constructs are accurate, it is necessary to examine the secondary cognitive constructs involved in task performance in addition to the variations in response format that are unique to each subtest.

When low scores or scores that are not commensurate with what is known about the examinee emerge on any of the STI subtests, the clinician must analyze the contributions of the secondary cognitive constructs while simultaneously considering item-level responses and behaviors observed during administration. Low-level performance on Delayed Symbol Translation and/or on Recognition Symbol Translation is likely to be attributed to an underlying deficit in the consolidation and/or retrieval of verbal-visual pairings in long-term memory; however, clinicians who appreciate that a low score on the Delayed and/or Recognition Symbol Translation subtests may be the result of difficulties with secondary cognitive constructs rather than the primary constructs targeted for assessment are in a better position to translate assessment results into meaningful instructional and learning recommendations via item-level and cognitive construct-level analyses. Appendix 6.B provides a summary of the interpretations associated with behaviors observed during administration of the Symbol Translation and Naming Speed subtests that can be used to enhance hypothesis testing about what cognitive constructs are, or are not being used to perform subtests. Appendix 6.D provides a worksheet to aid in the interpretation of symbol translation subtest scaled score comparisons.

Examiners also can make use of the scaled score contrast scores available for enhancing interpretation of the Symbol Translation Subtests and base rate tables for score comparisons (Immediate Symbol Translation versus Delayed Symbol Translation, Immediate Symbol Translation versus Recognition Symbol Translation, and Delayed Symbol Translation versus Recognition Symbol Translation). See Table 6.3 for the list and location of the Symbol Translation Subtests contrast scores and pairwise comparisons base rate tables.

When interpreting performance on the Symbol Translation subtests it is important to keep in mind the inter-related nature of these three tasks. For instance, an examinee who exhibits difficulty encoding visual-verbal stimuli during administration of the Immediate Symbol Translation Subtest will be exposed to fewer visual-verbal pairings and, thus, will engage in fewer recall items on the Delayed and Recognition Symbol Translation subtests because only items presented during the immediate item administration are assessed during the delayed and recognition administrations. Performance on the Delayed and Recognition Symbol Translation subtests therefore must be interpreted in light of cognitive constructs not intended to be the primary focus of these tasks, such as the examinee's successful ability to register and hold differentially coded visual-verbal stimuli in immediate memory. It follows that meaningful interpretation of the STI subtests needs to include interpretation of contrast-level comparisons in order to determine whether there are unusual differences among scores obtained on subtests that purport to measure immediate visual-verbal learning, delayed recall of visual-verbal associations, and/or the retrieval of visual-verbal pairings from long-term storage. Appendix C of the *WISC-V Technical and Interpretive Manual* (Wechsler, 2014a) offers an in-depth discussion of methods for contrasting scores on the Immediate, Delayed and Recognition Symbol Translation subtests and interpreting the results of such contrasts.

CONCLUSION

Expanding upon the process-oriented approach to interpretation of assessment data, this chapter applies neuropsychological concepts within the context of an Interpretative Levels Framework to analyze and interpret performance on the WISC-V. This hierarchical framework consists of a series of levels representing degrees of aggregation, or disaggregation, of data collected *during* administration and evaluated *after* administration. The implication of the framework is that performance cannot be interpreted adequately from the perspective of a single level because the aggregate of information at each successive level obscures the details embedded in each level below it. While top-down analysis, emphasizing the FSIQ and Indexes, will not necessarily result in faulty conclusions, the premise of this chapter is that bottom-up analysis (Cognitive Construct, Item, and Subtest levels) enables clinicians to characterize a child's performance in the most effective and accurate manner possible within the context of a neuropsychologically oriented perspective.

Neuropsychological interpretation of the WISC-V begins at the Cognitive Constructs level, thereby acknowledging that performance on factorially complex tasks cannot be explained only by the contributions of a single, targeted mental construct. Instead, performance of a task reflects the use of one or more primary cognitive constructs that the task purports to measure as well as the use of one or more secondary cognitive constructs that may not have been targeted for assessment but that nevertheless may be required for effective performance. Given that cognitive tasks are not "pure" measures of a single cognitive construct, poor performance of a task cannot be attributed solely to a deficit in the primary cognitive construct targeted for assessment without a thorough exploration of the role of additional primary and secondary cognitive constructs that may have been involved in task performance. This exploration must incorporate careful observation of task performance in order to generate hypotheses about how the examinee is, or is not, employing specific cognitive constructs when responding to particular items. It is critical to note that the cognitive constructs employed by individual examinees are self-selected, often reflecting inherent preferences or biases of the examinee, and may not be consistent with the cognitive constructs targeted for measurement. Prudent observations combined with clinical acumen, therefore, are not only vital ingredients in discerning the nature of low or inconsistent scores but are necessary in order to avoid interpretive inaccuracies.

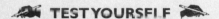 **TEST YOURSELF**

1. **Which of the following is a key focus of a process-oriented approach according to the authors?**
   a. FSIQ
   b. Observation of examinee performance on each WISC-V subtest item
   c. Statistically significant differences between index scores
   d. Complementary Subtest Scores

2. **Which of the following is true about levels of interpretation on the WISC-V?**
   a. Global composite-level interpretation highlights the contribution of the separate indexes and subtests to the global score.
   b. Primary indexes are an accurate representation of the multiple cognitive constructs that are needed to perform the aggregated tasks of each index.
   c. Performance on WISC-V subtests involves the use of multiple cognitive constructs.
   d. Only the cognitive constructs thought to be required for item performance are being assessed on each individual WISC-V item.

3. **Analysis of item response patterns yields information that can be very useful in testing hypotheses about the specific cognitive constructs likely to be involved in Subtest performance.**
   a. True
   a. False

4. **Which subtests should a clinician administer if he or she wanted to know more about an examinee's ability to reason with verbal information?**
   a. Vocabulary and Similarities
   b. Similarities and Comprehension
   c. Information and Vocabulary
   d. Comprehension and Information

5. **Which of the following is not a secondary cognitive construct engaged during assessment of verbal comprehension?**

   a. Auditory Attention

   b. Expressive Language

   c. Working Memory

   d. Motor Functioning

6. **The WISC-V Fluid Reasoning Domain consists of the Matrix Reasoning, Picture Concepts, Arithmetic, and Figure Weights subtests.**

   a. True

   b. False

7. **Are language abilities engaged while completing Fluid Reasoning and Visual Spatial subtests?**

   a. No, only nonverbal reasoning is engaged.

   b. Yes, it is a secondary cognitive construct that is necessary for successful performance.

   c. Possibly, but it is not a required secondary cognitive construct for successful performance.

   d. Yes, but only if the examinee is deaf and communicates using sign language.

8. **Which of the following constructs do the Working Memory Domain subtests assess?**

   a. Reasoning with orally presented verbal information

   b. Mental manipulation of information

   c. Speed of information processing

   d. Retrieval from recent long-term storage

9. **Which subtest not included in the WISC-V Working Memory Domain primarily assesses working memory?**

   a. Block Design

   b. Delayed Symbol Translation

   c. Arithmetic

   d. Coding

10. **The WISC-V Processing Speed tasks directly apply to academic tasks such as fluent reading, writing, and completion of math calculations.**

    a. True

    a. False

Answers: 1. b; 2. c; 3. a; 4. b; 5. d; 6. a; 7. c; 8. b; 9. d; 10. b

REFERENCES

Arnsten, A. F. T., & Robbins, T. W. (2002). Neurochemical modulation of prefrontal cortical functioning in humans and animals. In D. T. Stuss & R. T. Knight (Eds.), *Principles of frontal lobe function* (pp. 31–50). Oxford, UK: Oxford University Press.

Berninger, V. W. (1994). *Reading and writing acquisition: A developmental neuropsychological perspective.* Boulder, CO: Westview.

Berninger, V. W., & Richards, T. L. (2002). *Brain literacy for educators and psychologists.* San Diego, CA: Academic Press.

Carroll, J. B. (1993). *Human cognitive abilities: A survey of factor-analytic studies.* Cambridge, UK: Cambridge University Press.

Dehaene, S. (1997). *The number sense: How the mind creates mathematics.* Oxford, UK: Oxford University Press.

Dehaene, S. (2009). *Reading in the brain: The new science of how we read.* New York, NY: Penguin.

Dehaene, S. (2011). *The number sense: How the mind creates mathematics* (2nd ed.). Oxford, UK: Oxford University Press.

Dehaene, S. (2014). *Consciousness and the brain: Deciphering how the brain codes our thoughts.* New York, NY: Viking.

Dehn, M. J. (2013). Enhancing SLD diagnoses through the identification of psychological processing deficits. *Australian Educational and Developmental Psychologist, 30*(02), 119–139.

Flanagan, D. P., Alfonso, V. C., & Ortiz, S. O. (2012). The cross-battery assessment (XBA) approach: An overview, historical perspective, and current directions. In D. P. Flanagan & P. L. Harrison (Eds.), *Contemporary intellectual assessment: Theories, tests, and issues* (3rd ed., pp. 459–483). New York, NY: Guilford.

Flanagan, D. P., Alfonso, V. C., Ortiz, S. O., & Dynda, A. M. (2010). Best practices in cognitive assessment for school neuropsychological evaluations. In D. C. Miller (Ed.), *Best practices in school neuropsychology: Guidelines for effective practice, assessment, and evidence-based intervention* (pp. 101–140). Hoboken, NJ: Wiley.

Hale, J. B., & Fiorello, C. A. (2004). *School neuropsychology: A practitioner's handbook.* New York, NY: Guilford.

Kaplan, E. (1988). A process approach to neuropsychological assessment. In T. Boll & B. K. Bryant (Eds.), *Clinical neuropsychology and brain functions: Research, measurement, and practice* (pp. 125–167). Washington, DC: American Psychological Association.

Kaplan, E., Fein, D., Morris, R., Kramer, J. H., & Delis, D. C. (1999). *The WISC-III as a processing instrument.* San Antonio, TX: Psychological Corporation.

Korkman, M., Kirk, U., & Kemp, S. L. (1998). *NEPSY: A developmental neuropsychological assessment.* San Antonio, TX: Psychological Corporation.

Kosslyn, S. M. (1992). *Wet mind: The new cognitive neuroscience.* New York, NY: Simon and Schuster.

Levine, M. D. (1994). *Educational care: A system for understanding and helping children with learning problems at home and in school.* Cambridge, MA: Educators Publishing Service.

Levine, M. D., Gordon, B. N., & Reed, M. S. (1998). *Developmental variation and learning disorders* (2nd ed.). Cambridge, MA: Educators Publishing Service.

Luria, A. R. (1973). *The working brain: An introduction to neuropsychology.* New York, NY: Basic Books.

Luria, A. R. (1980). *Higher cortical functions in man.* New York, NY: Basic Books.

McCloskey, G. (2009a). The WISC-IV Integrated. In D. P. Flanagan & A. S. Kaufman, *Essentials of WISC-IV Assessment* (2nd ed., pp. 310–467). Hoboken, NJ: Wiley.

McCloskey, G. (2009b). Clinical applications I: A neuropsychological approach to interpretation of the WAIS-IV and the use of the WAIS-IV in learning disability assessments. In E. O. Lichtenberger & A. S. Kaufman, *Essentials of WAIS-IV assessment* (pp. 208–244). Hoboken, NJ: Wiley.

McCloskey, G., & Maerlender, A. (2005). The WISC-IV Integrated. In A. Prifitera, D. H. Saklofske, & L. G. Weiss, *WISC-IV clinical use and interpretation: Scientist-practitioner perspectives* (pp. 102–149). San Diego, CA: Academic Press.

McCloskey, G., Slonim, J., & Hartz, E. (2016). Interpreting the WISC-V using George McCloskey's neuropsychologically oriented process approach to psychoeducational evaluations. In A. S. Kaufman, S. E. Raiford, & D. L. Coalson. *Intelligent testing with the WISC-V* (pp. 493–547). Hoboken, NJ: Wiley.

Miller, D. C. (2011). *Essentials of school neuropsychological assessment* (2nd ed.). Hoboken, NJ: Wiley.

Posner, M. I., & Raichle, M. E. (1994). *Images of mind*. New York, NY: Scientific American Library/Scientific American Books.

Posner, M. I., & Rothbart, M. K. (2007). *Educating the human brain*. Washington, DC: American Psychological Association.

Sporns, O. (2011). *Networks of the brain*. Cambridge, MA: MIT Press.

Stuss, D. T., & Knight, R. T. (Eds.). (2002). *Principles of frontal lobe function* (2nd ed.). Oxford, UK: Oxford University Press.

Temple, C. (1997). *Developmental cognitive neuropsychology*. East Sussex, UK: Psychology Press.

Wechsler, D. (2011). *Wechsler Abbreviated Scale of Intelligence* (2nd ed.). Bloomington, MN: Pearson.

Wechsler, D. (2014). *Wechsler Intelligence Scale for Children–Fifth Edition*. Bloomington, MN: Pearson.

Wechsler, D., & Kaplan, E. (2015). *Wechsler Intelligence Scale for Children–Fifth Edition Integrated*. Bloomington, MN: Pearson.

Wechsler, D., Kaplan, E., Fein, D., Kramer, J., Morris, R., Delis, D., & Maerlender, A. (2004). *Wechsler Intelligence Scale for Children–Fourth Edition Integrated*. Bloomington, MN: Pearson.

Appendix 6.A

COGNITIVE CONSTRUCTS ASSESSED WITH THE WISC-V SUBTESTS

Appendix 6.A identifies the cognitive constructs likely to be used to complete each WISC-V Subtest. Content is arranged according to the domains of functioning assessed by the WISC-V: Verbal Comprehension, Fluid Reasoning and Visual Spatial, Working Memory, Processing Speed, and the Complementary subtests. The Fluid Reasoning and Visual Spatial domains are addressed together because of the large amount of overlap of the cognitive constructs likely to be used. Likewise, the Arithmetic and Immediate Symbol Translation subtests are included with the Working Memory Domain subtests. The five complementary subtests are listed together in the final section. Discussion within each section focuses on primary and secondary cognitive constructs and executive functions.

Primary Cognitive Constructs
Primary constructs are those capacities that are the focal point of assessment with the subtest.

Secondary Cognitive Construct
Secondary constructs are those capacities that were not intended to be the primary focus of assessment, but that may be affecting performance to varying degrees depending on the specific cognitive strengths and weaknesses of the examinee and how the examinee is approaching the task.

Executive Functions
As a class of cognitive constructs, executive functions are responsible for cueing and directing the use of other mental capacities that are used for the purposes of perceiving, feeling, thinking, and acting. As such, they are intricately involved in the performance of all the tasks of the WISC-V. The degree of involvement of specific executive functions in the performance of specific subtests, however, is highly variable and dependent on many factors, including the directions provided to the examinee about how to perform the task and the input, processing, and output demands of the task. It is important to understand the role of executive functions in cueing and directing the use of primary and secondary cognitive constructs. For most subtests, demands for the use of executive functions are reduced greatly through the use of explicit directions and teaching examples that model how to perform a task and/or the kind of

response that is desired. For some examinees, however, even these executive function aids do not help to ameliorate the effects of their severe executive function deficits, and the effects of these deficits often can be observed in the examinee's efforts to perform tasks.

Verbal Comprehension Domain Subtests

The Verbal Comprehension Domain subtests assess many primary and secondary constructs.

Primary Cognitive Constructs

The two primary cognitive constructs assessed by the Verbal Comprehension Domain comprise Retrieval of Verbal Content from Remote Long-Term Storage and Reasoning with Auditorily Presented Verbal Content.

Retrieval of Verbal Content from Remote Long-Term Storage

This cognitive capacity is essential for effective performance of the Vocabulary and Information subtests. In the case of the Similarities and Comprehension Subtests, the relative importance of retrieval of information from remote long-term storage can vary greatly. If an examinee is not familiar with words that are presented as part of the directions or the items of the subtest, then lack of retrieval of semantic information will have a limiting effect on performance with the Similarities subtest and the Comprehension subtest, but this is much less likely to occur with the WISC-V than the WISC-IV, because the test development team made a concerted effort to avoid the use of words such as *lumber* and *advantages* that may not be known to younger examinees. Beyond understanding of subtest directions and item content, an examinee may have stored specific knowledge that can be retrieved and expressed as responses to test items. In the case of the Vocabulary and Similarities subtests, the type of verbal content retrieved is semantic knowledge; for the Information subtest, specific content area factual knowledge is retrieved; for the Comprehension subtest, the type of content retrieved is specific knowledge of social conventions and rules or the reasons for practical behaviors.

Reasoning with Auditorily Presented Verbal Content

This cognitive construct most often is required for success with the Similarities and Comprehension subtests. Reasoning with language is not assessed directly by the Vocabulary and Information subtests; individuals who have not registered and stored the needed specific word meanings or content area facts prior to administration of the Vocabulary and Information subtests cannot apply reasoning ability to "figure out" the meaning of specific vocabulary words or to induce the answer to factual information questions during test administration. Examinees with extensive semantic and content area knowledge stores, however, can access these while responding to specific Similarities and Comprehension subtest items, thereby bypassing the use of reasoning abilities on those items.

Secondary Cognitive Constructs

There are multiple Secondary Cognitive Constructs assessed by the Verbal Comprehension Domain as described below.

Auditory Acuity

While listening to the directions and the items presented by the examiner, the examinee must have adequate auditory acuity. If the examinee cannot hear all of the speech sounds made by the examiner, directions may be misunderstood. Typically, an examinee's auditory acuity should be assessed and verified to be within normal limits with or without the use of assistive devices prior to test administration, thereby reducing the likelihood that poor auditory acuity will be a factor in performance. If overlooked, however, a deficit in auditory acuity can significantly affect task performance with all verbal subtests.

Attention to Auditorily Presented Verbal Information

While listening to the directions and the items presented by the examiner, the examinee must have the capacity to attend to auditorily presented verbal information. A lack of adequate attention can compromise auditory discrimination, auditory comprehension, and the initial registration of information and lead to inconsistent or ineffective performance of test items.

Auditory Discrimination

The examinee must be able to listen to and effectively process the language used by the examiner when directions are being provided before he or she responds to the items of each Verbal Comprehension subtest. If the examinee is prone to auditory discrimination errors when listening to others speak, specific words may be misunderstood resulting in incorrect responses or no response at all.

Auditory Comprehension (Receptive Language)

Not only must the examinee be able to hear and discriminate the individual sounds of words spoken by the examiner, the examinee must also grasp the meaning of the sentences that are being spoken as subtest directions or items. Increasing complexity in the grammar and syntax used in subtest directions and items increases the demand for well-developed auditory comprehension. Although all of the Verbal subtests require the use of auditory comprehension to some degree, the Comprehension and Information subtests make greater demands on this construct than the Similarities and Vocabulary subtests. It should be noted, however, that the WISC-V test development team made a concerted effort to simplify the grammar and syntax of test directions in an attempt to minimize the possibility that auditory comprehension difficulties would be interfering with the understanding of test directions.

Auditory Processing Speed
The speed with which an examinee can register auditory information can greatly affect the examinee's ability to register all the information that is presented in a short period of time. Although the items of each Verbal Comprehension subtest are read to the examinee at a normal conversational pace, an examinee with slow auditory processing speed may not be able to register all of the information provided in each item; this is especially true for the Comprehension and Information subtests.

Initial Registration of Auditorily Presented Verbal Information
An examinee who is not able to initially register auditorily presented information and hold it for a brief time will not be able to effectively engage with the processing of the intended input or be able to formulate an adequate response. The ability to initially register and briefly hold information (typically referred to as short-term or immediate memory) is distinct from the other auditory capacities discussed here and is also different from working memory that involves the manipulation of information after it has been registered, and different from the executive functions that are needed to cue the effective initial registration and holding of information.

Auditory Working Memory
When directions are long or make use of complex grammar and syntax and/or the examinee requires more than a few seconds to retrieve or compose a response, the examinee may find it necessary to hold in mind and reference the auditorily presented item content while attempting to retrieve relevant information and/or compose a response. Although working memory capacity may need to be accessed for any of the Verbal Comprehension subtests, it is most likely to be used when attempting the items of the Comprehension and Information subtests.

Expressive Language
After hearing, comprehending, and processing subtest directions and items, the examinee is required to use expressive language abilities to communicate a response. Although all of the Verbal Comprehension subtests require a vocal

response, the Vocabulary and Comprehension subtests typically require more in the way of expressive language production than the Similarities and Information subtests in order for a response to be judged correct. Responses to the Similarities subtest items also may require greater expressive language capacity if the examinee is unable to provide a concise single word concept response to identify how two words are alike.

Executive Functions

For the Verbal Comprehension subtests, accurate responding depends in part on the effective use of one or more of the following executive functions:

- Cueing the appropriate considerations of the cognitive demands of a task and the amount of mental effort required to effectively perform the task (Gauge Cue)
- Cueing and directing auditory perception and discrimination (Perceive Cue)
- Cueing and directing the focusing and sustaining of attention to auditory stimuli (Focus/Select and Sustain Cues)
- Cueing and directing auditory processing speed (Pace Cue)
- Cueing and directing efficient retrieval from long-term storage (Retrieve Cue)
- Cueing and directing the use of reasoning abilities (Generate and/or Associate Cues)
- Cueing and directing the initiation and sustaining of on-demand (i.e., at the request of the examiner) use of expressive language capacities (Sustain and Execute Cues)
- Cueing and directing the flexible shifting of cognitive mind-set to consider and respond to the specific demands of the task (Flexible and Shift Cues)
- Cueing and directing the use of working memory resources (Hold and Manipulate Cues)
- Recognizing that a cue for retrieval of additional information (i.e., examiner saying "Tell me more . . .") can aid performance (Awareness of external Retrieve Cues)
- Coordinating the use of reasoning and retrieval capacities, and possibly working memory, to produce a response (Integration of Multiple Cues)
- Cueing the inhibition of impulsive responding (Inhibit Cue)

COGNITIVE CONSTRUCTS ASSESSED WITH THE FLUID REASONING AND VISUAL SPATIAL SUBTESTS

The Fluid and Visual Spatial Domain subtests assess many primary and secondary constructs.

NOTE

· ·

See Rapid Reference 6.8 for the complete list of the Cognitive Constructs Assessed with the Arithmetic subtest.

Primary Cognitive Constructs

The Fluid and Visual Spatial Domain assesses a single primary cognitive construct: Reasoning with Nonverbal Visual Material.

Reasoning with Nonverbal Visual Material

This cognitive capacity is essential for effective performance of most of the items of the Matrix Reasoning, Figure Weights, and Block Design subtests and many of the items of the Picture Concepts subtest. Although Carroll (1993) and the WISC-V test development team (Wechsler, 2014) consider the Visual Puzzles subtest an assessment of reasoning, clinicians should be open to the possibility that the Visual Puzzles subtest may be a stronger measure of basic visual perceptual processing than a measure of reasoning with nonverbal visual stimuli, especially when performance on the Visual Puzzles subtest deviates significantly from performance on the Block Design, Matrix Reasoning, Figure Weights, and Picture Concepts subtests.

For the Figure Weights subtest, realizing that solutions for the more difficult items always require the application of reasoning with quantitative information rather than simply looking for an answer that "looks right" will increase the likelihood of correct responses beyond the level of chance.

It is important to keep in mind that reasoning with nonverbal visual stimuli does not necessarily involve nonverbal reasoning. Reasoning with visual stimuli can involve nonverbal reasoning, verbal reasoning, quantitative reasoning, or various combinations of these different ways to reason. Examinees often are observed talking to themselves about Matrix Reasoning, Figure Weights, and Picture Completion items, and occasionally talking themselves through the placement of blocks on the Block Design subtest. (In contrast, clinicians are likely to note a lack of such verbalization when examinees are performing the Visual Puzzles subtest items.) The type of reasoning abilities that are engaged to perform the Fluid Reasoning and the Visual Spatial subtests will depend on the individual examinee and his or her perceptions of what abilities are required to succeed with the task.

Secondary Cognitive Constructs

There are multiple Secondary Cognitive Constructs assessed by the Visual Spatial Domain as described below.

Visual Acuity

While attempting to perform the Fluid Reasoning and the Visual Spatial subtests, visual acuity is necessary to ensure that all of the visual elements of each item can be accurately viewed. If the examinee cannot see clearly all of the visual information provided in each item, incorrect responses may result. Typically, an examinee's visual acuity is assessed and verified to be within normal limits with or without the use of corrective lenses prior to test administration so that this capacity should not be a factor in performance. If overlooked, however, visual acuity problems can significantly affect task performance with any of the subtests that use visual stimuli.

Attention to Visual Stimuli

To perform Fluid Reasoning and the Visual Spatial subtest tasks, an examinee must have the capacity for focusing and sustaining attention for the visual stimuli of each item.

Visual Perception and Representation

To perform Fluid Reasoning and the Visual Spatial subtests, the examinee must have the perceptual capacity to form relatively accurate visual representations of the stimuli presented. Some visually impaired examinees or examinees with severe visual perception deficits might have difficulty making sense of the information being presented, especially the more abstract geometric representations of the Matrix Reasoning, Block Design, and Visual Puzzles subtests. In the case of the Picture Concepts subtests, some examinees may not be able to recognize what common object or scene is being depicted.

Visual Discrimination

Many of the items of the Fluid Reasoning and the Visual Spatial subtests require careful application of visual discrimination abilities (i.e., the ability to see visual similarities and differences in the visual stimuli being presented). As is the case with Visual Perception, some visually impaired examinees or examinees with severe visual perception deficits might have difficulty seeing the visual similarities and differences in the visual images being presented, especially the more detailed visual elements of the Figure Weights subtest or the abstract geometric representations of the Matrix Reasoning, Visual Puzzles, and Block Design subtests. In the case of the Picture Concepts subtest, examinees may miss important details in the drawings of common objects or scenes that would enable them to identify the common characteristic shared with other objects or scenes.

Visualization

The ability to generate visual images (i.e., visual mental representations "in the mind's eye") is essential to effective performance only on the Visual Puzzles subtest. For Block Design and the Fluid Reasoning subtests, visualization may help with performance but is not essential for success. Individuals lacking in visualization capacity will find the Visual Puzzles items extremely difficult to complete within the specified time limits. Although some examinees will attempt to apply analysis and synthesis and reasoning abilities to the solution of Visual Puzzles items, these efforts are likely to require an inordinate amount of time to "talk through" the correct positioning of the visual elements. Examinees completing items much sooner than the 30-second time limit appear to be able to quickly "see" how the various visual elements would fit together rather than engaging in elaborate thought routines involving analysis and synthesis and reasoning. For the Matrix Reasoning, Block Design, Figure Weights, and Picture Concepts items, a lack of visualization can be compensated for as discussed in the next section on working memory.

Working Memory: Visual (mentally manipulating visually presented stimuli)

There should be little doubt that being able to hold and manipulate visualized mental representations can enhance greatly an examinee's performance with many items of the Fluid Reasoning and Visual Spatial subtests. For some Visual Puzzles and Matrix Reasoning items, solutions can be derived much more quickly if the examinee can mentally rotate visual images that are being held in working memory to envision how elements would look if rotated or repositioned, or if the examinee can hold in mind specific visual element relationships of a Matrix Reasoning item while examining and comparing response options.

For the more difficult items of the Figure Weights subtest, it appears essential for an examinee to be able to hold and compare quantitative equivalence hypotheses and the objects that were included in each equivalence hypothesis and keep track of the hypotheses that have been generated and apply them to deduce the correct response within 30 seconds. For Block Design, performance can be enhanced when a visual image of the model can be held in mind to guide the placement of blocks in the examinee's construction. For the Picture Concepts subtest, the examinee will benefit from the ability to hold, compare, and keep track of multiple hypotheses and the images of objects or scenes that were included in each hypothetical grouping.

What is open to debate, however, is whether the use of working memory capacity is a necessary precondition for successful performance with any or all of the items of the Fluid Reasoning or Visual Spatial subtests. It is certainly conceivable that an examinee with very poor working memory capacity can succeed with many of the Matrix Reasoning, Visual Puzzles, and Picture Concepts items and some of the less difficult Figure Weights items by repetitively rescanning the visual stimuli of the items to refresh the visual mental representations rather than trying to hold them in working memory for prolonged periods of time. In the case of Block Design, an examinee with poor working memory capacity can frequently compare the model design with the construction in progress to judge the accuracy of block placements and guide further performance. The need for such repeated scanning of images will, however, increase the time needed for item completion, which may affect scores on the Block Design, Visual Puzzles, and Figure Weights subtests because of individual item time limits.

Manual Motor Dexterity

The Block Design subtest requires the examinee to handle 4–9 blocks and move them about on a flat surface to construct 2×2 or 3×3 designs. Scoring criteria stipulate the specific placement of blocks required to earn credit for a design. All designs must be completed within a specified amount of time, and for the four most difficult items, bonus points are awarded for speed of performance. Examinees who may be lacking in motor coordination for a variety of reasons may find it difficult to handle the blocks, resulting in inaccurate block placements, rotated or fragmented designs, slowed production and disruption of the use of analysis and synthesis, reasoning, and/or other constructs due to overfocusing on motor coordination difficulties.

Visual Processing Speed

The Visual Puzzles and Figure Weights subtests have specific time limits for delivery of item responses. For these subtests, visual processing speed plays a critical role in task performance; slow visual processing speed will increase the time required to mentally represent all of the visual information being presented in an item, thereby affecting the amount of time required to identify a solution.

Mental Processing Speed

The slow processing of thoughts about item solutions also increases the time needed to arrive at a response. For the Visual Puzzles and Figure Weights subtests, mental processing speed can play a critical role in performance because of individual item time limits. In the case of Block Design, all designs must be completed within a specified amount of time, and for the four most difficult items, bonus points are awarded for speed of correct responding.

Motor Processing Speed

For the Block Design subtest, the examinee must use blocks to construct a design that matches a model. Slow motor processing speed, therefore, can affect item performance. Slower processing speed with Block Design items can be the result of slow speed of visual processing, slow speed of thinking about how to solve an item, slow speed of motor movement, or slow speed only when required to integrate visual processing with motor movement. Processing speed should not be thought of as a unitary trait; examinees are not either uniformly fast, average, or slow. Processing speed can vary with each task that requires speeded performance. Although some examinees may be fast with all tasks or slow with all tasks, it is much more common to find examinees whose processing speeds vary greatly from one task to another.

Language Representation of Visual Stimuli

Although the Picture Concepts subtest can be completed without the use of reasoning with language, a verbal mediation strategy is modeled for all examinees when explaining the task in the subtest directions. Examinees who have strong preferences for the use of verbal abilities are likely to follow the pattern modeled for them in the subtest directions and apply verbal labels to objects and scenes and then apply reasoning with language to identify the common physical characteristics or conceptual similarity that links two or more objects or scenes. A verbal mediation strategy also is demonstrated during the directions for the Matrix Reasoning Subtest, again providing examinees who prefer verbal processing with examples of the use of a strategy for verbally labeling the visual stimuli presented in test items.

Executive Functions

For the Fluid Reasoning and Visual Spatial subtests, accurate responding depends in part on the effective use of one or more of the following executive functions:

- Cueing and directing efficient perception of visual stimuli (Perceive Cue)
- Cueing the appropriate consideration of the cognitive demands of a task and the amount of mental effort required to effectively perform the task (Gauge Cue)

- Cueing and directing the focusing of attention to visual details and task demands
- Cueing and directing sustained attention to task (Sustain Cue)
- Cueing and directing the use of reasoning abilities (generating novel solutions or making associations with prior knowledge that lead to problem solutions) (Generate and/or Associate Cues)
- Cueing and directing the inhibition of impulsive responding (Inhibit Cue)
- Cueing and directing the flexibility to recognize the need to change and the shifting of cognitive mindset needed to consider and respond to the specific, and at times further changing, demands of the task (Flexible and Shift Cues)
- Cueing and directing the use of working memory resources (Hold and Manipulate Cues)
- Cueing and directing the organization of information (Organize Cue)
- Cueing and directing the execution of motor routines (Block Design only) (Execute Cue)
- Cueing and directing mental, visual, motor, and visual-motor processing speeds (Pace Cue)
- Cueing and directing the balance between pattern (global) and detail (local) processing (Balance Cue)
- Cueing and directing the monitoring of work progress and the correcting of errors (Monitor and Correct Cues)
- Cueing and directing the coordination of the use of multiple mental constructs simultaneously (Integration of Multiple Cues)

COGNITIVE CONSTRUCTS ASSESSED WITH THE WORKING MEMORY SUBTESTS AND THE ARITHMETIC AND IMMEDIATE SYMBOL TRANSLATION SUBTESTS

Primary Cognitive Constructs

The Primary Cognitive Constructs assessed by the Working Memory, Arithmetic and Immediate Symbol Translation subtests vary depending on the specific subtest as described below.

Initial Registration of Auditorily Presented Verbal Information

This cognitive construct is essential for effective performance of all of the items of the Digit Span, Letter-Number Sequencing (LNS), Arithmetic, and Immediate Symbol Translation subtests. Before examinees can respond to any of the items of these subtests, they must effectively register the auditorily presented verbal information and hold it at least for 1–3 seconds. It also is important to note that some examinees will immediately tag the visual input pictures of the Picture Span subtest with verbal labels that they initially register auditorily thereby transforming this subtest into a visual-verbal input task.

Initial Registration of Visually Presented Nonverbal Information

This cognitive construct is essential for effective performance of the Picture Span and Immediate Symbol Translation subtests. Before examinees can respond to any of the items of these subtests, they must effectively register the visually presented nonverbal information (pictures and abstract symbols) and hold it for at least 1–3 seconds.

Working Memory: Auditory (manipulating auditorily presented verbal information or manipulating visually presented information that is being auditoriy represented in mind)

This cognitive construct is essential for effective performance of the items of the Digit Span Backward, Digit Span Sequencing, Letter-Number Sequencing, Arithmetic, and Immediate Symbol Translation subtests and can be very helpful, but not essential, in the performance of the Digit Span Forward items. Items requiring mental manipulation cannot be completed by a simple "dumping" of the information being held in the initial registration buffer. The information must be held for more than 1–3 seconds and manipulated in some way in order for a correct response to be constructed.

Although all of these tasks except Digit Span Forward require the use of Initial Registration and Working Memory, the contributions of these two capacities to task performance are distinct but are not dissociable. A examinee with extremely poor initial registration capacity for a certain type of stimuli will not be able to perform effectively on a task that requires mental manipulation of that same type of stimuli (note that this is not the same as saying that an examinee who scores poorly on a task involving initial registration of stimuli also will score poorly on a task involving initial registration and working memory of the same stimuli, as discussed in the text of this chapter).

In the case of the Arithmetic subtest, the directions have been changed such that for items 20 to 34 the examiner may repeat the item once. For younger children with working memory or math skill deficits, this change is unlikely to have an impact on their performance. For some older children the repetition of an item may reduce, but not completely eliminate, the working memory demands of the item.

In the case of the Immediate Symbol Translation subtest, each item makes successively greater demands on working memory as the number of symbol-word associations that must be held in mind increases. As administration of the task increases beyond a few minutes, it is very likely that the examinee has transferred some of the symbol-word associations to recent long-term storage and is now retrieving them from recent long-term storage to respond to additional items.

In the case of the Picture Span subtest, examinees who initially tagged the pictures with verbal labels are likely to be using the articulatory loop during the remainder of the 5-second exposure interval to verbally rehearse the picture sequence before choosing their response options when the page is turned.

Working Memory: Visual (manipulating visually presented nonverbal information or manipulating auditorily presented information that is being visually represented in mind)

This cognitive construct may be used for effective performance of the items of the Picture Span and Immediate Symbol Translation subtests. Items requiring mental manipulation cannot be completed by a simple "dumping" of the information being held in the initial registration buffer. The information must be held for more than 1–3 seconds and manipulated in some way in order for a correct response to be constructed.

After initially registering the visual stimuli of Picture Span items, some examinees may choose to continue to hold the visual images in visual working memory until they respond. After initially registering the symbol-word associations of Immediate Symbol Translation subtest items, some examinees may choose to emphasize visual elements in their attempts to hold and manipulate the symbol-word associations in working memory.

After initially registering the auditory input of Arithmetic Subtest items, some examinees may choose to create visual images of numbers and their relationships while attempting to perform the mental calculations in working memory. After hearing the numbers (or numbers and letters) of the Digit Span and Letter-Number Sequencing subtests, some examinees may choose to "see" the numbers and letters as visual images in mind as they manipulate them to prepare a response.

Secondary Cognitive Constructs

There are multiple Secondary Cognitive Constructs assessed by the Working Memory, Arithmetic, and Immediate Symbol Translation subtests.

Auditory Acuity

While listening to the directions and the individual test items spoken by the examiner, the examinee must have adequate auditory acuity. If the examinee cannot hear all of the speech sounds made by the examiner, directions may be misunderstood and/or items may not be heard accurately. Typically, an examinee's auditory acuity is assessed and verified to be within normal limits with or without the use of assistive devices prior to test administration so that this capacity should not be a factor in performance. If overlooked, however, a deficit in auditory acuity can significantly affect task performance with all verbal subtests.

Visual Acuity

While attempting to perform the Picture Span and Immediate Symbol Translation subtests, visual acuity is necessary to ensure that all of the visual elements of each item can be accurately viewed. If the examinee cannot see clearly all of the visual information provided in each item, incorrect responses may result. Typically, an examinee's visual acuity is assessed and verified to be within normal limits with or without the use of corrective lenses prior to test administration so that this capacity should not be a factor in performance. If overlooked, however, visual acuity problems can significantly affect task performance with any of the subtests that use visual stimuli.

Auditory Discrimination

Before responding to the items of each auditorily presented subtest, the examinee must be able to listen to and effectively process the language used by the examiner when directions and test items are being provided. If the examinee is prone to auditory discrimination errors when listening to others speaking, specific letters, numbers, or words may be misunderstood, resulting in incorrect responses or no response at all. The WISC-V test development team made modifications to the stimuli of the Digit Span and Letter-Number Sequencing tasks in an effort to reduce the likelihood of auditory discrimination errors (e.g., using only non-rhyming letter and number name combinations in each item; therefore, the rhyming letters v and b and the number 3 would not be used in the same item).

Visual Perception and Representation

To perform the Picture Span and Immediate Symbol Translation subtests, the examinee must have the perceptual capacity to form relatively accurate visual representations of the stimuli presented. Some visually impaired examinees or examinees with severe visual perception deficits might have difficulty making sense of the information being presented, especially the more abstract geometric representations of the Immediate Symbol Translation subtest. In the case of the Picture Span subtest, some visually impaired examinees might not be able to recognize what common object is being depicted.

Visual Discrimination

The items of the Immediate Symbol Translation subtest require careful application of visual discrimination abilities (i.e., the ability to see visual similarities and differences in the visual stimuli being presented). As is the case with Visual Perception, some visually impaired examinees or examinees with severe visual perception deficits might have difficulty seeing the visual similarities and differences in the more detailed visual symbols presented.

Attention to Auditory Stimuli

To perform auditorily presented Working Memory subtest tasks, the examinee must have the capacity for focusing and sustaining attention for the auditory stimuli of each item.

Attention to Visual Stimuli

To perform the Picture Span and Immediate Symbol Translation subtest tasks, an examinee must have the capacity for focusing and sustaining attention for the visual stimuli of each item.

Auditory Processing Speed

The speed with which an examinee can register auditory information can greatly affect the examinee's ability to register all the information that is presented in a short period of time. Although Digit Span and Letter Number Sequencing item stimuli are presented at the relatively slow rate of one stimulus unit per second, an examinee with extremely slow auditory processing speed may not be able to keep up with this rate of information delivery, thereby reducing the examinee's capacity for registering all of the stimuli. Similarly, although the Arithmetic Subtest items are read to the examinee at a normal conversational pace, an examinee with slow auditory processing speed may not be able to register all of the information provided in each word problem.

Visual Processing Speed

The Picture Span subtest has specific time limits for the presentation of item stimuli. For this subtest, visual processing speed may play a critical role in task performance, especially as the number of objects presented increases during the 5-second exposure time. Slow visual processing speed will increase the time required to initially register all of the stimuli of each item.

Mental Processing Speed

The speed with which an examinee can manipulate information while holding it in mind can greatly affect an examinee's performance with the Arithmetic subtest. An examinee with slow mental processing speed may not be able to complete

Arithmetic items within the 30-second time limit despite the ability to correctly solve the problem. Similarly, individuals with slow mental processing speed may have difficulties with completing all the mental manipulations required to assemble a response to items of the Digit Span, Letter-Number Sequencing, Picture Span, and Immediate Symbol Translation subtests.

Processing speed should not be thought of as a unitary trait; examinees are not either uniformly fast, average or slow. Processing speed can vary with each task that requires speeded performance. Although some examinees may be fast with all tasks or slow with all tasks, it is much more common to find examinees whose processing speeds vary greatly from one task to another.

Retrieval of Verbal Information from Remote Long-Term Storage

The Arithmetic and Letter-Number Sequencing subtests and the Digit Span Sequencing task all require the retrieval of verbal information from long-term storage. The requirement for the retrieval of math facts, procedures, and/or problem-solving routines is fairly obvious; the examinee must have knowledge of mathematics in order to solve the auditorily presented math word problems. No matter how effective the examinee is at holding and manipulating information in mind, such holding and manipulating will not result in a correct response unless the examinee has stored and can retrieve information about the math procedures needed to solve the word problem. Perhaps less obvious but no less critical to performance is the need for the examinee to be able to retrieve the correct sequence of the letters of the alphabet and the order of the numbers from 1 to 10 while holding and manipulating the specific series of number and letter stimuli for each item of the Letter-Number Sequencing subtest and the Digit Span Sequencing task.

Retrieval of Information from Recent Long-Term Storage

In the case of the Immediate Symbol Translation subtest, each item makes successively greater demands on working memory as the number of symbol-word associations that must be held in mind increases. As administration of the task increases beyond a few minutes, it is very likely that the examinee has transferred some of the symbol-word associations to recent long-term storage and is now retrieving them from recent storage to respond to additional items.

Math Calculation and Problem-Solving Skills

Before engaging in the retrieval from long-term storage of knowledge about how to perform calculations and solve problems, an examinee must have learned how to perform the math calculations and have had some exposure to math problem solving exercises. If the examinee does not possess the requisite math skills, effective performance of Arithmetic items is not likely.

Expressive Language Ability

The Digit Span, Letter-Number Sequencing, Arithmetic, and Immediate Symbol Translation subtests all require the examinee to orally respond to items. Although the expressive language response demands of these tasks appear to be minimal in nature, some examinees with language processing difficulties or limited English proficiency may find it difficult to produce an accurate response while attempting to hold and manipulate item content.

Sequencing Ability

The Digit Span, Picture Span, Letter-Number Sequencing, and Arithmetic subtests all require the examinee to either maintain the sequence of the information as provided (Digit Span Forward, Picture Span), to re-sequence the information (Digit Span Backward, Digit Span Sequencing, Letter-Number Sequencing), or to correctly sequence the steps in solving a math problem (Arithmetic). Careful recording of responses enables the examinee to identify sequencing errors with these subtests.

Executive Functions

For the subtests discussed in this section, accurate responding depends in part on the effective use of one or more of the following executive function capacities:

- Cueing and directing efficient perception of auditory or visual stimuli (Perceive Cue)
- Cueing the appropriate consideration of the cognitive demands of a task and the amount of mental effort required to effectively perform the task (Gauge Cue)
- Cueing the modulation of effort while performing tasks (Modulate Cue)
- Cueing and directing the focusing of attention to the auditory and/or visual details of the stimuli being presented (Focus Cue)
- Cueing and directing sustained attention to task (Sustain Cue)
- Cueing the inhibition of impulsive responding (Inhibit Cue)
- Cueing and directing the use of initial registration capacities (Hold Cue)
- Cueing and directing the use of mental manipulation (working memory) capacities (Manipulate Cue)
- Cueing and directing the use of reasoning abilities (generating novel solutions or making associations with prior knowledge that lead to Arithmetic problem solutions) (Generate and/or Associate Cues)
- Cueing and directing the organization of information (Organize Cue)

- Cueing and directing the execution of sequencing routines (Execute Cue)
- Cueing and directing auditory, visual, and mental processing speed (Pace Cue)
- Cueing and directing a shift to more extensive detail (local) processing rather than pattern (global) processing (Shift Cue)
- Cueing and directing the retrieval of information from remote or recent long-term storage (Retrieve Cue)
- Cueing and directing the monitoring of work and the correcting of errors (Monitor and Correct Cues)
- Cueing and directing the coordination of the use of multiple mental constructs simultaneously (Integration of Multiple Cues)

COGNITIVE CONSTRUCTS ASSESSED WITH THE PROCESSING SPEED SUBTESTS

The Processing Speed Domain subtests assess many primary and secondary constructs.

Primary Cognitive Constructs

Visual Processing Speed

As the name given to this Index implies, processing speed is the primary capacity assessed with the Processing Speed subtests. Each of these subtests must be completed within a specified amount of time, and the tasks are relatively simple and clearly demonstrated so as to require no reasoning to figure out how to complete them. Low scores often reflect slow visual processing speed, but other forms of slow processing speed (grapho-motor or motor) may be affecting performance as well. The visual processing demands of each of these subtests are substantial. The Coding subtest requires rapid visual processing of the relationships between 9 symbols and 9 numbers and the rapid visual monitoring of the production of the symbols that match the numbers. The Symbol Search subtest requires rapid visual discrimination of two target stimuli and sets of 5 response stimuli. The Cancellation subtest requires rapid visual discrimination among rows of stimuli to locate targeted response images.

Motor and/or Grapho-motor Processing Speed

The three Processing Speed Domain subtests all require the use of pencil and paper during performance, but they vary substantially in the extent to which motor movement and/or grapho-motor speed are likely to affect performance.

The Coding subtest makes the greatest demands on motor movement and motor speed as the examinee must continually reproduce the symbols associated with numbers. In contrast, the Symbol Search and Cancellation subtest require only occasional pencil strokes to mark targeted visual responses. The Coding subtest therefore is likely to be affected the most by motor processing speed problems. Factors other than processing speed, however, can influence performance on these subtests, especially the Cancellation subtest.

Secondary Cognitive Constructs

There are multiple Secondary Cognitive Constructs assessed by the Processing Speed subtests.

Visual Acuity

While attempting to perform the Processing Speed subtests, visual acuity is necessary to ensure that all of the visual elements of each task can be accurately viewed. If the examinee cannot see or is struggling to see clearly all of the visual information provided for each task, poor performance marked by slowed speed or incorrect responses may result. Typically, an examinee's visual acuity is assessed and verified to be within normal limits with or without the use of corrective lenses prior to test administration so that this capacity should not be a factor in performance. If overlooked, however, visual acuity problems can significantly affect task performance with any or all of the Processing Speed subtests.

Attention to Visual Stimuli

To perform Processing Speed subtest tasks, the examinee must have the capacity for focusing and sustaining attention for the visual stimuli of each task.

Visual Perception/Representation

To perform Processing Speed subtest tasks, the examinee must have the perceptual capacity to form relatively accurate visual representations of the stimuli presented. Some visually impaired examinees and severely perceptually impaired examinees might lack this capacity and have difficulty visually organizing the information being presented, especially the more abstract geometric representations of the Symbol Search subtest.

Visual Discrimination

All of the Processing Speed subtest tasks require careful application of visual discrimination processes, that is, the ability to see visual similarities and differences in the visual stimuli being presented. As is the case with Visual Perception, some younger examinees and severely perceptually impaired older examinees might lack this capacity and have difficulty seeing the visual similarities and differences in the visual images being presented, especially the more abstract geometric representations of the Symbol Search subtest.

Grapho-motor Functioning

The Coding subtest requires the examinee to handle a pencil to transcribe code symbols into empty boxes continuously for a 2-minute period. Although not as demanding on the motor system, the Symbol Search subtest requires the examinee to draw a slash through the matching symbol or the "No" box to complete each item for a period of 2 minutes, and the Cancellation subtest requires the examinee to draw a slash through as many animal pictures as possible in 45 seconds. Examinees who may be lacking in motor coordination for a variety of reasons may find it difficult to transcribe the coding symbols at all or to continue the transcription process for 2 minutes. Slowed performance, poorly formed symbols, or coding errors may result from motor coordination difficulties and or motor fatigue. Slowed performance, poorly formed symbols, or coding errors resulting from grapho-motor difficulties are likely to be encountered somewhat more frequently with the WISC-V Coding subtest than was the case with the WISC-IV Coding subtest. The reason for this is that the code symbols were revised to make them more unique and more easily recognized by digital media processes. Examinees with grapho-motor challenges are likely to find three of these revised symbols (the symbols associated with the numbers 1, 5, and 9) difficult and time-consuming to produce.

Visualization and Working Memory Applied to Visual Stimuli

For all three of the Processing Speed subtests, the examinee must hold in mind the directions for task completion for either 2 minutes (Coding and Symbol Search) or 45 seconds (Cancellation), but it could be argued that such holding of information does not require mental manipulation of the directions and the repetitious nature of the tasks continually reinforces the initial registration of the directions, thereby eliminating the necessity for working memory. Other than the possible minimal involvement in holding subtest directions, working memory capacities do not really need to be engaged in order for an examinee to perform well with any of the Processing Speed tasks. An examinee who is exceptionally fast can continually refer back to the code key when doing the Coding subtest or update the visual images of the target and choice symbols by continually rescanning the stimuli of each Symbol Search item, thereby minimizing the need for any involvement of working memory capacities.

There should be little doubt, however, that being able to generate visual images "in the mind's eye" and hold and manipulate such visual images can enhance an examinee's performance with all of the Processing Speed Domain subtests. For the Coding subtest, movement can be reduced and time might be saved if the examinee can hold in mind the number-symbol associations. For the Symbol Search subtest, being able to hold in mind the visual images of the target symbols while inspecting the symbols to the right of the targets can reduce the need for repeated back-and-forth scanning with each item. It is important to realize, however, that choosing to involve working memory to support the completion of these tasks does not necessarily ensure effective task performance.

Language Representation of Visual Stimuli

An examinee may find it useful to verbally label the Coding subtest symbols and symbol-number associations and recite these during performance of the task, to verbally describe visual features of the Symbol Search stimuli, or to verbally state the rule for the Cancellation tasks. Although such verbal mediation may enhance performance for examinees who choose to use it, it is by no means a necessity for successful performance.

Executive Functions

For the Processing Speed Domain subtests, accurate responding depends in part on the effective use of one or more of the following executive functions:

- Cueing and directing efficient perception of visual stimuli (Perceive Cue)
- Cueing the appropriate consideration of the cognitive demands of a task and the amount of mental effort required to effectively perform the task (Gauge Cue)
- Cueing and directing the focusing of attention to visual details and task demands (Focus Cue)
- Cueing and directing sustained attention to task (Sustain Cue)
- Cueing and directing the organization and/or planning of work strategies (Plan and Organize Cues)
- Cueing and directing the execution of motor routines (Execute Cue)
- Cueing and directing visual, motor, and visual-motor processing speed (Pace Cue)
- Cueing and directing a work pace that can achieve the needed balance between speed and accuracy (Balance Cue)
- Cueing and directing the monitoring of work and the correcting of errors (Monitor and Correct Cues)

- Cueing and directing the coordination of the use of multiple mental constructs simultaneously (Integration of Multiple Cues)
- Cueing and directing the inhibition of impulsive responding (Inhibit Cue)
- Cueing and directing the use of working memory resources (Manipulate Cue)
- Cueing and directing the generating of novel solutions or making associations with prior knowledge that lead to problem solutions; for example, referring back to his or her own work instead of looking up at the coding key (Generate and/or Associate Cues)

COGNITIVE CONSTRUCTS ASSESSED WITH THE NAMING SPEED SUBTESTS

Primary Cognitive Constructs

The Primary Cognitive Constructs assessed by the Naming Speed subtests vary depending on the specific subtest as described below.

Initial Registration of Auditorily Presented Verbal Information

This cognitive construct is essential for effective performance of the items of the Immediate and Recognition Symbol Translation subtests. Before an examinee can respond to any of the items of these subtests, he or she must effectively register the auditorily presented verbal information.

Initial Registration of Visually Presented Nonverbal Information

This cognitive construct is essential for effective performance of Naming Speed subtests and the Immediate Symbol Translation subtests. Before an examinee can respond to any of the items of these subtests, he or she must effectively register the visually presented nonverbal information (pictures and abstract symbols).

Working Memory: Auditory (manipulating auditorily presented verbal information or manipulating visually presented information that is being auditoriy represented in mind)

This cognitive construct is essential for effective performance of the Immediate Symbol Translation subtest. Items requiring mental manipulation cannot be completed by a simple "dumping" of the information being held in the initial registration buffer. The information must be held for more than a few seconds and manipulated in some way in order for a correct response to be constructed.

In the case of the Immediate Symbol Translation subtest, each item makes successively greater demands on working memory as the number of symbol-word associations that must be held in mind increases. As administration of the task increases beyond a few minutes, it is very likely that the examinee has transferred some of the symbol-word associations to recent long-term storage and is now retrieving them from recent long-term storage to respond to additional items.

Working Memory: Visual (manipulating visually presented nonverbal information or manipulating auditorily presented information that is being visually represented in mind)

This cognitive construct may be used for effective performance of the items of the Immediate Symbol Translation subtest. Items requiring mental manipulation cannot be completed by a simple "dumping" of the information being held in the initial registration buffer. The information must be held for more than a few seconds and manipulated in some way in order for a correct response to be constructed. After initially registering the symbol-word associations of Immediate Symbol Translation subtest items, some examinees may choose to emphasize visual elements in their attempts to hold and manipulate the symbol-word associations in working memory.

Retrieval of Verbal Labels for Size, Colors, and Objects From Remote Long-Term Storage

The Arithmetic and Letter-Number Sequencing subtests and the Digit Span Sequencing tasks all require the retrieval of verbal information from long-term storage. The requirement for the retrieval of math facts, procedures, and/or problem-solving routines is fairly obvious; the examinee must have knowledge of mathematics in order to solve the auditorily presented math word problems. No matter how effective the examinee is at holding and manipulating information in mind, such holding and manipulating will not result in a correct response unless the examinee has stored and can retrieve information about the math procedures needed to solve the word problem. Perhaps less obvious but no less critical to performance is the need for the examinee to be able to retrieve the correct sequence of the letters of the alphabet and the order of the numbers from 1 to 10 while holding and manipulating the specific series of number and letter stimuli for each item of the Letter-Number Sequencing subtest and the Digit Span Sequencing task.

Retrieval of Verbal Labels for Objects From Remote Long-Term Storage

The Naming Speed Color-Object and Size-Color-Object items require quick, efficient retrieval of verbal labels associated with sizes, colors, and specific objects.

Retrieval of Verbal Labels for Numbers and Letters From Remote Long-Term Storage

The Naming Speed Letter-Number items require quick, efficient retrieval of verbal labels associated with letters and numbers.

Retrieval of Verbal Labels for Quantities From Remote Long-Term Storage

The Naming Speed Quantity items require quick, efficient retrieval of verbal labels associated with quantities.

Retrieval of Information From Recent Long-Term Storage

In the case of the Immediate Symbol Translation subtest, each item makes successively greater demands on working memory as the number of symbol-word associations that must be held in mind increases. As administration of the task increases beyond a few minutes, it is very likely that the examinee has transferred some of the symbol-word associations to recent long-term storage and is now retrieving them from recent storage to respond to additional items.

Secondary Cognitive Constructs

There are several Secondary Cognitive Constructs assessed by the subtests of the Naming Speed subtests.

Auditory Acuity

While listening to the directions and the individual test items spoken by the examiner, the examinee must have adequate auditory acuity. If the examinee cannot hear all of the speech sounds made by the examiner, he or she may misunderstood directions and/or may not hear items accurately. Typically, an examinee's auditory acuity is assessed and verified to be within normal limits with or without the use of assistive devices prior to test administration so that this capacity should not be a factor in performance. If overlooked, however, a deficit in auditory acuity can significantly affect task performance with all verbal subtests.

Visual Acuity

While attempting to perform the Naming Speed and Immediate Symbol Translation subtests, visual acuity is necessary to ensure that all of the visual elements of each item can be accurately viewed. If the examinee cannot see clearly all of the visual information provided in each item, incorrect responses may result. Typically, an examinee's visual acuity is assessed and verified to be within normal limits with or without the use of corrective lenses prior to test administration so that this capacity should not be a factor in performance. If overlooked, however, visual acuity problems can significantly affect task performance with any of the subtests that use visual stimuli.

Auditory Discrimination

Before responding to the items of the Symbol Translation subtests, the examinee must be able to listen to and effectively process the language used by the examiner when directions and test items are being provided. If the examinee is prone to auditory discrimination errors when listening to others speaking, specific words may be misunderstood, resulting in incorrect responses or no response at all.

Visual Perception/Representation

To perform the Symbol Translation subtests, the examinee must have the perceptual capacity to form relatively accurate visual representations of the stimuli presented. Some visually impaired examinees or examinees with severe visual perception deficits might have difficulty making sense of the information being presented, especially the more abstract geometric representations of the Symbol Translation subtests.

Visual Discrimination

The items of the Immediate Symbol Translation subtest require careful application of visual discrimination abilities (i.e., the ability to see visual similarities and differences in the visual stimuli being presented). As is the case with Visual Perception, some visually impaired examinees or examinees with severe visual perception deficits might have difficulty seeing the visual similarities and differences in the more detailed visual symbols presented.

Attention to Auditory Stimuli

To perform auditorily presented Working Memory subtest tasks the examinee must have the capacity for focusing and sustaining attention for the auditory stimuli of each item.

Attention to Visual Stimuli

To perform the Picture Span and Immediate Symbol Translation subtest tasks, an examinee must have the capacity for focusing and sustaining attention for the visual stimuli of each item.

Auditory Processing Speed

The speed with which an examinee can register auditory information can greatly affect the examinee's ability to register all the information that is presented in a short period of time. Although the Symbol Translation item stimuli are presented at the relatively slow rate, an examinee with extremely slow auditory processing speed may not be able to keep up with this rate of information delivery, thereby reducing the examinee's capacity for registering all of the stimuli.

Visual Processing Speed

For the Naming Speed and Symbol Translation subtests, visual processing speed may play a critical role in task performance. Slow visual processing speed will increase the time required to initially register all of the stimuli of each item.

Oral-Motor Sequencing

Successful performance of the Naming Speed subtests depends in part on the physical capacity to conduct oral-motor movements in a coordinated manner.

Expressive Language Ability

Although the expressive language response demands of the Symbol Translation subtests appear to be minimal, examinees with language processing difficulties or limited English proficiency may find it particularly challenging to articulate the words that are used to form connected discourse on the Delayed Symbol Translation subtest.

Executive Functions

For the Naming Speed and Symbol Translation subtests, accurate responding depends in part on the effective use of one or more of the following executive functions:

- Cueing and directing the shifting between automatic retrieval of number names and automatic retrieval of letter names (Shift Cue)
- Cueing and directing efficient perception of visual-verbal stimuli (Perceive Cue)
- Cueing the appropriate consideration of the cognitive demands of a task and the amount of mental effort required to effectively perform the task (Gauge Cue)
- Cueing the modulation of effort while performing tasks (Modulate Cue)
- Cueing and directing the focusing of attention to the details of the stimuli being presented (Focus Cue)
- Cueing and directing sustained attention to task (Sustain Cue)
- Cueing and directing the pace of oral motor production (Pace Cue)
- Cueing and directing the retrieval of visual-verbal information from long-term storage (Retrieve Cue)
- Cueing and directing the monitoring of work and the correcting of errors (Monitor and Correct Cues)
- Cueing and directing the coordination of the use of multiple mental constructs simultaneously (Integration of Multiple Cues)

COGNITIVE CONSTRUCTS ASSESSED WITH THE SYMBOL TRANSLATION TASKS

Primary Cognitive Constructs

Visual-Verbal Associative Memory

This cognitive capacity is critical for the effective performance on the Delayed Symbol Translation and the Recognition Symbol Translation subtests. In order to respond to any of the items on these subtests, the examinee must have successfully encoded the verbal label that corresponds to each visual stimulus.

Consolidation of Visual-Verbal Stimuli

In order to demonstrate adequate performance on the Symbol Translation Tasks, visual-verbal pairings must be efficiently stored in memory. The extent to which the examinee has efficiently encoded the visual-verbal pairings in memory will directly affect the strength of the visual-verbal associates and the subsequent recall of one pair following exposure to the other in addition to recognition when provided with an array of word choices to accompany each visual stimulus.

Visual-Verbal Retrieval Efficiency

This cognitive capacity is necessary in order to successfully complete the Delayed Symbol Translation and Recognition Symbol Translation subtests. Each of the aforementioned subtests provides information regarding the precision with which visual-verbal associations have been retained over time. The latency between stimulus presentation and response provides valuable insight into the automaticity of recall/recognition.

Secondary Cognitive Constructs

There are several Secondary Cognitive Constructs assessed by the Symbol Translation tasks as described below.

Auditory Discrimination

The examinee must be able to listen to and effectively process the words spoken by the examiner when directions and test items are delivered. If the examinee is prone to auditory discrimination errors when listening to discourse, then words may be misunderstood, resulting in incorrect responses or no response at all.

Auditory Processing Speed

The speed with which an examinee can register auditory information can greatly affect the individual's ability to register all the information that is presented in a short period of time. An examinee with extremely slow auditory processing speed may not be able to keep up with the rate at which information is delivered, thereby reducing the examinee's capacity for registering all of the stimuli. Thus, slow auditory processing speed may constrain the examinee's ability to register the verbal response choices provided during the Recognition Symbol Translation subtest even though the response choices are provided at a normal conversational pace.

Attention to Visual Stimuli

The examinee must have the capacity to focus and sustain attention to the visual stimuli presented in order to successfully associate the pictographs with verbal labels during the learning phase of the task. Furthermore, the examinee must attend to the visual stimulus presented in order to retrieve the verbal associate on the Delayed Symbol Translation subtest and to effectively recognize the verbal label on the Recognition Symbol Translation subtest.

Attention to Verbal Stimuli

The examinee must have the capacity to focus and sustain attention to the auditory stimuli presented in order to actively associate the auditorily presented words with the visually presented stimuli during the learning phase of the task. Moreover, the examinee must attend to the selection of orally presented response options read aloud by the examiner in order to perform adequately on the Recognition Symbol Translation subtest.

Encoding of Differentially Coded (visual-verbal) Stimuli

Successful performance on the Delayed Symbol Translation and on the Recognition Symbol Translation subtests require the ability to effectively integrate visual-verbal associates in order to encode the pairings at the onset. Examinees who evidence marked impairment in their ability to encode visual-verbal associates will be unable to demonstrate competence on the cued recall paradigm (Delayed Symbol Translation) or on the forced-choice recognition paradigm (Delayed Symbol Recognition).

Expressive Language Ability

The Symbol Translation subtests impose an oral response format. Although the expressive language response demands of the aforementioned tasks appear to be minimal, examinees with language processing difficulties or limited English proficiency may find it particularly challenging to articulate the words that are used to form connected discourse on the Delayed Symbol Translation subtest.

Executive Functions

In addition to encoding and retrieval processes, the capacity to learn visual-verbal associations requires a number of implicit executive functions that vary based upon the characteristics of the task. For the Symbol Translation subtests, accurate responding depends in part on the effective use of one or more of the following executive functions:

- Cueing and directing efficient perception of auditory and visual stimuli (Perceive Cue)
- Cueing the appropriate consideration of the cognitive demands of a task and the amount of mental effort required to effectively perform the task (Gauge Cue)
- Cueing the modulation of effort while performing tasks (Modulate Cue)
- Cueing and directing the focusing of attention to the details of the stimuli being presented and ignoring extraneous information (Focus Cue)
- Cueing and directing sustained attention to task (Sustain Cue)
- Cueing and directing the use of working memory capacities (recalling words read on the DST Subtest in order to formulate a coherent sentence in the event of uncertainty of the verbal label) (Manipulate Cue)
- Cueing and directing the use of reasoning abilities (making associations with prior knowledge that lead to the production of a coherent sentence on the DST Subtest) (Associate Cue)
- Cueing and directing auditory processing speed (Pace Cue)
- Cueing and directing the retrieval of verbal information from long-term storage (Retrieve Cue)
- Cueing and directing the monitoring of work and the correcting of errors (Monitor and Correct Cues)
- Cueing and directing the coordination of the use of multiple mental constructs simultaneously (Integration of Multiple Cues)

Appendix 6.B

BEHAVIOR OBSERVATIONS AND PROCESS-ORIENTED ASSESSMENT AT THE SUBTEST, ITEM, AND COGNITIVE CONSTRUCT LEVELS

Behaviors observed during administration of subtests can be used to enhance hypothesis testing about what cognitive constructs are, or are not, being used to perform subtests. This appendix discusses behavior observations related to each subtest within each domain.

Special considerations apply when attempting to determine the extent to which subtest performance is being affected by a lack of use of executive functions. The examiner needs to keep in mind that direct observations of behavior often cannot determine the extent of involvement of executive functions in task performance. It is necessary to generate and test hypotheses regarding the role of executive functions in poor subtest performance. This is because poor performance on any subtest may be caused by a number of executive function difficulties. Within each domain, a list is provided of executive functions that could adversely affect performance if not utilized when needed.

When an examinee performs poorly on a subtest, follow-up with testing of the limits can help to determine whether the poor performance is caused by a lack of facility with the cognitive constructs that are being assessed or the poor performance is caused by a lack of use of executive functions needed to effectively perform the task. The process involved for testing the limits is to readminister the subtest while providing additional executive function scaffolds intended to cue the examinee as to the cognitive constructs needed to perform the task. At the least intrusive level, the examiner asks the examinee a vague, general question about task performance intended to offer a very subtle cue about what the examinee should do to perform the task as effectively as possible. In the case of the Similarities Subtest, this first question could take the form of a reflective question. For example, when returning to the Similarities subtest after completing the standard administration of the WISC-V, the examiner could state the following, "You answered several questions correctly, but when you got to _____ and _____, you said, 'I don't know'; okay, but let me ask you a question: 'Is there any way that you could know the answer?'" This vague cue is intended to help the examinee realize that there might be other ways to think about the item that might lead to a correct solution. If the examinee grasps the intention of the cue, she or he is likely to engage the reasoning capacities needed to at least make an effort to figure out how the two words are alike. If the examinee does not pick up on the first cue, additional, more specific cues can be provided in a scaffold-like manner in an effort to prompt the examinee to engage in reasoning with language.

Regardless of the score obtained, when an examinee performs inconsistently (difficult items completed correctly, but relatively easy items completed incorrectly), it is highly likely that executive functions are not being applied as effectively as possible. In these instances, additional information should be gathered to confirm or refute hypotheses about executive function difficulties.

VERBAL COMPREHENSION SUBTESTS

When taking the Verbal Comprehension subtests, examinees should record all responses as close to verbatim as possible and note the amount of time elapsed before he or she offers a response and the amount of time required to deliver a response. Beyond the recording of verbal responses, examiners should note additional aspects of the examinee's behavior, including:

- The quality of the responses provided in terms of the use of grammar, syntax and morphology; articulation, intonation pattern, prosody, and phrasing;
- Interpersonal social communication style;
- Comments about the testing process;
- Examinee statements about their perceptions of what is needed to complete a task; and
- Emotional reactions.

This recorded information can help examiners develop and test hypotheses about the mental constructs that are, or are not, being used to produce an examinee's responses.

It is critical to keep in mind that the same specific behavior can have different implications regarding the cognitive constructs being engaged. For example, a long latency period followed by a relatively inarticulate response to an item from the Similarities subtest often signals the accessing of reasoning ability to generate a response, but such hesitancy and inarticulateness may indicate a need for more time to try to organize a coherent verbal response because of expressive language difficulties or difficulties with the effective accessing of information from long-term storage.

It is also important to recognize that many examinees will not be uniform in their use of a specific cognitive capacity as they progress through the items of a single subtest. Cognitive capacity use will vary depending on the examinee's perceptions and judgments about what constructs are needed to produce an accurate response; the cognitive constructs most likely to be required to complete the item effectively (these can vary greatly for the items of a single subtest); the degree to which various cognitive constructs are accessible to the examinee; and the degree of competency the examinee is able to demonstrate in the use of various cognitive constructs. For example, in the case of the Similarities subtest, a majority of examinees will be reflexively retrieving stored associations when responding to the easiest items (these easy items naturally elicit such reflexive associative responding). As items get more difficult and likely to be less familiar, the examinee needs to use executive functions to become aware of the need to engage reasoning abilities and cue the shift from retrieval to reasoning in an attempt to respond effectively.

In the case of the Vocabulary subtest, items will be more uniformly perceived as requiring the retrieval of previously learned information from long-term storage. Occasionally, however, an examinee faced with an unfamiliar word might attempt to reason out the word's meaning; such attempts usually, but not always, fail even in cases where the examinee has a wealth of knowledge about prefixes, suffixes, word roots, and the derivations of words from other cultures.

An examinee who struggles to provide an adequate response to the most basic of word relationships on the Similarities subtest may be demonstrating the effects of (1) a poor store of knowledge; (2) a poor ability to reason with verbal concepts; (3) poor knowledge and poor reasoning ability; (4) adequate stored knowledge but difficulties with retrieval of that knowledge; or (5) adequate reasoning and retrieval constructs but compromised expressive language abilities.

In contrast, an examinee may have stored so much information about word relationships that he or she goes much further into the Similarities subtest using only retrieval from long-term storage. When challenged by much more difficult items to use reasoning to "figure out" a relationship on the spot, the examinee now avoids engaging reasoning by simply saying "I don't know."

Hypotheses to be considered in such a situation include:

1. Good knowledge store and good access of knowledge but poor reasoning ability;
2. Good knowledge store and good access to knowledge store and good reasoning but
   2a. inadequate executive function cueing of the need to engage reasoning and/or
   2b. inadequate cueing of the mental effort required to generate a novel response and/or
   2c. inadequate mental energy available to engage reasoning.

Determining the most likely match between behavior and cognitive capacity use requires diligent testing of hypotheses; the more carefully an examinee's behavior is observed and the more a consistent pattern of behavior emerges within one subtest as well as across several subtests, the more likely the generation of a confirmable hypothesis. In many cases, testing the limits after completion of all WISC-V subtest standardized testing can help to confirm or refute specific hypotheses.

Behaviors related to the specific cognitive constructs most likely to be used with the tasks of the Verbal Comprehension Index are described below.

Observations Related to the Use of Reasoning With Verbal Information

The capacity to reason with verbal information is most likely to be assessed by an item when an examinee does not immediately offer a very specific response and/or requires more than 1–3 seconds to offer the response to the items of a subtest that requires the use of reasoning. Examinees who need to reason out the relationship between the two words (Similarities subtest) or think about the reasons for social conventions of behavior (Comprehension subtest) often offer longer, less articulate, more convoluted responses during which they add more information as they speak that either clarifies the relationship or introduces a new line of reasoning that may or may not be more accurate than the initial portion of the response. The use of the prompt "Tell me more" will be required with examinees who need to apply reasoning, because their explanations may be vague and nonspecific. Examinees who resist the effort needed to engage reasoning processes or who are ineffective at cueing themselves to apply their reasoning abilities will be more likely to offer quick "I don't know" responses. When observing a person who is attempting to use reasoning, one feels a qualitative sense of mental effort that comes through in the behaviors displayed.

Observations Related to the Use of Retrieval of Information From Long-Term Storage

The capacity to retrieve information from long-term storage is most likely to be assessed when the examinee shows no hesitation in initiating a response and provides an immediate, concise response such as offering a synonym for the meaning of a word (Vocabulary subtest), a basic fact (Information subtest), stating a single concept word or brief phrase that conceptually links the two stimulus words of an item (Similarities subtest), or reflexively reciting a very concise, well-organized, well-articulated rationale or offering a seemingly rote phrase to explain the reason(s) for social conventions of behavior (Comprehension subtest). When observing a person who is retrieving information from long-term storage effectively, one usually feels a qualitative sense of effortlessness that comes through in the behaviors displayed (e.g., relaxed body posture and facial expression).

For some examinees with generalized or specific retrieval problems, however, there may be signs of great mental effort as they attempt in vain to recall the meaning of a word (Vocabulary subtest), a relationship between words that they believe they know (Similarities subtest), or an isolated fact (Information subtest). Some examinees will verbally express great consternation with such struggles to retrieve information that they are certain they have stored at some time in the past. These difficulties with recall can have a more generalized effect of shaking the examinee's confidence in her or his ability to engage the cognitive constructs needed to perform the various WISC-V Subtest tasks, including those that do not require the retrieval of information from long-term storage. When observing a person who is having difficulty retrieving information from long-term storage, one usually feels a qualitative sense of struggle that comes through in the behaviors displayed (e.g., hunched body posture, looking upward for prolonged periods of time, and contorted facial expressions such as frowning, brow furrowing, or grimacing).

Observations Related to Difficulties With the Use of Auditory Processes

Examinees who have difficulty with one or more of the auditory processes required for accurately perceiving and representing auditory input are at risk of offering incorrect responses because of subtle misperceptions or even a complete lack of comprehension of what was said when directions and/or individual items were being presented.

Examinees who are experiencing difficulties with auditory acuity, auditory attention, auditory discrimination, or auditory comprehension, or who have slow auditory processing speed, often engage in behaviors that reflect these difficulties, such as:

- Tilting of the head to favor one ear when listening;
- Requests for repetition of directions, items, or specific words;
- Incorrect restatement of single words from directions or items ("Did you say _____?");
- Direct statements reflecting lack of comprehension of directions or an item ("I don't understand" or "I don't know what you mean"); and
- Signs of inattentiveness, such as looking away from the examiner and focusing attention on other aspects of the environment while directions and items are being presented.

The greater the number of times these behaviors occur, the greater the likelihood that auditory process deficits are present. Hypothetically, the effects of auditory process deficits can be minimized through repetition of directions and items; this hypothesis can be confirmed as accurate when repetitions of directions and items are followed by correct responses, indicating that initial difficulties with auditory processing were the most likely source of the initial confusion about the auditory input or the cause of the initially incorrect response. Hypotheses regarding the specific nature of auditory process deficits cannot be fully tested using only the information obtained in administration of the WISC-V, necessitating the use of additional measures specifically designed to assess the use of auditory processes. Special note should be made of attention difficulties that might indicate the need for ADHD (Attention-Deficit/Hyperactivity Disorder) or ADD (Attention Deficit Disorder) assessment.

Observations Related to the Use of Expressive Language Abilities

For all of the Verbal Comprehension subtests, the examinee is required to provide a vocal response. In the case of the Vocabulary, Information, and Similarities subtests, full credit can be earned for many items simply by stating a single word. For the remainder of the items of these subtests and all of the items of the Comprehension subtest, responses can vary from a single phrase to multiple sentences. For some examinees, low item scores may reflect an inability to adequately articulate information they were able to retrieve from long-term storage or an inability to articulate the product of their reasoning. It is important to note, however, that responses need not be well phrased or grammatically, syntactically, or morphologically correct in order for an examinee to earn full credit. As a result, some examinees with significant expressive language difficulties can score in the average range or above on any of the four Verbal Comprehension subtests. In such cases, picking up on and justifying the need for a more detailed speech and language evaluation will depend more on the careful observation and description of the examinees expressive language difficulties than on the attainment of one or more low subtest scores.

Specific difficulties observed during administration of the Verbal Comprehension subtests that might reflect an inability to express the product of reasoning or information that was retrieved, or that might indicate the need to refer for further assessment of speech and language on the basis of poor quality or poor production of language include the following:

- Item responses limited to single words or 2–3-word phrases even when greater production is needed to earn partial or full credit;

- Frequent poor use of grammar, syntax, and morphology, regardless of whether full or partial credit was earned;
- Circumlocutions (the examinee "talks around" a specific word or point, providing long narrative descriptions that do not quite hit the mark exactly);
- Paraphasias (the examinee makes unusual word substitutions);
- Articulation difficulties (speech is hard to understand);
- Excessive use of filler verbalizations such as "um," "ah," "like";
- Excessive production resulting in spoiled responses from conflicting information;
- Word-finding difficulties (the examinee cannot produce the specific word(s) he or she wants to describe an object or situation);
- Problems with information retrieval ("I know that. ..." or "Wait ... wait ... um, um, um");
- Vague general responses that are lacking in any specific content ("It's one of those things");
- Lack of adequate response despite an apparent understanding of the contexts in which the word would be used (e.g., knows where repairs are made—"like at the auto shop,"—and what is used to make them—"It's using tools"— but cannot accurately describe how the stimulus word would be different from other words used in those contexts);
- Inconsistent item response pattern (can't provide an adequate verbal response to easy items, but provides adequate responses for items that are more difficult);
- Unusual or atypical responses (offers opinions instead of responses such as "I know a lot of people might think they are alike but I know that they aren't");
- Frequent production of only 1-point responses for items when 0, 1, or 2 points are possible; and
- Never able to provide more than one reason, even after prompting, when two reasons are required for full credit on Comprehension items.

Observations Related to the Use of Working Memory Applied to Auditory Stimuli

The short directions and one- or two-word item stimuli of the Similarities and Vocabulary subtests make few working memory demands on examinees. Some of the Information subtest items and most of the Comprehension subtest items are much longer utterances and therefore somewhat more susceptible to the effects of weak working memory capacity. It is possible that examinees may find it difficult to hold the question in mind while attempting to locate the desired information in long-term storage (Information) or while attempting to construct an adequately reasoned response (Comprehension). When such disruption occurs, the most common result is a distorted response that does not really fit the original question. Based on the content of the response, the examiner may be able to identify what part of the question was not retained during mental efforts at retrieval or reasoning. If working memory disruption is suspected, it will be necessary to test such a hypothesis by finding ways to rule out the possible effects of other cognitive constructs, including difficulties with auditory acuity, auditory discrimination, auditory comprehension, and/or auditory attention.

Observations Related to the Use of Executive Functions

The highly specific subtest directions of the Verbal Comprehension subtests do much to reduce unwanted executive function involvement in the process of understanding what is required in order to perform items effectively. Even the highly structured format of the WISC-V, however, cannot completely eradicate the need for engagement of executive functions during task performance. Observance of the following behaviors may be indicative of difficulties with some of the executive functions involved in Verbal Comprehension Index task performance that are listed in Rapid Reference 6.6:

- Qualitatively poor effort or an overly nonchalant or overly confident attitude toward the Verbal Comprehension Index tasks may indicate difficulties with cueing the appropriate considerations of the cognitive demands of these tasks and the amount of mental effort required to effectively perform the tasks.
- Difficulties with retrieval despite statements or behaviors of the examinee suggesting that the examinee believes that she or he stored the information being requested may indicate difficulties with the cueing and directing of efficient retrieval from long-term storage. This hypothesis can be tested after standardized testing is complete by using a modified, cued recall procedure when readministering the items where these difficulties were noted. This process involves the examiner giving the examinee a hint about where to "find" the answer in their long-term stores ("You probably learned this in Science class in fourth or fifth grade"). Such cues are the equivalent of pointing out to the

examinee where in their knowledge stores they should be looking for the response. When this cueing procedure produces a correct response, it strongly suggests that the incorrect response was caused by an inability to direct retrieval processes efficiently rather than a lack of knowledge of the correct response.

• Examinees who over-rely on retrieval of information from long-term storage when attempting to respond to the Similarities and Comprehension items may in fact have the capacity to apply reasoning ability to produce correct responses but are not doing so, suggesting that the problem is not a lack of reasoning ability but rather a lack of adequate cueing and directing of the use of reasoning abilities or a lack of cueing and directing the flexible shifting of cognitive mind-set to consider and respond to the specific demands of the task. This hypothesis can be tested after standardized testing is complete by using an external prompting approach to the statement of questions. For example, for a Similarities item in which reasoning was thought to be avoided during standard administration, the examiner can introduce the item saying, "When I asked you how __ and __ are alike, you said 'I don't know,' is there any way you could know?" Or "Let's try one of these again; you may not have heard before how these two words are alike, so try right now to think about how the two words might be related and give me the best answer you can come up with."

FLUID REASONING AND VISUAL SPATIAL SUBTESTS

When administering the Fluid Reasoning and Visual Spatial subtests, examiners should record all responses and note the amount of time elapsed before the examinee offers a response and other response behaviors such as changing responses.

Observations Related to Reasoning With Nonverbal Visual Stimuli

This cognitive construct is essential for effective performance of most of the items of the Matrix Reasoning, Block Design, and Figure Weights subtests and some of the items of the Picture Completion subtest. It is important to keep in mind that reasoning with nonverbal visual stimuli does not necessarily involve nonverbal reasoning. Reasoning with visual stimuli can involve either nonverbal or verbal reasoning, or some combination of the two. Examinees often can be observed talking to themselves about Matrix Reasoning and Figure Weights items, and occasionally talking themselves through the placement of blocks on the Block Design subtest or trying to talk themselves through the spatial perception needed to complete Visual Puzzles items. The type of reasoning abilities that are engaged to perform Fluid Reasoning or Visual Spatial tasks will depend on the individual examinee's preferences and/or his or her perceptions of what abilities are required to do the task.

Timing items enables the examiner to test hypotheses about the kinds of reasoning that are being employed by the examinee. Quick accurate performance of items of the Matrix Reasoning and Figure Weights subtests (e.g., under 5 seconds for relatively easy items, under 10 seconds for mid-range difficulty items, under 15 seconds for difficult items) strongly suggests that the examinee is using nonverbal reasoning to complete these items because the engagement of verbal reasoning increases the amount of time required to complete items. As completion times increase, however, the more difficult it becomes to determine whether the additional time is caused by slow perception and organization of the visual information presented or by the use of language to assign verbal labels to the visual elements of the item. Overt verbalizations by the examinee will help to confirm the latter hypothesis, but in the absence of such overt cues, testing beyond the WISC-V would be needed to further test these hypotheses.

Observations Related to Difficulties With the Use of Visual Processes

Although the visual materials used with the WISC-V have been designed for ease of viewing, examinees who have difficulty with one or more of the visual processes required for accurately perceiving and representing visual input are at risk of offering incorrect responses because of subtle misperceptions or even a complete lack of understanding of what they are looking at when attempting to perform individual subtest items.

Examinees who are experiencing difficulties with visual acuity, visual attention, visual perception/representation, or visual discrimination often engage in behaviors that reflect these difficulties, such as:

- Eye rubbing, squinting, and related facial contortions that suggest a lack of visual acuity;
- Leaning forward and moving the eyes very close to the easel page;
- Leaning backward or moving their chair away from the table to increase the distance from the easel page;
- Continuous shifting of gaze from one part of the easel page to another with no apparent fixations (i.e., brief pauses) on any specific feature(s);
- Verbalizations related to a lack of understanding of the visual stimuli ("I have no clue what I am looking at here." "What is this?");

- Direct statements suggesting a real or perceived lack of acuity ("I can't see any of that");
- Signs of inattentiveness, such as looking away from the easel page and focusing visual attention on other aspects of the environment while directions and items are being presented; and
- Extremely quick but incorrect responding, suggesting a lack of attention to the item and/or the response options.

The greater the number of times these behaviors occur, the greater the likelihood that visual process deficits are present. The effects of some visual perception and discrimination problems (or the effects of poor executive direction of visual perceptions and discrimination) can be tested using a testing of the limits approach (after completion of standard administration of the WISC-V) wherein the examiner "perceptually guides" the examinee through an organized input of the visual information on the easel page. An example of this technique would be guiding the examinee through Matrix Reasoning by facilitating the examinee's visual processing of each cell in the item and each item response. For each Matrix Reasoning item, point to each image as you say the following: "Look at the first one here. This one goes with this one the way this one goes with which one of these? Look at the first choice. Now look at the second choice; now look at this one, now look at this one; now look at this one. Now, which one of these [point to each of the response choices] goes here?" Hypotheses regarding the specific nature of visual process deficits cannot be fully tested using only the information obtained in administration of the WISC-V; it is necessary to use additional measures specifically designed to assess the use of visual processes. Special note should be made of attention difficulties that might indicate the need for Attention-Deficit/ Hyperactivity Disorder or Attention Deficit Disorder assessment.

Observations Related to the Use of Working Memory Applied to Visual Stimuli

Being able to generate visual images "in the mind's eye" and hold and manipulate such visual images may be essential to the performance of the more difficult items of the Matrix Reasoning, Visual Puzzles, and Figure Weights subtests and certainly can enhance greatly an examinee's performance with many or all items of the Block Design subtest. It is certainly conceivable that an examinee with very poor visualization and/or very poor working memory capacities can succeed with most or all of the Block Design and Picture Concepts items, many of the Matrix Reasoning items, and at least some of the Visual Puzzles and Figure Weights items by frequently and repetitively rescanning the visual stimuli of the items. In the case of Block Design, an examinee with poor visualization and/or poor working memory can frequently compare the design model with the construction in progress to judge the accuracy of block placements and guide further performance. Observation for testing hypotheses about the use of working memory involves careful monitoring of the examinee's eye movements and gaze fixations and timing of individual item performance. Examinees who are attempting to by-pass the use of, or compensate for a lack of, working memory resources will exhibit frequent shifting of gaze between various locations on the easel page, especially between elements of the item stimulus and the multiple choice response options. The greater the number of changes in gaze fixation, the more likely it is that the examinee is having difficulty holding enough visual information in working memory to enable efficient problem solving, thereby necessitating continual re-registering of visual elements for use in working memory. These inefficiencies will increase the amount of time required to work on an item, thereby reducing the likelihood of success with difficult items that have strict time limits (Visual Puzzles, Figure Weights, and the more difficult Block Design items).

In contrast, examinees who are making the most efficient use of working memory tend to scan the stimuli to initially register and represent the item's visual contents, then shift gaze to the response options at the bottom of the page (or to the blocks), rarely, if ever, looking back up at the item or block model before delivering a correct response. When such behavior is observed, it strongly supports the hypothesis that the examinee was able to hold the initially registered stimuli or block design in working memory while choosing from among the response options or while constructing an accurate copy of the Block Design model.

Careful observation can help identify when it is necessary to test hypotheses about the extent to which performance with Fluid Reasoning and Visual Spatial tasks is being adversely affected by working memory difficulties. The Figure Weights subtest is especially well suited for testing hypotheses through adaptive readministration procedures wherein the examinee is allowed to use pencil and paper to aid in problem solving. Improvement of performance using pencil and paper increases the likelihood that the relatively poorer performance during the standard administration of the WISC-V was caused by the need to hold information in working memory rather than an inability to apply quantitative reasoning with visually presented nonverbal stimuli. Similar adaptive procedures could be used with Matrix Reasoning and Visual Puzzles items when behavior observations suggest that these subtests also are being adversely affected by a lack of use of working memory.

Observations Related to Manual Dexterity Difficulties

Completion of Block Design items requires adequate use of fine motor movements for accurate placement of the blocks into the properly oriented 2 × 2 or 3 × 3 configuration. Examinees who may be lacking in motor coordination for a variety of reasons may find it difficult to handle the blocks, resulting in inaccurate block placements, rotated or fragmented designs, slowed production and disruption of reasoning and other capacities because of an over-focusing on motor coordination. Careful observation is required to determine the full impact of such difficulties on performance of each item.

Observation of Difficulties With Visual, Motor, and/or Visuo-motor Processing Speed

Although the *WISC-V Technical and Interpretive Manual* (Wechsler, 2014) states that the effect of processing speed on Fluid Reasoning and Visual Spatial Index scores has been reduced due to a reduction of the number of Block Design items offering bonus points for speed (four items instead of six), the use of per item time limits on all Fluid Reasoning and Visual Spatial Index subtests except Matrix Reasoning and Picture Concepts makes processing speed a critical element in performance in this domain. This manual also points out that time limits were necessary to obtain item difficulty gradients with the Visual Puzzles and Figure Weights subtests, noting that many more examinees were able to perform many of the items of these subtests when no time limit was enforced. This fact strongly supports the hypothesis that processing speed, independent of reasoning ability or visual perception and discrimination, can greatly affect task performance. Contrasting scores on the Matrix Reasoning subtest and Picture Concepts with scores on the other FRI and VSI subtests can offer some evidence for the effect of processing speed (see Rapid Reference 6.9). Item-level observations and timing of individual item performance, however, can offer even stronger support when slow processing speed is thought to be affecting performance.

When an examinee is requiring relatively longer periods of time to complete Matrix Reasoning items (e.g., 10 seconds or more for the easiest items, 20 seconds or more for mid-range items, and more than 30 seconds for difficult items) and "times out" on multiple Figure Weights, Visual Puzzles, and/or Block Design items, hypotheses regarding the effects of slower processing speed can be tested using a testing of the limits approach after standard administration of the WISC-V by readministering items without time limits. When such procedures are used, completion times should be recorded; knowing how much time is required for obtaining correct responses offers a great deal of insight into the impact that strict, short time limits may have on the examinee.

Full consideration of the issue of the effect of processing speed on FRI and VSI subtest performance requires a discussion of the "30-second guideline" for administration of Matrix Reasoning subtest items. The *WISC-V Administration and Scoring Manual* indicates examiners can use clinical judgment in determining how long to allow an examinee to work on any individual Matrix Reasoning item, but 30 seconds per item can be used as a guideline in order to maintain a reasonable pace of administration. Examiners therefore must make judgments as to how long examinees are allowed to work on items. Adhering too closely to the 30-second guideline may restrict some examinees' opportunities for successful completion of items. Carefully timing and recording individual item performance times can provide important information that can be used in the process of deciding how much time to allow an examinee on each item. When a slow but accurate work pace is established early, examiners should consider allowing more than 30 seconds for difficult items when the examinee appears to be actively engaged with problem-solving efforts.

Observations Related to the Use of Executive Functions

The highly specific subtest directions of the Fluid Reasoning and Visual Spatial subtests do much to reduce unwanted executive function involvement in the process of understanding what is required in order to perform items effectively. The directions of the Matrix Reasoning subtest were revised to offer greater structure to examinees and the number of different Matrix Reasoning item types was reduced from four to two, thereby reducing further the need for examinees to "figure out" for themselves what kind of problem-solving strategies should be engaged. Even the highly structured format of the WISC-V directions and items, however, cannot completely eradicate the need for engagement of executive functions during task performance. Observance of the following behaviors may be indicative of difficulties with some of the executive functions involved in Fluid Reasoning task performance that are listed in Rapid Reference 6.7:

- Qualitatively poor effort or an overly nonchalant or overly confident attitude toward the Fluid Reasoning and Visual Spatial tasks may indicate difficulties with cueing the appropriate considerations of the cognitive demands of these tasks and the amount of mental effort required to effectively perform the tasks.

- A pattern of quick responding that does not consistently produce correct responses may be indicative of difficulties with any of a number of executive functions responsible for cueing and directing capacities such as focusing attention on important visual details or organizing efforts to initially register all of the visual information provided, sustaining attention and effort, inhibiting impulsive responding, monitoring work for errors, correction of errors, and balancing the processing of specific details and global patterns. For example, clinicians who carefully observe for these behaviors will note the difference between engaging in impulsive responding followed by efforts at monitoring and correcting responses (quick response followed almost immediately with a second response thought to be more accurate than the first; e.g., "1 . . . no, 3") and impulsive responding without such efforts. When a pattern of quick, inconsistent responses is obtained for one or more of the multiple-choice Fluid Reasoning and/or Visual Spatial subtests, the examiner should consider testing hypotheses related to inadequate use of executive functions to direct task performance. The effects of lack of adequate executive function engagement can be tested using a testing of the limits approach (after completion of standard administration of the WISC-V) wherein the examiner readministers items using a series of specific prompts that cue the examinee to carefully consider all of the visual information provided in the item and carefully consider all five of the response options at the bottom of the easel page. The number and type of prompts can vary depending on the degree of severity of the perceived executive function difficulties. Some examinees may require only a single general prompt for increased engagement and attention focusing, with additional prompts provided only if needed (e.g., "Let's try this again, but this time I want you to work more slowly and carefully consider all the information provided and all the choices at the bottom of the page"). Other examinees may require extensive prompting on every item in order to maintain adequate engagement (e.g., with a 2 × 2 Matrix Reasoning item: "Look at this; look at this; look at this; which one down here goes with this one? Wait, don't answer yet; Look at this; look at this; look at this; look at this; look at this. Now which one goes here?").

Examiners also should consider readministration of multiple-choice tasks when examinees demonstrate an inconsistent pattern of responses (e.g., easy items answered incorrectly but difficult items answered correctly) without any behaviors indicative of impulsive responding.

WORKING MEMORY DOMAIN AND ARITHMETIC AND SYMBOL TRANSLATION SUBTESTS

When administering the Working Memory Domain subtests, and/or the Arithmetic, Symbol Translation subtests, examiners should record all responses verbatim and note the amount of time elapsed before the examinee offers a response as well as the amount of time required to deliver a response. Beyond the recording of verbal responses, examiners should note additional aspects of the examinees' behavior, including the quality of the responses provided in terms of the use of intonation patterns, prosody and phrasing; interpersonal social communication style, body position, and comments about the testing process or statements about their perceptions of what is being required of them; and emotional reactions. This recorded information can help examiners develop and test hypotheses about the mental capacities that are, or are not, being used to produce an examinee's responses.

Determining the most likely match between behavior and cognitive construct use requires diligent testing of hypotheses; the more carefully an examinee's behavior is observed and the more a consistent pattern of behavior emerges within one subtest as well as across several subtests, the more likely the generation of confirmable hypotheses.

Behaviors related to the specific cognitive constructs most likely to be used with the tasks of the Working Memory Domain and the Arithmetic and Immediate Symbol Translation subtests follow. Initial registration of auditory (or visual) stimuli and application of working memory with auditory (or visual) stimuli are the primary cognitive constructs intended to be assessed with all of these subtests. It should be noted, however, that an examinee's capacity for initially registering the stimuli presented and manipulating the information in working memory are reflected directly in the number of correct responses delivered only when no other cognitive constructs are constraining performance. This means that efforts first should be made to determine the adequacy of the use of secondary cognitive constructs that can act as constraints on task performance.

Observations Related to Difficulties With the Use of Auditory Processes

Examinees who have difficulty with one or more of the auditory processes required for accurately perceiving and representing auditory input are at risk of offering incorrect responses because of misperceptions or even a complete lack of registration of what was said when directions and/or individual items are being presented. Examinees who are experiencing difficulties with auditory acuity, auditory attention, auditory discrimination, or auditory comprehension, or who have slow auditory processing speed, often engage in behaviors that reflect these difficulties, such as:

- Tilting of the head to favor one ear when listening;
- Requests for repetition of directions, items, or specific words;
- Incorrect restatement of single words from directions or items ("Did you say _____?");
- Direct statements reflecting lack of comprehension of directions or an item ("I don't understand" or "I don't know what you want me to say"); and
- Signs of inattentiveness, such as looking away from the examiner and focusing attention on other aspects of the environment while directions and items are being presented.

The greater the number of times these behaviors occur, the greater the likelihood that auditory process deficits are present. Hypothetically, the negative effects of auditory process deficits can be minimized through repetition of items, at least in the case of some of the items of the Arithmetic subtest. For the Letter-Number Sequencing subtest, repetition of directions may help to improve task performance for examinees with poor auditory comprehension. Administration of the Digit Span and Letter-Number Sequencing subtest items, however, prohibit examiners from repeating items, thereby eliminating repetition as a means of testing hypotheses about the effects of auditory process deficits on item performance. For Digit Span and Letter-Number Sequencing items, the careful observation for the presence of the behaviors mentioned previously is the only way to generate and test hypotheses about the effects of auditory process deficits on task performance. Hypotheses regarding the specific nature of auditory process deficits however cannot be fully tested using only the information obtained in administration of the WISC-V, necessitating the use of additional measures specifically designed to assess the use of auditory processes when difficulties are suspected. Special note should be made of attention difficulties that might indicate the need for ADHD or ADD assessment.

Observations Related to the Use of Sequencing Ability

Although expressive language response demands appear to be minimal for all of the working memory tasks, some examinees may experience difficulty with the demand for verbatim, sequential repetition or precise sequential reordering of the stimuli. Sequencing difficulties are readily apparent in the responses provided by examinees; individuals with sequencing difficulties often provide all of the correct numbers or letters and numbers that were presented but do not deliver them in the correct order. In other cases, sequencing errors are accompanied by omissions and/or additions. It is important for examiners to recognize the qualitative difference between incorrectly sequenced responses that offer all of the right numbers or numbers and letters and incorrect responses that fall short of providing all of the original stimuli. An examinee whose output reflects only a sequencing error was able to initially register and manipulate the information in working memory, but somewhere in the transition from initial registration to verbal output a misrepresentation of the information occurred. Examinees who are unable to reproduce all of the original stimuli are much less effective in their efforts at initial registration and/or in their use of working memory than those who make sequencing errors. Sequencing errors represent inefficient use of existing capacities rather than a lack of existence of such capacities.

Observations Related to the Use of Math Calculation and Problem-Solving Skills

Before engaging in the retrieval from long-term storage of knowledge about how to perform calculations and solve problems while holding the math problem in working memory, an examinee must have learned how to perform the necessary math calculations and have had some exposure to math problem solving exercises. If an examinee's math skills are deficient, no amount of working memory capacity will enable a correct response. When a low score is obtained on the Arithmetic subtest, multiple hypotheses can be generated: (1) poor math skills; (2) poor initial registration capacity; (3) poor working memory capacity; (4) poor retrieval of math knowledge from long-term storage; (5) a combination of two or more of any of these four. Although the WISC-V does not offer a means for effectively testing these competing hypotheses, the WISC-V Integrated will provides this capability. Without the WISC-V Integrated, examiners can use improvised testing of the limits which would involve re-administration of the Arithmetic items in various formats (showing printed versions of the items while the examinee attempts to complete the item; offering pencil and paper to use to figure out answers; providing written math calculation problems that represent the math calculations involved in each item).

Observations Related to the Use of Executive Functions

The highly specific subtest directions of the Working Memory subtests do much to reduce unwanted executive function involvement in the process of understanding what is required in order to perform items effectively. Even the highly structured format of the WISC-V, however, cannot completely eradicate the need for engagement of executive functions during task performance.

Qualitatively poor effort or an overly nonchalant or overly confident attitude toward the Working Memory tasks may indicate difficulties with cueing the appropriate considerations of the cognitive demands of the Working Memory Subtest tasks and the amount of mental effort required to effectively perform the tasks. Problems with gauging the amount of effort needed and/or initiating effort and/or sustaining effort to produce accurate responses can result in inconsistent performance within a task (getting longer span items correct after failing shorter span items; incorrectly responding on the first or second trial of a span length while correctly responding on the other trial of that span length) or across tasks (performing better with Digit Span Backward and/or Digit Span Sequencing than with Digit Span Forward; performing better with Letter-Number Sequencing than with Digit Span).

When performance on Digit Span Backward and/or Digit Span Sequencing is better than performance on Digit Span Forward, the most likely source of difficulty is the poor use of one or more of the executive function capacities needed to cue and direct efficient performance. Such paradoxical results most often involve poor use of one or more of the following executive function capacities:

- Cueing the appropriate consideration of the cognitive demands of a task and the amount of mental effort required to effectively perform the task;
- Cueing the modulation of effort while performing tasks;
- Cueing and directing efficient perception of auditory stimuli;
- Cueing and directing the focusing of attention to the auditory details of the stimuli being presented;
- Cueing and directing sustained attention to task; and
- Cueing and directing the use of initial registration capacities.

Although any of these six executive function capacities could be involved in paradoxical performance with Digit Span items, the likelihood that problems will occur only with Digit Span Forward items and not Digit Span Backward items is unlikely for the last four capacities listed. Some combination of the first two executive function capacities listed, however, is highly likely to be the source of difficulty when performance on Digit Span Backward is significantly better than performance on Digit Span Forward. Many examinees underestimate the difficulty involved in merely repeating digits forward but accurately perceive the difficult nature of repeating digits in reverse order; as a result, they do not cue the appropriate consideration of the cognitive demands of Digit Span Forward and/ or do not cue the appropriate level of mental effort needed to effectively perform Digit Span Forward. These examinees under10activate resources for Digit Span Forward then appropriately activate resources for Digit Span Backward with the result being better performance on Digit Span Backward than Digit Span Forward. Similar performance paradoxes may be observed with any of the Process Subtest span tasks when they are used in an assessment.

The adaptive use of executive functions to improve performance can be seen when examinees offer responses in chunked units as reflected in their intonation and phrasing patterns. For example, an examinee who is provided the digits 8-1-4-9-2-6 delivered in a monotone with about 1 second between each responds with prosodic groupings of "814, 926" has just demonstrated the use of executive functions to cue the use of a chunking strategy to reduce the difficulty of the item. In essence, the examinee was able to reduce a six registration-slot item into a two registration-slot item by employing this strategy, thereby increasing the likelihood of performing better overall than if the strategy had not been cued.

Observations Related to the Initial Registration of Auditorily Presented Verbal Information

All of the tasks of the Working Memory Index require the examinee to initially register auditory stimuli. When an examinee appears to be free of auditory acuity, discrimination and/or comprehension difficulties, appears to be attending to the presentation of each item, and a consistent response pattern is obtained, the examiner can hypothesize with greater certainty that the number of items answered correctly represents the examinee's capacity for initially registering the type of stimuli presented (i.e., random number series, random number/letter series, math word problems).

Observations Related to the Application of Working Memory with Auditory Stimuli

All of the tasks of the Working Memory Index except Digit Span Forward require the examinee to hold and manipulate auditory stimuli. When an examinee appears to be free of auditory acuity, discrimination and/or comprehension difficulties, appears to be attending to the presentation of each item, and a consistent response pattern is obtained, the examiner can hypothesize with greater certainty that the number of items answered correctly represents the examinee's capacity for holding and manipulating in working memory the type of stimuli presented (i.e., random number series, random number/letter series, math word problems).

PROCESSING SPEED SUBTESTS

When administering the Processing Speed subtests, examinees should closely observe the examinee's efforts at task completion. For the Coding and Symbol Search subtests, close observation is enhanced greatly through the use of time interval response recording procedures.

Time interval response recording can be used with the Coding and Symbol Search subtests to assess the extent to which an examinee is able to focus and sustain effort and/or direct the focusing and sustaining of effort for simple, repetitive tasks for a period of 2 minutes. Time interval response recording involves counting and recording the number of items completed during specific time intervals throughout the total 2-minute total time period. Although examiners can choose the time intervals they use (e.g., 15-second or 30-second), normative data have been collected with other editions of the Wechsler Scales (e.g., WISC-IV Integrated, 2004) using 30-second time intervals.

To obtain time interval data, the examiner records the number of symbols coded for the Coding subtest or the number of items marked for the Symbol Search subtest at the end of each 30-second interval after subtest timing begins. The 30-second response recording interval approach enables the clinician to view a set of four data points that can be used to evaluate the examinee's response pattern.

The clinically relevant information that can be gleaned from the recording of time interval production is the pattern of performance across the full 2-minute work period. Unfortunately, the 30-second response recording procedure was not used to collect data during the standardization of the WISC-V, precluding the offering of 30-second time interval raw score means and standard deviations for either the Coding or Symbol Search subtest, but these data likely will be included in the WISC-V Integrated.

Observations Related to Difficulties With the Use of Visual Processes

Although the visual materials used with the WISC-V have been well designed for ease of viewing, examinees who have difficulty with one or more of the visual processes required for accurately perceiving and representing visual input are at risk of offering incorrect responses because of subtle misperceptions or even a complete lack of understanding of what they are looking at when attempting to perform individual subtest items. Examinees who are experiencing difficulties with visual acuity, visual attention, visual perception/representation, or visual discrimination often engage in behaviors that reflect these difficulties, such as:

- Eye rubbing, squinting, and related facial contortions that suggest a lack of visual acuity;
- Leaning forward and moving the eyes very close to the booklet;
- Leaning backward or moving their chair away from the table to increase the distance from the booklet;
- Comments about difficulty seeing the materials or about the need to have their eyes checked for problems or the need to remember to bring or buy glasses (or contact lenses);
- Signs of inattentiveness, such as looking away from the booklet and focusing visual attention on other aspects of the environment while directions are being presented and/or items are being attempted;
- Interruptions of ongoing work by making comments, posing questions, or attempting to engage in conversation with the examiner; and
- Extremely quick but incorrect responding suggesting a lack of attention to the visual information represented in the items or random responding.

The greater the number of times these behaviors occur, the greater the likelihood that visual process deficits are present. The effects of some visual perception and discrimination problems (or the effects of poor executive direction of visual perceptions and discrimination) can be tested using a testing of the limits approach (after completion of standard administration of the WISC-V) wherein the examiner "perceptually guides" the examinee through an organized input of the visual information on the easel page.

Hypotheses regarding the specific nature of visual process deficits cannot be fully tested using only the information obtained in administration of the WISC-V; it is necessary to use additional measures specifically designed to assess the use of visual processes. Special note should be made of visual attention difficulties that might indicate the need for Attention-Deficit/Hyperactivity Disorder or Attention Deficit Disorder assessment.

Observations Related to Difficulties With the Use of Grapho-motor Capacities

Although all three of the Processing Speed subtests require examinees to use a pencil to provide responses, the specific grapho-motor demands of each Subtest vary greatly. The Coding Subtest places the greatest demands on grapho-motor capacities, requiring continuous production for the entire 2-minute period. Slowed performance, poorly formed symbols, or coding errors may result from motor coordination difficulties and or motor fatigue. Examiners should also look for signs of difficulties with basic pencil-handling skills, such as poor pencil grip or extremely heavy or light pressure on the pencil. Use of the time interval response coding procedures described previously can be useful in helping to identify examinees who are exhibiting grapho-motor difficulties despite earning scores in the average or above average range. Such examinees may start out performing very effectively for one to three 30-second intervals but then drop to and remain at a very low level of production for the remaining intervals. When such sudden drops in performance are noted, competing hypotheses regarding grapho-motor fatigue or difficulties with executive function cueing and directing of sustained effort should be considered.

Observations Related to the Use of Initial Registration and Working Memory Capacities Applied to Visual Stimuli

Being able to generate visual images "in the mind's eye" and hold and manipulate such visual images can enhance an examinee's performance with all of the Processing Speed subtests. For the Coding subtest, movement can be reduced and time might be saved if the examinee can hold in mind the digit-symbol associations shown in the coding key. The revised format of the WISC-V Coding subtest however, wherein each of the digits 1–9 appears randomly with equal frequency in each row of top boxes, makes it less likely that examinees will adapt the use of working memory capacities for the WISC-V Coding as quickly as they may have with the WISC-IV, where digits 1–4 are repeated more frequently at the beginning of the task and digits 5–9 are gradually introduced into the mix later. Examiners who observe task performance closely will be able to note the point at which the examinee no longer looks up at the code key or back at his or her own work, but rather relies completely on working memory for access to the digit-symbol associations. In contrast, examinees who make little or no effort to engage visual memory beyond basic initial registration of the digits in the top box will continually look back up at the code to determine the digit-symbol relationship to fill in each empty box.

Effective use of visual memory capacities can aid examinees in the quick inspection of Symbol Search items. Careful observation of examinee eye and head movements during performance will reveal the frequency with which the examinee refers back to the target symbols while inspecting the response option symbols. Examinees who are extremely effective at applying visual memory capacities will show a slight latency period while initially registering the target symbols, then move to inspect the response symbols and make their choice without ever looking back at the target symbols. In contrast, examinees having difficulty initially registering and holding the target symbols in mind while inspecting the response options will frequently look back and forth from target to option.

Careful observation of examinees' behaviors associated with the use of, or lack of use of, initial registration and working memory capacities applied to visual stimuli during performance of the PSI subtest tasks can provide valuable information that can be compared with information from other subtest observations for the purpose of testing hypotheses about memory capacity use or disuse.

Observations Related to the Use of Visual, Motor, and Visuo-motor Processing Speed

Inarguably, examinees who earn above-average scores on a Processing Speed subtest have demonstrated above average processing speed. Such scores, however, do not preclude the possibility that the examinee is inefficiently and/or inadequately employing his or her processing speed capacities. Additionally, examinees who earn scores in the average and below ranges also may be inefficiently or inadequately employing their processing speed capacities, resulting in underestimates of these capacities. Use of the time interval recording procedures described previously can be very useful in helping to generate hypotheses about how an examinee is, or is not, employing his or her processing speed capacities and the cognitive difficulties that might be interfering with efficient production. Because each of the PSI subtests requires the use of processing speed capacities across a somewhat prolonged time frame, the effects of cognitive capacities other than processing speed often become more pronounced as time progresses. These effects can be quantified and explored using the time interval recording procedure.

Observations Related to the Use of Executive Functions

Although the highly specific subtest directions of the Processing Speed subtests do much to reduce unwanted executive function involvement in the process of understanding what is required in order to perform items effectively, executive functions will need to be engaged in order for an examinee to sustain attention and effort consistently for the duration of a Processing Speed task and to avoid making errors. Use of the time interval response recording procedures can help greatly with the generation and testing of hypotheses about the effects of executive function difficulties on task performance.

Qualitatively poor effort or an overly nonchalant attitude toward the timed aspect of the Processing Speed tasks may indicate difficulties with cueing the appropriate considerations of the cognitive demands of the Processing Speed subtest tasks and the amount of mental effort required to perform the tasks effectively. Examinees with such difficulties are likely to produce consistently low scores across all four 30-second response intervals. Problems with gauging the amount of effort needed and/or initiating effort and/or sustaining effort to produce accurate responses can result in inconsistent performance within a task. When an examinee's efforts do not produce a pattern of consistent numbers of responses within time intervals, one of the most likely sources of difficulty beyond grapho-motor control problems is the poor use of one or more of the executive function capacities needed to cue and direct efficient performance. Following are the executive function capacities most likely to be involved in task performance and the observed behavior patterns obtained from the interval response recording that are most closely related with each:

- Cueing and directing efficient perception of visual stimuli and/or Cueing and directing the focusing of attention to visual details and task demands;
- Examinees who have demonstrated adequate use of visual processes on other subtests such as Matrix Reasoning but who commit errors on the Coding and/or Symbol Search Subtests may not be effectively cueing and directing the use of their visual processes during PSI subtest performance; and
- Cueing the appropriate consideration of the cognitive demands of a task and the amount of mental effort required to effectively perform the task.

These difficulties often result in consistently low production across intervals despite observed use of faster processing speed for other WISC-V subtests or other tasks administered in the assessment or reports from other sources. When these difficulties are short term, problems with initially activating to the required level may be observed. Slow gauging of task demands and/or slow initiation of effort will result in decreased production in the first to third intervals relative to performance in the remaining 30-second intervals after the relatively slower start.

- Cueing and directing sustained attention and effort to task

These difficulties often result in inconsistent production across the four time intervals of the task.

- Cueing and directing the organization and/or planning of work strategies and/or cueing and directing the generating of novel solutions or making associations with prior knowledge that lead to problem solutions

Some examinees are adept at actively engaging executive function capacities in an effort to make task performance more efficient and effective. These examinees will alter their work strategies from that suggested in the subtest directions, such as employing working memory resources to hold the Coding digit-symbol associations in mind while working instead of continuously looking back at the code key for each item, or referring back to own work instead of looking up at the coding key. For Symbol Search, some examinees choose to divide the task into two separate search routines, scanning the response options once to look for the first target and then again to look for the second target if a match was not found for the first target. During tryouts of the Cancellation subtest, many examinees attempted to employ a "corn-rowing" strategy of working across the first row from left to right and then working back across the second row in a right to left direction to ensure that they would maintain their place and not lose time in the process of reorienting by moving all the way back to the left-hand side of the page to start the second row. Specific directions had to be inserted into the standardization directions to ensure that this strategy was not employed by examinees—an alteration that reduced the likelihood that use of these executive functions would be affecting Cancellation performance. In contrast, some examinees do only what they are told and do not make any effort to further engage executive functions to alter their response strategy.

- Cueing and directing the execution of motor routines

Some examinees experience great difficulty with the cueing and directing of the use of motor routines to complete fine motor tasks involving the use of a pencil. The observed effect may be very poorly formed symbols or excessively long or short slashes or an inability to keep symbol drawings inside a single box, random search movements that do not contribute to task performance, or overly careful drawing of symbols.

- Cueing and directing a work pace that can achieve the needed balance between speed and accuracy

Examinees may demonstrate difficulty with adjusting their performance to the demands of these speeded tasks, working too fast or too slowly despite indications that an appropriate work pace could be engaged as demonstrated with other tasks or reports. When an exceptionally fast work pace is countered by several task errors, the likelihood is great that the examinee was not adjusting work pace to meet the demands of the task. Conversely, examinees who engage in overly careful productions of symbols or slash marks and frequent checking of work for accuracy throughout the task even though they have been performing very accurately are likely to be having difficulty adjusting their work pace to match the relatively simple demands of the task.

- Cueing and directing the monitoring of performance and the correcting of errors

Although the WISC-V manuals do not report the number of errors made by WISC-V standardization examinees, Coding subtest data from the WISC-III-PI reflected a surprisingly stable error rate for children ages 6 to 16. For the WISC-III Coding subtest, fewer than 2 percent of children at each age range made more than four to five errors, and fewer than 25 percent made more than one error. Assuming that examinees included in the WISC-V standardization sample are at least as capable as those in the WISC-III standardization sample, WISC-V examiners should expect to see similar error rates on the Coding subtest.

Similarly, using four errors as a rule of thumb for the Symbol Search subtest would provide a very conservative estimate for an excessive error rate considering the fact that the typical production rate for Symbol Search items was about half that of coding items for the WISC-III standardization sample. Examinees that make an excessive number of errors on the Coding and/or Symbol Search subtests are likely having difficulty with cueing and directing the use of cognitive capacities involved in monitoring for errors and/or cueing the cognitive capacities involved in correcting errors once they have been detected.

- Cueing and directing the coordination of the use of multiple mental capacities simultaneously

Some examinees find it difficult to use executive functions to coordinate the multitasking demands of the Coding subtest. These individuals often show good processing speed and efficient performance with the Symbol Search subtest, but earn scores on the Coding subtest that are 3 or more scaled score points lower than the score they earn on the Symbol Search subtest. Examiners wishing to further test the hypothesis of multi-tasking coordination difficulties have the option of administering the WISC-V Integrated Coding Copy subtest. When the Coding Copy subtest score is 3 or more scaled score points better than the Coding subtest Scaled Score, there is a greater likelihood that difficulties with executive function direction of multi-tasking are negatively affecting performance on the Coding subtest.

- Cueing and directing the inhibition of impulsive responding

Undetected errors on the Coding subtest accompanied by a relatively quick work pace are likely to be reflective of difficulties with inhibiting impulsive responding. Errors on the Symbol Search subtest that reflect selection of visual near-matches to target symbols accompanied by a relatively fast work pace also often can be indicators of a lack of inhibition of impulsive responding. When lack of inhibition is observed with other WISC-V tasks, however, the likelihood is that commission errors on the Cancellation subtest also are reflecting such difficulties increases proportionately with the number of Cancellation subtest commission errors being made.

- Cueing and directing the use of working memory resources

Examiners may find it useful to note when an examinee who demonstrates the effective use of working memory with multiple WISC-V subtests does not appear to be applying working memory resources to hold the digit-symbol relationships in mind while working on the Coding subtest.

NAMING SPEED SUBTESTS

The naming speed subtests require quick and efficient retrieval of verbal labels. Because most children age 6 and older have been using the verbal labels associated with the sizes, colors, objects, letters and numbers, and quantities used for these items, retrieval is tapping into highly automated naming processes that are part of an examinee's remote long-term storage. To perform these tasks effectively, the examinee must have adequate expressive language, visual processing, attention, and processing speed capacities. Difficulties with any of these will result in less than optimal performance.

For each Naming Speed task, examiners are instructed to record the completion time, which is then used as the raw score for deriving a normative scaled score. Examiners need to be aware of the fact that although only completion time is used to derive a scaled score, there can be substantial qualitative differences among examinees in terms of the accuracy of performance, and these variations in accuracy of responses are not factored into the obtained scores. It is essential, therefore, that the examiner carefully record the number of errors made by the examinee and compare this number to the base rates obtained with the standardization sample (Table C.18 in the *Administration and Scoring Supplement*). Additionally, examiners should note the occurrence of the following behaviors, as these offer great insight into difficulties that a score based solely on completion time may be masking. Also recommended is the practice of recording the completion time for each row of stimuli within an item so as to have a better understanding of the pace of production throughout task performance.

It is important to note that the Naming Speed Literacy tasks, unlike the Naming Speed Quantity tasks, are not simply measures of the speed of automaticity of retrieval from singular modules within remote long-term storage (i.e., rapid automatic naming tasks of a single dimension, such as naming letters only). Rather, these tasks require the examinee to shift between modular stores of automated information. Effective performance of these tasks therefore requires the use of executive functions to direct the shifting between the knowledge stores as quickly as possible. Inefficient use of executive functions can result in several distinct types of errors with these tasks as described following.

When poor performance is observed on all items of the Naming Speed Literacy task that are administered (two tasks for ages 6–8; only one task for ages 9–16), hypotheses related to rapid naming difficulties should be tested by administering more basic Rapid Automatic Naming (RAN) tasks that require the naming of a single attribute (e.g., letter names only, numbers only, object names only, color names only). If poor performance is observed on these more basic RAN tasks, attention should be focused on basic language deficits rather than on executive control of rapid automatic switching.

Observations Related to Processing Speed

Relatively slow, but error-free performance with Naming Speed Literacy across the Size-Color-Object items and Letter-Number items for ages 6–8 and with Letter-Number naming for ages 9–16 is likely to be reflecting a relative lack of automaticity with the retrieval of verbal labels.

Observations Related to Oral-Motor Sequencing

Successful performance of the Naming Speed subtests depends in part on the physical capacity to conduct oral-motor movements in a coordinated manner. Difficulties with oral-motor sequencing are likely to result in one or more of the following:

- Slurred speech;
- Incomplete articulation of words;
- Consistent misarticulating of specific words;
- Production of sounds other than the required verbal labels;

- Frequent pauses between naming efforts;
- Mouth movements unaccompanied by any sound;
- Excessive swallowing between naming efforts; and
- Facial contortions.

Observations Related to Expressive Language Ability

Most examinees within the WISC-V age range are able to handle the expressive language demands of the Naming Speed tasks. When asked to label size, color, and object name, most examinees will naturally follow the example of the examiner and find it most effective to perform the naming activity in the order of size, then color, then object name. This natural flow of size-color-object represents an innate sense of grammar and syntax that appears to be shared by native speakers of the English language and is quickly imitated by examinees who speak English as a second language.

Examiners may occasionally encounter an examinee who is unable to maintain, or who does not use at all, this natural grammatical sequencing of attributes (e.g., saying "red, big, door" or "car, little, yellow" or "big, duck, blue"). When this type of expressive language difficulty is observed, the examinee should be referred for a more in-depth speech/language assessment.

Observations Related to the Use of Executive Functions

Listed below are the executive function capacities most likely to be compromised in task performance and related behavior observations.

- Cueing of the use of processing speed

In some cases, the slow rate of production may be the result of the lack of use of executive functions (the Pace Cue) to increase the rate of production to match the instructions provided ("Name them as fast as you can without making any mistakes"). When an unusual number of errors are observed along with slow production time, additional difficulties involving the use of other executive functions are likely to be present. When naming errors are observed in concert with average or fast naming speed, the errors most likely are related to ineffective use of executive functions other than the Pace Cue.

- Directing the shifting between automatic retrieval of number names and automatic retrieval of letter names (Rapid Automatic Switching) (Shift Cue)

The Speeded Naming Literacy subtest requires examinees age 7 and older to complete the Letter-Number Naming item that requires the use of executive functions to shift between naming numbers and naming letters. This is especially likely to be the case when performance on the Letter-Number switching task contains many more errors than performance on the Size-Color-Object task or other basic rapid automatic naming tasks. Difficulties with the direction of this rapid automatic shifting (typically referred to as rapid automatic switching) can result in any or all of the following:

- Excessive pauses when shifting between letters and numbers;
- An unusual number of corrected errors;
- Repetition of the label(s) prior to the shift (e.g., repeating one or more letter names before saying the number that follows or repeating one or more number names before saying the letter name that follows);
- Production of sounds other than the required verbal labels;
- Frequent pauses between naming efforts;
- Mouth movements unaccompanied by any sound;
- Excessive swallowing between naming efforts; and
- Facial contortions.

- Cueing the modulation of effort

Some examinees may find the performance of Speeded Naming tasks to be so exceptionally challenging that they are unable to maintain control of their actions during performance of these tasks. When an examinee cannot modulate his activity level effectively during task performance, one or more of the following behaviors are likely to be observed:

- Inability to maintain voice control resulting in delivery of responses in a very loud or very soft voice;
- Excessive, often repetitive movements (motor overflow) such as banging a hand on the table with the production of each response;
- Head bobbing or nodding with each response, rhythmic intonation patterns across multiple responses; and
- Standing up or moving about while seated.

- Cueing the monitoring of responses and the correcting of errors

The occurrence of corrected or uncorrected errors is likely to reflect difficulties with the effective use of executive functions to monitor responses and to correct them when necessary. The number of errors made can be compared to the errors made in the standardization sample to determine whether or not the errors represent an unusual response pattern. The greater the number of errors, the greater the likelihood that executive function difficulties are present. Failure to monitor performance and/or to correct errors when they are detected are difficulties that can have a great impact on classroom performance. When excessive errors are noted, hypotheses related to executive function difficulties should be confirmed or refuted with additional testing or the gathering of additional information from situations outside of the testing environment.

Appendix 6.C

CLUSTER ANALYSIS INTERPRETATION

The WISC-V subtests can be subjected to the clinically based cluster analysis procedures described here to identify composite-level cognitive strengths and/or weaknesses as reflected in the patterns of subtest scores earned by an examinee in conjunction with hypotheses generated about the cognitive capacities used by an examinee to complete the items across multiple subtests.

STEPS FOR COMPLETING SUBTEST CLUSTER ANALYSES

1. Use the information gathered from careful observation of item performance to generate hypotheses about the mental capacities that are, or are not, being used to perform item-level tasks of the various subtests within each Index.
2. Cluster subtests by placing together those subtests thought to be assessing the same singular mental capacity or the same set (or subset) of mental capacities. These subtests all can be from a single Index or from multiple Indexes. The interpretive tables provided in Rapid References 6.6, 6.7, 6.8, 6.9, and 6.10 can be used to generate hypotheses about commonalities of cognitive construct assessment across subtests within each Index or across multiple Indexes.

Example Using the Verbal Comprehension Subtests

Verbal Comprehension Subtest Scaled Scores
Similarities 12
Vocabulary 8
Comprehension 12
Information 8

In this case, most of the Similarities and Comprehension subtest items appeared to be assessing reasoning with verbal information as well as effective expressive language ability; Vocabulary and Information items appeared to be assessing a lack of effective retrieval of verbal information from long-term storage and/or a lack of stored verbal knowledge; because similar expressive language demands were present for the Vocabulary, Similarities, and Comprehension subtest items, expressive language abilities are not likely to be associated with any differences found across the scores of these three subtests. Additionally, although the expressive language demands are different for the items of the Vocabulary and Information subtests, performance on these two subtests was at a consistent level, negating the need for hypotheses about performance variation because of expressive language demands. Based on these item and cognitive capacity analyses, the Similarities and Comprehension subtests were clustered together as measures of reasoning with long-term storage and the Vocabulary and Information subtests were clustered together as measures of retrieval from remote long-term storage.

3. Determine whether the clinically derived clusters can be supported empirically by the presence of significant differences between the scaled scores of the clusters.

Example: The scaled scores presented in Step 2 (Similarities 12, Vocabulary 8, Comprehension 12, Information 8) are graphed as shown in Figure 6C.1

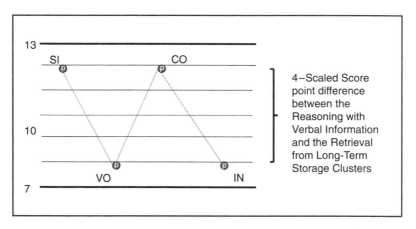

Figure 6C.1 Example of Subtest Cluster Analysis

4. Apply a rule of thumb of 3–scaled score point difference to identify statistically significant differences between subtest clusters.

Example: There is a 4–scaled score point difference between the Reasoning Cluster of Similarities and Comprehension and the Retrieval Cluster of Vocabulary and Information, which exceeds the 3–scaled score point rule of thumb.

5. Interpret statistically significant differences as composite cognitive strengths and/or weaknesses when all subtest scores of one cluster are above the mean and all of the subtest scores of another cluster are below the mean, and the two clusters are separated by 3 scaled score points or more, the above-mean cluster can be considered a relative cognitive strength and the below-mean cluster can be considered a relative cognitive weakness.

   Example: For the profile introduced in Step 2, the subtest scaled scores at the upper end of the average range on tasks involving reasoning with verbal information represent a relative strength; the subtest scaled scores at the lower end of the average range on tasks involving retrieval of information from long-term storage represent a relative weakness.

VERBAL COMPREHENSION CLINICAL CLUSTERS AND CLUSTER CONTRASTS

The Verbal Comprehension subtests can be subjected to a clinically based cluster analysis to identify composite-level cognitive strengths and/or weaknesses for the examinee using the general procedures described in Steps 1–5 above.

The clinical clusters most likely to be identified with the VCI subtests follow. Clinicians need to keep in mind that although the clusters are reflected in scaled score discrepancies, the scaled score discrepancies alone do not substantiate the existence of the differences between the cognitive capacities represented by each cluster. For example, a significant difference between low scores on the VO/CO cluster and higher scores on the SI/IN cluster represents a contrast based on expressive language demands only if the item and cognitive capacity-level analyses generated a supportable hypothesis related to the differential effects of expressive language demands on subtest item performance on these subtests.

Verbal Comprehension Clinical Cluster Contrasts

- Similarities and Comprehension (Reasoning with Language) versus Vocabulary and Information (Retrieval from Remote Long-Term Storage)
- Vocabulary, Similarities, Information (Retrieval from Remote Long-Term Storage) versus Comprehension (Reasoning with Language)

In this instance, it must be verified through process analysis that Similarities is reflecting primarily the use of retrieval from long-term storage rather than reasoning.

- Vocabulary and Comprehension (high demand for verbal expression) versus Similarities and Information (low demand for verbal expression)

FLUID REASONING AND VISUAL SPATIAL CLINICAL CLUSTERS AND CLUSTER CONTRASTS

The Fluid Reasoning and Visual Spatial subtests can be subjected to a clinically based cluster analysis to identify composite-level cognitive strengths and/or weaknesses for the examinee using the general procedures described in Steps 1–5 earlier.

The clinical clusters most likely to be identified with the Fluid Reasoning and Visual Spatial subtests follow. Clinicians need to keep in mind that although the clusters are reflected in scaled score discrepancies, the scaled score discrepancies alone do not substantiate the existence of the differences between the cognitive capacities represented by each cluster. For example, a significant difference between low scores on the Block Design/Coding cluster and higher scores on the Visual Puzzles/Symbol Search cluster represents a contrast based on high demands for visual-motor integration versus low demands for visual-motor integration only if the item and cognitive capacity-level analyses generated a supportable hypothesis related to the differential effects of visual-motor demands on subtest item performance on these subtests.

Fluid Reasoning/Visual Spatial Clinical Cluster Contrasts

- Matrix Reasoning and Figure Weights (Visual with Reasoning) versus Visual Puzzles and Block Design (Visual Spatial) (standard contrast mirroring the Fluid Reasoning Index versus Visual Spatial Index contrast)
- Visual Puzzles and Figure Weights and Symbol Search (Speeded Visual Processing) versus Matrix Reasoning and Picture Concepts (Non-speeded Visual Processing)
- Block Design and Coding (Strong Visual-Motor) versus Visual Puzzles and Symbol Search (Little or no Visual-Motor)
- Figure Weights and Visual Puzzles and Arithmetic (Working Memory demands within time constraints) versus Matrix Reasoning and Picture Concepts (Working Memory demands without time constraints)

- Visual Puzzles (Visualization necessary) versus Matrix Reasoning and Figure Weights and Picture Concepts (little or no Visualization necessary)

WORKING MEMORY CLINICAL CLUSTERS AND CLINICAL CLUSTER CONTRASTS

The Working Memory subtests can be subjected to a clinically based cluster analysis to identify composite-level cognitive strengths and/or weaknesses for the examinee using the general procedures described previously. The clinical clusters most likely to be identified with the Working Memory subtests follow. Clinicians need to keep in mind that although the clusters are reflected in scaled score discrepancies, the scaled score discrepancies alone do not substantiate the existence of the differences between the cognitive capacities represented by each cluster. For example, a significant difference between low scores on the Digit Span/ Letter-Number Sequencing cluster and a higher score on the Arithmetic subtest represents a contrast based on demands for initially registering and manipulating decontextual, nonmeaningful random sequences versus demands for initially registering and manipulating contextual, meaningful information in the form of everyday math problems only if the item- and cognitive capacity-level analyses generated a supportable hypothesis related to the differential effects of decontextual and contextual demands on subtest item performance on these subtests.

Working Memory Clinical Clusters

- Arithmetic (contextual, meaningful) versus Digit Span and Letter-Number Sequencing and possibly Immediate Symbol Translation (decontextual, nonmeaningful)
- Digit Span (Rote Repetition and minimal Working Memory demand) versus Letter-Number Sequencing and Arithmetic and possibly Immediate Symbol Translation (increased Working Memory demand)
- Arithmetic and Letter-Number Sequencing and Digit Span and possibly Immediate Symbol Translation (auditory working memory) versus Picture Span (visual working memory provided process analysis results support the likelihood that PS was attempted using visual rather than auditory working memory resources)

Appendix 6.D

SUBTEST AND PROCESS SCORE COMPARISON WORKSHEETS

Verbal Comprehension Subtest Scaled Score Comparison Worksheet

Subtest Comparison	Subtest 1		Subtest 2		Scaled Score Analyses	
	Raw Score	Scaled Score	Raw Score	Scaled Score	Scaled Score Diff (b-d)	Scaled Score Difference Significant?
	a	b	c	d	e	e > 3
SI vs VC						Y N
SI vs IN						Y N
SI vs CO						Y N
CO vs VC						Y N
CO vs IN						Y N
VC vs IN						Y N

Note: SI = Similarities; VC = Vocabulary; IN = Information; CO = Comprehension.

Fluid Reasoning and Visual Spatial Subtest Scaled Score Comparison Worksheet

Subtest Comparison	Subtest 1		Subtest 2		Scaled Score Analyses	
	Raw Score	Scaled Score	Raw Score	Scaled Score	Scaled Score Diff (b-d)	Scaled Score Difference Significant?
	a	b	c	d	e	e > 3
MR vs BD						Y N
MR vs VP						Y N
MR vs PCn						Y N
MR vs FW						Y N
BD vs VP						Y N

(continued)

(continued)

Subtest Comparison	Subtest 1		Subtest 2		Scaled Score Analyses	
	Raw Score	Scaled Score	Raw Score	Scaled Score	Scaled Score Diff (b-d)	Scaled Score Difference Significant?
BD vs PCn						Y N
BD vs FW						Y N
VP vs PCn						Y N
VP vs FW						Y N
PCn vs FW						Y N
	Process Score		**BD Subtest Score**			
						e > 1?
BDn vs BD						Y N
BDp vs BD						Y N

Note: MR = Matrix Reasoning; BD = Block Design; VP = Visual Puzzles; PCn = Picture Concepts; FW = Figure Weights; BDn = Block Design No Time Bonus; BDp = Block Design Partial Score.

Working Memory Subtest Comparison Worksheet

Subtest Comparison	Task 1	Task 2	Scaled Score Analyses			
	Raw Score	Scaled Score	Raw Score	Scaled Score	Scaled Score Diff (b-d)	Scaled Score Difference Significant?
	a	b	c	d	e	e > 3
DS vs AR						Y N
DS vs LNS						Y N
AR vs LNS						Y N
DS vs PS						Y N

(continued)

(continued)

	Task 1		Task 2		Scaled Score Analyses	
Process Task Comparison	Raw Score	Scaled Score	Raw Score	Scaled Score	Scaled Score Diff (b-d)	Scaled Score Difference Significant?
	a	b	c	d	e	e > 3
DSf vs DSb						Y N
DSf vs DSs						Y N
DSb vs DSs						Y N

	Task 1		Task 2		Scaled Score Analyses	
Subtest versus Process Task Comparison	Raw Score	Scaled Score	Raw Score	Scaled Score	Scaled Score Diff (b-d)	Scaled Score Difference Significant?
	a	b	c	d	e	e > 3
DSf vs AR						Y N
DSf vs LNS						Y N
DSb vs AR						Y N
DSb vs LNS						Y N
DSs vs AR						Y N
DSs vs LNS						Y N
DSf vs PS						Y N
DSb vs PS						Y N
DSs vs PS						Y N

Note: DS = Digit Span; AR = Arithmetic; LNS = Letter-Number Sequencing; PS = Picture Span; DSf = Digit Span Forward; DSb = Digit Span Backward; DSs = Digit Span Sequencing.

Processing Speed Subtest Comparison Worksheet

	Task 1		Task 2		Scaled Score Analyses	
Subtest Comparison	Raw Score	Scaled Score	Raw Score	Scaled Score	Scaled Score Diff (b-d)	Scaled Score Difference Significant?
	a	b	c	d	e	e > 3
CD vs SS						Y N
CD vs CA						Y N
SS vs CA						Y N

(continued)

(continued)

Process Task Comparison	Task 1 Raw Score	Task 1 Scaled Score	Task 2 Raw Score	Task 2 Scaled Score	Scaled Score Diff (b-d)	Scaled Score Difference Significant?
	a	b	c	d	e	e > 3
CAr vs CAs						Y N

Note: CD = Coding; SS = Symbol Search; CA = Cancellation; CAr = Cancellation Random; CAs = Cancellation Structured.

Complementary Subtest Comparison Worksheet

Subtest Comparison	Task 1 Raw Score	Task 1 Scaled Score	Task 2 Raw Score	Task 2 Scaled Score	Scaled Score Diff (b-d)	Scaled Score Difference Significant?
	a	b	c	d	e	e > 3
NSL vs NSQ						Y N
NSQ vs AR						Y N
IST vs DST						Y N
IST vs RST						Y N
DST vs RST						Y N

Process Task Comparisons	Task 1 Raw Score	Task 1 Scaled Score	Task 2 Raw Score	Task 2 Scaled Score	Scaled Score Diff (b-d)	Scaled Score Difference Significant?
	a	b	c	d	e	e > 3
NSco vs NSsco						Y N
NSsco vs NSln						Y N

Note: NSL = Naming Speed Literacy; NSQ = Naming Speed Quantity; AR = Arithmetic; IST = Immediate Symbol Translation; DST = Delayed Symbol Translation; RST = Recognition Symbol Translation; NSco = Naming Speed Color-Object; NSsco = Naming Speed Size-Color-Object; NSln = Naming Speed Letter-Number.

Seven

USE OF THE WISC-V IN THE IDENTIFICATION OF SPECIFIC LEARNING DISABILITIES

The purpose of this chapter is to provide guidance to those who use the WISC-V in the identification of specific learning disability (SLD). Guidelines are offered within the context of a researched-based operational definition of SLD that is consistent with the federal definition of SLD (34 CFR Part 300.8[c]10; see Don't Forget "2004 IDEIA Definition of SLD") and the third option specified in the procedures for identifying SLD (34 CFR Part 300.309; see Don't Forget "Federal Regulations Permit the Use of a PSW Model for SLD Identification") included in the 2006 regulations that accompany the Individuals with Disabilities Education Improvement Act of 2004 (IDEIA). This third option involves the evaluation of a pattern of strengths and weaknesses (PSW) that is consistent with the SLD construct via a combination of tests of cognitive and academic abilities and neuropsychological processes (see Fiorello, Flanagan, & Hale, 2014). Flanagan and colleagues' Dual Discrepancy/Consistency (DD/C) operational definition of SLD is used as the basic conceptual structure for the independent evaluation of SLD (i.e., Flanagan, Ortiz, & Alfonso, 2013; Flanagan, Ortiz, Alfonso, & Mascolo, 2002; McDonough & Flanagan, 2016). The utility of the WISC-V in SLD identification and diagnosis is demonstrated using the data from the case study presented in Chapter 8.

Specifically, after describing the DD/C operational definition of SLD (referred to as "DD/C model" for short), this chapter demonstrates how to enter WISC-V and *Wechsler Individual Achievement Test–Third Edition* (WIAT-III; Pearson, 2009) data (along with data from other batteries) into X-BASS and conduct a PSW analysis that is consistent with the DD/C model. The information in this chapter serves as a research-based approach for conducting comprehensive evaluations for suspected SLD using the WISC-V and related instruments, such as the WIAT-III.

DON'T FORGET

2004 IDEIA Definition of SLD

A disorder in one or more of the basic psychological processes involved in understanding or using language, spoken or written, which manifests itself in the imperfect ability to listen, think, speak, read, write, spell, or do mathematical calculations. Such terms include such conditions as perceptual disabilities, brain injury, minimal brain dysfunction, dyslexia, and developmental aphasia.

DON'T FORGET

Federal Regulations Permit the Use of a PSW Model for SLD Identification

Evaluation documentation must consider whether the student exhibits a pattern of strengths and weaknesses
- In performance, achievement or both
- Relative to age, state-approved grade-level standards, or intellectual development
- That is determined by the group to be relevant to the identification of SLD using appropriate instruments

(34 CFR 300.311(a)(5)), (34 CFR 300.309(a)(2(ii))

THE DUAL DISCREPANCY/CONSISTENCY OPERATIONAL DEFINITION OF SLD

Cognition is a complex process, involving multiple mental activities operating individually and in conjunction with one another. A weakness in any one or combination of these mental activities can result in learning difficulties for a student. Using the lens of a "pattern of strengths and weaknesses" rather than global scores more accurately identifies the nature of those learning difficulties, and helps plan specially designed instructional activities for individual students. (Alston-Abel, and Berninger, in press)

Flanagan and colleagues first proposed their operational definition of SLD 15 years ago (Flanagan et al., 2002). Since that time they have modified and refined their operational definition periodically to ensure that it reflects the most current theory, research, and thinking with regard to (1) the nature of SLD; (2) the methods of evaluating various elements and concepts inherent in SLD definitions; and (3) criteria for establishing SLD as a discrete condition separate from undifferentiated low achievement and overall below average ability to think and reason, particularly for the purpose of acquiring, developing, and applying academic skills (e.g., Flanagan, Alfonso, & Mascolo, 2011; Flanagan, Alfonso, & Ortiz, 2012; Flanagan, Ortiz, Alfonso, & Mascolo, 2006). The most recent iteration of Flanagan and colleagues' operational definition of SLD (i.e., the DD/C model) is presented in Rapid Reference 7.1.

This definition encourages a continuum of data-gathering methods, beginning with Curriculum-Based Measures (CBM) and progress monitoring and culminating in norm-referenced tests of cognitive and academic abilities and neuropsychological processes for students who demonstrate an inadequate response to high quality instruction and intervention—a process long advocated (e.g., Reynolds & Shaywitz, 2009). This type of systematic approach to understanding learning difficulties can emanate from any well-researched theory (see Flanagan, Alfonso, Mascolo, & McDonough, in press; Hale, Wycoff, & Fiorello, 2011; McCloskey, Whitaker, Murphy, & Rogers, 2012; McDonough & Flanagan, 2016). The DD/C definition is grounded primarily in Cattell-Horn-Carroll (CHC) theory, but has been extended to include important neuropsychological functions that are not explicit in CHC theory (e.g., executive functions, orthographic processing).

DON'T FORGET

The DD/C operational definition of SLD encourages a continuum of data-gathering methods, beginning with CBM and progress monitoring and culminating in a comprehensive evaluation of cognitive and academic abilities and neuropsychological processes for students who demonstrate an inadequate response to high-quality instruction and intervention.

The DD/C model provides a framework for organizing data from the WISC-V, and other batteries included in the assessment, to evaluate whether an individual's PSW is consistent with the SLD construct. The essential elements in evaluation of

Rapid Reference 7.1

The Dual Discrepancy/Consistency (DD/C) Operational Definition of SLD

Level	Nature of SLD[1]	Focus of Evaluation	Examples of Evaluation Methods and Data Sources	Criteria for SLD	SLD Classification and Eligibility
I	Difficulties in one or more areas of academic achievement, including[2] Basic Reading Skill, Reading Comprehension, Reading Fluency, Oral Expression, Listening Comprehension, Written Expression, Math Calculation, and Math Problem Solving.	**Academic Achievement:** Performance in specific academic skills (e.g., *Grw (reading decoding, reading fluency, reading comprehension, spelling, written expression), Gq (math calculation, math problem solving), and Gc (communication ability, listening ability)*].	Response to quality instruction and intervention via progress monitoring, performance on norm-referenced, standardized achievement tests, evaluation of work samples, observations of academic performance, teacher/parent/student interview, history of academic performance, and data from other members of the Multidisciplinary Team (MDT) (e.g., speech-language pathologist, interventionist, reading specialist).	Performance in one or more academic areas is *weak or deficient[3]* (despite attempts at delivering quality instruction) as evidenced by converging data sources.	Necessary
II	SLD does not include a learning problem that is the result of visual, hearing, or motor disabilities; of intellectual disability or disorder; or of environmental, educational, cultural, or economic disadvantage.	**Exclusionary Factors:** Identification of potential primary causes of academic skill weaknesses or deficits, including intellectual disability, cultural or linguistic difference, sensory impairment, insufficient instruction or opportunity to learn, organic or physical health factors, social/emotional or psychological difficulty or disorder.	Data from the methods and sources listed at Levels I and III; Behavior Rating Scales; medical records; prior evaluations; interviews with current or past professionals such as counselors, psychiatrists, etc.	Performance is not *primarily* attributed to these exclusionary factors, although one or more of them may contribute to learning difficulties. [Consider using the *Exclusionary Factors Form*, which is included in Rapid Reference 7.4.]	
III	A disorder in one or more of the basic psychological/neuro-psychological processes involved in understanding or in using language, spoken or written; such disorders are presumed to originate from central nervous system dysfunction.	**Cognitive Abilities & Processes:** Performance in cognitive abilities and processes (e.g., *Gv; Ga, Glr, Gsm, Gs*), specific neuropsychological processes (e.g., attention, executive functioning, orthographic processing; rapid automatic naming) and learning efficiency (e.g., associative memory; free recall memory, meaningful memory).	Performance on norm-referenced tests, evaluation of work samples, observations of cognitive performance, task analysis, testing limits, teacher/parent/student interview, history of academic performance, and records review.	Performance in one or more cognitive abilities and/or neuropsychological processes (related to academic skill deficiency) is *weak or deficient[3]* as evidenced by converging data sources.	

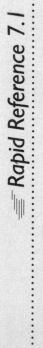

				Sufficient For SLD Identification
IV	The specific learning disability is a discrete condition differentiated from generalized learning deficiency by generally average or better ability to think and reason and a learning skill profile exhibiting significant variability, indicating pattern of cognitive and academic strengths and weaknesses.	**Pattern of Strengths and Weaknesses (PSW) Marked by a Dual-Discrepancy/Consistency (DDC)** Determination of whether academic skill weaknesses or deficits are *unexpected* and related to *domain specific* cognitive weaknesses or deficits; pattern of data reflects a below average aptitude-achievement *consistency* with at least *average ability* to think and reason.	Data gathered at all previous levels as well as any additional data following a review of initial evaluation results (e.g., data gathered for the purpose of hypothesis testing; data gathered via demand analysis and limits testing).	Circumscribed below average aptitude-achievement consistency; circumscribed ability-achievement and ability-cognitive aptitude *discrepancies*, with at least average ability to think and reason; clinical judgment supports the impression that the student's overall ability to think and reason will enable him or her to benefit from tailored or specialized instruction/intervention, compensatory strategies, and accommodations, such that his or her performance rate and level will likely approximate more typically achieving, non-disabled peers. Use the Cross-Battery Assessment Software System (X-BASS v2.0; Ortiz, Flanagan, & Alfonso, 2017) to conduct the PSW analysis.
V	Specific learning disability has an adverse impact on educational performance.	**Special Education Eligibility[4]** Determination of Least Restrictive Environment (LRE) for delivery of instruction and educational resources.	Data from all previous levels and MDT meetings.	Student demonstrates significant difficulties in daily academic activities that cannot be remediated, accommodated, or otherwise compensated for *without* the assistance of individualized special education services. Necessary for Special Education Eligibility

Source: Adapted from Flanagan, Ortiz, and Alfonso (2013).

[1] This column includes concepts inherent in the federal definition (IDEIA, 2004), Kavale, Spaulding, and Beam's (2009) definition, Harrison and Holmes's (2012) consensus definition, and other prominent definitions of SLD (see Sotelo-Dynega, in press). Thus, the most salient prominent SLD markers are included in this column.

[2] Poor spelling with adequate ability to express ideas in writing is often typical of dyslexia and/or dysgraphia. Even though IDEIA 2004 includes only the broad category of written expression, poor spelling and handwriting are often symptomatic of a specific writing disability and should not be ignored (Wendling & Mather, 2009).

[3] Weak performance is typically associated with standard scores in the 85–89 range, whereas deficient performance is often associated with standard scores that are greater than 1 SD below the mean. Interpretations of weak or deficient performance based on standard scores that fall in the weak and deficient ranges are bolstered when they have ecological validity (e.g., when there is evidence that the abilities or processes identified as weak or deficient manifest in everyday classroom activities that require these abilities and processes).

[4] The major specific learning disability may be accompanied by secondary learning difficulties that should be considered when planning the more intensive, individualized special education instruction directed at the primary problem. For information on linking assessment data to intervention, see Mascolo, Alfonso, and Flanagan (2014).

SLD in the DD/C definition, as illustrated in Rapid Reference 7.1, comprise (1) academic ability analysis, (2) evaluation of mitigating and exclusionary factors, (3) cognitive ability and processing analysis, (4) pattern of strengths and weaknesses (PSW) analysis, and (5) evaluation of interference with learning for purposes of special education eligibility. These elements are depicted as distinct levels in Rapid Reference 7.1 and together form the DD/C operational definition of SLD. The WISC-V and related batteries (e.g., WIAT-III, *Kaufman Test of Educational Achievement–Third Edition* [KTEA-3; Kaufman & Kaufman, 2014]) can be used effectively to gather information and test hypotheses at each level of this operational definition.

It is assumed that the levels of evaluation depicted in Rapid Reference 7.1 are undertaken after pre-referral assessment activities have been conducted and when a focused evaluation of specific abilities and processes through standardized testing is deemed necessary. Evaluation of the presence of a learning disability is based on the assumption that an individual has been referred for testing specifically because of observed learning difficulties. However, prior to formal testing, it is expected that remediation of academic skill weaknesses via an RTI service delivery model or a Multi-Tiered System of Support (MTSS) was attempted with little success. Moreover, prior to beginning SLD assessment with the WISC-V, other significant data sources should have already been gathered and considered within the context of the intervention activities. These data may include results from informal testing, direct observation of behaviors, work samples, reports from people familiar with the individual's difficulties (e.g., teachers, parents), and information provided by the individual him- or herself.

The various levels of the DD/C operational definition of SLD include a number of terms and concepts, such as strengths, weaknesses, unexpected underachievement, and consistency, all of which are referenced in X-BASS (Cross-Battery Assessment Software System), particularly with regard to the DD/C PSW analysis that is conducted by the software. Appendix E provides definitions of important terms that are used throughout this chapter and in X-BASS and clarifies some concepts that have been misunderstood or overlooked in the PSW literature (see Flanagan & Schneider, 2016). This appendix may be particularly useful as a quick reference until users of X-BASS become familiar with the DD/C model and how the criteria therein are operationalized by this software.

DON'T FORGET

The DD/C operational definition of SLD is automated in X-BASS.

Level I: Analysis of Specific Academic Skills

Level I focuses on the basic concept of SLD: that underlying ability and processing deficits affected skill development adversely, which contributed to underachievement. In other words, intrinsic cognitive weaknesses or deficits often manifest in observable phenomena, particularly academic achievement. Thus, the first component of the DD/C operational definition of SLD involves documenting that some type of *learning* dysfunction exists. In the DD/C definition, the presence of a *weakness* or *normative weakness/deficit* (see Rapid Reference 7.2 for definitions) established through standardized testing, and supported through other means such as clinical observations of academic performance, work samples, and parent and teacher reports, is a necessary but insufficient condition for SLD determination. Level I includes the first criterion that is considered necessary for determining the presence of SLD. When criteria are met at Levels I through IV, practitioners can be reasonably confident that a diagnosis or classification of SLD is appropriate.

Level I involves comprehensive measurement of the major areas of academic achievement (i.e., reading, writing, math, and oral language abilities) or any subset of these areas that is the focus and purpose of the evaluation. The academic abilities depicted at this level are organized according to the eight areas of achievement specified in IDEIA (2004). These eight areas are math calculation, math problem solving, basic reading skills, reading fluency, reading comprehension, written expression, listening comprehension, and oral expression. Typically, the eight areas of academic achievement (which include language-related areas: oral expression and listening comprehension) are measured using standardized, norm-referenced tests. The WIAT-III, KTEA-3, and *Clinical Evaluation of Language Fundamentals-Fifth Edition* (CELF-5; Wiig, Semel, & Secord, 2013) batteries combined provide for measurement of all eight areas (see Rapid Reference 7.3). Nevertheless, it is important to realize that data on academic performance should come from multiple sources (see Rapid Reference 7.1, Level I, column 4). Following the collection of data on academic performance, it is necessary to determine whether the student has a weakness or normative weakness/deficit in one or more specific academic skills.

Determining whether a student has a weakness or normative weakness/deficit usually involves making normative-based comparisons of the student's performance against a representative sample of same-age or -grade peers from the general population. If weaknesses in the student's academic performance are not found (i.e., all scores suggest generally average or better performance relative to most people), then the issue of SLD may be moot because such weaknesses are a necessary component for SLD identification/diagnosis.

≡ Rapid Reference 7.2

Definition of Weakness and Normative Weakness or Deficit

Term or Concept	Meaning Within the Context of DD/C	Comments
Weakness	Performance on standardized, norm-referenced tests that falls *below average* (where average is defined as standard scores between 90 and 110 [inclusive], based on a scale having a mean of 100 and standard deviation of 15). Thus, a weakness is associated with standard scores of 85 to 89 (inclusive).	Interpreting scores in the very narrow range of 85–89 requires clinical judgment, as abilities associated with these scores may or may not pose significant difficulties for the individual. Interpretation of any cognitive construct as a weakness for the individual should include ecological validity (i.e., evidence of how the weakness manifests in real-world performances, such as classroom activities).
Normative Weakness or Deficit	Performance on standardized, norm-referenced tests that falls greater than one standard deviation below the mean (i.e., standard scores < 85). This type of weakness is often referred to as "population relative" or "inter-individual." The terms "normative weakness" and "deficit" are used interchangeably.	The range of 85–115, inclusive, is often referred to as the range of *normal limits* because it is the range in which nearly 70% of the population falls on standardized, norm-referenced tests. Therefore, scores within this range are sometimes classified as *within normal limits* (WNL). As such, any score that falls outside and below this range is a normative weakness *as compared to most people*. Notwithstanding, the meaning of any cognitive construct that emerges as a normative weakness is enhanced by ecological validity.

DON'T FORGET

Weakness: Standard scores between 85 and 89, inclusive
Normative Weakness/Deficit: Standard scores < 85

≡ Rapid Reference 7.3

Correspondence Between Subtests From the WIAT-III, KTEA-3, and CELF-5 and the Eight Areas of SLD Listed in the Federal Definition

SLD Area	WIAT-III	KTEA-3	CELF-5
Basic Reading Skills	Early Reading Skills Pseudoword Decoding Word Reading	Decoding Fluency Letter and Word Recognition Nonsense Word Decoding Phonological Processing	
Reading Fluency Skills	Oral Reading Fluency	Silent Reading Fluency Word Recognition Fluency	
Reading Comprehension	Reading Comprehension	Reading Comprehension Reading Vocabulary	Reading Comprehension
Mathematics Calculations	Math Fluency—Addition Math Fluency—Multiplication Math Fluency—Subtraction Numerical Operations	Math Computation Math Fluency	
Mathematics Problem Solving	Math Problem Solving	Math Concepts and Applications	
Written Expression	Alphabet Writing Fluency Essay Completion Sentence Composition Spelling	Spelling Written Expression Writing Fluency	Structured Writing
Oral Expression	Oral Expression	Associational Fluency Object Naming Facility Oral Expression	Formulated Sentences

(continued)

(continued)

SLD Area	WIAT-III	KTEA-3	CELF-5
Listening Comprehension	Listening Comprehension	Listening Comprehension	Following Directions Linguistic Concepts Semantic Relationships Sentence Comprehension Understanding Spoken Paragraphs Word Structure

Nevertheless, some students who struggle academically, particularly very bright students, might not demonstrate academic weaknesses or deficits on standardized, norm-referenced tests of achievement for a variety of reasons. For example, some students may have figured out how to compensate for their processing deficit(s). Therefore, it is important not to assume that a student with a standard score in the upper 80s or low 90s, for example, on a "broad reading" composite is "okay," particularly when a parent, teacher, or the student him- or herself expresses concern. Under these circumstances, a more focused assessment of the CHC abilities and neuropsychological processes related to reading should be conducted. Conversely, the finding of low scores on norm-referenced achievement tests does not guarantee that there will be corresponding low scores on norm-referenced cognitive tests in areas that are related to the achievement area—*an important fact that was ignored in a recent investigation of the DD/C method* (i.e., Kranzler, Floyd, Benson, Zaboski, & Thibodaux, 2016). Below average achievement may be the result of a host of factors, only one of which is weaknesses or deficits in related cognitive processes and abilities. Most practitioners know this to be true. See Flanagan and Schneider (2016) for a discussion.

As Rapid Reference 7.1 demonstrates, the presence of an academic weakness or normative weakness/deficit established through standardized testing, for example, and corroborated by other data sources, such as CBM, clinical observations of academic performance, work samples, and so forth, is a necessary (but insufficient) condition for SLD determination (Level I in Rapid Reference 7.1). At this initial level then, a student's academic performance is compared to that of other individuals included in the WIAT-III or KTEA-3 normative samples. When weaknesses or normative weaknesses/deficits in academic performance are found, and are corroborated by other data sources, the process advances to Level II.

DON'T FORGET

Academic Performance on Norm-Referenced Tests	Data-Gathering Methods	Examples of Factors That Inhibit Academic Performance	Examples of Factors That Facilitate Academic Performance
Weakness: SS = 85–89, inclusive	Standardized tests (individual and group)	Exclusionary factors that are contributory, such as social/emotional, psychological, and culture and language difference	Familial support; good teacher/ student relationship; others who believe in student's capabilities
Deficit: SS < 85	Progress monitoring data; CBM data	Lack of sufficient resources	Self-determination, effort, perseverance
	Work samples, classroom observations	Poor communication between home and school	Adequate resources at the individual and classroom level
	Parent, teacher, and student interviews	Instruction not matched to student's instructional level	Good home-school collaboration/ partnership
	Criterion referenced: Benchmark assessment		Instruction matched to student's instructional level

Note: SS = Standard Score.

Level II: Evaluation of Exclusionary Factors as Potential Primary and Contributory Reasons for Academic Skill Weaknesses or Deficits

Level II involves evaluating whether any documented weaknesses or deficits found through Level I evaluation are or are not primarily the result of factors that may be, for example, largely external to the individual, non-cognitive in nature, or the result of a condition other than SLD. Because there can be many reasons for weak or deficient academic performance, reasonable hypotheses related to potential reasons for academic weaknesses should be developed. For example, cultural and linguistic differences are two common factors that can affect test performance and academic skill acquisition adversely and result in achievement data that appear to suggest SLD (see Chapter 9 this volume). In addition, lack of motivation and effort, social-emotional disturbance, performance anxiety, psychiatric disorders, sensory impairments, intellectual disability, and medical conditions (e.g., hearing or vision problems) also need to be ruled out as potential explanatory correlates to (or *primary* reasons for) any weaknesses or deficits identified at Level I. Rapid Reference 7.4 provides an example of an Exclusionary Factors form that can be used to document systematically and thoroughly that the exclusionary factors listed in the federal definition of SLD (as well as other factors) were evaluated.

Note that because the process of SLD determination does not necessarily occur in a strict linear fashion, evaluations at Levels I and II often take place concurrently, because data from Level II are often necessary to understand performance at Level I. The circular arrows between Levels I and II in Rapid Reference 7.1 are meant to illustrate the fact that interpretations and decisions that are based on data gathered at Level I may need to be informed by data gathered at Level II. Ultimately, at Level II, the practitioner must judge the extent to which any factors other than cognitive impairment can be considered the *primary* reason for academic performance difficulties. If performance cannot be attributed primarily to other factors, then the second criterion necessary for establishing SLD according to the operational definition is met and assessment may continue to the next level.

CAUTION

There are many exclusionary factors to consider in an evaluation of suspected learning disability. The work of the practitioner is to determine whether any that are present are likely to be the *primary* reason for academic learning failure.

It is important to recognize that, although factors such as having English as a second language, may be present and may affect performance adversely, SLD can also be present. Certainly, students who have vision problems, chronic illnesses, limited English proficiency, and so forth, may also have SLD. Therefore, when these or other factors at Level II are present or when they are determined to be *contributing* to poor performance, SLD should not be ruled out. Rather, only

≡ Rapid Reference 7.4

. . . .

Evaluation and Consideration of Exclusionary Factors for SLD Identification

An evaluation of specific learning disability (SLD) requires an evaluation and consideration of factors, other than a disorder in one or more basic psychological processes that may be the primary cause of a student's academic skill weaknesses and learning difficulties. These factors include vision/hearing,[1] or motor disabilities, intellectual disability (ID), social/emotional or psychological disturbance,environmental or economic disadvantage, cultural and linguistic factors (e.g., limited English proficiency), insufficient instruction or opportunity to learn and physical/health factors. These factors may be evaluated via behavior rating scales, observations, classroom interviews, teacher and parent records, attendance social/developmental history, family history, vision/hearing exams,[1] medical records, prior evaluations, and interviews with current or past counselors, psychiatrists, and paraprofessionals who have worked with the student. Noteworthy is the fact that students with (and without) SLD often have one or more factors (listed below) that **_contribute_** to academic and learning difficulties. However, the practitioner must rule out any of these factors as being the **_primary_** reason for a student's academic and learning difficulties to maintain SLD as a viable classification/diagnosis.

Vision (Check All that Apply):

☐ Vision test recent (within 1 year)

☐ Vision test outdated (> 1 year)

☐ Passed

☐ Failed

☐ Wears Glasses

☐ History of visual disorder/disturbance

☐ Diagnosed visual disorder/disturbance

Name of disorder: _____

☐ Vision difficulties suspected or observed (e.g., difficulty with far or near point copying, misaligned numbers in written math work, squinting or rubbing eyes during visual tasks such as reading, computers)

NOTES:____ _____
_____
_____

Hearing (Check All that Apply):[2]

☐ Hearing test recent (within 1 year)

☐ Hearing test outdated (> 1 year)

☐ Passed

☐ Failed

☐ Uses Hearing Aids

☐ History of auditory disorder/disturbance

☐ Diagnosed auditory disorder/disturbance

☐ Name of disorder:_____

☐ Hearing difficulties suggested in the referral (e.g., frequent requests for repetition of auditory information, misarticulated words, attempts to self-accommodate by moving closer to sound source, obvious attempts to speech read)

NOTES:_____
_____
_____

Note: Constructed in collaboration with Jennifer T. Mascolo, PsyD.

(continued)

(continued)

Motor Functioning (Check All that Apply):

☐ Fine Motor Delay/Difficulty

☐ Gross Motor Delay/Difficulty

☐ Improper pencil grip (Specify type: _____)

☐ Assistive devices/aids used
(e.g., weighted pens, pencil grip, slant board)

☐ History of motor disorder

☐ Diagnosed motor disorder

Name of disorder: _____

☐ Motor difficulties suggested in the referral
(e.g., illegible writing; issues with letter or number
formation, size, spacing; difficulty with fine motor
tasks such as using scissors, folding paper)

NOTES:_____
_____
_____

Cognitive and Adaptive Functioning (Check All that Apply):

☐ Significantly "subaverage intellectual functioning" (e.g., IQ score of 75 or below)

☐ Pervasive cognitive deficits (e.g., weaknesses or deficits in many cognitive areas, including *Gf and Gc*)

☐ Deficits in adaptive functioning (e.g., social, communication, self-care)

Areas of significant adaptive skill weaknesses (check all that apply):

☐ Motor Skill   ☐ Communication   ☐ Socialization

☐ Daily Living Skills   ☐ Behavior/Emotional Skills   ☐ Other

NOTES:_____
_____
_____

Social-Emotional/Psychological Factors (Check All that Apply):

☐ Diagnosed psychological disorder (Specify: _____)

☐ Date of Diagnosis

☐ Family history significant for psychological difficulties

☐ Disorder presently treated - specify treatment modality (e.g., counseling, medication): _____

☐ Reported difficulties with social/emotional functioning (e.g., social phobia, anxiety, depression)

☐ Social-Emotional/Psychological issues suspected or suggested by referral

☐ Home-School Adjustment Difficulties

☐ Lack of Motivation

☐ Emotional Stress

Note: Constructed in collaboration with Jennifer T. Mascolo, PsyD.

☐ Autism

☐ Present Medications (type, dosage, frequency, duration) _____

☐ Prior Medication Use (type, dosage, frequency, duration) _____

☐ Hospitalization for psychological difficulties (date(s): _____)

☐ Deficits in social, emotional, or behavioral [SEB] functioning (e.g., as assessed by standardized rating scales)

Significant scores from SEB measures: _____

NOTES:_____
_____
_____

Environmental/Economic Factors (Check All that Apply):

☐ Limited access to educational materials in the home

☐ Caregivers unable to provide instructional support

☐ Economic considerations precluded treatment
of identified issues (e.g., filling a prescription,
replacing broken glasses, tutoring)

☐ Temporary Crisis Situation

☐ History of educational neglect

☐ Frequent transitions (e.g., shared custody)

☐ Environmental space issues (e.g., no space
for studying, sleep disruptions due to shared
sleeping space)

NOTES:_____
_____
_____

Cultural/Linguistic Factors (Check All that Apply):[3]

☐ Limited Number of Years in U.S. (___)

☐ No History of Early or Developmental
Problems in Primary Language

☐ Current Primary Language Proficiency:
(Dates: _____ Scores: _____)

☐ Acculturative Knowledge Development
(Circle one: High – Moderate – Low)

☐ Language(s) Other than English Spoken in Home

☐ Lack of or Limited Instruction in Primary Language
(# of years _____)

☐ Current English Language Proficiency:
(Date: _____ Scores: _____)

☐ Parental Educational and Socio-Economic Level
(Circle one: High – Moderate – Low)

NOTES:_____
_____
_____

Note: Constructed in collaboration with Jennifer T. Mascolo, PsyD.

(continued)

(continued)

Physical/Health Factors (Check All that Apply):

☐ Limited access to healthcare   ☐ Minimal documentation of health history/status

☐ Chronic health condition (Specify: _____)   ☐ Migraines

☐ Temporary health condition (Date/Duration: _____)   ☐ Hospitalization (Dates: _____)

☐ History of Medical Condition (Date Diagnosed _____)

☐ Medical Treatments (Specify: _____)

☐ Repeated visits to the school nurse   ☐ Repeated visits to doctor

☐ Medication (type, dosage, frequency, duration: _____)

NOTES:_____

_____

_____

Instructional Factors (Check All that Apply):

☐ Interrupted schooling (e.g., mid-year school move)   Specify why: _____

☐ New teacher (past 6 months)   ☐ Retained or advanced a grade(s)

☐ Nontraditional curriculum (e.g., homeschooled)   ☐ Accelerated curriculum (e.g., AP classes)

☐ Days Absent _____

NOTES:_____

_____

_____

Determination of Primary and Contributory Causes of Academic Weaknesses and Learning Difficulties (Check One):

☐ Based on the available data, it is reasonable to conclude that one or more factors is *primarily* responsible for the student's observed learning difficulties. Specify: _____

☐ Based on the available data, it is reasonable to conclude that one or more factors *contributes* to the student's observed learning difficulties. Specify: _____

☐ *No* factors listed here appear to be the primary cause of the student's academic weaknesses and learning difficulties

Note: Constructed in collaboration with Jennifer T. Mascolo, PsyD.

[1] **For vision and hearing disorders,** it is important to understand the nature of the disorder, its expected impact on achievement, and the time of diagnosis. It is also important to understand what was happening instructionally at the time the disorder was suspected and/or diagnosed. **With regard to hearing,** even mild loss can affect initial receptive and expressive skills as well as academic skill acquisition. When loss is suspected, the practitioner should consult professional literature to further understand the potential impact of a documented hearing issue (see American Speech-Language-Hearing Association guidelines, http://www.asha.org). **With regard to vision,** refractive error (i.e., hyperopia and anisometropia), accommodative and vergence dysfunctions, and eye movement disorders are associated with learning difficulties, whereas other vision problems are not (e.g., constant strabismus and amblyopia). As such, when a vision disorder is documented or suspected, the practitioner should consult professional literature to further understand the impact of the visual disorder (e.g., see American Optometric Association, http://www.aoa.org).

[2] When there is a history of hearing difficulties and a learning disability diagnosis is being considered, hearing testing should be recent (i.e., conducted within the previous 6 months).

[3] When evaluating the impact of language and cultural factors on a student's functioning, the practitioner should consider whether and to what extent other individuals with similar linguistic and cultural backgrounds as the referred student are progressing and responding to instruction in the present curriculum (e.g., if an limited English proficiency (LEP) student is not demonstrating academic progress or is not performing as expected on a class- or district-wide assessment when compared to his or her peers who possess a similar level of English proficiency and acculturative knowledge, it is unlikely that cultural and linguistic differences are the sole or primary factors for the referred student's low performance). In addition, it is important to note that as the number of cultural and linguistic differences in a student's background increase, the greater the likelihood that poor academic performance is attributable primarily to such differences rather than a disability.

Note: All 50 U.S. states specify eight exclusionary criteria. Namely, learning difficulties cannot be primarily attributed to (1) visual impairment; (2) hearing impairment; (3) motor impairment; (4) intellectual disability; (5) emotional disturbance; (6) environmental disadvantage; (7) economic disadvantage; and (8) cultural difference. Noteworthy is the fact that certain states have adopted additional exclusionary criteria including autism, (California, Michigan, Vermont, and Wisconsin), emotional stress (Louisiana and Vermont), home or school adjustment difficulties (Louisiana and Vermont), lack of motivation (Louisiana and Tennessee), and temporary crisis situation (Louisiana, Tennessee, and Vermont). The present authors have integrated these additional criteria under "social-emotional/psychological factors" and "environmental/economic factors" and have added two additional categories, namely, "instructional factors" and "physical/health factors" to this form.

when such factors are determined to be *primarily* responsible for weaknesses in learning and academic performance, not merely contributing to them, should SLD, as an explanation for dysfunction in academic performance, be discounted. Examination of exclusionary factors is necessary to ensure fair and equitable interpretation of the data collected for SLD determination and as such, is not intended to *rule in* SLD. Rather, careful examination of exclusionary factors is intended to rule out other possible explanations for deficient academic performance.

One of the major reasons for placing evaluation of exclusionary factors at this (early) point in the SLD assessment process is to provide a mechanism that is efficient in both time and effort and that may prevent the unnecessary administration of additional tests. However, it may not be possible to rule out all of the numerous potential exclusionary factors at this stage in the assessment process. For example, the data gathered at Levels I and II may be insufficient to draw conclusions about such conditions as developmental disabilities and intellectual disability, which often require more thorough and direct assessment (e.g., administration of an intelligence test and adaptive behavior scale). When exclusionary factors have been evaluated carefully and eliminated as possible *primary* explanations for poor academic performance—at least those that can be evaluated at this level—the process may advance to the next level.

Level III: Analysis of Cognitive Abilities and Processes

The criterion at this level is similar to the one specified in Level I except that it is evaluated with data from an assessment of cognitive abilities and processes. Analysis of data generated from the administration of standardized tests represents the most common method available by which cognitive and neuropsychological functions in individuals are evaluated. However, other types of information and data are relevant to cognitive performance (see Rapid Reference 7.1, Level III, column 4). Practitioners should seek out and gather data from other sources as a means of providing corroborating evidence for standardized test findings. For example, when test findings are found to be consistent with the student's performance in the classroom, a greater degree of confidence may be placed on test performance because interpretations of cognitive weakness have ecological validity—an important condition for any diagnostic process (Flanagan et al., 2012; Hale & Fiorello, 2004; Mascolo et al., 2014).

Rapid Reference 7.5 includes information that may assist practitioners in understanding whether or not specific cognitive weaknesses or deficits affect performance in real-world settings adversely. This rapid reference includes information about (1) seven broad CHC cognitive abilities and processes that are important for learning and academic achievement; and (2) how weaknesses or deficits in these cognitive domains manifest in general as well as in specific academic areas. Identification of the manner in which cognitive weaknesses or deficits manifest in an academic setting, in particular, provides ecological validity for cognitive test findings. The information contained in Rapid Reference 7.5 has been incorporated into a form that may be filled out by teachers and parents with or without the aid of a practitioner. This form is included in Appendix D and may be copied, disseminated, and used at the practitioner's discretion. Note that once evidence of ecological validity is obtained, there are a number of factors that may assist in minimizing the effects of a cognitive weakness on the individual's ability to access the curriculum, for example. These factors are listed in Appendix 7.A.

Because new data are gathered at Level III, it is possible to evaluate the exclusionary factors that could not be evaluated earlier (e.g., Intellectual Disability). The circular arrows between Levels II and III in Rapid Reference 7.1 are meant to illustrate the fact that interpretations and decisions that are based on data gathered at Level III may need to be informed by data gathered at Level II. Likewise, data gathered at Level III are often necessary to rule out (or in) one or more exclusionary factors listed at Level II in Rapid Reference 7.1. Reliable and valid identification of SLD depends in part on being able to understand academic performance (Level I), cognitive performance (Level III), and the many factors that may facilitate or inhibit such performances (Level II).

Level IV: The Dual Discrepancy/Consistency Pattern of Strengths and Weaknesses (DD/C PSW)

This level of evaluation revolves around a theory- and research-guided examination of performance across academic skills, cognitive abilities, and neuropsychological processes to determine whether the student's pattern of strengths and weaknesses is consistent with the SLD construct. When the process of SLD identification has reached this level, three necessary criteria for SLD identification have already been met: (1) one or more weaknesses or deficits in academic performance; (2) one or more weaknesses or deficits in cognitive performance; and (3) exclusionary factors determined not to be the primary cause of the academic and cognitive weaknesses or deficits. What has yet to be determined is whether the pattern of results is marked by an empirical or ecologically valid relationship between the identified cognitive and academic weaknesses, whether the individual's cognitive weakness or deficit is domain-specific, whether the individual's academic weakness or deficit (underachievement) is unexpected, and whether the

Rapid Reference 7.5

General and Specific Manifestations of Weaknesses or Deficits in Cognitive Abilities and Processes

General and Specific Manifestations of a Fluid Reasoning (Gf) Weakness

CHC Broad Cognitive Abilities/ Neuropsychological Functions	Brief Definition[1]	General Manifestations of the Cognitive/ Neuropsychological Weakness	Specific Manifestations of the Cognitive/ Neuropsychological Weakness
Fluid Reasoning (Gf)	• Novel reasoning and problem solving; ability to solve problems that are unfamiliar • Processes are minimally dependent on prior learning • Involves manipulating rules, abstracting, generalizing, and identifying logical relationships • Fluid reasoning is evident in inferential reasoning, concept formation, classification of unfamiliar stimuli, categorization, and extrapolation of reasonable estimates in ambiguous situations (Schneider & McGrew, 2012) • Narrow Gf abilities include Induction, General Sequential Reasoning (Deduction), and Quantitative Reasoning	**Difficulties With:** • Higher-level thinking and reasoning • Transferring or generalizing learning • Deriving solutions for novel problems • Extending knowledge through critical thinking • Perceiving and applying underlying rules or process(es) to solve problems	**Reading Difficulties** • Drawing inferences from text • Abstracting main idea(s) **Math Difficulties** • Reasoning with quantitative information (word problems) • Internalizing procedures and processes used to solve problems • Apprehending relationships between numbers **Writing Difficulties** • Essay writing and generalizing concepts • Developing a theme • Comparing and contrasting ideas

General and Specific Manifestations of a Crystallized Intelligence (Gc) Weakness

CHC Broad Cognitive Abilities/ Neuropsychological Functions	Brief Definition[1]	General Manifestations of the Cognitive/ Neuropsychological Weakness	Specific Manifestations of the Cognitive/ Neuropsychological Weakness
Crystallized Intelligence (Gc)	• Breadth and depth of knowledge and skills that are valued by one's culture • Developed through formal education as well as general learning experiences • Stores of information and declarative and procedural knowledge • Reflects the degree to which a person has learned practically useful knowledge and mastered valued skills (Schneider & McGrew, 2012) • Narrow Gc abilities include General Verbal Information, Language Development, Lexical Knowledge, Listening Ability, Information about Culture, Communication Ability, and Grammatical Sensitivity	**Difficulties With:** • Vocabulary acquisition • Knowledge acquisition • Comprehending language or understanding what others are saying • Fact-based/ informational questions • Using prior knowledge to support learning • Finding the right words to use/say	**Reading Difficulties** • Decoding (e.g., word student is attempting to decode is not in his or her vocabulary) • Comprehending (e.g., poor background knowledge about information contained in text) **Math Difficulties** • Understanding math concepts and the "vocabulary of math" **Writing Difficulties** • Grammar (syntax) • Bland writing with limited descriptors • Verbose writing with limited descriptors • Inappropriate word usage **Language Difficulties** • Understanding class lessons • Expressive language: "poverty of thought"

(continued)

General and Specific Manifestations of an Auditory Processing (Ga) Weakness

CHC Broad Cognitive Abilities/ Neuropsychological Functions	Brief Definition[1]	General Manifestations of the Cognitive/ Neuropsychological Weakness	Specific Manifestations of the Cognitive/ Neuropsychological Weakness
Auditory Processing (Ga)	• Ability to analyze and synthesize auditory information • One narrow aspect of Ga is a precursor to oral language comprehension (i.e., parsing speech sounds or Phonetic Coding) • In addition to Phonetic Coding, other narrow Ga abilities include, Speech Sound Discrimination, Resistance to Auditory Stimulus Distortion, Memory for Sound Patterns, (and others related to music)	**Difficulties With:** • Hearing information presented orally • Initially processing oral information • Paying attention especially in the presence of background noise • Discerning the direction from which auditory information is coming • Discriminating between simple sounds • Foreign language acquisition	**Reading Difficulties** • Acquiring phonics skills • Sounding out words • Using phonetic strategies **Math Difficulties** • Reading word problems **Writing Difficulties** • Spelling • Note taking • Poor quality of writing

General and Specific Manifestations of a Long-Term Storage and Retrieval (Glr) Weakness

CHC Broad Cognitive Abilities/ Neuropsychological Functions	Brief Definition[1]	General Manifestations of the Cognitive/ Neuropsychological Weakness	Specific Manifestations of the Cognitive/ Neuropsychological Weakness
Long-Term Retrieval (Glr)	• Ability to store information (e.g., concepts, words, facts), consolidate it, and fluently retrieve it at a later time (e.g., minutes, hours, days, and years) through association • In Glr tasks, information leaves immediate awareness long enough for the contents of primary memory to be displaced completely. In other words, Glr tasks (unlike Gsm tasks) do not allow for information to be maintained continuously in primary memory (Schneider & McGrew, 2012) • Glr abilities may be categorized as either "learning efficiency" or "fluency". Learning efficiency narrow abilities include Associative Memory, Meaningful Memory, and Free Recall Memory; fluency narrow abilities involve either the production of ideas (e.g., Ideational Fluency, Associational Fluency), the recall of words (e.g., Naming	**Difficulties With:** • Learning new concepts • Retrieving or recalling information by using association • Performing consistently across different task formats (e.g., recognition versus recall formats) • Rapid retrieval of information • Learning information quickly • Paired learning (visual-auditory) • Recalling specific information (words, facts)	**Reading Difficulties** • Accessing background knowledge to support new learning while reading • Slow to access phonological representations during decoding • Retelling or paraphrasing what one has read **Math Difficulties** • Memorizing math facts • Recalling math facts and procedures **Writing Difficulties** • Accessing words to use during essay writing • Specific writing tasks (compare and contrast; persuasive writing) • Note-taking • Idea generation/production

(continued)

CHC Broad Cognitive Abilities/ Neuropsychological Functions	Brief Definition[1]	General Manifestations of the Cognitive/ Neuropsychological Weakness	Specific Manifestations of the Cognitive/ Neuropsychological Weakness
	Facility, Word Fluency), or the generation of figures (e.g., Figural Fluency, Figural Flexibility) (Schneider & McGrew, 2012)	· Generating ideas rapidly	**Language Difficulties** · Expressive: circumlocutions, speech fillers, "interrupted" thought, pauses · Receptive: making connections throughout oral presentations (e.g., class lecture)

General and Specific Manifestations of a Processing Speed (Gs) Weakness

CHC Broad Cognitive Abilities/ Neuropsychological Functions	Brief Definition[1]	General Manifestations of the Cognitive/ Neuropsychological Weakness	Specific Manifestations of the Cognitive/ Neuropsychological Weakness
Processing Speed (Gs)	· Speed of processing, particularly when required to focus attention for 1–3 minutes	**Difficulties With:** · Efficient processing of information	**Reading Difficulties** · Slow reading speed, which interferes with comprehension

- Usually measured by tasks that require the ability to perform simple repetitive cognitive tasks quickly and accurately
- Narrow Gs abilities include Perceptual Speed, Rate-of-Test-Taking, Number Facility, Reading Speed, and Writing Speed (note that the latter two abilities are also listed under other broad CHC domains, including Grw)

- Quickly perceiving relationships (similarities and differences between stimuli or information)
- Working within time parameters
- Completing simple, rote tasks quickly

- Need to reread for understanding

Math Difficulties
- Automatic computations
- Computational speed is slow despite accuracy
- Slow speed can result in reduced accuracy due to memory decay

Writing Difficulties
- Limited output due to time factors
- Labored process results in reduced motivation to produce

Language Difficulties
- Cannot retrieve information quickly; slow, disrupted speech; cannot get out thoughts quickly enough
- Is slow to process incoming information, puts demands on memory store, which can result in information overload and loss of meaning

(continued)

General and Specific Manifestations of a Visual Processing (Gv) Weakness

CHC Broad Cognitive Abilities/ Neuropsychological Functions	Brief Definition[1]	General Manifestations of the Cognitive/ Neuropsychological Weakness	Specific Manifestations of the Cognitive/ Neuropsychological Weakness
Visual Processing (Gv)	• Ability to analyze and synthesize visual information • The ability to make use of simulated mental imagery (often in conjunction with currently perceived images) to solve problems (Schneider & McGrew, 2012) • There are many narrow Gv abilities, some of which include Visualization, Speeded Rotation, Closure Speed, Flexibility of Closure, Visual Memory, and Spatial Scanning	**Difficulties With:** • Recognizing patterns • Reading maps, graphs, and charts • Attending to fine visual detail • Recalling visual information • Appreciation of spatial characteristics of objects (e.g., size, length) • Recognition of spatial orientation of objects	**Reading Difficulties** • Orthographic coding (using visual features of letters to decode) • Sight-word acquisition • Using charts and graphs within a text in conjunction with reading • Comprehension of text involving spatial concepts (e.g., social studies text describing physical boundaries, movement of troops along a specified route) **Math Difficulties** • Number alignment during computations • Reading and interpreting graphs, tables, and charts **Writing Difficulties** • Spelling sight words • Spatial planning during writing tasks (e.g., no attention to margins, words that overhang a line) • Inconsistent size, spacing, position, and slant of letters

General and Specific Manifestations of a Short-Term (Working) Memory (Gsm) Weakness

CHC Broad Cognitive Abilities/ Neuropsychological Functions	Brief Definition[1]	General Manifestations of the Cognitive/ Neuropsychological Weakness	Specific Manifestations of the Cognitive/ Neuropsychological Weakness
Short-Term (Working) Memory (Gsm)	Ability to hold information in immediate awareness and use or transform it within a few seconds	**Difficulties With:** • Following multistep oral and written instructions • Remembering information ong enough to apply it • Remembering the sequence of information • Rote memorization • Maintaining one' place in a math problem or train of thought while writing	**Reading Difficulties** • Reading comprehension (i.e., understanding what is read) • Decoding multisyllabic words • Orally retelling or paraphrasing what one has read **Math Difficulties** • Rote memorization of facts • Remembering mathematical procedures • Multistep problems and regrouping • Extracting information to be used in word problems **Writing Difficulties** • Spelling multisyllabic words • Redundancy in writing (word and conceptual levels) • Identifying main idea of a story • Note taking

(continued)

General and Specific Manifestations of an Attention Weakness

CHC Broad Cognitive Abilities/ Neuropsychological Functions	Brief Definition[1]	General Manifestations of the Cognitive/ Neuropsychological Weakness	Specific Manifestations of the Cognitive/ Neuropsychological Weakness
Attention	Attention is a complex and multifaceted construct used when an individual must focus on certain stimuli for information processing. In order to regulate thinking and to complete tasks of daily living such as schoolwork, it is necessary to be able to attend to both auditory and visual stimuli in the environment. Attention can be viewed as the foundation of all other higher-order processing. Attention can be divided into five subareas: selective/focused attention, shifting attention, divided attention, sustained attention, and attentional capacity (Miller, 2010) It is important to identify the exact nature of the attentional problem(s) prior to selecting an intervention, teaching strategies, modifying the curriculum, or making accommodations	• Easily distracted • Lacks attention to detail; makes careless mistakes • Difficulty discerning demands of a task (e.g., where to begin or how to get started) • May only be able to attend to task in short intervals • Difficulty changing activities • Difficulty applying a different strategy when task demands change • Difficulty attending to more than one thing or task at a time • Cannot perform well when faced with multiple stimuli or an abundance of detail	**Reading Difficulties** • Loses one's place easily • Easily distracted while reading • Does not pick up important details in text **Math Difficulties** • Does not consistently attend to math signs • Frequent mistakes on word problems **Writing Difficulties** • Has difficulty completing long assignments; difficulty following timelines

General and Specific Manifestations of Weaknesses in Executive Functions

CHC Broad Cognitive Abilities/ Neuropsychological Functions	Brief Definition[1]	General Manifestations of the Cognitive/ Neuropsychological Weakness	Specific Manifestations of the Cognitive/ Neuropsychological Weakness
• Executive Functioning	Executive functioning is often understood as two broadly conceptualized areas that are related to the brain's frontal lobes: cognitive control and behavioral/emotional control. The *cognitive* aspects of executive functioning include concept generation (Gc/Glr); problem solving (Gf); attentional shifting (attention; Gs); planning; organizing; working memory (Gsm); and retrieval fluency (Glr). The *behavioral/emotional* aspects of executive functioning relate to the inhibitory controls of behavior (e.g., impulsivity, regulation of emotional tone, etc.). (see Miller, 2010; www.school neuropsych.com)	**Difficulty With:** • Learning new activities, generating concepts, and solving problems • Identifying goals and setting goals • Planning (e.g., begins project without necessary materials; does not allocate sufficient time to complete task) • Sequencing (e.g., may skip steps in multistep problems) • Prioritizing (e.g., not sure what's important when taking notes)	**Reading Difficulties** • Sequencing; telling a story chronologically • Prioritizing; extracting main idea and other important information • Problem solving; drawing inferences from text **Math Difficulties** • Sequencing; remembering order of operations • Prioritizing; figuring out what is importing when solving word problems • Shifting; attending to math signs on a page **Writing Difficulties** • Generating ideas to write about

(continued)

433

CHC Broad Cognitive Abilities/ Neuropsychological Functions	Brief Definition[1]	General Manifestations of the Cognitive/ Neuropsychological Weakness	Specific Manifestations of the Cognitive/ Neuropsychological Weakness
		• Organization (e.g., loses important papers; fails to turn in completed work; creates unrealistic schedule)	• Sequencing a story
			• Prioritizing main events in a story
		• Initiation (e.g., has difficulty getting started on tasks, assignments, etc.)	
		• Pace (e.g., often runs out of time on seatwork and exams; has difficulty completing homework due to unrealistic timeline)	
		• Shifting between activities flexibly; coping with unforeseen events	

- Self-monitoring (e.g., doesn't check to ensure that each step was completed; doesn't check work before submitting it)
- Emotional control (e.g., may exhibit inappropriate or over-reactive response to situations)

[1]Most all definitions were originally derived from Carroll (1993). Two-letter factor codes (e.g., RG) are primarily from Carroll. More detailed definitions are reported in Schneider and McGrew (2012).

Source: Examples were adapted from Packer and Pruitt's book, *Challenging Kids, Challenged Teachers* (Bethesda, MD: Woodbine Press, 2010)

individual displays at least average ability to think and reason. These four conditions form a specific PSW that is marked by two discrepancies and a consistency (DD/C). *X-BASS is needed to determine whether the data demonstrate the DD/C pattern because specific formulae and regression equations are necessary to make the determination.* Each condition is described below.

DON'T FORGET

The DD/C PSW analysis in X-BASS is simple to conduct and requires the following: (1) entering data that represent seven areas of cognitive ability or processing (i.e., Gf, Gc, Glr, Gsm, Gv, Ga, Gs) and one or more areas of academic achievement; (2) transferring estimates of those cognitive and academic areas to a "Data Organizer" tab by clicking a button next to each estimate; (3) selecting estimates from the Data Organizer tab for inclusion in the PSW analysis by checking a box next to the estimate, which automatically transfers those estimates to a "Strengths and Weaknesses" tab; and (4) designating each of the cognitive and academic estimates as either a strength or a weakness. Upon completion of those steps, the DD/C PSW analysis is automatically calculated and interpreted. These steps are demonstrated in the last section of this chapter using scores from the WISC-V, WIAT-III, and other batteries used in Amanda's evaluation (see Chapter 8).

Relationship Between Cognitive and Academic Weaknesses

A student with an SLD possesses specific cognitive and academic weaknesses or deficits. When these weaknesses are related empirically or when there is an ecologically valid relationship between them, the relationship is referred to as a *below average cognitive aptitude-achievement consistency* in the DD/C definition. This consistency is a necessary marker for SLD because SLD is *presumably* caused by cognitive processing weaknesses or deficits (e.g., Fletcher, Lyon, Fuchs, & Barnes, 2007; Hale et al., 2010). Thus, there is a need to understand and identify the underlying cognitive ability or processing problems that contribute significantly to the individual's academic difficulties.

CAUTION

The term *causal* as used within the context of the DD/C model has been misconstrued to mean "deterministic." That is, if we know the causal inputs, we can predict the outcome *perfectly* (Kranzler et al., 2016). However, just because the causal inputs may be known, the outcomes clearly cannot be predicted perfectly. Cognitive abilities are indeed causally related to academic abilities, but the relationship is *probabilistic*, not deterministic, and is of moderate size (Flanagan & Schneider, 2016). The finding of cognitive weaknesses *raises the risk* of academic weaknesses; it does not guarantee academic weaknesses (Flanagan & Schneider). Likewise, it should not be assumed that the finding of academic weaknesses means that there are related cognitive weaknesses. In many cases there are no cognitive correlates. Academic weaknesses may be related to numerous factors, only one of which is a cognitive weakness.

The term *cognitive aptitude* within the context of the DD/C definition represents the specific cognitive ability or neuropsychological processing weaknesses or deficits that are empirically related to the academic skill weaknesses or deficits. For example, if a student's basic reading skill deficit is related to cognitive deficits in phonological processing (a narrow Ga ability) and rapid automatic naming (a narrow Glr ability), then the combination of below average narrow Ga and Glr performances represents his or her *below average cognitive aptitude for basic reading*, meaning that these below average performances *raise the risk* of a weakness in basic reading skills. Moreover, the finding of below average performance on measures of phonological processing, rapid automatic naming, and basic reading skills together represents a *below average cognitive aptitude-achievement consistency*.

The concept of a below average cognitive aptitude-achievement consistency reflects the notion that there are documented relationships between specific cognitive abilities and processes and specific academic skills. Empirically supported cognitive-achievement relationships are summarized in Rapid Reference 7.6. The finding of below average performance in related cognitive and academic areas is an important marker for SLD in the DD/C model and seemingly in other alternative research-based approaches (e.g., Hale et al., 2011; McCloskey et al., 2012).

In the DD/C model, the criteria for establishing a below average cognitive aptitude-achievement *consistency* are as follows:

1. "Below average" performance (i.e., less than 90, and more typically at least a standard deviation or more below the mean) in the specific cognitive *and* academic areas that are considered weaknesses or deficits; and

2. Evidence of an empirical relationship between the specific cognitive and academic areas of weakness and/or an ecologically valid relationship between these areas. To validate the relationship between the cognitive and academic areas of weakness, practitioners can document

Rapid Reference 7.6.

Summary of Relationships Between Cognitive Abilities and Processes and Specific Academic Skills

	Reading Achievement	Math Achievement	Writing Achievement
Gf	Inductive (I) and general sequential reasoning (RG) abilities play a moderate to strong role in reading comprehension. Executive functions, such as planning, organization, and self-monitoring, are also important.	Reasoning inductively and deductively with numbers (RQ) is very important for math problem solving at all ages. Executive functions, such as set shifting and cognitive inhibition, are also important.	Inductive (I) and general sequential reasoning abilities (RG) are consistently related to written expression at all ages. Executive functions, such as attention, planning, and self-monitoring, are also important.
Gc	Language development (LD), lexical knowledge (VL), general information (KO), and listening ability (LS) are important at all ages for reading acquisition and development. These abilities become increasingly important with age. Oral Language, Listening Comprehension, and EF (Executive Function: planning, organization, self-monitoring) also important for reading comprehension.	Language development (LD), lexical knowledge (VL), general information (KO), and listening abilities (LS) are important at all ages. These abilities become increasingly important with age. Number representation (e.g., quantifying sets without counting, estimating relative magnitude of sets) and number comparisons related to overall Number Sense.	Language development (LD), lexical knowledge (VL), and general information (KO) are important primarily after about the second grade. These abilities become increasingly important with age. Level of knowledge of syntax, morphology, semantics, and VL has a significant impact on clarity of written expression and text generation ability.
Gsm	Memory span (MS) and working memory capacity (WM) are important for overall reading success. Phonological memory or WM for verbal and sound-based information may also be important.	Memory span (MS) and working memory capacity (WM) or attentional control. Gsm important for math problem solving and overall success in math.	Memory span (MS) is important to writing, especially spelling skills, whereas working memory is related to advanced writing skills (e.g., written expression; synthesizing multiple ideas, ongoing self-monitoring). Gsm is important for overall writing success.

	Reading	Mathematics	Writing
Gv	Orthographic processing (often measured by tests of perceptual speed that use orthographic units as stimuli) is related to reading rate and fluency.	Visualization (VZ), including mental rotation, is important primarily for higher level (e.g, geometry; calculus) and math problem solving.	Orthographic processing (often measured by tests of perceptual speed that use orthographic units as stimuli) is related to spelling. Visualization (VZ) is also important for written expression.
Ga	Phonetic coding (PC) or "phonological awareness/processing" is very important during the elementary school years for the development of basic reading skills. Phonological memory or WM for verbal and sound-based information may also be important.		Phonetic coding (PC) or "phonological awareness/processing" is very important during the elementary school years for both basic writing skills and written expression (primarily before about Grade 5).
Glr	Naming facility (NA) or "rapid automatic naming" (also called speed of lexical access) is very important during the elementary school years for reading rate and fluency. Associative memory (MA) is also important.	Naming facility (NA; or speed of lexical access); Associative memory (MA)–memorization and rapid retrieval of basic math facts; accurate and fluent calculation.	Naming facility (NA) or "rapid automatic naming" (also called speed of lexical access) has demonstrated relations with written expression, primarily writing fluency. Storing and retrieving commonly occurring letter patterns in visual and motor memory are needed for spelling.
Gs	Perceptual speed (P) abilities are important during all school years, particularly the elementary school years.	Perceptual speed (P) important during all years, especially the elementary school years for math calculation fluency.	Perceptual speed (P) abilities are important during all school years for basic writing and related to all ages for written expression.

Source: The information in this table was compiled based on a number of syntheses of the literature on cognitive-achievement relationships (viz, Flanagan et al., 2013; McDonough, Flanagan, Sy, & Alfonso, in press; McGrew & Wendling, 2010).

the manner in which the cognitive weakness or deficit manifests in real world performances, as discussed previously (see Rapid Reference 7.5).

It is important to understand that these criteria are operationalized further in X-BASS. Rapid Reference 7.7 provides a more detailed explanation of how a consistency between cognitive and academic weaknesses is determined by the software.

When the criteria for a below average cognitive aptitude-achievement consistency are met, there may or may not be a nonsignificant difference between the scores that represent the cognitive and academic areas of weakness. That is, in the DD/C model, "consistency" refers to the fact that an empirical or ecologically valid relationship exists between the areas of identified cognitive and academic weakness, but not necessarily a nonsignificant difference between these areas. While a nonsignificant difference between the areas of cognitive and academic weakness would be expected, it need not be an inclusionary criterion for SLD. Because many factors facilitate and inhibit performance, a student may perform better or worse academically than his or her cognitive weaknesses may suggest, as mentioned at Level 1 above (see also Flanagan et al., 2013, for a discussion).

Discovery of consistencies among cognitive abilities and processes and academic skills in the below average (or lower) range could result from intellectual disability, pervasive developmental disorders, or generally below average cognitive ability, which would negate two important markers of SLD: that cognitive weaknesses are domain specific and that underachievement is unexpected. Therefore, identification of SLD should not rest on below average cognitive aptitude-achievement consistency alone. A student with SLD typically has many cognitive capabilities. Therefore, in the DD/C model, the student must demonstrate a pattern of strengths or an estimate of overall intellectual ability that is at least average.

At Least Average Ability to Think and Reason (g)

A specific learning disability is just that: *specific*. It is not general. As such, the below average cognitive aptitude-achievement consistency ought to be circumscribed and represent a significantly different level of functioning as compared to the student's cognitive capabilities or strengths in other areas. Indeed, the notion that students with SLD are of generally average or better overall cognitive ability is well known and has been written about for decades (e.g., Hinshelwood, 1917; Orton, 1937). In fact, the earliest recorded definitions of learning disability were developed by clinicians based on their observations of individuals who experienced considerable difficulties with the acquisition of basic academic skills, despite their average or above average general intelligence. According to Monroe

Rapid Reference 7.7

Description of the Consistency Component of the DD/C Model and How It Is Determined Using X-BASS

Term or Concept	DD/C	X-BASS	Comments
Below Average Aptitude-Achievement Consistency	Areas of cognitive and academic weakness are below average and there is an empirical and/or ecologically valid relationship between them.	For this component of the PSW analysis, X-BASS answers two specific questions and based on the answers to those questions, provides a statement about the presence of Below Average Aptitude-Achievement Consistency. The first question is, "Are the scores that represent the cognitive and academic areas of weakness actually weaknesses as compared to most people (i.e., below average or lower compared to same-age peers from the general population)?" The program parses the cognitive and academic weakness scores into three levels, < 85, 85–89 inclusive, and ≥ 90. Scores that are less than 85 are considered *normative* weaknesses; scores that are between 85 and 89 (inclusive) are considered weaknesses because they are below average; and scores of 90 or higher are not considered to be weaknesses. Next, the two scores (academic and cognitive) are examined relative to each other. When both scores are less than 85, the program reports a "Yes," meaning that both scores are normative weaknesses. If one score is less than 85 and the other is between 85 and 89, the program reports "Likely." If both scores are between 85 and 89 (inclusive), the program reports "Possibly" (because the scores are within normal limits, despite being classified as below average).	In some cases, the question of whether or not an individual's pattern of strengths and weaknesses is marked by a below average aptitude-achievement consistency may not be clear based on the quantitative data alone. As such, it is always important to interpret an individual's pattern of strengths and weaknesses within the context of all available data sources (e.g., including exclusionary factors, behavioral

(continued)

441

Term or Concept	DD/C	X-BASS	Comments
		The program also reports "Possibly" when one score is less than 85 and one is 90 or higher. If one score is between 85 and 89 (inclusive) and the other is 90 or higher, the program reports "Unlikely," and when both scores are 90 or higher, the program reports "No," indicating that the scores cannot be considered weaknesses as compared to most people. The second question is, "Are the areas of cognitive and academic weaknesses related empirically?" The strength of the relationship between the cognitive and academic areas of weakness is reported automatically by X-BASS as either LOW (median intercorrelation < .3), Moderate (i.e., MOD) (median intercorrelation between .3 and .5), or HIGH (median intercorrelation > .5), based on a review of the literature (see Flanagan, Ortiz, & Alfonso, 2013; McGrew & Wendling, 2010) and the technical manuals of cognitive batteries (e.g., WJ IV, WISC–V). Information regarding where the cognitive and academic weakness scores fall as compared to most people and the strength of the relationship between the two areas is used to answer the question, "Is there a below average aptitude-achievement consistency?" The answer automatically generated by X-BASS is either "Yes, Consistent," "No, Not Consistent," or "Possibly, Use Clinical Judgment." For example, if the cognitive and academic areas selected by the evaluator as weaknesses are associated with scores that fall below 85 and if the strength of the relationship between the areas of cognitive and academic weakness is moderate or high, then the program reports "Yes, Consistent."	observations, work samples) and render a judgment about SLD based on the totality of the data.

(1939), "The children of superior mental capacity who fail to learn to read are, of course, spectacular examples of specific reading difficulty since they have such obvious abilities in other fields" (p. 23; cf. Mather, 2011). Indeed, "all historical approaches to SLD *emphasize the spared or intact abilities* that stand in stark contrast to the deficient abilities" (Kaufman, 2008, pp. 7–8, emphasis added).

Current definitions of SLD also recognize the importance of generally average or better overall ability as a characteristic of individuals with SLD. For example, the official definition of learning disability of the Learning Disabilities Association of Canada (LDAC) states, in part, "Learning Disabilities refer to a number of disorders which may affect the acquisition, organization, retention, understanding or use of verbal or nonverbal information. These disorders affect learning in individuals who *otherwise demonstrate at least average abilities essential for thinking and/or reasoning*" (http://www.ldac-acta.ca/learn-more/ld-defined, emphasis added; see also Harrison & Holmes, 2012).

Unlike some definitions of SLD, such as Canada's (Harrison & Holmes, 2012), the 2004 IDEIA definition does make reference to overall cognitive ability level. However, the 2006 federal regulations contain the following phrasing: "(ii) The child exhibits a pattern of strengths and weaknesses in performance, achievement, or both, relative to age, State-approved grade-level standards, or intellectual development, that is determined by the group to be relevant to the identification of a specific learning disability. . ." Given the vagueness of the wording in the federal regulations, one could certainly infer that this phrase means that the cognitive and academic areas of concern are significantly lower than what is expected relative to same-age peers or relative to otherwise average intellectual development. Indeed, there continues to be considerable agreement that a student who meets criteria for SLD has *some* cognitive capabilities that are at least average relative to most people (e.g., Berninger, 2011; Feifer, 2012; Fiorello et al., 2014; Flanagan & Alfonso, in press; Flanagan et al., 2011; Geary, Hoard, & Bailey, 2011; Hale & Fiorello, 2004; Hale et al., 2011; Harrison & Holmes, 2012; Kaufman, 2008; Kavale & Forness, 2000; Kavale & Flanagan, 2007; Kavale et al., 2009; Mather & Wendling, 2011; McCloskey et al., 2012; Naglieri, 2011; Shaywitz, 2003). Moreover, the criterion of overall average or better cognitive ability (despite specific cognitive processing weaknesses) is necessary for differential diagnosis.

By failing to diagnose SLD from other conditions (i.e., differential diagnosis) that impede learning, such as intellectual disability, pervasive developmental disorders, and overall below average ability to learn and achieve (sometimes referred to as "slow learner"), the SLD construct loses its meaning and there is a tendency (albeit well intentioned) to accept anyone under the SLD category who has learning difficulties for reasons other than specific cognitive dysfunction (e.g., Kavale & Flanagan, 2007; Kavale, Kauffman, Bachmeier, & LeFever 2008; Mather & Kaufman, 2006; Reynolds & Shaywitz, 2009). Although the underlying and varied causes of the learning difficulties of all students who struggle academically *should be investigated and addressed*, an accurate SLD diagnosis is necessary because it informs instruction (e.g., Hale et al., 2010). When practitioners adhere closely to the DD/C model, SLD can be differentiated from other disorders that also manifest as academic difficulty (e.g., Berninger, 2011; Della Toffalo, 2010; Flanagan et al., 2013).

While it may be some time before consensus is reached on what constitutes "at least average overall cognitive ability" for the purpose of SLD identification, a student with SLD, *generally speaking*, ought to be able to perform academically at a level that approximates that of his or her more typically achieving peers when provided with individualized instruction as well as appropriate accommodations, curricular modifications, and the like. In addition, for a student with SLD to reach performances (in terms of both rate of learning and level of achievement) that approximate his or her non-disabled peers, he or she must possess the ability to learn compensatory strategies and apply them independently, which often requires higher level thinking and reasoning, including intact executive processes (e.g., Maricle & Avirett, 2012; McCloskey, Perkins, & Van Divner, 2009).

Determining otherwise average or better ability to think and reason (or average or better *g*) for a student who has a below average cognitive aptitude-achievement consistency is not a straightforward task, however, and there is no agreed upon method for doing so. The main difficulty in determining whether or not an individual with *specific* cognitive weaknesses has otherwise average overall ability or *g*, is that the global ability score or scores that are available on a cognitive or intelligence battery may be attenuated by the cognitive processing weakness(es). Most batteries have a total test score that is an aggregate of *all* (or nearly all) abilities and processes measured by the instrument. As such, in many instances, the individual's specific cognitive weaknesses or deficits attenuate the total test score on these instruments. This problem with ability tests was noted as far back as the 1920s, when Orton stated, "It seems probably that psychometric tests as ordinarily employed give an entirely erroneous and unfair estimate of the intellectual capacity of these [learning disabled] children" (1925, p. 582; cf. Mather, 2011). Perhaps for this reason intelligence and cognitive ability batteries have become more differentiated, offering a variety of specific cognitive ability composites and options for global ability estimates.

DON'T FORGET

Many scholars use the term "overall cognitive/intellectual ability" interchangeably with the first factor that emerges in a factor analysis of cognitive tests—that is, Spearman's g. The estimates of overall intellectual ability referred to in this chapter are consistent with this conceptualization.

The WISC-V offers the General Ability Index (GAI) as an alternative to the FSIQ (Full Scale IQ) because it may be useful in making decisions about overall intellectual ability within the context of an SLD evaluation. The GAI contains the same subtests as the FSIQ with the exception of Digit Span (a Working Memory subtest) and Coding (a Processing Speed subtest). Students with SLD often perform lower on tests of cognitive proficiency (i.e., working memory and processing speed) compared to tests that reflect higher level thinking and reasoning (e.g., crystallized intelligence, fluid reasoning, and visual processing) (Raiford, Weiss, Rolfhus, & Coalson, 2005, 2008). Lower cognitive proficiency compared to higher-level reasoning abilities attenuates the FSIQ, rendering the GAI a viable alternative for the purpose of describing overall intellectual ability. An analysis of the FSIQ, GAI, and Cognitive Proficiency Index (CPI) can assist in understanding whether overall intellectual ability was lowered by the inclusion of tests of working memory and processing speed (see Chapter 4 for specific information on the purpose of comparing the FSIQ, GAI, and CPI and guidance on how to report and discuss differences among these scores).

The criterion of at least average ability to think and reason as described in the DD/C model is determined by X-BASS. To understand how X-BASS makes the determination of at least average overall cognitive ability, it is necessary to understand three terms as they are used in the DD/C model and in X-BASS: "strength," "g-value," and "Facilitating Cognitive Composite (FCC)." These terms are defined in Rapid Reference 7.8 and elaborated upon in the last section of this chapter. Essentially, X-BASS calculates a proxy for g (i.e., the FCC) based on the cognitive areas that the user indicated were strengths for the individual. This estimate takes into account how many cognitive areas are designated as strengths, which ones are designated as strengths, and where the scores representing these cognitive areas fall relative to most people.

Rapid Reference 7.8

Terms Used in the DD/C Model and in X-BASS Necessary to Understand How "At Least Average Overall Ability" Is Conceptualized and Calculated

Term or Concept	DD/C	X-BASS	Comments
Strength	Performance on standardized, norm-referenced tests that falls in the *average range* (standard scores between 90 and 110 [inclusive], based on a scale having a mean of 100 and standard deviation of 15) or higher. Thus, a strength is associated with standard scores of about 90 or higher.	On the "Strengths and Weaknesses Indicator" tab, users must classify scores as either a strength or a weakness. The general guideline for a strength is that the farther a score falls above 90, the greater the probability that the construct it represents (e.g., short-term memory) facilitates performance in some way. **Caution:** *The user may classify any score as a strength on the Strengths and Weaknesses Indicator tab, including scores that fall below average or lower. Selecting a score as a strength, regardless of where it falls relative to most people, does not guarantee that it will meet criteria for PSW.*	Note that the term *strength* is typically only assigned to scores that are *average* (e.g., standard scores of ≥ 90) for the purpose of conducting a PSW analysis within the context of the DD/C operational definition. Ordinarily, average scores are just that, *average*, reflecting adequately developed skills or abilities. They are not strengths in the normative sense, although they may be strengths in the relative sense (both of which are described below). When the term *strength* is used to describe average performance in a PSW analysis, it simply means that the ability area associated with the average score *does not appear to interfere with or adversely affect the individual's learning*. No other meaning should be ascribed to the word *strength* in the PSW analysis, as operationalized by DD/C.

| g-Value | Not discussed in the DD/C definition, but is used to determine whether or not an estimate of overall cognitive or intellectual ability is calculated. | The g-value is automatically calculated by X-BASS and assists in answering the question, "How likely is it that the individual's pattern of cognitive strengths represents at least average overall ability?" The higher the g-value, the greater the likelihood that the individual's overall cognitive or intellectual ability (i.e., estimate of g) is at least average, despite one or more specific cognitive weaknesses. The g-value was calculated via the use of "g-weights" for broad CHC abilities—values that indicate the relative contribution of each broad ability to overall intellectual ability (see Quick Reference E.1 in Appendix E for details). | A low g-value (e.g., not enough areas designated as strengths) suggests that overall intellectual ability is below average or lower. In other words, a low g-value suggests that in all likelihood the individual's cognitive weaknesses are more pervasive or *global* rather than *specific*. In this case, an estimate of overall intellectual ability is not calculated and the PSW analysis is not conducted. **Don't Forget:** Individuals with low overall cognitive or intellectual ability and achievement are in need of services, but do not meet the SLD criteria set forth in the DD/C definition. These individuals are perhaps best served at Tiers II and III of an RTI model. |
| **Cognitive Strengths that constitute at least average overall ability to** | The DD/C definition requires that the examiner assess a minimum of seven CHC areas: Gf, Gc, Gsm, Glr, Gv, Ga, and Gs. Based on the CHC areas that were designated as strengths, a g-value is calculated. If the g-value is of sufficient magnitude, a composite is calculated | When the g-value is of sufficient magnitude, a standard formula is used in X-BASS to calculate a composite based on all CHC scores that were designated as strengths by the user. The composite is called the FCC. Steps and formulae used in X-BASS to calculate a composite are summarized in Quick | If too few CHC scores were designated as strengths, then X-BASS will not calculate an FCC. A sufficient breadth of cognitive abilities must be designated as strengths for the FCC to be calculated because the FCC is expected to be an estimate of g or general intelligence without the attenuating effects of specific cognitive weaknesses. |

(continued)

Term or Concept	DD/C	X-BASS	Comments
think and reason— The Facilitating Cognitive Composite (FCC)	and is considered a proxy for g or overall cognitive ability. **Don't Forget:** In addition to the seven CHC areas, common neuropsychological domains that are often assessed in cases of suspected SLD include orthographic processing (OP), speed of lexical access (LA), cognitive efficiency (CE), and executive functions (EF). If any of these neuropsychological domains is evaluated, it may also be included in the PSW analysis.	Reference E.2 in Appendix E. See also the "PSW-A Notes" tab in X-BASS for more information.	For example, if an individual had relative weaknesses in working memory and processing speed, the FCC would be akin to using the WISC-V GAI as an estimate of general intelligence rather than the FSIQ, because the GAI does not include explicit measures of working memory or processing speed. Also, if the areas that are designated as strengths by the user are sufficient in number, yielding a g-value that suggests at least average overall cognitive or intellectual ability, but the scores representing those areas are in the mid to upper 80s, for example, the FCC may fall below 85. In v1.2 of X-BASS, when *an FCC fell below 85, the program did not report it and the PSW analysis was not conducted.* The assumption here was that the individual's weaknesses were more pervasive and global, rather than specific. Below average cognitive and academic ability in and of itself is not consistent with the SLD construct. However, clinical judgment may suggest

that multiple data sources support SLD, despite a below average FCC, versions 1.4 and 2.0 of X-BASS allow the user to continue with the PSW analysis by overriding the "at least average overall ability" criterion. However, when the FCC falls below 85, X-BASS conducts the PSW analysis automatically *but reports that such an analysis is not consistent with the DD/C model.*

Don't Forget: Although neuropsychological domains (e.g., CE, EF) may be included in the PSW analysis, they are not included in the calculation of the FCC.

Even when it is determined that a student has overall average ability to think and reason along with a below average cognitive aptitude-achievement consistency, these findings alone do not satisfy the criteria for a pattern of strengths and weaknesses consistent with the SLD construct in the DD/C model. This is because it is not yet clear whether the differences between the score representing overall ability and those representing specific cognitive and academic weaknesses or deficits are statistically significant, meaning that such differences are reliable differences (i.e., not due to chance). Moreover, it is not yet clear whether the cognitive area(s) of weakness is domain-specific and whether the academic area(s) of weakness (or underachievement) is unexpected.

Domain-Specific Cognitive Weaknesses or Deficits: The First Discrepancy in the DD/C Definition of SLD

SLD has been described as a condition that is domain specific. In other words, areas of cognitive weakness or deficit are circumscribed, meaning that while they interfere with learning and achievement, they are not pervasive and do not affect all or nearly all areas of cognition. According to Stanovich (1993), "The key deficit must be a vertical faculty rather than a horizontal faculty—a domain-specific process rather than a process that operates across a variety of domains" (p. 279). It is rare to find an operational definition that specifies a criterion for determining that the condition is "domain specific." Some suggest that this condition is supported by a statistically significant difference between a student's overall cognitive ability and a score representing the individual's cognitive area of weakness (e.g., Naglieri, 2011).

However, a statistically significant difference between two scores means only that the difference is not due to chance; it does not provide information about the *rarity* or infrequency of the difference in the general population. Some statistically significant differences are common in the general population; others are not. Therefore, to determine whether the cognitive area that was identified as a weakness by the evaluator is domain specific, the difference between the individual's actual and expected performance in this area should be uncommon in the general population. Rapid Reference 7.9 summarizes the specific criteria used in X-BASS to determine whether a cognitive area designated as a weakness is also domain-specific. This rapid reference introduces a new term that is used in X-BASS: the Inhibiting Cognitive Composite or ICC. The ICC is an aggregate of the estimates of cognitive abilities and processes that the evaluator designated as weaknesses.

Rapid Reference 7.9

Terms Used in the DD/C Model and in X-BASS Necessary to Understand How a "Domain Specific Weakness" Is Conceptualized and Calculated

Term or Concept	DD/C	X-BASS	Comments
Discrepancy I: Cognitive weaknesses that are *domain specific* and the Inhibiting Cognitive Composite (ICC)	The concept of at least average overall cognitive or intellectual ability that implies that any cognitive weaknesses that are observed are "circumscribed" or domain specific, not general or more pervasive.	In the PSW analysis conducted automatically in X-BASS, any scores designated as weaknesses, regardless of magnitude, are labeled "Actual." The Facilitating Cognitive Composite (FCC) is used in a regression equation to calculate a "Predicted" score. For a cognitive weakness to be considered domain specific, two conditions must be met: (1) the difference between the FCC and Actual (weakness) score must be statistically significant ($p < .05$); and (2) the difference between the Predicted and Actual scores must be considered unusual or rare in the general population. *Note that X-BASS corrects for false negatives — this means that the program guards against missing SLD when the condition is present.* When more than one cognitive weakness (among the seven CHC areas) is identified, then an ICC is automatically calculated. The purpose of the ICC is simply to provide a summary of the individual's cognitive weaknesses. For the purpose of the PSW analysis, the user may select either the ICC or an individual cognitive ability or processing composite to represent "cognitive weakness."	Even if a weakness is considered domain specific, the actual score may not be below average. The actual score must be below average to meet part of the criteria for "consistency" in the DD/C definition.

451

Unexpected Underachievement: The Second Discrepancy in the DD/C Definition of SLD

The traditional ability-achievement discrepancy analysis was used to determine whether an individual's underachievement (e.g., reading difficulty) was unexpected (i.e., the individual's achievement was not at a level that was commensurate with his or her overall cognitive ability). A particularly salient problem with the ability-achievement discrepancy approach was that a total test score from a cognitive or intelligence test (e.g., FSIQ) was used as the estimate of overall ability. However, for individuals with SLD, the total test score was often attenuated by one or more specific cognitive weaknesses or deficits and therefore may have provided an unfair or biased estimate of the individual's actual overall intellectual capacity. Furthermore, when the total test score was attenuated by specific cognitive weaknesses or deficits, the ability-achievement discrepancy was often not statistically significant, which frequently resulted in denying the student much needed academic interventions and special education services (e.g., Aaron, 1995; Hale et al., 2011). For this reason, as stated earlier, the WISC-V includes the GAI as an alternative to the FSIQ for use in comparison (discrepancy) procedures—an alternative that Flanagan and her colleagues have advocated for many years (e.g., see Appendix H in Flanagan, McGrew, & Ortiz, 2000, and Appendix H in Flanagan et al., 2013). Rapid Reference 7.10 summarizes the specific criteria used in X-BASS to determine whether an academic area designated as a weakness represents unexpected underachievement.

In sum, an individual's scores from a comprehensive evaluation are assessed at this level of the DD/C model (Level IV) to determine whether they represent a pattern of strengths and weaknesses that is consistent with SLD. The pattern that suggests SLD is characterized by *two discrepancies*—one that defines SLD as a domain-specific condition and one that further defines SLD as unexpected underachievement—that is concomitant with a below average cognitive aptitude-achievement *consistency.* Thus, a DD/C pattern of strengths and weaknesses is the overarching diagnostic marker of SLD.

Level V: Evaluation of Interference With Learning

When the SLD determination process reaches this point, presumably the criteria at each of the previous levels were met. In addition to the PSW requirement for SLD identification, a basic eligibility requirement contained in the legal and clinical prescriptions for diagnosing SLD refers to whether the suspected learning problem(s) result in significant or substantial academic failure or other restrictions or limitations in daily life functioning.

Rapid Reference 7.10

Terms Used in the DD/C Model and in X-BASS Necessary to Understand How "Unexpected Underachievement" Is Conceptualized and Calculated

Term or Concept	DD/C	X-BASS	Comments
Discrepancy 2: Academic weaknesses that represent *unexpected underachievement*	Individuals with at least average overall cognitive or intellectual ability are expected to perform at about an average level academically, particularly when no other obvious factors are inhibiting academic performance. When a general ability > academic achievement pattern is observed in the absence of any factors that may provide an explanation for the pattern, it is typically termed *unexpected underachievement*—the most salient diagnostic feature of SLD.	In the PSW analysis, an academic weakness represents *unexpected underachievement* when two conditions are met: (1) the difference between the Facilitating Cognitive Composite (FCC) and Actual Composite (academic weakness) score is statistically significant (*p* < .05); and (2) the difference between the Predicted and Actual academic scores is unusual or rare in the general population. *Note that X-BASS corrects for false negatives – this means that the program guards against missing SLD when the condition is present.*	Even if a weakness represents unexpected underachievement, the actual score may not be below average. The actual score must be below average to meet part of the criteria for "consistency" in the DD/C definition. **Don't Forget:** Because individuals benefit from explicit instruction, evidence-based interventions, strategy instruction, and the like, those individuals who have received such instruction and services may very well perform in the average range academically, which should not automatically rule out SLD, particularly when all other criteria are met. Results of a PSW analysis must *always* be considered within the context of the entire case history and current level and type of services provided to the individual.

453

The legal and diagnostic specifications of SLD necessitate that practitioners review the whole of the collected data and make a professional judgment about the extent of the adverse impact that any measured deficit has on an individual's performance in one or more areas of learning or academic achievement. Essentially, Level V analysis serves as a kind of quality control feature designed to prevent the application of an SLD diagnosis in cases in which "real-world" functioning is not in fact impaired or substantially limited as compared to same-age peers in the general population, regardless of the patterns seen in the data.

This final criterion requires practitioners to take a very broad survey not only of the entire array of data collected during the course of the assessment, but also of the real-world manifestations and practical implications of any presumed disability. In general, if the criteria at Levels I through IV were met, it is likely that in the vast majority of cases, Level V analysis serves only to support conclusions that have already been drawn. However, in cases where data may be equivocal or when procedures or criteria other than those specified in the DD/C model have been utilized, Level V analysis becomes an important safety valve, ensuring that any representations of SLD suggested by the data are indeed manifest in observable impairments in one or more areas of functioning in real-life settings.

The final section of this chapter walks the reader through three simple steps that ensure that the data necessary for conducting a PSW analysis following the DD/C model have been entered into X-BASS appropriately. Following these three steps, guidance on how to view and understand program output is provided.

USING X-BASS FOR SLD IDENTIFICATION: THREE STEPS TO PSW OUTPUT

While reading the information in this section, having the X-BASS program open will be helpful. Also, for reference, the data that are used here are those from the case of Amanda (Chapter 8) and are found in Rapid Reference 7.11.

Getting Started

1. X-BASS opens to a "Welcome" screen (see Figure 7.1). This tab allows you to select one of three modes of operation: Beginner, Intermediate, and Advanced. The Beginner mode provides maximum guidance and explanation of program functionality through extensive pop-up messages. When more familiar with X-BASS, the mode may be changed to Intermediate, and eventually Advanced, with the latter option containing the fewest number of pop-ups. From the Welcome

Rapid Reference 7.11

. . . .

WISC-V, WIAT-III, and CTOPP-2 Data From the Case of Amanda (Chapter 8, "Illustrative Case Report")

Composites	Scores	Percentile Rank	Classification
Full Scale IQ Score	91	27	**Average**
Verbal Comprehension Index (VCI or Gc)	100	50	**Average**
Similarities	10		Average
Vocabulary	10		Average
Fluid Reasoning Index (FRI or Gf)	97	42	**Average**
Matrix Reasoning	9		Average
Figure Weights	10		Average
Visual Spatial Index (VSI or Gv)	81	16	**Low Average**
Block Design	6		Below Average
Visual Puzzles	7		Low Average
Working Memory Index (WMI or Gsm)	85	16	**Low Average**
Digit Span	8		Average
Picture Span	7		Low Average
Processing Speed Index (PSI or Gs)	92	30	**Average**
Coding	8		Average
Symbol Search	9		Average
Naming Speed Index (NSI)	99	47	**Average**
Naming Speed Literacy	98		Average
Naming Speed Quantity	102		Average
Symbol Translation Index (STI)	102	55	**Average**
Immediate Symbol Translation	102		Average
Delayed Symbol Translation	102		Average
Recognition Symbol Translation	104		Average

(continued)

(continued)

Composites	Scores	Percentile Rank	Classification
Storage and Retrieval Index (SRI or Glr)	**100**	**50**	**Average**
Oral Language	**96**	**53**	**Average**
Listening Comprehension	96	39	Average
Oral Expression	98	45	Average
Total Reading	**76**	**5**	**Well Below Average**
Basic Reading	**81**	**10**	**Below Average**
Word Reading	77	6	Well Below Average
Pseudoword Decoding	85	16	Low Average
Reading Comprehension and Fluency	**73**	**4**	**Well Below Average**
Reading Comprehension	79	8	Well Below Average
Oral Reading Fluency	74	4	Well Below Average
Mathematics	**90**	**25**	**Average**
Math Problem Solving	83	13	Below Average
Numerical Operations	99	47	Average
Math Fluency	**89**	**23**	**Average**
Math Fluency- Addition	89	23	Average
Math Fluency- Subtraction	91	27	Average
Written Expression	**82**	**12**	**Below Average**
Spelling	74	4	Well Below Average
Sentence Composition	94	34	Average
Phonetic Coding: Analysis	**85**	**16**	**Low Average**
Phoneme Isolation	7	16	Low Average
Segmenting Nonwords	8	25	Average
Phonetic Coding: Synthesis	**49**	**< 0.1**	**Extremely Below Average**
Blending Words	2	0.1	Extremely Below Average
Blending Nonwords	1	0.1	Extremely Below Average

Note: CTOPP-II = Comprehensive Test of Phonological processing, Second Edition

Cross-Battery Assessment Software System (X-BASS® v2.0)

Conceptualization by D.P. Flanagan, S.O. Ortiz, V.C. Alfonso; Programming by S.O. Ortiz and A.M. Dynda   Release: 2.0

Copyright © 2017 Samuel O. Ortiz, Dawn P. Flanagan & Vincent C. Alfonso. All Rights Reserved

Essentials
of **Cross-Battery Assessment**
Third Edition

- Clear guidance on integrating cognitive, academic and neuropsychological tests
- Expert advice on identifying specific learning disabilities
- Conveniently formatted for rapid reference

Dawn P. Flanagan
Samuel O. Ortiz
Vincent C. Alfonso

Alan S. Kaufman & Nadeen L. Kaufman, *Series Editors*

Essentials of Cross-Battery Assessment, 3rd Edition remains the reference document necessary for understanding Cross-Battery Assessment (XBA) and the principles upon which the X-BASS is based.

X-BASS is an automated Cross-Battery data management system with integrated, single-entry data management across all programs (XBA Analyzer, PSW Analyzer, and C-LIM Analyzer) that facilitates data analysis and enhances interpretation. In addition, X-BASS includes enhanced features for data entry and organization, program navigation, composite and subtest selection, and automatic and selective graphing of scores. Special provisions for determination of specific learning disability via interactive PSW analyses and assistance with understanding test score validity for English language learners are also included.

Beginner Mode:
If you are new to XBA or X-BASS, click the "Beginner Mode" button for step by step guidance and assistance in using X-BASS. This option is strongly recommended for first time users of X-BASS.

[Beginner Mode]

Quick Start:
Users familiar with X-BASS can manually select the desired User Mode and go directly to the Start or Index tab.

(Start)   (Index)

What's New?
Click here to find out more about the new features and changes to the current version of X-BASS.

[What's New]

User Mode
○ Beginner
○ Intermediate
● Advanced

X-BASS
Cross-Battery Assessment
Software System

ACCESS CARD

Cross-Battery XBA
Assessment

NOTE: THIS SOFTWARE IS BEST VIEWED AT 100% MAGNIFICATION AND WIDE SCREEN RESOLUTIONS.
LOWER MAGNIFICATION SETTINGS MAY RESULT IN FORMAT CHANGES AND TEXT THAT IS HIDDEN OR UNREADABLE.

For best results, adjust your window to the same width as the line above.

Welcome | Authors | Guide | Help | Start | Index | Test List | XBA | XBA Graph | Integrated Graph | Data Organizer | Data Organizer Graph | Data Entry - Other | S&W Indical ...

Figure 7.1 X-BASS Welcome Screen

screen, click on the "Guide" tab at the bottom of the screen for general operating instructions (see Figure 7.2). This tab provides all the information needed to get started and also contains a number of frequently asked questions about X-BASS. The User Guide may be printed for easy reading and reference. Note that navigation via the tabs at the bottom of each screen will not provide pop-up messages. In order the receive pop-up messages, you must navigate via the buttons.

2. On the User Guide tab, click the round "Start" button in the upper right corner, which takes you to the "Start and Data Record Management" tab (see Figure 7.3). Identifying information is entered on this tab and the examinee's age is automatically calculated. Figure 7.3 shows the identifying information that was entered for Amanda. Once this information is entered, click on the "Create New Record" button, which is the top button in the far right column. The program will take a few seconds to create the new record and then automatically advance to the "Test Index and Main Navigation" tab (or "Index" tab for short; see Figure 7.4). As may been seen by the number of buttons on the Index tab, X-BASS has many functions and all of them can be accessed by clicking the appropriate button. Although this chapter focuses only on the DD/C PSW component of X-BASS, individual video tutorials are available at http://www.crossbattery.com that demonstrate additional functions of the software.

Step 1. Enter Individual Test Data and Cross-Battery Data into X-BASS and Transfer the Best Estimates of Cognitive and Academic Performance to the Data Organizer Tab

1.1 *WISC-V Data:* Click on the "WISC-V" button on the Index tab, which will automatically advance to the "WISC-V Data Analysis" tab (see Figure 7.5). All WISC-V data may be entered on this tab. Once data are entered, the program provides information regarding whether the indexes and global ability scores are cohesive and whether or not follow up assessment is considered necessary. The meaning of *cohesion* and *follow up* were discussed in Chapter 4. Note that Figure 7.5 shows only the top of the WISC-V Data Analysis tab. Scrolling down this tab will reveal all of the WISC-V Indexes, global scores, and new clinical composites.

After entering all WISC-V data, evaluate the results of the cohesion and follow up analyses. If indexes are cohesive and follow up is not considered necessary, then click on the "Transfer to Data Organizer"

Cross-Battery Assessment Software System (X-BASS® v2.0)

Index **Start**

Data Organizer	XBA Analyzer
S&W Indicator	PSW Analyzer
PSW-A Data Summary	C-LIM Analyzer

| WISC-V | WPPSI-IV | WAIS-IV | WIAT-III | WJ IV COG | WJ IV ACH | WJ IV OL | KABC-II | KTEA-3 | CAS2 | DAS-II | SB5 |

User Guide

Conceptualization by D.P. Flanagan, S.O. Ortiz, V.C. Alfonso; Programming by S.O. Ortiz and A.M. Dynda
Copyright © 2017 Samuel O. Ortiz, Dawn P. Flanagan & Vincent C. Alfonso. All Rights Reserved

NOTE: X-BASS does NOT use or calculate subtest raw scores and is NOT a test scoring program. Users of this software are responsible for following all test publishers' administration and scoring guidelines. All scores entered into X-BASS must be derived from use of each test's respective norms and via the specific procedures provided by the respective test publishers. All instructions regarding operation of X-BASS must be reviewed carefully prior to use.

FOR BEST VIEWING, SET YOUR WINDOW TO CORRESPOND TO THE WIDTH OF THIS LINE

User Guide and General Operating Instructions

New users should begin by scrolling down to read all the instructions and specific tab notes and click 'Beginner Mode' before proceeding.
Users may click on the button below to the right to print the User Guide and General Operating Instructions for reference.
Experienced users may set the desired mode manually and then click the Start button to go to the main tab and begin program operation.

Beginner Mode

User Mode
○ Beginner - show all messages
○ Intermediate - show most messages
● Advanced - hide most messages

Troubleshooting **Print User Guide**

X-BASS may now be run in three user modes. The default setting is the "Beginner Mode" which will display step by step guidance in using the program and applying XBA rules, in addition to the typical error, confirmation, results, and warning messages. This setting is recommended for first time users or users who are not yet very familiar with X-BASS operations and XBA procedures. "Intermediate Mode" displays only typical messages without much guidance. "Advanced Mode" suppresses all messages except results and critical ones or those that require user input. This mode is recommended only for experienced users of X-BASS, however, the mode can be changed at any time during program operation.

Quick Start Instructions and Notes:

• Each time the program is opened, if an internet connection is available, it will automatically check for an updated version. If one is found, a pop up message will occur recommending download and installation of the update. Any pop up "Security Warning: Data connections disabled" messages can be dismissed or enabled. In addition, a black button at the bottom right of the Start tab allows for manually checking to see if an update to X-BASS is available.

• Clicking the Start button takes you to the "Start and Data Record Management" tab. There you can either enter new demographic information and create a new record or open a saved data record.

• Creating a new record takes you to the "Test Index and Main Navigation" tab; opening a saved record populates all data from that record and prompts you to click on the Index tab or stay on the Start tab.

• Select the core battery used in your assessment (or for ELLs, the C-LIM Index) and click on its button it to go to the tab for that battery.

• If entering data for a new record, enter the examinee's obtained composite and subtest scores on all appropriate tabs.

• X-BASS automatically evaluates or analyzes most composites for cohesion and provides a statement regarding whether the composite is cohesive. A recommendation for

Figure 7.2 User Guide Tab in X-BASS (Top Portion of tab)

Cross-Battery Assessment Software System (X-BASS® v2.0)

Start and Data Record Management

Conceptualization by D.P. Flanagan, S.O. Ortiz, V.C. Ortiz; Programming by S.O. Ortiz and A.M. Dynda
Copyright © 2017 Samuel O. Ortiz, Dawn P. Flanagan & Vincent C. Alfonso. All Rights Reserved

| Guide | Tab Help | | | | | | | | | | | Next Step | Index |

| WISC-V | WAIS-IV | WPPSI-IV | WIAT-III | WJ IV COG | WJ IV ACH | WJ IV OL | KABC-II | KTEA-3 | CAS2 | DAS-II | SB5 |

To SET or change user mode for X-BASS, use the buttons to the right. Beginner Mode displays additional guidance and assistance in using the program. Intermediate mode displays typical informational and confirmational messages. Advanced mode suppresses all except critical messages.

1. ENTER NAME (if new case)

*Name of Examinee:	Amanda Farris
Name of Evaluator:	Dr. Erin McDonough
Examinee's Age:	8 years 3 month(s)

2. ENTER DATES/GRADE

*Date of Evaluation:	1/4/2016	Use mm/dd/yyyy
*Date of Birth:	10/1/2007	If an error occurs, try yyyy/mm/dd.
*Examinee's Grade:	2	PK,K,1-12,12+

User Mode ○ Beginner ○ Intermediate ● Advanced

3. CREATE NEW DATA RECORD

Create New Record

Check box if examinee is current or former ELL ☐

DATA RECORD IS ACTIVE

OPEN SAVED DATA RECORD

Amanda Farris ▼

Save Current Record

To OPEN and activate a saved record from the database, select it from the dropdown menu on the right. Data records are listed in alphabetical order by first name. Once selected, all data associated with the record will be populated in the appropriate locations. Click the Index button at the upper right corner of this tab to begin reviewing and updating the saved data. The program can store and retrieve data for up to 500 cases.

To SAVE or update the current data record, click the blue "Save Current Record" button and continue working. Frequent saves are recommended.

Export Current Database

Import Saved Database

To EXPORT and save the current database (for importation to a newer version of X-BASS), click the "Export Current Database" button. This action creates a file that can be used by updated versions of X-BASS to automatically transfer and merge the current database for use with the new version.

To IMPORT a saved database (for use in a newer version of X-BASS), click the "Import Saved Database" button. Note that you must have already exported the previous database using the older version of X-BASS. Once the older database has been properly saved, use this button to import it.

Clear Data/Reset Program

To CLEAR all scores, selections, and tab data in current use from the program, click the "Clear Data/Reset Program" button. CAUTION: This action is not reversible, removes data in current use, and resets the program to default values. Unsaved data and information will be permanently erased.

Delete Record

To DELETE a saved data record, select the record from the dropdown menu and click the "Delete Record" button. CAUTION: Make sure this is what you want to do because this action is not reversible.

Figure 7.3 Start and Data Record Management Tab in X-BASS

Cross-Battery Assessment Software System (X-BASS® v2.0)

Test Index and Main Navigation

Conceptualization by D.P. Flanagan, S.O. Ortiz, V.C. Alfonso; Programming by S.O. Ortiz and A.M. Dynda
Copyright © 2017 Samuel O. Ortiz, Dawn P. Flanagan & Vincent C. Alfonso. All Rights Reserved

The demographic information below will be automatically carried over to all other tabs.

Name of Examinee:	Amanda Farris	Date of Evaluation:	1/4/2016
Name of Evaluator:	Dr. Erin McDonough	Date of Birth:	10/1/2007
Examinee's Age:	8 years 3 month(s)	Examinee's Grade:	2

Click on any of the buttons below to navigate directly to any of the tabs to begin score entry, analyze data, or examine graphs.

COGNITIVE & LANGUAGE BATTERIES

WISC-V	WJ IV COG	CAS2
WAIS-IV	WJ IV OL	KABC-II
WPPSI-IV	DAS-II	SB5

ACADEMIC BATTERIES

| WJ IV ACH |
| WIAT-III |
| KTEA-3 |

ANALYSES

| XBA Analyzer |
| PSW Analyzer |
| C-LIM Analyzer |

TEST SCORE SUMMARY GRAPHS

WISC-V Graph	WJ IV COG Graph	CAS2 Graph
WIAT-III Graph	WJ IV ACH Graph	KABC-II Graph
WAIS-IV Graph	WJ IV OL Graph	KTEA-3 Graph
WPPSI-IV Graph	DAS-II Graph	SB5 Graph

SCORE MANAGEMENT

| Data Organizer |
| Data Entry – Other |
| S&W Indicator |
| PSW-A Data Summary |

DATA GRAPHS

| Integrated Graph |
| XBA Analyzer Graph |
| Data Organizer Graph |
| C-LIM Summary |

REFERENCE & INFORMATION

XBA-CHC Test List	C-LTC Reference	Selecting PSW-A Scores
C-LIM Notes	C-LIM Interpretation	PSW-A Notes
C-LIM Statements	About the Authors	Welcome

INDEX

| g-Value |
| C-LIM Index |
| Help |

REPORTS

| WISC-V Report |

Figure 7.4 Test Index and Main Navigation Tab in X-BASS

461

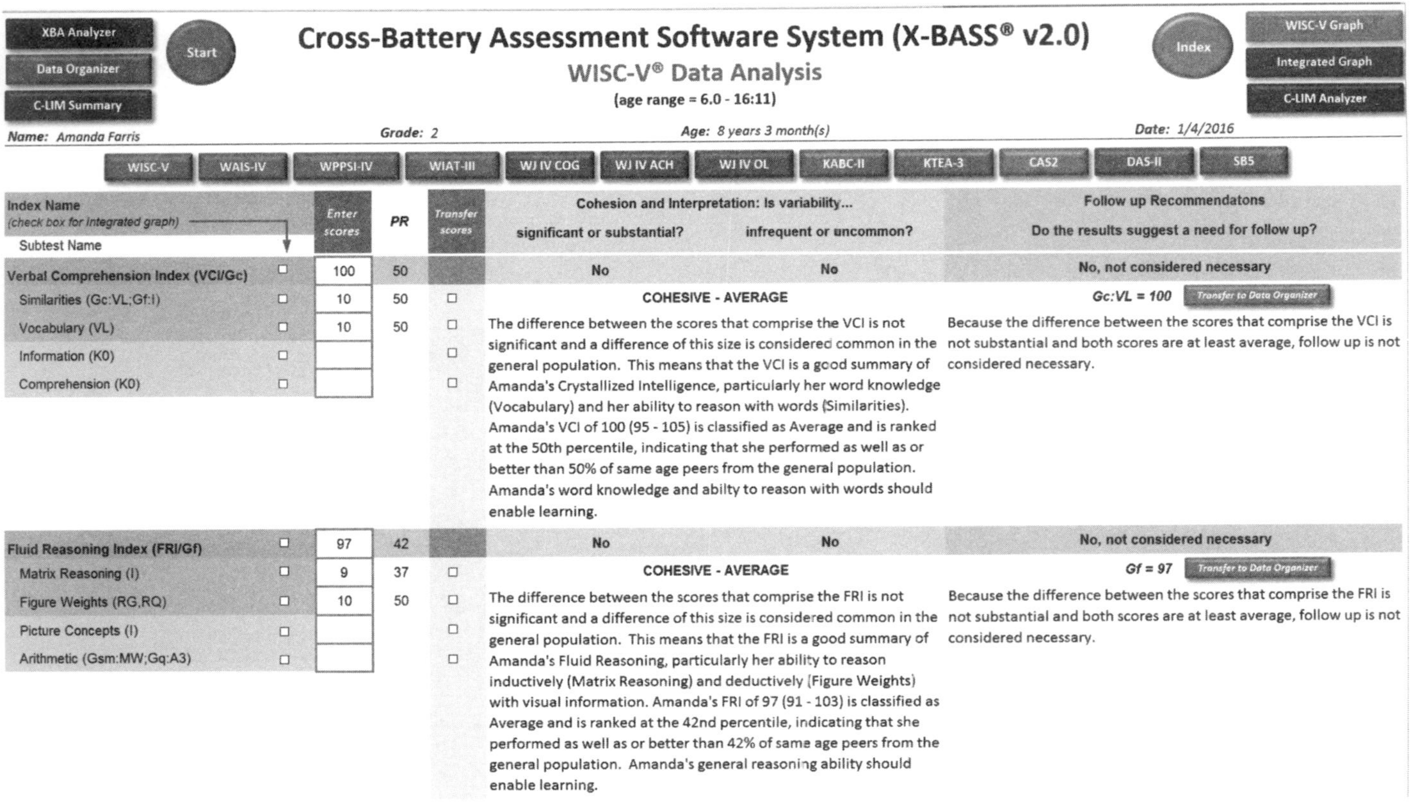

Cross-Battery Assessment Software System (X-BASS® v2.0)

WISC-V® Data Analysis

(age range = 6.0 - 16:11)

Start · Index

XBA Analyzer · Data Organizer · C-LIM Summary

WISC-V Graph · Integrated Graph · C-LIM Analyzer

WISC-V · WAIS-IV · WPPSI-IV · WIAT-III · WJ IV COG · WJ IV ACH · WJ IV OL · KABC-II · CAS2 · KTEA-3 · DAS-II · SB5

Name: Amanda Farris   **Grade:** 2   **Age:** 8 years 3 month(s)   **Date:** 1/4/2016

Index Name (check box for integrated graph) Subtest Name	Enter scores	PR	Transfer scores	Cohesion and Interpretation: Is variability...

Cohesion and Interpretation: Is variability...
significant or substantial?   infrequent or uncommon?   Do the results suggest a need for follow up?

Follow up Recommendations

Verbal Comprehension Index (VCI/Gc)				No	No	No, not considered necessary
Similarities (Gc:VL;Gf:I)	100	50	☐			
Vocabulary (VL)	10	50	☐			
Information (K0)	10	50	☐			
Comprehension (K0)			☐			

COHESIVE - AVERAGE   Gc:VL = 100   *Transfer to Data Organizer*

The difference between the scores that comprise the VCI is not significant and a difference of this size is considered common in the general population. This means that the VCI is a good summary of Amanda's Crystallized Intelligence, particularly her word knowledge (Vocabulary) and her ability to reason with words (Similarities). Amanda's VCI of 100 (95 - 105) is classified as Average and is ranked at the 50th percentile, indicating that she performed as well as or better than 50% of same age peers from the general population. Amanda's word knowledge and ability to reason with words should enable learning.

Because the difference between the scores that comprise the VCI is not substantial and both scores are at least average, follow up is not considered necessary.

Fluid Reasoning Index (FRI/Gf)	97	42	☐	No	No	No, not considered necessary
Matrix Reasoning (I)	9	37	☐			
Figure Weights (RG;RQ)	10	50	☐			
Picture Concepts (I)			☐			
Arithmetic (Gsm:MW;Gq:A3)			☐			

COHESIVE - AVERAGE   Gf = 97   *Transfer to Data Organizer*

The difference between the scores that comprise the FRI is not significant and a difference of this size is considered common in the general population. This means that the FRI is a good summary of Amanda's Fluid Reasoning, particularly her ability to reason inductively (Matrix Reasoning) and deductively (Figure Weights) with visual information. Amanda's FRI of 97 (91 - 103) is classified as Average and is ranked at the 42nd percentile, indicating that she performed as well as or better than 42% of same age peers from the general population. Amanda's general reasoning ability should enable learning.

Because the difference between the scores that comprise the FRI is not substantial and both scores are at least average, follow up is not considered necessary.

Figure 7.5 WISC-V Data Analysis and Interpretation Tab in X-BASS (Top Portion of tab)

Visual Spatial Index (VSI/Gv)	☐	81	10	☐	No	No	No, not considered necessary
Block Design* (Vz)	☐	6	9	☐			
Visual Puzzles (Vz)	☐	7	16	☐ ☐			Gv:Vz = 81 Transfer to Data Organizer

*Additional process scaled scores can be generated for Block Design (see WISC-V Administration and Scoring Manual Supplement). These subtest processes are available in the XBA Analyzer Gv drop down menu.

COHESIVE - HIGH PRIORITY CONCERN

The difference between the scores that comprise the VSI is not significant and a difference of this size is considered common in the general population. This means that the VSI is a good summary of Amanda's Visual Processing, particularly her ability to perceive complex patterns and mentally simulate how they might look when transformed in some way (e.g., rotated). Amanda's VSI of 81 (76 - 89) is classified as Below Average and is ranked at the 10th percentile, indicating that she performed as well as or better than 10% of same age peers from the general population. Amanda's difficulty with analyzing and synthesizing visual information is not only a personal weakness for her, but it is also a weakness relative to her same age peers. The difference between her VSI and the average of all of her primary index scores is so large that it is not commonly found in the general population (i.e., < 10%). Taken together, these results suggest that Amanda's visual processing difficulty may contribute to learning difficulties and is, therefore, a high priority concern. Minimizing the effects of Amanda's visual processing difficulties on learning should play an essential role in intervention planning.

Because the difference between the scores that comprise the VSI is not substantial, indicating similar subtest performances, follow up is not considered necessary.

Figure 7.5 (continued)

button corresponding to each index. This button is located in the far right column of the WISC-V Data Analysis tab. For example, Figure 7.5 shows that the WISC-V VCI, FRI, and VSI are all cohesive, meaning that each provides a good summary of the theoretically related abilities it was intended to represent. In addition, follow up was not considered necessary for any of these Index Scores. If the evaluator is confident that these indexes adequately represent the individual's performance in these cognitive domains (i.e., Gc: VL [Lexical Knowledge] for VCI; Gf [Fluid Reasoning] for FRI and Gv:Vz [Visualization] for VSI), then she or he may transfer the estimates of these abilities to the Data Organizer tab. In the case of Amanda, all of her Index Scores were cohesive and did not require follow up. Therefore, in addition to the VCI, FRI, and VSI, the WMI (Gsm), PSI (Gs), and SRI (Glr) were transferred to the Data Organizer tab.

Note that the Data Organizer tab "holds" all the best estimates of the cognitive, academic, and neuropsychological constructs that were evaluated and transferred there until the user is ready to move forward with analysis of the data (see Step 2). When follow up is considered necessary in any given domain, more than one estimate of performance in that domain may be transferred to the Data Organizer tab. For example, in the area of Glr, the individual may have performed in the Average range on tests of Associative Memory (MA; Symbol Translation Index [STI]) and in the Well Below Average range on tests of Naming Facility (NA; Naming Speed Index [NSI]). In this case, two estimates of Glr (STI and NSI) may be transferred to the Data Organizer tab in lieu of the SRI to represent best the individual's range of performance in the area of Glr.

1.2   *CTOPP-2 Data:* Because the WISC-V measures six of the required seven areas necessary to conduct a PSW analysis following the DD/C model, selected subtests of the CTOPP-2 were administered to measure the seventh area (i.e., Ga). Given the substantial variation in Amanda's performance on the CTOPP-2 (i.e., 2 and 2/3 standard deviation difference between her highest and lowest scores), these data were analyzed via the XBA Analyzer tab (see Figure 7.6). From the XBA Analyzer tab, two auditory processing scores were transferred to the Data Organizer tab via the button labeled "Transfer XBA Comp(s) to Data Organizer," one that represents Phonetic Coding: Analysis (SS = 85) and one that represents Phonetic Coding: Synthesis (SS = 49). For an explanation of how the CTOPP-2 data were analyzed, see Chapter 4 and the case study in Chapter 8.

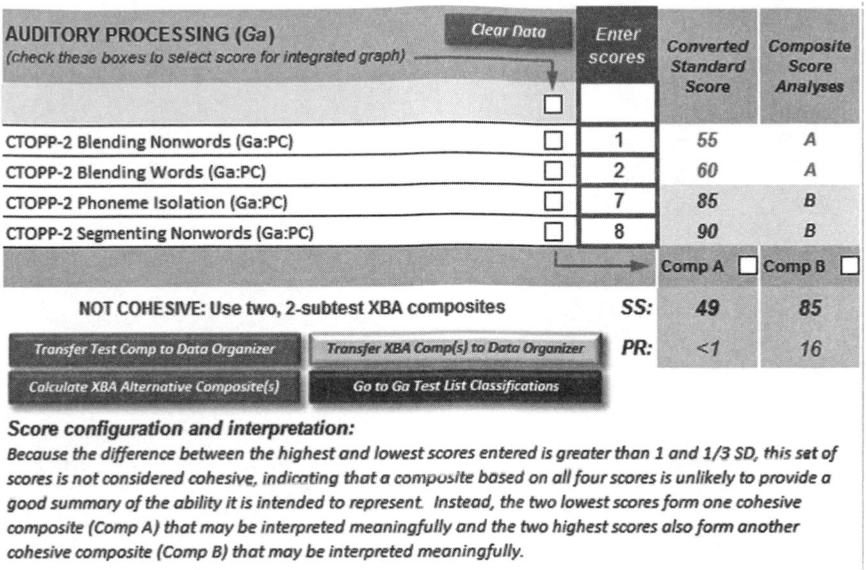

Figure 7.6 Analysis of Selected Subtests From the CTOPP-2 on the XBA Analyzer Tab of X-BASS

1.3 *WIAT-III Data:* Click on the "WIAT-III" button located at the top of any of the tabs already mentioned. All WIAT-III data may be entered on the "WIAT-III Data Analysis" tab. Once data are entered, the program provides information regarding whether the composites are cohesive and whether or not follow up assessment is considered necessary. Figure 7.7 shows the WIAT-III Data Analysis tab with Amanda's data. Of note, there are composites on all achievement batteries that summarize different aspects of a broad domain, such as reading. For example, as may be seen in Figure 7.7, the WIAT-III Total Reading composite includes tests of basic reading skills (BRS), reading comprehension (RC), and reading fluency (RF). While summary scores are useful in some instances and are often reported in psychoeducational evaluations, in X-BASS all achievement tests are classified according to the eight IDEIA-specific areas of SLD. Therefore, achievement scores can only be transferred to the Data Organizer tab when they align with one of the eight areas. This is why there is no button in the far right column of Figure 7.7 for the Total Reading score on the WIAT-III that would allow it to be transferred to the Data Organizer tab. However, because the WIAT-III Basic Reading Composite is comprised of two subtests that were

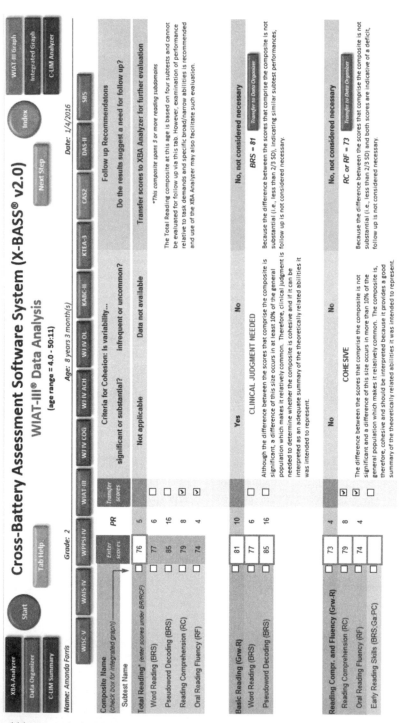

Figure 7.7 WIAT-III Data Analysis Tab in X-BASS

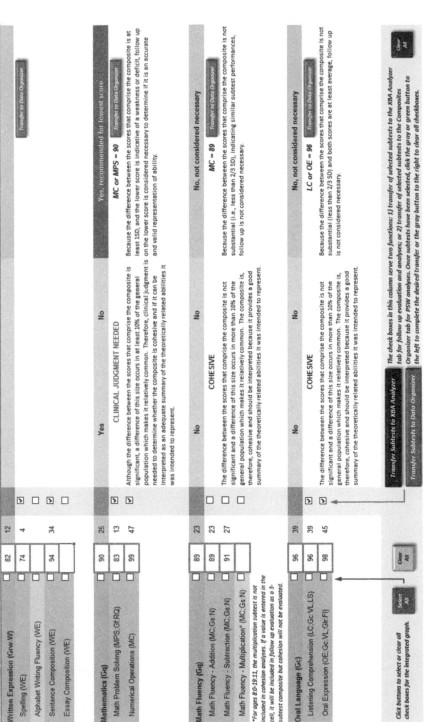

Figure 7.7 (continued)

classified as BRS, the program allows the composite to be transferred to the Data Organizer tab (via the button in the far right column next to "BRS = 81" in Figure 7.7).

Note that the WIAT-III Reading Comprehension and Fluency composite is made up of a test of RC and a test of RF. Although this composite may be transferred to the Data Organizer tab, when the "Transfer to Data Organizer" button is pressed, a pop-up message appears asking the evaluator whether she or he wants to transfer the composite to the RC or RF section of the Data Organizer tab. If the evaluator prefers to transfer each subtest separately, then she or he should click on the box in the "Transfer Scores" column to the right of the subtest scores and then scroll to the bottom of the tab and click on the "Transfer Subtests to Data Organizer" button (seen at the bottom of Figure 7.7). When the evaluator clicks on this button, the Reading Comprehension subtest score appears in the RC section of the Data Organizer tab and the Oral Reading Fluency subtest score appears in the RF section of this tab. Figure 7.7 also shows that the subtests that make up the Mathematics and Oral Language composites were selected for transfer to the Data Organizer tab, rather than the composites themselves, for the same reason—that is, these composites are each made up of subtests that measure two different IDEIA-specific SLD areas.

Notice that the Written Expression (WE) composite in Figure 7.7 consists of subtests that have all been classified as the IDEIA-specific SLD area of written expression. As such, a cohesive WE composite may be transferred to the Data Organizer tab. In the case of Amanda, however, the WE composite was not cohesive and therefore the boxes next to the subtest scores were selected for independent transfer to the Data Organizer tab.

DON'T FORGET

It is assumed prior to transferring the individual subtest scores to the Data Organizer tab that these scores are good representations of the individual's actual ability in the areas represented by the scores. In other words, other data sources should be available that corroborate these scores. If other data are not available, follow up assessment may be warranted to investigate further score performances that suggest a weakness or deficit for the individual.

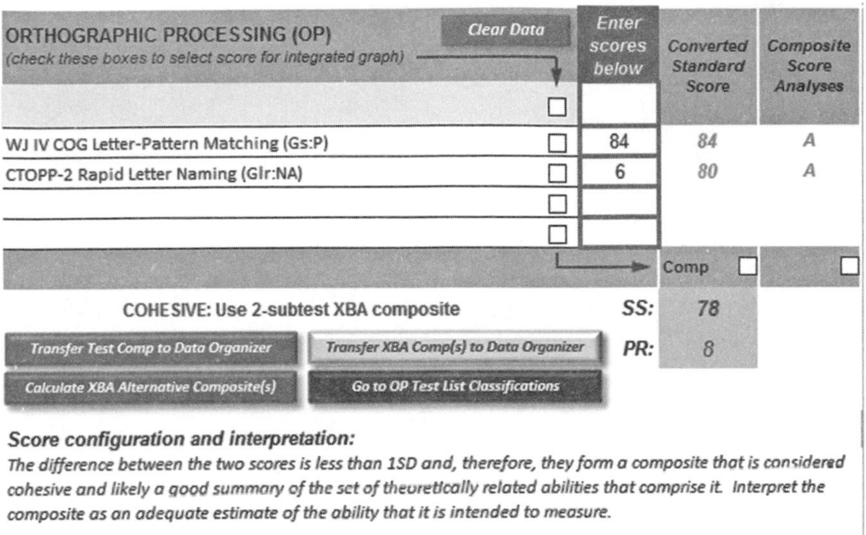

ORTHOGRAPHIC PROCESSING (OP) (check these boxes to select score for integrated graph)	Clear Data		Enter scores below	Converted Standard Score	Composite Score Analyses
		☐			
WJ IV COG Letter-Pattern Matching (Gs:P)		☐	84	84	A
CTOPP-2 Rapid Letter Naming (Glr:NA)		☐	6	80	A
		☐			
		☐			
			Comp ☐		☐

COHESIVE: Use 2-subtest XBA composite   **SS:** 78

Transfer Test Comp to Data Organizer	Transfer XBA Comp(s) to Data Organizer
Calculate XBA Alternative Composite(s)	Go to OP Test List Classifications

PR: 8

Score configuration and interpretation:
The difference between the two scores is less than 1SD and, therefore, they form a composite that is considered cohesive and likely a good summary of the set of theuretically related abilities that comprise it. Interpret the composite as an adequate estimate of the ability that it is intended to measure.

Figure 7.8 Analysis of Selected Subtests on the XBA Analyzer Tab of X-BASS

1.4   *Cross-Battery (XBA) Data:* Amanda's evaluator administered a test from the WJ IV and an additional test from the CTOPP-2 to follow up on her hypothesis that Amanda's reading difficulties may be related in part to an orthographic processing weakness or deficit. These data were entered into the "Orthographic Processing (OP)" section of the XBA Analyzer tab (see Figure 7.8). The OP XBA composite of 78 was transferred to the Data Organizer tab by clicking on the "Transfer XBA Comp(s) to Data Organizer" button.

Step 2. Select Scores From the Data Organizer Tab for Inclusion in the PSW Analysis

In Step 1, the best estimates of cognitive abilities and processes, academic achievement, and neuropsychological processes were transferred to the Data Organizer tab. Figure 7.9 shows the Data Organizer tab with all of Amanda's data that were transferred from the WISC-V, WIAT-III, and XBA Analyzer tabs. Specifically, test composites (such as the WISC-V indexes) appear in the top row of each CHC domain on this tab and XBA composites, if calculated, appear in the bottom portion of each domain.

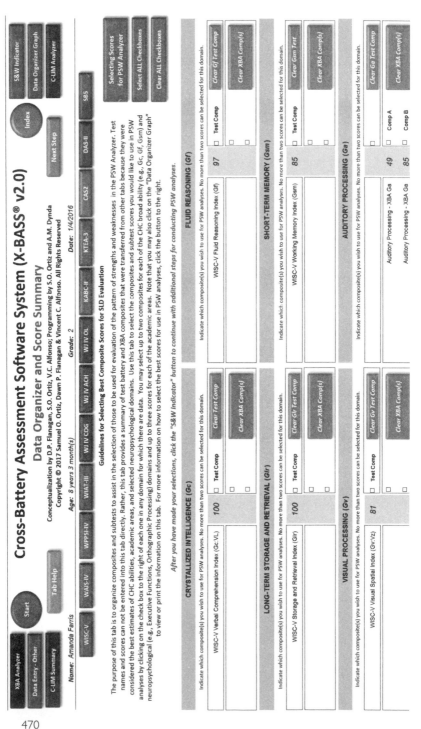

Figure 7.9 XBA Score Summary and Data Organizer Tab in X-BASS

PROCESSING SPEED (Gs)

Indicate which composite(s) you wish to use for PSW analyses. No more than two scores can be selected for this domain.

			Test Comp	Clear Gs Test Comp
WISC-V Processing Speed Index (Gs)	92		☐	Clear XBA Comp(s)
			☐	
			☐	

Grw-R: BASIC READING SKILLS (BRS)

Indicate which composite or subtests you wish to use for PSW analyses. All three scores may be selected for this domain.

		Test Comp	Clear Score 1
WIAT-III Basic Reading Skills (BRS)	81	☐	Clear Score 2
		☐ Subtest	Clear Score 3
		☐	

Grw-R: READING FLUENCY (RF)

Indicate which composite or subtests you wish to use for PSW analyses. All three scores may be selected for this domain.

		Subtest	Clear Score 1
WIAT-III Oral Reading Fluency (RF;Grw-R:RS)	74	☐	Clear Score 2
		☐	Clear Score 3
		☐	

Gq: MATH CALCULATION (MC)

Indicate which composite or subtests you wish to use for PSW analyses. All three scores may be selected for this domain.

		Test Comp	Clear Score 1
WIAT-III Math Fluency (MC)	89	☐	Clear Score 2
WIAT-III Numerical Operations (MC;Gq:A3)	99	☐ Subtest	Clear Score 3
		☐	

ORAL EXPRESSION (OE)

Indicate which composite or subtests you wish to use for PSW analyses. All three scores may be selected for this domain.

		Subtest	Clear Score 1
WIAT-III Oral Expression (OE;Gc:VL,Glr:FI)	98	☐	Clear Score 2
		☐	Clear Score 3
		☐	

DOMAIN SPECIFIC KNOWLEDGE (Gkn)

Indicate which composite(s) you wish to use for PSW analyses. No more than two scores can be selected for this domain.

		Clear Gkn Test
	☐	Clear XBA Comp(s)
	☐	
	☐	

Grw-R: READING COMPREHENSION (RC)

Indicate which composite or subtests you wish to use for PSW analyses. All three scores may be selected for this domain.

		Subtest	Clear Score 1
WIAT-III Reading Comprehension (RC;Grw-R:RC)	79	☐	Clear Score 2
		☐	Clear Score 3
		☐	

Grw-W: WRITTEN EXPRESSION (WE)

Indicate which composite or subtests you wish to use for PSW analyses. All three scores may be selected for this domain.

		Subtest	Clear Score 1
WIAT-III Spelling (WE;Grw-W:SG)	74	☐	Clear Score 2
WIAT-III Sentence Composition (WE;Grw-W:EU,WA)	94	☐ Subtest	Clear Score 3
		☐	

Gq: MATH PROBLEM SOLVING (MPS)

Indicate which composite or subtests you wish to use for PSW analyses. All three scores may be selected for this domain.

		Subtest	Clear Score 1
WIAT-III Math Problem Solving (MPS;Gf:RQ)	83	☐	Clear Score 2
		☐	Clear Score 3
		☐	

LISTENING COMPREHENSION (LC)

Indicate which composite or subtests you wish to use for PSW analyses. All three scores may be selected for this domain.

		Subtest	Clear Score 1
WIAT-III Listening Comprehension (LC;Gc:VL,LS)	96	☐	Clear Score 2
		☐	Clear Score 3
		☐	

Figure 7.9 (continued)

471

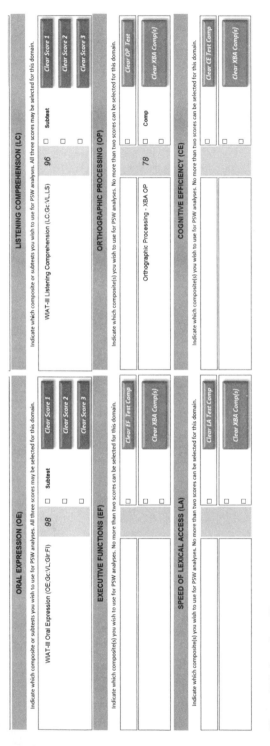

Figure 7.9 (continued)

DON'T FORGET

A composite is listed on the Data Organizer tab as an "XBA" composite if it was generated by the XBA Analyzer tab in either of the two following conditions: (1) based on test scores that represent similar aspects of the same construct (e.g., two or more tests of Gf) that come from different batteries and therefore do not share a norm group; or (2) based on test scores that represent similar aspects of the same construct that come from the same battery (i.e., share a common norm group), but a composite is not available for that particular combination of scores.

Step 2 requires that the evaluator select the scores from the Data Organizer tab that will be included in the PSW analysis by clicking the small box to the right of each score. Alternatively, the evaluator may click on the "Select ALL Checkboxes" button on this tab. Once selected, a check mark appears automatically in each small box and the score itself is highlighted (see Figure 7.10). In the overwhelming majority of cases, all scores that were transferred to the Data Organizer tab are selected for inclusion in the PSW analysis. There may be times, however, when three scores are transferred to one or more of the CHC cognitive domains. Only two scores per CHC cognitive domain may be selected for inclusion in the PSW analysis. Up to three scores may be transferred to any of the IDEIA-specific SLD areas, and up to three scores in each SLD area may be selected for inclusion in the PSW analysis. Figure 7.10 shows that all cognitive scores that were transferred from the WISC-V tab to the Data Organizer tab were selected for inclusion in the PSW analysis. Although not shown in Figure 7.10, the estimate of Gs (i.e., the PSI) was also selected.

When a score is selected on the Data Organizer tab, it is automatically transferred to the "Strengths and Weaknesses" Indicator tab. After selecting all scores for inclusion in the PSW analysis, click on the top button in the far right corner of the Data Organizer tab labeled "S&W Indicator."

Step 3. Indicate Whether the Scores on the Strengths and Weaknesses Indicator Tab Represent a Strength or Weakness for the Individual

An individual's pattern of strengths and weaknesses ought to encompass the totality of the data gathered to the extent possible. The DD/C model encourages this perspective. Therefore, rather than simply selecting a single "strength" and a single "weakness" among many scores (as some PSW models require) the DD/C model requires that all scores representing cognitive, academic, and neuropsychological constructs be categorized by the evaluator as one or the other (as discussed earlier in this chapter). The general guidelines

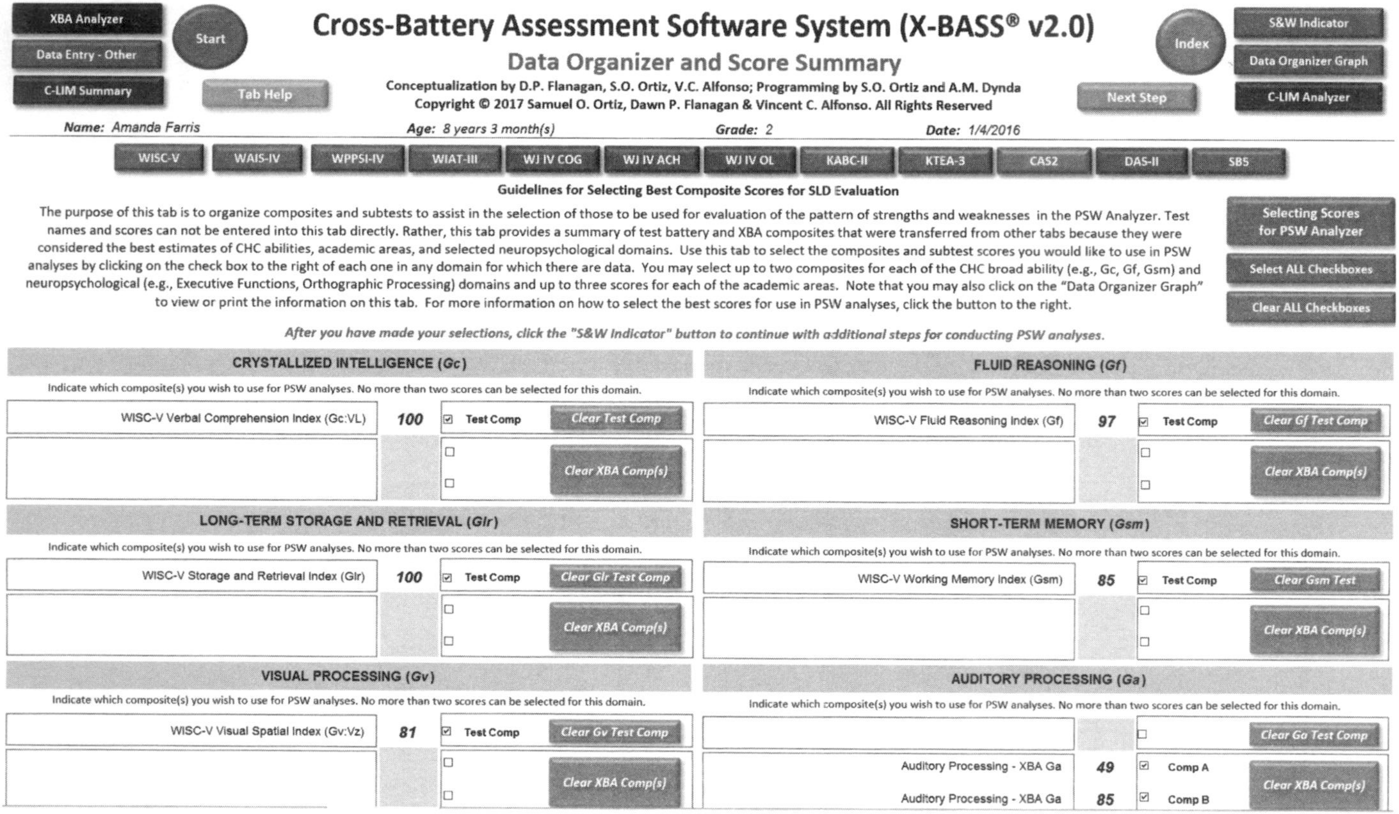

Figure 7.10 Top Portion of Data Organizer Tab in X-BASS Showing That Scores Have Been Selected for Inclusion in PSW Analysis

for categorizing a cognitive score as either a strength or a weakness are as follows:

1. If the standard score representing a cognitive domain is *around* 90 or higher, and in the evaluator's clinical judgment the individual's cognitive performance in this domain does not appear to impact learning or academic achievement adversely, then the score may be categorized as a strength (*for the purpose of the PSW analysis*). In cases where the standard score is greater than 90, and perhaps much higher than 90, it is likely that the cognitive domain represented by this score *facilitates* learning and academic performance and, therefore, should be categorized as a strength.

2. If the standard score representing a cognitive domain is *less than* 90, and in the evaluator's clinical judgment the individual's cognitive performance in this domain appears to impact learning or academic achievement adversely, then the score may be categorized as a weakness. In cases where the standard score is less than 85, it is likely that the cognitive domain represented by this score *inhibits* learning and academic performance and, therefore, should be categorized as a weakness.

3. Because some cognitive domains with corresponding scores in the upper 80s and low 90s may be among the individual's highest scores, then even scores in the upper 80s may be judged by the evaluator to be "strengths" for the individual. Likewise, because some cognitive domains with corresponding scores in the upper 90s and lower 100s may be among the individual's lowest scores, then even scores in these ranges may be judged by the evaluator to be "weaknesses" for the individual. There is no "cut point" in X-BASS on this tab that designates a score as a strength or weakness. Due to a multiplicity of factors that affect an individual's score performances, clinical judgement it not only encouraged when making determinations about strengths and weaknesses, it is necessary.

Categorizing all score performances as either strengths or weaknesses, taking into consideration where the scores fall relative to most people, and where the scores fall relative to the individual's own capabilities is important in understanding whether or not the individual meets criteria for SLD. Nevertheless, categorizing an individual's scores as either strengths or weaknesses is only one of many important considerations that assist in making an SLD determination.

Figure 7.11 shows Amanda's strengths and weaknesses in cognitive, achievement, and neuropsychological processing domains as indicated by her evaluator.

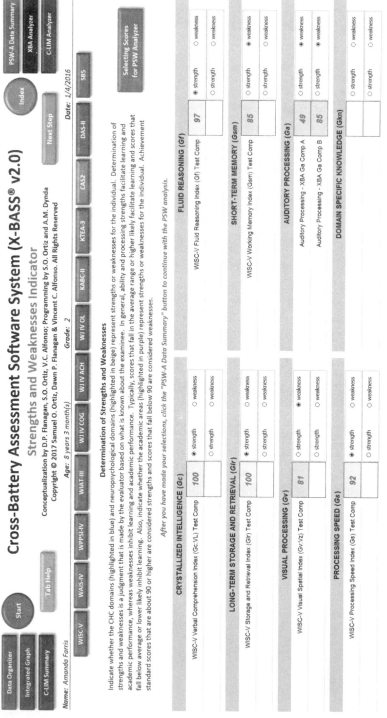

Figure 7.11 Strengths and Weaknesses Indicator Tab of X-BASS

Grw-R: BASIC READING SKILLS (BRS)

	Score		
WIAT-III Basic Reading Skills (BRS) Test Comp	81	○ strength	● weakness
		○ strength	○ weakness
		○ strength	○ weakness

Grw-R: READING FLUENCY (RF)

	Score		
WIAT-III Oral Reading Fluency (RF:Grw-R:RS) Subtest	74	○ strength	● weakness
		○ strength	○ weakness
		○ strength	○ weakness

Gq: MATH CALCULATION (MC)

	Score		
WIAT-III Math Fluency (MC) Test Comp	89	● strength	○ weakness
WIAT-III Numerical Operations (MC:Gq:A3) Subtest	99	● strength	○ weakness
		○ strength	○ weakness

ORAL EXPRESSION (OE)

	Score		
WIAT-III Oral Expression (OE:Gc:VL,Glr:Fl) Subtest	98	● strength	○ weakness
		○ strength	○ weakness
		○ strength	○ weakness

EXECUTIVE FUNCTIONS (EF)

		○ strength	○ weakness
		○ strength	○ weakness

SPEED OF LEXICAL ACCESS (LA)

		○ strength	○ weakness
		○ strength	○ weakness

Grw-R: READING COMPREHENSION (RC)

	Score		
WIAT-III Reading Comprehension (RC:Grw-R:RC) Subtest	79	○ strength	● weakness
		○ strength	○ weakness
		○ strength	○ weakness

Grw-W: WRITTEN EXPRESSION (WE)

	Score		
WIAT-III Written Expression (WE) Test Comp	82	○ strength	● weakness
WIAT-III Spelling (WE:Grw-W:SG) Subtest	74	○ strength	● weakness
WIAT-III Sentence Composition (WE:Grw-W:EU,WA) Subtest	94	● strength	○ weakness

Gq: MATH PROBLEM SOLVING (MPS)

	Score		
WIAT-III Math Problem Solving (MPS:Gf:RQ) Subtest	83	○ strength	● weakness
		○ strength	○ weakness
		○ strength	○ weakness

LISTENING COMPREHENSION (LC)

	Score		
WIAT-III Listening Comprehension (LC:Gc:VL,LS) Subtest	96	● strength	○ weakness
		○ strength	○ weakness
		○ strength	○ weakness

ORTHOGRAPHIC PROCESSING (OP)

	Score		
Orthographic Processing - XBA OP Comp	78	○ strength	● weakness
		○ strength	○ weakness

COGNITIVE EFFICIENCY (CE)

		○ strength	○ weakness
		○ strength	○ weakness

Figure 7.11 (continued)

As may be seen in Figure 7.11, Amanda's strengths and weaknesses appear to follow the "around 90" criterion pretty closely, as most scores were at least a few points above or below 90 and corroborating data sources were available to support the evaluator's designations. One exception was Amanda's WIAT-III Math Fluency score of 89. If X-BASS was programmed to designate every score below 90 as a "weakness," then this score would have showed up in Figure 7.11 as a weakness. Because X-BASS was designed deliberately to allow for clinical judgment, Amanda's Math Fluency score of 89 was considered a strength. The evaluator categorized Math Fluency as a strength because math is a personal strength for Amanda, the teacher reported math to be a relative strength for Amanda and indicated that she was performing as well as most students in the class in the area of mathematics, and Amanda reported that she likes math and is confident in her math skills. In light of this information coupled with her other solid average math performances and her average processing speed, Amanda's evaluator judged Math Fluency to be a strength, indicating that her ability in this area is not likely to interfere with the continued development of her math skills.

After designating all scores as either strengths or weakness, X-BASS conducts a PSW analysis via an operationalization of the criteria set forth in the DD/C definition of SLD. The PSW output generated by X-BASS and guidance on how the user can select cognitive and academic areas of strength and weakness for the PSW analysis are presented next. To review a summary of the data that provide the input for the PSW analysis, click on the "PSW-A Data Summary" button at the top right of the Strengths and Weaknesses Indicator tab.

PSW-A DATA SUMMARY

The PSW-A Data Summary tab displays a few important terms, which were defined in Rapid References 7.8 and 7.9 earlier. In the majority of cases, no additional information needs to be added to this tab, and no data need to be changed on this tab. The top portion of this tab (shown in Figure 7.12) summarized the CHC ability domains that were identified by the evaluator as strengths and weaknesses. In X-BASS, areas of strength are printed and highlighted in green and areas of weakness are printed and highlighted in red. Also shown at the top of this tab are three estimates: (1) the *g*-value; (2) the Facilitating Cognitive Composite or FCC; and (3) the Inhibiting Cognitive Composite or ICC.

Figure 7.12 shows that Amanda's *g*-value is .72, which is high. A high *g*-value (i.e., $\geq$ .60) indicates that despite Amanda's cognitive areas of weakness (i.e., those printed in red and labeled with a W on this tab), it is very likely that her overall cognitive ability is at least average. When the *g*-value is high, X-BASS

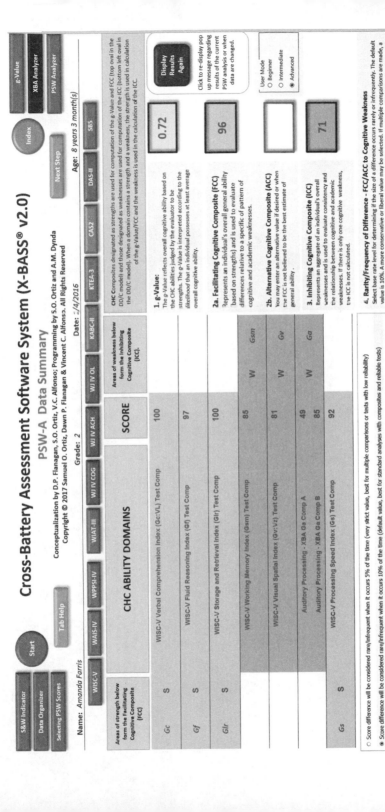

Figure 7.12 The PSW-A Data Summary Tab of X-BASS

479

		WIAT-III Subtest/Composite	Score		
		WIAT-III Basic Reading Skills (BRS) Test Comp	81	W	Grw-R BRS
		WIAT-III Reading Comprehension (RC;Grw-R:RC) Subtest	79	W	Grw-R RC
		WIAT-III Oral Reading Fluency (RF;Grw-R:RS) Subtest	74	W	Grw-W RF
Grw-W WE	S	WIAT-III Written Expression (WE) Test Comp	82	W	Grw-W WE
		WIAT-III Spelling (WE;Grw-W:SG) Subtest	74	W	Grw-W WE
		WIAT-III Sentence Composition (WE;Grw-W:EU,WA) Subtest	94		
Gq MC	S	WIAT-III Math Fluency (MC) Test Comp	89		
		WIAT-III Numerical Operations (MC;Gq:A3) Subtest	99		
		WIAT-III Math Problem Solving (MPS;Gf:RQ) Subtest	83	W	Gq MPS
OE	S	WIAT-III Oral Expression (OE;Gc:VL;Glr:FI) Subtest	98		
LC	S	WIAT-III Listening Comprehension (LC;Gc:VL,LS) Subtest	96		

○ Score difference will be considered rare/infrequent when it occurs 5% of the time (very strict value, best for multiple comparisons or tests with low reliability)

○ Score difference will be considered rare/infrequent when it occurs 10% of the time (default value, best for standard analyzes with composites and reliable tests)

● Score difference will be considered rare/infrequent when it occurs 15% of the time (very liberal value, increases false positive rate–not recommended)

5. Rarity/Frequency of Difference - FCC/ACC to Academic Weakness
Select base rate level for determining whether the size of a difference occurs rarely or infrequently. The default value is 10%. A more conservative or liberal value may be selected. If multiple comparisons are made, a stricter value may be appropriate.

Figure 7.12 (continued)

automatically calculates an FCC. Amanda's FCC is 96, indicating that, without the attenuating effects of her cognitive weaknesses, her overall intellectual capacity is in the Average range. Another way of conceptualizing the FCC is that it provides an indication that Amanda has at least average ability to think and reason—a defining characteristic of the PSW component in the DD/C model. Amanda's FCC suggests that she has a number of cognitive abilities and processes that ought to facilitate learning and academic performance. (For information on how the FCC was calculated, go to the "Index" tab and click on "PSW-A Notes" in the "References and Information" section.)

DON'T FORGET

The FCC is akin to a total test score from a cognitive or intelligence battery, or a proxy for psychometric g, because it is an aggregate of a sufficient breadth of cognitive abilities that are typically part of global test scores or alternative estimates of global ability, such as the GAI on the WISC-V and the Gf-Gc composite on the WJ IV. However, it is different from alternative estimates of global ability on current batteries because it always consists of only the individual's cognitive strengths and it will be calculated only when the individual has a sufficient breadth of cognitive strengths in the "right" areas (i.e., those most closely related to academic success at the individual's grade level; see the PSW-A Notes tab for more information).

Also listed in the top portion of the PSW-A Data Summary tab in Figure 7.12 is Amanda's ICC of 71, which is in the Well Below Average range. The ICC is an aggregate of Amanda's cognitive ability and processing weaknesses and suggests that such weaknesses will likely inhibit learning and academic achievement unless they are accommodated or compensated for in some way.

Notice that Figure 7.12 shows that the PSW-A Data Summary tab includes a space next to the Alternative Cognitive Composite or ACC. In some instances, the user may "override" the FCC with another composite. The ACC refers to any cognitive composite derived from a cognitive or intelligence battery that is considered to be a good estimate of overall ability and a better estimate than the FCC. Typically, if either the g-value or FCC is reported in yellow there exists a question regarding whether or not the individual is of at least generally average overall cognitive ability. In this situation, clinical judgment is necessary to make that determination. If an alternative composite is considered a better estimate of overall ability as compared to the FCC, then it may be entered on this tab in the space provided.

The PSW analysis calculates the difference between Amanda's ICC, or any one of the scores that make it up, and a score that was predicted by the FCC using a regression equation (as described below). The difference is considered rare if it occurs in about 10% of the population or less, which is the default value set in X-BASS. Figure 7.12 shows that this option is selected and highlighted automatically. The evaluator may change the default value a priori (i.e., prior to advancing to the results of the PSW analysis) under certain circumstances. However, 10% is the preferred value for examining score differences for the purpose of SLD identification (e.g., Evans, 1990; Reynolds, 1985; Wright, 2002) and, therefore, has not been changed for Amanda's analysis.

The next section of the PSW-A Data Summary tab in Figure 7.12 shows the Achievement or IDEIA-specific SLD areas that were categorized by the evaluator as strengths and weaknesses for Amanda. Note that the PSW analysis calculates the difference between Amanda's academic weaknesses and a score that was predicted by the FCC using a regression equation (as described below). In this comparison, as in the actual and predicted score comparison for a cognitive area of weakness, the difference is considered rare if it occurs in about 10% of the population or less. Figure 7.12 shows that the default value was changed from 10% to 15% for this comparison. The evaluator changed the default value a priori (i.e., prior to conducting the PSW analysis) for the following reasons. First, Amanda has undergone at least two years of intervention services for reading difficulties and has reportedly made progress. Second, when Amanda began taking medication for ADHD her basic reading skills reportedly improved. Given these two factors, the evaluator suspected that her reading performance may be somewhat higher than it would have been without the added benefit of two years of intervention and medication. Therefore, a more liberal value was selected to ensure that any improvements she may have made in reading would not lead to a false negative (not identifying SLD in error) because Amanda is still below expectation (in academic performance) despite intervention, and other data sources suggest that she may have a learning disability.

CAUTION

Without a compelling reason to change the *Frequency of the Difference* for the actual and predicted cognitive comparison or the actual and predicted achievement comparison, the default difference should remain at 10%—the recommended default value.

The final section of the PSW-A Data Summary tab shows other ability and processing domains that were not included in the previous sections. These domains are Domain-Specific Knowledge (or Gkn; see Appendix A for more information), Executive Functions (EF), Orthographic Processing (OP), Speed of Lexical Access (LA), and Cognitive Efficiency (CE). As may be seen in the bottom portion of Figure 7.12, Amanda's OP score of 78 was reported as a weakness. Note that these five additional areas may be included in the PSW analysis, but they do not contribute to the FCC if identified as strengths or to the ICC if identified as weaknesses. Once the information on the PSW-A Data Summary tab has been reviewed, the user may click on the top right button on this tab titled "g-value."

PSW-A g-VALUE DATA SUMMARY

The PSW-A g-Value Data Summary tab is shown in Figure 7.13. This tab is informational only. It provides an interpretation of the g-value (e.g., "g-value = .72, Average overall ability is very likely"), the scale used to determine the likelihood that the g-value represents at least average overall ability (e.g., ≥ .60 = average overall ability is very likely), and the specific cognitive abilities and processes used to calculate the g-value, FCC, and ICC. The bottom of this tab answers the following question that is specific to the g-value: "How likely is it that the individual's pattern of strengths indicates at least average overall ability?" The answer to this question assists in understanding the importance of at least average overall ability in the learning process. Figure 7.13 shows that the answer to this question based on Amanda's g-value is: *Despite the presence of weaknesses in one or more cognitive ability domains, this individual displays average or better functioning in cognitive ability domains considered important for acquiring the academic skills typical for this grade level. The individual's overall cognitive ability is very likely to be average or better and, therefore, ought to enable learning and achievement, especially when specific cognitive weaknesses are minimized through compensatory efforts, accommodations, and the like.*

Once the g-value information has been reviewed, the user may click on the "PSW Analyzer" button located at the top right of the PSW-A g-value tab. Note that this button is not visible in Figure 7.13.

DUAL DISCREPANCY/CONSISTENCY MODEL: PSW ANALYSES FOR SLD

The "Dual Discrepancy/Consistency Model: PSW Analyses for SLD" tab (or "PSW Analyzer [PSW-A]" tab for short; see Figure 7.14) provides the results of the PSW analysis following the DD/C model. There are three ovals on the

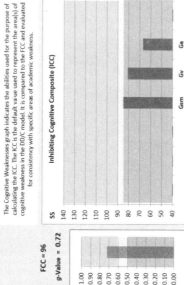

Figure 7.13 The g-Value Tab of X-BASS

PSW-A tab. The top oval represents Amanda's cognitive strengths and includes the FCC of 96. Note that the top oval also includes a drop-down menu in which Amanda's supporting academic strengths are listed. Because the FCC represents Amanda's cognitive capabilities that are anticipated to facilitate learning and achievement, it is expected that individuals with SLD would demonstrate areas of achievement that are consistent with their cognitive capabilities. Clicking on the drop-down menu in the top oval reveals the following areas of strength for Amanda that are consistent with her FCC: a specific area of Written Expression (i.e., Sentence Composition), (shown in Figure 7.14), Oral Expression, Listening Comprehension, and Math Calculation.

The bottom left oval in Figure 7.14 represents the individual's cognitive weakness. The first PSW analysis is automatically conducted using the ICC because it is the default area of cognitive weakness (as shown in Figure 7.14). However, the user may select any area that was designated as a cognitive weakness from the drop-down menu located in the bottom left oval. For Amanda, this drop-down menu includes the WISC-V WMI and VSI, two auditory processing composites, and an orthographic processing composite.

The bottom right oval in Figure 7.14 represents the individual's academic weakness. Like the cognitive weakness component of the PSW analysis, the academic weakness component is automatically conducted using the first area that was marked as a weakness on the Strengths and Weaknesses Indicator tab following the order in which the IDEIA-specific SLD areas are listed (i.e., BRS, RC, RF, WE, MC, MPS, OE and LC). Because Amanda had a weakness in BRS, her WIAT-III Basic Reading Skills composite appears in the bottom right oval in Figure 7.14. The other areas of academic weakness included in the drop-down menu of the bottom right oval for Amanda include WIAT-III Reading Comprehension, Oral Reading Fluency, Spelling, and Math Problem Solving.

Because X-BASS automatically conducts a PSW analysis, it is important to decide a priori what cognitive strengths and weaknesses will be analyzed. The ICC is a good choice for the area of cognitive weakness because it provides an aggregate of all weaknesses. However, the ICC may contain estimates of cognitive abilities or processes that are not closely related to the academic area of weakness, which will lower the strength of the relationship between the ICC and the area of academic weakness. In that situation, it is important to select an alternative cognitive weakness.

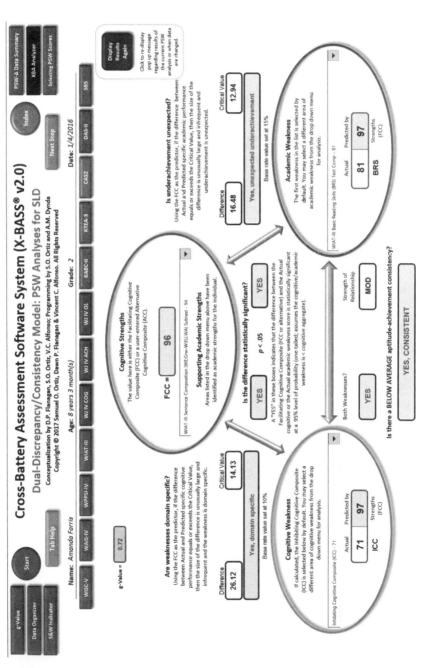

Figure 7.14 The PSW Analyzer Tab in X-BASS with ICC as the Default Cognitive Weakness

CAUTION

The ICC may contain estimates of cognitive abilities or processes that are not closely related to the academic area of weakness, which will lower the strength of the relationship between the ICC and the area of academic weakness. For example, the ICC may be made up of Gsm, Glr, and Ga and the academic area may be Math Calculation. The strength of this relationship (i.e., ICC-Math Calculation) may be Low, primarily because Ga does not have a strong relationship with Math Calculation. If a situation such as this occurs, it is important to select an alternative cognitive weakness from the drop-down menu (i.e., one from the ICC that is related to the academic area of weakness, such as Gsm in this case, or a neuropsychological domain, such as cognitive efficiency).

Figure 7.14 shows the default values for the initial PSW analysis for Amanda (i.e., an ICC of 71 and the WIAT-III Basic Reading Skills composite of 81). The results of this analysis show that Amanda's PSW is consistent with SLD because the following conditions were met:

1. *At least average overall ability:* FCC of 96
2. *Domain-specific cognitive weakness:* The difference between the FCC of 96 and the ICC of 71 is statistically significant (as indicated by the "yes" in the left center of the ovals in Figure 7.14) and the difference between the predicted (97) and actual (71) ICC is rare in the general population (about 10%), indicating that Amanda's cognitive areas of weakness are domain specific.
3. *Unexpected underachievement:* The difference between the FCC of 96 and the WIAT-III Basic Reading Skills composite of 81 is statistically significant (as indicated by the "yes" in the right center of the ovals in Figure 7.14) and the difference between the predicted (97) and actual (81) Basic Reading Skills composite is rare in the general population (about 15%), indicating that Amanda's academic area of weakness is unexpected.
4. *Below Average aptitude-achievement consistency:* The scores that represent the areas of cognitive and academic weakness are below average as compared to most people and there is an empirically established relationship between at least some of the areas that make up the ICC and basic reading skills. Amanda's ICC is made up of estimates of working memory, visual processing, and auditory processing. Although working memory and auditory processing (viz., phonological process-

ing) are related to basic reading skills, visual processing (as measured by the WISC-V VSI) is not. Therefore, it is likely that the strength of the relationship between the ICC and basic reading skills was tempered by the inclusion of visual processing in the ICC. Nevertheless, the data are sufficient to support a consistency between Amanda's areas of cognitive and academic weakness.

Amanda's evaluator decided a priori to run two analyses on the PSW-A tab, one with phonological processing and basic reading skills as the areas of cognitive and academic weakness and the other with orthographic processing and oral reading fluency as the areas of cognitive and academic weakness, respectively. Figure 7.15 shows the results of this latter comparison. Note that whereas the strength of the relationship between the ICC and basic reading skills was moderate (see Figure 7.14), the strength of the relationship between phonological processing and basic reading skills is high (see Rapid Reference 7.6) and the strength of the relationship between orthographic processing and oral reading fluency is high (as may be seen in Figure 7.15). The results of the PSW analyses conducted with Amanda's data provided support for an SLD classification in basic reading skills and reading fluency.

The results of the PSW analyses are provided in written form as answers to four specific questions:

1. Did the individual's observed cognitive and academic performance meet criteria within the DD/C model consistent with PSW-based SLD identification?
2. Is there evidence of domain-specific weaknesses in cognitive functioning?
3. Is there evidence of unexpected underachievement?
4. Is there evidence of below average aptitude-achievement consistency?

The answers to these four questions for Amanda, when orthographic processing and basic reading skills were selected as the areas of cognitive and academic weakness, respectively, are provided in Figure 7.16. Noteworthy is the fact that if the answer to the first question (i.e., Did the data meet criteria for a PSW that is consistent with SLD?) is "yes," the output clearly states, "This pattern of results does not automatically confirm the presence of SLD. . ." and if the answer is "no," the output clearly states, "This pattern of results does not automatically rule out the presence of SLD. . ." The reason for these clarifications is that a classification or diagnosis of SLD should not rest on quantitative data alone. Other data gathered through multiple methods and multiple sources need to be considered and must corroborate any conclusions that are drawn from the PSW analyses.

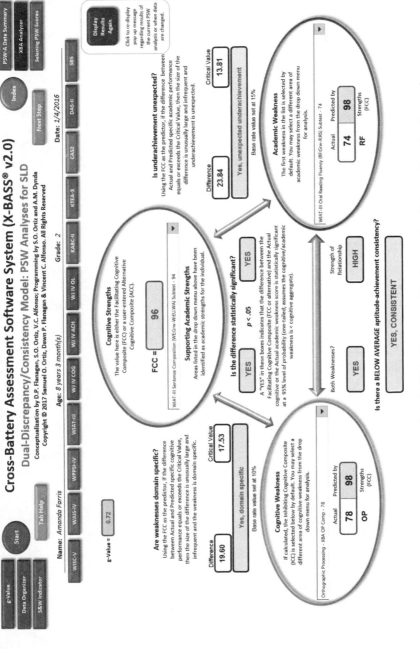

Figure 7.15 PSW Analyzer Tab of X-BASS With Orthographic Processing Selected as the Area of Cognitive Weakness

Dual-Discrepancy/Consistency Model: Summary of PSW Analyses for SLD

Name: *Amanda Farris* **Age:** *8 years 3 month(s)* **Grade:** *2* **Date:** *1/4/2016*

Did the individual's observed cognitive and academic performances meet criteria within the DD/C model consistent with PSW-based SLD identification?

YES. Based on the data selected for use in the PSW Analyzer, specific criteria for establishing a PSW consistent with SLD have been met. However, this pattern of results does not automatically confirm the presence of SLD. This pattern must be considered within the context of the entire case history of the individual. In addition, other data gathered through multiple methods need to be considered (e.g., information regarding exclusionary factors) when identifying or diagnosing SLD (see chapter 4 in Essentials of Cross-Battery Assessment, 3rd Ed.).

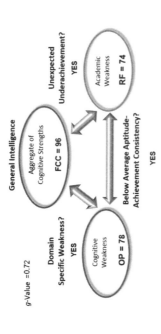

g-Value =0.72

General Intelligence

Aggregate of Cognitive Strengths

FCC = 96

Unexpected Underachievement?

YES

Academic Weakness

RF = 74

Domain Specific Weakness?

YES

Cognitive Weakness

OP = 78

Below Average Aptitude-Achievement Consistency?

YES

1. Is there evidence of domain specific weaknesses in cognitive functioning?

YES. The difference between the individual's estimate of intact cognitive abilities (FCC=96) and the score representing the area of specific cognitive weakness (OP=78) is statistically significant. This finding means that there is likely a true or real difference between the estimate of overall cognitive strengths and the identified area of specific cognitive weakness for the individual. In addition, there is an unusually large difference between actual performance in the specific cognitive area (SS=78) and expected performance (SS=98) as predicted by overall cognitive strengths. That is, based on the individual's estimate of cognitive strengths, it was predicted that the individual would perform much better in the specific cognitive area. In fact, the size of the difference between the individual's actual and predicted performance in the specific cognitive area occurs very infrequently. The results of these analyses suggest that the individual's PSW consists of a domain-specific cognitive weakness (particularly when the actual SS<90), an inclusionary criterion for SLD.

2. Is there evidence of unexpected underachievement?

YES. The difference between the individual's estimate of intact cognitive abilities (FCC=96) and the score representing the area of specific academic weakness (RF=74) is statistically significant. This finding means that there is likely a true or real difference between the estimate of overall cognitive strengths and the identified area of specific academic weakness for the individual. In addition, there is an unusually large difference between actual performance in the specific academic area (SS=74) and expected performance (SS=98) as predicted by overall cognitive strengths). That is, based on the individual's estimate of cognitive strengths, it was predicted that the individual would perform much better in the specific academic area. In fact, the size of the difference between the individual's actual and predicted performance in the specific academic area occurs very infrequently. The results of these analyses suggest that the individual's PSW is marked by unexpected underachievement (particularly when the actual SS < 90), an inclusionary criterion for SLD.

3. Is there evidence of a below-average aptitude-achievement consistency?

YES. The specific cognitive (SS=78 for OP) and academic (SS=74 for RF) scores are indicative of normative weaknesses or deficits compared to same age peers (SS<85). There is research that supports a high relationship between OP (Orthographic Processing) and Reading Fluency which indicates that they are related. This combination of scores provides evidence that assists in explaining the nature of the individual's observed learning difficulties. Based on all of these considerations, these findings appear to indicate overall support for the criterion regarding below average aptitude-achievement consistency.

Figure 7.16 Specific Questions about PSW Results Answered in X-BASS

CONCLUSION

The DD/C operational definition of SLD presented in this chapter provides a guide to the process of using and interpreting the WISC-V, WIAT-III, and data from other batteries effectively within the context of SLD referrals. X-BASS provides an efficient means of conducting the PSW component of the DD/C model. When the criteria at each level of the DD/C model are met, including the exclusionary factors component, it may be concluded that the data are sufficient to support a diagnosis of SLD.

TEST YOURSELF

1. **IDEIA 2004 considers dyslexia as a disorder in one or more of the basic psychological processes involved in understanding or using language, spoken or written, which manifests itself in the imperfect ability to listen, think, speak, read, write, spell, or do mathematical calculations.**
   a. True
   b. False

2. **According to the DD/C operational definition of SLD, which of the following are defining characteristics or markers for SLD?**
   a. At least average overall ability despite specific areas of cognitive processing weakness
   b. A below average aptitude-achievement consistency
   c. A specific pattern of cognitive weaknesses and below average overall ability
   d. a and b only

3. **Which of the following is a common component of third-method approaches to SLD identification?**
   a. Below average cognitive-achievement consistency
   b. Academic strengths
   c. Behavioral difficulties
   d. Self-efficacy

4. **There are many exclusionary factors to consider in an evaluation of suspected learning disability. The work of the practitioner is to determine whether any that are present is likely to be the *primary* reason for academic learning failure.**
   a. True
   b. False

5. **In the DD/C model, the criteria for establishing a below average cognitive aptitude-achievement *consistency* are as follows:**
   a. Below average performance in the specific cognitive *and* academic areas that are considered weaknesses or deficits
   b. Evidence of an empirical relationship between the specific cognitive and academic areas of weakness and/or an ecologically valid relationship between these areas
   c. Neither a nor b
   d. a and b

6. **The GAI contains the same subtests as the FSIQ with the exception of the following:**
   a. Digit Span and Coding
   b. Digit Span and Figure Weights
   c. Similarities and Vocabulary
   d. Matrix Reasoning and Figure Weights

7. **The *g*-value is automatically calculated by X-BASS and assists in answering which question?**
   a. What is the individual's IQ?
   b. What is the individual's probability of academic success?
   c. How likely is it that the individual's pattern of cognitive strengths represents at least average overall ability?
   d. How likely is it that the individual's pattern of cognitive weaknesses represents a specific learning disability?

8. **In the PSW analysis, an academic weakness represents *unexpected underachievement* when:**
   a. The difference between the FCC and Actual (weakness) score is statistically significant ($p < .05$)
   b. The difference between the Predicted and Actual scores is unusual or rare in the general population
   c. a and b
   d. Neither a nor b

9. **The WISC-V provides measures of six of the required seven areas necessary to conduct a PSW analysis following the DD/C model.**
   a. True
   b. False

10. Which is/are true of the PSW-A component of X-BASS?

   a. Automatically conducts PSW analyses in a manner consistent with the DD/C model

   b. Corrects for false negatives

   c. Uses a statistical rarity criterion to determine domain-specific cognitive weaknesses and unexpected underachievement

   d. All of the above

Answers: 1. a; 2. d; 3. a; 4. a; 5. d; 6. a; 7. c; 8. c; 9. a; 10. d

REFERENCES

Aaron, P. G. (1995). Differential diagnosis of reading disabilities. *School Psychology Review, 24*, 345–360.

Alston-Abel, N. L., & Berninger, V. (in press). Integrating instructionally relevant SLD diagnoses, patterns of strengths and weaknesses, and positive home-school partnerships: FAPE for all. In D. P. Flanagan & V. C. Alfonso (Eds.), *Essentials of specific learning disability identification* (2nd ed.). Hoboken, NJ: Wiley.

Berninger, V. W. (2011). Evidence-based differential diagnosis and treatment of reading disabilities with and without comorbidities in oral language, writing, and math: Prevention, problem-solving consultation, and specialized instruction. In D. P. Flanagan & V. C. Alfonso (Eds.), *Essentials of specific learning disability identification* (pp. 203–232). Hoboken, NJ: Wiley.

Carroll, J. B. (1993). *Human cognitive abilities: A survey of factor analytic studies.* New York, NY: Cambridge University Press.

Della Toffalo, D. A. (2010). Linking school neuropsychology with response-to-intervention models. In *Best practices in school neuropsychology: Guidelines for effective practice, assessment, and evidence-based intervention* (pp. 159–183). Hoboken, NJ: Wiley.

Evans, L. D. (1990). A conceptual overview of the regression discrepancy model for evaluating severe discrepancy between IQ and achievement scores. *Journal of Learning Disabilities, 23*, 406–412.

Feifer, S. G. (2012, May 11). *Integrating RTI with cognitive neuropsychology: A scientific approach to reading.* Presentation given at the Fordham University 4th Annual Assessment Conference. New York, NY.

Fiorello, C. A., Flanagan, D. P., & Hale, J. B. (2014). Response to the special issue: The utility of the pattern of strengths and weaknesses approach. *Learning Disabilities: A Multidisciplinary Journal, 20*(1), 55–59.

Flanagan, D. P., & Alfonso, V. C. (Eds.). (in press). *Essentials of specific learning disability identification* (2nd ed.). Hoboken, NJ: Wiley.

Flanagan, D. P., & Alfonso, V. C. (Eds.). (2011). *Essentials of specific learning disability identification.* Hoboken, NJ: Wiley.

Flanagan, D. P., Alfonso, V. C., & Mascolo, J. T. (2011). A CHC-based operational definition of SLD: Integrating multiple data sources and multiple data gathering methods. In D. P. Flanagan & V. C. Alfonso (Eds.), *Essentials of specific learning disability identification* (pp. 233–298). Hoboken, NJ: Wiley.

Flanagan, D. P., Alfonso, V. C., Mascolo, J. T., & McDonough, E. M. (in press). A CHC-based operational definition of SLD: Integrating multiple data sources and multiple data gathering methods. In D. P. Flanagan & V. C. Alfonso (Eds.), *Essentials of specific learning disability identification* (2nd ed.). Hoboken, NJ: Wiley.

Flanagan, D. P., Alfonso, V. C., & Ortiz, S. O. (2012). The cross-battery assessment approach: An overview, historical perspective, and current directions. In D. P. Flanagan & V. C. Alfonso (Eds.), *Contemporary intellectual assessment: Theories, tests, and issues* (3rd ed., pp. 459–483). New York, NY: Guilford.

Flanagan, D. P., McGrew, K. S., & Ortiz, S. O. (2000). *The Wechsler intelligence scales and Gf-Gc theory: A contemporary approach to interpretation.* Boston, MA: Allyn and Bacon.

Flanagan, D. P., Ortiz, S. O., & Alfonso, V. C. (2013). *Essentials of cross-battery assessment* (3rd ed.). Hoboken, NJ: Wiley.

Flanagan, D. P., Ortiz, S. O., Alfonso, V. C., & Mascolo, J. (2002). *The Achievement Test Desk Reference (ATDR): Comprehensive assessment and learning disabilities.* Boston, MA: Allyn & Bacon.

Flanagan, D. P., Ortiz, S., Alfonso, V. C., & Mascolo, J. (2006). *The Achievement Test Desk Reference (ATDR): A guide to learning disability identification* (2nd ed.). Hoboken, NJ: Wiley.

Flanagan, D. P., & Schneider, W. J. (in press). A commentary on Kranzler and colleagues' classification agreement analysis of cross-battery assessment in the identification of specific learning disorders in children and youth. *International Journal of School and Educational Psychology.*

Fletcher, J. M., Lyon, G. R., Fuchs, L. S., & Barnes, M. A. (Eds.) (2007). *Learning disabilities: From identification to intervention.* New York, NY: Guilford.

Geary, D. C., Hoard, M. K., & Bailey, D. H. (2011). Fact retrieval deficits in low achieving children and children with mathematical learning disability. *Journal of Learning Disabilities, 45*(4), 291–307. doi:10.1177/0022219410392046

Hale, J. B., & Fiorello, C. A. (2004). *School neuropsychology: A practitioner's handbook.* New York, NY: Guilford.

Hale, J. B., Wycoff, K. L., & Fiorello, C. A. (2011). RTI and cognitive hypothesis testing for identification and intervention of specific learning disabilities: The best of both worlds. In D. P. Flanagan & V. C. Alfonso (Eds.)., *Essentials of specific learning disability identification* (pp. 173–201). Hoboken, NJ: Wiley.

Harrison, A. G., & Holmes, A. (2012). Easier said than done: Operationalizing the diagnosis of learning disability for use at the postsecondary level in Canada. *Canadian Journal of School Psychology, 27,* 12–34.

Hinshelwood, J. (1917). *Congenital word-blindness.* London, UK: H. K. Lewis.

Individuals with Disabilities Education Improvement Act of 2004, 20 U.SC. §§ 1401 et seq. (2004).

Kaufman, A. S. (2008). Neuropsychology and specific learning disabilities: Lessons from the past as a guide to present controversies and future clinical practice. In E. Fletcher-Janzen & C. Reynolds (Eds.), *Neuropsychological perspectives on learning disabilities in an era of RTI: Recommendations for diagnosis and intervention* (pp. 1–13). Hoboken, NJ: Wiley.

Kaufman, A. S., & Kaufman, N. L. (2014). *Kaufman test of educational achievement* (3rd ed.). Bloomington, MN: Pearson.

Kavale, K. A., & Flanagan, D. P. (2007). Ability-achievement discrepancy, response to intervention, and assessment of cognitive abilities/processes in specific learning disability identification: Toward a contemporary operational definition. In *Handbook of response to intervention: The science and practice of assessment and intervention* (pp. 130–147). New York: NY: Springer Science + Business Media. doi: 10.1007/978–0–387–49053–3_10

Kavale, K. A., & Forness, S. R. (2000). What definitions of learning disability say and don't say: A critical analysis. *Journal of Learning Disabilities, 33*, 239–256.

Kavale, K. A., Kauffman, J. M., Bachmeier, R. J., & LeFever, G. B. (2008). Response-to-intervention: Separating the rhetoric of self-congratulation from the reality of specific learning disability identification. *Learning Disability Quarterly, 31*, 135–150.

Kavale, K. A., Spaulding, L. S., & Beam, A. P. (2009). A time to define: Making the specific learning disability definition prescribe specific learning disability. *Learning Disability Quarterly, 32*(1), 39–48.

Kranzler, J. H., Floyd, R. G., Benson, N., Zaboski, B., & Thibodaux, L. (2016). Classification agreement analysis of cross-battery assessment in the identification of specific learning disorders in children and youth. *International Journal of School and Educational Psychology, 4 (3)*, 124–136.

Maricle, D. E., & Avirett, E. (2012). The role of cognitive and intelligence tests in the assessment of executive functions. In *Contemporary intellectual assessment: Theories, tests, and issues* (3rd ed., pp. 820–828). New York: NY: Guilford.

Mascolo, J. T., Alfonso, V. C., & Flanagan, D. P. (2014). *Essentials of planning, selecting, and tailoring interventions for unique learners.* Hoboken, NJ: Wiley.

Mather, N. (2011). *Let's stop monkeying around: What we know about reading disabilities.* Verona, NY: New York Association of School Psychologists.

Mather, N., & Kaufman, N. (2006). Introduction to the Special Issue, Part Two: It's about the what, the how well, and the why. *Psychology in the Schools, 43*(8), 829–834. doi: 10 .1002/pits.20199

Mather, N., & Wendling, B. J. (2011). How SLD manifests in writing. In D. P. Flanagan & V. C. Alfonso (Eds.), *Essentials of specific learning disability identification* (pp. 65–88). Hoboken, NJ: Wiley.

McCloskey, G., Perkins, L. A., & Van Divner, B. (2009). *Assessment and intervention for executive function difficulties.* New York, NY: Routledge.

McCloskey, G., Whitaker, J., Murphy, R., & Rogers, J. (2012). Intellectual, cognitive, and neuropsychological assessment in three-tier service delivery systems in schools. In D. P. Flanagan & P. L. Harrison (Eds.), *Contemporary intellectual assessment: Theories, tests and issues* (3rd ed., pp. 852–881). New York, NY: Guilford.

McDonough, E. M., & Flanagan, D. P. (2016). Use of the Woodcock-Johnson IV in the identification of specific learning disabilities in school-age children. In D. P. Flanagan & V. C. Alfonso (Eds.), *WJ IV clinical use and interpretation: Scientist-practitioner perspectives* (pp. 211–252).

McDonough, E. M., Flanagan, D. P., Sy, M., & Alfonso, V. C. (in press). Specific Learning Disorder. In S. Goldstein & M. DeVries (Eds.), *Handbook of DSM-5 disorders in children.* New York, NY: Springer.

McGrew, K. S., & Flanagan, D. P. (1998). *The Intelligence Test Desk Reference (ITDR): CHC cross-battery assessment.* Boston, MA: Allyn & Bacon.

McGrew, K. S., & Wendling, B. L. (2010). CHC cognitive-achievement relations: What we have learned from the past 20 years of research. *Psychology in the Schools, 47*, 651–675.

Miller, D. C. (Ed.). (2010). *Best practices in school neuropsychology: Guidelines for effective practice, assessment, and evidence-based intervention.* Hoboken, NJ: Wiley.

Monroe, M. (1932). *Children who cannot read: The analysis of reading disabilities and the use of diagnostic tests in the instruction of retarded readers.* Chicago, IL: University of Chicago Press.

Naglieri, J. A. (2011). The discrepancy/consistency approach to SLD identification using the PASS theory. In D. P. Flanagan & V. C. Alfonso (Eds.), *Essentials of specific learning disability identification* (pp. 145–172). Hoboken, NJ: Wiley.

Ortiz, S. O. (in press). Assessment of culturally and linguistically diverse individuals with the WISC-V. In D. P. Flanagan & V. C. Alfonso (Eds.), *Essentials of WISC-V assessment*. Hoboken, NJ: Wiley.

Ortiz, S. O., Flanagan, D. P., & Alfonso, V. C. (2016). *Cross-Battery Assessment Software System (X-BASS)* (Versions 1.3, and 1.4) [Computer software]. Hoboken, NJ: Wiley.

Ortiz, S. O., Flanagan, D. P., & Alfonso, V. C. (2017). *Cross-Battery Assessment Software System (X-BASS)* (Version 2.0) [Computer software]. Hoboken, NJ: Wiley.

Orton, S. T. (1937). *Reading, writing and speech problems in children*. New York, NY: Norton.

Packer, L. E., & Pruitt, S. K. (2010). *Challenging kids, challenged teachers*. Bethesda, MD: Woodbine House.

Pearson. (2009). *Wechsler Individual Achievement Test* (3rd ed.). Bloomington, MN: Author.

Raiford, S. E., Weiss, L. G., Rolfhus, E., & Coalson, D. (2005/2008). *General ability index*. WISC-IV Technical Report #4 (updated December 2008). San Antonio, TX: Pearson Education. http://images.pearsonclinical.com/images/assets/WISC-IV/80720 _WISCIV_Hr_r4.pdf

Reynolds, C. R. (1984–85). Critical measurement issues in learning disabilities. *Journal of Special Education, 18*, 451–474.

Reynolds, C. R., & Shaywitz, S. A. (2009). Response to intervention: Prevention and remediation, perhaps. Diagnosis, no. *Child Development Perspectives, 3*, 44–47.

Schneider, W. J., & McGrew, K. (2012). The Cattell-Horn-Carroll model of intelligence. In D. Flanagan & P. Harrison (Eds.), *Contemporary intellectual assessment: Theories, tests, and issues* (3rd ed., pp. 99–144). New York, NY: Guilford.

Shaywitz, S. (2003). *Overcoming dyslexia*. New York, NY: Knopf.

Sotelo-Dynega, M. (in press). Overview of specific learning disabilities. In D. P. Flanagan & V. C. Alfonso (Eds.), *Essentials of specific learning disability identification* (2nd ed.) Hoboken, NJ: Wiley.

Stanovich, K. E. (1993). Romance and reality. *Reading Teacher, 47*(4), 280.

Wagner, R. K., Torgesen, J. K., Rashotte, C. A., & Pearon, N. A. (2013). *Comprehensive Test of Phonological Processing, Second Edition* (CTOPP-II). Austin, TX: Pro-Ed.

Wendling, B. J., & Mather, N. (2009). *Essentials of evidence-based academic interventions*. Hoboken, NJ: Wiley.

Wiig, E. H., Semel, E., & Secord, W. A. (2013). *Clinical evaluations of language fundamentals* (5th ed.). Bloomington, MN: Pearson.

Wright, J. (2002). *Best practices in calculating severe discrepancies between expected and actual academic achievement scores: A step-by-step tutorial*. http://www.kasp.org/documents /discrepancies.pdf

Appendix 7.A

FACTORS THAT MAY FACILITATE LEARNING AND AID IN BYPASSING OR MINIMIZING THE EFFECTS OF DEFICITS

Table 1 Factors That May Facilitate Learning and Aid in Bypassing or Minimizing the Effects of a Fluid Reasoning (Gf) Deficit

Classroom Instructional Factors	Instructional Materials	Environmental	Strategies
Use demonstrations to externalize the reasoning process (think-alouds)	Expanded answer keys containing the "reason" for correct/incorrect choices Use metacognitive strategies (mnemonics that are *memorable* and that *accurately represent* the learning task)	Problem-solving charts (hanging or taped to desk)	Use tools that help students categorizes objects and concepts to assist in drawing conclusions (e.g., graphic organizers, concept maps)
Gradually offer guided practice (e.g., guided questions list) to promote internalization of procedures or process(es)	Guided lists for implementing procedures, formulas	Procedural charts/lists (hanging or taped to desk)	Listen to and separate the steps in completing a problem from the content used in a problem
Offer targeted, explicit feedback	Models/examples	Preferred seating arrangements that provide easy access to a peer model with strong reasoning skills (e.g., for cooperative learning activities)	
Offer opportunities for learning formats that allow for reasoning to be modeled for the student (e.g., cooperative learning, reciprocal teaching)	Text features (boldface, italics)		
Compare new concepts to previously learned concepts (same vs. different)	Graphic organizers that allow for a visual depiction of relationships between and among concepts		
Use analogies, similes, metaphors, paired with concrete explanations to support understanding when presenting tasks (e.g., "We are going to learn our math facts with *lightning speed*, that means we are going to learn them *fast*.")	Manipulatives to demonstrate relationships (e.g., part to whole relationships)		

Table 2 Factors That May Facilitate Learning and Aid in Bypassing or Minimizing the Effects of a Crystallized Intelligence (Gc) Deficit

Classroom Instructional Factors	Instructional Materials	Environmental Factors	Strategies
Provides an environment rich in language and experiences	Contains chapter glossaries	Word-of-the-day calendar	Use *Know-What to Know-Learned* (KWL) strategy to increase background knowledge
Incorporates frequent practice with and exposure to words	E-glossaries available	Word walls	Use context when reading to ascertain meaning
Reads aloud to children	Provides vocabulary building activities (print or online)	Distraction-free seating	Capitalize on opportunities to practice new words (listening for their use in television shows and other media, purposely using them in conversation)
Varies reading purpose (leisure, information)	Contains tools for priming background knowledge (e.g., Harcourt)	Closed doors	Engage in activities such as word searches containing related terms (e.g., travel terms) and crosswords (note: puzzlemaker.com can create customized puzzles)
Works on vocabulary building	Includes story starters	Closed windows	Write a new word and its definition along with a drawing
Teaches morphology	Includes text features (boldface, italics)		
Capitalizes on opportunities to define words within instruction (e.g., "the *composition* of igneous rock, that is, *what it is made of*, is . . .")	Availability of video clips		

(continued)

499

Table 2 (continued)

Classroom Instructional Factors	Instructional Materials	Environmental Factors	Strategies
Includes supportive modalities (e.g., visuals, gestures) to increase understanding of language used	Audio glossaries		
Embeds instruction within a meaningful context (e.g., relating words to learner experiences, increasing listening ability through game-like format)	Dictionaries		
Develops vocabulary through naturalistic extension of language (e.g., if a student asks, "Can I *start* my work?," the teacher might respond, "Yes, you can *begin* your work," naturally building synonym knowledge)	Thesaurus		
Uses extension and expansion strategies (Mather, Goldstein, Lynch, & Richards, 2001)	Encyclopedias		
	Use vocabulary cartoons (Burchers, Burchers, & Burchers, 2000)		
	Use text talks		

Table 3 Factors That May Facilitate Learning and Aid in Bypassing or Minimizing the Effects of an Auditory Processing (Ga) Deficit

Classroom Instructional Factors	Instructional Materials	Environmental Factors	Strategies
Enunciates sounds in words in an emphatic manner when teaching new words for reading or spelling	Video clips	Rules for talking and listening	Use comprehension monitoring (e.g., Does the word I heard/read make sense in context?)
Uses instructional techniques (e.g., work preview/text preview) to clarify unknown words	Read-aloud texts/features	Spelling lists	Engage in self-advocacy (e.g., asking for information to be repeated and/or clarified in regard to the misheard part)
Provides instructional supports (e.g., guided notes) during note-taking activities	Audio glossaries	Closed doors	Physically positioning oneself toward/close to the speaker
Builds in time for clarification questions related to "missed" or "misheard" items during lecture	Supplement oral instructions with written instructions	Closed windows	Attending to speaker's mouth and/or gestures, facial expressions, during the delivery of information
Shortens instructions	Phonemic awareness activities	Distraction-free seating	Recording notes via audio methods to allow a mechanism for being able to fill in notes for completeness
Makes an effort to minimize background noise via the use of instructional commands (e.g., work quietly, refrain from talking with your neighbor)	Electronic textbooks	Noise minimizers (carpet, noise-reducing headphones)	Following along with written directions/text during the provision of oral instruction

(continued)

Table 3 (continued)

Classroom Instructional Factors	Instructional Materials	Environmental Factors	Strategies
Repeats or rephrases questions asked by other students to ensure that all students "hear" the question that is associated with the teacher's given response	Guided notes, graphic organizers	Preferential seating (close to teacher, away from heaters, fans)	Practicing spelling lists with visually based techniques
Emphasizes sight-word reading		Localize sound source for student by standing closer when delivering instructions	Use visualization strategies to remember things
Pauses when delivering oral instruction to allow time for student to process auditory information			Use written mediums (e.g., e-mail, text) to preserve content/integrity of information communicated

502

Table 4 Factors That May Facilitate Learning and Aid in Bypassing or Minimizing the Effects of a Long-Term Retrieval (Glr) Deficit

Classroom Instructional Factors	Instructional Materials	Environmental Factors	Strategies
Uses closed-ended questions, yes/no, true/false	Guided lists for implementing procedures, formulas	Procedural charts	Organizes material to be learned using visual aids (e.g., diagrams, flowcharts), auditory aids (e.g., chunking), or other tangibles (e.g., flash cards)
Uses consistent instructional routines	Practice guides	Word walls	Makes connections by relating material to be learned to oneself
Offers repeated practice with and review of newly presented information	Online review	Creates a schedule for distributed practice of material to be learned	Desk organizers
Teaches memory strategies and encourages their use (verbal rehearsal to support encoding, use of mnemonic devices; Dehn, 2010)	Glossaries (electronic, audio, printed)	Calendars with visual references to due dates	Relates concepts to be learned to one another via tools such as a concept map
	External memory aids (lists, audible timers)		Plans for regular review of material
Uses multiple modalities when teaching new concepts (pair written or visual with verbal information) to support dual recoding (Dehn, 2010)	Study guides		

(continued)

Table 4 (continued)

Classroom Instructional Factors	Instructional Materials	Environmental Factors	Strategies
Limits the amount of new material to be learned; introduces new concepts gradually and with a lot of context	Review sheets	Visual reminders (sticky notes, color-coded systems)	Rehearses material to be learned via recitation, repetition
Is mindful of when new concepts are presented	Dictionaries (to support word retrieval)	Studies and completes homework in a designated location with necessary materials	Uses active learning strategies (note taking, flash cards, concept maps, chunking) in review sessions
Makes associations between newly learned and prior information explicit	Quiet environment or noise-reduction aids (headphones, cubicles, study carrels)	Preferential seating to minimize distractions when encoding	Studies and reviews learning material immediately prior to sleeping
Uses lists to facilitate recall (prompts)	Thesaurus (to build vocabulary and minimize impact of retrieval weaknesses)		Uses organizational strategies such as semantic clustering (Dehn, 2010)
Expands vocabulary to minimize impact of word retrieval deficits			Uses verbal association strategies (e.g., elaboration, Dehn, 2010)
Builds in wait-time for student when fluency of retrieval is an issue			Implements dual coding strategies (visual to verbal and vice versa)
Uses text previews to "prime" knowledge			Engages in self-testing
Provides background knowledge first before asking a question to "prime" student for retrieval			Uses specific strategies for academic tasks (e.g., PQRST, for reading comprehension; Dehn, 2010)

Table 5 Factors That May Facilitate Learning and Aid in Bypassing or Minimizing the Effects of a Processing Speed (Gs) Deficit

Classroom Instructional Factors	Instructional Materials	Environmental Factors	Strategies
Focuses on features of work products that are unrelated to time parameters (e.g., quality or accuracy of a response)	Practice guides	Clocks	Preview important parts of text (end-of-chapter questions, title, subtitles, glossary of terms) to facilitate reading speed
Repeated practice	Plan for long-term projects by using a realistic schedule that allows for consistent movement toward completion	Written schedules	Apply planning and time management strategies
	Online review	Desk organizers	Use techniques such as skimming and scanning for reading activities
Offers speed drills	Use computer activities that require quick, simple decisions		Use an outlining strategy for note taking
Extended time	Books on tape		
Reduces the quantity of work required (including homework)	Online activities/games (e.g., http://www.arcademicskillbuilders.com/games/)		
Increases wait-times both after questions are asked and after responses are given			
Choral repeated reading			

Table 6 Factors That May Facilitate Learning and Aid in Bypassing or Minimizing the Effects of a Visual Processing (Gv) Deficit

Classroom Instructional Factors	Instructional Materials	Environmental Factors	Strategies
Provide oral explanation for visual concepts	Video clips	Color-coded Information	Uses orthographic strategies for decoding (e.g., word length, shape of word); Uses "cover-copy-compare" technique—go to: http://www.amblesideprimary.com/ambleweb/lookcover/lookcover.html
Reviews spatial concept and supports comprehension through use of hands-on activities and manipulatives (e.g., using models to demonstrate the moon's orbital path)	Enlarged text (via online zoom feature or alternative print copy of textbook, worksheet)	Preferential seating aimed at allowing the student to access visual material (e.g., smart board manipulatives, visual aids, and other materials to support learning	Capitalizes on intact or strong auditory skills during learning/studying (e.g., uses phonemic skills for decoding tasks)
Provides verbal label for visual representations (e.g., "The shaded red bars represent women's votes, the green bars represent men's votes")	Highlights margins during writing tasks	Assigned note-taking buddy	Pairs visual information with verbal (mnemonics)
Provides written copies of oral instructions, lectures	Provides direct handwriting practice	Readers or scribes, where needed	Labels visual charts/graphs with verbal labels
Auditory cueing to supplement visual information/cues (e.g., "Look at the bar graph for weekly sales")	Provides visual supports (graphic organizers, graph paper)	Reduce visual distraction	Highlights or color codes important information
	Provides graph paper to assist with number alignment	Alternative lighting (natural light, non-fluorescent lighting)	Uses aids to support visual tracking (finger, index card, ruler)
			Spaces items on a page
	Books on tape		
	Text-to-speech technology (screen and text readers)		Uses applications or supports that allow for enlargement of fonts
	Reading/scanning pens		Uses note-taking strategies (e.g., Cornell, outlining)

Table 7 Factors That May Facilitate Learning and Aid in Bypassing or Minimizing the Effects of a Short-Term Memory (Gsm) Deficit

Classroom Instructional Factors	Instructional Materials	Environmental Factors	Strategies
Offers repetition of information	Practice guides	Apply rote strategies (e.g., basic rehearsal, simple repetition) for information to be learned in the short term	Semantic rehearsal (creating a sentence using things to be remembered)
Reviews information and newly presented concepts often	Color-coded Information	Encourage use of relational strategies (e.g., mnemonics)	Chunking
	Guided study	Written schedules	Paraphrasing
Delivers information in manageable parts	Math-facts tables (e.g., multiplication)	Visual schedules (e.g., pictures) Written reminders (homework)	Visual mnemonics (imagery, pegwords, loci, keyword method; Dehn, 2010)
	Online review		Chaining
Evidences use of consistent instructional routines	Use elaborative rehearsal (associating new information with prior knowledge)		First-letter mnemonics
Uses meaningful stimuli to assist with encoding and allow for experiential learning (i.e., learning while doing)	Flash cards		Use tangible reminders (alarms, to-do lists, calendar schedules)
Provides opportunities for repeated practice and review	Multisensory materials to facilitate encoding		Apply specific academic strategies (e.g., write out all math computations, use a calculator, spellchecker)

(continued)

Table 7 (continued)

Classroom Instructional Factors	Instructional Materials	Environmental Factors	Strategies
Provides supports (e.g., lecture notes, guided notes, study guides, written directions) to supplement oral instruction			
Breaks down instructional steps for student			
Provides visual support (e.g., times table) to support acquisition of basic math facts			
Outlines math procedures for student and provides procedural guides or flashcards for the student to use when approaching problems			
Highlights important information within a word problem			
Has students write all steps and show all work for math computations			
Uses writing programs or techniques that emphasize drafting first (e.g., Draft Builder 6)			
Teaches chunking strategies			

REFERENCES

Burchers, S., Burchers, M., & Burchers, B. (2000). *Vocabulary cartoons: Building an educated vocabulary with sight and sound memory aids.* Punta Gorda, FL: New Monic Books.

Dehn, M. J. (2010). *Long-term memory problems in children and adolescents: Assessment, intervention, and effective instruction.* Hoboken, NJ: Wiley.

Mather, N., Lynch, K., & Richards, A. M. (2001). The thinking blocks: Language, images and strategies. In S. Goldstein & N. Mather (Eds.), *Learning disabilities and challenging behaviors: A guide to intervention and classroom management.* Baltimore, MD: Brookes.

Eight

ILLUSTRATIVE CASE REPORT

Erin M. McDonough

This chapter includes the results of a psychoeducational evaluation that was conducted following Cross-Battery Assessment (XBA) principles and procedures and interpreted within the context of the Cattell-Horn-Carroll (CHC) theory of cognitive abilities. The evaluation is of a student who was referred because of purported reading difficulties. The WISC-V and WIAT-III were the core batteries used in this evaluation. Determination of specific learning disability (SLD) was guided by the Dual-Discrepancy/Consistency (DD/C) operational definition of SLD described in Chapter 7 and the Pattern of Strengths and Weaknesses Analyzer component of the Cross-Battery Assessment Software System (X-BASS v2.0; Ortiz, Flanagan, & Alfonso, 2017). Additional case reports using WISC-V as the core battery are included in Appendix C.

PSYCHOEDUCATIONAL EVALUATION REPORT

Privileged & Confidential

EXAMINEE: Amanda Farris **ETHNICITY:** Eastern European-American
BIRTHDATE: 10/1/2007 **REPORT DATE:** 01/24/2016
AGE: 8 years, 3 months **EVALUATION DATES:** 1/4/16, 1/11/16, 1/14/16
GRADE: Second **EXAMINER:** Erin M. McDonough, PhD

Reason for Referral

Amanda was referred by her mother, Ms. Beth Farris, for a psychoeducational evaluation in order to determine the nature and etiology of Amanda's academic difficulties, specifically in reading. Ms. Farris would like the evaluation to identify any diagnoses, specifically dyslexia. The evaluation is also intended to generate appropriate recommendations to address any cognitive, academic, or social-emotional concerns, regardless of any potential diagnoses.

Background Information

The following sections provide information about Amanda's family background, developmental history, health history, social behavior and temperament, and educational history.

Family Background

Amanda is an 8-year-old girl who was adopted outside of the United States. She resides with her adoptive mother and her mother's partner, Mr. Sean Delaney, who is Amanda's father. Ms. Farris is a tour guide, and her partner is a computer programmer. Amanda was born to an 18-year-old woman. According to adoption records, it was a difficult birth in which Amanda may have suffered from anoxia. Supplemental oxygen was provided for an unknown length of time. It was reported that Amanda's birth mother used alcohol and nicotine during the pregnancy. Amanda's birth mother reportedly left the hospital after the birth, so Amanda was cared for in the early months of her life by her maternal grandmother but was removed from her guardianship because of undernourishment. At that point, Amanda was placed in a hospital for appropriate care until she could be transferred to an orphanage, which occurred when Amanda was 11 months of age. Amanda was adopted at age 2 years 4 months, and although there is not a great deal known about the biological family, Ms. Farris was told that Amanda's biological mother dropped out of school after the fifth grade. Ms. Farris reported that care in the orphanage seemed appropriate and nurturing and that it seemed that the women in the orphanage genuinely cared for Amanda and the other children.

Developmental History

Although little is known about attainment of developmental milestones, Ms. Farris reported that Amanda was walking without assistance at 15 months and was speaking some words at the time of her adoption. Ms. Farris also reported that Amanda quickly learned the English language when she came to the United States. An evaluation performed when Amanda was 2 years 8 months revealed no significant deficits warranting early intervention services. Amanda was described by Ms. Farris as athletic with well-developed gross motor skills, but fine motor skills might be mildly delayed. Ms. Farris described that Amanda experienced mild difficulties buttoning her clothing and added that Amanda's drawing skills developed more slowly than those of her peers. Amanda receives occupational therapy for these difficulties.

Ms. Farris reported that during Amanda's early childhood, she experienced difficulties in several developmental areas. Amanda was underweight at the time of her adoption; she is currently at the 55th percentile for body mass index (BMI). Although sleep has not been a problem for Amanda in the past, it has become more of a challenge since beginning the medication *Concerta* for Attention-Deficit/Hyperactivity Disorder (ADHD), which was diagnosed last spring.

Health History

Amanda has had some minor illnesses. As a young child, she had three or four ear infections, and Ms. Farris described them as "bad ones" resulting in a perforated eardrum. Antibiotics were prescribed and the perforated eardrum was described as "mostly healed." Amanda sees an ear, nose, and throat (ENT) physician every 6 months, and her hearing is reportedly within normal limits. Ms. Farris also reported that Amanda experienced some high fevers when she was younger. The most serious illness experienced was a bout of pneumonia at age 5 with a hospitalization that lasted less than 48 hours.

Amanda was diagnosed with ADHD by a pediatric neurologist in the spring of 2015. Initially, Amanda was prescribed *Ritalin*, but now takes 27 mg of *Concerta* once daily in the morning. Although Ms. Farris noted an improvement in Amanda's attention, the medication has not entirely ameliorated her academic problems. Amanda is under the regular care of a pediatrician, whom she sees annually. Her hearing and vision were reported to be normal. During the time of this evaluation, Amanda was examined by a developmental ophthalmologist who determined that there were no visual anomalies contributing to academic problems.

Social Behavior and Temperament

Ms. Farris also described Amanda's behavior and temperament. She described her as having a short attention span and stated that she can be overly energetic and overstimulated in play. Amanda was also described as impulsive and prone to overreact when faced with a problem. Ms. Farris also endorsed that Amanda needs a lot of parental attention and has become more oppositional and more irritable recently. She requires much parental attention and has fears, including not wanting to fall asleep unless her mother is in the room.

Ms. Farris also stated that Amanda does not have significant problems in developing or maintaining peer relationships. She described her daughter as very friendly and outgoing, but noted that Amanda can sometimes be "too much" for other children. When asked to clarify, Ms. Farris stated that Amanda sometimes gets too close to other children and doesn't observe typical physical boundaries and sometimes is "overly friendly."

Ms. Farris described Amanda as very interested in athletic activities. She plays tennis, does Tae Kwan Do, rides her bicycle, plays soccer, and rides her scooter. She enjoys watching television, playing dress-up, and performing songs and skits. She also has a rock collection and loves science.

Educational History

Amanda attended preschool starting at the age of 2½. She initially attended 3 days per week for 8 hours each day; as she became older, she increased to 5 days per week for 8 hours a day. There were no problems noted during preschool. She attended public elementary school for kindergarten, at which time her academic problems were first noted. She completed first grade, but was still struggling with reading and she was retained. It was noted that she had difficulty spelling, blending words, and writing letters correctly. There was some improvement in reading noted when Amanda began taking *Concerta*. Ms. Farris reported that Amanda is sounding out most words and has difficulty recognizing sight words. Despite extra reading help for nearly 2 years, Amanda is in danger of being retained a second time. Ms. Farris noted that her academic difficulties were affecting her self-esteem.

Amanda was evaluated in the fall of 2013 by a neuropsychologist. She was administered the *Dean-Woodcock Neuropsychological Battery*, the *Conners Rating Scales-Third Edition* (Conners-3), and the *Beery Buktenica Test of Visual Motor Integration* (Beery VMI). Findings of the neuropsychological battery indicated performance generally within normal limits with the exception of near point visual acuity, which was moderately impaired. Her performance on the Beery VMI fell within the Average range. Parent reports on the Conners-3 indicated clinically significant inattention and hyperactivity/impulsivity. The recommendations of the neuropsychologist included referral to a psychiatrist for medication consultation for ADHD, placement in a Collaborate Team Teaching (CTT) classroom, resource room for reading instruction, and a behavior modification plan.

Two Individualized Education Programs (IEPs) were available for review. The first was dated December 13, 2013. Specific testing results indicated that Amanda was administered the *Wechsler Intelligence Scale for Children-Fourth Edition* (WISC-IV) at some time prior to the first IEP. Those results revealed a Full Scale IQ (FSIQ = 83) and Verbal Comprehension Index (VCI = 83) in the Low Average range and a Perceptual Reasoning Index (PRI = 92), Working Memory Index

(WMI = 94), and a Processing Speed Index (PSI = 94) in the Average range (PSI = 94). No subtest scores were reported. Academic testing revealed Average Word Reading and Spelling, Low Average Pseudoword Decoding, and "Borderline" Reading Comprehension. The IEP stated that "Amanda's phonetic and word attack skills do not appear to be on [grade] level." Amanda was classified for special education services as Other Health Impaired. Special Education Teacher Support Services (SETSS) were recommended for English Language Arts. She was also given a Behavioral Intervention Plan to address out of seat and crawling behavior.

The second IEP, dated November 6, 2015, referred to the Teacher's College Reading Assessments, the Go Math Assessment, and the Beery VMI. Her reading level was determined to be below Grade 2 standards. Math performance was below grade level in the area of problem solving. The Beery VMI findings were in the Average range. The IEP indicated that Amanda's second-grade placement is in an Integrated Co-Teaching classroom for all academic subjects with SETSS, Occupational Therapy, and Speech-Language Therapy. There was improvement noted in behavior, attention, and reading skills following her medication for ADHD. It was noted that Amanda continued to display significant difficulties decoding and spelling, although her reading skills reportedly were improving slowly. Testing accommodations included extended time, a separate location, revised test directions, and questions read aloud.

Current Evaluation Procedures

Wechsler Intelligence Test for Children-Fifth Edition (WISC-V)
Woodcock-Johnson Tests of Cognitive Abilities-Fourth Edition (WJ IV)-Selected subtest
Comprehensive Test of Phonological Processing-Second Edition (CTOPP-2)-Selected subtests
Wechsler Individual Achievement Test-Third Edition (WIAT-III)
Test of Silent Word Reading Fluency-Second Edition (TOSWRF-2)
Comprehensive Behavior Rating System (CBRS)-Parent and Teacher Reports
Thematic Apperception Test (TAT)-Selected cards

Behavioral Observations

Amanda arrived at testing sessions accompanied by her mother. Upon initial introduction to the examiner, she seemed shy, as evidenced by her hiding behind her mother. She was also hesitant to speak with the examiner. In response to questions, initially she nodded. After several minutes, she began providing one-word answers, and then after several more minutes, she began speaking in longer, more elaborate sentences. At that point, rapport was quickly established and easily maintained. Amanda felt comfortable enough to joke with and tease the examiner; she was charming and engaging.

During formal testing, Amanda was more attentive during visual tasks than verbal tasks, but even on visual tasks, she was somewhat inattentive and distractible. She made comments on harder items such as "That's a hard one" and "That's the trickiest." During verbal tasks, she played with her shirt sleeves, but this did not appear to interfere with her performance. She demonstrated adequate frustration tolerance, persisting on even more difficult items.

Statement of Validity

The results presented in this report were compiled from tests that do not share a common norm group; however, test results have been interpreted following the Cross-Battery Assessment (XBA) approach and integrated with data from other sources, including educational records, parent–teacher interviews, behavioral observations, work samples, and other test findings to ensure ecological validity. Standardization was followed for all test administrations. No single test or procedure was used as the sole criterion for classification, eligibility, or educational planning. Unless otherwise noted, the results of this evaluation are considered reliable and valid estimates of Amanda's demonstrated skills and abilities at this time.

Evaluation of Cognitive Abilities and Processes

Amanda's cognitive abilities and processes were assessed across seven domains of cognitive functioning through the use of the WISC-V and CTOPP-2. The WISC-V yields a Verbal Comprehension Index (VCI), Fluid Reasoning Index (FRI), Visual Spatial Index (VSI), Working Memory Index (WMI), Processing Speed Index (PSI), and Storage and Retrieval Index (SRI). These Index Scales provide estimates of cognitive abilities and processes that are related to learning and academic achievement, namely Crystallized Intelligence (Gc), Fluid Reasoning (Gf), Visual Processing (Gv), Short-Term Memory (Gsm), Processing Speed (Gs), and Long-Term Storage and Retrieval (Glr), respectively. The CTOPP-2 yields a Phonological Awareness composite that provides an estimate of (Ga), which is also related to achievement, namely basic reading skills. Selected subtests from other batteries were administered to test hypotheses about Amanda's performance in certain cognitive domains. Amanda's performance in each cognitive domain is described later in this report.

Individual composites and subtest scores are referred to throughout this report and appear in a separate table at the end of this report. The mean standard score for all indexes (and certain subtests) on the WISC-V, as well as the composites on the CTOPP-2, is 100, with a standard deviation of 15. WISC-V and CTOPP-2 subtest scaled scores are based on a mean of 10 and a standard deviation of 3. Standard scores between 85 and 115 (and scaled scores between 7 and 13) are considered to be within normal limits because nearly 70% of the general population performs within this range. Table 8.1 provides more specific information about how scores were classified in this evaluation.

Table 8.1 Score Classifications

Standard Score	Scaled Score	Percentile Range	Classification
<70	1–3	< 2nd	Normative Weakness/Extremely Below Average
70–79	4–5	2nd to 8th	Normative Weakness/Well Below Average
80–84	6	9th to 14th	Normative Weakness/Below Average
85–89	**7**	**16th to 23rd**	**WNL/Low Average**
90–109	**8–11**	**25th to 73rd**	**WNL/Average**
110–115	**12–13**	**75th to 84th**	**WNL/High Average**
116–119	–	86th to 90th	Normative Strength/Above Average
120–129	14–15	91st to 97th	Normative Strength/Well Above Average
≥130	16–19	≥ 98th	Normative Strength/Extremely Above Average

Note: On standardized norm-referenced tests, most people (almost 70%) perform within normal limits (WNL; standard scores of 85 to 115, inclusive). This range is highlighted in bold.

Crystallized Intelligence (Gc)

Crystallized intelligence refers to the breadth and depth of a person's acquired knowledge of a culture and the effective application of this knowledge. This store of primarily verbal or language-based knowledge represents those abilities that are acquired during educational and general life experiences. The WISC-V measures Crystallized Intelligence via two primary subtests; namely, Similarities and Vocabulary, which make up the VCI. The Similarities Subtest measured lexical knowledge and reasoning with verbal information. This subtest required Amanda to listen to two words and draw conceptual or concrete similarities between the two words based on her understanding of the two words. Amanda earned a Similarities subtest scaled score of 10, which is in the Average range. The Vocabulary subtest measured lexical knowledge and required Amanda to define vocabulary words. Amanda earned a Vocabulary subtest scaled score of 10, which also falls in the Average range. Overall, Amanda's VCI of 100 is Average, indicating that her Crystallized Intelligence likely facilitates learning and academic performance.

Fluid Reasoning (Gf)

Fluid reasoning is the ability to reason, form concepts, and solve problems that often include novel information or procedures. In addition, Fluid Reasoning tasks tend to involve basic reasoning processes that depend minimally on learning and acculturation. The WISC-V measures fluid reasoning via the Matrix Reasoning and Figure Weights Subtests. The Matrix Reasoning subtest measured inductive reasoning by requiring Amanda to complete complex matrix patterns. Amanda earned a Matrix Reasoning scaled score of 9, which fell in the Average range. It should be noted that Amanda chose responses somewhat impulsively on this subtest, occasionally missing important visual details; therefore, her Matrix Reasoning score may slightly underestimate her ability to reason inductively. The Figure Weights subtest measured general sequential reasoning and quantitative reasoning and required Amanda to view two scales, one with missing weights, and choose one from a set of options that balanced the scales. Amanda earned a Figure Weights subtest scaled score of 10, which fell in the Average range. Overall, Amanda's FRI of 97 is Average, indicating that her Fluid Reasoning likely facilitates learning and academic performance.

Visual Processing (Gv)

Visual processing is the ability to analyze and synthesize visual information including perceiving, storing, manipulating, and thinking with visual patterns. The VSI on the WISC-V is made up of two subtests: namely, Block Design and Visual Puzzles. The Block Design subtest measured the ability to analyze and synthesize visual information by requiring Amanda to recreate designs using blocks. Amanda earned a Block Design scaled score of 6, which fell in the Below Average range. She made two dimension errors and one rotation error when recreating the visual designs. The number of dimension errors Amanda made occurred in less than 5% of the normative sample. The Block Design Partial and No Time Bonus scaled scores did not differ significantly from the Block Design scaled score, suggesting time did not affect her performance. Amanda commented during this subtest that the items were difficult for her, and she appeared to recognize that the items were progressively becoming more difficult. The Visual Puzzles Subtest also measures the ability to analyze and synthesize visual information and required Amanda to view a completed puzzle and choose the three pieces that combine to recreate the puzzle. Amanda performed in the Low Average range on this subtest as well, earning a scaled score of 7. Overall, Amanda's VSI of 81 is Below Average and is a normative weakness relative to same age peers from the general population. Amanda's difficulty with visual processing may be a contributing factor to her learning difficulties.

Short-Term Memory (Gsm)

Short-term memory (also called *short-term working memory*) refers to the ability to hold information in immediate awareness and then use it within a few seconds. Short-term memory tasks often require that information in immediate awareness be manipulated or transformed in some way. The WISC-V assesses short-term memory via the Digit Span and Picture Span subtests, which make up the WMI. The Digit Span subtest required Amanda to listen to the examiner state a series of digits and then repeat those numbers in the same order (Forward task), reverse order (Backward task), and ascending order (Sequencing task). Digits Forward measured memory span, while Digits Backward and Sequencing measured working memory. Amanda earned a scaled score of 8 on the Digit Span subtest, which fell in the Average range with no significant differences among the three memory tasks. The Picture Span subtest required Amanda to look at a set of pictures and then identify them in sequential order among a set of distractor pictures. Amanda earned a scaled score of 7 on this subtest, indicating Low Average performance. Overall Amanda's WMI of 85 is Low Average. It is possible that Amanda's weakness in working memory contributes to her learning and academic difficulties.

Processing Speed (Gs)

Processing speed refers to the efficiency of cognitive processing and is based on the speed of mental activity. It involves the ability to perform simple clerical-type tasks quickly, especially when under pressure to maintain attention and concentration. The WISC-V measures Processing Speed with two subtests, Coding and Symbol Search, which make up the PSI. The Coding subtest required Amanda to copy symbols that correspond to specific numbers as quickly as possibly within a 2-minute time limit. Amanda earned a scaled score of 8 on this subtest, which fell in the Average range. The Symbol Search task required Amanda to quickly scan a set of symbols and identify whether the target shape was repeated in the stimulus shapes. Amanda earned a scaled score of 9 on this subtest, which also fell in the Average range. Overall Amanda's PSI of 92 is within the Average range and, therefore, is not likely to be contributing to her academic difficulties.

Long-Term Storage and Retrieval (Glr)

The ability of *long-term storage and retrieval* involves the mental processes of encoding, storing, and retrieving information. Specifically, it reflects the efficiency with which information is initially stored and later retrieved by using association. The WISC-V contains subtests that measure two aspects of Long-Term Storage and Retrieval, namely associative memory and speed of lexical access. The Immediate Symbol Translation subtest required Amanda to pair new symbols with a word and then to "read" sentences made up only of those symbols; this subtest measured Associative Memory, or the ability to remember previously unrelated information as having been paired, an essential skill for learning. Amanda earned a standard score of 102 on this subtest, which fell in the Average range. Delayed Symbol Translation was administered 20-30 minutes after Immediate Symbol Translation and measured long-term recall of information acquired through associative learning; Amanda earned a standard score of 102 on this subtest, which also fell in the Average range. Recognition Symbol Translation measured the ability to recognize, rather than freely recall, information acquired through associative learning. Amanda earned a standard score of 104 on this subtest, which fell in the Average range. The Naming Speed Literacy subtest required Amanda to identify letters and numbers quickly and measured speed of lexical access or how quickly she was able to rapidly recall (i.e., retrieve) objects, letters, and numbers by their names. The Naming Speed Quantity subtest required Amanda to identify quickly the quantity of blue squares inside boxes and measured speed of lexical access and number facility, or the speed at which simple arithmetic operations are performed accurately. Amanda earned standard scores of 98 and 102, respectively, on these subtests, which fell in the Average range. Overall, Amanda's Long-Term Storage and Retrieval likely facilitates learning.

However, it is important to note that Amanda's standard score of 89 on the Letter-Number portion of the Naming Speed Literacy subtest was in the Low Average range. In light of Amanda's reading difficulties, this performance suggested that Amanda may have a weakness in orthographic processing. To follow up on this hypothesis, the WJ IV Letter Pattern Matching test was administered. Amanda earned a standard score of 84 on this test, which fell in the Below Average range and is a normative weakness. In addition, the CTOPP-2 Rapid Letter Naming subtest was administered. Amanda obtained a scaled score of 6 on this subtest, which also fell in the Below Average range. The scores from these two subtests were combined to form an Orthographic Processing composite using X-BASS. Amanda's Orthographic Processing standard score of 78 fell in the Well Below Average range and is a normative weakness. This orthographic processing weakness most likely contributes to Amanda's reading difficulties.

Auditory Processing (Ga)

Auditory processing involves auditory perception and includes a wide range of abilities needed to discriminate, analyze, synthesize, comprehend, and manipulate sounds. The WISC-V does not have subtests that measure this cognitive processing domain explicitly. As a result, Auditory Processing was measured with selected subtests from the CTOPP-2. On the Blending Words and Blending Nonwords subtests Amanda was required to combine separate sounds to make a whole word and a nonword after listening to a series of separate sounds, respectively. On the Phoneme Isolation and Segmenting Nonwords subtests Amanda was required to identify specific phonemes within presented words and repeat nonwords one sound at a time after listening to a series of nonwords, respectively. These four subtests measured Amanda's awareness of and access to the sound structure of her oral language, also known as phonological processing. Because of the substantial variation in scores across these subtests, which ranged from Average (Segmenting Nonwords) to Extremely Below Average (Blending Nonwords), X-BASS was used to gain a better understanding of Amanda's strengths and weaknesses in phonological processing. Specifically, Phoneme Isolation and Segmenting Nonwords produced a Phonetic Coding: Analysis standard score of 85, which is Low Average. Blending Words and Blending Nonwords produced a Phonetic Coding: Synthesis standard score of 49, which is Extremely Below Average. Amanda's skill in analyzing phonemes or segmenting larger units of speech sounds into smaller units of speech sounds (Phonetic Coding: Analysis) is much better developed than her skill in synthesizing phonemes into whole words or blending smaller units of speech together into larger units of speech (Phonetic Coding: Synthesis). It is possible that the difference in Amanda's ability to analyze and synthesize phonemes is related to the type of intervention she has been receiving as well as the increased working memory demands involved in the synthesis tasks. The observed weakness in blending, in particular, is a significant contributing factor to Amanda's reading difficulties.

Tables 8.2 and 8.3 include the results of Amanda's evaluation of her cognitive abilities and processes.

Table 8.2 Results of Amanda's Performance on the WISC-V

Composite Subtest	Scaled/ Standard Score	Percentile Rank	Classification
Full Scale IQ	**91**	**27**	**Average**
Verbal Comprehension Index (VCI or Gc)	**100**	**50**	**Average**
Similarities	10		Average
Vocabulary	10		Average
Fluid Reasoning Index (FRI or Gf)	**97**	**42**	**Average**
Matrix Reasoning	9		Average
Figure Weights	10		Average
Visual Spatial Index (VSI or Gv)	**81**	**16**	**Low Average**
Block Design	6		Below Average
Visual Puzzles	7		Low Average
Working Memory Index (WMI or Gsm)	**85**	**16**	**Low Average**
Digit Span	8		Average
Picture Span	7		Low Average
Processing Speed Index (PSI or Gs)	**92**	**30**	**Average**
Coding	8		Average
Symbol Search	9		Average
Naming Speed Index	**99**	**47**	**Average**
Naming Speed Literacy	98		Average
Naming Speed Quantity	102		Average
Symbol Translation Index	**102**	**55**	**Average**
Immediate Symbol Translation	102		Average
Delayed Symbol Translation	102		Average
Recognition Symbol Translation	104		Average
Storage and Retrieval Index	**100**	**50**	**Average**

Table 8.3 Results of Amanda's Performance on the CTOPP-2

Composite Subtest	Scaled/Standard Score	Percentile Rank	Classification
Phonetic Coding: Analysis[1]	**85**	**16**	**Low Average**
Phoneme Isolation	7	16	Low Average
Segmenting Nonwords	8	25	Average
Phonetic Coding: Synthesis[1]	**49**	**< 0.1**	**Extremely Below Average**
Blending Words	2	0.1	Extremely Below Average
Blending Nonwords	1	0.1	Extremely Below Average

[1] These composites were generated using X-BASS.

Evaluation of Academic Achievement

To assess Amanda's academic achievement, the WIAT-III was administered. Amanda's performance in Oral Language, Reading, Mathematics, and Written Expression were evaluated and are described next.

Oral Language

Amanda was administered two subtests measuring Oral Language skills; namely, Listening Comprehension and Oral Expression. Listening Comprehension measured Amanda's skill in identifying objects by listening to words spoken on a recording (Receptive Vocabulary, standard score [SS] = 90) and her skill in comprehending spoken language (Oral Discourse Comprehension, SS = 104). Amanda earned a standard score of 96 on the Listening Comprehension Subtest, which fell in the Average range. The Oral Expression Subtest consisted of Expressive Vocabulary, Oral Word Fluency, and Sentence Repetition tasks. Amanda's standard score on the Oral Expression Subtest of 98 also fell in the Average range. These results suggest that Amanda's skills in understanding and producing spoken language are in the Average range relative to her same age peers. Therefore, Amanda's oral language may facilitate her learning. Table 8.4 includes the results of Amanda's oral language scores.

Table 8.4 Results of Amanda's Performance on Oral Language Subtests

Composite	Standard Score	Percentile Rank	Classification
Oral Language	96	53	Average
Subtest	**Standard Score**	**Percentile Rank**	**Classification**
Listening Comprehension	96	39	Average
Oral Expression	98	45	Average

Reading

Amanda was administered four subtests to measure her reading ability. The first, Reading Comprehension, measured the ability to derive meaning from text. Amanda's standard score of 79 fell in the Well Below Average range. She understood one brief passage and answered four out of six questions correctly. It appeared to the examiner that Amanda was unable to read two additional passages and guessed on the comprehension questions. It is suspected that her inability to comprehend the passages was due to inadequate basic reading skills rather than a deficit in comprehension. Amanda was also administered a subtest, Word Reading, which required her to read words in isolation. Her standard score of 77 on this subtest fell in the Well Below Average range. She recognized few words with automaticity, and the speed of her word reading is at the 5th percentile. Amanda's poor sight word recognition and slow reading speed further support an orthographic processing weakness. Amanda also completed the Pseudoword Decoding subtest, which required her to read non-real words using phonetic principles. Her standard score of 85 on this subtest fell in the Low Average range. Amanda also completed the Oral Reading Fluency subtest, which required her to read aloud while being timed. Based on Amanda's performance on the first passage, standard administration procedures required that the Grade 1 item set be administered. Her standard score of 74 on the Oral Reading Fluency subtest fell in the Well Below Average range.

Because of the observed difficulty with automatic recognition of sight words, Amanda completed the TOSWRF-2, which is a word recognition test that required her to draw lines between words that did not have spaces between them as quickly as possible. This test measured automatic sight word recognition under timed conditions. In 3 minutes, Amanda correctly identified 16 words by sight. She earned a standard score of 75, which fell in the Well Below Average range. This finding further supports an orthographic processing weakness as a contributing factor to Amanda's reading difficulties. Table 8.5 includes the results of Amanda's reading evaluation.

Table 8.5 Results of Amanda's Reading Evaluation

Composites	Standard Score	Percentile Rank	Classification
Total Reading	76	5	Well Below Average
Basic Reading	81	10	Below Average
Reading Comprehension and Fluency	73	4	Well Below Average
Subtest	**Standard Score**	**Percentile Rank**	**Classification**
Word Reading	77	6	Well Below Average
Pseudoword Decoding	85	16	Low Average
Reading Comprehension	79	8	Well Below Average
Oral Reading Fluency	74	4	Well Below Average

Mathematics

Amanda was administered subtests measuring her abilities to solve mathematical problems, perform numerical operations, and complete simple math computations under timed conditions. On the Math Problem Solving subtest, Amanda completed oral math problems with pictorial cues. She completed many of the problems, but had difficulty with those related to the value of currency and those with graphs (which may be related to her weakness in Visual Processing). Her standard score of 83 on the Math Problem Solving subtest fell in the Below Average range. Her performance on the Numerical Operations subtest resulted in a standard score of 99, which fell in the Average range. On tasks requiring Amanda to solve simple addition and subtraction problems quickly, Amanda earned standard scores of 89 and 91, respectively. Overall, Amanda's mathematics abilities ranged from Below Average to Average and are generally considered relative academic strength for her. Table 8.6 includes the results of Amanda's mathematics evaluation.

Table 8.6 Results of Amanda's Mathematics Evaluation

Composite	Standard Score	Percentile Rank	Classifications
Mathematics	90	25	Average
Math Fluency	89	23	Low Average
Subtest	**Standard Score**	**Percentile Rank**	**Classifications**
Math Problem Solving	83	13	Below Average
Numerical Operations	99	47	Average
Math Fluency-Addition	89	23	Low Average
Math Fluency- Subtraction	91	27	Average

Written Expression

Amanda completed three subtests to evaluate her written expression abilities. She was administered the Sentence Composition subtest, which consists of two components, Sentence Combining and Sentence Building. The Sentence Combining component required her to combine two sentences into one sentence. Her performance on this task was in the Average range (SS = 104). The Sentence Building component of this subtest required her to write sentences using a different target word in each sentence. Her performance on this task fell in the Low Average range (SS = 87). Overall, Amanda's Sentence Composition subtest standard score of 94 fell in the Average range. Of note, she performed only two of six of the sentences on the Sentence Building task; however, she performed them well enough to earn an Average score. Amanda also completed the Spelling subtest, which measured her ability to spell words spoken by the examiner. Her performance fell in the Well Below Average range (SS = 74). Her spelling performance is consistent with her orthographic and phonological processing weaknesses, noted earlier in this report. Table 8.7 includes the results of Amanda's written expression evaluation.

Table 8.7 Results of Amanda's Written Expression Evaluation

Composite	Standard Score	Percentile Rank	Classification
Written Expression	82	12	Below Average
Subtest	**Standard Score**	**Percentile Rank**	**Classification**
Spelling	74	4	Well Below Average
Sentence Composition	94	34	Average

Social-Emotional/Behavioral Evaluation

During the initial parent interview, Ms. Farris discussed two areas of social-emotional and behavioral functioning that warranted evaluation, specifically inattentiveness and distractibility. Amanda was previously diagnosed with ADHD and currently takes medication to help control her symptoms. Amanda's mother, father, and teacher, Ms. Bellow, completed the appropriate forms of the CBRS. Because of Amanda's reading difficulties, it was deemed too burdensome for Amanda to complete the self-report version of the CBRS.

The CBRS report provides information about Amanda's behavior, how she compares to other youth her age, and which scales are elevated. The scales are Emotional Distress, Aggressive Behaviors, Worrying, Upsetting Thoughts, Social Problems, Academic Difficulties, Language, Math, Hyperactivity/Impulsivity, Separation Fears, Perfectionistic and Compulsive Behaviors, Violence Potential, and Physical Symptoms. The scales have a mean of 50 (standard T-score) and a standard deviation of 10. Standard T-scores above 60 (or 1 standard deviation above the mean) are considered elevated and clinically significant. (See Appendix 8.A for CBRS scores. Note that P1 = Ms. Farris's report, P2 = Mr. Delaney's report, and T = Ms. Bellow's report).

Validity Indices

Validity indices on the CBRS consist of the Inconsistency Index, Negative Impression scale, and Positive Impression scale. The Inconsistency Index is a score based on how the respondent answered pairs of items similar in content. The Negative Impression scale indicates when the respondent reports an unusually high number of maladaptive behaviors, suggesting an overly negative impression of the individual. The Positive Impression scale indicates that the respondent endorsed an unusually high number of positive attributes, suggesting that the respondent views the individual in an overly positive manner. All three reporters responded in a way that suggests that the current results are reliable and valid.

Content Scales

The Emotional Distress, Worrying, Social Problems, and Separation Fears scales were elevated on Mr. Delaney's report. The Academic Difficulties scale was very elevated on Mr. Delaney's and Ms. Bellow's reports; this scale was also elevated on Ms. Farris's report. The Language scale was very elevated on Mr. Delaney's and Ms. Bellow's reports; this scale was not elevated on Ms. Farris's report. The Math scale was very elevated on Mr. Delaney's and Ms. Bellow's reports. The Hyperactivity/Impulsivity scale was very elevated on Mr. Delaney's and Ms. Farris's reports; the Hyperactivity scale was not elevated on Ms. Bellow's report.

DSM-5 Symptom Scales and Symptom Counts

The CBRS also provides information to assist evaluators in making diagnoses; this information consists of Symptom Scales and Symptom Counts. Amanda's results suggest that she probably meets criteria for ADHD-Combined Type because of elevations on the Hyperactivity/Impulsivity and Inattentive scales. Mr. Delaney reported behavior consistent with a diagnosis of Oppositional Defiant Disorder; however, neither the teacher nor Amanda's mother's report indicated behavior consistent with that diagnosis. Ms. Farris and Mr. Delaney reported behavior consistent with a manic episode; however, upon closer inspection, these items seem related to ADHD symptoms. Mr. Delaney's responses resulted in a very elevated score on the Generalized Anxiety Disorder scale, while Ms. Farris's responses were consistent with Separation Anxiety Disorder.

Impairment

Based on reports from Amanda's parents and teacher, it appears that Amanda's difficulties result in impairment in the academic setting as "often" or as "very frequently." Amanda's parents rated her impairment in the social setting as "occasional." Mr. Delaney rated Amanda's impairment in the home setting as "very frequently," while Ms. Farris rated her impairment in the home setting as "occasional."

In general, all three raters reported significant academic difficulties, with two raters reporting clinically significant problems in language (i.e., reading) and two raters reporting clinically significant problems in math. Amanda's parents reported clinically significant hyperactivity and impulsivity and inattentiveness. Manic symptoms appear to be related to ADHD, rather than a mood disorder. There do appear to be symptoms of Separation Anxiety or Generalized Anxiety. These disorders were explored further with her parents, and Amanda did not meet criteria for Separation Anxiety. There do appear to be symptoms of mild anxiety, but not enough to warrant a diagnosis of Generalized Anxiety. In general, Mr. Delaney reported more significant concerns than either Ms. Farris or

Ms. Bellow, but the results of all three reports are consistent with Amanda's history of ADHD and learning problems.

In addition to the CBRS, a projective measure of emotional and behavioral functioning was administered; Amanda responded to several cards on the TAT. In general, themes in Amanda's responses centered on relationships. One of her stories included reference to a child being abandoned and being found by police and a family who "loved him so much." Most of Amanda's responses were descriptions of the card rather than an imaginative elaboration of the cards, but with prompting, she provided some conclusion. Most stories included reference to happy relationships between individuals either as friends or families. Adults were portrayed as caring, nurturing, and limit setting. Children were described as generally happy with mild discontent at limit setting. Conflicts were usually resolved with the assistance of adult figures. No signs of significant mood or anxiety difficulties were evident in Amanda's stories. None of the characters in her stories engaged in disruptive or aggressive behavior.

Interpretation and Clinical Impressions

Amanda Farris is a cooperative, charming 8-year-old girl who was referred by her mother, Ms. Beth Farris, for a psychoeducational evaluation to determine whether Amanda has a learning disability or another diagnosis that might be contributing to her academic difficulties. To answer these questions, background information was obtained and reviewed through a variety of sources, including a developmental history interview with Ms. Farris and a record review of previous evaluations and progress reports. In addition, cognitive and academic tests were administered to Amanda. Finally, diagnostic questionnaires were completed by Amanda's mother, father, and teacher.

Amanda was born to a mother who reportedly used alcohol and nicotine during pregnancy. Amanda's birth was complicated due to anoxia, and early care experiences in the first three months of life were reportedly neglectful. She was cared for in a hospital until 11 months of age and then lived in an orphanage until 2 years of age. She was adopted by Ms. Farris and brought to the United States at age 2 years 4 months. Biological family history is significant for learning difficulties. Amanda was evaluated for early intervention services after arriving in the United States and did not qualify for these services. Developmental milestones are for the most part unknown, although it was reported that she quickly learned English. Academic problems were first noted in kindergarten, and behavioral problems were evident as well. Amanda was diagnosed with ADHD and although she has had a positive response to medication treatment, academic difficulties persist.

Cognitive testing revealed that Amanda has Average cognitive abilities and processes in Crystallized Intelligence, Fluid Reasoning, Long-Term Storage and Retrieval, and Processing Speed. There were also cognitive abilities and processes that are considered weaknesses. Amanda demonstrated Below Average Working Memory abilities on the WISC-V, Low Average Phonetic Coding: Analysis and Extremely Below Average Phonetic Coding: Synthesis on the CTOPP-2. In addition, Amanda's performance on the Letter-Number portion of the WISC-V Naming Speed Literacy Subtest suggested the need to investigate orthographic processing as a potential contributing factor to her reading difficulties. Overall, specific data gathered from the CTOPP-2 revealed a phonological processing deficit, and data from the CTOPP-2, WISC-V, and WJ IV revealed an orthographic processing deficit. These deficits were corroborated by other data sources.

Academic testing revealed Below Average performance across domains with some relative strengths in specific skills. Generally, math performance fell in the Average range with a relative strength in numerical operations and a relative weakness in math problem solving. Amanda's reading and writing skills were Below Average while her Oral Language skills were Average. Notably, the difference between Amanda's Oral Language composite and her Reading Comprehension and Fluency composite was 23 points. This difference is rare, occurring in less than 10 percent of the population and provides support for a specific learning disability in reading.

Because Amanda's evaluation results appear consistent with a specific learning disability in reading, her cognitive and academic test performances were evaluated in terms of a Patterns of Strengths and Weaknesses (PSW) model for identifying learning disabilities. This model of learning disability identification is research based and allowable under federal regulations. This model also helps to inform intervention recommendations as specific cognitive processing and academic weaknesses are considered in relation to one another. Amanda's PSW was evaluated using X-BASS. Results are consistent with the classification category of Specific Learning Disability in Basic Reading Skills and Reading Fluency in accordance with the Individuals with Disabilities Education Improvement Act (IDEIA).

More specifically, Amanda's Orthographic Processing and Auditory Processing scores were evaluated separately in terms of discrepancy from her overall average cognitive ability estimate and in terms of their relationship to her reading skills. The findings from these analyses supported domain-specific deficits in orthographic and phonological processing as compared to same-age peers and relative to her generally Average overall cognitive ability and a strong consistent relationship between these processing areas and her basic reading skills. These results support a diagnosis of mixed dyslexia, which is a combination of orthographic (also called *dyseidetic* or *surface*) and phonological (also called *dysphonetic*) dyslexia subtypes.

Overall, although Amanda's cognitive ability and processing strengths have facilitated her learning and academic performance in some areas, such as math, her phonological and orthographic processing weaknesses and her weakness in working memory have interfered significantly with her ability to acquire and develop basic reading skills in a manner consistent with the majority of her peers. (See Appendix 8.B for results of PSW Analysis.)

In addition to mixed dyslexia, Amanda demonstrated symptoms consistent with a diagnosis of ADHD. Direct observations and teacher and parent reports as well as historical information all support a continued diagnosis of ADHD-Combined Type. Although her ADHD symptoms likely exacerbate academic difficulties, they did not appear to be primarily responsible for her reading difficulties. It is important that one consider ADHD symptoms as a contributory factor to learning problems when making treatment and educational recommendations; Amanda will require a smaller learning environment to increase the likelihood that she will respond well to an intervention.

Based on the current results, there did not appear to be significant social-emotional difficulties. Data suggestive of manic symptoms were more consistent with ADHD symptoms, and there was no other evidence of any mood related disorder. While Amanda may experience mild anxiety symptoms, particularly related to academic issues, psychiatric disorders were ruled out as accounting for academic problems.

According to the most recent IEP, the school district is recommending Integrated Co-Teaching (ICT) services in a general education classroom in a community school. Based on the current evaluation findings, this examiner strongly disagrees with this recommendation. Amanda has cognitive deficits in orthographic processing, phonological processing (particularly, phonetic coding synthesis), and working memory, all of which manifest in academic difficulties in reading skills (i.e., sight word recognition, reading fluency, reading comprehension); these deficits require that specialized instructional methods be implemented. In addition to specific cognitive deficits, Amanda exhibits hyperactivity, impulsivity, and inattentiveness, which contribute to learning difficulties. All of these factors combine to make learning difficult for Amanda and her learning needs quite complex. As a result, she requires a small-class, full-time special education setting to address her learning needs adequately. In the opinion of this examiner, her cognitive, academic, and attentional needs cannot be addressed adequately in an ICT classroom because of the demands on the teacher's time that Amanda's learning needs require.

Amanda has completed first grade twice and is now completing second grade. She has reportedly received intensive reading interventions for approximately one and a half academic years. She is currently at an H reading level according to her mother's report. Despite repeating first grade with special education supports and receiving reading interventions for at least one and a half academic years, an "H" reading rating indicates that Amanda is at a Level 1 for January of second grade, according to the Teachers College Reading Levels. She is reportedly in danger of being retained a second time because of her lack of responsiveness to previous reading interventions. A second retention would not only have a strong likelihood of being ineffective in remediating her reading skills, but it would also be very likely to cause harm to Amanda's social-emotional development.

In addition to placement considerations, this examiner is also recommending that an evidence-based reading intervention for students with orthographic and phonological processing deficits be implemented. This program should be delivered by a certified special education teacher with experience teaching children with specific learning disabilities in reading. This intervention should be delivered with full adherence to the program guidelines. If a small-group intervention is utilized, there should be no more than three children total in the group and all children should have similar learning profiles. Otherwise, an individual intervention approach may be warranted.

Strengths (Abilities, characteristics, and circumstances that are likely to facilitate learning and academic performance)

- Verbal knowledge
- Fluid reasoning skills
- Invested, committed parents
- Friendly, sociable
- Cooperative, persistent

Weaknesses (Cognitive processes and academic weaknesses that will very likely inhibit learning and academic progress)

- Orthographic Processing
- Phonological Processing (i.e., Phonetic Coding: Synthesis, such as blending words)
- Working Memory
- Poor sight word recognition
- Poor reading comprehension and fluency

Recommendations for Intervention and Remediation

General

- Placement in a small class in a special education school specifically for children with learning disabilities that can provide Amanda with specialized instruction and the individualized attention her cognitive and academic weaknesses require
- Continued psychiatric consultation for medication management for ADHD symptoms

Accommodations

- Extended time on tests because of attentional deficit, or replace timed tests with an alternative assessment procedure
- Testing in separate location because of symptoms of inattention and distractibility
- Directions and questions read aloud on all tests
- Provide extra time to complete in-class assignments, or shorten assignments
- Modified homework assignments

Auditory Processing (Ga)

- Speech-language therapy to address poor phonetic synthesis (i.e., blends), three times weekly in small group or individually

Reading

- Because of Amanda's deficient basic reading skills, specifically in sight-word recognition, an intensive *multi-modal, evidence-based reading intervention* is necessary. This program should be delivered consistently and with integrity by a certified special education teacher in a small-group setting with no more than three students. All students should have similar reading difficulties.
- A fold-in technique using vocabulary flash cards should be used to increase Amanda's sight-word vocabulary so that she is less reliant on her phonetic synthesis. Word lists such as *Dolch Basic Sight Words* or *1000 Instant Words* contain high-frequency words used in reading materials.
  - http://www.k12reader.com/fry-word-list-1000-high-frequency-words/
- Elkonin boxes help students identify each phoneme when reading a word. This intervention is warranted to help Amanda attend to each grapheme when decoding unfamiliar words.

- When assigning independent reading activities, ensure that the book or passage is at Amanda's independent reading level.
- Additional resources:
  - http://www.readingrockets.org
  - Earobics (available from Cognitive Concepts)
  - WORDS: Integrated Decoding and Spelling Instruction Based on Word Origin and Word Structure (available from PRO-ED)

Writing

- Facilitate generation of ideas for writing tasks using story starters, brainstorming, and so on.
- Do not penalize for poor spelling. Provide correction.
- Provide opportunities for practice of writing skills, focusing on expression of ideas, semantics, and mechanics.
- Continued speech-language therapy to improve expression of ideas.

Respectfully Submitted,

_____   _____
Erin M. McDonough, PhD   Date
Licensed Psychologist

REFERENCE

Ortiz, S. O., Flanagan, D. P., & Alfonso, V. C. (2017). *Cross-battery assessment software system* (X-BASS v2.0). Hoboken, NJ: Wiley.

Appendix 8.A

CBRS SCORES

Conners CBRS Content Scale Detailed Scores: Comparison across Raters

The following table summarizes the results for each scale, as well as any statistically significant ($p < .10$) differences in T-scores between pairs of raters. If a pair of ratings is not noted in the "Statistically Significant Differences" column, then the difference between those two raters did not reach statistical significance.

Scale	T- score (percentile) Guideline			Statistically Significant Differences
	P1	P2	T	
Emotional Distress	52 (66) Average	69 (99) Elevated	54 (83) Average	P2 > T; P2 > P1
Upsetting Thoughts[1,2]	46 (42) Average	46 (42) Average	55 (79) Average	No significant differences
Worrying[1]	59 (82) Average	70 (94) Very Elevated	-	P2 > P1
Social Problems[1]	57 (77) Average	73 (97) Very Elevated	53 (65) Average	P2 > P1; P2 > T
Separation Fears[3]	52 (60) Average	68 (93) Elevated	46 (40) Average	P2 > P1; P2 > T
Social Anxiety[3]	-	-	59 (88) Average	Comparison not possible
Defiant/Aggressive Behaviors	49 (65) Average	64 (94) High Average	47 (60) Average	P2 > P1; P2 > T
Academic Difficulties	66 (95) Elevated	90 (99) Very Elevated	74 (97) Very Elevated	P2 > T; P2 > P1; T > P1
Language[4]	63 (90) High Average	90 (98) Very Elevated	72 (94) Very Elevated	P2 > T; P2 > P1; T > P1
Math[4]	59 (90) Average	70 (98) Very Elevated	90 (96) Very Elevated	T > P2; T > P1; P2 > P1
Hyperactivity/ Impulsivity[5]	70 (98) Very Elevated	84 (99) Very Elevated	59 (86) Average	P2 > P1; P2 > T; P1 > T
Perfectionistic and Compulsive Behaviors	45 (47) Average	42 (18) Average	58 (86) Average	T > P1; T > P2
Violence Potential Indicator	56 (81) Average	61 (91) High Average	49 (63) Average	P2 > T; P1 > T
Physical Symptoms	63 (91) High Average	63 (91) High Average	45 (41) Average	P1 > T; P2 > T

Note(s):
[1]Subscale of Emotional Distress on the Parent form.
[2]Upsetting Thoughts/Physical Symptoms, subscale of Emotional Distress on the Teacher form.
[3]Subscale of Emotional Distress on the Teacher form.
[4]Subscale of Academic Difficulties on the Parent and Teacher forms.
[5]Hyperactivity on the Teacher form.

Detailed Scores: Comparison across Raters

The following table summarizes the results for each DSM-5 Symptom scale, as well as any statistically significant ($p < .10$) differences in T-scores between pairs of raters. If a pair of ratings is not noted in the "Statistically Significant Differences" column, then the difference between those two raters did not reach statistical significance.

Scale	T- score (percentile) Guideline			Statistically Significant Differences
	P1	P2	T	
ADHD Predominantly Inattentive Presentation	81 (99) Very Elevated	90 (99) Very Elevated	63 (86) High Average	P2 > P1; P2 > T; P1 > T
ADHD Predominantly Hyperactive-Impulsive Presentation	70 (98) Very Elevated	84 (99) Very Elevated	62 (89) High Average	P2 > P1; P2 > T; P1 > T
Conduct Disorder	57 (85) Average	64 (91) High Average	46 (39) Average	P2 > T; P1 > T
Oppositional Defiant Disorder	59 (80) Average	83 (99) Very Elevated	51 (73) Average	P2 > P1; P2 > T; P1 > T
Major Depressive Episode	49 (62) Average	57 (81) Average	55 (82) Average	No significant differences
Manic Episode	72 (94) Very Elevated	72 (94) Very Elevated	58 (82) Average	P1 > T; P2 > T
Generalized Anxiety Disorder	61 (91) High Average	89 (98) Very Elevated	59 (82) Average	P2 > P1; P2 > T
Separation Anxiety Disorder	54 (68) Average	65 (88) Elevated	45 (37) Average	P2 > P1; P2 > T
Social Anxiety Disorder (Social Phobia)	47 (44) Average	59 (85) Average	56 (86) Average	No significant differences
Obsessive-Compulsive Disorder	44 (39) Average	44 (39) Average	57 (89) Average	T > P1; T > P2
Autism Spectrum Disorder	42 (37) Average	55 (77) Average	53 (68) Average	P2 > P1

Appendix 8.B

CROSS-BATTERY ASSESSMENT SOFTWARE SYSTEM (X-BASS): DUAL-DISCREPANCY/ CONSISTENCY MODEL: PSW RESULTS FOR AMANDA FARRIS

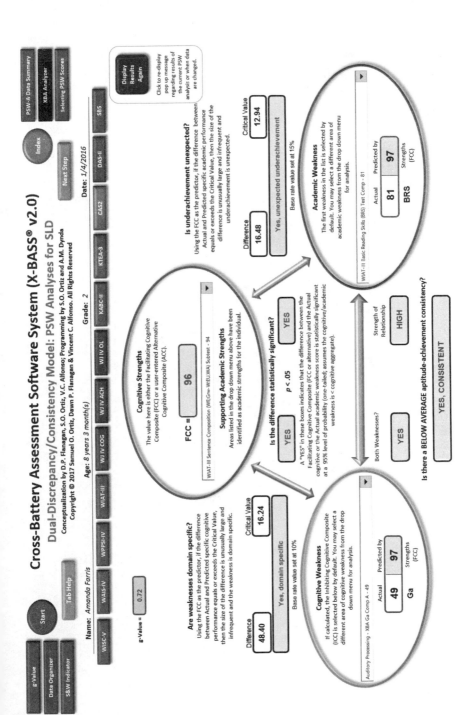

Cross-Battery Assessment Software System (X-BASS® v2.0)

Dual-Discrepancy/Consistency Model: PSW Analyses for SLD

Conceptualization by D.P. Flanagan, S.O. Ortiz, V.C. Alfonso; Programming by S.O. Ortiz and A.M. Dynda
Copyright © 2017 Samuel O. Ortiz, Dawn P. Flanagan & Vincent C. Alfonso. All Rights Reserved

Name: *Amanda Farris*   Age: 8 years 3 month(s)   Grade: 2   Date: 1/4/2016

g-Value = 0.72

Are weaknesses domain specific?
Using the FCC as the predictor, if the difference between Actual and Predicted specific cognitive performance equals or exceeds the Critical Value, then the size of the difference is unusually large and infrequent and the weakness is domain specific.

Difference 48.40   Critical Value 16.24

Yes, domain specific

Base rate value set at 10%

Cognitive Weakness
If calculated, the Inhibiting Cognitive Composite (ICC) is selected below by default. You may select a different area of cognitive weakness from the drop down menu for analysis.

Auditory Processing - XBA Ga Comp A - 49

Actual 49 | Predicted by 97
Ga | Strengths (FCC)

Cognitive Strengths
The value here is either the Facilitating Cognitive Composite (FCC) or a user-entered Alternative Cognitive Composite (ACC).

FCC = 96

Supporting Academic Strengths
Areas listed in the drop down menu above have been identified as academic strengths for the individual.

WIAT-III Sentence Composition (WE-GrW-WE-LWA) Subtest - 94

Is the difference statistically significant?

YES   p < .05   YES

A "YES" in these boxes indicates that the difference between the Facilitating Cognitive Composite (FCC or alternative) and the Actual cognitive or the Actual academic weakness score is statistically significant at a 95% level of probability (one-tailed; assumes the cognitive/academic weakness is < cognitive aggregate).

Both Weaknesses?   Strength of Relationship

YES   HIGH

Is there a BELOW AVERAGE aptitude-achievement consistency?

YES, CONSISTENT

Is underachievement unexpected?
Using the FCC as the predictor, if the difference between Actual and Predicted specific academic performance equals or exceeds the Critical Value, then the size of the difference is unusually large and infrequent and underachievement is unexpected.

Difference 16.48   Critical Value 12.94

Yes, unexpected underachievement

Base rate value set at 15%

Academic Weakness
The first weakness in the list is selected by default. You may select a different area of academic weakness from the drop down menu for analysis.

WIAT-III Basic Reading Skills (BRS) Test Comp - 81

Actual 81 | Predicted by 97
BRS | Strengths (FCC)

Start   Tab Help

Next Step

Index

Display Results Again
Click to re-display pop up message regarding results of the current PSW analysis or when data are changed.

g-Value
Data Organizer
S&W Indicator

PSW-A Data Summary
XBA Analyzer
Selecting PSW Scores

WISC-V | WAIS-IV | WPPSI-IV | WIAT-III | WJ IV COG | WJ IV ACH | WJ IV OL | KABC-II | KTEA-3 | CAS2 | DAS-II | SBS

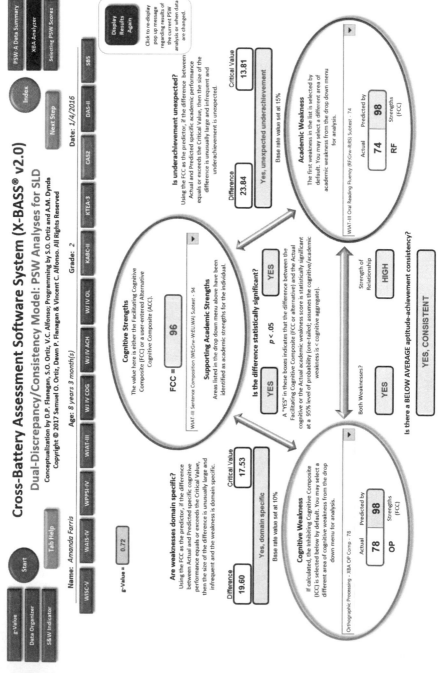

Nine

ASSESSMENT OF ENGLISH LEARNERS WITH THE WISC-V

Samuel O. Ortiz, Kristan E. Melo, and Meghan A. Terzulli

Assessment of individuals from diverse cultural and linguistic backgrounds is an activity that has been ongoing for over a century. Despite the lengthy attention devoted to the endeavor, research-based principles that might be used to guide best practice for assessing diverse individuals remains relatively vague and poorly understood. Perhaps a large part of the reason may be due rightly to the wide range and complexity of variables involved in the assessment of individuals, particularly children, from culturally and linguistically diverse backgrounds. Such variables include the language in which the assessment is administered, the individual's English language proficiency, the modality of assessment (i.e., nonverbal versus verbal), the introduction or use of modifications or adaptations to testing, and so forth. These variables interact with other variables that relate to the developmental experiences of the individual, such as the age at which the individual was first exposed to English, type of educational programming received and for how long, opportunity for the acquisition of "mainstream" acculturative knowledge, and possible interruptions in the development of the individual's native language and culture, among others (Harris & Llorente, 2005; Ortiz, 2008). Given the multitude of factors present in the context of evaluating diverse individuals that one must consider in order to make appropriate decisions when testing, it becomes less surprising that translation of research into practical guidelines has progressed relatively little in more than 100 years.

There is arguably no test more frequently used in the cognitive evaluation of children than the Wechsler scales (Flanagan & Kaufman, 2009; Weiss, Prifitera, & Munoz, 2015), and this is no exception for the evaluation of culturally and linguistically diverse children (Ortiz, 2009). In a survey of school psychologists' cognitive assessment practices, Sotelo-Dynega and Dixon (2014) found that the majority of school psychologists selected the *Wechsler Intelligence Scale for Children-Fourth Edition* (WISC-IV) regardless of the reason for referral. The advent of the WISC-V is unlikely to alter this pattern considering the sheer proportion of monolingual English-speaking psychologists. For example, a survey of members of the National Association of School Psychologists (NASP) indicates that only 13.9% indicated fluency in a language other than English (Klotz, 2016). Likewise, only 27 languages other than English are represented in this sample, compared to the 400 languages spoken by families living in the United States (Klotz, 2016; U.S. Census Bureau, 2015). Such statistics indicate that it is highly likely that non-native English-speaking children (or simply English learners [ELs]) will invariably continue to be evaluated in English (most often with a Wechsler Scale) by English speakers—a pattern that has remained rather consistent historically (Ochoa, Powell, & Robles-Piña, 1996).

The mismatch between the language of administration and the native language of the examinee has not been entirely overlooked. The popularity of the Wechsler Scales and their inherent dual modality framework (i.e., Verbal IQ tests vs. Performance IQ tests) provided a convenient methodology that has resulted in favoring the use of "nonverbal" tests for ELs in attempts to increase the validity of ability measurements by deliberately excluding verbal tests that are more likely to be attenuated by the effects of limited English proficiency than nonverbal ones (Cathers-Schiffman, & Thompson, 2007; Lohman, Korb, & Lakin, 2008; see also Chapter 4). Accordingly, the Wechsler Nonverbal Scale of Ability (WNV; Wechsler & Naglieri, 2006) was developed precisely for use with children from culturally and linguistically diverse backgrounds and has since become the second most frequently used cognitive assessment battery by school psychologists for evaluating this population (Sotelo-Dynega & Dixon, 2014). It is important to note, however, that despite the ubiquitous nature of the Wechsler Scales, their popularity is not a result of any exceptional or inherent characteristics regarding fairness or cross-cultural validity that other batteries lack. Rather, the popularity of its administration with diverse children can in part be attributed to more pedestrian factors, such as simply being the most frequently used test in any application as well as the relative absence of any better alternatives (Ortiz & Melo, 2015).

Compounding the issue of testing ELs is the relative lack of professional agreement regarding systematic frameworks to guide such evaluations (Ortiz, 2014). Policies that are beginning to broach the process of evaluation with ELs, albeit still in a very general manner, have only recently emerged (e.g., American Educational Research Association, American Psychological Association, & National Council on Measurement in Education, 2015; NASP, 2016). One of the more persistent stumbling blocks in advancing consensus in the evaluation of diverse individuals is attributable to seemingly conflicting research findings, erroneous interpretations of such findings, and misconceptions regarding test bias and fairness (Ortiz, 2014; Ortiz, Ortiz, & Devine, 2016; Rhodes, Ochoa, & Ortiz, 2005). Nevertheless, it is research that must guide any approach that seeks to evaluate diverse individuals because it is the only manner in which the process can be deemed to be both fair and valid.

The purpose of this chapter is to examine how and in what manner the WISC-V may be used to assess the intelligence and cognitive abilities of children from diverse cultural and linguistic backgrounds in a manner that can be defended as being both fair and valid. To accomplish this goal, issues regarding fairness and bias in testing will be discussed initially along with specific attention to the systematic attenuating impact that developmental language proficiency (and to a lesser extent, opportunity for acquisition of acculturative knowledge) has on test performance (Cormier, McGrew, & Ysseldyke, 2014; Flanagan, Ortiz, & Alfonso, 2013; Ortiz, 2014; Sotelo-Dynega, Ortiz, Flanagan, & Chaplin, 2013). Next, current and common approaches to evaluation of diverse individuals that rely on standardized testing is presented that demonstrates their insufficiency with regard to yielding valid test scores. And last, a framework for best practice using the WISC-V is presented that offers all practitioners (including those who speak English only) a practical approach that uses time and resources efficiently, meets all legal and regulatory requirements, and establishes the validity of test scores, resulting in defensible interpretation (Flanagan et al., 2013; Mpofu & Ortiz, 2009; Ortiz & Melo, 2015; Ortiz et al., 2016).

The foundation of the proposed framework addresses the core objective in assessment: validity. Any approach to assessment of diverse individuals must provide direct evaluation of obtained scores to determine whether they were affected by cultural and linguistic factors to an extent that may have rendered them invalid indicators of the abilities they were intended to represent (Ortiz, 2009; Ortiz & Melo, 2015). In other words, the assessment must ask the question, "To what extent has the validity of test results been compromised by factors that do not actually constitute or suggest an intrinsic lack of ability?" Only when the validity of test results has been established credibly can an examiner begin to synthesize test scores with other sources of data to formulate conclusions and interpretations that are truly nondiscriminatory (Ortiz, 2014; Ortiz & Melo, 2015; Ortiz et al., 2016).

FAIRNESS, BIAS, AND TRADITIONAL ASSESSMENT APPROACHES

The scientific *zeitgeist* in which psychological testing arose was wedded solely to an immutable and hierarchically based notion of superiority in intelligence resulting from a simple difference in genetics, primarily as a function of skin color (Brigham, 1923). This meant that notions regarding the complete and unalterable inherited basis of intelligence automatically chained IQ test use to the misconception that administration without any alteration or modification represented a fair and appropriate assessment method for evaluating any individual, irrespective of linguistic or cultural differences (Goddard, 1917). This idea persisted for decades and was given additional credence when systematic research in the 1970s and 1980s on test bias (as defined from a purely psychometric point of view) consistently failed to find any such bias when testing individuals from different races and ethnicities (Figueroa, 1983; Reynolds & Ramsay, 2003; Sandoval, Frisby, Geisinger, Scheunemann, & Grenier, 1998; Valdes & Figueroa, 1994). However, given the manner that bias has been defined traditionally (i.e., primarily as related to problems with test reliability) it would have been very surprising if bias had been found, as such results would have meant that an IQ or cognitive ability test somehow loses its accuracy solely on the basis of the color of a person's skin. This would be akin to having a scale that suddenly cannot accurately gauge weight when the person using it has dark skin rather than light skin. Bias, defined as such, should not and in fact does not exist. But reliability is not a guarantee of validity. And when the focus of bias shifts from reliability to validity, the results are much different.

Research addressing bias in testing has largely conceptualized "race and ethnicity" as the target variable that should presumably confound test scores. This does not, however, appear to be a reasonable conceptualization. For example, the racial or ethnic category of "Hispanic" covers an extremely wide range of individuals of various races, language fluencies (including languages beyond Spanish and English, such as Nahautl of Mexico or Taíno of the Caribbean), and opportunities for the acquisition of mainstream U.S. acculturative knowledge (the type that typically appears on tests). Further, while identifying as Hispanic certainly increases the likelihood that the individual would have been exposed to another language (i.e., Spanish), it by no means makes it certain.

Consider, for example, the following three individuals: (1) a second- generation, 12-year-old Colombian American child born in the United States to parents who immigrated here, who is a bilingual English-Spanish speaker with greater proficiency in English and who has been schooled entirely in English since kindergarten; (2) a first-generation, 12-year-old Colombian American child with no prior formal education who immigrated to the United States from Colombia with his/her parents a year ago and who has been learning English for only one school year; and (3) a fifth-generation native-English-speaking, 12-year-old born to Colombian parents who are fully acculturated to the U.S. mainstream and have been educated entirely in English. All three individuals are 12 years old, all are residing in the United States and attending U.S. schools, and all are classified as Hispanic. But it is unlikely that one would assume that all three of these 12-year-olds would perform similarly on tests of intelligence or cognitive abilities administered to them in English.

All things other than exposure to English and U.S. culture being equal, the first 12-year-old, by virtue of his/her superior English proficiency and education, would do significantly better on an intelligence test than the second 12-year-old who has yet to gain even minimal comprehension of English and who has received only one year of formal education in English. Moreover, neither of the first two 12-year-olds would be expected to fare so well on the test compared to the third 12-year-old who has had every experiential advantage, including fully acculturated parents and grandparents who are native speakers of English, and who has had far more opportunity to acquire the typical types of incidental mainstream U.S. acculturative knowledge that is inherent in intelligence tests. Yet research on bias related to race (i.e., using race/ethnicity as an independent variable) assumes that the performance of all three of these 12-year-olds should in fact be equivalent because they are all of the same age (and therefore development) and all belong to the same group: Hispanic. Thus, differences in their performance on an intelligence test relative to non-Hispanics would be attributed erroneously to race.

Given the preceding example, it should be clear that it is not race or ethnicity that affect test performance but rather each individual's *developmental English language proficiency* and *opportunity for the acquisition of incidental mainstream U.S. acculturative knowledge.* Differences in these two variables, particularly developmental language proficiency in English, have powerful attenuating effects on test performance (Cormier et al., 2014; Dynda, 2008; Sotelo-Dynega et al., 2013). Accordingly, we would expect that the second-generation Colombian American 12-year-old would perform better than the first-generation Colombian American 12-year-old but not so well as the fifth-generation native-English-speaking 12-year-old on tests given in English and on whom the tests were primarily normed. Thus, despite simplistic notions of skin color and assumptions of comparability related to development, differences in test performance between racial and ethnic groups is influenced by the extent to which individuals, such as the 12-year-olds described here, differ in *experiential background* (i.e., developmental language proficiency and opportunity for acculturative knowledge acquisition) as compared to the experiential backgrounds of those on whom the test was normed (Salvia & Ysseldyke, 1991). Current research supports and extends this notion by illustrating that test performance is affected proportionally and in accordance with the degree to which a given test measures or requires age-appropriate development of language or acculturative knowledge, albeit the results are more robust for language (Cormier et al., 2014; Dynda, 2008; Sotelo-Dynega et al., 2013).

There is a considerable body of research using various historical and contemporary versions of the WISC that support the principle described. This is especially true when studies are examined that have specifically avoided using race as an independent variable and instead focused on language proficiency. Research specifically undertaken with ELs and not racial categories consistently demonstrates that linguistically diverse individuals perform much lower on tests of cognitive abilities than monolingual native English speakers, particularly on tests that either measure or rely heavily on language-based abilities (Borghese & Gronau, 2005; Cathers-Schiffman & Thomson, 2007; Dynda, 2008; Nieves-Brull, 2006; Sanchez-Escbedo, 2012; Sotelo-Dynega, 2013; Styck & Watkins, 2013, 2014).

Because the tests employed in all of these studies were normed in a manner that ignored language proficiency as a stratification variable, the vast majority of the standardization samples were comprised of monolingual, native English speakers. Even when linguistically diverse individuals are included, albeit not in any systematic way, they are often of a level of English proficiency that allows them to understand test directions with ease, as determined by the examiner (or test publisher), so as not to compromise test administration or norming procedures. Despite what is clearly a restricted range in English language proficiency, the results from these studies remain consistent in demonstrating that children who are significantly "different" in English language proficiency (and presumably acculturative knowledge acquisition) as compared to the tests' norm samples display scores that are below the expected mean (i.e., SS = 100).

If an examiner were unaware of this effect, it is likely that no consideration regarding the attenuating effect of language proficiency on test performance would be made, and it might be concluded invalidly that such students have below average intelligence or possess some type of disability. Interpretations such as these, because of the lack of construct validity, would likely lead to decisions that are erroneous and that may cause harm to the individual (e.g., inappropriate identification of disability, incorrect placement in special education). To prevent inequitable outcomes and to make interpretations defensible and fair requires that practitioners evaluate the *validity* of the test scores before drawing any conclusions about the ability levels of an individual or his or her general intelligence. In other words, the question—To what extent do test scores reflect experiential differences rather than intrinsic disorders?—must be carefully considered and examined systematically before any valid inferences can be drawn from the data.

In the attempt to establish validity of test scores so as to permit interpretation, various assessment procedures have been undertaken by psychologists. The goal of these approaches is always the same: increase the fairness and validity of test scores obtained from evaluations conducted on diverse individuals. Some of the more common and current methods include modifications and adaptations to administration or scoring, primary or exclusive use of tests or test batteries that are considered nonverbal, and testing in the native language (Ortiz, 2014; Ortiz & Dynda, 2013). The relative success or failure of these methods with respect to the degree to which they actually ensure fairness and yield valid results are discussed next.

Modified Methods of Evaluation: Modified or Altered Assessment

One of the more common approaches to testing diverse individuals is simply to modify or alter the test in a manner that allows the examinee to demonstrate his or her true ability and reduces potential bias inherent in strict administration of the test. Such methods may include allowing the lengthening of or completely eliminating time limits (such as on Block Design), accepting responses in languages other than English, repeating instructions or translating instructions to the native language, pre-teaching task concepts, skipping inappropriate items (e.g., "Who was Christopher Columbus?"), and use of a translator or interpreter for administration. The intention is, of course, noble in that the alterations should assist the individual by providing better opportunities to demonstrate his or her abilities. And although one can assume that some of these modifications (e.g., removal of time limits) would certainly improve performance (as they would even with non-ELs), all of these methods violate standardization procedures, and thus render the test scores invalid by undermining the psychometric properties of the test. Violating standardization introduces new and unquantifiable amounts of error (which could have either helped or hindered performance) and which can no longer be discerned by the examiner or the test's publisher due to the altered administration. This would be particularly problematic in the diagnosis of a specific learning disability (SLD), because accurate diagnosis of SLD requires a valid and nuanced profile of strengths and weaknesses across many domains. As such, modified assessment, while well intended, is not a sufficient approach to generating test scores that are valid and permit interpretation. This is not to say that modifications or alterations should never be used, however, because information derived from this method can yield important and valuable *qualitative* information. However, if the purpose of a standardized test is to yield valid *quantitative* representations of an individual's cognitive abilities, modified assessment by itself will not serve this purpose adequately. This suggests that when practitioners decide to employ standardized tests that they should consider administering them in the specified standardized manner first and modify or alter the administration only later in follow-up efforts to derive qualitative data. In this way, it leaves the original scores from the original administration unaltered and potentially subject to examination regarding the influence of linguistic and cultural variables. Scores obtained from any nonstandardized administration of a test cannot ever be determined to be valid and will effectively preclude any interpretation.

Nonverbal Methods of Evaluation: Language Reduced Assessment

Perhaps the most common method for assessing children from diverse backgrounds involves the administration of a nonverbal test or battery. In a survey of 323 school psychologists, Sotelo-Dynega and Dixon (2014) found that 88.6% of the school psychologists use a measure of nonverbal intelligence such as the WNV. This method has also been recommended by various researchers (Cathers-Schiffman & Thompson, 2007; Kranzler, Flores, & Cody, 2010) as well as by the developers of the WISC-V (Wechsler, Raiford, & Holdnack, 2014). Despite its widespread adoption in practice, nonverbal assessment does not appear to provide a satisfactory or complete solution to the issue of test score validity.

It has long been standard clinical practice for psychologists to administer and interpret only the subtests that made up the old Performance IQ and to simply disregard use of the Verbal IQ Subtests in the Wechsler Scales (Figueroa, 1990). Given that the PIQ and VIQ originally reflected the name and structure as drawn from the Army Mental Tests (Yerkes, 1921) and were considered initially by Wechsler to represent a range of interchangeable tests (Wechsler, 1944), it is not surprising that these indexes have been eliminated beginning with the WISC-IV and continuing in the WISC-V. Nevertheless, for the WISC-V, Wechsler and colleagues still recommend that the "NVI [Nonverbal Index] may provide a more appropriate estimate of intellectual ability for children who are English language learners but who can comprehend English subtest instructions" (2014; p. 141). The NVI consists of the subtests that make up the Visual Spatial Index (VSI; Block Design and Visual Puzzles), the Fluid Reasoning Index (FRI; Matrix Reasoning and Figure Weights), and the Processing Speed Index (PSI; Coding and Symbol Search).

At face value, it stands to reason that a nonverbal measure of intellectual ability would be a fairer estimate of intelligence for children from diverse backgrounds. For one, it seems logical that children who have limited English proficiency would perform better on subtests that either reduce or attempt to eliminate language demands. Of course, it is an erroneous assumption to believe that a nonverbal measure is wholly "nonverbal," because it is impossible to administer any test without any communication whatsoever. That the communication may well be gestural rather than verbal does not eliminate the purpose of language in testing that is based on communication and comprehension (Mpofu & Ortiz, 2009; Ortiz et al., 2012). And although many tests exist that permit administration solely through the use of gestures, none of them provides guidance on how the meaning of the gestures are to be conveyed to and learned by the examinee in the absence of any verbal communication. Moreover, the test content and stimuli, and even the very act of testing itself, is a cultural artifact that is not completely removed from the testing situation (Ortiz & Melo, 2015). For these reasons, nonverbal tests might be more accurately referred to as "language-reduced" tests. And whereas it has been demonstrated that performance of diverse individuals on such language-reduced tests is much closer to the normative mean than on language-embedded tests (Cathers-Schiffman & Thompson, 2007), the scores remain narrow in scope and of limited interpretive applicability. For example, research has demonstrated that nonverbal tests have relatively poor predictive validity for overall academic performance (Lohman et al., 2008), which is likely due to the lack of measurement of abilities that are most relevant and pertinent to school success (i.e., language abilities related to the acquisition and development of reading and writing skills). Given the ubiquitous nature of reading and writing difficulties as the presumptive concerns for evaluation referrals involving suspected SLD, the use of tests that do not provide any information in this regard will have little utility.

The movement toward nonverbal tests may have been driven in large part by the need to establish an individual's overall intellectual level. For example, Cathers-Schiffman and Thompson (2007) found that, on the WISC-III, Spanish-speaking children scored highest on the Perceptual Organizational Index (POI) and comparably to English speakers. However, on the VCI and the GAI, Spanish speakers scored significantly lower than English speakers. This led them to conclude that nonverbal measures are a fairer and more valid estimate of general intellectual ability, or g. This is only true, however, if one adheres to the concept of g (a debatable proposition, cf., Horn & Knoll, 2007) and if one finds current utility in the concept of g—a notion that is disappearing quickly in the wave of developments in SLD and use of approaches rooted in patterns of strengths and weaknesses (PSW) in cognitive functioning. As testing moves further away from broad indexes such as IQ and closer to distinct cognitive abilities with specific relations to academic functioning (Schneider & McGrew, 2012), nonverbal tests will likely become less and less relevant as well. The fact that within the context of CHC theory, nonverbal tests will, by definition, be restricted to measurement of a very narrow range of abilities (e.g., in the case of the NVI only Fluid Reasoning [Gf], Visual Processing [Gv], and Processing Speed [Gs] are measured among the seven generally needed to evaluate for SLD). If a child's abilities in these areas are intact, then the WNV would yield an estimate of intelligence that might falsely suggest overall average intelligence by having overlooked other abilities in which the child could actually have deficits. Similarly, if the child's performance yields a low WNV, it would suggest low overall intelligence, when the child might have significant strengths in abilities that went unmeasured by the test. In recognition of this potential problem, Weiss and colleagues (2006) assert that "the inclusion in the WNV of nonverbal tasks that are typically verbally mediated . . . , may further increase construct coverage of the various domains of intelligence measured nonverbally" (p. 49). Despite the claim, use of a nonverbal test that may or may not require internal verbal mediation is a poor substitute for direct measurement of the verbal ability. Abilities such as Crystallized Intelligence (Gc) and Auditory Processing (Ga), which represent the two best predictors of the development and acquisition of reading and writing skills, simply cannot be measured adequately or validly in a nonverbal manner.

When these shortcomings are combined with the one problem that plagues all tests in general (i.e., lack of norm sample stratification by language proficiency), it must be seen that language-reduced tests are also an insufficient and incomplete solution to the problem of test score validity. Whereas such tests clearly reduce the attenuating effect of language proficiency on test performance, the resulting narrow focus on abilities, over-reliance on the validity of general estimates of intelligence, and lack of predictive value in academic achievement, makes them no different than the tests (of Gv, Gf, and Gs) that appear on more comprehensive batteries that also include verbal tests. To be sure, nonverbal tests are good and useful tests for various purposes, but they do not differ in any meaningful way from nonverbal tests found on comprehensive batteries. Thus, psychologists looking for an assessment method that provides valid estimates of general intelligence or a broad range of specific cognitive abilities cannot rely on nonverbal tests exclusively.

Dominant Language Evaluation: Native Language Assessment

With the introduction of the WISC-IV Spanish (Wechsler, 2004), Spanish-speaking professionals who were competent and qualified had the option of conducting an assessment with Spanish speakers in Spanish, that is, their dominant language, using a contemporary instrument. Native language tests, such as the WISC-IV Spanish, give the appearance of being able to solve all the problems inherent in evaluation of children from diverse backgrounds, at least for those who are Spanish speakers. Generally speaking, the decision to use a native language test often comes after testing the individual's language dominance in both English and the native language. When the individual is dominant in English, testing is done in English. When the individual is found to be dominant in the native language, in this case Spanish, the testing is done in the native language. One of the problems with this approach, however, is the assumption that if the individual is dominant in the native language, then the individual's level of proficiency in that language is comparable to other age- or grade-matched peers and thus scores obtained via the native language would be automatically valid (Esparza-Brown, 2007). The same problem holds if the individual is dominant in English. Dominance, however, is not an indicator of proficiency or development in a language. It merely indicates which language is better developed at that point. One can easily be dominant in a language and still lack significant proficiency in it as compared to another language. Dominance and proficiency are therefore not equivalent, and establishing dominance only serves to indicate in which language the individual is likely to perform better but not necessarily comparable to other children of the same age or grade. How well-developed specific skills and abilities are in a particular individual is not described by dominance and thus fails to provide valid information on whether that individual in fact possesses age- or grade-appropriate development in that language (Ortiz et al., 2016). Beyond this issue lies the fact that little research exists that may be used to guide and inform psychologists' interpretations of test scores obtained via native language administration (Ortiz, 2014; Ortiz et al., 2016). Even when an individual is tested in his or her native or dominant language, the type of educational programming the individual has received and for how long, as well as the parents' own literacy level in both the native language and English, all play a role in the language development of the individual (Rhodes et al., 2005). Their impact is not altered by the presence or absence of dominance. Still other potentially problematic issues in the implementation of native-language tests is that they require psychologists to be qualified and competent to administer and score the test in the native language. Such "bilingual" psychologists, as noted previously, are relatively uncommon and become exceedingly scarce for languages other than Spanish.

One basic problem with native-language testing that also plagues English-language testing is the lack of adequate representation in the norm sample along the lines of developmental language proficiency. It should be noted, for example, that the WISC-IV Spanish norms are *equated* to the WISC-IV norms and that, as such, the WISC-IV Spanish does not actually represent a completely separate and independent norm sample of 2,200 Spanish-speaking children. Rather, developers of the WISC-IV Spanish tested a subsample of about 500 ELs and then statistically equated their score distribution to the larger (and presumably more normally distributed) English normative sample to create a set of scores that could be used in place of direct normative comparisons. There is nothing inherently wrong with this statistical approach to norming but it highlights the limitations of the sample and how it was constructed. More concerning than use of equated norms is that the developers did not attempt to stratify or control for variables that affect native language development for children here in the United States. For example, the type of education being received by ELs in the United States can vary from no differentiated instruction for ELs to ESL services to bilingual programs to dual-language programs. Likewise, an individual's current level of English language proficiency and parental education and SES were not factors used to determine appropriate and expected levels of performance (Braden & Iribarren, 2007).

The end result is that by equating the Spanish norms to the English norms (which are stratified primarily by age), the nonlinear trajectory of language acquisition as well as the non-normative distribution of language proficiency by age is not adequately controlled. Neither is the issue of differential language proficiency controlled as a function of country of origin. The preceding example regarding the three different 12-year-old Colombian children highlights this issue—that although they are all of the same age and the same country of origin, their language skills in both English and Spanish are vastly different. If they were tested with the WISC-IV Spanish, it is likely that the pattern of performance would be the exact reverse of what had been found previously with the first-generation 12-year-old scoring best, followed by the second-generation 12-year-old, and with the English-only-speaking 12-year-old bringing up the rear. Of course, psychologists would instantly recognize the inherent problems in testing a native English speaker in Spanish, yet there seems to be little recognition of the same problems when native Spanish speakers are tested in English. To be fair, there was some attempt in development of the WISC-IV Spanish to control for language proficiency issues, but it was a rather broad stroke that does not adequately address the issue. This is why the WISC-IV Spanish is recommended only for children who have not been in the United States for more than 5 years—if so, the recommendation is to use the English version. Such a recommendation implies the existence of a rather homogenous level of language proficiency across the equated sample, which cannot be true or even possible with the sampling techniques that were used. But it does restrict the variability in language proficiency and suggests that the norms are applicable only to children with fewer than 5 years of learning English. Thus, test performance for children of the same age is less likely to be based on intrinsic individual differences and more likely to be based on varying levels of formal education in the native language.

It should be noted that such problems in norm sample representation is not limited to the WISC-IV Spanish. A truly adequate and representative EL norm sample would need to utilize only ELs in the United States, not native speakers in other countries, and would have to be stratified by the examinee's level of English language proficiency across each age group. This is a complicated and difficult process that has not yet been accomplished in the development of any comprehensive test of intelligence or cognitive ability to date and should, therefore, not be construed as a technical deficiency as much as a practical limitation.

Despite the presence of these issues, native-language evaluation problems could well be mitigated substantially if there were an established literature base regarding the manner in which ELs in the United States perform on tests given to them in their native languages. Unfortunately, this is an area that has been significantly overlooked, and there is precious little data on which to base expectations of performance for U.S. bilinguals. What data do exist seem to suggest that the effects of linguistic proficiency continue to have a linear and predictable effect on test performance (Esparza-Brown, 2007). Not only does it appear that language proficiency moderates performance on tests as a function of the degree to which the tests require or rely upon linguistic development, but the pattern is similar for both children receiving native-language instruction as for those receiving English only, albeit the pattern of decline is less steep for the former (Esparza-Brown, 2007). Nevertheless, without a body of literature upon which practice can be based, it must be concluded that native-language evaluation also remains an unsatisfactory solution for addressing issues of test score validity.

Dominant Language Evaluation: English Language Assessment

As noted previously, the most widely used assessment method in the evaluation of diverse individuals is to administer a test in English, largely irrespective of the examinee's proficiency. On the surface, this method appears rather counterintuitive considering the history of poor performance of ELs on tests administered to them in English as well as the fact that the three methods described in the preceding sections arose precisely because of the questionable validity of scores obtained via English-language administration of tests. Research has consistently shown that ELs perform about 15-20 points lower on verbal tasks and about 3-5 points lower on language-reduced tasks when tests are administered in English (DiCerbo & Barona, 2000; Neisser et al., 1997; Ortiz & Melo, 2015; Valdes & Figueroa, 1996), so suggesting such a method seems only to perpetuate the inherent bias in this assessment approach. It was also noted, however, that the vast majority of psychologists in the United States continue to assess children from linguistically diverse backgrounds in the only manner in which they are capable of doing so—in English. Coupled with the relative lack of accepted guidelines of practice, apart from a general framework for nondiscriminatory assessment (Ortiz, 2014), and the limited attention provided to the development of such competency in graduate psychological training, many psychologists probably see themselves as having no other real option. For example, in a survey of school psychologists, only 11.6% identified themselves as "bilingual/multicultural school psychologists," but 87.2% of the sample reported that they routinely evaluated students who were culturally and linguistically diverse with significant reliance on "nonverbal" tests administered in English (Sotelo-Dynega & Dixon, 2014). Given the problems with validity that surround over-reliance on nonverbal tests of cognitive ability and intelligence, such a finding is rather alarming but not entirely surprising. Not only do recent statistics suggest that about 20% or more of the student population is composed of current and former ELs (O'Bryon & Rogers, 2010), the numbers are expected to increase rapidly, far outpacing the number of qualified bilingual psychologists. Moreover, if a child is considered to be "fluent" in English according to State standards, and thus no longer receives English as a Second Language services, IDEA (2004) permits testing solely in English and without any consideration regarding the child's native language or the fact that the child is not a native English speaker and never will be.

It must be understood that a child who learns two languages (i.e., is bilingual) does not stop being bilingual simply because they have become dominant in English. The child is still bilingual, and still has varying and likely unequal levels of proficiency in English and the native language. Once two languages were introduced into the child's life, they were no longer monolingual speakers of either language and remain different from their monolingual peers. Whereas an individual may reach "English proficiency" after a few years in an English educational environment, this does not mean that he or she has "caught up" to, from a developmental perspective, his or her monolingual peers in any meaningful way (Thomas & Collier, 2002).

Given this landscape, it is hard to see the merits of English language assessment, but there is one major advantage to this approach: the evaluator does not have to speak any other language than English. It should not be thought, however, that being able to speak another language renders one automatically qualified and competent as a bilingual evaluator. The process of nondiscriminatory assessment and the ability to interpret data fairly and drawing valid, defensible conclusions from test scores must be taught, learned, and practiced every bit as much as any other psychological skill. Professional knowledge regarding the various techniques necessary to discern the manner in which linguistic and cultural variables could be affecting test performance must be acquired—it is not imbued automatically as a facet of bilingualism.

Despite these drawbacks, English language assessment has one extremely significant advantage that the other methods do not have—there is a century's worth of research that describes the test performance of ELs. This body of research provides the needed context through within which practitioners may be able to evaluate the validity of test scores generated via testing in English. As such, it is recommended that testing of ELs *begin* with standardized administration of cognitive ability tests given in English, followed, if necessary, by the administration of native language cognitive ability tests for the purposes of cross-linguistic confirmation and validation. The practical features of this framework and the rationale for its development and implementation is described in the section below.

A RECOMMENDED BEST PRACTICE APPROACH

This section provides best practice recommendations for practitioners who evaluate students who are learning to speak English. Emphasis is placed on the validity of test results for these students in light of their unique culture and language backgrounds.

General Considerations

An in-depth discussion of all aspects of nondiscriminatory assessment is beyond the scope of this chapter and the reader is referred to other sources for information (Ortiz, 2014). But in general, evaluation of students from diverse backgrounds using standardized tests rests on the degree to which validity of the scores can be established, specifically the construct validity of the obtained test scores. When an EL obtains a low score on a test administered in English (or even the native language), it becomes necessary to determine if the scores represent a difference in experiential background (because of language or opportunity for acculturative knowledge acquisition) or whether they constitute evidence of an intrinsic disorder. In terms of validity, one must decide if the test scores actually represent what they were intended to represent (the level of ability in the domain intended to be measured by the specific subtest) or if the test score might instead represent the extraneous and confounding influence of factors that were not intended to be measured (e.g., linguistic proficiency). If one can establish that the obtained test scores are valid and truly measure the intended areas of cognitive functioning (unencumbered by external influences), then one can make claims about the presence of a disorder. However, if the validity of test scores cannot be established (or is simply ignored), then one cannot make any such claims or provide any such interpretations. A psychologist must carefully consider and defend the validity of obtained test scores, particularly with respect to the presence and impact of factors that constitute a difference (e.g., limited English development) whenever an EL is being evaluated. Without such due consideration and defense, interpretation of test scores is specious and indefensible, regardless of hollow admonitions that the results were interpreted with "extreme caution." Attempts to interpret test scores without establishing their validity violates basic psychometric standards of practice and renders such conclusions drawn from those interpretations as, at best, useless, and at worst, harmful to the examinee.

Consideration regarding procedures for assessment must necessarily involve consideration of the reason and purpose of testing. The use of standardized tests in often employed in evaluation as an efficient means of identifying deficits in cognitive abilities as by comparing them to a normative standard. As such, the major focus of testing and interpretation typically rests on whether scores are normatively *low*, rather than being average or above average. It is easily understood that scores which reflect poor performance are relatively easy to obtain since there are myriad reasons having nothing to do with lack of ability that can readily explain why an individual may have underperformed on a standardized test. For example, being hungry, tired, emotionally upset, sick, nervous, angry, distracted, and so forth are all simple explanations regarding why someone managed to perform at a level below their actual or true ability. The same cannot be said, however, for scores that are *above* one's own ability as it is extremely unlikely that one would manage to demonstrate a level of ability that they do not actually possess. This is especially true for cognitive ability tests where simple guessing is unlikely to have any effect on improving performance. Therefore, it can be assumed that if an examinee scores in the Average range or above on a given test of ability, it must mean that his/her ability is at least in the average range—it could very well be higher, but it cannot be lower and by definition, cannot be an indication of possible disability and does not, for the purposes of most evaluations, require any further validation. Conversely, if testing results in low scores, the need to consider and establish validity is essential in determining whether the scores are reflections of true deficits and the extent to which subsequent interpretations and conclusions can be drawn and defended. For this reason, standardized administration becomes a requirement as it assists in ensuring that many of the factors that could confound test results have been controlled or eliminated. In the case of ELs, standardization is insufficient, however, because it does not address the possibility that the presence of factors related to language proficiency and acculturative knowledge acquisition could potentially have attenuated test performance nonetheless—factors that are specifically identified as exclusionary variables in the identification of a Specific Learning Disability (SLD) according to IDEA (2004).

Because the fundamental goal of evaluation with ELs is to establish the validity of the obtained test scores, an approach that starts with standardized administration of tests in English takes on additional advantages. As noted previously, evaluation in English represents the only current, evidence-based method for assessment as it can be guided by more than a century of research on the performance of ELs on such tests. This means that it is the only approach where the possibility exists of being able to evaluate the validity of test scores for ELs by comparing them to that found in the literature exists. In this way, the body of research serves as a sort of de facto and appropriate "norm" sample that does not currently exist for any given test. At the very least, and assuming a largely nondisabled population, it can allow determination of whether scores obtained from testing in English are somehow comparable to scores generated via research. In contrast, if the evaluation process began with native language testing, the lack of any substantive body of research on the performance of ELs would preclude evaluation of the validity of such scores. Thus, it is only with an approach that begins with tests administered in English that the lack of adequate norm representation can be ameliorated by turning to the existing research evidence.

Beginning an evaluation in English also means that any evaluator, whether monolingual or bilingual, can conduct the initial testing without assistance. Furthermore, if the evaluation is conducted for the purposes of identifying a possible disability, and should all of the obtained test scores suggest average or higher functioning, it can then be reasonably concluded that, as far as the test data are concerned, the examinee has no cognitive deficits in the areas assessed. This means that no further testing is necessary and that, in the absence of other compelling evidence to the contrary, the evaluation could effectively end as having provided sufficient information that the individual does not possess any identifiable cognitive-based disability. This does not mean that no intervention or other action is required or that the examinee will simply return to the general education environment and suddenly start to succeed academically. Because the most common purpose for an evaluation is linked to intervention, such a finding not only rules out the presence of a disability but also strongly suggests the need to examine instructional and other factors that are affecting school performance. It is more likely, however, that evaluation of one or more cognitive domains via testing in English first are likely to result in low scores. Such a result now requires direct evaluation of the validity of the test scores. Because the testing was conducted in English, psychologists may use research on the performance of ELs to assist in evaluating the extent to which linguistic and cultural factors may have affected and potentially invalidated the resulting test performance. This is the singular purpose of the Culture-Language Interpretive Matrix (C-LIM)—a framework that systematically collates the research in a way that facilitates comparisons of individual performance to the collective research-based normative performance. This evaluative process is not possible for tests administered in the native language because of the lack of sufficient research with which to make such comparisons and further highlights the rationale for administering tests in English first. It is important to understand the significance of the word *first* as used herein. Whenever evaluation of test score with the C-LIM suggests that the results are possibly or likely to be valid, additional evidence of their validity becomes necessary. The most appropriate and direct manner for providing this additional validation must come from follow-up administration of native-language tests (either directly by a bilingual evaluator or via the use of an interpreter/translator). But the process of follow-up evaluation is relatively efficient because it is not necessary to re-evaluate every domain but rather, only those that were found to be below average (or suggestive of deficits in functioning). Test scores obtained in English that are found to be within the average range or higher need not be re-tested for reasons stated earlier. Thus, follow-up evaluation in the native language will, in most cases, be quicker and more efficient that initial testing in English and the primary purpose of such is to provide cross-linguistic confirmation of the original test scores obtained in English. Cross-linguistic confirmation refers to the general consensus that cognitive deficits transcend language. That is, if there is a true cognitive deficit, the deficit will appear in *both* languages, not just one (Bialystok, 1991; Grosjean, 1989; Paradis, 2014). With respect to testing, if a low score is obtained via English-language administration of a test, then that deficit in performance should appear in the same domain even when testing is conducted in the native language. Conversely, if the domain in which a deficit has been observed in testing conducted in English but is not observed when that domain is evaluated in the native language, it can be concluded that the original score was in fact invalid after all (for reasons that may or may not be due to language) and that the native language score represents a valid indicator of at least average ability in the domain that was measured.

It is important to emphasize the logical and rational aspects of this approach as they are integral to the development of the process. If testing begins in English and all scores are found to be in the average range or higher, then testing can cease because the examinee has demonstrated at least average ability in all areas measured. Thus, the *absence* of a disability can be confirmed via English-language administration alone and can save significant time and resources. Not only does it not require a bilingual evaluator, it also prevents needless native language testing of children from diverse backgrounds. If any low scores are obtained via testing conducted via English-language administration, and after having been judged to be possibly or likely valid when examined within the C-LIM, then follow-up in the native language is necessary for cross-linguistic confirmation but not for all areas that were assessed. Instead, the evaluator only needs to follow-up with native-language tests that measure the same abilities in which low scores were obtained in English, thus streamlining the assessment process. This also means that *presence* of a disability can only be confirmed with a combination of both English- and native-language evaluation.

It is important to note that native-language follow-up on low scores obtained from testing in English need not and should not be concerned primarily with quantitative scores. For one, when testing outside of English and Spanish, native-language tests are few and far between, so the generation of quantitative normative scores is only possible via use of a translator/interpreter. Further, since the native-language tests lack proper sampling and linguistic stratification necessary to adequately represent ELs in the United States, the generation of scores from such tests are not likely to be valid anyway. This is also why psychologists need not be concerned about practice effects; the purpose of follow-up is to confirm or disconfirm the validity of scores obtained via testing English and not to generate valid measures of cognitive ability. However, despite these problems, should test scores from native language evaluation be within the average range or higher, it begins to suggest that the original scores from testing in English are unlikely to be valid. For the most part, however, psychologists should pay particular attention to the qualitative and observational information that can be readily gleaned from testing as such test behavior may well inform the nature and extent of necessary and appropriate instructional accommodations and curricular modifications.

BEST PRACTICES IN THE EVALUATION OF ELS WITH THE WISC-V

Given the preponderance of research evidence of EL test performance on the Wechsler Scales and the best practices framework outlined in the preceding section, the WISC-V is a very reasonable battery for beginning an evaluation of ELs. The WISC-V represents an even more advanced instrument than its predecessor and a more defensible factor structure than ever before. Yet, its similarity to previous editions also makes it relatively straightforward for the purposes of evaluating ELs as the need to maintain somewhat parallel testing in both languages is still quite feasible. Implementation of the WISC-V in this regard is much like that for any other battery and includes strict adherence to standardized protocol and procedures for reasons that have already been described. Whenever testing in English first results in scores that suggest low functioning, it becomes necessary to determine the extent that linguistic and cultural factors may have had in attenuating the obtained scores. It was mentioned that this is the very purpose of the C-LIM and its use in addressing test score validity is outlined in the section below

Use of the C-LIM With the WISC-V

The Culture-Language and Interpretive Matrix (CLIM; Flanagan, Ortiz, & Alfonso, 2013; Ortiz & Mclo, 2015; Ortiz, Flanagan, & Alfonso, 2015) is based on an aggregation of research on the test performance of ELs. By collating results from a wide variety of studies conducted on ELs who were tested in English, the C-LIM provides a simple, evidence-based method that facilitates analysis of the extent to which linguistic and cultural variables may have affected test performance. When that impact is reflected by a broad and systematic attenuation of scores, it suggests that the test scores are more likely to be reflections of linguistic/cultural variables rather than actual ability and thus likely invalid. When there is no observance of a general attenuating effect on test scores, it suggests that the results are more likely to be reflections of true ability (or lack thereof) than reflections of linguistic/cultural variables, and thus likely to be valid. Given the limited scope of this chapter, the C-LIM will be discussed primarily with respect to its use and application with the WISC-V, and with the assumption that its basic principles, guidelines, purpose, and rationale are already familiar to the reader via the original sources. It should be noted as well that the automated C-LIM is no longer a separate software application and has instead been integrated with other Cross-Battery tools (i.e., Data Management and Interpretive Assistant [DMIA] and Pattern of Strengths and Weaknesses Analyzer [PSW-A]) to form the Cross-Battery Assessment Software System (X-BASS; Ortiz, Flanagan, & Alfonso, 2015).

The C-LIM is a two dimensional matrix that consists of nine cells representing various degrees of linguistic demand and cultural loading. Originally, classifications of subtests was based on the test's characteristics regarding each dimension (Flanagan & Ortiz, 2001). However, since 2007 classifications have been based on actual mean values aggregated across a wide range of research studies on EL test performance found in the literature (Flanagan, Ortiz, & Alfonso, 2007, 2013). Because the C-LIM is concerned with basic construct validity, only subtests are classified as it makes no sense to determine the validity of composites if the validity of the subtests that comprise the composites has not been determined to be valid themselves. Each subtest of the WISC-V is classified in one of the nine available cells. Given the recent publication of the WISC-V, its current classifications (see Figure 9.1) are necessarily based on both research as well as expert consensus. Subtests that were carried over from the WISC-IV (e.g. Block Design, Similarities, Coding, etc.) have retained their previous classifications and have substantial empirical evidence based on the aggregate subtest means obtained from current and previous research. New subtests have been tentatively classified based on expert consensus and after careful evaluation of the intended construct, task demands, and similarity to other current subtests on the same and other batteries. Of particular note is that these classifications, as are all classifications within the C-LIM, are subject to modification pending the results of ongoing and future research. The C-LIM is dynamic in this regard and it is intended to be molded on the basis of studies that administer tests in English to ELs who are not disabled and of generally average ability.

To use the C-LIM, practitioners simply enter the subtest scores into the appropriate cells and the program automatically generates an aggregate value for each cell as well as a series of graphs of the pattern of aggregate values for all cells in which data are entered. The aggregate values in the matrix, and more importantly the resulting bar graphs that are generated from the results, display the individual's pattern of performance and permits comparison to the "average" values culled from the literature. In general, if linguistic and cultural factors are broadly and systematically attenuating an EL's test scores, then the pattern of test scores should be relatively consistent with the expected pattern of decline (or attenuation) as depicted in the C-LIM. This pattern involves not only an overall pattern of decline, but aggregate scores for cells with data that are of the same or similar magnitude as that obtained by normal ELs according to the literature. The observance of such a pattern would then indicate that performance was likely subject to the systematic attenuating effect of limited English proficiency and lack of opportunity for the acquisition of acculturative knowledge. Furthermore, if this is the case, and if the primary purpose of the evaluation was to identify a potential disability, then it means that testing can now cease and the examiner may reasonably conclude that the test scores do not support the presence of any type of cognitive disability. That is, the individual's performance was commensurate with the performance of other ELs who are known to be non-disabled and of generally average ability.

On the other hand, when there is an absence of an overall pattern of decline, or when one or more of the cell aggregates is seen to be below the expected level

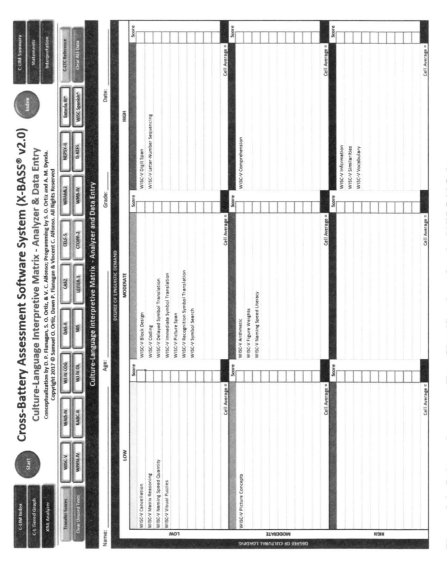

Figure 9.1 Culture-Language Test Classifications for the WISC-V Subtests

of performance as established by normal ELs in the literature, then it suggests that the results are not primarily due to linguistic/cultural influences and the results are possibly valid (pending further validation via native-language evaluation). In such cases, linguistic and cultural influences may well remain contributory in nature, but they have been determined not to be the primary reason for the low performance. This suggests that not only are the results possibly valid, they cannot be explained by linguistic/cultural factors and thus some other factor must be present to account for the observed scores—one possible explanation may well be a true deficit if cross-validated with native-language evaluation and other convergent data. The process of cross-linguistic validation using native-language evaluation is described in the following section.

Native Language Follow-Up Evaluation With the WISC-V

One minor complication regarding evaluation of diverse children in the native language with the Wechsler Scales is the temporary absence of an identical, alternate language version of the WISC-V for use in the United States. It is our understanding that a Spanish version of the WISC-V is already in development and should appear soon. The recommended approach for evaluation outlined in this chapter relies on the use of native-language tests as follow-up measures to low scores obtained via English administration for the purposes of cross-linguistic validation and confirmation of suspected deficits. The structure of the WISC-V differs significantly from that of the WISC-IV making pure "parallel" follow-up testing impossible. For example, new subtests have been introduced on the WISC-V and the number of subtests that comprise some of the indexes has changed from three to two. Thus, until a WISC-V Spanish version is available, follow-up on low scores from administration of the WISC-V in English will need to be conducted in a manner that closely approximates the indexes using the same subtests (if available) and the same number of subtests. When the same subtest is not available on the WISC-IV Spanish, a subtest that most closely matches the new subtest should be selected. Likewise, when a WISC-V index is based only on two subtests but the old WISC-IV Spanish index is based on three, only the two same or most similar subtests should be used for follow-up. In cases where such two-subtest composites may not exist on the WISC-IV Spanish, users will need to rely on software to generate appropriate composites from the obtained scores.

With respect to differences between the WISC-IV Spanish and WISC-V, some broad abilities (Gc as measured by the VCI, and Gs as measured by the PSI) continue to use the same subtests and will permit follow-up native-language evaluation. However, the VCI on the WISC-V is comprised only of Similarities and Vocabulary with Information no longer required as it is for the VCI on the WISC-IV Spanish. Follow-up testing need only administer Similarities and Vocabulary and a composite value can be generated by entering the subtest scores on the XBA Analyzer tab of X-BASS. For Gsm as measured by the WMI on the WISC-V, Picture Span has replaced Letter-Number Sequencing despite the fact that Letter-Number Sequencing remains available on the battery. Thus, follow-up testing in the area of Gsm can be accomplished via administration of one of the same subtests from the WISC-IV Spanish (i.e., Digit Span) and combining it with Letter-Number Sequencing which will form a norm-based composite (WMI) that is highly comparable to the WMI on the WISC-V. With respect to Gv, the WISC-V now has a new VSI which does not exist on the WISC-IV Spanish and which was formed via the addition of a new Gv subtest—Visual Puzzles. Moreover, the only *Gv* subtest that exists on the WISC-IV Spanish is Block Design. Thus, follow-up of potential problems noted on the VSI via native-language evaluation with the WISC-IV Spanish can only be accomplished with Block Design and the supplemental Picture Completion subtest. Although this combination provides an adequate *Gv* composite comparable to the VSI, careful attention should be paid to performance on Picture Completion due to its relatively high cultural loading. Finally, *Gf* on the WISC-V is measured by the new Fluid Reasoning Index (FRI) and includes Matrix Reasoning from the WISC-IV Spanish but combines it with a new subtest, Figure Weights. To follow-up in the domain of Gf using the WISC-IV Spanish, Matrix Reasoning will need to be combined with Picture Concepts as the best alternative and the composite value will need to be generated via the XBA Analyzer tab in X-BASS or other software. A potential problem for Gf, however, is that on the WISC-V, it consists of Matrix Reasoning, which measures the narrow ability, *induction* (I), and Visual Puzzles, which measures the narrow ability, *general sequential reasoning* (RG). The WISC-IV Spanish combination of Matrix Reasoning and Picture Concepts are both measures of the narrow ability, *induction.* Therefore, if a low score via testing in English is obtained on the WISC-V and the low score is attributable primarily to performance on Figure Weights (which measures RG), it may be better to go "outside" the battery and use a *Gf* cluster that better represents both narrow abilities (e.g., the *Gf* cluster from the Batería III). Alternatively, another option for remaining "within" the battery would be to rely on the last resort method previously discussed (i.e., translating the subtest informally). In such cases, practitioners must rely much more heavily on the qualitative data than the quantitative. At the very least, such differences in performance should guide subsequent interpretations as well as the collection of additional data necessary to firmly establish validity of the test scores. See Table 9.1 for a list of the WISC-IV Spanish and WISC-V subtests and their broad/narrow ability classifications.

This process is further detailed in the case study that appears at the end of the chapter. Obviously, when the WISC-V Spanish becomes available and assuming its structure is not changed, practitioners will then have no difficulty simply utilizing fully parallel tests in both English and for follow-up Spanish evaluation. It should be remembered, however, that this option will be available solely for examinees for whom follow-up testing can be conducted in Spanish. The lack of parallel WISC-V batteries for use in the United States in other languages means that follow-up testing in these cases will need to rely predominantly on the only feasible method left available, use of translators/interpreters for informal translation of English language tests. In addition, this approach will likely need to be employed by evaluators who are not bilingual and who have no access to a bilingual evaluator for assistance. Therefore, although it cannot be denied that psychometric problems are rampant when it comes to the use of translators/interpreters and informal translation of the administration of tests, it can be

Table 9.1 Broad and Narrow Ability Classifications of the WISC-V and WISC-IV Spanish Subtests

Broad Ability	Narrow Ability	WISC-V Subtest	WISC-IV Spanish Subtest
Gc	VL	Similarities Vocabulary	Similarities Vocabulary
	K0	Comprehension Information	Comprehension Information
Gf	I	Matrix Reasoning Picture Concepts	Matrix Reasoning Picture Concepts
	RG	Figure Weights	n/a
Gv	Vz	Block Design Visual Puzzles	Block Design n/a
	CF	n/a	Picture Completion
Gsm	MS	Digit Span (MW, MS) Picture Span	Digit Span (MW, MS) n/a
	MW	Digit Span (MW, MS) Letter-Number Sequencing	Digit Span (MW, MS) Letter-Number Sequencing Arithmetic
Gs	R9	Coding	Coding
	P	Symbol Search Cancellation	Symbol Search Cancellation

considered a lesser concern given that the point of follow-up testing is primarily to obtain *qualitative* information for cross-linguistic confirmation, not necessarily valid quantitative scores. Furthermore, should performance improve significantly, or rise to the average range, for abilities tested in the native language (as compared to having been in the deficit range when tested in English) it should be construed as strong evidence of both excellent learning potential on the part of the individual as well as ability that is likely to be at least average and possibly even higher. In such cases, practice effects would be diagnostic and constitute considerable evidence that learning problems must reside in the classroom and not in the child. In addition, since scores in the average range obtained via cognitive testing are very unlikely to occur by chance or for spurious reasons, such patterns of performance must be viewed as evidence of abilities that are intact and not indicative of deficit or disability.

Additional Considerations in Test Score Validity

The main purpose of follow-up evaluation in the native language of low test scores originally obtained in English is to provide cross-linguistic confirmation/disconfirmation of those scores. As such, this process can result in two possible outcomes. The first outcome is that the follow-up native-language test scores also suggest deficits in functioning because they are at the same or similar levels of performance (i.e., below average range). The second outcome is that the follow-up native-language test scores instead do not suggest deficits in functioning because they are at a higher level of performance than the scores originally obtained in English (i.e., average or above average range).

In cases where follow-up native-language test scores are similar or within the same range of functioning as the original English language test scores, it would be reasonable to conclude that the individual has a true and valid deficit in the domain that was measured as supported by the presence of cross-linguistic confirmatory evidence (i.e., the deficit appears in both languages, not just one). The original scores obtained from testing in English can then be considered to be likely valid and further interpretations and conclusions can be drawn from the English score(s) if additional converging evidence supports them. Low scores in both English and the native-language may occur for reasons other than true deficits—for example, in cases where an EL has received all instruction in English. To avoid making interpretive errors or discriminatory judgments regarding the meaning of test scores, even when cross-linguistic support is present, requires consideration of additional ecological factors that includes the referral concerns, teacher/parent observations, work samples, progress monitoring data, and the degree to which the observed and suspected cognitive deficits provide reasonable and empirically associated explanations for the reported academic difficulties. Such contextual evaluation is part and parcel of a nondiscriminatory approach and is the final consideration necessary to definitively establish the validity of test scores and the subsequent clinical inferences and interpretations that may emanate from them.

In cases where follow-up native-language test scores are significantly higher than the English scores and when such scores are observed to be in the average or higher range, cross-linguistic validation and confirmation has not occurred. Because a disorder cannot exist in only one language, and because average or higher scores are unlikely to occur by chance (as compared to low scores that may well be spurious), average or higher scores in follow-up native-language testing effectively serve to invalidate the original test score obtained in English. It can thus, be reasonably concluded that the original English test score is *invalid* (for reasons that may or may not be due to linguistic or cultural factors) and that the follow-up native-language test score is *valid* and better represents the individual's true ability in this domain. In essence, the follow-up native-language score replaces the original score from testing in English. As noted, average or better scores are highly unlikely to have occurred by chance and while the increase in performance may not be entirely explainable in all cases, it must nevertheless be accepted as evidence of at least average ability and in no way an indication of cognitive dysfunction. Note that the C-LIM is designed to investigate the effects of culture and language on test scores only and that there are an infinite number of other extraneous variables that could account for low test scores obtained in English. The absence of such factors in follow-up testing may therefore increase performance, not because of the use of the native language, but merely because they were present in the original but not the follow up testing situation. Whatever the case, whenever follow-up native language test results provide sufficient data to indicate that performance in a given domain has risen to the point that it denotes average or better performance, it stands to reason that it represents a better and more valid estimate of the individual's true ability than does the original scores obtained from testing the same domain in English.

On a final note, native-language test scores should not be considered a definitive method for evaluating the validity of English language test scores. Qualitative analysis can and should be used in the assessment of test score validity. In cases where there is no native-language version of the test, this type of analysis becomes critical as it is the only means by which to validate the test scores obtained via English-language administration. Moreover, low performance in both English and the native language may occur for reasons other than a true deficit, for example, the typical absence of native language instruction. And as with any aspect of assessment, conclusions drawn from such data should be based on converging information from multiple sources of data as described previously and as related to referral concerns, progress monitoring data, parent/teacher observations, and the extent to which any presumed cognitive deficits provide logical or empirically driven explanations of reported academic deficits.

The Gc Caveat

While the method for cross-linguistic confirmation described in the previous section can be employed to validate test scores in any cognitive domain, there is a notable exception for Gc. By its very definition, Gc comprises various aspects of language development as well as the amount of cultural knowledge one has acquired. It is, therefore, impossible to separate Gc from the influence of linguistic/cultural factors because Gc is itself, nothing more than culture and language. The overwhelming majority of culture-bound information representative of Gc is acquired in both formal educational settings as well as incidentally in social settings typical of a particular culture. This is one reason why Gc correlates so highly with formal education (Schrank, McGrew, & Mather, 2015). And because both language and the acquisition of acculturative knowledge occur in a known developmental manner associated closely with and measurable by age, it would be unreasonable to expect an EL, irrespective of English language proficiency, to possess comparable knowledge or language skill as compared to same-age, native-English speaking peers. By definition, ELs have been exposed to culture-specific and English language environments for a shorter period of time, in some cases considerably shorter, than their native-English speaking peers. Such comparisons would be tantamount to comparing the vocabulary of a 5-year-old to that of a 10-year-old or expecting the general knowledge of a 10-year-old to be comparable to the knowledge of a 15-year-old.

Therefore, when interpreting abilities in the domain of Gc, scores for an EL should be evaluated only relative to the selected pattern of expected performance that corresponds to the degree of difference indicated in the C-LIM. Normative comparisons to batteries or tests in either English or the native language will always remain inherently discriminatory and the only manner in which a fair and equitable assessment of Gc can be obtained is relative to other ELs. ELs generally score poorly on Gc tests because of the high reliance on age-appropriate development of language and acculturative knowledge. The attenuation can be as high as nearly 2 full standard deviations below the mean depending on their level of English proficiency (Sotelo-Dynega et al., 2013). Thus, in many cases, ELs will present with a score for Gc that may be considerably below average (SS < 90) from a test's normative perspective. But when that same aggregate score is viewed within the context of the expected range in the

C-LIM (a comparison that is made only to other ELs with similar experiential backgrounds), it may still fall within the range that is considered normal or average for an EL as specified by research. To avoid potentially discriminatory interpretation of test scores measuring Gc, psychologists should only examine the extent to which a Gc score (as indicated by the aggregate value for the "high/high" cell since all Gc tests are invariably classified in this category) is within or above the specified range of performance generated via the accumulated research and as represented by the shaded region at the far right side of the C-LIM. In addition, the magnitude of the aggregate value represents a good guide regarding the need for follow-up testing in the native language. If the magnitude of the Gc aggregate score is within or above the shaded range in the C-LIM, then Gc should be considered to be within the average range and no further testing in this area is necessary. Only when the aggregate value for Gc is below the shaded range in the C-LIM is follow-up testing in the native language determined to be appropriate and necessary. Note that it is even possible that a low English Gc score might result in a high average native-language Gc score and that both can be simultaneously valid as each represents the degree of relative proficiency in each language. However, such contrasting results do not indicate the presence of a disability as language skills are not deficient in the native language. It merely indicates that the examinee's language abilities are better developed in one language than in the other, likely as a function of differences in experience and education in each one. Extremely low scores in Gc (below the shaded band), particularly if coupled with low native-language Gc scores (especially in the narrow ability areas related to listening ability [LS] or communication ability [CM]), may be a red flag for a speech and language impairment (SLI), as opposed to SLD. Appropriate bilingual speech-language referrals should be made if such is the case. Recent updates to X-BASS have largely automated consideration of these and other issues related to Gc in evaluation of ELs and will be illustrated in the case study that follows.

CASE STUDY: JOSE MARIA

Jose Maria is a 9-year-old fourth grader of Nicaraguan heritage who was evaluated for suspected learning disability by the school's psychologist. Jose's teacher reported that he was having significant difficulty in a variety of academic areas as compared to his classmates. The problems appeared to be related primarily to reading and writing and no concerns regarding math skills were noted. Jose was born in a rural area of Nicaragua and came to the United States at the age of 1 with his mother and father (including a brother 5 years older) and moved around the southwestern parts of the United States until finding a more permanent residence near Denver, Colorado. His parents have little formal education and both work daily to support the family as much as possible, with his father employed primarily in construction and his mother as a maid in the hotel industry. Jose and his family speak Spanish predominantly and while his parents can only understand rudimentary English, Jose's English is advanced enough that he no longer receives ESL services from his district. In fact, Jose's experiences from having been raised primarily in the United States and the fact that all of his education has been in English since kindergarten has led to substantial conversational proficiency in English and he speaks without a trace of accent. The final testing conducted by the district's ESL department indicated that he had long been dominant in English and his recent score on the state's proficiency examination (i.e., WIDA: ACCESS for ELLs 2.0) was above the necessary cutoff and provided the impetus to withdraw his ESL services last year. Although his teacher and other educators involved in the case suggest that Jose's English abilities are now advanced enough to make language a negligible factor in explaining his academic difficulties, the psychologist assigned to the case recognized that an accent is not an indicator of developmental proficiency and that even after being declassified as a limited English speaker, his language development in English was unlikely to be commensurate with that of his same age or grade native-English-speaking peers. Nevertheless, the extent to which Jose's observed academic difficulties might be attributable to simple developmental differences in English language proficiency or the acquisition of acculturative knowledge rather than reflections of potential disability (e.g., manifestation of a specific learning disability [SLD]), was not clear given the available information and remained a question that could benefit from a comprehensive evaluation.

Having developed competency in the recently published WISC-V, the psychologist decided to use it as the core battery for evaluation. The psychologist noted that the WISC-V provides adequate measures of Gc (VCI), Gf (FRI), Gv (VSI), Gsm (WMI), and Gs (PSI). And although Glr is now measurable via the new Naming Speed and Symbol Translation subtests, the psychologist's unfamiliarity with these tests led to the decision to measure Glr and Ga via Cross-Battery methods using the WJ IV. In this manner, the psychologist would be able to begin the evaluation using tests to be administered in English and which cover the seven major CHC broad abilities necessary to implement the district's pattern of strengths and weaknesses (PSW) model for identification of SLD. Such a battery would provide both a general idea regarding overall ability but more importantly it would provide a comprehensive examination of the full range of cognitive abilities, including those that might be most related to the reported reading and writing difficulties in the classroom. In addition, the WISC-V is co-normed with the WIAT-III which would provide an ideal assessment of Jose's current levels of academic functioning. Jose's teacher had reported that his problems were primarily in the area of reading comprehension and retention. Although he seemed to be able to decode words efficiently and sounded as if he were reading somewhat fluently, Jose was often observed to have trouble recalling the meaning of the paragraphs and passages he just read. His teacher also reported that Jose displayed inconsistent patterns in learning where he often seemed unable to remember or recall things he had learned on a consistent basis whereas at other times his knowledge seemed solid. These problems in reading and retention were beginning to put Jose at a significant disadvantage given the increasing reading demands of the curriculum and it was clear to his teacher that he was struggling more and more to keep up with the rest of the class and the assigned work. The teacher reported similar concerns with written language—inconsistent learning, trouble expressing his thoughts clearly, not remembering what his topic was when he was writing, and so on. Accordingly, the psychologist chose to evaluate distinct aspects of reading, including basic reading skills and reading comprehension, as well as written expression. Despite the lack of concern with mathematics, the psychologist included evaluation of match calculation and concepts as a way of highlighting Jose's strengths in these areas relative to the reported weaknesses in reading and writing. There were no strong indications of any behavioral problems reported by Jose's teacher, although she did mention that this year he did seem to be more distracted and disruptive than in the past. She is unsure whether this is simple frustration, evidence of some other type of dysfunction, or whether it constitutes some aspect of his language and cultural difference.

Results from administration of the WISC-V, WIAT-III, and the selected clusters/subtests from the WJ IV Tests of Cognitive Ability (Schrank et al., 2014) are presented in Table 9.2 in a format that is typical of the way results are presented in tabular form in reports. Such tables are invariably intimidating as the sheer number of tests and scores can easily overwhelm non-professionals. Still, even an experienced psychologist is unlikely to be able to examine results in this manner and make headway in evaluating the effect of cultural and linguistic influences on teste performance. It is for this reason that the C-LIM exists. In accordance with the specified instructions and guidance gleaned from readings on use of the C-LIM, the psychologist utilized the C-LIM Analyzer tab in X-BASS and began by entering the obtained subtest scores from all batteries. The first step was to click the WISC-V button from the top menu bar to populate the matrix with the corresponding WISC-V subtests and their correct classifications. Once the scores

Table 9.2 Test Scores From WISC-V, WIAT-III, and WJ IV COG for Jose Maria

Wechsler Intelligence Scale for Children-Fifth Edition

Verbal Comprehension Index	76	Fluid Reasoning Index	82	Visual-Spatial Index	95
Similarities	5	Matrix Reasoning	7	Block Design	9
Vocabulary	6	Figure Weights	7	Visual Puzzles	9
Working Memory Index	79	Processing Speed Index	94		
Digit Span	5	Coding	9		
Picture Span	7	Symbol Search	8		

Wechsler Individual Achievement Test-III

Basic Reading	94	Reading Comprehension	76	Written Expression	92
Word Reading	92	Reading Comprehension	76	Spelling	100
Pseudoword Decoding	98	Oral Reading Fluency	80	Sentence Composition	86
				Essay Composition	93

Woodcock Johnson IV Tests of Cognitive Ability

Auditory Processing	91	LT Storage/Retrieval	77
Phonological Processing	99	Story Recall	79
Nonword Repetition	84	Visual-Auditory Learning	75

for the subtests that were administered were entered, the psychologist clicked on the WJ IV COG button at the top and the subtests from that battery were now populated in the matrix and any WISC-V subtests for which no score had been entered were removed to make space for the WJ IV COG subtests. Once the scores for the WJ IV COG were entered, the psychologist use the "Clear Unused Tests" button to remove the names of subtests from the WJ IV COG that had not been administered and for which no score existed. The C-LIM automatically calculates cell aggregates and graphs the results for analysis that permitted the psychologist to examine the validity of the test scores from a perspective that accounts for the impact of cultural and linguistic differences on performance. The main matrix, tiered graph, and primary culture-language graph generated by the C-LIM with Jose Maria's subtest data are depicted in Figures 9.2, 9.3, and 9.4, respectively.

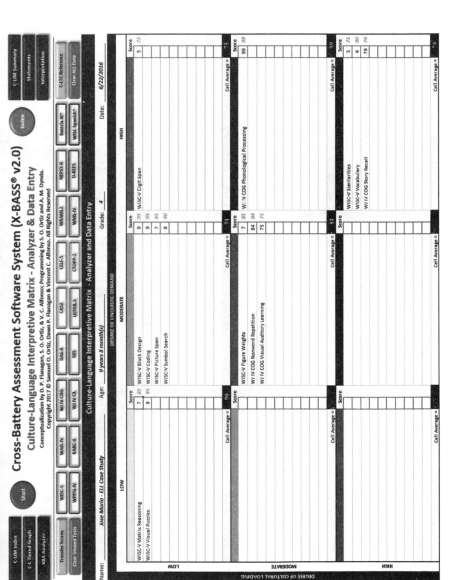

Figure 9.2 Culture-Language Interpretive Matrix for Jose Maria Case Study

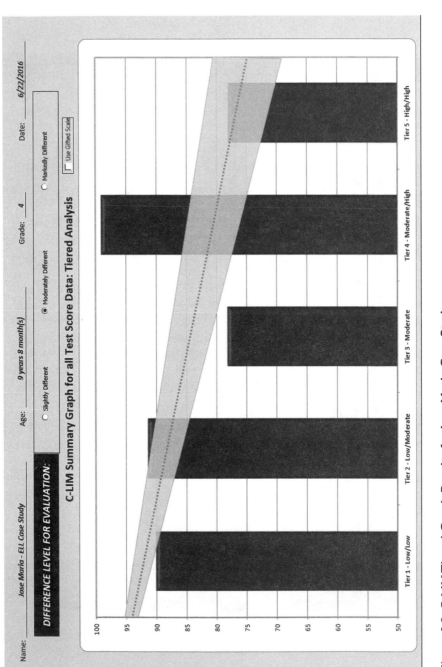

Figure 9.3 C-LIM Tiered Graph Results for Jose Maria Case Study

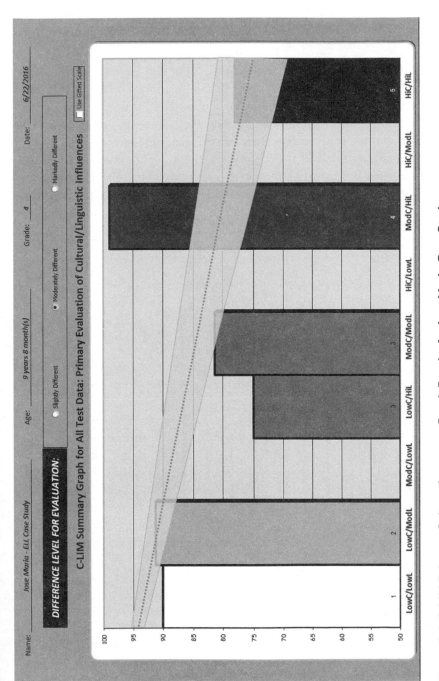

Figure 9.4 C-LIM Primary Culture-Language Graph Results for Jose Maria Case Study

Prior to examining the pattern of scores, the psychologist obtained and confirmed information from the pre-referral team and the ESL department regarding Jose's language proficiency and development. As noted, Jose had recently taken and passed the federally mandated English proficiency testing required for assessing and demonstrating progress in English language acquisition for the district's EL population. Careful examination of the information contained in Jose's records revealed no unusual events or circumstances in his development. Jose was only a year old when he came to the United States, had learned Spanish at home almost exclusively and up until starting kindergarten. Upon entering school, Jose was instructed only in English and was given ESL support services (which are, of course, rendered in English). Overall, the psychologist concluded that Jose's developmental history and his experiences in language and educationally were rather typical of other ELs born in the United States or who come to the United States at an early age as did Jose. Furthermore, the records available to the psychologist indicated that his parents were of very modest means and could be classified as low SES (Jose was enrolled in the school's free/reduced lunch program). Again, Jose's background and experience appeared to be very comparable to other children who also first began to learn English upon entering school at the age of five and who received ESL services but never any form of native-language instruction. Accordingly, the psychologist determined that the most appropriate basis for evaluating Jose's test performance within the C-LIM was best represented by the category of "moderately different" and thus this level of difference was indicated by selection of the appropriate radio button visible at the top left of each graph in Figures 9.3 and 9.4.

Upon evaluation of the pattern of scores from the perspective regarding research that demonstrates an attenuation of performance as tests require increased developmental acculturative knowledge acquisition and English language proficiency, the school psychologist concluded that there did not appear to be an overall or general pattern of decline across all scores and that there were some cell aggregates where the subtests that comprise them did not reach the expected range for ELs of average ability and similar "moderately different" backgrounds. This indicated that there did not appear to be a primary effect of these cultural and linguistic variables on Jose's test performance and consequently, the results were declared to be valid. The psychologist noted, however, that the impact of linguistic and cultural differences evaluated within the C-LIM did not simply disappear. Rather, these variables and their effect remains present and likely continues to exert some degree of contributory influence on Jose's test performance, albeit not to the extent that it is systematic across all test scores or powerful enough to constrain the test scores within or above the expected range. As such, the psychologist could not reasonably consider the alternative that the pattern of test scores suggested that they were likely to be invalid. To the contrary, evaluation within the C-LIM appeared to provide clear support that the results were possibly valid and that evaluation should therefore proceed.

Having declared the results possibly valid, the psychologist proceeded to evaluate the data using XBA principles to carefully evaluate and enhance the theoretical and psychometric validity of the obtained results. The DMIA module within X-BASS provided the functionality necessary to carry out these procedures. When the subtest data were transferred from the C-LIM and the composites entered into their respective cells on each test tab (including entry of all WIAT-III scores as well) in X-BASS, the only cluster that failed to demonstrate the requisite cohesion for which XBA follow-up was recommended was in the Auditory Processing (Ga) domain. Close inspection of the composition of the subtests that comprise the Ga cluster in the WJ IV COG reveals that of the two subtests that comprise it (Phonological Processing and Nonword Repetition), the latter is classified as having a primary loading on Short-Term Memory (Gsm) and only a secondary loading on Ga. Further examination of the data also indicated that Gsm could not be determined reliably to be an area of strength or weakness given that the Phonological Processing score was average (SS = 99) but the Nonword Repetition score was low average and outside normal limits (SS = 84). The problem was resolved via supplemental testing using the Sound Blending subtest from the WJ IV OL battery. The resulting score (SS = 88) was combined via XBA methods to form an XBA Ga composite of 92 which suggested no real difficulties in this domain. Moreover, there had been no reported concerns with decoding difficulties in reading on Jose's part and his performance in the Basic Reading Skills (BRS) domain of the WIAT-II corroborated the lack of any problems with this aspect of reading (e.g., Word Reading SS = 92, Pseudoword Decoding SS = 98). As such, it was clear that Jose's auditory processing ability was in reality a strength, not a weakness, and that the presence of a low score on Nonword Repetition was likely attributable to deficits in Gsm as indicated by the low score on the WMI of the WISC-V (SS = 79).

In addition to a possible weakness in the area of Gsm, the psychologist noted potential deficits in Gf (FRI SS = 82), Glr (SS = 77), and Gc (VCI SS = 76). The psychologist then decided to conduct follow-up native-language evaluation of these areas to provide the necessary cross-linguistic confirmation that they are indeed domains that represent areas of true weaknesses. In recognition of the Gc caveat discussed previously, the psychologist first sought to determine whether this ability actually required re-evaluation or not. This was accomplished by examining the magnitude of the aggregate value for Gc within the context of the C-LIM graphs as reflected by the high/high cell in the matrix (bottom right location) (see

Figure 9.2) and the bars at the far right-hand side of the graphs (see Figure 9.3 and Figure 9.4). The psychologist noted that although the magnitude of the Gc cluster was low (SS = 76), performance in the high culture/high language (Tier 5) cell was well within the shaded and expected range. The psychologist recognized that this finding indicated that Jose's Gc abilities were in fact comparable to other ELs with comparable experiential and developmental backgrounds and that it should therefore be considered a "strength" within the context of assigning meaning and for the purposes of identifying SLD as well via the district's PSW model. This obviated the need for follow-up testing in the native language for Gc and instead, the psychologist conducted follow-up evaluation in the native language only for Gsm, Glr and Gf. Because the psychologist was competent and qualified to evaluate in Spanish, it was not necessary to rely on the assistance of a bilingual evaluator or a translator/interpreter. Had this not been the case, the appropriate procedure would have been to either secure the assistance of a bilingual evaluator for the follow-up testing or else to engage the services of a translator/interpreter for re-administration of the tests via the native language. Also, because the original data were collected in a manner consistent with XBA procedures (using two batteries), the need to provide reasonably parallel testing meant that Gsm was evaluated using the WMI from the WISC-IV Spanish, albeit only the Digit Span subtest was the same for both domains. Likewise, Gf was also re-evaluated using subtests from the WISC-IV Spanish albeit only the Block Design subtest was common in both domains. As for Glr, it was re-evaluated using the Glr cluster from the Batería III since it has originally been evaluated using the WJ IV COG. In these cases, the new clusters only use one of the two tests from the old clusters and the corresponding subtests from the old clusters were used to create composites that mirror the same domains but which did not use the exact same tests. Again, this is a concession to the fact that there is no current WISC-V Spanish or Batería IV. If and when such tests become available and assuming that they retain the same structure, future applications of the WISC-V and WJ IV COG in testing with ELs will become more straightforward and strictly parallel. Results from follow-up evaluation are provided in Figure 9.5.

While acknowledging the slight differences in subtest composition between the Gf, Gsm and Glr clusters from the WISC-V/WISC-IV Spanish and WJ IV COG/Batería III, it was nevertheless clear that performance in the area of Gf increased significantly when evaluated in the native language (SS = 91) as compared to English (SS = 82). Because the native-language score was now within the average range, the psychologist concluded that the original score must have been attenuated by factors other than cultural and linguistic difference. In fact, the psychologist was able to recall that the English administration of the two subtests

Wechsler Intelligence Scale for Children-V

Verbal Comprehension Index	76	_Fluid Reasoning Index_	82	_Visual-Spatial Index_	95
Similarities	5	Matrix Reasoning	7	Block Design	9
Vocabulary	6	Figure Weights	7	Visual Puzzles	9
Working Memory Index	79	_Processing Speed Index_	94	_WISC-IV Spanish (Gf)_	91
Digit Span	5	Coding	9	Matrix Reasoning	8
Picture Span	7	Symbol Search	8	Picture Concepts	9
WISC IV Spanish WMI	72				
Digit Span	5				
Letter-Number Sequencing	4				

Wechsler Individual Achievement Test-III

Basic Reading	94	_Reading Comprehension_	76	_Written Expression_	92
Word Reading	92	Reading Comprehension	76	Spelling	100
Pseudoword Decoding	98	Oral Reading Fluency	80	Sentence Composition	86
				Essay Composition	93

Woodcock Johnson IV Tests of Cognitive Ability

Auditory Processing	91	_LT Storage/Retrieval_	77
Phonological Processing	99	Story Recall	79
Nonword Repetition	84	Visual-Auditory Learning	75
		Batería III LT Retrieval	79
		Visual-Auditory Learning	81
		Retrieval Fluency	78

Figure 9.5 Test Scores From WISC-V, WIAT-III, and WJ IV COG With Follow-Up Native Language Scores for Jose Maria

from this cluster had been administered immediately preceding lunch and a recess break and that this may have caused Jose to rush through items and lose some concentration in an effort to ensure that he wouldn't miss being able to eat and play with his friends. Regardless of the reason, the native-language Gf cluster clearly represents a better and more valid indication of his true ability in this domain and it renders the original score from English testing as invalid. Thus, the psychologist chose to use the new composite instead of the original cluster to ensure fair and equitable interpretation and for use in later PSW analysis as correctly representing an area of "strength," rather than one of weakness as was implied by the original score. In contrast, Jose's performance in the area of Gsm on the WISC-IV Spanish was actually found to be slightly lower (WMI SS = 72) than what was originally found when evaluated in English (SS = 79). Similarly, Jose's performance in the area of Glr on the Batería III was only slightly higher (SS = 79) but still within the deficit range as was his original score obtained from testing in English (SS = 77). In both cases, the psychologist properly concluded that these results served to provide cross-linguistic confirmation of the validity of the original scores obtained from testing in English. Therefore, in the absence of any other extraneous variables that might be recognized or identified, follow-up testing in the domains of Gsm and Glr strongly suggest that that the original scores are likely to be valid and true indicators of deficits in these domains.

To complete the assessment, the psychologist next conducted a PSW-based evaluation of SLD using the model and analyses operationalized in the X-BASS and which is based on a PSW approach known as the Dual-Discrepancy/Consistency model of SLD identification (Flanagan et al., 2013). This included selection of the most defensible and valid representations of ability in each domain and indication of each ability (both cognitive and academic) as either a strength or weakness. A summary of the data as so indicated and organized for the purpose of this analysis is presented in Figure 9.6. Note that the summary indicates that Jose does not meet the criteria necessary for establishing SLD within the framework of this model largely because the g-Value (an indicator of overall general ability) is .38 and falls well below the necessary .51 lower limit for acceptable defense of generally average ability. The psychologist was at first a bit surprised but then rightly realized that Gc had been erroneously marked as a weakness rather than as a strength based on the Gc caveat its evaluation within the C-LIM. The psychologist corrected this error in designation and the new results are presented in Figure 9.7 which now demonstrates that Jose does indeed have sufficient general ability to meet the criterion necessary for establishing overall general ability as required by most consensus definitions of SLD. In this case, the g-Value is now a robust .64 and the FCC (which was not calculated or displayed previously) is now shown to be SS = 91. The summary also correctly shows that the only areas of suspected weakness are seen in the Gsm and Glr domains.

The psychologist next examined the data within the PSW Analyzer in X-BASS and, in this case, the results indicated that the pattern of strengths and weaknesses for Jose were indeed fully consistent with probable SLD. This analysis and a summary of the operational criteria used to establish SLD are provided in Figure 9.8. It should be noted that this analysis does not require any alterations or modifications subject to evaluation of ELs. All such necessary accommodations have already been accomplished via automatic guidance within X-BASS. For example, although the psychologist "forgot" to mark Gc as a strength, the current version of X-BASS provides a pop up message that reminds practitioners that the value should rightly be considered a strength, not a weakness, whenever the value meets certain specific criteria (the case involves an EL, the value of the Gc composite falls within or above the shaded range in the C-LIM corresponding to the selected range of difference, and the value of the Gc composite is below 90). Likewise, when all of these criteria are met and Gc is marked as a strength (despite the low magnitude of the score),

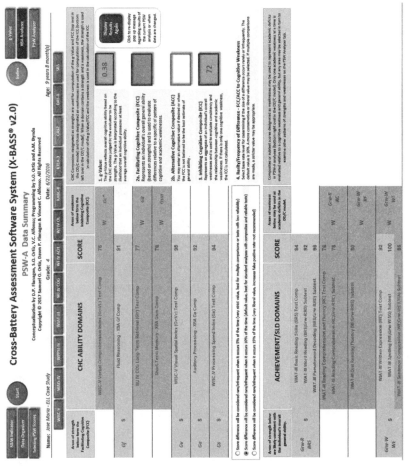

Figure 9.6 Data Summary and Preliminary PSW Analysis for Jose Maria Case Study With Incorrect Designation of Gc

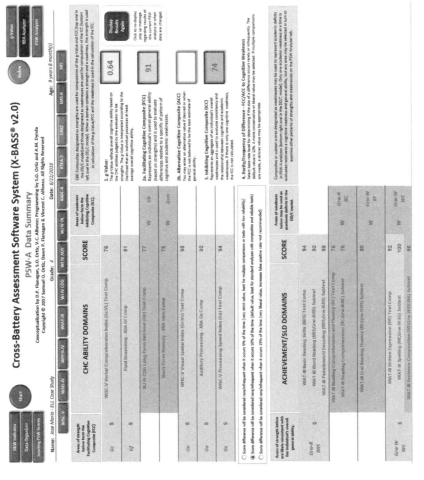

Figure 9.7 Data Summary and Preliminary PSW Analysis for Jose Maria Case Study With Correct Designation of Gc

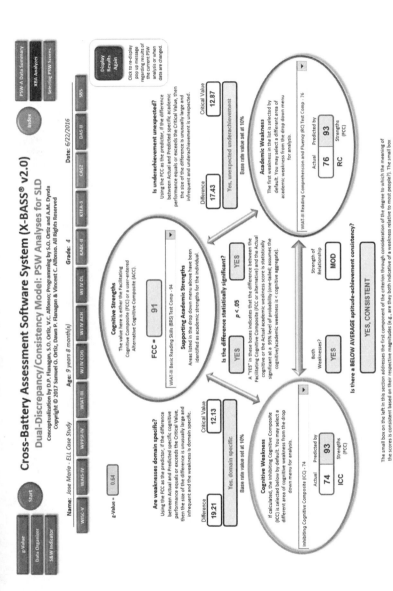

Figure 9.8 Final PSW Analysis and Determination of SLD for Jose Maria Case Study

X-BASS will automatically exclude the value from calculation of the FCC to prevent discriminatory attenuation that suggests less than average general ability. By incorporating these guiding principles within X-BASS use of the WISC-V (or any other battery for that matter) in the evaluation of ELs is greatly simplified and adds extra protection against potentially discriminatory decisions or oversights.

Based on the information provided by the PSW Analyzer, the psychologist ultimately concluded that Jose's overall pattern of strengths and weaknesses were consistent with SLD and that all necessary criteria for establishing a learning disorder had been adequately met. Moreover, the observed deficits in Gsm and Glr were very consistent with the teacher's reports regarding inconsistent learning and trouble remembering the meaning of passages that had just been read by Jose. Given the consistency and further support of this ecological data and information, the psychologist concluded that Jose met the district's standards for identification as having SLD within the requisite PSW model and that coupled with his observed educational needs in the areas of reading comprehension, oral reading fluency, and written expression (notably sentence composition), he was likely to be eligible for special education and related services. At the IEP meeting, the psychologist advocated for culturally and linguistically appropriate goals and objectives as well as interventions within the general education setting for Jose to help him manage and ameliorate his deficits in Gsm and Glr, as well as his specific difficulties in reading comprehension and written language. By ensuring that Jose receives culturally and linguistically relevant support in the special and general education environments, it is expected that he will be afforded sufficient opportunity necessary to maximize his success in the classroom (Brown & Ortiz, 2014).

CONCLUSION

Although the preceding case study, to a large extent, tended to somewhat simplify the process of evaluation of ELs with the WISC-V and WISC-IV Spanish, care was taken to illustrate some of the more critical points and decisions that are likely to cause the most problems for psychologists. For example, had the evaluation been undertaken in a manner that did not follow the recommended best practice framework, the psychologist would have been in problematic situations from which escape may not have been possible. Use of native-language tests at the beginning of the evaluation would have resulted in an inability to evaluate or assess the impact of linguistic/cultural variables on test performance—thereby wasting precious time and resources. Had the psychologist conducted follow-up evaluation of all areas of functioning that were initially assessed in English, more time and resources would have been spent unnecessarily in the evaluation of abilities that were already known to be strengths for the individual. Had the psychologist failed to consider the Gc caveat and maintained a strict normative interpretation for Gc, Jose would not have met criteria for SLD any may well have been thought, at best, not to be disabled, or at worst, possibly intellectually disabled. And had the psychologist not utilized the C-LIM to evaluate the impact of linguistic and cultural factors on test performance, it would have been impossible to continue with any type of evaluation because the test scores used in identifying SLD must be first established as being valid. The entire process of evaluation described by the case study sought to examine and ensure validity of the obtained results so as to permit valid and defensible interpretations and conclusions. Use of the recommended best practice approach, along with XBA principles and procedures and utilization of the automated processes and analyses contained in X-BASS (e.g., C-LIM, PSW Analyzer, etc.) provided a comprehensive and systematic approach to evaluation that is easily defensible from a legal, theoretical, and psychometric standpoint. Had the psychologist not followed all of the procedures described in the case study, it is likely that the results would have been discriminatory. And without any attempt to establish validity, the obtained test scores could not have been given any meaning and attempts to do so would be no more valid than merely guessing. Clearly, the adherence to the proposed best practice framework assisted greatly in preventing a wide range of potentially critical mistakes in the evaluation process—most of which would likely have had rather negative consequences for Jose.

It is worth mentioning that although SLD was the outcome in this case, it is entirely possible that the results from initial testing in English could have formed a pattern that was consistent with the levels of performance typical of ELs who are non-disabled and of average ability or higher. That is, when the results follow the type of systematic decline and the magnitude of the aggregate scores in each cell are within the range consistent with what has been found in the research, the only reasonable conclusion is that the obtained test scores are invalid because they reflect primarily the influence of linguistic and cultural variables rather than the individual's true level of ability. For reference purposes, an example of what such likely "invalid" results might look like in the C-LIM graphs is presented in Figure 9.9. But the determination of invalid test scores carries with it the benefit of being able to cease further testing as the resulting pattern is consistent with performance of other individuals with comparable backgrounds who are of average ability or higher and who are also not disabled. This significantly enhances

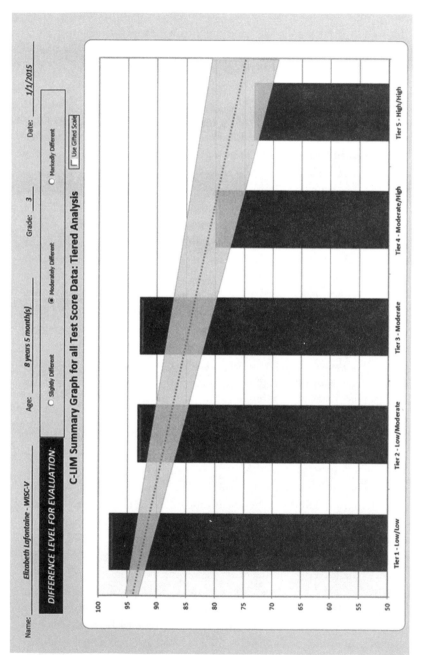

Figure 9.9 C-LIM Tiered Graph Results Suggesting Likely Invalid Test Scores and the Primary Influence of Linguistic/Cultural Variables

the efficiency of the approach and again reduces the possibility of discriminatory conclusions and indefensible attempts to ascribe meaning to invalid data. This is not to say, however, that the presence of such a pattern means that the assessment is invalid—only that the test scores are invalid. In fact, by invalidating the test scores in this manner (should the pattern suggest it) the assessment maintains its validity because it provides a defensible position that the individual is in fact, not disabled.

In conclusion, the methods for nondiscriminatory evaluation of diverse individuals outlined in this chapter are not necessarily specific to use of the WISC-V. They do illustrate, however, that it can be used as an effective tool for evaluation of ELs, particularly when supplemented with tests from the WISC-IV Spanish. Even when the examinee's heritage language is something other than Spanish, the framework proposed herein can be utilized via the aid of a translator/interpreter. As such, the WISC-V continues to be a viable tool to evaluate diverse individuals when applied within the best practice approach outlined in this chapter, which is arguably necessary to achieve fairness and promote equitable and nondiscriminatory practices.

TEST YOURSELF

1. **There is widespread consensus in psychology regarding specific guidelines and procedures for evaluating English learners with standardized tests.**
   a. True
   b. False

2. **The most critical issue necessary for evaluation of English learners is rooted primarily in the concept of:**
   a. Reliability
   b. Validity
   c. Item bias
   d. Racial differences

3. **When bias is defined traditionally with respect to the psychometric properties of a test, research has provided strong evidence of bias in which of the following areas?**
   a. Reliability
   b. Factor structure
   c. Prediction
   d. None of the above

4. **Test performance of English learners is influenced by the presence of differences relative to the norm sample primarily with regard to:**

   a. Gender

   b. Experience/development

   c. Ethnicity

   d. Geographical location

5. **The factor that is responsible for the observation that English learners score well below the normative mean on tests that measure verbal ability is:**

   a. Limited English proficiency

   b. Intelligence

   c. Scoring errors

   d. Genetics

6. **Which of the following methods of assessment, when used with English learners, automatically results in valid scores for comprehensive abilities that can be interpreted and defended?**

   a. Modified or altered testing

   b. Nonverbal testing

   c. Native-language testing

   d. None of the above

7. **Although testing in English seems counterintuitive, it is the only method where scores may be evaluated and determined to be valid because:**

   a. It can be conducted by any evaluator including those who are not bilingual.

   b. English-language tests have norms that are entirely appropriate for English learners.

   c. A large body of empirical research exists that can guide expectations of performance.

   d. Language is not an important factor in the test performance of English learners.

8. **The primary purpose of the C-LIM is to:**

   a. Reduce the psychometric bias found in tests.

   b. Evaluate the impact of cultural and linguistic differences on test performance so that a decision regarding the validity of the test results can be made systematically.

   c. Assist bilingual psychologists in performing evaluations in the native language.

   d. Eliminate the need for clinical judgment or collection of data regarding cultural, linguistic, and educational background.

9. **When using the C-LIM, which of the following general interpretive statements is incorrect?**

    a. When test performance increases diagonally across the cells from the upper left to the bottom right, scores should be deemed to be likely invalid and should not be interpreted.

    b. When test performance increases diagonally across the cells from the lower left to the top right, scores should be deemed to be likely invalid and should not be interpreted.

    c. When test performance decreases diagonally across the cells from the upper left to the bottom right, scores should be deemed to be likely invalid and should not be interpreted.

    d. When test performance decreases diagonally across the cells from the lower left to the top right, scores should be deemed to be likely invalid and should not be interpreted.

10. **The validity of test scores obtained from administration of the WISC-V to English learners requires the accumulation of evidence that should include, at a minimum:**

    a. Scores that have been found validated via use of the C-LIM

    b. Cross-validation from native-language testing to confirm areas of deficit

    c. Ecological information and data from converging sources

    d. All of the above

Answers: 1. b; 2. b; 3. d; 4. b; 5. a; 6. d; 7. c; 8. b; 9. c; 10. d

REFERENCES

American Educational Research Association, American Psychological Association, & National Council on Measurement in Education. (2015). *Standards for educational and psychological testing.* Washington, DC: Author.

Bialystok, E. (1991). *Language processing in bilingual children.* New York, NY: Cambridge University Press.

Borghese, P., & Gronau, R. C. (2005). Convergent and discriminant validity of the universal nonverbal intelligence test with limited English proficient Mexican-American elementary students. *Journal of Psychoeducational Assessment, 23,* 128–139.

Braden, J. P., & Iribarren, J. A. (2007). Test review: Wechsler, D. (2005). Wechsler Intelligence Scale for Children-Fourth Edition Spanish. *Journal of Psychoeducational Assessment, 25,* 292–299.

Cathers-Schiffman, T. A., & Thompson, M. S. (2007). Assessment of English- and Spanish-speaking students with the WISC-III and Leiter-R. *Journal of Psychoeducational Assessment, 25,* 41–52.

Cormier, D. C., McGrew, K. S., & Ysseldyke, J. E. (2014). The influences of linguistic demand and cultural loading on cognitive test scores. *Journal of Psychoeducational Assessment, 32*(7), 610–623.

DiCerbo, K. E., & Barona, A. (2000). A convergent validity study on the Differential Ability Scales and the Wechsler Intelligence Scale for Children-Third Edition with Hispanic children. *Journal of Psychoeducational Assessment, 18*, 344–352.

Dynda, A. M. (2008). *The relation between language proficiency and IQ test performance.* Unpublished manuscript. New York, NY: St. John's University.

Esparza-Brown, J. (2007). *The impact of cultural loading and linguistic demand on the performance of English/Spanish bilinguals on Spanish language cognitive tests.* Unpublished manuscript. Portland, OR: Portland State University.

Figueroa, R. A. (1983). Test bias and Hispanic children. *Journal of Special Education, 17*, 431–440.

Figueroa, R. A. (1990). Assessment of linguistic minority group children. In C. R. Reynolds & R. W. Kamphaus (Eds.), *Handbook of psychological and educational assessment of children: Vol. 1. Intelligence and achievement.* New York, NY: Guilford.

Flanagan, D. P., & Harrison, P. L. (Eds.). (2005). *Contemporary intellectual assessment: Theories, tests, and issues* (2nd ed.). New York, NY: Guilford.

Flanagan, D. P., & Kaufman, A. S. (2009). *Essentials of WISC-IV assessment* (2nd ed.). Hoboken, NJ: Wiley.

Flanagan, D. P., Ortiz, S. O., Alfonso, V. C., & Mascolo, J. T. (2002). *The Achievement in Test Desk Reference (ATDR): Comprehensive assessment and learning disability identification.* New York, NY: Wiley.

Flanagan, D. P., Ortiz, S. O., & Alfonso, V.C. (2007). *Essentials of cross-battery assessment* (2nd ed.) New York, NY: Wiley.

Flanagan, D. P., Ortiz, S .O., & Alfonso, V. C. (2013). *Essentials of cross-battery assessment* (3rd ed.). New York, NY: Wiley.

Goddard, H. H. (1914). Mental tests and the immigrant. *Journal of Delinquency, 2*, pp. 243–277.

Grosjean, F. (1989). Neurolinguists beware!: The bilingual is not two monolinguals in one person. *Brain and Language, 36*, 3–15.

Harris, J. G., & Llorente, A. M. (2005). Cultural considerations in the use of the Wechsler Intelligence Scale for Children-Fourth Edition. In A. Prifitera, D. H. Saklofske, & L. G. Weiss (Eds.), *WISC-IV clinical use and interpretations: Scientist-practitioner perspectives* (pp. 382–416). San Diego, CA: Academic Press.

Individuals with Disabilities Education Act, 20 U.S.C. § 1400 (2004).

Kranzler, J. H., Flores, C. G., & Coady, M. (2010). Examination of the cross-battery approach for the cognitive assessment of children and youth from diverse linguistic and cultural backgrounds. *School Psychology Review, 39*, 431–446.

Lohman, D. F., Korb, K., & Lakin, J. (2008). Identifying academically gifted English language learners using nonverbal tests: A comparison of the Raven, NNAT, and CogAT. *Gifted Child Quarterly, 52*, 275–296.

Mpofu, E., & Ortiz, S. O. (2009). Equitable assessment practices in diverse contexts. In E. L. Grigorenko (Ed.), *Multicultural psychoeducational assessment* (pp. 41–76). New York, NY: Springer.

Neisser, U., Boodoo, G., Bouchard, T. J., Boykin, A. W., Brody, N., Ceci, et al. (1996). Intelligence: Knowns and unknowns. *American Psychologist, 51*, 77–101.

Nieves-Brull, A. (2006). *Evaluation of the Culture-Language Matrix: A validation study of text performance in monolingual English speaking and bilingual English/Spanish speaking populations.* Unpublished manuscript. New York, NY: St. John's University.

O'Bryon, E. C., & Rogers, M. R. (2010). Bilingual school psychologists' assessment practices with English language learners. *Psychology in the Schools, 47*, 1018–1034.

Ochoa, S. H., Powell, M. P., & Robles-Piña, R. (1996). School psychologists' assessment practices with bilingual and limited-English-proficient students. *Journal of Psychoeducational Assessment, 14*, 250–275.

Ortiz, S. O. (2001). Assessment of cognitive abilities in Hispanic children. *Seminars in Speech and Language, 22(1)*, 17–37.

Ortiz, S. O. (2008). Best practices in nondiscriminatory assessment. In A. Thomas & J. Grimes (Eds.), *Best practices in school psychology V* (pp. 661–678). Washington, DC: National Association of School Psychologists.

Ortiz, S. O. (2009). Bilingual-multicultural assessment with the WISC-IV. In D. P. Flanagan & A. S. Kaufman (Eds.), *Essentials of WISC-IV assessment* (2nd ed., pp. 295–309). Hoboken, NJ: Wiley.

Ortiz, S. O. (2014). Best practices in nondiscriminatory assessment. In A. Thomas & J. Grimes (Eds.), *Best practices in school psychology VI*. Washington, DC: National Association of School Psychologists.

Ortiz, S. O. (2015). CHC Theory of Intelligence. In S. Goldstein & J. Naglieri (Eds.), *Handbook of intelligence: Evolutionary theory, historical perspective, and current concepts* (pp. 209–228). New York, NY: Springer.

Ortiz, S .O., & Dynda, A. M. (2013a). *Cross-Battery Assessment Culture-Language Interpretive Matrix, version 2.0 (XBA C-LIM v2.0) – PC and Mac versions*. Available on CD published with *Essentials of Cross-Battery Assessment* (3rd ed.). Hoboken, NJ: Wiley.

Ortiz, S. O., & Dynda, A. M. (2013b). *Cross-Battery Assessment Data Management and Interpretive Assistant, version 2.0 (XBA DMIA v2.0) – PC and Mac versions*. Available on CD published with *Essentials of Cross-Battery Assessment* (3rd ed.). Hoboken, NJ: Wiley.

Ortiz, S. O., & Dynda, A. M. (2013c). *Cross-Battery Assessment Processing Strengths and Weaknesses Analyzer, version 1.0 (XBA PSW-A v1.0) – PC and Mac versions*. Available on CD published with *Essentials of Cross-Battery Assessment* (3rd ed.).Hoboken, NJ: Wiley.

Ortiz, S. O., Flanagan, D. P., & Alfonso, V. C. (2015). *Cross-Battery Assessment Software System (X-BASS v1.0) PC and Mac versions*. Hoboken, NJ: Wiley.

Ortiz, S. O., & Melo, K. (2015). Evaluation of intelligence and learning disability with Hispanics. In K. Geisinger (Ed.), *Psychological testing of Hispanics* (pp. 109–134). Washington, DC: APA Books.

Ortiz, S. O., Ochoa, S. H., & Dynda, A. M. (2012). Testing with culturally and linguistically diverse populations: Moving beyond the verbal-performance dichotomy into evidence-based practice. In D. P. Flanagan & P. L. Harrison (Eds.), *Contemporary intellectual assessment: Theories, tests, and issues* (3rd ed., pp. 526–552). New York, NY: Guilford.

Ortiz, S. O., Ortiz, J. A., & Devine, R. I. (2016). Use of the WJ IV with English Language Learners. In D. P. Flanagan & V. C. Alfonso (Eds.), *WJ IV clinical use and interpretation* (pp. 317–354). New York, NY: Elsevier.

Paradis, M. (2014). *The assessment of bilingual aphasia*. New York, NY: Psychology Press.

Reynolds, C. R., & Ramsay, M. C. (2003). Bias in psychological assessment: An empirical review and recommendations. In J. R. Graham & J. A. Naglieri (Eds.), *Handbook of psychology: Vol. 10. Assessment psychology* (pp. 67–94). Hoboken, NJ: Wiley.

Rhodes, R., Ochoa, S. H., & Ortiz, S. O. (2005). *Assessment of culturally and linguistically diverse students: A practical guide*. New York, NY: Guilford.

Salvia, J., & Ysseldyke, J. E. (1991). *Assessment* (5th ed.). New York, NY: Houghton Mifflin.

Sanchez-Escobedo, P., Hollingworth, L., & Fina, D. F. (2012). A cross-cultural, comparative study of the American, Spanish, and Mexican versions of the WISC-IV. *TESOL Quarterly, 45,* 781–792.

Sandoval, J., Frisby, C. L., Geisinger, K. F., Scheunemann, J. D., & Grenier, J. R. (Eds.). (1998). *Test interpretation and diversity: Achieving equality in assessment*. Washington, DC: American Psychological Association. http://dx.doi.org/10.1037/10279-000

Schneider, J., & McGrew, K. S. (2012). The Cattell-Horn-Carroll Model of intelligence. In D. P. Flanagan & P. L. Harrison (Eds.), *Contemporary Intellectual Assessment* (3rd Ed., pp. 99–143). New York, NY: Guilford.

Schrank, F. A., McGrew, K. S., & Mather, N. (2015). The WJ IV Gf-Gc Composite and its use in the identification of specific learning disabilities. *Assessment Service Bulletin Number 3*. Rolling Meadows, IL: Riverside.

Sotelo-Dynega, M., & Dixon, S. G. (2014). Cognitive assessment practices: A survey of school psychologists. *Psychology in the Schools, 51*(10), 1031–1045.

Sotelo-Dynega, M., Geddes, L., Luhrs, A., & Teague, J. (2009). *What is a bilingual school psychologist? A national survey of the credentialing bodies of school psychologists.* Poster presented at the National Association of School Psychologists Annual Conference, Boston, MA.

Sotelo-Dynega, M., Ortiz, S. O., Flanagan, D. P., & Chaplin, W. (2013). English language proficiency and test performance: Evaluation of bilinguals with the Woodcock-Johnson III Tests of Cognitive Ability. *Psychology in the Schools, 50*(8), 781–797.

Styck, K. M., & Watkins, M. W. (2013). Diagnostic utility of the Culture-Language Interpretive Matrix for the Wechsler Intelligence Scales for Children–Fourth Edition among referred students. *School Psychology Review, 42*(4), 367–382.

Styck, K. M., & Watkins, M. W. (2014). Discriminant validity of the WISC-IV Culture-Language Interpretive Matrix. *Contemporary School Psychology, 18*, 168–188.

Thomas, W. P., & Collier, V. P. (2002). *A national study of school effectiveness for language minority students' long-term academic achievement.* http://www.usc.edu/dept/education/CMMR/CollierThomasExReport.pdf

U.S. Census Bureau. (2015). Current Population Survey, released 2015. Retrieved October 22, 2015, from http://www.census.gov/cps/

Valdes, G., & Figueroa, R. A. (1994). *Bilingualism and testing: A special case of bias.* Norwood, NJ: Ablex.

Vukovich, D., & Figueroa, R. A. (1982). *The validation of the System of Multicultural Pluralistic Assessment: 1980-1982.* Unpublished manuscript, University of California at Davis, Department of Education. In D. P. Flanagan, S. O. Ortiz, & V. C. Alfonso (2013). *Essentials of cross-battery assessment* (3rd ed.). Hoboken, NJ: Wiley.

Wechsler, D. (1944). *The measurement of adult intelligence* (3rd ed.). Baltimore, MD: Williams & Wilkins.

Wechsler, D. (2003). *Wechsler Intelligence Scale for Children-Fourth Edition (WISC-IV).* San Antonio, TX: Pearson.

Wechsler, D. (2004). *Wechslder Intelligence Scale for Children-Fourth Edition Spanish (WISC-IV).* San Antonio, TX: Pearson.

Wechsler, D. (2014). *Wechsler Intelligence Scale for Children-Fifth Edition (WISC-V).* San Antonio, TX: Pearson.

Wechsler, D., & Naglieri, J. A. (2006). *Wechsler Nonverbal Scale of Ability.* San Antonio, TX: Pearson.

Wechsler, D., Raiford, S. E., & Holdnack, J. A. (2014). *WISC-V technical and interpretive manual.* Bloomington, MN: Pearson Psychological Corporation.

Weiss, L., Prifitera, A., & Munoz, M. (2015). In K. F. Geisinger (Ed.), *Psychological testing of Hispanics* (2nd ed., pp. 81–108). Washington, DC: American Psychological Association.

Weiss, L. G., Harris, J. G., Prifitera, A., Courville, T., Rolfhus, E., Saklofske, D. H., et al. (2006). WISC-IV interpretation in societal context. In L. G. Weiss, D. H. Saklofske, & J. Holdnack (Eds.), *WISC-IV advanced clinical interpretation* (pp. 1–57). Burlington, MA: Academic Press.

Yerkes, R. M. (1921). *Psychological examining in the United States Army.* Memoirs of the National Academy of Sciences, Vol. 15. Washington, DC: NASP.

Ten

WISC-V AND Q-INTERACTIVE

Carlea Dries, Ron Dumont, and Kathleen D. Viezel

This chapter presents a review of the Q-interactive platform for administering tests published by Pearson Education, Inc. Although Q-interactive provides accessibility to a wide range of assessment tools, this chapter focuses on the platform in general, and the WISC-V (Wechsler, 2014a) in particular. In order to review the Q-interactive program the authors administered several iPad WISC-Vs to volunteers. To compare the two types of WISC-V administrations (iPad vs. traditional), in at least one case, an iPad administration was conducted by an experienced examiner while at the same time another experienced examiner sat in on the testing session and recorded all responses using the standard record form and stopwatch timing procedures. In another situation, a reviewer worked with a practicing examiner who had neither used the Q-interactive system nor administered a WISC-V. This volunteer found it difficult to learn the assessment tool and the digital platform simultaneously. Overall, among these authors, the iPad WISC-V was administered at least 20 times to age-appropriate volunteers.

It should be noted that the information was current as of our initial evaluation of the system. Issues reported may have been corrected by Pearson in the time since publication. Please refer to the company's website for the most current information.

DIGITAL PLATFORM

Use of technology is a continuing trend within the school setting. Pearson Education offers examiners two distinct computer and Web-based systems: Q-interactive, a tablet-based digital platform for administering and scoring a vast array of Pearson assessment products, and Q-global, a Web-based scoring and reporting platform. At the time of this review, the only tablet that supports Q-interactive is the iPad. Throughout this review we refer to the use of Q-interactive as "iPad administration" and to the more traditional administration as "paper-and-pencil administration."

Assessments available on Q-interactive include the *Clinical Evaluation of Language Fundamentals–Fifth Edition* (CELF-5), *Children's Memory Scale* (CMS), *California Verbal Learning Test–Second Edition* (CVLT-II), *California Verbal Learning Test–Children's Version* (CVLT-C), *Delis-Kaplan Executive Function System (D-KEFS), Goldman-Fristoe Test of Articulation–Third Edition* (GFTA-3), *Khan-Lewis Phonological Analysis–Third Edition* (KLPA-3), *Kaufman Test of Educational Achievement–Third Edition* (KTEA-3), *A Developmental NEuroPSYchological Assessment–Second Edition* (NEPSY-II), *Peabody Picture Vocabulary Test–Fourth Edition* (PPVT-4), *Wechsler Adult Intelligence Scale–Fourth Edition* (WAIS-IV), *Wechsler Individual Achievement Test–Third Edition* (WIAT-III), *Wechsler Intelligence Scale for Children–Fourth Edition* (WISC-IV), *Wechsler Intelligence Scale for Children–Fifth Edition* (WISC-V), *Wechsler Memory Scale–Fourth Edition* (WMS-IV), and the *Wechsler Preschool and Primary Scale of Intelligence–Fourth Edition* (WPPSI-IV). Rapid Reference 10.1 lists the tests available through Q-interactive along with the names of the authors and dates of publication. It is important to note that not all subtests are available for each assessment tool.

≡ Rapid Reference 10.1

Pearson Tests Available Through Q-interactive

Cohen, M. (1997). *Children's Memory Scale.*

Delis, D. C., Kaplan, E., & Kramer, J. H. (2001). *Delis-Kaplan Executive Function System.*

Delis, D. C., Kramer, J. H., Kaplan, E., & Ober, B. A. (1994). *California Verbal Learning Test–Children's Version.*

Delis, D. C., Kramer, J. H., Kaplan, E., & Ober, B. A. (2000). *California Verbal Learning Test–Second Edition.*

Dunn, L. M., & Dunn, D.M. (2007). *Peabody Picture Vocabulary Test–Fourth Edition.*

Goldman, R., & Fristoe, M. (2015). *Goldman-Fristoe Test of Articulation–Third Edition.*

Kaufman, A. S., & Kaufman, N. L. (2014). *Kaufman Test of Educational Achievement–Third Edition.*

Khan, M. O., & Lewis, N.P. (2015). *Khan-Lewis Phonological Analysis–Third Edition.*

Korkman, M., Kirk, U., & Kemp, S. (2007). *A Developmental NEuroPSYchological Assessment–Second Edition.*

Wechsler, D. (2003). *Wechsler Intelligence Scale for Children–Fourth Edition.*

Wechsler, D. (2008). *Wechsler Adult Intelligence Scale–Fourth Edition*.
Wechsler, D. (2009a). *Wechsler Individual Achievement Test–Third Edition*.
Wechsler, D. (2009b). *Wechsler Memory Scale–Fourth Edition*.
Wechsler, D. (2012). *Wechsler Preschool and Primary Scale of Intelligence–Fourth Edition*.
Wechsler, D. (2014). *Wechsler Intelligence Scale for Children–Fifth Edition*.
Wiig, E. H., Semel, E., & Secord, W. A. (2013). *Clinical Evaluation of Language Fundamentals–Fifth Edition*.

Note: Not all subtests are available for each assessment tool. All tests are published by Pearson.

Some tests still require the purchase of certain response booklets even if the subtests are available on the iPad. For example, when using the Q-interactive platform, examiners still need the Symbol Search, Coding, and Cancellation response booklets for the WISC-V. Additionally, the current Q-interactive system does not include scoring templates for subtests (e.g., Coding, Symbol Search). However, these scoring templates and response booklets, along with the Block Design cubes and eraserless pencils (one red, one yellow #2), are available within the Starter Kit that is sent with an initial purchase of a Q-interactive license.

The Q-interactive website has posted eight equivalency studies that compare test results obtained using traditional administration techniques versus the Q-interactive system administration. The results from these studies suggest that, although there may be some differences between scores based on the administration presentation, these differences are generally small and provide initial evidence that the two formats will yield clinically equivalent scores. The most recent study (Daniel, Wahlstrom, & Zhang, 2014) compared the equivalency of WISC-V results for a large sample of children who were administered the test either in traditional paper format (*n* = 175) or Q-interactive format (*n* = 175).

Fifteen of the 18 subtests evaluated were statistically equivalent. Only three subtests (i.e., Arithmetic, Block Design, and Comprehension) showed statistically significant format effects, with examinees scoring lower on Arithmetic and Comprehension and higher on Block Design when using the iPad version. Although statistically significant, the effect sizes were small (J. Cohen, 1988), and no difference exceeded the effect size threshold (.20) set by the researchers. Overall, examiners should expect examinees to receive approximately the same score regardless of the format by which the WISC-V is administered. Because all of the equivalency studies were conducted with nonclinical populations, it remains to be seen whether examinees with disabilities obtain equivalent scores using Q-interactive. Three special group study technical reports have been published (http://www.helloq.com/research.htm) specific to assessment results of students identified as gifted, or with an intellectual disability, attention-deficit/hyperactivity disorder, autism, or specific learning disability in reading or math.

When using the Q-interactive system, it is important to note that the tests themselves are exactly the same as the traditional paper-and-pencil version; what is new is how the examiner administers them.

DON'T FORGET

It is important to note that the Q-interactive versions of tests are exactly the same as the traditional paper-and-pencil versions; what is new is how the examiner administers them.

During iPad administration, examiners and examinees use synced, wireless iPads. The examiner's iPad is essentially the test's administration manual and record form all in one. The examiner can read the instructions, time and capture response information (including the ability to audio-record and/or transcribe most responses), score individual items, and view and control the examinee's iPad. The examinee's iPad is used as an interactive stimulus booklet that has the capability of capturing an examinee's touch responses for certain items. For example, on the Matrix Reasoning subtest, if the examinee points at and touches the stimuli on his or her iPad screen, the response shows up as a digital signal, or fingerprint, on the examiner's iPad. However, the selection does not remain visible on the examinee's iPad for an extended period. One examinee commented that it was difficult for her to be sure that what she selected registered on the examiner's device or whether she needed to be more forceful with her touch. When the examiner has completed a subtest, it is automatically scored and results are available for instant review. Process scores (e.g., Block Design No Time Bonus, Longest Digit Forward, Picture Span Response) are also tabulated automatically. Once the entire test is complete, results are not only available on the iPad, but are sent to a database that is accessible via the Q-interactive companion website.

One important aspect of the Q-interactive system is the ability to receive test and program updates. Users will receive a notification when a new update is available. The update can then be downloaded to reflect the most recent version of an assessment instrument or an improvement to the application. Additionally, the HelloQ website contains a note that a user has access to new assessments for the first 30 days they are available on Q-interactive. Technical support access is unlimited, and includes training such as live and prerecorded webinars and video tutorials.

HARDWARE

Use of this digital platform requires two Apple iPads (version 2 or newer). A capacitive stylus is highly recommended. The use of a stylus certainly makes the assessment process more efficient and the resulting test record more accurate. If examiners wish to write verbatim responses, the stylus provides the familiarity of a pen or pencil for writing instead of the clumsiness of trying to write with a finger. A capped or closed pen does not work on the device. Also, attempting to use fingers instead of a stylus to record answers generally requires more time and may lead to long delays between test items. It should be noted that iPad 2s and the new iPad Air have screens that are 9.7 inches on the diagonal while the iPad mini's screen is about 2 inches smaller at 7.9 inches on the diagonal. Because of the need to present stimuli at the same size as was done during standardization, if one does use an iPad mini it is highly recommended that the mini serve only as the examiner's tool and not be used as the stimulus book. Trainers and examiners should be mindful of this recommendation, because during the review process, we were technically able to utilize an iPad mini for the examiners' administration manual as well as for the examinee's stimulus book.

DON'T FORGET

Because of the need to maintain standardization, if an iPad mini is used, it should be used only as the examiner's tool and never as the stimulus book.

Because examiners may be sharing an iPad with other adults and examinees, we highly recommend a protective screen cover. Examinees have a tendency to touch the iPad during administration because of their fascination with the technology. A sturdy case, preferably one that would cover the "home" button on the examinee's device, is also recommended. Be sure to clean the iPad screen before testing. Fingerprints and smudges on the screen could detract from the administration and affect the result.

CAUTION

Be sure to clean the iPad screen before testing because fingerprints and smudges on the screen could detract from the administration and affect the results.

On a positive note, the battery length of the iPad is generally sufficient to cover a standard school day. Nonetheless, it is recommended that both devices be plugged in each night to be sure enough charge is available for the first assessment of the day.

SOFTWARE

Each iPad needs to have the Q-interactive app (Assess), which is free to download from the iTunes store. During test administration, the two iPads must be connected via Bluetooth. If Bluetooth connectivity is lost or interrupted, the session will be delayed because there is no way to advance to another item. This can be a critical concern during timed tasks (e.g., Figure Weights, Visual Puzzles) or those with a specific exposure length (i.e., Picture Span). During this process, each reviewer experienced at least some difficulty getting the iPads to connect successfully and maintain connectivity. The Frequently Asked Questions (FAQs) section of the HelloQ website has some recommendations on how to reestablish connectivity if it is lost during a session. Setting up the Bluetooth correctly requires more than just a basic knowledge of how to use an iPad. The user must be familiar (and comfortable) with manipulating iPad settings, but once all settings are adjusted properly, the use of the iPads was easy and we encountered only minor annoyances and problems. For example, when first learning to use the Q-interactive system, these authors neglected to turn off all notification for the iPad in use. During a practice test administration an alert sounded and a scheduled appointment appeared on the screen. Although minor in nature, it did disrupt the flow of the administration. Although it is not needed when actually administering a test, Wi-Fi is required in order to run certain aspects of the Q-interactive system.

SET-UP

Although Q-interactive is an iPad application-based assessment system, some of the examiner's work needs to be done outside of the Assess application. It should be noted that the Q-interactive system has two websites that can be accessed from a Wi-Fi-enabled iPad or from any device with access to the Internet. One website (http://www.helloq.com) contains an overview of products, research, webinars, and news. The companion website (http://www .qiactive.com) provides a portal through which assessments can be set up (through your "dashboard") and through which the examinee database is accessible.

DON'T FORGET

· ·

http://www.helloq.com has an overview of products, research, webinars, and news. http://www.qiactive.com is the portal through which assessments can be set up and the examinee database can be accessed.

In order to test an examinee, a profile must be created on the website. The Q-interactive interface for creating a new examinee for the database is generally a smooth and intuitive process, but it did present us with some minor inconveniences. For example, an examinee ID number is required. Additionally, the Date of Birth field may be counterintuitive to many American users because it utilizes a day/month/year format rather than month/day/year. (The Q-global scoring system uses the month/day/year format.) These formats are different from pencil-and-paper protocols that typically use a year/month/day order. A user can edit the examinee information after the fact, in the event of an incorrect entry (e.g., birth date).

Once an examinee's profile has been created, all tests that are intended for use with the examinee are selected. If a particular assessment is selected that is inappropriate for the specific examinee (e.g., choosing the WISC-V for a 4-year-old), an alert appears on screen offering the opportunity to continue with the selection or make a new one. The user has the flexibility to choose individual subtests instead of a full battery. For example, for a WISC-V, the examiner may, for cost- or time-saving purposes, choose to administer only the seven subtests required to tabulate a Full Scale IQ, Ancillary, Complementary, or other subtests, used in certain circumstances such as obtaining domain indices, require an additional cost.

Additional tests or subtests can be included even after setting up an initial testing battery from either the Q-interactive website or the Assess application. From Assess, you can "edit" in the Test tab of the current examinee and resume the assessment more quickly than if you followed the multiple-step process from the website. Within the website, you can navigate from any of the main tabs (i.e., Dashboard, Clients, Batteries, Assessments) and use the step-by-step guide. In order to add more subtests during the session, Wi-Fi connectivity is not needed. An alert will appear reiterating the need for Bluetooth connection and the recommendation to disable Wi-Fi on the examinee's device, but the newly selected test is added and usable. This allows an examiner to add a replacement subtest immediately (e.g., if a subtest is spoiled during administration) even if working in a building that does not have Wi-Fi access. Should a user try to add a subtest that has already been administered, a warning will appear and give the opportunity to reconsider the selection.

After the initial battery is selected on the website and while the iPad has Wi-Fi available, the assessment information can be downloaded onto the Assess application on the examiner's iPad. Once the Assess application is opened, the user must "sync" the iPad to be able to access the selected materials. This adds extra steps in the testing process, and there is currently no way to create a new examinee directly through the Assess application.

Therefore, if an examiner is testing multiple examinees in a short period of time, care should be taken to plan all batteries in advance; spontaneous testing sessions may be more difficult than the traditional paper-and-pencil model. Another note is that simply being logged in to the Q-interactive website does not suffice; the user must also log in to the Assess application. All usernames and passwords are case sensitive and, in an apparent effort to be more secure, passwords require a combination of uppercase and lowercase letters, numbers, and special characters. The information does not automatically save or become stored on the iPads. Such measures for security's sake are appreciated on a global level, but in the minute-to-minute can be considered a time-consuming annoyance.

CAUTION

If an examiner intends to test several examinees in a short period of time, care should be taken to plan all batteries in advance because spontaneous testing sessions may be more difficult than the traditional paper-and-pencil model.

Once an assessment is started on one iPad, it cannot be resumed on another, even if the same user account is being utilized and the iPad is synced with the website. Although Q-interactive does allow for multiple-user accounts, the inability to transfer assessments from one iPad to another may present a potential difficulty if the original iPad was broken, lost or stolen, or replaced with a newer model.

When setting up the iPads for use in an actual administration, certain settings must be accurately configured. For example, it's important to maximize the brightness of the screen, to set the autolock to 15 minutes or never, to set a passcode so that things cannot be entered without your acknowledgment or approval, to lock the rotation of the screen, and to turn off multi-tasking and notifications (see Rapid Reference 10.2). If notifications are not disabled (i.e., in "Do Not Disturb" mode), the examiner or examinee may receive calendar alerts for meetings, reminders, phone or FaceTime calls, and so on. We learned this the hard way—while testing a student the calendar notification appeared in the middle of a subtest, resulting not only in slight embarrassment but a delay and break in the test administration. In order to communicate, the two iPads being used must be set to the same case-sensitive Bluetooth name. If an agency or school has more than one set of iPads, each should have an independent name so that information does not get transmitted to the wrong device. These configurations are discussed in the portable document formats (.pdfs) available from the Support tab of the Q-interactive website. A new user would be wise to review these documents prior to any testing session.

≡ Rapid Reference 10.2

iPad settings must be accurately configured. Be sure to:

- Maximize the brightness of the screen;
- Set the autolock to 15 minutes or never;
- Set a passcode so that things cannot be entered without your acknowledgment or approval;
- Lock the rotation of the screen; and
- Turn off multi-tasking and notifications.

CAUTION

Failure to disable notifications (i.e., the devices are not in "Do Not Disturb" mode) may result in the examiner or examinee receiving calendar alerts for meetings, reminders, phone or FaceTime calls, and so on.

Although some of these setting configurations may seem trivial, neglecting them can cause frustration and disrupt a smooth administration of a test. For example, if the autolock is not set properly, the examinee's iPad may go to "sleep" during tasks in which it is not needed for displaying information (e.g., Similarities, Digit Span). After those tasks, if the iPad has gone to sleep mode, the transition to the next subtest will be delayed until the iPad is reawakened. Additionally, the examinee's screen could fade or go black when taking time to respond to a prompt on an untimed task. If for some reason the examiner does not fully close out of the examinee's device after the evaluation session, the last presented image (e.g., specific trial for Picture Span) will appear when the iPad is reawakened again.

This does not automatically correct itself when another examinee or battery is synced. In short, it is recommended to always close the application after the session to avoid what could be lengthy delays in beginning the next appointment. Another important consideration is disabling the home button on the examinee's iPad. Examinees may be tempted to push this button during a testing session, which would exit the application and return to the iPad home screen. Using the iPad's "Guided Access" feature will help with this issue, as might the protective case described earlier.

Many iPad covers allow the iPad to stand up on a table. For some tests, the stimulus books are presented flat on the table (e.g., WISC-V), while other tests present the stimuli in an upright, easel format (e.g., WIAT-III). In order to maintain standardization procedures, examiners must be acutely aware of the stimulus book and, therefore, the iPad's presentation style. For ease in administration, for the examiner's iPad, we suggest obtaining a cover that will mimic a slant board. This not only prevents the examinee from seeing the information on the main screen, but the slanting makes it easier for writing responses with the stylus.

ADMINISTRATION

Our experiences suggest that examiners who wish to use the Q-interactive digital system first should be able to administer flawlessly the more traditional paper-and-pencil version of the WISC-V (and, in fact, any test they wish to administer using this platform). Although the Assess application contains all subtest-specific administration instructions, the purchase of a Q-interactive license does not include hard copy versions of the traditional administration and technical manuals. Digital versions of the WISC-V administration, scoring, and technical manuals are available under the Support tab on the website. This is certainly a plus, but examiners cannot directly access the manuals while administering tests without switching from the Assess application to the website (and having to log in again). Additionally, the iPad administration and scoring instructions may not include some of the finer points of administration and the nuances of scoring. From within the Assess application, the examiner can access components of the administration manual from the information button near the top of the screen (signaled by a lowercase *i* in a circle). This dropdown gives the specific requirements (e.g., materials needed, administration instructions, timing guidelines) for the current subtest. This list ends with the reminder to refer to the test's administration and scoring manual for additional information.

To use the WISC-V manual as an example, Rapid Reference 10.3 provides an excerpt of the information that is available in the standard manuals but not in the

Assess application. If an examiner is completely knowledgeable about these and other specific issues, the use of the actual or online manuals will not be a problem while testing. (*Note:* The examples provided in Rapid Reference 10.3 are only selected omissions and do not constitute a comprehensive list.)

≋ Rapid Reference 10.3

Examples of information that is available in the standard manuals but not in the Assess application:

- Suggested seating arrangement
- Guidelines for how an examiner is to praise effort without providing feedback about the examinee's performance
- Specific instruction to the examiner regarding how to time subtests properly (e.g., whether or not to stop timing in order to repeat instructions or provide prompts)
- Descriptions of when examiners can readminister items to which the examinee previously provided an "I don't know" response
- Guidelines for when to query and how to score queried responses
- How to determine and score a spoiled response
- How to score multiple responses
- Description of how and when to scramble blocks on Block Design

---

Besides these differences, examiners wishing to use the Q-interactive system are encouraged to "practice, practice, practice." We found that the ease and comfort with the technology grew as experience increased. The most technologically savvy reviewer required practice to become comfortable with the nuances of the application, and even the least technologically savvy reviewer became comfortable and fluent with the administration after four or five practice administrations. Some components of the application are not intuitive such that practice is essential for fluid administration.

Timing

One potentially helpful feature of the iPad administration is the built-in stopwatch. Examiners no longer have to carry a stopwatch on which they have somehow disabled the sound or try to use a watch or clock. Instead, with a tap, examiners turn the stopwatch feature on and off and the time is automatically recorded. Additionally, the timer turns red to alert the examiner that time is about to run out, which can be helpful. The user must be aware that the change in color does not signify that time has expired; instead, it is a warning. A secondary indication appears within the stopwatch when time has elapsed. Examiners have the option of having the stopwatch count up or count down. The timer continues even if the screen is changed. For instance, if the user would like to return to a task in the "To Do" list (created automatically within the Assess application) while the examinee completes the Coding activity, she may do so and the stopwatch will continue to time the task. However, the timer is not visible with the "To Do" list open or when on another screen so the examiner must be mindful of the end of the time period. The stopwatch is not present for all tests, only for those that have a specified time limit. Some subtests for which the timer would be useful do not have a timer at all. For example, on the Matrix Reasoning subtest, after 30 seconds an examiner should ask "Do you have an answer?" but there is no timer to help keep track of that time. However, on the Figure Weights and Visual Puzzles subtests (*note:* these are timed tasks for which the stopwatch does appear), a reminder to prompt for a response appears at the appropriate time. Another timer appears to keep track of the amount of time between the conclusion of Immediate Symbol Translation and the corresponding tasks of Delayed Symbol Translation and Recognition Symbol Translation; this clock is easily overlooked and, although it is extremely useful in tracking the time interval, it can, in fact, be ignored. Nothing prevents the examiner from continuing with the administration regardless of the time lapse.

DON'T FORGET

A timer is not always available during iPad administration. During the Matrix Reasoning subtest, an examiner should, after 30 seconds, ask the examinee "Do you have an answer?" but there is no visible timer to help keep track of that time.

On the Picture Span subtest, the examiner sends the image to the examinee's device, gives the direction to "Remember these pictures in order," and then starts the stopwatch. The timer automatically keeps track of the exposure limit (e.g., 5 seconds) and then advances to the response page. This is very useful in that it can maintain standardization and reduce timing errors. However, if the examiner does not start the timer after sending the image to the examinee's iPad and giving the appropriate instruction, there is no other way to advance to the response page when the time limit expires. The only way to advance to the item is to start the timer. Swiping does not work, nor does selecting the "Hide image" button. An examiner's mistake in not utilizing the timer would provide the examinee the benefit of a prolonged exposure, which could invalidate the item.

Despite these benefits, one of the most difficult aspects of the iPad administration for one of these reviewers (RPD) to become accustomed to was how to keep the timing accurate. Experienced examiners who were familiar with using a traditional stopwatch may forget to stop the built-in timer until many seconds passed, therefore leading to inaccurate times. These are automatically recorded on the electronic protocol as "OTL" (over time limit). It may take several practice administrations before use of the stopwatch feature becomes natural. However, in anticipation of this learning curve, the developers added a feature to adjust time after it has been stopped. The examiner is able to tap the area that shows the time and use the toggles to correct the error. There are no reminders to start the timer and an examiner might not notice until time lapsed. It is also important to note that the timer may continue even after points are awarded (e.g., Block Design). The examiner needs to turn off the stopwatch or swipe to the next item in order to cease timing. Further, for example on the Visual Puzzles subtest, the examiner can begin timing without showing the image on the examinee's device. This can be an issue when the Bluetooth connectivity has been lost, because an OTL notation will be made on the electronic protocol despite the fact that the examinee had not yet been presented with the item.

A significant strength of the iPad administration over the traditional paper-and-pencil testing is the management of basal and ceiling rules. Examiners are reminded of suggested start points, and if a reversal rule is triggered, a pop-up message appears alerting the examiner and suggesting which item to administer next. A similar note appears when a ceiling rule is triggered. Examiners are given the choice to discontinue the test or proceed to "test the limits." It is likely these pop-ups will reduce examiner error while still giving experienced examiners flexibility to administer additional items. Examiners used to testing the limits should be aware of some constraints. Testing the limits can be done only at the immediate end of a subtest—examiners cannot go back at the end of the assessment. Once the examiner selects "Discontinue" he or she no longer has the ability to return to a section. Further, examiners can only readminister the most recent item or go forward in the subtest.

One potential problem with the automated alerts and scoring for basals and ceilings is the "Wechsler giveth and Wechsler taketh away" phenomenon. The Wechsler administration manual makes it clear that examinees can be started at an earlier start point than suggested for their ages if they are suspected of intellectual disability. Regardless of an examinee's performance on items preceding the usual start point, full credit is awarded for all of these items if perfect scores are obtained on the age-appropriate start point and subsequent item (for full explanation of this scoring rule, see pages 35–41 in the *WISC-V Administration and Scoring Manual*). The Q-interactive interface manages this by awarding credit for items failed below the suggested start point. The score for the failed item is automatically rescored to receive full credit.

Scoring

Item-level scoring is easy to use and designed to minimize administration time and examiner error. The reviewers enjoyed the options for recording the examinee's response on most nonverbal tasks. For example, with some practice, it is easy to copy the examinee's actual reproduction on Block Design. The examiner's iPad displays an empty block configuration of each item. By tapping a specific block, the display changes the color of the block (white to red) and/or the design of the block (solid color or split color). There is no way to change the dimension or shape of an incorrect response, but examiners can record Dimension Errors and indicate the number of correctly placed blocks to generate a partial score automatically. There is also the capability to rotate the block to represent the actual reproduction (errors and rotations) given by the examinee, but at least one reviewer was unable to make this feature work. Additionally, the extra tapping and overt screen manipulation can be a signal to a savvy examinee that an incorrect response was given. We found that recording the designs (and certain verbal responses) using the stylus pen was a bit time consuming, which may affect the testing situation if an examinee is particularly restless. Completing a record form by hand was faster and more efficient than using the stylus.

The scoring procedure for the Complementary subtests is inconsistent. For the Naming Speed subtests (Literacy and Quantity), the examiner taps only when the provided response is incorrect or in the event of a self-correction. However, for the Symbol Translation subtests such as Immediate Symbol Translation, the examiner taps the item for which the examinee responded correctly. There is no way to record a verbatim response or note a self-correction. For Delayed Symbol Translation, the score is automatically tabulated unless the individual earns zero points, in which case the examiner needs to tap the "0 point" button. Further, for Recognition Symbol Translation, the examiner must select a point value for the score to be recorded. Similarly, there is no way to note a self-correction or verbatim response without using the notepad feature (to be discussed later).

For tasks in which the examinee selects a response by touching the appropriate multiple-choice item on the iPad (e.g., Matrix Reasoning), the selection is automatically highlighted on the examiner's iPad. At times, there can be a lag between the examinee's selection and its recognition on the examiner's device. This can cause confusion if the examinee offers multiple responses or self-corrects. The system records both (or all) responses, but lists them in order from least to greatest (e.g., 2 then 4) even if the examinee selected 4 then 2. The user must be wary of which is chosen as the final answer.

CAUTION

In situations in which an examinee selects multiple responses or makes self-corrections, the examiner must be mindful of the selection order. The system will record all responses in sequence from least to greatest regardless of the order in which the examinee made the selection.

Recording verbal responses presents with some potential difficulties. Similar to a traditional manual, the iPad provides examples of common 0-, 1-, and 2-point responses to items on the examiner's display, and the examiner may select (by tapping) one of these as the examinee's response. Not all of these options are visible on the screen given the location of the area to handwrite verbatim responses. On items to which an examinee gives multiple responses, the examiner could easily choose the multiple responses; however, during our initial assessment period, the order in which responses were given was not noted. For example, if an examinee gives a verbal response that includes a 0-point response, followed by a 2-point response, and finally ended with a 1-point response, and the examiner taps the 0-, 2-, and 1-point responses in that order, the responses are recorded as a 2-, 1-, and 0-point sequence. It should be noted that Pearson has corrected this issue such that the order in which the examinee selects responses is recorded. There is also the potential that, with the desire to shorten administration time, examiners will begin to select the closest response rather than record the examinee's exact, verbatim response with the stylus pen. The examiner does not have to record anything other than a point value for the response.

From the Assess application, there is no easy way to view the whole electronic protocol. Examiners wishing to review a particular subtest's verbatim responses must log in to the Q-website and search for the item-level results view of the protocol (to be discussed later). Within Assess an examiner can review individual items for audio or written records.

We predict the practice of recording verbatim responses will decline with the use of iPad administrations, resulting in the loss of much valuable clinical assessment information. For example, during our review, when the iPad administration was accompanied by the traditional pencil-and-paper recording, much information potentially useful to interpretation was lost because of the lack of a verbatim recording. Throughout the administration of the WISC-V, the iPad administrator simply chose the closest appropriate listed response to try and match what the examinee said. Although this did allow for correct score agreement between the two administrators, there were significant qualitative differences between the two recordings. For example, for one item the examinee responded, "Both like sumpton, like words for numbers . . . like first . . . came in first . . . like sumptom . . . numbers." The iPad examiner simply chose the response "Numbers" missing the nuances of the misarticulations, the time gaps between phrases, and the overall verbal presentation. Later, on another subtest, the examinee's response of "Um . . . to see if they have a good book or an idea about one" was recorded as "Indicates fundamental misconception." For the now-optional Comprehension subtest, the examiner cannot select the closest option from the menu of general concepts or write while the menu screen is open. A nice touch, however, is that there is a visible cue to query for the second general concept if only one correct concept is provided initially.

One other concern about recording verbatim responses or even notes related to an examinee's behaviors is that not all subtests provide space for the written notes. On subtests where a verbal response is not expected (e.g., Block Design, Picture Concepts), there is no place to record notes except to open, through a menu choice at the top of the window within the Assess application, a notepad. This feature was a bit cumbersome. Not only does it take extra time to open the new window to write a note, but also the note completely obscured from view the rest of the test on the iPad, making it difficult to follow the examinee's responses. The examiner can use a color-coding option to denote a particular test item or subtest-specific comment. This capability is available only when working within the current subtest; once the subtest has ended (e.g., the user has already swiped to begin the next subtest), the color-coding feature is no longer accessible. Without updating the color, or if a comment is added after the discontinue has been met, the notes are considered "general," so the examiner would need to provide specific detail(s) to keep track of when a particular note was recorded (e.g., a subtest name or a time period). All notes, regardless of color coding, are stored sequentially. The overall process was awkward. We found ourselves writing notes on a piece of paper instead.

Even experienced examiners make incorrect item-level judgment calls, which are usually corrected after the examiner later reviews the examinee's verbatim response. Similarly, although examiners can indicate whether they queried by tapping a button on their iPad screens, there is no way to indicate multiple queries without writing a verbatim response sequence. The system does allow for the recording and playback of all verbal responses. Although the audio-recording feature is an attractive option and was used often during our review to double check the item-level scoring, examiners should be advised that the audio-recordings are deleted as soon as the completed assessment is removed from the iPad to be stored in the electronic database. There is no way to transfer and save the audio-recordings separately. The reduction in transcribing verbatim responses is not a technology flaw, but our concern is that it may increase the potential of user scoring error. The Wechsler manuals still clearly advise that all responses be recorded verbatim; therefore, in our opinion, users of Q-interactive should obtain a stylus pen and write all examinee responses and other significant verbalizations on their electronic record forms.

CAUTION

Although Q-interactive provides the capability of having the iPad record the actual testing session, the audio-recordings are deleted as soon as the completed assessment is removed from the iPad to be stored in the cloud. There is no way to transfer and save the audio-recordings separately.

Writing with the stylus is also a learning experience. For examinees who talk a lot, and especially for those who talk quickly, the stylus writing can be a chore compared to the ease of recording with paper and pencil. Examiners cannot erase when using a stylus. Increasing the size of the writing space requires additional steps and time, but can be managed. At times, not all of the markings (e.g., crosses of t) were recorded by the system such that the evaluator needed to rewrite certain components. However, the handwriting capture technology was surprisingly accurate and easy to read if the examiner wrote carefully.

Although examiners can select and record an examinee's 2-, 1-, or 0-point responses (depending upon the item), examiners must still assign the actual score to the individual items separately. Pearson should be lauded for maintaining examiner freedom in scoring; however, these reviewers believe they may have missed an opportunity to prevent errors in scoring. If, for example, a 2-point response is selected (or a 0-point and a 2-point response), but the examiner scores the item as worth 1 point, it would be useful to have a pop-up message appear informing the examiner of the potential conflict between the selected response and the score awarded. This would also be a useful check in the situation when an examiner might accidentally hit an active button while swiping to the next screen. For instance, on verbal subtests, swiping sometimes resulted in accidentally selecting a response the examinee did not give. Examiners should be mindful of this potential user error.

TRAINING AND TECH SUPPORT

As discussed earlier, regardless of their level of familiarity with traditional paper-and-pencil administrations, examiners should receive training and/or extensive practice prior to using Q-interactive technology in a real assessment situation. Pearson has recognized this concern by providing webinars and other supports for examiners. Webinars are scheduled for participants to attend live, and the helloq.com website states archived webinars are available for users who have purchased a license. Unfortunately, it was hard for these reviewers to access the archived webinars except for the "On-Board" series. We cannot say whether the other presentations will be easy to access for the typical subscriber. Within the Support tab of Q-interactive (accessible after logging in) user guides and video tutorials specific to the platform are available for download or view. There are also test administration video tutorials available for specific instruments or individual subtests. Pearson also offers a monthly virtual "office hour" to answer any concerns, as well as a technical support hotline. We utilized these resources, and found the staff to be helpful and courteous.

DON'T FORGET

User guides and video tutorials are available for download or view within the Support tab of Q-interactive (accessible after logging in to http://www.qiactive.com).

OUTPUT

For examiners and trainers used to reviewing a completed record form, the Q-interactive output can be a slight disappointment and occasionally confusing. As in the traditional form, the user can modify the results by selecting such specifics as the confidence interval (e.g., 95%), base rate reference group (e.g., overall sample), critical significance value (e.g., .05), and comparison group (e.g., mean of FSIQ subtests). There are options to review output online or to print results. A full report can be generated similar to the one that is available on Q-global. This report is exported to a .doc format so that it can be copied and pasted. Of note is that some of the graphs and score representations seen on the screen have unexplained information. For the score profile graphs, each subtest scaled score or composite index is plotted against a number line with a vertical line indicating the confidence interval, but there is an additional horizontal line plotted. No explanation is given for what this line represents.

Downloading the SLK or Excel file is preferred, although, unfortunately, there is no one file format that contains all of the necessary information in a user-friendly format. The SLK file provides two easy-to-read tables on one page. The first table contains the composite standard score, percentile rank, and 90% and 95% confidence intervals. The second table contains the subtest raw and scaled scores. The file contains no process-level analysis information. The exported Excel file is less easy to read and, perhaps because of all information being in several narrow columns, takes several printed pages. Information includes raw scores, scaled scores, "contextual events" such as the number of queries or "don't know" responses, subtest completion time, and whether discontinue and reversal rules were triggered (either yes or no). This file also contains all of the index- and subtest-level comparisons, as well as the process-level analysis information; however, these tables are difficult to read without reformatting the file.

It is also possible to print out every subtest's item-level response, but the results are again occasionally difficult to read and when printed (landscape orientation is recommended), take up several pages, some of which are blank. Reading the printout is confusing because, except for the very first page (Block Design), the subtest names are not visible and there are no page numbers or identifying details (e.g., date of the assessment, examinee name, examinee ID). Each subtest page contains information related to that specific subtest, including where appropriate the item number, raw score, completion time, "picklist" responses for verbal items, verbatim response (if recorded), and events (e.g., self-correction). These printouts, although somewhat useful, still do not match the detail and ease of use that an actual record form provides—particularly to a university trainer or school-based supervisor. For example, the Block Design pages are missing partial scores and time limits for specific bonus points for speed. University trainers and supervisors will have no way to tell whether the examiner awarded the correct number of raw score points based on the time limits. Additionally, for several subtests, the correct responses are not given on this printout. This is problematic for trainers. For example, the Digit Span, Picture Span, and Letter-Number Sequencing subtest pages each provide raw scores and verbatim responses; however, the correct target numbers or sequences are not provided. This can make it difficult to confirm accurate scoring, because there is no way to know why an examiner scored an item as 1 or 0.

SECURITY AND LEGAL ISSUES

Regardless of the practice setting, examiners will undoubtedly be concerned about the security of hosting confidential assessment information in an online database. Pearson provides sufficient security details on the HelloQ website. Notably, Q-interactive is compliant with Health Insurance Portability and

Accountability Act (HIPAA) security regulations. Examiners may wish to consult with their district's legal representative prior to adopting the Q-interactive method of assessment to ensure security safeguards meet their specific requirements. For example, it remains uncertain how Q-interactive assessments will be regulated under Family Educational Rights and Privacy Act (FERPA); specifically, what components of an iPad assessment and potential output will be considered part of the examinee's educational record versus the examiner's private notes and administration tools. Finally, examiners should be cognizant of their use of the audio-recording feature of the iPad administration. In some settings, use of audio- or video-recording devices requires an additional consent. Examiners are encouraged to consult their local and state guidelines.

CONSIDERATIONS FOR UNIVERSITY TRAINERS

University trainers may find the Q-interactive modality difficult for training purposes. Because many training programs require students to administer full batteries of tests and then hand in the record forms for correction, the introduction of Q-interactive presents several distinct concerns. First, there are really no record forms to hand in, aside from the item-level response "protocol" and the response booklets (e.g., Coding, Symbol Search). Unless students are required to record all answers verbatim using a stylus (and they should be), trainers will be able to see only which answer choices the student actually selected. Additionally, the format of the output (described earlier) may present further difficulties for trainers who wish to review a student's scoring and interpretation.

There may also be practical hurdles to teaching the Q-interactive technology in a traditional assessment class. On a positive note, at present, there is no longer a student license fee. Further, a free Starter Kit is available with the classroom license so the relevant materials for each accessed test do not need to be purchased. Although this is helpful for the response booklets, the training site would need to purchase other materials, such as the Block Design cubes. Further, because each administration requires two iPads, a training program would have to purchase either multiple iPads or cope with the logistical problems of a full class sharing what equates to virtually one test kit. Although some students may have their own iPads to use, there is a potential fairness issue for students who are not so economically advantaged as their peers.

A benefit to the trainer/student program offered by Pearson is that a trainer has access to all students' electronic dashboards. Time will tell if trainers find grading electronic administrations easier or more difficult than paper-and-pencil administrations. Will Q-interactive alleviate some of the administration and scoring errors that are common to students learning these tests, or does adminis-tration using iPads introduce a whole new set of errors?

Pricing

Price is typically a major factor to consider when determining which assessment tools or instruments an individual examiner or district should select for his or her practice. Therefore, it may be prudent to compare the cost of assessment using the Q-interactive system to the cost of traditional paper-and-pencil administration. For the purpose of a pricing evaluation, we estimated the initial cost to procure all of the testing materials necessary as well as the cost of common administration practices. It is presumed by the authors that the user already has two iPads. Therefore, the purchase of the devices was not included in the comparison.

Initial Costs of Test and Scoring Materials

The total price of a new WISC-V kit is $1,145.00. This includes the *Administration and Scoring Manual* (Wechsler, 2014b), the *Technical and Interpretive Manual* (Wechsler, 2014c), three stimulus books, scoring keys, and a set of blocks. In addition to these materials, a new WISC-V kit comes with 25 copies of each of the Record Forms and the Response Booklets.

In order to administer a WISC-V using the Q-interactive system, an annual license needs to be purchased. The price of the license varies depending on the num-ber of users and the number of instruments that will be used. For this comparison, the lowest rate (1 to 4 users with 1 to 3 instruments) was used. The annual license fee for this category is $200.00. With the first license, the Starter Kit, including the specific materials needed to administer and score the test, is sent for free.

Another option for an examiner using the traditional pencil-and-paper admin-istration is to use the computerized scoring report package available from Q-global instead of manually scoring and reporting. In addition to the current per-report price of $2.00, there are three unlimited-use scoring and reporting subscription options: 1 year ($35.00), 3 years ($99.00), and 5 years ($149.00). If a user wishes to obtain interpretative reports, the fee schedule changes to the per-report price of $3.50, or the subscription rates of 1 year for $45.00, 3 years for $129.00, or 5 years for $199.00. Based upon these estimates, not including the purchase of the two iPads and selecting the 1-year level of unlimited scoring and interpretative subscription option, the cost of the initial set-up for testing using the traditional administration versus the Q-interactive administration supports using the iPads ($1,190 vs. approximately $200).

Cost of Administration

In order to determine a fair comparison between the cost of administering a WISC-V using either of the two methods, the cost of administering 7, 10, 15, and 21 subtests was calculated. These variations allow cost estimates for administering just the 7 subtests required to obtain the FSIQ; the 10 subtests required to obtain the FSIQ and the 5 primary indexes; the 15 subtests required to obtain the FSIQ, 5 primary and 5 ancillary indexes; and finally 21 subtests required to obtain the FSIQ, 5 primary and 5 ancillary indexes, and the complementary indexes. Rapid Reference 10.4 shows cost estimates for the various subtest combinations. Record Forms and Response Booklets are typically sold in packages of 25. The cost for a traditional paper-and-pencil WISC-V administration, depending on the number of subtests administered, ranged from $8.24 (7 or 10 subtests) to $10.28 (15 or 21 subtests).

When administering the test through the Q-interactive system, subtests are purchased individually at a cost of about $1.50 each. Discounts are offered for the purchase of subtests in bulk. Additionally, Response Booklet #1, which includes Coding and Symbol Search, costs $3.24, and Response Booklet #2, which includes Cancellation, costs $2.04. The total cost for administering the 7, 10, 15, or 21 subtests and the response booklets ranges from $13.74 (7 × $1.50 plus $3.24) to $31.50 (21 × $1.50 plus $5.28). In all cases, after initial start-up costs are factored in, the use of the iPad costs more than the traditional paper-and pencil administration.

≡ Rapid Reference 10.4

Pricing Comparison Between Q-interactive and Traditional WISC-V Administrations

Number of Subtests	Q-interactive			Traditional		
	Subtest	Response Booklets	Total Cost	Sub-test	Response Booklets	Total Cost
7	10.50	3.24	13.74	5.00	3.24	8.24
10	15.00	3.24	18.24	5.00	3.24	8.24
15	22.50	5.28	27.78	5.00	5.28	10.28
21	31.50	5.28	36.78	5.00	5.28	10.28

Note: Cost per subtest for Q-interactive is $1.50. Response Booklet #1 = $3.24, Response Booklet #2 = $2.04. Number of subtests: 7 = Core, 10 = Primary, 15 = Primary and Ancillary, 21 = Primary, Ancillary, and Complementary.

Pricing Conclusion

Although the initial start-up cost is less when using the Q-interactive system if the examiner already owns two iPads, the cost of giving 7, 10, 15, or 21 subtests is substantially greater than the traditional pencil-and-paper administration. There are many variables that could affect the prices using the Q-interactive system, such as purchasing subtests in bulk and the number of users and instruments on the license. Also, users should remember the annual licensing fee that bears the additional cost of renewal each year to access the Q-interactive system. Unused assessments may now roll over indefinitely, providing the license remains active. The Q-interactive system includes automatic scoring as well as cloud-based storage of results. If these services are important to you, they may make the cost differential between the two administration types seem much more reasonable.

OVERALL IMPRESSIONS AND RECOMMENDATIONS

Assessment-related fields will most likely continue to move toward using technology to administer test batteries. Strengths of the Q-interactive system include the reduction in the physical bulk of the materials needed to be transported between testing sites; the positive reaction and attraction that examiners and examinees have for the use of the technology; the potential for the reduction in certain administration errors, most notably basal and ceiling rules, prompt reminders (e.g., Visual Puzzles' "Do you have an answer?"), and automated exposure time limits; and the potential for more accurately obtained scores and interpretive data because of the automatic scoring done by the program (alleviating the need to look up scores and base rate information).

Potential issues with the use of the Q-interactive platform include the cost structure that may be problematic or prohibitive for examiners or agencies (schools) with limited budgets; the loss of important interpretive information because of the temptation to limit the number of subtests administered (and bought), as well as the potential loss of verbatim response recordings; and the substandard format and presentation of the data output and results. We highly recommend that anyone wishing to use this new and innovative means of testing do two things: first, become thoroughly trained in the traditional paper-and-pencil administration of any test before administering it on the iPad, *and* practice repeatedly with the new technology before ever attempting its use with an actual examinee.

✍ TEST YOURSELF ✍

1. **Assessments available on Q-interactive include all of the following except**
   a. CELF-5
   b. WJ IV
   c. WISC-V
   d. PPVT-4

2. **The Q-interactive versions of tests are exactly the same as the traditional paper-and-pencil version; what is new is how the examiner administers them.**
   a. True
   b. False

3. **All of the following statements are true of Q-interactive except**
   a. Q-interactive requires the use of two iPads.
   b. http://www.helloq.com and http://www.qiactive.com are two websites that are available to assist examiners in test administration.
   c. a Wi-Fi connection is necessary throughout the administration of tests via Q-interactive.
   d. raw scores are automatically generated through Q-interactive.

4. **Q-interactive audio-recordings are automatically deleted as soon as the completed assessment is removed from the iPad and are stored in the cloud.**
   a. True
   b. False

5. **Strengths of the Q-interactive system include all of the following except**
   a. data output and results are user-friendly and easily understood.
   b. bulk of materials needed for testing is reduced.
   c. use of technology is appealing to many examiners and examinees.
   d. exposure time to stimuli is automated.

Answers: 1. b; 2. a; 3. c; 4. a; 5. a

REFERENCES

Cohen, J. (1988). *Statistical power analysis for the behavioral sciences* (2nd ed.). Hillsdale, NJ: Erlbaum.

Cohen, M. (1997). *Children's Memory Scale.* San Antonio, TX: Pearson.

Daniel, M. H., Wahlstrom, D., & Zhang, O. (2014). *Q-interactive technical report 8: Equivalence of Q-interactive® and paper administrations of cognitive tasks: WISC®–V.* San Antonio, TX: Pearson. http://www.helloq.com/research.html

Delis, D. C., Kaplan, E., & Kramer, J. H. (2001). *Delis-Kaplan Executive Function System.* San Antonio, TX: Pearson.

Delis, D. C., Kramer, J. H., Kaplan, E., & Ober, B. A. (1994). *California Verbal Learning Test, Children's Version.* San Antonio, TX: Pearson.

Delis, D. C., Kramer, J. H., Kaplan, E., & Ober, B. A. (2000). *California Verbal Learning Test* (2nd ed.). San Antonio, TX: Pearson.

Dunn, L. M., & Dunn, D. M. (2007). *Peabody Picture Vocabulary Test* (4th ed.). San Antonio, TX: Pearson.

Goldman, R., & Fristoe, M. (2015). *Goldman-Fristoe Test of Articulation* (3rd ed.). San Antonio, TX: Pearson.

Kaufman, A. S., & Kaufman, N. L. (2014). *Kaufman Test of Educational Achievement* (3rd ed.). San Antonio, TX: Pearson.

Khan, M. L., & Lewis, N. P. (2015). *Khan-Lewis Phonological Analysis* (3rd ed.). San Antonio, TX: Pearson.

Korkman, M., Kirk, U., & Kemp, S. (2007). *A Developmental NEuroPSYchological Assessment* (2nd ed.). San Antonio, TX: Pearson.

Wechsler, D. (2003). *Wechsler Intelligence Scale for Children* (4th ed.). San Antonio, TX: Pearson.

Wechsler, D. (2008). *Wechsler Adult Intelligence Scale* (4th ed.). San Antonio, TX: Pearson.

Wechsler, D. (2009a). *Wechsler Individual Achievement Test* (3rd ed.). San Antonio, TX: Pearson.

Wechsler, D. (2009b). *Wechsler Memory Scale* (4th ed.). San Antonio, TX: Pearson.

Wechsler, D. (2012). *Wechsler Preschool and Primary Scale of Intelligence* (4th ed.). San Antonio, TX: Pearson.

Wechsler, D. (2014a). *Wechsler Intelligence Scale for Children* (5th ed.). San Antonio, TX: Pearson.

Wechsler, D. (2014b). *WISC-V Administration and scoring manual.* San Antonio, TX: Pearson.

Wechsler, D. (2014c). *WISC-V Technical and interpretive manual.* San Antonio, TX: Pearson.

Wiig, E. H., Semel, E., & Secord, W. A. (2013). *Clinical evaluation of language fundamentals* (5th ed.). San Antonio, TX: Pearson.

Epilogue

DOROTHEA MCCARTHY REMEMBERED

Alan S. Kaufman

Dawn Flanagan and Vinny Alfonso asked me to write a few pages to include in *Essentials of WISC-V Assessment*, a book I had coauthored in earlier editions. They proposed an Epilogue on the topic of my choice. I decided to talk about one of my unsung mentors, Dr. Dorothea McCarthy, one of the first female PhDs in psychology in the 1930s and '40s. She was author of the best, most child-oriented preschool test ever, the all-but-forgotten McCarthy Scales of Children's Abilities for ages 2½ to 8½ years (McCarthy, 1972). Why should I devote my few pages to anyone but Dr. Wechsler in a book that features the fifth incarnation of his beloved WISC? Because I have remembered the great man over and over in my career, both when lecturing (Kaufman, 1996, 2005) and writing (Kaufman, 1992; Kaufman, Raiford, & Coalson 2016), but I have given Dr. McCarthy short shrift for the past 40 years, ever since Nadeen and I wrote our first book about her scales (Kaufman & Kaufman, 1977).

In fact, Dr. McCarthy was an innovator in test development, with her conceptions reflecting the precursors of CHC theory. She was an uncanny clinician who could see into the souls of young children. She taught me so much about being a clinician. But we didn't like each other very much, so I have unconsciously neglected her in my keynote addresses and books. When I met her in 1968, as a brash 24-year-old know-it-all, I was given the task of crafting her bucketful of 40+ tests into a practical test kit and to get it published promptly. Dr. McCarthy, at age 60, was dealing with some personal dramas. Her McCarthy Scales was supposed to be published in 1959, as per its contract, but it had been subjected to a decade's worth of pilot tests and tryouts (and was not published until 1972!), while Dr. Wechsler's WPPSI, without so much as a field trial, was published in 1967. "That man wouldn't recognize a preschooler if it was his grandchild," she said to me, privately, about the great man. "Promise me you will *never* work with Wechsler on the WISC or WAIS—promise me that." (A bit like Lady Catherine de Bourgh telling Lizzie to promise that she will never marry Mr. Darcy.) I didn't respond.

But Dr. Wechsler was only one of her nemeses at that time. She was married to an alcoholic, she told me, and she was being forcibly retired at age 65 by Fordham University—where she wasn't even the most famous woman professor (that was Anne Anastasi). And yet Dr. McCarthy was a born clinician with the knack for capturing the heart and soul of the young or shy or nonverbal child. She had the insight to replace the boring Knox Cubes ("Tap these blocks in the same order that I do") with a colorful toy xylophone. She arranged the test sequence to gradually bring the young nonverbal child on board. Start with an all-nonverbal copying task in which even 2½-year-olds earn half-credit (Block Building). Then go to a nonverbal task that requires a little bit of thinking and encourages spontaneous verbalization (Puzzle Solving). Require verbalization on the third task, but only to repeat the names of pictures that are shown. Then have the child define spoken words on part 3 of the fourth task—but only after the child first points to pictures that are named by the examiner (part 1) and then tells the names of pictures (part 2). Dr. McCarthy built a test that almost guaranteed gaining rapport with nearly all children by carefully orchestrating the order of a few cognitive tasks.

But she wasn't just thinking about establishing rapport—she wanted to maintain it throughout the evaluation. The children, who are getting a bit tired, need a built-in break. She met that goal by opting to measure gross motor ability, not just mental ability. As one of the leading developmental psychologists and language specialists of her day, Dr. McCarthy knew that gross motor ability should be measured alongside language and nonverbal abilities because of their synchronous development at ages 2½ to 5, followed by asynchrony at ages 6 to 8½. So she put all gross motor tasks, such as hopping and aiming a beanbag at a target, right in the middle of the test sequence to provide a built-in recess for everyone, the examiner included. Then she would bring the child back to the table cautiously: a simple imitative gross motor task (copying the examiner's movements such as hand clasping), followed by two convergent nonverbal paper-and-pencil tasks. Only then did Dr. McCarthy challenge children with cognitively complex tests such as verbal fluency, number concepts, and concept formation. I was awed when I realized there was a plan behind every decision she made; nothing happened by chance. Even more awed when, time and again, Nadeen was able to obtain valid cognitive and motor profiles from young emotionally disturbed children who had been declared "untestable."

Yet when I think of Dr. McCarthy today I am just as impressed by her theoretical approach to intelligence as I am by her clinical acumen. She wanted to use an array of ability scales to best depict a child's profile. She believed that most tasks measure multiple abilities and gave some of them dual-scale membership. Tapping Sequence, for example, was included on *both* the Perceptual-Performance and Memory scales. (That task was originally called Musical Memory, but that name quickly became a joke to standardization examiners, who were frustrated trying to tap out "tunes" on the cheap xylophone; so we changed it to Tapping Sequence.) Similarly, the two drawing tests were included on both the Perceptual-Performance and Motor scales.

Dr. McCarthy was truly thinking Thurstone (1938) and Cattell (1941) while Wechsler (1949, 1967) and Terman and Merrill (1960) were still locked into Spearman's (1904) *g*. She analyzed children's abilities in terms of broad and narrow abilities at the same time that Horn (1965) was coming to the multi-ability conclusion in his doctoral dissertation. Her scales measured Gc, Gsm, Gq, and Gf/Gc before these names were in everyday clinical jargon. I was proud to be the one to help develop the McCarthy Scales, write most of the manual, and see it published in 1972. But there was almost a blooper. Only a last-minute burst of laughter by an otherwise serious editor, when she was reading the manual page proofs, kept us from nicknaming the Perceptual-Performance Scale the P-P scale. ("Sorry, Mr. Gomez, it seems that your daughter has a weakness in pee-pee.")

But true to her word, Dr. McCarthy would not forgive me for working closely with Dr. Wechsler on the WISC-R, starting in 1970, when I "belonged" to her. She made my life difficult, complaining to secretaries at the company, and anyone who would listen to her, that I was ruining her test. When the test was finally published in 1972 to outstanding reviews by clinicians and children alike, she started to warm up to me again. Then she died suddenly of a heart attack at age 66 in September 1974. I found out about it a few days after our youngest child, James, was born on September 21. Desperately, I wanted to know *exactly* when Dr. McCarthy died. To my relief, it was on September 22. Just in case the Eastern religion belief in reincarnation was correct, I wasn't taking any chances! (True story.)

In retrospect, I realize that much of the fault in my relationship with Dr. McCarthy was my own. At 24 I thought I knew it all, or at least I acted like I did. My degree of empathy to the trials in Dr. McCarthy's life would have emerged as a weakness in my personal profile. She taught me so much about clinical assessment, young children's thinking and behavior, and about the need to depart from the conventional Wechsler system of V-P discrepancies to truly understand children's patterns of strengths and weaknesses. She has not been given enough credit as a pioneer in the field of theory-based assessment or as one of my key mentors. She was both.

REFERENCES

Cattell, R. B. (1941). Some theoretical issues in adult intelligence testing. *Psychological Bulletin, 38*, 592.

Horn, J. L. (1965). *Fluid and crystallized intelligence: A factor analytic and developmental study of the structure among primary mental abilities.* Unpublished doctoral diss. University of Illinois, Urbana-Champaign.

Kaufman, A. S. (1992). Dr. Wechsler remembered. *School Psychologist, 46*(2), 45, 17.

Kaufman, A. S. (1996, August). *David Wechsler: The man and his impact.* Invited Division 12 address presented at the meeting of the American Psychological Association, Toronto, Ontario, Canada.

Kaufman, A. S. (2005, April). *From David Wechsler to the new IDEA guidelines: 35 years in the eye of the IQ storm.* Invited Legends Address presented at the meeting of the National Association of School Psychologists, Atlanta, GA.

Kaufman, A. S., & Kaufman, N. L. (1977). *Clinical evaluation of young children with the McCarthy Scales.* New York, NY: Grune & Stratton.

Kaufman, A. S., Raiford, S. E., & Coalson, D. L. (2016). *Intelligence testing with the WISC-V.* Hoboken, NJ: Wiley.

McCarthy, D. (1972). *Manual for the McCarthy Scales of Children's Abilities.* New York, NY: Psychological Corporation.

Spearman, C. E. (1904). "General intelligence," objectively determined and measured. *American Journal of Psychiatry, 15*, 201–293.

Terman, L. M., & Merrill, M. A. (1960). *Stanford-Binet Intelligence Scale: Manual, Form L-M.* Boston, MA: Houghton Mifflin.

Thurstone, L. L. (1938). Primary mental abilities. *Psychometric Monographs* (1). Chicago, IL: University of Chicago Press.

Wechsler, D. (1949). *Manual for the Wechsler Intelligence Scale for Children (WISC).* New York, NY: Psychological Corporation.

Wechsler, D. (1967). *Manual for the Wechsler Preschool and Primary Scale of Intelligence (WPPSI).* New York, NY: Psychological Corporation.

About the Authors

Dawn P. Flanagan, PhD, is professor of psychology at St. John's University and affiliate clinical professor of psychology at Yale Child Study Center, Yale University School of Medicine. She serves as an expert witness, learning disabilities consultant, and psychoeducational test/measurement consultant and trainer for national and international organizations. Dr. Flanagan is an author and editor of numerous publications, including more than 20 books on assessment and learning disabilities. She is best known for her development of the Cross-Battery Assessment approach and the Dual Discrepancy/Consistency operational definition of specific learning disabilities.

Vincent C. Alfonso, PhD, is the dean of the School of Education at Gonzaga University. He is past president of Division 16 (School Psychology) of the American Psychological Association (APA), fellow of Divisions 5, 16, and 43 of the APA, and a certified school psychologist and licensed psychologist. He has been providing psychoeducational services to individuals across the life span for more than 25 years. He is the coeditor with Dawn Flanagan of *Essentials of Specific Learning Disability Identification*, (2nd edition) and coauthor of *Essentials of Cross-Battery Assessment* (3rd edition).

Contributors

Jamie Chaffin, EdD
Eastern Washington University

Gail Cheramie, PhD
University of Houston–Clear Lake

Carlea Dries, PsyD
Allendale Public Schools

Ron Dumont, EdD, NCSP
Fairleigh Dickinson University

Alan S. Kaufman, PhD
Yale University School of Medicine

Samantha Kaufman
Philadelphia College of
Osteopathic Medicine

Robert Lichtenstein, PhD
William James College

George McCloskey, PhD
Philadelphia College of
Osteopathic Medicine

Erin M. McDonough, PhD
St. John's University

Kristan E. Melo, MS
St. John's University

Naoko Nagoshi, PhD
SAITAMA University

Samuel O. Ortiz, PhD
St. John's University

Susie Engi Raiford, PhD
Pearson Clinical Assessment
San Antonio, Texas

W. Joel Schneider, PhD
Illinois State University

Jamie Slonim
Philadelphia College of
Osteopathic Medicine

Meghan A. Terzulli, BA
St. John's University

Kathleen D. Viezel, PhD
Fairleigh Dickinson University

Robert Whitaker, PsyS, NCSP, ABSNP
Gallaudet University

Index

A

Aaron, P. G., 452
Alfonso, V. C., 1, 21–22, 168, 178, 216, 218, 221, 228, 249, 287, 405, 407, 511, 541, 552, 617
Alston-Abel, N. L., 406
American Educational Research Association, 540
American Psychological Association, 540
American Speech-Language-Hearing Association, 421
Army Alpha Test, 12
Army Mental Tests, 546
Arnstein, A.F.T., 287
Assess (Q-interactive app), 596, 590, 600–602, 605, 606
Avirett, E., 444

B

Bachmeier, R. J., 444
Bailey, D. H, 443
Barnes, M. A., 436
Barona, A., 551
Beam, A. P., 443
Behavior observations and process-oriented assessment at the subtest, item, and cognitive construct levels, 363–394; difficulties with visual, motor, and/or visuo-motor processing speed, 375–376; Fluid Reasoning and Visual Spatial Subtests, 371–378; related to difficulties with use of auditory processes, 367–368, 378–379; related to difficulties with use of visual processes, 372–373; related to manual dexterity difficulties, 373; related to reasoning with nonverbal visual stimuli, 371–372; related to use of executive functions, 370–371, 376–378; related to use of expressive language abilities, 368–369; related to use of reasoning with verbal information, 366; related to use of retrieval of information from long-term storage, 366–367; related to use of working memory applied to auditory stimuli, 369–370; related to use of working memory applied to visual stimuli, 373–374; Verbal Comprehension Subtests, 364–366; Working Memory Domain and Arithmetic and Symbol Translation Subtests, 378–383
Benson, N., 405
Berninger, V. W., 287, 406, 443, 444
Bialystok, E., 556
Binet, A., 1, 6–9, 12
Boodoo, G., 551
Borghese, J. P., 544
Bouchard, T. J., 551
Boykin, A. W., 551
Braden, J. P., 284, 550
Brody, N., 551
Burchers, B., 500
Burchers, M., 500
Burchers, S., 500

C

California, 421
California Verbal Learning Test, Children's Version (Delis, Kramer, Kaplan, and Ober), 592
California Verbal Learning Test, Second Edition (Delis, Kramer, Kaplan, and Ober), 592
Canivez, G. L., 23, 37, 41, 47
Carroll, J. B., 1
Carson, J., 6
Cathers-Schiffman, T. A., 540, 544, 546, 547
Cattell, R. B., 619
Cattell-Horn-Carroll Theory of Cognitive Abilities (CHC Theory), 4, 34, 36, 37, 40, 287, 407
CELF-5. *See Clinical Evaluation of Language Fundamentals-Fifth Edition* (CELF-5; Wiig, Semel, and Secord)
Chaplin, W., 543
Chen, H., 37
Children's Memory Scale (Cohen), 592
Chronologist age, 8
C-Lim. *See* Culture-Language Interpretive Matrix (C-LIM)

Clinical clusters. *See* Cluster analysis interpretation (Appendix 6.C)

Clinical Composites, 167

Clinical Evaluation of Language Fundamentals-Fifth Edition (CELF-5; Wiig, Semel, and Secord), 411, 413, 592

Cluster analysis interpretation (Appendix 6.C): example of subtest cluster analysis, 396 Fig. 1.1; fluid reasoning and visual spatial clinical clusters and cluster contrasts, 398; steps for completing, 395–397; verbal comprehension clinical clusters and cluster contrasts, 3397–398; working memory clinical clusters and clinical cluster contrasts, 399

Coady, M., 540, 546

Coalson, D. L., 23, 30, 32, 135, 180, 184, 200, 249, 442, 617

Cognitive aptitude, 437

Cognitive constructs, assessed with WISC-V Subtests-Appendix 6.A: executive functions, 304–305; with Fluid Reasoning and Visual Spatial Subtests, 339–344; with Naming Speed Subtests, 355–359; primary cognitive constructs, 334; with Processing Speed Subtests, 351–355; secondary cognitive constructs, 334; with symbol translation tasks, 360–362; Verbal Comprehension Subtests, 335; with Working Memory Subtests and Arithmetic and Immediate Symbol Translation Subtests, 344–351

Cognitive Proficiency Index (CPI), 442

Cohen, J., 593

Cohen, M., 592

Collier, V. P., 552

Comprehensive Test of Phonological Processing-Second Edition (CTOPP-2), 455, 464, 515

Comrey, A. L., 218

Cormier, D. C., 541, 543–544

Courville, T., 548

Crawford, J. R., 134

Cross-Battery Assessment approach (XBA), 4, 21, 168

Cross-Battery Assessment Software Program (X-BASS), 29, 168, 410, 436

Cross-Battery Assessment Software Program (X-BASS), use of for SLD identification: analysis of selected subsets from CTOPP-2 on XBA analyzer tab of X-BASS, 465

Fig. 7.6; analysis of selected subsets on XBA analyzer tab of X-BASS, 469 Fig. 7.8; data organizer tab in X-BASS, 470—472 Fig. 7.9; dual discrepancy/consistency model: PSW analyses for SLD, 483–490; FStart and data record management tab in X-BASS, 460; getting started, 454—460; g-value tab of X-BASS, 484 Fig. 7.13; PSW analyzer tab in X-BASS with ICC as default cognitive, 486 Fig. 7.14; PSW analyzer tab of X-BASS with orthographic processing selected as area of cognitive weakness, 489 Fig. 7.15; PSW-A Data Summary tab, 483; PSW-A *g*-Value Data Summary, 483; specific questions about PSW results answered in X-BASS, 490 Fig. 7.16; step 1: enter individual test data and cross-battery data into X-BASS and transfer best estimates of cognitive and academic performance to data organizer tab, 458; step 2: select scores from data organizer tab for inclusion in PSW analysis, 469—473; step 3: indicate whether scores on strengths and weaknesses indicator tab represent strength or weakness for individual, 473–478; strengths and weaknesses indicator tab of X-BASS, 476—477 Fig. 7.11; test index and main navigation tab in X-BASS, 461 Fig. 7.4; top portion of data organizer tab in X-BASS showing that scores have been included in PSW analysis, 474 Fig. 7.10; user guide tab in X-BASS, 459 Fig. 7.2; WIAT-III data analysis tab in X-BASS, 466—467 Fig. 7.7; WISC-V, WIAT-III, and CTOPP-2 data from case of Amanda, 455—456 Rapid Reference 7.11; WISC-V data analysis tab in X-BASS, 462–463 Fig. 7.5; X-BASS welcome screen, 457 Fig. 7.1

Crystallized Intelligence (Gc), 33

CTOPP-2. *See Comprehensive Test of Phonological Processing-Second Edition* (CTOPP-2)

Culture-Language Interpretive Matrix (C-LIM), 556–559, 569, 575, 583

D

Daniel, M. H., 180, 593

Data Management and Interpretive Assistant (DMIA), 552, 575

DD/C. *See* Dual Discrepancy/
    Consistency (DD/C)
Deary, I. J., 2, 6
Dehaene, S., 287
Dehn, M. J., 287, 500, 504
Delis, D. C., 287, 592
Delis-Kaplan Executive Function System (D-KEFS;
    Delis, Kaplan, and Kramer), 592
Della Toffalo, D. A., 444
Denver, Colorado, 568
*Developmental NEuroPSYchological Assessment,
    Second Edition* (NEPSY-II; Korkman, Kirk,
    and Kemp), 592
Devine, R. I., 541
DiCerbo, K. E., 551
Dixon, S. G., 539, 546, 552
DMIA. *See* Data Management and Interpretive
    Assistant (DMIA)
Dombrowski, S. C., 23, 41
Dries, Carlea, 591
Drozdick, L., 33, 268
Dual Discrepancy/Consistency (DD/C), 405, 407
Dumont, R., 23, 32, 249, 591
Dunn, D. M., 592
Dunn, L. M., 592
Dynda, A. M., 62, 287, 543–539

E

Empathy, 3
English learners, assessment of: additional
    considerations in test score validity,
    564–566; best practices, 557–559; broad
    and narrow ability classifications of WISC-V
    and WISC-IV Spanish subtests, 563 Tab.
    9.1; case study: Jose Maria, 567–582;
    dominant language evaluation: English
    language assessment, 551–553; dominant
    language evaluation: native language
    assessment, 548–551; fairness, bias, and
    traditional assessment approaches, 541–544;
    Gc caveat, 566–567; modified or altered
    assessment, 544–546; native language
    follow-up evaluation, 561–561; nonverbal
    methods of evaluation: language reduced
    assessment, 546–548; overview, 539–541;
    recommended best practice approach,
    553–557; use of C-LIM, 558–559
Esparza-Brown, J., 543, 551
Evans, L. D., 482
Explanation, 3

F

Facilitating Cognitive Composite (FCC), 442
Family Educational Rights and Privacy Act
    (FERPA), 610
Fancher, R. E., 1
Fantuzzo, J. W., 41
Farris, Amanda, psychoeducational evaluation
    report: auditory processing (Ga), 521–522;
    background information, 512–515;
    behavioral observations, 515–516; Conners
    CBRS content scale detailed scores:
    comparison across raters, 534–535; content
    scales, 527; Cross-Battery Assessment
    Software System (X-BASS): Dual-
    Discrepancy/Consistency model: PSW
    results for Amanda Farris, 536; crystallized
    intelligence (Gc), 517–518; current
    evaluation procedures, 515; developmental
    history, 512–513; DSM-5 symptom scales
    and symptom counts, 527; education
    history, 514–515; evaluation of academic
    achievement, 523–524; evolution of
    cognitive abilities and processes, 516–517;
    family background, 512; fluid reasoning
    (Gf), 518; health history, 513; impairment,
    527–528; interpretation and clinical
    impressions, 527–531; long-term storage
    and retrieval (Glr), 520–521; mathematics,
    524–525; oral language, 523; processing
    speed (Gs), 519–520; reading, 523–524;
    reason for referral, 511–512; recommenda-
    tions for intervention and remediation,
    532–533; results of Amanda's performance
    on CTOPP-2, 522 Tab. 8.3; results of
    Amanda's performance on WISC-V, 522
    Tab. 8.2; score classifications, 517 Tab. 8.1;
    short-term memory (Gsm), 519; social
    behavior and temperament, 513–514;
    social-emotional/behavioral evaluation,
    526–527; statement of validity, 516;
    validity indices, 526; visual processing
    (Gv), 518–519; written expres-
    sion, 525–526
Feifer, S. G., 40, 443
Fein, D., 287
Felske, Florence, 6
Figueroa, R. A., 542, 546, 551
Fina, D. F., 544
Fiorello, C. A., 287, 405, 407, 422, 443
Fitzer, K. R., 40

Flanagan, D. P., 1, 4, 21–22, 29, 40, 168, 178–180, 216, 218, 221, 227, 247, 287, 405–407, 410, 414, 422, 437, 440, 444, 452, 511, 539, 541, 558, 578, 617
Fletcher, J. M., 436
Flores, C. G., 540, 546
Floyd, R. G., 414
Fluid reasoning and visual spatial subtests, behavioral observations, and process-oriented assessment: difficulties with visual, motor, and/or visuo-motor processing speed, 375–376; related to difficulties with use of visual processes, 372–373; related to manual dexterity difficulties, 375; related to reasoning with nonverbal visual stimuli, 371–373; related to use of executive functions, 376–378; related to use of working memory applied to visual stimuli, 371–372
Flynn, J. R., 47
Fordham University, 617–618
Forness, S. R., 443
Fox, H. C., 2
Frisby, C. L., 542
Fristoe, M., 592
FSIQ. See Full Scale IQ
Fuchs, L. S., 436
Full Scale IQ (FSIQ), 9, 133, 287; indexes and, 137—139

G

GAI. See General Ability Index (GAI)
Garthwaite, P. H., 134
Gault, C. B., 134
Geary, D. C., 443
Geddes, L., 543
Geisinger, K. F., 542
General Ability Index (GAI), 167, 288, 386, 442; as alternative to FSIQ, 199—209; Amanda: referred for suspected learning disability, 204—205; Beth: referred for Gifted and Talented Program, 208—209; Omar: referred for suspect learning disabilities, 207; Rhonda: referred for suspected autism spectrum disorder, 206; and specific learning disability, 200; and students who are gifted and talented, 200—203; and students with intellectual disability, 203—204

General intelligence, 10
Gerhardstein Nader, R., 40
Glue, P., 3
Glutting, J. J., 41, 47
Goddard, H. H., 542
Goldman, R., 592
Goldman-Fristoe Test of Articulation, Third Edition (Goldman and Fristoe), 592
Goldstein, S., 500
Gordon, M. N., 287
Gottfredson, L. S., 2
Grenier, J. R., 542
Gronau, R. C., 544
Grosjean, F., 556

H

Hale, J. B., 287, 405, 407, 422, 436, 437, 444, 452
Harris, J. G., 539
Harrison, A. G., 409, 443
Hartz, E., 287
Health Insurance Portability and Accountability Act (HIPAA), 609–610
HelloQ website, 593, 609
Helloq.com, 596
Hicks, K., 40
High Priority Concern (HPC), 263
Hinshelwood, J., 440
HIPAA. See Health Insurance Portability and Accountability Act (HIPAA)
Hoard, M. K., 443
Holdnack, J. A., 184, 249, 546
Hollingworth, L., 544
Holmes, A., 443
Horn, J. L., 547, 619
Hulbert, S., 180

I

IDEIA. See Individuals with disabilities Education Improvement Act of 2004 (IDEIA)
Individuals with disabilities Education Improvement Act of 2004 (IDEIA), 405, 411, 443, 552, 555; definition of SLD, 406
Inhibiting Cognitive Composite (ICC), 450
Intellectual disability, 7
Intelligence quotient (IQ), 2, 7
Intelligent Testing (Kaufman), 192, 269
Intelligent Testing with the WISC-III (Kaufman), 192

Interpretation, neuropathological, of performance, 300–321; cognitive constructs likely to be assessed by Complementary Subtests, 323–325 Rapid Reference 6.10, 323–325 Rapid Reference 6.10; cognitive constructs likely to be assessed by Fluid Reasoning Subtests, Visual Puzzles (VP), and Picture Span (PS)Subtests, 306–308 Rapid Reference 6.7; cognitive constructs likely to be assessed by Verbal Comprehension Domain Subtest, 302–303 Rapid Reference 6.6; cognitive constructs likely to be assessed by working memory domain tasks and Arithmetic (AR) and Immediate Symbol Translation (IST) Subtests, 312–314 Rapid Reference 6.8; Complementary Subtests, 321–329; Fluid Reasoning and Visual Spatial Domains, 305–311; Naming Speed Subtests, 322–327; Processing Speed Domain, 317–321; Symbol Translation Subtests, 327–329; Verbal Comprehension Domain, 301–305; Working Domain (including Arithmetic and Immediate Symbol Translation Subtests), 311–317

Interpretation, neuropathological approach, 287; global level of interpretation, 289; interpretive levels framework applied to WISC-V, 288 Fig. 6.1; item level of interpretation, 297—298; key facts about global composite level, 285 Rapid Reference 6.1; key facts about item level of interpretation, 298 Rapid Reference 6.4; key facts about subtest level of interpretation, 297 Rapid Reference 6.3; levels of interpretation, 288—296; process score, scaled score, and raw norms available in WISC-V manuals, 294—296 Tab. 6.3; specific composite (index and subtest cluster) level of interpretation, 290; subtest level of interpretation, 293–297; subtest scaled score pairwise comparisons and subtest scaled scores contrast scores available in WISC-V manuals, 294 Tab. 6.2; task-specific cognitive construct level of interpretation, 299—300; WISC-V indexes and alternate subtest clinical clusters model based on neuropsychological constructs, 288 Tab. 6.1

Iribarren, J. A., 550

J

Jose Maria: ELS case study, 567–582; C-LIM primary culture-language graph results for, 573 Fig. 9.4; C-LIM tiered graph results for, 572 Fig. 9.3; C-LIM tiered graph results suggesting likely invalid test scores and primary influence of linguistic/cultural variables, 584 Fig. 9.9; Culture-Language Interpretive Matrix (C-LIM) for, 571 Fig. 9.2; data summary and preliminary PSW Analysis with correct designation of Gc, 580 Fig. 9.7; data summary and preliminary PSW Analysis with incorrect designation of Gc, 579 Fig. 9.6; final PSW analysis and determination of SLD, 581 Fig. 9.8; test scores from WISC-V, WIAT-III, and WJ IV COG, 570 Tab. 9.2; test scores from WISC-V, WIAT-III, and WJ IV COG with follow-up native language scores for, 577 Fig. 9.5

K

Kamphaus, R. W., 3, 203
Kaplan, E., 287, 592
Kauffman, J. M., 444
Kaufman, A. S., 2, 4–6, 10, 29, 135, 137, 172—173, 178–180, 182, 184, 192, 200, 249, 269, 410, 443, 444, 539, 592, 617
Kaufman, N. L., 172—173, 410, 592, 617
Kaufman, S., 287
Kaufman Test of Educational Achievement-Third Edition (KTEA-3; Kaufman and Kaufman), 172—173, 173 Rapid Reference 4.5, 281, 410, 411, 413, 592
Kavale, K. A., 443, 444
Keith, T. Z., 21, 23, 37, 218, 221, 283
Kemp, S. L., 287, 592
Key Asset (KA), 263
Kim, S., 3, 203
Kirk, U., 287, 592
Knight, R. T., 287
Konold, T. R., 41
Korb, K., 547
Korkman, M., 287, 592
Kosslyn, S. M., 287
Kramer, J. H., 287, 592
Kranzler, J. H., 436, 540, 546
KTEA-3. *See Kaufman Test of Educational Achievement, Third Edition*)

L

Lakin, J., 547
Lamiell, J. T., 2
Learning, factors to facilitate: and minimizing effects of Auditory Processing (Ga) deficit, 501–502 Tab. 3; and minimizing effects of Crystallized Intelligence (Gc) deficit, 499–500 Tab. 2; and minimizing effects of Fluid Reasoning (Gf) deficit, 498 Tab. 1; and minimizing effects of Long-Term Retrieval (Glr) deficit, 503–504 Tab. 4; and minimizing effects of Processing Speed (Gs) deficit, 505 Tab. 5; and minimizing effects of Short-Term Memory (Gsm) deficit, 507–508 Tab. 7; and minimizing effects of Visual Processing Speed (Gv) deficit, 506 Tab. 6
Learning Disabilities of Canada (LDAC), 443
LeFever, G. B., 444
Levine, A., 172
Levine, M. D., 287
Lichtenberger, E. O., 55
Llorente, A. M., 539
Lohman, D. E., 1–2, 13
Lohman, D. F., 547
Louisiana, 421
Luhrs, A., 543
Luria, A. R., 287
Lynch, K., 500
Lyon, G. R., 436

M

Maerlender, A., 287
Maricle, D. E., 444
Marks, L., 172
Mascolo, J. T., 221, 228, 405, 407, 417, 422
Mather, N., 5, 173, 177, 443, 444, 500
McCarthy, D., 617–619
McCarthy Scales of Children's Abilities (McCarthy), 617
McCloskey, G., 287, 407, 437, 443, 444
McDermott, P. A., 41
McDonough, E. M., 221, 405, 407, 511
McGrew, K. S., 4, 5, 173, 177, 178, 204, 218, 221, 452, 541, 547, 566
Mean of the Index Scores (MIS), 254–266
Melo, K., 539–541, 547, 551
Mental age, 8

Merrill, M. A., 619
Messick, S., 218, 221
Miller, D. C., 287
Monroe, M., 440, 443
Morgan, A. W., 3
Morris, J., 548
Morris, R., 287
Mpofu, E., 541, 547
Munoz, M, 539
Murphy, R., 407

N

Naglieri, J. A., 443, 450, 540
Nagoshi, N., 287
Naming Speed Subtests, behavioral observations and process-oriented assessment: related to expressive language ability, 392; related to oral-motor sequencing, 391–392; related to processing speed, 391; related to use of executive functions, 392–394
NASP. *See* National Association of School Psychologists (NASP)
National Association of School Psychologists (NASP), 540
National Council on Measurement in Education, 540
Neisser, U., 551
Nelson, J. M., 47
NEPSY-II. *See Developmental NEuroPSYchological Assessment-Second Edition* (NEPSY-II)
Niebling, B. C., 284
Nieves-Brull, A., 544
Niileksela, C. R., 221
Nonverbal Index (NVI), 167, 288
Normative Strength (NS), 263
Normative Weakness (NW), 263
NVI, 288. *See* Nonverbal Index

O

Ober, B. A., 592
O'Bryon, E. C., 552
Ochoa, S. H., 62, 540, 541
Opperman, M. A., 539
Orsini, S. O., 180
Ortiz, J. A., 541
Ortiz, S. O., 4, 21–22, 62, 168, 178, 218, 249, 287, 405, 407, 452, 511, 539–541, 545, 547, 543, 551–553, 552
Orton, S. T., 440, 444

P

Packer, L. E., 432
Paradis, M., 556
Pattern of strength and weakness (PSW), 405; permitted use of, for SLD identification, 406
Pattern of Strengths and Weaknesses Analyzer (PSW-A), 552
Patterson, T., 3
Peabody Picture Vocabulary Test, Fourth Edition (Dunn and Dunn), 592
Pearson Education, Inc., 281, 405, 591–593, 607, 609
Perkins, L. A., 444
Personal Strength (PS), 263
Personal Weakness (PW), 263
Petoskey, M. D., 3
Pezzuti, L., 180
Pitner, R., 172
Point scales, 12
Posner, M. I., 287
Powell, M. P., 540
Prediction, 3
Prifitera, A., 184, 249, 539
Principal Axis Factor Analysis (Sattler et al.), 30
Processing Speed Subtests, behavioral observations, and process-oriented assessment: related to difficulties with use of grapho-motor capacities, 384–385; related to difficulties with use of visual processes, 383–384; related to use of executive functions, 386–390; related to use of initial registration and working memory capacities applied to visual stimuli, 385–386; related to use of visual, motor, and visuo-motor processing speed, 386
Pruitt, S. K., 432
Psychometric properties: strengths, 282–284; weaknesses, 283-284

Q

Q-global (Pearson Education, Inc.), 591–592, 596
qiactie.com, 608
Q-interactive (Pearson Education, Inc.): administration, 600–601; application (Assess), 596; considerations for university trainers, 610–613; cost of administration, 612; digital platform, 591–594; hardware, 595–596; initial costs of tests and scoring materials, 611; iPad settings for, 599 Rapid Reference 10.2; output, 608–609; overall impressions and recommendations, 613; Pearson tests available through, 592–593 Rapid Reference 10.1; pricing, 611; pricing comparison between Q-Interactive and traditional WISC-V administrations, 612 Rapid Reference 10.4; pricing conclusion, 613; scoring, 604–607; security and legal issues, 609–610; set-up, 596–600; software, 596; standard manual for, 601 Rapid Reference 10.3; timing, 601–604; training and tech support, 608
Quantitative Reasoning Index (QRI), 35
Querying: in administration of WISC-V, 76—78; and meaning of "I don't know," 76; repeating items, 77—78

R

Radwan, S., 221
Raichle, M. E., 287
Raiford, S. E., 33, 35, 135, 180, 184, 200, 249, 268, 442, 546, 617
Ramsay, M. C., 542
Range of Human Capacities (Wechsler), 6
Rapport, with examinee: appropriate feedback and encouragement, 58 Rapid Reference 2.3; establishing, 55—58; keys to establishing positive report, 57 Rapid Reference 2.2; keys to maintaining rapport, 60 Rapid Reference 2.4; maintaining, 58—61; what to remember when preparing to administer WISC-V, 55 Rapid Reference 2.1
Rapsey, C., 3
Raw score, 133
Reed, M. S., 287
Responses, recording, 71—74; abbreviations for recording responses on WISC subtests, 73 Rapid Reference 2.6
Reynolds, M. R., 21, 23, 203, 216, 218, 221, 283, 407, 444, 482, 542
Reynolds Intellectual Ability Scales-Second Edition (RAIS-2), 203
Rhodes, R., 541, 543
Richards, A. M., 500
Richards, T. L., 287
Robbins, T. W., 287
Robles-Piña, R., 540

Rogers, J., 407
Rogers, M. R., 552
Rolfhus, E., 200, 442
Rothbart, M. K., 287

S

Saklofske, D. H., 10, 184, 249
Salvia, J., 543
Sanchez-Escobedo, P., 544
Sandoval, J., 542
Sattler, J. M., 23, 29, 32, 36, 41, 249
Scheunermann, J. D., 542
Schneider, J., 547
Schneider, W. J., 1, 4, 23, 178, 410, 414, 437
Schrank, F. A., 173, 566, 569
Schrank, R. A., 5
Secord, W. A., 593
Semel, E., 593
Shaywitz, S. A., 407, 443, 444
Simon, T., 1, 6, 7, 9
SLD. *See* Specific learning disabilities (SLD)
Slonim, J., 287
Sotelo-Dynega, M., 221, 539, 543–544, 546, 552, 566
Spaulding, L. S., 409
Spearman, C. E., 10, 41, 619
Special needs, testing individuals with, 61—63
Specific learning disabilities (SLD): correspondence between subtests from WIAT-III, KTEA-3, and CELF-5 and the eight areas of SLD listed in federal definitions, 413—414 Rapid Reference 7.3; definition of weakness and normative weakness or deficit, 412 Rapid Reference 7.2; description of consistency component of DD/C model and how it is determined using X-BASS, 441–442 Rapid Reference 7.7; domain-specific cognitive weaknesses of deficits: first discrepancy in DD/C definition of SLD, 450; dual discrepancy/consistency operational definition of, 406–411; evaluation and consideration of exclusionary factors for SLD identification, 417–421 Rapid Reference 7.4; general and specific manifestations of weakness or deficits in cognitive abilities and processes, 424—435 Rapid Reference 7.5; IDEA definition of (2004), 406; at least average ability to think and reason, 440–450 Rapid Reference 7.6; Level 1: analysis of specific academic skills, 411–415; Level II: evaluation of exclusionary factors as potential primary and contributory reasons for academic skill weaknesses or deficits, 414—422; Level III: analysis of cognitive abilities and processes, 421–423; Level IV: dual discrepancy/consistency pattern of strengths and weaknesses (DD/C PSW), 423—452; Level V: evaluation of interference with learning, 452—454; relationship between cognitive and academic weaknesses, 436—440; summary of relationships between cognitive abilities and processes and specific academic skills, 438–439 Rapid Reference 7.6; terms used in DD/C model and in X-BASS necessary to understand how "at least average overall ability" is conceptualized and calculated, 446—449 Rapid Reference 7.8; terms used in DD/C model and in X-BASS necessary to understand how a "domain specific weakness" is conceptualized and calculated, 451 Rapid Reference 7.9; terms used in DD/C model and in X-BASS necessary to understand how "unexpected underachievement" is conceptualized and calculated, 453 Rapid Response 7.10; unexpected underachievement: second discrepancy in DD/C definition of, 449; use of WISC-V in identification of, 405
Sporns, O., 287
Standard scores, 8, 133
Stanford-Binet, 11, 172
Stanovich, K. E., 450
Starr, J. M., 2
Stern, W., 2, 7
Stuss, D. T., 287
Styck, K. M., 544
Subtest administration, rules for primary subtests: behaviors to note on Block Design, 80—81; behaviors to note on Coding, 90—91; behaviors to note on Digit Span, 88—89; behaviors to note on Figure Weights, 95; behaviors to note on Matrix Reasoning, 85—86; behaviors to note on Picture Span, 98; behaviors to note on Similarities, 83—84; behaviors to note on Symbol Search, 100—101; behaviors to note on Visual Puzzles, 96; behaviors to note on Vocabulary, 92–93; Block Design (Visual

Spatial Index), 78—81; changes in administration from WISC-IV to WISC-V: Subtest 1, Block Design, 79; changes in administration from WISC-IV to WISC-V: Subtest 2, Similarities, 83; changes in administration from WISC-IV to WISC-V: Subtest 3, Matrix Reasoning, 85; changes in administration from WISC-IV to WISC-V: Subtest 4, Digit Span, 87—88; changes in administration from WISC-IV to WISC-V: Subtest 5, Coding, 90; changes in administration from WISC-IV to WISC-V: Subtest 6, Vocabulary, 92; changes in administration from WISC-IV to WISC-V: Subtest 10, Symbol Search, 100; Coding (Processing Speed Index), 89—91; common errors on Block Design subtest, 122; common errors on Coding subtest, 125; common errors on Digit Span subtest, 124; common errors on Figure Weights subtest, 123; common errors on Matrix Reasoning subtest, 122; common errors on Picture Span subtest, 124; common errors on Similarities subtest, 120–121; common errors on Symbol Search subtest, 125; common errors on Visual Puzzles subtest, 122; common errors on Vocabulary subtest, 121; Digit Span (Working Memory Index), 86—89; Figure Weights (Fluid Reasoning Index), 93–95; Matrix Reasoning (Fluid Reasoning Index), 84—86; Picture Span (Working Memory Index), 97–98; seating arrangement for Block Design Subtest, 82; Similarities (Verbal Comprehension Index), 82—84; Symbol Search (Processing Speed Index), 99–101; Visual Puzzles (Visual Spatial Index), 95–97; Vocabulary (Verbal Comprehension Index), 91–93

Subtest administration, rules for secondary and complementary subtests: Arithmetic (Fluid Reasoning Index, Secondary), 116–118; behaviors to note on Arithmetic, 117–118; behaviors to note on Cancellation, 109; behaviors to note on Comprehension, 115–116; behaviors to note on Delayed Symbolic Translation, 119; behaviors to note on Immediate Symbol Translation, 113; behaviors to note on Information, 102–103; behaviors to note on Letter-Number Sequencing, 106–107; behaviors to note on Naming Speed Literacy, 111; behaviors to note on Naming Speed Quantity, 112; behaviors to note on Picture Concepts, 104–105; behaviors to note on Recognition Symbol Translation, 120; Cancellation (Processing Speed Index, Secondary), 108–109; changes in administration from the WISC-IV to the WISC-V: Subtest 11, Information, 102; changes in administration from the WISC-IV to the WISC-V: Subtest 12, Picture Concepts, 104; changes in administration from the WISC-IV to the WISC-V: Subtest 18, Comprehension, 115; changes in administration from the WISC-IV to the WISC-V: Subtest 19, Arithmetic, 117; common errors on Arithmetic Subtest, 123; common errors on Cancellation Subtest, 125; common errors on Comprehension Subtest, 121; common errors on Delayed Symbol Translation Subtest, 126; common errors on Immediate Symbol Translation Subtest, 126; common errors on Information Subtest, 121; common errors on Letter-Number Sequencing Subtest, 124; common errors on Naming Speed Literacy Subtest, 126; common errors on Picture Concepts Subtest, 123; common errors on Recognition Symbol Translation Subtest, 126–127; Comprehension (Verbal Comprehension Index, Secondary), 114–116; Delayed Symbol Translation (Complementary), 118–119; Immediate Symbol Translation (Complementary), 112–113; Information (Verbal Comprehension Index, Secondary), 101–103; Letter-Number Sequencing (Working Memory Index, Secondary), 105–107; Naming Speed Literacy (Complementary), 109–111; Naming Speed Quantity (Complementary), 111–112; Picture Concepts (Fluid Reasoning index, Secondary), 103–105; Recognition Symbol Translation (Complementary), 119–120

Subtest and process score comparison worksheets (Appendix 6.D): complementary subtest comparison worksheet, 403; Fluid

Reasoning and Visual Spatial subtest scaled score, 401–402; Processing Speed subtest, 402–403; Verbal Comprehension subtest scaled score comparison worksheet, 401; Working Memory subtest, 402–403

Subtests, rules for starting and discontinuing, 64—71; behaviors to note on Coding, 90—91; starting points and whether reverse rules apply, 64—67 Rapid Reference 2.5; summary of WISC-V subtest discontinue rules, 70 Table 2.3; summary of WISC-V subtest reverse rules, 67—68 Table 2.2

Sy, M., 221

T

Temple, C., 287

Tennessee, 421

Terman, L. M., 172, 619

Test development and content: strengths, 279—280; weaknesses, 281

Testing conditions, appropriate: testing environment, 54; testing materials, 54—55

Thibodaux, L., 414

Thomas, W. P., 552

Thompson, M. S., 540, 544, 546, 547

Thurstone, L. L., 619

Timing: in administration of WISC-V, 74—75; nine timed subtests on WISC-V, 75; what to remember when using stopwatch on timed tests, 75 Rapid Reference 2.7

Tulsky, D. S., 10

U

Uncommon Personal Strength (PS/ Uncommon), 263

Uncommon Personal Weakness (PW/ Uncommon), 263

U.S. Army, 12

U.S. Census Bureau, 540

V

Valdes, G., 542, 551

Van Divner, B., 444

Verbal Comprehension Subtests, behavioral observations and process-oriented assessment: related to difficulties with use of auditory processes, 367–368; related to use of executive functions, 370–371; related to use of expressive language abilities, 368–369; related to use of reasoning with verbal information, 366; related to use of working memory applied to auditory stimuli, 369–370

Verbal Expanded Crystallized Index (VECI; Raiford, Drozdick, Zhang, and Zhu), 33

Viezel, K. D., 591

W

Wahlstrom, D., 593

WAIS. See Wechsler Adult Intelligence Scale (WAIS)

Watkins, M. W., 23, 37, 41, 47, 544

Wechsler, D., 4–14, 34, 38–41, 49, 55—56, 71, 135, 137, 183, 184, 200—201, 203, 216—217, 540, 593, 603, 607, 617, 619

Wechsler Adult Intelligence Scale (WAIS), 5

Wechsler Adult Intelligence Scale-Fourth Edition (WAIS-IV), 287, 592

Wechsler Individual Achievement Test-Third Edition (WIAT-III), 173, 405, 410, 411, 413, 468

Wechsler Individual Achievement Test-Third Edition (WIAT-III, Pearson), 281, 569, 570, 577, 592

Wechsler Intelligence Scale for Children-Fifth Edition (WISC-V). See WISC-V

Wechsler Intelligence Scale for Children-Fourth Edition (WISC-IV), 287, 540, 592

Wechsler Intelligence Scale for Children-IV Spanish (WISC-IV Spanish), 548–550, 561, 562, 566–567

Wechsler Intelligence Scale for Children-Third Edition (WISC-III), 13

Wechsler Nonverbal Scale of Ability (WNV), 540

Wechsler Performance IQ, 8

Wechsler Preschool and Primary Scale of Intelligence (WPPSI), 5

Wechsler Verbal IQ, 9

Wechsler-Bellevue battery, 11

Weiss, L. G., 37, 184, 200, 249, 442, 539, 548

Wendling, B. J., 221, 443

Werder, J. K., 177

Whalley, L. J., 2

Whitaker, J., 407

Whitaker, R., 287

Whiteman, M. C., 2

WIAT-III. See Wechsler Individual Achievement Test-Third Edition

Wiig, E. H., 593

Winsor, A. P., xvi

WISC-III. *See Wechsler Intelligence Scale for Children-Third Edition* (WISC-III)

Wisconsin, 421

WISC-R, 6

WISC-V, administration: appropriate feedback and encouragement, 58—59 Rapid Reference 2.3; appropriate testing conditions, 53—55; considerations, 63—64; deciding on, *versus* another battery for 6-and 16-year-olds, 64 Tab. 2.1; frequently asked questions, 127–129; querying, 76—78; rapport with examinee, 55—61; recording responses, 71—74; rules for starting and discontinuing subtests, 64—71; special considerations for testing children at extreme ends of age range, 63—64; subtest administration, 127—132; subtest-by-subtest rules, for primary subtests, 78—101; subtest-by-subtest rules, for secondary and complementary subtests, 101—127; testing individuals with special needs, 61—63; timing, 74—76

WISC-V, interpretation: Amanda's performance on WISC-V, 169—170 Rapid Reference 4.2; bottom portion of test-specific tabs on X-BASS: confidence interval for score reporting, 176 Fig. 4.1; classification system for, 172 Rapid Reference 4.4; generic classification system to classify all scores in psychoeducational report, 174 Rapid Reference 4.6; getting started, 169; location of information in WISC manuals needed for score conversions, 171 Rapid Reference 4.3; note about classification intervals, 175—178; note about classification systems, 171—172 Rapid Reference 4.3; overview, 167—169; score report from X-BASS with Amanda's data displayed with 68% confidence, 176 Fig. 4.2; score report from X-BASS with Amanda's data displayed with 95% confidence, 177 Fig. 4.3; some reasons for using 68% confidence intervals for score reporting, 177—178 Rapid Reference 4.7; step-by-step, 178—180; summary of, step-by-step, 168—169 Rapid Reference 4.1

WISC-V, interpretation, step 1: determine best way to describe overall intellectual ability, 182—209; composition of FSIQ and selected primary and ancillary index scales for describing overall intellectual ability, 183 Rapid Reference 4.9; data for Alysia, 198 Rapid Reference 4.16; definition of cohesion and clinical meaningfulness, 185 Rapid Reference 4.10; example of decision making process for NVI *versus* FSIQ, 198—199; example of X-BASS output for determining best estimate of global ability for Alysia, 199 Fig. 4.4; FSIQs cohesive, but not considered clinically meaningful, 195—196; GAI as alternative to FSIQ, 199—209; is NVI or FSIQ best estimate of overall intellectual ability for ELS or language related disorder-summary of steps, 186—191 Rapid Reference 4.12; nature and meaning of global ability composites, 196—197 Rapid Reference 4.15; note about clinical meaningfulness, 193—194; NVI as alternative to FSIQ, 184—193; percentage of standardized sample obtaining high minus low scaled score difference between 5 and 9, inclusive, 193 Rapid Reference 4.13; sample statement by X-BASS for individual who is WL or suspected of having language-related disorder, 186 Rapid Reference 4.11; two children with same FSIQ but different scaled scores, 195 Rapid Reference 4.14; why detailed analyses are necessary to determine best estimate of global ability, 192—193

WISC-V, interpretation, step 2: analyze Primary Index Scales, 209; CHC broad and narrow abilities measured by Primary Index Scales, 210—217; cohesion analysis of Primary Index Scales using X-BASS, 222 Rapid Reference 4.22; criteria used in X-BASS for follow-up analysis for composites that are made up of two scores, 230 Tab 4.1; example of cohesion and follow-up statements for Amanda's VCI and FRI in X-BASS, 223 Fig. 4.5; example of cohesion and follow-up statements for Amanda's VSI and WMI in X-BASS, 224 Fig. 4.6; example of non-cohesive composite reported and interpreted for Marie, 227 Fig. 4.8; example of X-BASS output when follow-up may be necessary for the FRI, 247 Fig. 4.9; examples of cohesion analysis for Fluid Reasoning Index (FRI), 226 Rapid Reference 4.23; examples of what is meant by "follow-up" in X-BASS, 228—229 Rapid Reference 4.24; follow-up assessment, 227; guidance provided by X-BASS based on follow-up analysis, 243—244 Rapid Reference 4.26; guidelines for index score interpretation based on cohesion and follow-up analysis, 244—246 Rapid Reference 4.27; note about construct representation, 218—221; portion of interpretive output summary for Amanda from X-BASS, 225 Fig. 4.7; Primary Index Scale cohesion, 221—228 ; summary of five Primary Indexes, 210 Rapid Reference 4.19; two-subtest composites, 231—242 Rapid Reference 4.25

WISC-V, interpretation, step 3: analyze the Ancillary Index Scales: Quantitative Reasoning Index (QRI), Auditory Working Memory (AWMI), and Cognitive Proficiency Index (CPI), 248—249; clinical utility of selected Ancillary Index Scales, 249 Rapid Reference 4.29; summary of three Ancillary Indexes, 248 Rapid Reference 4.28

WISC-V, interpretation, step 4: analyze the Complimentary Index Scales: Naming Speed Index (NSI), Symbol Translation Index (STI), and Storage and Retrieval Index (SRI), 250—251; clinical utility of Complementary Index Scales, 251–252 Rapid Reference 4.31; summary of the three Ancillary Indexes, 251 Rapid Reference 4.30

WISC-V, interpretation, step 5: determine normative strengths and weaknesses in Index Scale profile, 249—251; chart for Categorizing Index Scale scores from a normative perspective, 253 Rapid Reference 4.32

WISC-V, interpretation, step 6 (optional): determine personal strengths, personal weaknesses, key assets, and high priority concerns among Primary Index scores: chart for Categorizing Index Scale scores from a normative perspective, 254–266; determination of strengths and weaknesses using overall sample comparisons, 255 Tab. 4.2; determining strengths and weaknesses

using FSIQ 80—89, 257 Tab. 4.4; determining strengths and weaknesses using FSIQ 90—109, 258 Tab. 4.5; determining strengths and weaknesses using FSIQ 110—119, 259 Tab. 4.6; determining strengths and weaknesses using FSIQ 120 and higher, 260 Tab. 4.7; determining strengths and weaknesses using FSIQ less than 80 composite, 256 Tab. 4.3; interpretation of strengths and weaknesses in Primary Index Scale profile, 264–266 Rapid Reference 4.34; note about personal strengths and weaknesses, 254–266; terms used in strengths and weaknesses analysis of Primary Index Scales, 263 Rapid Reference 4.33

WISC-V, interpretation, step 7 (optional): determine whether new clinical composites are cohesive and add clinically relevant information beyond that provided by Primary, Ancillary, and Complementary Scales, 266; cohesion analysis for clinical composites made of three or more subtest, 273 Tab. 4.10; cohesion analysis for new clinical composites made up of two subtests, 272 Tab. 4.9; internal consistency reliability coefficients and SEMs, 270–271 Tab. 4.8; summary of new clinical composites, 267–268 Rapid Reference 4.35

WISC-V, overview of, 1–50; Alfred Binet and "first" intelligence tests, 6–7; ancillary and complementary index scales, 22 Fig. 1.3; broad CHC classifications of WISC-V subtests according to various data sources, 23 Rapid Reference 1.2; changes from WISC-IV to WISC-V, 16–17; classification of WISC-V subtest g-loadings, 32 Tab. 1.6; composition of WISC-V Full Scale IQ, 20 Fig. 1.1; description, 13; descriptions of WISC-V subtests, 18–20 Tab. 1.4; from explanation to enduring empathy, 3; General Intelligence $\neq$, 9–11; g-loadings of WISC-V subtests, 30–32; intelligence test interpretation general trends, 3–4; from mental ages to intelligence quotients to standard scores, 7–9; new subtests on WISC-V, 18 Tab. 1.3; from prediction to prevention, 2–3; previous editions, 13; Primary Index Scales, 21 Fig. 1.2; structure, 32; structure of WISC-V composite scores and corresponding internal consistency coefficients, 31 Tab. 1.5; subtest structure of previous editions, 14 Tab. 1.1; suggested abilities and processes measured by WISC-V subtests and possible influences on subtest performance, 24–29 Rapid Reference 1.3; value of history of Wechsler Scales, 4–5; Wechsler's subtests, 11–12; WISC-V at a glance, 14–16 Tab. 1.2; Yerkes Point Scales, 12–13

WISC-V, scoring: allowable subtest substitutions for deriving FSIQ, 139 Tab. 3.1; appropriate situations for calculating index scores and FSIQ when raw scores of zero are obtained on subtests, 142; Arithmetic (FRI, Secondary) keys, 160; Block Design (VSI, Primary) key, 148 Tab. 3.5; Cancellation (PCI, Secondary) keys, 155—156; changes in scoring: Subtest 1, Block Design (VSA, Primary), 146 Tab. 3.2; changes in scoring: Subtest 2, Similarities (VCI, Primary), 147 Tab. 3.3; changes in scoring: Subtest 3, Matrix Reasoning (FRI, Primary), 147 Tab. 3.4; changes in scoring: Subtest 4, Digit Span (WMI, Primary), 147—148; changes in scoring: Subtest 5: Coding (WMI, Primary), 148—149; changes in scoring: Subtest 6, Vocabulary (VCI, Primary), 151 Tab. 3.7; changes in scoring: Subtest 10: Symbol Search (PSI, Primary), 153 Tab. 3.8; changes in scoring: Subtest 11: Information (VCI, Secondary), 154 Tab. 3.9; changes in scoring: Subtest 12: Picture Concepts (FRI, Secondary), 154 Tab. 3.10; changes in scoring: Subtest 14: Cancellation (PSI, Secondary), 156 Tab. 3.11; changes in scoring: Subtest 18: Comprehension (VCI, Secondary), 160 Tab. 3.12; common errors in calculating total raw scores, 135–136; Comprehension (VCI, Secondary) keys,160; Delayed Symbol Translation (Complementary) keys, 161–162i; Digit Span (WMI, Primary) keys, 147—148; Flight Weights (FRI, Primary) keys, 151; frequently asked questions, 162—164 Rapid Reference 3.2; Immediate Symbol Translation (Complementary) keys, 158—159; indexes

and FSIQ, 137—139; Information (VCI, Secondary) keys, 154; Letter-Number Sequencing (VMI, Secondary) keys, 155; Matrix Reasoning (FRI, Primary) key, 147; most frequent errors in obtaining scaled scores, 136—137; Naming Speed Literacy (Complementary) keys, 156—158; Naming Speed Quantity (Complementary) keys, 158–159; Picture Concepts (FRI, Secondary) keys, 154; Picture Span (WMI, Primary) keys, 151—152; prorating FSIQ on WISC-V, 142—143; Recognition Symbol Translation (Complementary) keys, 162; scoring subtests requiring judgement, 143—144; Similarities (VCI, Primary) key, 146; special considerations for calculating index scores and FSIQ using supplemental subtests, 139—140; special considerations for indexes and FSIQ with subtest raw scores of zero, 141—142; standard scores, 134 Rapid Reference 3.1; subtest raw scores and raw process scores, 134—136; subtest scaled, standard, standardized process scores, and contrast scores, 136—137; subtests composing WISC-V Ancillary Indexes, 141; subtests composing WISC-V complementary indexes, 141; subtests composing WISC-V Primary Indexes and FSIQ, 138; Symbol Search (PSI, Primary) keys, 152—153; types of scores, 133—134; Visual Puzzles (VSI, Primary) keys, 151; Vocabulary (VCI, Primary), 149—150

WISC-V, theoretic structure, 32; exploratory factor analysis of WISC-V subtests, 36 Tab. 1.7; Fluid Reasoning Subtests: Matrix Reasoning, Picture Concepts, Figure Weights, and Arithmetic, 35—37; Long-Term Storage and Retrieval subtests, 40; new Gc clinical composites for WISC-V, 33 Rapid Reference 1.4; new Gf clinical composite for, 35 Rapid Reference 1.5; new Glr clinical composite for, 41 Rapid Reference 1.8; new Gs clinical composite for, 39 Rapid Reference 1.7; new Gsm clinical composites for, 38 Rapid Reference 1.6; Processing Speed Subtests: Coding, Symbol Search, and Cancellations, 39—40; relations with other variables, 41; summary of criterion validity studies for Primary Index Scales and FSIQ, 43—46;

summary of special group studies for Primary Index Scales and FSIC, 42; Verbal Comprehension Subtests: Similarities, Vocabulary, Information, and Comprehension, 33—35; Visual Spatial Processing Subtests: Block Design and Visual Puzzles, 37; Wechsler's IQ *versus* Spearman's *g*, 41—48; Working Memory Index Subtests: Digit Span, and Letter-Number Sequencing, 37—39

WISC-V Administration and Scoring Manual (Wechsler), 61, 62, 64, 72, 76, 78, 82, 84, 87, 89, 91, 94, 97, 99, 101, 103, 105, 108, 109, 111, 112, 114, 116, 118, 133, 136, 137, 139

WISC-V Administration and Scoring Manual Supplement (Wechsler), 135–137

WISC-V Technical and Interpretive Manual (Wechsler), 13, 36, 37, 72, 135, 137, 171, 254, 280, 285, 304, 311, 328—329, 375

Within Normal Limits (WNL), 263

WJ IV COG. *See Woodcock-Johnson IV Tests of Cognitive Ability*

Woodcock, R. W., 5, 21, 177, 202

Woodcock-Johnson IV Tests of Cognitive Ability (WJ IV COG; Schrank, Mather, and McGrew), 5, 172—173, 569, 570, 577

Working Memory Domain and Arithmetic and Symbol Translation Subtests, behavioral observations and process-oriented assessment, 378; related to application of Working Memory with Auditory Stimuli, 382–383; related to difficulties with use of auditory processes, 378–379; related to initial registration of auditorily presented verbal information, 382; related to use of executive functions, 380–382; related to use of math calculation and problem-solving skills, 378; related to use of sequencing ability, 379–380

WPPSI. *See* Wechsler Preschool and Primary Scale of Intelligence (WPPSI)

Wright, J., 482

Wycoff, K. L., 407

X

XBA. *See Cross-Battery Assessment* approach (XBA)

X-BASS. *See Cross-Battery Assessment Software System* (X-BASS)

Y

Yerkes, R. M., 12, 546

Ysseldyke, J. E., 541, 543

Z

Zaboski, B., 414

Zhang, O., 33, 268, 593

Zhou, X., 33, 268

Zhu, J., 10, 37